**FIFTH
EDITION**

ECONOMICS
A Tool for Critically Understanding Society

The Addison-Wesley Series in Economics

FIFTH EDITION

ECONOMICS
A Tool for Critically Understanding Society

Tom Riddell
Smith College

Jean Shackelford
Bucknell University

Steve Stamos
Bucknell University

With Contributions by
Bill Cooper

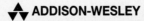 **ADDISON-WESLEY**

An imprint of Addison Wesley Longman, Inc.

Reading, Massachusetts • Menlo Park, California • New York • Harlow, England
Don Mills, Ontario • Sydney • Mexico City • Madrid • Amsterdam

Senior Editor: Denise Clinton
Senior Development Manager: Sylvia Mallory
Editorial Assistant: Rebecca Ferris
Managing Editor: Jim Rigney
Production Supervisor: Billie Porter
Senior Manufacturing Supervisor: Hugh Crawford
Cover Designer: Diana Coe
Cover Photo: Image © 1998 PhotoDisc, Inc.
Text Design, Composition, and Project Coordination: Elm Street Publishing Services, Inc.

Economics: A Tool for Critically Understanding Society, Fifth Edition

Library of Congress Cataloging-in-Publication Data

Riddell, Tom, 1944–
    Economics: a tool for critically understanding society / Tom Riddell, Jean Shackelford, Steve Stamos with contributions by Bill Cooper.—5th ed.
      p.   cm.—(Addison-Wesley series in economics)
    Includes index.
    ISBN 0-201-55714-2 (paper)
    1.Economics. I. Shackelford, Jean A. II. Stamos, Steve, 1947– . III. Title. IV. Series.
HB171.5.R43   1998
330—dc21

97-34257

1 2 3 4 5 6 7 8 9 10 —MA— 99 98 97

CONTENTS IN BRIEF

■ PART 4   MACROECONOMICS   291

■ PART 5   INTERNATIONAL ECONOMICS AND FINANCE   441

CONTENTS

■ PART 2   ECONOMIC HISTORY AND THE DEVELOPMENT OF MODERN ECONOMIC THOUGHT   47

Chapter 3   The Evolution of Economic Systems   49

Chapter 10   Noncompetitive Markets and Inefficiency   189

Chapter 11   Resource Markets and the Distribution of Income   212

Chapter 18   Aggregate Demand and Aggregate Supply   402

Chapter 19   Unemployment, Inflation, and Stabilization Policy in a Global Economy   419

FOREWORD

Approaching the turn of the century, the U.S. economy finds itself in moderately good shape. The 1990s has not been a period of rampant prosperity, nor has the decade seen wrenching recession. Although the 1990s began with a recession (reduced economic activity and rising unemployment), the economy has since then experienced a mild but steady recovery, with slow growth and very mild inflation (price increases). Overall, the economy has been on a gradual and continuing upward trend.

Despite the economic growth, economic issues remain. Bill Clinton, in his successful 1992 presidential campaign, placed economic growth, jobs, and investment among his primary concerns. The 1996 campaign also emphasized such issues as taxes, the federal budget, and health care.

The nation has been confronted with a number of intriguing economic problems in the 1990s. The growth in output and jobs has proceeded very slowly. Interest rates have remained at relatively low levels, thus holding out hope for increased consumer and business spending. More spending promises more jobs, higher standards of living, and prosperity. However, the slow growth has not made much of a dent in the unemployment rate. In addition, the federal budget deficit, mired in the range of $150 to $200 billion, has seemed unsolvable. In September 1993, the Clinton administration unveiled a plan to reorganize the increasingly criticized and expensive health care system. But the system's complexities and vested interests have prevented any fundamental reform.

The banking system has gone through an intense period of turmoil. In the late 1980s, hundreds of banks around the country failed; in the 1990s, bank mergers have literally changed the face of the industry.

In the labor force, there were relatively fewer high-paying jobs and more low-wage jobs. Increasingly, families have had to rely on multiple wage earners to make adequate family incomes. Discrimination against women and minorities (though decreasing) continues to rob them of the chance for full economic advancement. As the population and labor force become increasingly diverse, this problem will be an even greater challenge.

On the international scene, the United States moved from being the world's largest creditor to being its largest debtor in the 1980s. The United States continues to face sharp competition in domestic and international markets from other advanced nations and from some of the Newly Industrializing Countries. International debt problems potentially threaten the stability of the international financial system (as well as U.S. banks). Extensive poverty and hunger throughout the world assault our sensitivities and responsibilities. Environmental problems such as the disposal of toxic wastes, deforestation, global warming, and the depletion of the ozone layer require truly global solutions. The post–Cold War period, the dramatic changes sweeping Eastern Europe, and the rise of nationalism in many areas of the world present both challenges and chances for peace, as well as uncertainty about the future.

This list of problems is not all-inclusive, but it is suggestive. It highlights the reality of the U.S. and global economies at the end of the twentieth century. This combination of strengths and weaknesses provides fertile ground for politicians, the media, the public at large, and economists to try to understand what is going on. What accounts for economic successes and failures? How can we address these economic problems and preserve long-run economic growth and stability? How can we utilize the resources at our disposal to respond to human needs? How does one make one's way in this world and find gainful employment?

The recent experiences of the U.S. economy and its historical roots have produced ferment in the field of economics. There are many competing explanations for U.S. successes and failures. Economists even disagree about what to call a problem. Conservative economists have their explanations about what is wrong with the economy and how their policies will correct it. Monetarists chime in with their own theories and suggestions. Keynesian economists focus on the limitations inherent in these approaches and offer their solutions. Further to the left, based on their own assumptions and economic perspectives, other economists argue for industrial policy, public ownership, democratic economic planning, and increased attention to economic equity.

These debates are not sterile. They are a part of the public dialogue in this country—in the media, in political campaigns, in communities—about important problems and what to do about them. An informed position on these issues requires following events, paying attention to the discussion, and developing an understanding of how the economy works. In this context, the study of economics can contribute to our efforts to develop a critical understanding of our society and to work actively toward improving its performance in the future.

This introductory economics textbook is dedicated to promoting that effort. It attempts to develop fundamental economic tools of analysis in clear, simple, and understandable terms. It is designed to encourage the application of those tools to analyzing the most important economic issues facing the country, the world, and its peoples. And it emphasizes the variety of theories and ideas that economists and others have developed to explain U.S. and world economic events. We believe that the approach of this text helps students develop their critical ability to understand and analyze economic problems. It is readable, emphasizes relevant concerns, and does not avoid controversy. It is "user-friendly."

THE FIFTH EDITION

This edition of *Economics: A Tool for Critically Understanding Society* builds on the success of the first four editions, as well as the need to update economics textbooks regularly with current information and changing economic issues. To guide our revisions, we have also relied on feedback from colleagues, students, and faculty who have used the text. Their criticisms, suggestions, and advice have been instructive and helpful.

In the fifth edition, we have tried, in particular, to streamline and consolidate the text. A reorganized Part 1 begins with a chapter on economics as a social science and a new chapter on the emergence of the global economy. A reduced Part 2 focuses on the historical development of the modern economic system and the economic thought that accompanied it. Part 3 remains basically the same, but with increased emphasis on issues of race, gender, the global economy, and the environment. In Part 4, on macroeconomics, we have simplified the presentation of aggregate demand and supply, as well as emphasizing the operation of the macroeconomy in an international context. Part 5 maintains its focus on international trade, finance, development, and systems in transition. Previous editions discussed the future in Part 6; that material has been integrated into other sections of the text.

Economics: A Tool for Critically Understanding Society is still basically a one-semester text, although it may be appropriate for use in some full-year introductory economics courses. The scope of the book is less than that of most full-year texts. It does not try to cover everything. We emphasize the fundamentals of economics and focus on relevant applications of those concepts. In our experience, too much information, too much qualification, and too much supplementary material can get in the way of a solid foundation in the essential and relatively simple concepts. Furthermore, adequate examples from contemporary economic events are reported in the press every day to complement and enrich textbook economics.

Our objective through five editions has been to retain simplicity while at the same time adequately covering the basic micro- and macroeconomic concepts. Consequently, we are convinced (both in theory and in practice) that this text is suitable for use in either one-semester or full-year courses. The Preface to the Instructor contains suggested outlines for one-semester and two-semester courses. Obviously, in a full-year course, there is more time to use supplementary material on issues or themes in modern economics.

Throughout the text, we have continued to supplement the development of basic economic concepts with cartoons and articles. We have reduced the number of reproduced articles based on the conclusion that a multitude of examples is available from following current economic events and requiring (or encouraging) students to read a newspaper. To emphasize the development of critical thinking and the controversial nature of economics, each part of the text ends with a "Thinking Critically" section with different views of important issues. In addition, the chapters contain questions for students to answer as they read through and review the text. This feature is unique to our book, and we feel it provides a strong pedagogical contribution.

ACKNOWLEDGMENTS

Once again numerous staff members at Addison Wesley Longman have been supportive in their assistance, advice, and cooperation in this edition of *Economics: A Tool for Critically Understanding Society*. We appreciate their contributions. We are particularly indebted to Denise Clinton and Sylvia Mallory, our editors, for their encouragement and perseverance. The institutions where we have taught—Bucknell University, the University of Massachusetts/Amherst, and Smith College—have provided support for our work.

Colleagues who offered helpful criticisms and suggestions for improving the text include Dean Baker, Adrienne Birecree, Greg Krohn, John Pool, Charles Sackrey, Geoffrey Schneider, Frank Slavik, and David Wells. For past reviews of the text, we appreciate the work of Teresa Amott, Fikret Ceyhun, Norris Clement, James Cobbe, Robert Drago, Richard B. Hansen, Steve Hickerson, Stewart Long, Tom Maddox, Claron Nelson, Ned C. Pearlstein, Bruce Richard, Philip Schuchman, Larry Simmons, and Dale Warnke. For the fifth edition, we are grateful to Jeffrey Blais, Victor Brajer, E. R. Dietrich, Gary E. Francis, John R. Garrett, John A. Hansen, Bruce Roberts, Geoffrey Schneider, Steven L. Widener, and Michael Zweig for their comments. Over the course of five editions, we have received valuable research and preparation assistance from Brian Brinkman, Bob Brown, Chad Brown, Elizabeth Buchanan, Diane Collins, Beverly Griffith, Tony John, Jenae Johnson, Sharon Killian, Pam Paaso, Christie Rowe, Kaitlin Shepard, Letitia Sloan, Michell Walborn, and Ruth Wynkoop. We would also like to acknowledge the continuing contributions of Alice VanBuskirk, as well as those of Carol MacColl of Paradise Copies, Northampton, Massachusetts.

Dedication—In Memoriam, William Hawley Cooper, 1916–1997

Bill Cooper was our department chair, mentor, and friend. He brought the three of us to Bucknell in the early seventies and proceeded to convene meetings to produce a book of readings for our introductory economics course. Those readings eventually turned into the first edition of this text.

Bill was an innovative and inspirational teacher—with an uncanny ability to provoke students to think for themselves. He was particularly interested in taking students into the community to study and learn about real-life economic issues.

We will miss his wit and his Robin Hood greens. But the lessons we learned from him about teaching, trying to be ethical, and understanding the world remain.

T. R.
Northampton, Massachusetts

J.S., S.S.
Lewisburg, Pennsylvania

PREFACE TO THE INSTRUCTOR

Throughout the past three decades, teachers of introductory economics have expressed a good bit of dissatisfaction with the available textbooks. Not surprisingly, this discontent has led to the continual development of new textbooks for both one-semester and two-semester courses. Many of the new books, but not all, have attempted to cut down on the encyclopedic nature of the prototypical Samuelson text, and many have introduced readings and problems that are up-to-date and relevant to the current population of introductory economics students. This book is in that tradition. It also offers many singular contributions:

- It is intended primarily to be a one-semester book.
- It focuses on a particular set of basic economic concepts.
- It emphasizes active learning by the student.
- It includes different perspectives.
- It places a good bit of responsibility for teaching the course on the instructor.
- It encourages the development of critical thinking.

Many of the textbooks that were popular in the 1950s and 1960s were relatively easy to teach from; the material was all there, it was all relatively straightforward, and it was all familiar to anyone with a graduate degree in economics. Certainly, there was room for classroom innovation and experimentation to make learning economics exciting and lively. But the form and content of the two-semester textbook made it only too easy to lecture on the development of the theory in the text.

However, in the context of the continuing turmoil and confusion of the 1960s and 1970s, many economics teachers became dissatisfied with this approach to introductory economics. They wanted more relevance and applicability of economic concepts. Many were concerned with the lack of balance in the texts—one particular "brand" of economics would be emphasized to the exclusion of others. These teachers wanted their courses to provide more controversy and exposure to different points of view. They wanted less scope and less depth in the development of theory. They wanted to take a more active role in teaching their courses. These kinds of concerns originally inspired us to begin the effort of writing this textbook.

In the 1980s and into the 1990s, with continuing economic difficulties, the resurgence of monetarism, the rise of conservative economics, and expanding economics enrollments, a "countermovement" occurred. Many one-semester courses were replaced by full-year courses. Full-year textbooks proliferated. They strove for comprehensiveness, relevance, applications, and, sometimes, balance. In essence, they mimicked the Samuelson model; they tried to cover every new issue and every new theory and policy, and to do so in depth. They were often accompanied by slick packages with test banks, computer programs, transparency masters, and so forth. More recently, economics enrollments have declined, and the competition in the textbook market has intensified. This revised edition of *Economics: A Tool for Critically Understanding Society* maintains its commitment to focus on some of the most important, essential, and useful economic concepts. It provides up-to-date coverage, but not at the expense of overkill. In fact, this edition is shorter than the previous edition by almost 100 pages!

This text obviously does not cover every possible topic or economic concept that one might want to teach in the ideal introductory course. Nor are the articles and examples we have chosen the ones that everyone would select. The questions for the students as they read through the text might not be the ones that you would choose to emphasize the essence of a particular concept. However, we do think the book will help students to learn and practice economics and the economic way of thinking as they progress through your course. We believe this book leaves room for and, indeed, requires a substantial amount of imagination, work, and dedication on the part of the instructor. You will have to teach economics, and we hope this text will help you in your task.

One of the most important innovations we have made in teaching our courses is to require the students to read a daily newspaper. Because of our location and the College Service it offers, we have used the *New York Times* in this way. The *Wall Street Journal*, the *Christian Science Monitor*, and the *Washington Post Weekly* are also good supplementary resources and are mailed all over the country. Reading the paper helps students use and reinforce economics—to inform themselves, formulate questions in class, discuss controversial events or proposals, and gain insight into real, current examples of economic problems and the light that economics can throw on them. Combining current events and economics can enable students to develop a critical understanding of the world. Using a newspaper allows the instructor to keep the course relevant and up-to-date. It also confronts the results of a 1990 survey that revealed very low rates of newspaper readership by seventeen- to twenty-nine-year-olds in the United States.

We hope this text will encourage you and help you continue to be creative and imaginative in the way you teach introductory economics. It has been a lot of work for us—including many headaches and failed experiments. But then it has also been fun, exciting, and rewarding. Teaching's like that, isn't it?

Suggested One-Semester Course Outline
(Fourteen Weeks)

Part 1	Chapters 1–2	Week 1	
Part 2	Chapters 3–4	Week 2	
	Chapters 5–6	Week 3	
Part 3	Chapters 7–8	Week 4	
	Chapter 9	Week 5	Exam 1
	Chapters 10–11	Week 6	
	Chapters 12–13	Week 7	
Part 4	Chapters 14–15	Week 8	
	Chapter 16	Week 9	
	Chapter 17	Week 10	Exam 2
	Chapters 18–19	Week 11	
Part 5	Chapter 20	Week 12	
	Chapter 21	Week 13	
	Chapters 22–23	Week 14	Final Exam

Suggested One-Semester Micro Course Outline
(Fourteen Weeks)

Part 1	Chapters 1–2	Week 1	
Part 2	Chapters 3–4	Week 2	
	Chapters 5–6	Week 3	
Part 3	Chapter 7	Week 4	
	Chapter 8	Week 5	Exam 1
	Chapter 9	Week 6	
	Chapter 10	Week 7	
	Chapter 11	Week 8	
	Chapter 12	Week 9	
	Chapter 13	Week 10	Exam 2
Part 5	Chapter 20	Week 11	
	Chapter 21	Week 12	
	Chapter 22	Week 13	
	Chapter 23	Week 14	Final Exam

Suggested One-Semester Macro Course Outline
(Fourteen Weeks)

Part 1	Chapters 1–2	Week 1	
Part 2	Chapters 3–6	Week 2	
Part 3	Chapters 7–8	Week 3	
Part 4	Chapter 14	Week 4	
	Chapter 15	Week 5	Exam 1
	Chapter 16	Week 6	
	Chapter 17	Week 7	
	Chapter 18	Week 8	
	Chapter 19	Week 9	Exam 2
	Chapter 20	Week 10	
	Chapter 21	Week 11	
Part 5	Chapter 22	Week 12	
	Chapter 23	Week 13	
	Review	Week 14	Final Exam

PREFACE TO THE STUDENT

ECONOMICS: WHAT'S IN IT FOR YOU?

More than 200 years after the United States became an independent nation, it is one of the most technologically and economically advanced countries in the world. Its complex economic system produces and distributes goods and services daily and provides one of the world's highest standards of living. Yet we are not satisfied, because we, personally and collectively, have many economic problems. Can people find and keep jobs that provide them with the income to support themselves and their families? What are the prospects for improvements in people's economic well-being? Can you find a job that you like? What's more, the United States is not isolated from the rest of the world. Other peoples face similar, as well as different, problems. Inflation, unemployment, energy problems, downsizing, discrimination, deficits, debt, poverty, pollution, resource shortages, underdevelopment in the Third World, and corruption in business and politics are problems that have dominated global headlines in the last third of the twentieth century.

Economics, as one of the social sciences, helps us understand, think, and form opinions about and develop responses to these economic aspects of our social reality. Economics can be a tool that aids us in defining our successes and our failures, as well as in preserving success and correcting failure. It can contribute to our awareness. In an increasingly complex and confusing world, this tool can serve us personally and collectively as we strive to be responsible citizens of our communities, our nation, and our world. This book is dedicated to helping you to acquire that tool.

> We want to make economics as important as baseball and football scores. The minds are out there. It's a question of getting the attention.
>
> —Robert P. Keim, President of the Advertising Council, commenting on a public service campaign to "improve public understanding and awareness of the system," 1975.

> Acting is a business—no more than that—a craft, like plumbing, or being an economist; it's been a good living.
>
> —Marlon Brando, actor, in a television interview with Dick Cavett, 1973.

An inhabitant of cloud-cuckoo land; one knowledgeable in an obsolete art; a harmless academic drudge whose theories and laws are but mere puffs of air in face of the anarchy of banditry, greed, and corruption which holds sway in the pecuniary affairs of the real world.

—A definition of *economist* that won an award from the *New Statesman* in England, 1976.

The questions in this book are not rhetorical. Each is intended to make you pause and think. Try to answer each question as you go along. Or use them to review each chapter after you have finished reading it.

1. Would you like to be an economist? Why or why not?
2. Why are you taking economics?
3. "Economics has [usually] been a countercyclical discipline; it flourishes when the economy founders, and vice versa." Why do you suppose that is so?

OBJECTIVES, OR WHAT WE HAVE DESIGNED THIS BOOK TO ACCOMPLISH

Before you begin your formal study, we would like to share the following list of what we consider the most important objectives of an introduction to modern economics:

- To produce some "cognitive dissonance." By this, we mean that we hope to present you with some ideas, facts, and ways of thinking that are new or different to you. Our hope is that these will challenge you to think, to work a little, and to learn. Is capitalism better than socialism? It might be, but then again, it might not be! We hope to open your mind to thinking about alternatives. What is "investment"? It is *not* simply buying a share of stock in a corporation! Introductory economics may shake up some of your preconceived ideas and beliefs. And it may reorganize them into a *system* of thought.
- To give you perspective on the historical changes in the material conditions, economic institutions, and social relations of human society. The United States has not always been affluent, and capitalism has not always existed.
- To introduce you to a system of economic theories and ideas about the economic institutions of societies—and how those ideas and theories have changed over time. Even the conservative Republican Richard Nixon became a Keynesian in the 1970s. (We will learn more about Keynesian economics in Part 4, but basically it is an economic theory that suggests an important role for the government in guiding the overall economy.) But in the 1980s, Ronald Reagan's economic policies were based on a harsh critique of Keynesian economics; he emphasized the primary importance of business activity as opposed to the government.

Bill Clinton's economic policies in the mid-1990s have relied on an eclectic mixture of market-based, Keynesian theories and monetary policy that emphasized a positive role for government in influencing economic growth. The challenge of Newt Gingrich and the Republican Congress in the mid-1990s over the role of government and taxes and spending was based primarily on conservative thinking.

- To convey to you *some* of the economic theories that economists, or groups of economists, regard as accurate descriptions and predictors of economic activity. For example, how do the two sides of a market, the buyers and sellers, interact to determine prices? We do not intend to give you a survey of all of economics, but to expose you to some of the most basic and useful economic concepts. There is too much of economics to try to do all of it in one semester or even a year; time is *scarce* (that's an economic concept).

- To focus on some contemporary economic issues—inflation, unemployment, growth, resource shortages, international trade, the ecological crisis, poverty and income distribution, multinational corporations, economic growth and development, and others.

- To expose you to the various, and contending, schools of economic thought. Not all economists agree on which theories or even on which problems are the most important. We hope that you will at least appreciate the variety of economic opinion—no matter which, if any, particular set of economic ideas appeals to you.

- To give you practice using economic concepts. We don't want you just to "input" the concepts in your head and "print them out" on tests. We hope that this text gives you opportunities to use economic concepts in solving real-world problems. Our intention is to provide you with case studies that allow you to apply economic concepts, ideas, and theories so that you may come to better understand the world you live in (and perhaps to change it!). We enthusiastically recommend that you read a daily newspaper. Regularly reading the newspaper will provide numerous real-world examples of economic problems (to integrate theory and reality). And applying economic concepts will help you understand them and figure out their implications. We may even be able to suggest solutions to some of these problems. How would you eliminate poverty?

CALVIN AND HOBBES © 1992 Watterson. Dist. by UNIVERSAL PRESS SYNDICATE. Reprinted with permission. All rights reserved.

PREFACE TO THE STUDENT

- To give you a foundation in economic "literacy." You should be able to interpret some of the jargon of professional economists. You should also be able to identify the variables, ramifications, and possible explanations of and solutions to a variety of economic problems. We hope you develop a facility to evaluate economic ideas critically.
- To demystify economics so that you do not feel that the economy and its problems are too complex to understand and solve. Economics and economic policy ought not to be left only to the economists.
- To provide a foundation for future and continued learning. The world is complex. But economics will assist you in thinking critically and independently about our world. It can be one more tool that allows (and encourages) you to assume a creative stance in your community, your society, and your world.

Our hope is that we can excite you about economics, and that the insights you develop will make useful and creative contributions to your pursuit of a rich and meaningful life.

4. Are there any objectives we have missed? What are they? Do these objectives make sense to you? Why? Why not? In what ways are these objectives consistent with (different from) what you expected from introductory economics?

ECONOMICS AS A TOOL FOR CRITICAL THINKING IN A CHANGING GLOBAL ECONOMY

Will capitalism survive? How did the United States come to have a capitalist economic system? In the near future, how will the U.S. economy change? Will it retain world economic leadership? Or will it lag behind the rapid advance of Japan and Western Europe? With the collapse of the Soviet Union, will socialism survive? Will Eastern European economies become more like Western capitalism? Or will they retain some socialist goals while relying more heavily on markets? What will happen to economic reform in China—especially with the integration of Hong Kong?

Why does the United States have such an advanced economy? Yet, in the midst of relative affluence, why is there unemployment and poverty? Is there a reason that a black person is more likely than a white person to be poor and unemployed? Why do women earn, on the average, about 70 percent of what men earn? In the post–Cold War era, why does the United States devote almost $300 billion annually to military spending? How does the United States produce so much food when less than 5 percent of the population is involved in food production?

Can global hunger and starvation be eliminated? Are the threats of environmental degradation—global warming, the depletion of the ozone layer, deforestation, and the buildup of toxic wastes—irreversible? Will there be another energy crisis?

Will *you* be employed? Rich? Poor?

These are all predominantly economic questions that affect each and every one of us in our day-to-day lives—either directly or indirectly. We read about these problems in the newspapers, we hear about them on the radio and the television, politicians talk about them, and we discuss them with our friends and neighbors. They are important and interesting. We have opinions about them—and answers to some or all of them.

Economics is essentially an organized body of knowledge about all of these issues, some of which are current and some of which are perpetual. It seeks to understand and explain these problems and to assist us in solving them. It helps us to think about these problems by indicating important variables and relationships. We hope that, in this course, you will learn to use economics to consider the problems that interest and affect you.

1

Economics as a Social Science

INTRODUCTION

What is economics? And what can it do for us?

Economics is the study of how the productive and distributive aspects of human life are organized. The productive aspects include the activities that result in the goods and services that satisfy our day-to-day demands as human beings—for automobiles, cereal, clothes, movies, etc. The distributive aspects are the ways a society makes these goods and services available to people in the society who are willing to pay for them. Economics studies the history of production, distribution, and consumption of goods and services in different societies and countries, including the ways these aspects have changed over time. It seeks to help us understand the complexities of economic systems in the modern world.

Economics, as a social science, is thus an accumulation of human knowledge about one particular segment of social life: production, distribution, and consumption. Like the other social sciences, including geography, political science, psychology, and sociology, economics focuses on only one part of a rich and complex social reality.

DEFINITIONS IN THIS BOOK

Key economic concepts are indicated in the text by **bold type**. In addition, a glossary at the end of the text defines these important terms.

In this chapter, we examine economics as a social science. We will be concerned with its goals and methods, as well as its relevance to our lives. In addition, we will introduce briefly the different branches of economics and the kinds of things that economists do. Finally, we will see that economists have some disagreements about what economics is and ought to be.

WHAT IS ECONOMICS?

In recent years, teachers of economics have become concerned about how best to teach economics. Their concern stems from the importance of economic knowledge in the modern world and the difficulties of teaching that knowledge to students in a way that will prove useful to them. Out of this concern, many economists have attempted to define precisely what the key elements of economic understanding are and to concentrate on teaching these. A reasonable list of key elements of economic understanding would include the following:

- Practicing a reasoned approach to economic issues
- Mastering the basic economic concepts
- Possessing an overview of the economy
- Identifying important economic issues
- Applying the concepts to particular issues
- Reaching reasoned decisions on economic issues

These elements provide some insights into the nature of economics as the study of the productive and distributive aspects of human life. Economic understanding encompasses both a body of knowledge and a way of thinking about the economic aspects of social life. It is concerned with practicing a reasoned approach; that is, economics presents an organized and logical way of thinking about economic reality. It uses many basic concepts that focus our attention on key variables in economic activity. It provides us with an overall appreciation of the structure and complexity of the economic system in this country, as well as those in others and the global economy. It should help us identify the issues that will be important to us in our individual and social lives. In addition, economics helps us to reason and to draw conclusions about specific economic problems, their ramifications, and possible solutions.

In attempting to accomplish all of these tasks, one of the central concerns of economics is the development of **economic theory**. This task relates to the *method* of economics. While economics is concerned with social life and the vagaries of human beings, the development of theory requires that economics be as scientific as possible. An economic theory, for example, would try to explain why the prices of agricultural goods change from year to year, as well as to predict how prices might change in the future.

Economists attempt to measure and collect facts about economic activity. In doing so, they try to discover certain patterns in the relationships between different components of economic life. When the facts suggest that these patterns express a constant relationship (in normal circumstances), economists may use them as the basis for economic theories. An example of such a theory is the theory of supply and demand. This theory emerged out of observations of the behavior of prices of goods in markets and how the prices changed over time. The theories developed from efforts to explain these changes. We can use this economic theory to gain insight into how goods and services are valued by society's members, how costly they are to produce, and what price they will sell for in the society, given different circumstances.

The function of economic theory, therefore, is to allow us to examine certain aspects of economic life, discover more or less constant relationships between different economic variables, and predict possible economic events. For example, the theory of supply and demand tells us that, most of the time, a desired article in short supply will command a relatively high price. From this, we can conclude (theorize) that if the supply of that article is reduced, then its price is likely to go up even further.

Note that such statements are based on an **assumption**—an *if* statement— followed by a conditional conclusion. Economists love to make assumptions. Much of their theory is based on similar assumptions. In the final analysis, however, their theories must be judged by whether their conclusions and predictions conform with what actually happens in economic reality. In the case of supply-and-demand theory, frequent examples enable us to check the validity of the conclusions and predictions of this economic theory.

For example, in 1973, when the Middle Eastern oil-producing countries embargoed shipments of oil to the United States, Western Europe, and Japan, the supply of oil decreased, and the price *did* increase. Likewise, when there are good crops of wheat in the United States, the price of wheat is likely to go down; when crops are bad because of the weather, the price of wheat goes up. Extensive flooding in the Midwest in the early 1990s hampered farmers' ability to grow corn and led to sharply higher corn prices. Whenever a freeze occurs in Florida, it sharply reduces the supply of Florida oranges, and this is followed by an increase in the price of oranges. In the late 1980s, as a result of overexpansion in the industry, the price of personal computers decreased. In the mid-1990s, a paper shortage led to increased prices for newspapers, magazines, and photocopying. In each of these cases, economic reality conforms with economic theory.

These examples highlight the *relevance* of economics. Economics and economic theories are concerned with problems and activities that are important to all of us as individuals and to our societies. The scope of economics can be international, national, regional, local, or personal. The problems and activities that are the subject matter of economics include such pressing concerns as inflation, productivity, supplies of natural resources, efficiency, debt, unemployment, technological development, product distribution, advertising, poverty, alienation, the allocation of scarce resources, income redistribution, taxation, war, and a host of others. Economics identifies such economic problems, describes their ramifications, hypothesizes about their causes, predicts their future development, and prescribes solutions to them. In so doing, economics can build our understanding of the fundamental economic aspects of our social lives.

ONE METHOD FOR ECONOMIC THEORY

Milton Friedman, a Nobel Prize winner in economics, has argued for a particular method in the construction of economic theory. This methodology, which he calls "positive economics," has four basic components:

1. The process begins with a set of reasonable *assumptions* about some aspect of economic behavior. For example, in Part 3, one of the most important assumptions that we will make is that the primary objective of firms is the maximization of profits.
2. Next, we try to identify some important economic *concepts* and construct some variables to measure them. For the firm, we will measure profits, costs, revenues, marginal costs, marginal revenues, and other variables. These are all functions of the economic activity of the firm.
3. Based on the assumptions we have made and the concepts we have identified, we develop some *hypotheses* and logical deductions about economic behavior. In the case of the firm, we theorize that the firm maximizes profits at a rate of output where its marginal costs equal its marginal revenues. In Part 3, we will demonstrate this in more detail.
4. The final step is to *test the theory*. Does the hypothesis conform with observable events? When marginal costs do not equal marginal revenues, does the firm alter its decisions so that it can increase its profits?

Friedman emphasizes that this method produces abstract economic theory; it simplifies and generalizes. The purpose, however, is to create a model of the economy that will help us evaluate and analyze the real-world economy. A model is an abstraction, or simplification, of the economy, not an exact replica of it.

Economics and Economists

There are many branches of economics, some of which will be introduced in this book. Economic history reviewed briefly in Chapter 3 focuses on how and why economic activity has changed over time. Urban economics focuses on analyzing the economic operation and problems of cities. Microeconomics is concerned primarily with the activities of smaller economic units, such as the household or the firm, and markets for goods and services. Macroeconomics has the much broader subject of the operation and health of an entire national economy. International economics deals with economic relationships and activities on a global scale. Economic thought treats the development of ideas by economists through the years. Economic development concentrates on theories and problems associated with the economic growth and maturation of national economies. Public policy economics is concerned with the analysis of proposals for dealing with public problems. Political economy highlights the relationships between economic and political institutions and how they affect each other. This by no means exhausts the list of the different branches of economics.

Given this wide variety of branches of economics, economists do many different things. Many people trained in economics as a discipline become teachers of economics in high schools, colleges, or universities. Many work in businesses, informing decision makers on current and future economic realities. Since World War II, an increasing number of economists have found employment in government at the local, state, and federal levels. Economists also work for consulting firms, labor unions, public interest or lobbying groups, and international organizations.

With this diversity of employment experiences (and hence allegiances and perspectives), it should not be very surprising to find a healthy amount of "confusion" within the social science of economics. Economists, despite their efforts to build economic theory, often disagree with one another. They may differ about which problems are most important (or even, sometimes, that there are problems!), what the causes of a problem are, and which solutions to a problem are the best. Controversy in economics reflects controversy in life.

Nevertheless, most economists accept a large core of economic ideas. We will study many of these ideas in this book. In addition, economists are uni-

WHAT IS ECONOMICS?

fied by the goal of economics: building knowledge about the economic aspects of life.

Much of the debate among economists about what economics is and should be concerns its scope. The famous English economist Alfred Marshall (1842–1924) thought economics could be one of the most precise and scientific of the social sciences because it deals with observable and measurable data in the form of prices, quantities produced and sold, and incomes. In his *Principles of Economics*, he wrote:

> The advantage which economics has over other branches of social science appears then to arise from the fact that its special field of work gives rather larger opportunities for exact methods than any other branch. It concerns itself chiefly with those desires, aspirations and other affections of human nature, the outward manifestations of which appear as incentives to action in such a form that the force or quantity of the incentives can be estimated and measured with some approach to accuracy; and which therefore are in some degree amenable to treatment by scientific machinery. An opening is made for the methods and the tests of science as soon as the force of a person's motives—*not* the motives themselves—can be approximately measured by the sum of money, which he will just give up in order to secure a desired satisfaction; or again by the sum which is just required to induce him to undergo a certain fatigue.
>
> —Alfred Marshall, *Principles of Economics*
> (Macmillan Publishing Co., Inc., 1948).

Other economists, however, have been less convinced by this argument. They point out that economics, as one of the social sciences, cannot divorce itself from the society in which it exists. The efforts of human beings to understand reality must necessarily be influenced by morality, ideology, and value judgments. In other words, economics cannot be totally scientific because the economist's understanding of the subject matter is affected by his or her evaluation of, opinions about, and conclusions concerning social reality. Economics as a body of thought functions to preserve, protect, and/or challenge existing social reality—as well as help us to understand it. For some economists, then, economics should be a part of the effort to understand *and to improve* social existence. Joan Robinson (1903–1983), another English economist, wrote in *Freedom and Necessity*:

> The methods to which the natural sciences owe their success—controlled experiment and exact observation of continually recurring phenomena—cannot be applied to the study of human beings by human beings. So far, no equally successful method of establishing reliable natural laws has been suggested. Certainly, the social sciences should not be unscientific. Their practitioners should not jump to conclusions on inadequate evidence or propound circular statements that are true by definition as though they had some factual content; when they disagree they should not resort to abuse like theologians or literary critics, but should calmly set about to investigate the nature of the difference and to propose a plan of research to resolve it. . . . The function of social science is quite different from that of the natural sciences—it is to provide society with an organ of self-consciousness. Every interconnected group of human beings has to have an ideology—that is, a

Chapter 1 ECONOMICS AS A SOCIAL SCIENCE

conception of what is the proper way to behave and the permissible pattern of relationships in family, economic, and political life.

—Joan Robinson, *Freedom and Necessity* (Pantheon Books, 1970).

For Robinson, then, economics must attempt to be scientific and rigorous, but since it is also concerned with the effort to create a better society, it must also devote itself to exploring areas that are more philosophical. It must recognize its ideological elements, and that, as one of the social sciences, it is also involved as a tool of analysis in the formation of public policy.

Along these lines, economists often divide their discipline between "economics" and what is called "**political economy**." Economics in this sense is more concerned with explaining what can be measured and with developing theories about "purely" economic relationships. Political economy, on the other hand, is more concerned with the relationships of the economic system and its institutions to the rest of society and social development. It is sensitive to the influence of noneconomic factors such as political and social institutions, morality, and ideology in determining economic events. It thus has a broader focus than economics.

1. "The function of social science . . . is to provide society with an organ of self-consciousness." What does this mean? How does economics do this?
2. What, according to Robinson, is an ideology? What role do ideologies play in social development?
3. What does Robinson think is the task of economics as a social science? Do you agree with her or not? Would Alfred Marshall?

PARADIGMS AND IDEOLOGIES

Not only do economists disagree about what economics is and should be, they often disagree about what economic problems are important, what theories are correct, and what economic policies are best. This is especially true over time, as the economic problems a society is likely to face change with changing conditions. Along with changes in economic problems and economic institutions, economic theories have also changed. The changes in economic theory and the differences among economists have two results that are useful to keep in mind while studying economics: First, there are different and sometimes contesting kinds of economic theory. Second, there are different kinds of economists with different goals, values, and beliefs.

The Realm of Theory

Different periods of economic history (and different economic systems) have given rise to different types of economic theories. New types of economic conditions and economic institutions have required different systems of thought and explanation. Stated slightly differently, as crises have developed in economic matters when the old gave way to the new, economic institutions changed. The previous theories and notions became inadequate to explain the new conditions and problems, so economic thought also changed.

Thomas Kuhn, in *The Structure of Scientific Revolutions*, refers to such changes in scientific theory as changes in **paradigms**. A paradigm structures thought about a certain aspect of nature, life, or society. It delineates the scope of a discipline (the questions to be asked about a certain subject and the phenomena to be explained), as well as the method of the discipline (the criteria for accepting explanations).

Paradigms are usually widely accepted as providing a coherent and correct understanding of some aspect of life. However, as time passes, natural and social conditions may change, and new interpretations and new facts may become known. If so, the existing paradigm may be challenged or may be inadequate to explain reality, and a new and more widely accepted paradigm will eventually be developed. An example of this in the field of astronomy was the replacement of the Ptolemaic by the Copernican paradigm. The Copernican paradigm is now widely accepted, because it conforms with what we now know and observe—that the planets revolve around the sun. Another example is the explorer Christopher Columbus, who was sure (along with others) that the earth wasn't flat!

Likewise, as economic crises occur and economic conditions change, one economic paradigm replaces another. Before the Great Depression of the 1930s, the dominant economic theory was classical economics, which argued that a laissez-faire, self-regulating market economic system would eliminate economic instability through the flexibility of markets. If overproduction of goods led to a decrease in production and an increase in unemployment, then the markets would respond to correct the situation. Prices would fall and stimulate consumption of those goods, thus eliminating the surplus. Wages would fall and stimulate the hiring of unemployed workers. To explain why overproduction or underconsumption would be unlikely in a laissez-faire market economic system, classical economics relied on Say's law, developed by the French economist J. B. Say (1767–1832), which held that supply creates its own demand. Say theorized that incomes paid out in the process of production would always be sufficient to buy what was produced. The flexibility of prices and wages in self-regulating markets would ensure this result. However, when economists observed the severity and persistence of the Great Depression, they questioned Say's law. Consequently, they turned to a new paradigm, Keynesian economics (about which we will learn more in Part 4), which offered an explanation for why depressions occur and what can be done about them.

Not only do paradigms change over time, two contending paradigms sometimes seek to explain the same aspect of reality. Examining the same events and facts but differing in the use of key concepts and relationships, these contending paradigms offer conflicting (or at least differing) interpretations. At one time or another, or in different places, one or the other might be dominant.

An example of conflicting paradigms is the contrast between orthodox economics and Marxian economics. **Orthodox economics** accepts the institutional setting of the economy and builds a theory around how it works. **Marxian economics** assumes a critical stance toward the existing economic system and attempts to discover how it will and can be changed. Orthodox economics accepts capitalism, and Marxian economics criticizes capitalism and argues for socialism. A third paradigm, **institutional economics**, bridges Marxian and orthodox economics. It focuses on the role of changing institutions and power in influencing economic affairs.

Another example of conflicting paradigms occurs within orthodox economics between the Keynesian and monetarist approaches. The Keynesian view contends that it is most important to focus on the aggregate demand for goods and services to understand economic events. The monetarist view rejects this approach and argues that only through monetary changes can we understand the economy. Throughout this book, we will encounter these different paradigms as they attempt to explain economic reality.

The Realm of the Economist

Economists are human beings with differing ideas, theories, assumptions, and ideologies. As economic conditions and institutions have changed, so have economists' ideas, theories, assumptions, and ideologies. In different times and spaces, economists have differed. And in the *same* time and space, economists disagree. One way of clarifying this is to examine **ideology**. E. K. Hunt, in *Property and Prophets*, defines an ideology this way:

> [A set of] ideas and beliefs that tend to justify morally a society's social and economic relationships. Most members of a society internalize the ideology and thus believe that their functional roles, as well as those of others, are morally correct, and that the method by which society divides its produce is fair. This common belief gives society its cohesiveness and vitality. Lack of it creates turmoil and strife—and ultimately revolution if the differences are deep enough.

At different times, different ideologies may dominate. At one time, Confucianism was the ideology of China. Later, the dominant ideology in China was that of Maoism and socialism. Catholicism and a concern with the next world once dominated Western Europe; later, individualism and materialism held sway.

Ideologies influence the development of theory. For example, the ideology of individualism promoted the development of the economic theory of classical liberalism, and both accompanied the emergence of capitalism as an economic system. More recently, the combination of the ideologies of liberal democracy, the benevolent state, and individualism have promoted the acceptance of Keynesian economics along with the emergence of welfare or state capitalism. In the 1990s, with a large government presence in the economy and persistent budget deficits, some economists (and politicians) with a conservative ideology have argued for increased reliance on market forces and a significant reduction in government spending.

Different ideologies concerning the goals of a society and an economic system may conflict. For example, differences in ideology underlie the division of Western economists today into three broad groups: liberal, conservative, and radical. Each group has its own ideas, theories, and ideologies. These are described in the next section.

4. What is your ideology?
5. Compare and contrast Hunt's definition of ideology with that of Joan Robinson.

CONSERVATIVE, LIBERAL, AND RADICAL ECONOMICS

Adam Smith, in his day, was a radical. Karl Marx was a radical. John Maynard Keynes offered a liberal solution to the 1930s crisis of capitalism. Newt Gingrich (R., Georgia), Speaker of the House of Representatives and author of *Contract with America*, is a contemporary conservative.

What are some of the essential elements of conservative, liberal, and radical ideologies and theories? What are the differences among them? How do they interpret different economic issues, and what different solutions do they offer for economic problems?

Conservative economists focus on the operation of markets in a capitalist, free-market economic system. They argue that private ownership of resources under capitalism assures economic and political freedom for individuals in that society. Individuals make their own decisions for their own private gains. Markets, where goods and services are exchanged, will then operate to produce economic well-being and growth for the society and the individuals within it. Markets, through the action of competition, enforce a result that is the best for everyone and uses resources efficiently. Consequently, conservatives see the profit motive as being one of the most important and positive aspects of capitalism. Firms, to meet their own interests in competitive markets, must produce exactly what consumers want at the lowest price. One further implication of conservative economics is that, since markets operate efficiently and produce economic growth, the government need not take an active role in the operation of the economy (beyond some important, fundamental obligations—see Chapter 13). In fact, most conservatives argue that excessive government intervention in the economy is the source of many of our economic problems.

The roots of conservative economics can be found in eighteenth-century classical liberalism. Beginning in Chapter 3, we will encounter the emergence of this body of thought and explore this theory in more detail. Modern examples of conservative economics include "free-market" economics, supply-side economics, and monetarism. Conservative economists include Milton Friedman, author of *Capitalism and Freedom* and a Nobel Prize winner; Alan Greenspan, chairman of the Federal Reserve System; and

Senator Phil Gramm (R., Texas), who used to be an economics professor. Ronald Reagan, George Bush, Newt Gingrich, and Robert Dole are obvious examples of politicians who believe in the ideas and the theories of conservative economics. Much of the advertising and educational efforts of corporate America utilize the logic and conclusions of conservative economics. *The Wall Street Journal* takes a consistently conservative position in its editorials.

Liberal economists accept the structure of the capitalist economic system and its basic institutions of private property and markets. They also agree with conservatives that, for the most part, this free-market system tends to produce efficiency and economic growth and that it protects individual freedom. However, they admit that the operation of the market system inherently tends to produce a number of problems. For example, it fosters an unequal distribution of income and economic power, often neglects some of the by-products of economic production and exchange such as pollution, sometimes fails to provide necessary goods and services that can't be produced profitably, and can't guarantee economic stability. Liberals then usually point out that there is a solution to these problems that does not interfere with the basic structure of the economic system; they give the responsibility for addressing these problems to the government. The federal government, in particular, can attempt to redistribute income through its taxation and spending system, and it can attempt to regulate the production of pollution in the economy. All levels of government can provide "public" goods such as parks, roads, schools, and police and fire protection. Finally, the federal government can take responsibility for trying to achieve economic prosperity and price stability and to avoid economic depressions. For liberals, the market works economic wonders, but they are qualified wonders; the active involvement of governments in the economy can improve its performance.

The theoretical underpinnings of most liberal economists can be found in Keynesian economics. Some liberals also find the ideas of Thorstein Veblen and other institutionalist economists to be helpful in framing their understanding of the economy. We will encounter these theories again in Parts 2 and 4. John Kenneth Galbraith of Harvard University has written a number of important books about economics and the economy from a Keynesian and institutionalist perspective. Lester Thurow, who teaches at the Massachusetts Institute of Technology, is another liberal economist and the author of *The Zero-Sum Society* and *The Future of Capitalism*. Jimmy Carter, Walter Mondale, Michael Dukakis, and Bill Clinton are politicians who utilize the ideas and the theories of liberal economics. *Business Week* magazine usually presents a relatively liberal editorial policy.

Radical economists tend to be very critical of the structures, institutions, operation, and results of capitalist economic systems. They do not deny that capitalism has been quite successful over the past several centuries in increasing the productive capacity of Western nations and the average standard of living for their inhabitants. However, radical economists suggest that the very operation of a market system based on private ownership creates different classes of people in capitalist societies. On the one hand are those who own productive resources, organize and control productive activity, and have

■ Lower East Side of Manhattan, New York. *(Michael J. Folsol/SuperStock, Inc.)*

the goal of earning profits for themselves. On the other hand are people who do not own any productive property and who rely on the sale of their mental and/or physical labor to earn a living. Radicals are quick to point out that there are inherent conflicts between these two groups over wages, working conditions, product safety, and economic power. It is this basic class structure of the society, radicals argue, that produces economic inequality, exploitation, and alienation. In addition, they conclude that capitalist production and growth are inherently unable to provide for public goods, ignore the social costs of productive activity, and lead to economic instability. Consequently, the efforts of the state (all levels of government) to deal with these problems are merely Band-Aid solutions because they do not address the root causes—private ownership, production for profit, and a class society.

In the view of radical economists, solving modern economic problems such as poverty, income inequality, discrimination, and pollution requires alterations in the basic economic institutions of the society. Many radicals believe in nationalization, and many want to limit the existing power of corporations. Many would advocate much more significant redistribution of income in the United States (and the world). Some even call for social ownership and control of productive resources in pursuit of social goals of production.

Radical economics finds its roots in both institutional and Marxian economics. Although many radicals find the ideas of both Keynesian and conservative economics useful in understanding how capitalism and markets work, radicals depart in their evaluation of the operation and results of capitalism. For them, the negative aspects outweigh the positive. Samuel Bowles, (the late) David Gordon, and Thomas Weisskopf are radical economists who have written *Beyond the Wasteland: A Democratic Alternative to Economic Decline.* This book contains their analysis of recent U.S. economic experience and presents a radical economic program for restructuring the economy and addressing many of its long-run and more recent problems. Barry Bluestone and Bennett Harrison, authors of *The Deindustrialization of America,* have focused on the problem of plant closings and runaway shops from a radical perspective and have offered some solutions. *Mother Jones, Z, The Nation,* and *Dollars & Sense* are examples of periodicals that contain a radical point of view. Many of the ideas about economic priorities and policy articulated by Jesse Jackson in his presidential campaigns—for instance, increased income redistribution, significantly reduced military spending, and the promotion of full employment—are compatible with radical economics. The recently organized New Party has a radical platform.

Conservatives, Liberals, and Radicals on Poverty

From these brief descriptions of conservative, liberal, and radical economics, it should be possible to identify the basic approach that each would take to understanding a particular economic problem and suggesting solutions for it. But let's develop a single example: poverty. Conservatives tend to argue that poverty exists because of the particular attributes of individuals and their inability to earn high incomes in labor markets. Either they have the wrong skills or few skills, or they don't try or work hard enough. The solution, then, is either "It's appropriate that their economic rewards are low," or "They need to develop their marketable skills." If the society decides that it wants to facilitate the reduction of poverty, the most appropriate way might be through education. Individuals have to develop skills and work harder.

Liberals maintain that, very often, the poverty of individuals is a result of circumstances beyond their control. Consequently, not only would they support a public role for education (and job training) to increase people's marketable skills, but, in addition, they would favor direct income redistribution to increase the purchasing power of poor people. This would reduce the burdens of poverty, but it also might create the chance for people to move out of poverty. Liberals would support food stamps and welfare for the poor. Conservatives tend not to support these programs because they represent government interference with markets, and conservatives think that poverty can be reduced effectively only by the participation of responsible individuals in free markets.

Radicals generally would support governmental redistribution programs and certainly would oppose efforts to take economic benefits away from poor people. However, they would argue that redistribution programs have a very limited effect in eliminating poverty. Governmental programs have reduced poverty, but given the source of unequal incomes in private ownership of productive resources and the fundamental individualism of capitalism, the system cannot tolerate the amount of redistribution that would be necessary to eliminate poverty. Only massive redistribution of income to poor people or a radical restructuring of the institutions and goals of the economic system could significantly reduce the incidence of poverty in the United States.

The analyses of current economic problems are distinctive based on different ideologies and theories. And these differences are reflected in the variety of proposed solutions. One of the fascinating aspects of modern economics is the controversy that rages over our understanding of and efforts to deal with these problems. Conservative, liberal, and radical economics have all contributed to that process.

6. Which set of economic ideas do you think is dominant in the United States today?
7. Paul Sweezy, a U.S. Marxian economist, has written, "It seems to me that from a scientific point of view the question of choosing between approaches can be answered quite simply. Which more accurately reflects the fundamental characteristics of social reality which is under analysis?" Critically evaluate each of the different perspectives with respect to that statement. How are your answers affected by your own beliefs?
8. What is the difference between theory and ideology?

 CONCLUSION

There are many different branches of economics, the social science that focuses on building an understanding of how the economy—production, distribution, and consumption of goods of services—works. Economists do many different things, not the least of which is disagree with each other while at the same time working together to build economic theory. One observation that they would probably all agree on is the tremendous growth in an emerging global economy, to which we turn in the next chapter.

Review Questions

1. What is economics? Is that what you thought economics is (or should be)?
2. What is the goal of economic theory? What is the test of an economic theory?
3. Why do economists disagree?
4. What is a paradigm? In your life have you ever replaced one paradigm with another?
5. What are the main differences among conservative, liberal, and radical economists?
6. Paradigms can offer contending explanations of the same reality. Sometimes the contention can reflect intense political, social, and economic struggles. Develop some examples of new paradigms for which the people suggesting them have been subjected to neglect, harassment, ridicule, or even punishment.

2

Exploring the Emerging Global Economy

INTRODUCTION

Although we have come to take it for granted, virtually everything we do is directly or indirectly involved with the international economy. To understand how this affects your life, just look around. Take five minutes and list things that surround you in your room—shoes, clothes, stereo, furniture, radio, TV, VCR, lamps.

> 1. Where were the items in your room made? What about the coffee, tea, juice, or fruit you had for breakfast? How about lunch and dinner? Did you ride a bike or drive a car powered by petroleum today? Where do you work? Your parents? How much of this work is dependent on the foreign sector? Do you or your parents have investments or a pension fund with investments in international funds? Where do those funds originate? Now, make a list of all of the countries that are a part of your daily life. Impressive, isn't it?

Even a quick listing likely shows how truly interdependent the global economy has become. This trend is expected to accelerate in the coming years. As we will see throughout this book, the process of technological change and innovation is bringing the world closer and closer together every day.

This chapter will introduce a few fundamental concepts and explore the dynamics of the global economy, which we will develop in greater detail in later chapters. Without these concepts and this perspective, it would be hard to understand much of your daily life. Indeed, the changes taking place right now are creating a new global economy that will determine not only how you live, but also the kind of work you will be doing after you graduate. Most experts suggest that you will have not one but several distinct careers in the future, each largely shaped by the new global economy.

The chapter also explores some forces that have shaped the global economy. The global economy emerged in the post–World War II period, from 1944 to the mid-1970s, but it has undergone a fundamental transformation since then. Much of this change has been driven by technological developments. Technological advances have altered industries and careers, generating new jobs and making others obsolete. At the same time, growing resource use has created tensions between policymakers, producers, and environmentalists.

GLOBALIZATION: MAKING A BIG WORLD SMALLER

If you are a college student between the ages of eighteen and twenty-five, the world has changed significantly since you were born. The decade of the 1980s brought transitions in the political, economic, technological, and environmental arenas. Some of these changes continue to reshape our work and nonwork life, much as the early Industrial Revolution did during the mid-1800s. This revolution is fueling increased globalization.

Globalization has made a big world smaller. Globalization affects trade, finance, production, communications, and technological change. When we look at a world map (see Figure 2.1), we need to think about how this global community of people and nations is being systematically drawn closer together. At Distributed Service Systems, a small full-service computer company located in Reading, Pennsylvania, a technical consultant sits at a terminal and solves assembly line production problems at Carpenter Technology steel plants in India, China, Mexico, or Taiwan. At the same time, a major

■ FIGURE 2.1 The world

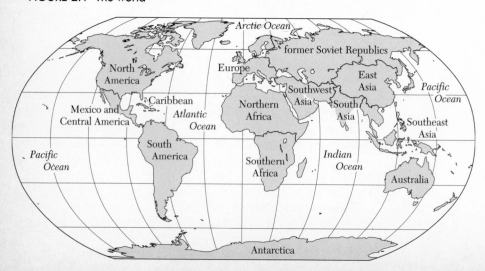

Chapter 2 EXPLORING THE EMERGING GLOBAL ECONOMY

U.S. global manufacturer in Green Bay, Wisconsin, has a small staff of foreign currency traders working twenty-four hours a day to manage the firm's global financial needs and resources.

Since 1980, world **exports** (goods leaving a country) have increased 167 percent, and U.S. **imports** (goods coming into the country) have tripled. In 1960, total U.S. trade equaled 9 percent of **gross domestic product (GDP)**, which is the annual output of goods and services; in the 1990s, it amounted to almost 23 percent. Twelve million U.S. workers' jobs are tied to exports, and global sales figure prominently in firms' production, investment, and hiring decisions. Nations have found it cheaper and more efficient to trade more with each other than to produce all their products at home.

In 1995, the global economy grew by an estimated 3.7 percent from the previous year's level. This robust year of growth was led by developing countries, whose output of goods and services expanded by 6 percent, more than double the 2.5 percent growth registered by the industrial countries. By 1995, world exports reached $4.5 trillion, compared to just over $2.0 trillion in 1980 and $1.3 trillion in 1970. The gross world product in 1995 reached a record level of $21 trillion, up from $10 trillion in 1970 and $15 trillion in 1980. In 1995, the industrialized countries of the United States, Germany, Japan, France, Italy, and the United Kingdom led the world in terms of gross domestic product, exports, and imports.

Another sign of growth is the increase in the annual average percentage growth of the gross domestic product over the period 1980–1995 for countries in Asia and South Asia compared to the twenty-two industrial countries (in Europe, North America, and Japan) that are members of the Organization for Economic Cooperation and Development (OECD). As shown in Figure 2.2,

■ FIGURE 2.2 GDP growth: Asian nations vs. OECD industrial nations

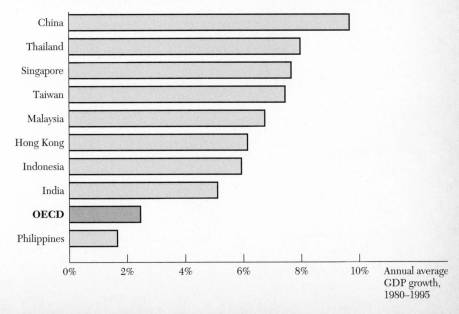

Annual average GDP growth, 1980–1995

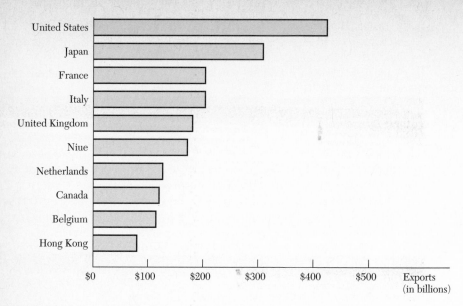

FIGURE 2.3 The global economy's biggest players: (a) 10 largest exporters

the OECD countries' cumulative GDP growth was 2.5 percent, while China's growth averaged 9.9 percent, and the rest of the countries (except for the Philippines) ranged between 5 and 8 percent. With respect to population, China and India led the world with 1.2 billion and 800 million respectively. (See Figure 2.3 for information on the largest national economies.)

FIGURE 2.3 The global economy's biggest players: (b) 10 largest importers

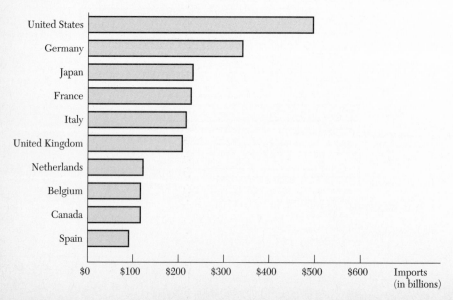

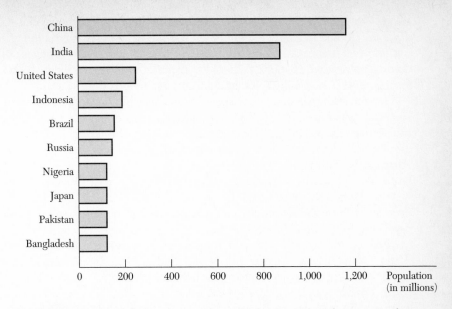

■ FIGURE 2.3 The global economy's biggest players: (c) 10 largest populations

New players have clearly emerged on the international scene. In 1970 only 29 percent of exports went to developing countries; by 1995 the figure reached 41 percent. You might be surprised to note that Brazil is the ninth largest economy, measured by gross domestic product, in the world. Do you

■ FIGURE 2.3 The global economy's biggest players: (d) 10 largest gross domestic products

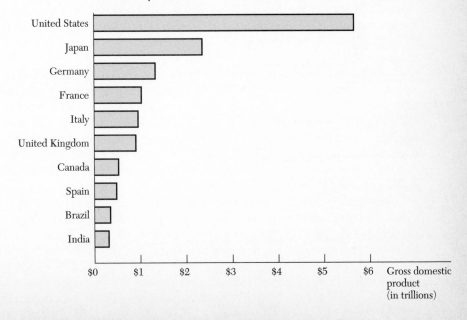

speak Portuguese, or Japanese or German? While international business is often conducted in English, understanding important differences in language and culture means knowing something about a variety of regions. Given demographic and economic changes, these countries are likely to remain strong sources of product demand and investment in the future.

Finance and investment have gone global as well. To finance trade among so many different nations, a foreign exchange market has emerged with daily transactions of over $1.2 trillion. But currency is not the only financial instrument traded internationally. The hot picks of Wall Street in the 1990s included stock in companies from the emerging market economies. During the late 1980s, global flows of foreign direct investment rose 29 percent annually—approximately three times the growth in world trade. Global expansion is driven partly by the search for new markets, but also by diversifying risk and searching for profits all over the world. By one estimate, roughly 40 percent of revenues of large investment houses are now made outside the United States. Big firms can borrow money in London or in Tokyo as easily as they can in New York. Electronic banking lets companies shift money from country to country with unprecedented ease. It also lets you withdraw money from a bank machine in Buenos Aires or Santiago with the same bank card used at your local bank. In Buenos Aires, you must decide if you want pesos or dollars from the bank machine.

2. There are advantages and disadvantages to the rapid movement of capital (money) in the new world of global finance. What do you suppose some of these may be?

In the 1950s and 1960s, many big companies had headquarters around the world, often with separate production facilities. Today, however, these firms find the source of their comparative advantage in being able to manage information and knowledge, linking their facilities and making strategic decisions about what to produce where. Production can be quickly moved from Detroit to Singapore to take advantage not only of lower wages but also movements in exchange rates.

Globalization has been facilitated by dramatic changes in communication. Managers in a plant in Mexico can access the same databases in Louisville, Kentucky, as a domestic manager does from a plant in California. Paper documents fly through fax machines, and advances in satellite communications make teleconferencing cheaper and more efficient than business trips. Globalization has made the world a bigger playing field, including many more players, yet with a smaller, more tightly knit international production system.

Globalization has also transformed the economic environment of individual consumers and employees. It has changed the products you buy. The orange you ate for breakfast was as likely to be from Brazil as Florida. The Ford Escort was one of the first genuine world cars in that it was built with parts from dozens of countries, such as the ones identified in Figure 2.4. Imagine the kind of organization, communication, management, transportation, labor, and technology required to accomplish such a project. As a

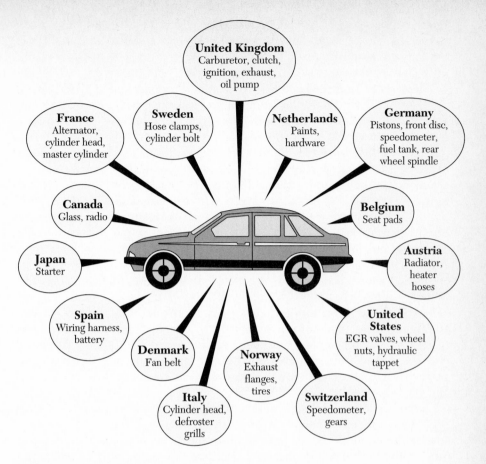

■ FIGURE 2.4 Ford Escort, the world car

Source: World Development Report, 1990; U.S. Automobile Industry, 1980 (Washington, D.C.: U.S. Government Printing Office, p. 57).

result, globalization has changed the kind of work you do—the U.S. worker today is more likely to be involved in information systems than assembly line production. And globalization opens up new opportunities for investment. Why limit yourself to lower returns at home if the rewards are great abroad? Many savings, retirement, and pension funds are being invested in foreign countries.

Globalization even reaches beyond the economy to culture. It has in some cases promoted cultural homogeneity (Arnold Schwarzenegger plays well in Rio) but also introduces new trends.

Globalization's Winners and Losers

Globalization is not good news for everyone. Some have gained in the global economy, but others have lost. If you were born in one of the great U.S. steel-producing cities like Youngstown, Ohio, you might have seen the city experience an economic depression in the mid- to late 1980s as many of the steel mills closed, thousands of workers lost their jobs, and the economic base of many communities died. This raised many questions. Why did the steel mills close or relocate? Where did they go? Why did they go?

These are complicated questions to answer. From the end of World War II (1945) to the early 1960s, the United States was the most powerful economic player in the world. The United States had the most advanced technologies, the most educated workforce, and access to inexpensive raw materials (especially oil) and markets. By the early 1970s, this had all begun to change. Western Europe (especially West Germany), Japan, and many countries called NICs (newly industrialized countries like Mexico, Brazil, Taiwan, South Korea, and Malaysia) began to seriously compete with the United States. These countries adopted and developed competitive technologies and new organizational and management approaches, giving them a decisive advantage over production in the United States. In addition, wage rates in the NICs range from $.60 to $1.00 per hour, making it nearly impossible for the advanced industrial countries to compete with wage rates (including benefits) of $12 to $36 per hour.

Revolutionary technological changes in production, transportation, communications, and information systems enable firms to produce and market a good or service anywhere in the world. With these advanced systems in place, the cost of labor became one of the most critical competitive variables. Developing countries have relatively low labor costs and no labor unions.

In the late 1980s, U.S. steelmakers were forced to confront nearly a decade of slow growth and the low demand for steel resulting from a highly valued U.S. dollar driving U.S. steel prices above the prices of foreign competitors. Steel mills in Ohio and Pennsylvania relocated to Mexico, Brazil, and South Korea, implementing new technology and using low-wage labor to produce the same, if not better, products.

This is but one example of the globalization of production. Most U.S. firms have had to become more and more global. These corporations in the sectors of manufacturing, transportation, communications, finance, and banking utilize computer and information systems to expand their operations all over the globe. They find themselves competing head-to-head with giants from every other country. In the early 1990s, the United States, Japan, and a unified Germany dominated the global economy, while the collapse of the former Soviet Union along with the transition to market economies in Eastern Europe, Asia, and Latin America symbolized the great transformation that is still under way.

If these changes have not caught up with your daily life, the more subtle daily impact of the changing global economy has no doubt left its mark. In the summer of 1993, if you lived in a small rural town in Ohio, you would have noticed that the U.S. dollar declined against the Japanese yen during the summer. How could you tell? The fewer yen a dollar is worth, the more dollars it takes to pay for a product imported from Japan. The new Nikon 300-millimeter lens at the local photo store sold for $750 at the beginning of the year, but by November it was priced at $1,000. Japanese cars averaged about $2,000 more per car than comparably equipped American cars. For firms in town that exported goods, the weak dollar made their products cheaper for foreigners who have strong currencies. But for local firms that imported goods from Japan, the weak dollar made goods they purchased harder to pay for. And the weak dollar (strong yen) made it attractive for Japanese firms to locate in small rural U.S. communities, giving them access to lower-cost production and important markets.

As a consumer, you might also have noticed the effects of the depreciation of the Mexican peso in late 1994. In December 1994, the peso went from a value of 3.5 pesos per dollar to 7.5 pesos per dollar. If you were a consumer of Mexican goods, this meant you got more pesos per dollar, so Mexican goods (exports) were less expensive and thus more attractive. Your purchasing power increased for Mexican goods. However, if you were a Mexican consumer, this depreciation of the peso meant you needed more pesos (about double) to buy a U.S. dollar. U.S. exports to Mexico were very expensive for you. It also meant you needed twice as many pesos to buy one dollar's worth of goods in Mexico.

> 3. Have you bought anything lately that was imported? What has been the U.S. dollar exchange rate with that particular country's currency? Has this made your purchase more or less expensive?

Making sense of this global economic revolution involves understanding some of the basic concepts of international trade and finance. Why do nations trade? How is trade financed? What are the institutional rules that guide trade and financial transactions between countries? Why does it make sense to produce the same product around the world? What are the costs of globalized production?

WHY NATIONS TRADE

International trade has a long and illustrious history. As far back as classical antiquity, nations have traded. The major reason for this is that both parties gain from the process. Another reason is that nations are increasingly interdependent. No nation can be truly self-sufficient without great expense or sacrifice. The United States, for example, is one of the most self-sufficient countries in the world, yet it depends on imports for virtually all of its bauxite, diamonds, tin, coffee, nickel, manganese, rubber, tungsten, bananas, gold, platinum, and chromium, to name but a few commodities. The last two—crucial in the production of jet engines and many other industrial processes—are nonexistent in the United States and come almost exclusively from South Africa.

Every nation needs imports, albeit some more than others. To pay for those imports, it need to export goods. All nations therefore need international trade. Indeed, it is now virtually impossible to buy anything in the United States that is not produced at least partially abroad. For example, about the only part of an IBM computer that is made in the United States is the outer case. Congresswoman Louise Slaughter (D., New York) once asked the Xerox Corporation to supply her with a copying machine that was completely produced in the United States. Xerox couldn't. Similarly, although VCR technology was invented in the United States, it has never been possible to purchase even one videocassette recorder made in the United States; all are made abroad, as are virtually all color television sets. Automobiles, once produced in Detroit, are now an amalgamation of parts produced around the world.

||| 4. Can you think of some imported products and resources that the United States depends on? List them.

The Theory of Comparative Advantage

In one sense international trade is very simple: one nation—given its natural resource endowment, level of technology, and level of development of its labor force—specializes in whatever it can produce most efficiently and trades that product to another nation for whatever the other nation can do best. Trading with others presumably leaves both parties better off than they would be otherwise. This reasoning, called the **theory of comparative advantage**, was first developed by English economist David Ricardo in the early 1800s. This venerable theory basically posits that every country gains by "putting its best foot forward," specializing in the goods it can produce most efficiently and trading them to other countries for what they can produce relatively more efficiently.

This principle is easier to understand on a personal level. Consider actor Harrison Ford (a.k.a. Han Solo, Indiana Jones, etc.), who is also a highly skilled carpenter. Indeed, he earned his living at carpentry before turning to acting. While Ford may be a better carpenter than most he could hire to do repair work around his house, it would be very expensive for him to do his own repairs because he would have to give up income he earns as a movie star—approximately $20 million per film. Economists use the term **opportunity cost** to express what someone gives up by making a choice. In this case, the opportunity cost of doing carpentry work is very high for Harrison Ford because he can earn so much money as a movie star. Meanwhile, the opportunity cost for Ford's carpenter, who has no other occupation, is very low; she gives up very little by choosing to do carpentry work. According to the theory of comparative advantage, Ford would specialize in acting and hire a carpenter because he has a comparative advantage in acting, while the carpenter has a comparative advantage in carpentry.

By the same reasoning, one nation can benefit from trading internationally even if it is more efficient (that is, it can "do better carpentry") in the production of all products than the nation with which it is trading. The United States might be more efficient than Mexico at producing both textiles and computers, but because the United States has limited resources, the opportunity cost of producing textiles is very high. If the United States chooses to devote resources to producing textiles, it will have fewer resources with which to produce computers (which generate relatively higher profits). Since Mexico can produce textiles with its resources, the United States is better off specializing in the production of computers and importing textiles from Mexico. This allows both countries to produce what they do best (i.e., to produce the good with the lowest opportunity cost). In this way, international trade pays off even if one nation has an advantage in cost efficiency over another in all goods. This, Ricardo argued, will always be true so long as each nation has different resource endowments. We will delve more deeply into the theory of comparative advantage in Chapter 20.

Free Trade versus Protectionism

When we consider trade issues, the debate about the pros and cons of free trade often occupies the stage. Free trade occurs when there are no obstacles to the free flow of goods and services between countries. This means the absence of **quotas** (physical limits) or **tariffs** (taxes) on imports or exports. While economic theory suggests that free trade is desirable and over time produces positive economic gains for individual nations as well as the larger global trading community, in the short run this is not always the case. Nor is it clear that, in practice, the benefits of free trade come without serious economic cost and consequence for particular sectors of the economy, regions of a country, and workers.

As nations strive to keep income in their country, they may engage in **protectionism**, which means putting up barriers to imports. It seems logical that if your objective is to maximize exports and limit imports to protect domestic jobs, then one simple way to do it is to put a tariff or a tax on imports, or to limit by law the quantity of imports allowed to enter the country by imposing a quota on them. Trade restrictions such as tariffs and quotas have the effect of increasing production in domestic industries by protecting them from foreign competition, which saves jobs at home. However, imposing trade restrictions also raises prices on imported goods and allows industries protected by tariffs to sell their products domestically for a higher price than they could if they had to face foreign competition.

Those who favor free trade (a group that includes the majority of economists) argue that international trade increases the overall level of income and consumption possibilities. Opponents argue that free trade comes at too high a cost, especially in terms of jobs lost to foreign competition. Others, as we shall see in Chapter 20, argue that what is needed is *fair* trade, on the assumption that for free trade to occur, countries need to be guaranteed full access to each other's markets.

Trade Liberalization and the North American Free Trade Agreement (NAFTA)

Recently there have been both global and regional movements toward trade liberalization policies, promoted at the world level by the General Agreement on Tariffs and Trade (GATT) and the World Trade Organization (WTO).

Europe and nations in Southeast Asia and Latin America have negotiated regional trade pacts with neighboring countries. Faced with regional trade blocs and increased competition, the United States, Canada, and Mexico in 1993 signed the North American Free Trade Agreement (NAFTA).

The goal of NAFTA is to promote free trade and expand the volume of goods and services among these three countries. The agreement was very controversial; economists argued about the costs and benefits of free trade for each country, as well as the more specific impacts on special economic sectors in each country. The agreement was signed with special parallel side agreements having to do with issues like worker health and safety, child labor, and environmental practices. In the year before the agreement was signed, the United States was exporting over $40 billion annually to Mexico and importing about $36 billion a year from Mexico. Mexico's exports to the United States represented about two-thirds of its total exports. Two years after the agreement was signed, exports and imports between both countries boomed to a level of over $50 billion. When the Mexican peso collapsed in late 1994, the devalued peso and resulting currency crisis led to further U.S. imports from Mexico. U.S. imports from Mexico rose to more than $60 billion, and U.S. exports to Mexico fell dramatically from over $50 billion to around $37 billion as the purchasing power of the peso declined.

It is still too soon to make a definitive judgment as to the success or failure of NAFTA. Most experts believe that it will take several years to reach an objective conclusion about the positive and negative consequences. As illustrated in Figure 2.5, U.S.–Mexican trade had already been increasing when NAFTA was signed.

FINANCING INTERNATIONAL TRADE

In the summer of 1990, 1 U.S. dollar could be exchanged for 128 Japanese yen, 2,753 Mexican pesos, 1.23 Canadian dollars, or 1,302 Italian lira. What makes one currency worth a certain amount when measured in terms of another?

Less than a month later, the U.S. dollar was worth 153 Japanese yen. What caused the change in the rate at which these two currencies could be traded? And what happened to the U.S. consumer wanting to purchase a VCR made in Japan during that month?

When nations engage in international trade, they do not generally trade goods for goods directly; international trade requires a system of paying for transactions. Nations must agree on what is acceptable to use as a medium of exchange and a unit of account for international transactions. Since every nation has its own currency, there has to be some way to determine the value at which currencies exchange for one another. This, among other things, is the role of international finance.

Exchange Rates

The foreign **exchange rate** is the rate at which one country's currency exchanges for another country's currency. These rates of exchange fluctuate

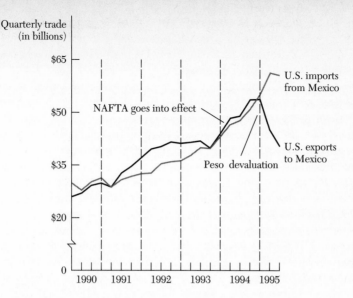

Quarterly trade
(in billions)

$65

$50   NAFTA goes into effect

$35   Peso devaluation

$20

U.S. imports
from Mexico

U.S. exports
to Mexico

0

1990   1991   1992   1993   1994   1995

■ FIGURE 2.5 Trade between the United States and Mexico

Source: U.S. Department of Commerce.

daily depending on economic circumstances within, and transactions between, countries. These shifts in exchange rates affect us in direct ways.

We don't think about it very often, but exchange rates come to your attention a little more dramatically if you are on a vacation or business trip in a foreign country. One day you cash a ten-dollar traveler's check in Japan and get, say, 1,000 yen for it—about enough to get into a movie. The next day, the value of the dollar falls, and you get only 800 yen for your ten dollars. Since prices have not changed in Japan, you have to come up with more dollars to see another movie.

Exchange rate fluctuations like that happen all the time. What causes them?

Within a country, when we purchase goods or services, only one currency is involved, so the process is fairly simple. You hand over the money to someone, who sells you what you want. The price you pay is, generally speaking, determined by the amount of the product available at the time and by consumers' demand for it. But when you buy a product made in another country, a more complicated exchange process is triggered. If, for example, you buy a Japanese automobile, you pay for it in dollars, and that's all you have to think about. However, the Japanese auto manufacturer can't pay its bills in dollars; it needs yen. Somewhere along the line, your dollars have to be changed (converted) into yen so the Japanese auto manufacturer can be paid in local currency.

This exchange takes place in the foreign exchange market, which is why foreign money is called foreign exchange. The number of yen a dollar will buy depends on a number of factors, but most involve how many yen

Americans want compared to how many dollars the Japanese demand. In 1995 the U.S. wanted (imported) $66 billion more of Japanese products than the Japanese wanted (imported) of ours. This was reflected in a weakening of the dollar and a strengthening of the yen.

The weakening of the dollar relative to the yen (or depreciation of the dollar) driven by an excess demand by U.S. consumers for Japanese goods should, however, eventually help to balance trade. As the dollar weakens and buys fewer yen, more dollars are needed to purchase Japanese electronics and cars. As Japanese imports become more expensive in the United States, consumers should respond by reducing their demand for them, taking pressure off the yen and bolstering the dollar. The United States both loses and gains in this process. It pays higher prices for the Hondas and the Sonys, but since Japanese goods are becoming more expensive, U.S. consumers should begin switching to lower-priced domestically produced goods. Then more jobs will be created in the United States. For Japan it's the opposite—lower prices for U.S. blue jeans or airplanes come at the cost of fewer jobs in Japan as Japanese consumers substitute lower-priced U.S. goods for more expensive Japanese goods.

As we have seen, the price of one country's goods in relation to another's depends on the rate of exchange between their currencies. If exchange rates are allowed to fluctuate freely according to market supply and demand, then they simply reflect each nation's demand for another's products—its exportable goods and services. This is because the demand for foreign currencies (foreign exchange) is in part a derived demand, derived from the demand for imports and exports. Thus, whenever two countries are trading, two markets are involved: the product market and the foreign exchange market. While this complicates the analysis, the key to understanding exchange systems is to recognize that the demand for foreign exchange is derived from the nation's demand for goods and services, financial instruments like stocks and bonds, and purchases of physical assets like production facilities. We will explore exchange rates further in Chapter 21.

TECHNOLOGICAL CHANGE AND COMPETITIVENESS

The process of economic growth and economic development, including globalization, owes its rapid pace to modern computer and information technology. Technology is thus one of the most important factors contributing to and underlying the globalization of economic activity.

Since the 1800s, economic activity has been driven by a set of changing new technologies. Steam power, cotton textiles, and iron defined the 1800–1850 period. Railways and steel shaped the period from 1850 to 1900. The first half of the twentieth century was marked by transformations in electricity, chemicals, and automobiles. Electronics, synthetic materials, and petrochemicals dominated the 1950s, and at present we are watching the integration of information and computer technology. These stages have been driven by the actions of entrepreneurs and innovators. We have seen technological revolutions in the fields of transportation, communications, information, electronics, and manufacturing. In today's rapidly changing global economy, the information revolution driven by the computer is bringing about changes and competitive pressures that are literally changing the lives of everyone on the planet.

The New Global Economy and Competitiveness

Manufacturing employment as a percentage of the U.S. labor force has been decreasing since the early 1900s, when it represented over 25 percent of the labor force. By the mid-1990s, it represented only 13 percent. Yet, U.S. manufacturing output almost doubled from 1970 to 1990 as employment fell dramatically. The period 1961 to 1991 witnessed a relocation of manufacturing within and outside of the United States as firms moved to the low-wage (nonunion) Southeast and Southwest as well as across the border to Mexico and other newly industrializing countries like South Korea, Taiwan, Singapore, Malaysia, Thailand, and Indonesia. Other industrialized countries, including Germany, Canada, France, and Britain, experienced the same decrease in manufacturing employment as a percentage of the total labor force. In these countries the service sector grew, as did new employment in the emerging high-technology industries.

In the United States, the buzzword of the mid-1990s was *downsizing*, which symbolized the systematic reduction of employees by some of the largest firms (AT&T, IBM, General Motors, and Citibank) in the U.S. corporate sector. These reductions in staff were driven by the stated need to reduce costs and improve productivity. Employment for the *Fortune* 500 companies declined from 1979 to 1993. Meanwhile, direct foreign investment from the United States to other nations increased from $50 billion in 1983 to $225 billion in 1990. Much of this increase went to developing nations, especially those in East Asia—particularly China, which experienced an inflow of $28 billion in 1993, compared to almost nothing in 1983.

Much direct foreign investment is in firms all over the world that are attempting to adapt to a modern form of production. The roots of the contemporary manufacturing process are in the evolution of automobile production in Japan. This form of manufacturing was engineered by Toyota, and the story has been articulated in a 1990 book by James P. Womack, Daniel T. Jones, and Daniel Roos, *The Machine That Changed the World: The Story of Lean Production—How Japan's Secret Weapon in the Global Auto Wars Will Revolutionize Western Industry*.

The Rise of Toyota and World-Class Manufacturing

Until the rise of Toyota in the early 1970s, the Big Three U.S. automobile producers—Ford, General Motors, and Chrysler—had dominated domestic and global markets. Their organizational and production model was based on assembly line methods derived from the pioneering days of Henry Ford in the 1920s. This model was a very bureaucratic and centralized system of automobile production. The mass production system was supported by a multilayered and complicated supplier system, and responsibilities were divided along functional lines: product design, inventory, production and assembly, distribution, marketing, and finance. This model worked because for decades the Big Three did not face genuine competition. However, the competitive environment was changing, and Japanese firms were discovering new ways to organize production and apply new technologies.

In 1973-1974 the Organization of Petroleum Exporting Countries (OPEC) instituted an oil embargo against the United States and Western Europe and quadrupled oil prices. As U. S. consumers grew more concerned about gas mileage, Japan and Germany entered the U.S. market selling fuel-efficient, quality automobiles at competitive prices. In particular, Toyota's world-class manufacturing model emerged.

What did Toyota do differently? By fundamentally reconceptualizing the way cars were made and the way the automobile firm was organized and managed, Toyota was able to produce quality cars efficiently. The company reorganized a production system and incorporated state-of-the-art technology with a highly educated, motivated, dedicated, and trained workforce. Toyota wanted to be a lean and flexible producer that could respond to particular consumer and market demands quickly. To be more efficient, Toyota found ways to reduce or eliminate waste and inefficiencies. This would reduce costs and improve quality. Everything changed, from the use of suppliers to the making of parts, the management of inventory with the "just-in-time" system, the design of products, the application of computerized manufacturing technologies and information systems to all functions, the development of special production and quality teams, and customer relations. This was the beginning of the world-class manufacturing model.

Toyota's initiatives challenged the world's other auto producers to reevaluate every aspect of their production and organizational systems. Automobile producers had to totally transform themselves or risk extinction. The U.S. auto industry took almost twenty years to learn and apply the fundamental lessons taught by Toyota and others who followed their footsteps. This transition has not been easy. But by the mid-1990s, a consensus emerged that the U.S. automobile industry had successfully adapted to the challenges brought forth by the need to establish a world-class manufacturing model to compete in the global economy. The universal challenge for all producers of goods and services, not just the automobile industry, is to design systems that provide for continuous improvement in a changing global economy.

Manufacturing Technology: On the Cutting Edge

In March 1994, *The Economist* magazine featured a special report titled "Manufacturing Technology: On the Cutting Edge." This article described the technological changes taking place in the area of manufacturing driven largely by the use of computer controls. These changes are possible because of a revolution in computer information systems. The rapid adoption and implementation of these new technologies is being forced by the competitive nature of the new global economy.

Technology has shortened product cycles (the period from the development and design of a product to its production, to its distribution, to its maturity, and finally to the end of its marketable life). New technologies are enabling firms to have smaller production runs and reduce the time that any manufacturing system designed for a single product remains useful. In short, the age of mass production may be over; producers now must meet specific customer needs and demands almost immediately. To do this, producers in many industries are using computer technologies to save money, customize products, and shorten cycle times. The automobile sector has successfully introduced robotics; on average, about 40 percent of the labor to assemble a car is done through automated processes. The aircraft and aerospace industry has utilized computer-assisted design (CAD) systems to design and simulate the building of the Boeing 747 and 777 aircraft.

While it takes machines to make other machines that will build products, the computer has become the new tool to make the machines that will build other machines that will make products. This has a profound impact on the way jobs are done and the ways in which firms compete. An apt example of this manufacturing technology revolution is found at the Ingersoll Milling Machine Company. In its research laboratory, it has built the octahedral hexapod, an unusual machine tool that looks a bit like an illustration in a geometry book, a bit like a sculpture, a bit like a time machine. Steel cylinders are joined in a framework with eight open, triangular faces: a top and a base held apart by six triangular sides, half of them pointing up and half pointing down. The three topmost corners are shoulders; from each of them,

■ Factory workers adjusting televisions in a production line, near Osaka, Japan. *(Charles Gupton/Tony Stone Images)*

two arms reach toward a platform that they hold in the center of the framework. On the platform is a light motor and a machine tool capable of cutting, drilling, or boring. When the six arms expand and contract—they do not bend—the platform moves. Its cutting edge can be positioned anywhere within a meter or so, pointing in any direction. The hexapod is exceptionally strong and rigid. It can be installed anywhere, with no special foundations. It can be made cheaply. The key technology is computer control.

As we will see in other sections of the book, new computer-driven technologies like this are changing every aspect of our lives. Producers have little choice but to apply these new technologies to create the flexible manufacturing systems necessary to satisfy customers and compete in the global economy.

MULTINATIONAL CORPORATIONS: THE GLOBAL FIRM

A **multinational corporation** (MNC), or transnational corporation, is a legal corporation that owns and controls enterprises in more than one country. It has a parent company based in the home country. The parent generally has one or more foreign affiliates, subsidiaries, or branches in one or more countries. The investment made by an MNC another country is called **direct private investment**.

The multinational firm of the 1950s and 1960s grew and expanded because of its size, capital assets, power in terms of marketing and sales, vertical and functional organization, control of technology and information, in-house research and development operations, access to markets, cheap resource inputs and foreign labor, and low-cost energy. By the early 1970s, the formerly dominant MNCs, especially those based in the United States, were being challenged by new players from Japan, Europe, and the newly industrialized countries like Brazil, Mexico, and South Korea. For many U.S. multinationals, this forced a painful long-term process of adjustment and restructuring that began in the mid-1970s and is still taking place today. It required for many a total rethinking and reengineering of the way the enterprise functioned and was managed, from resource inputs to production, mar-

TABLE 2.1 The Top Twenty Global Companies, 1996

| Rank | | | Market Value |
1996	1995	Company	Billions of U.S. Dollars
1	3	General Electric	U.S. 137.34
2	2	Royal Dutch/Shell	Neth/Britain 128.29
3	1	NTT	Japan 115.70
4	6	Coca-Cola	U.S. 115.07
5	8	Bank of Tokyo-Mitsubishi	Japan 110.29
6	4	Exxon	U.S. 105.27
7	5	AT&T	U.S. 99.72
8	7	Toyota Motor	Japan 85.78
9	13	Philip Morris	U.S. 82.09
10	16	Merck	U.S. 78.62
11	14	Roche Holding	Switzerland 73.31
12	20	Microsoft	U.S. 71.04
13	22	Johnson & Johnson	U.S. 64.88
14	10	Fuji Bank	Japan 62.99
15	21	Intel	U.S. 62.09
16	11	Sumitomo Bank	Japan 61.89
17	9	Industrial Bank of Japan	Japan 60.47
18	19	Procter & Gamble	U.S. 60.28
19	17	Wal-Mart Stores	U.S. 59.35
20	18	IBM	U.S. 57.61

Source: *Business Week*, July 8, 1996.

keting, sales, finance, human resource management, compensation, cultural and political context, and environmental considerations. By the late 1990s, it was clear that the most important competitive factor for a multinational firm in the global economy was its use of knowledge.

Table 2.1 lists the twenty largest global firms. The multinational corporation Nestlé, a Swiss-based confectionery firm, generated 98 percent of its annual revenues outside Switzerland. U.S. firms have access to much larger domestic markets, so it is not surprising that they have lower percentages of sales revenues coming from foreign sales. For example, Ford, General Motors, and General Electric are at the bottom of this category.

≡ NIKE'S INDONESIAN SWEATSHOPS

The clothing line of well-known television talk show host Kathie Lee Gifford became the center of public debate in 1996, when it was learned that the clothes were being made in U.S. and foreign sweatshops.

Looking for similar stories, reporters soon discovered that the Nikomas Gemilang factory in Serang, fifty miles west of Jakarta, Indonesia, made 1.2 million pairs of Nike sneakers a month. This factory paid a $2.23 daily wage for work performed in a repressive environment characterized by forced overtime, physical punishment, and the constant presence of the Indonesian military to support the actions of the factory owners against the workers.

These workers were making Pegasus running shoes, which retail for $75 but cost just $18.25 to put together and ship to the United States. Huge revenues and profits from shoes allow Nike to pay huge endorsement incomes to athletes like Michael Jordan and golf phenomenon Tiger Woods.

When confronted with these realities, Nike's chief executive Philip H. Knight defended Nike's use of subcontractors by acknowledging, "There's some things we can control and some things we can't control." For many American consumers and labor advocates, Nike's participation in and support of such practices raise major ethical and moral questions.

Clearly, rapid globalization is linking manufacturers, investors, and consumers in a way that raises issues like Nike's use of Asian sweatshops. Stories about sweatshops haunt U.S. consumers and damage public relations for participating firms. People understand why low-wage labor is attractive for foreign firms, but at what price? Should there be an international labor code of conduct to protect the rights of workers everywhere?

1. Does Nike's use of sweatshops that mistreat labor present itself as an ethical issue for you as a consumer? Explain your answer.
2. Would you be in support of an international labor code of conduct? Explain your answer.
3. Examine Nike's home page on the Internet to determine its financial performance and its position on the issue of sweatshops.

Source: "Pangs of Conscience," *Business Week,* July 29, 1996.

5. How can the concepts of lean and flexible production and continuous improvement be applied in the service sector? If you
have had work experience, think about how this management
revolution could be applied to your workplace.

ENERGY AND THE ENVIRONMENT

Globalization of production has increased demand for the world's energy
resources. It has also intensified the impact of local demand on the environment worldwide. As developing nations hope to increase growth and developed nations hope to improve on current living standards, more production
facilities are established, increasing pollution and resource use while destroying natural habitats. At the same time, information technology is enabling
greater emphasis on environmental issues.

Energy

Everything that we do requires energy. You cannot lift your finger without
expending energy. From an economic perspective, then energy sources of
greatest interest are fossil fuels such as petroleum used to generate electricity and provide transportation. Aside from the cost of labor, the availability
and price of petroleum are among the most critical determinants of the
availability and cost of the vast majority of the goods and services produced
in the world.

Until the early 1970s, citizens of industrial countries took for granted that
their affluence and material standard of living were based on easily available
and affordable (but nonrenewable) fossil fuels, especially petroleum. The
OPEC-generated oil crises of the 1970s made people more aware of the fact
that petroleum is nonrenewable, the product of a unique and singular historic
geologic process. The remaining petroleum reserves are concentrated in the
Middle East.

The United States currently utilizes about seventeen million barrels (each
barrel contains forty-two gallons) of petroleum a day and depends on foreign
imports for about 50 percent of this amount. This amount represents 1,029
gallons per person annually in the United States, compared to 700 gallons per
person in Japan and 481 gallons per person in Great Britain. Since 1991, after
Operation Desert Storm (when the United States and European countries
carried out a major military action against Iraq to protect Kuwait and oil
interests in the Middle East), petroleum conservation in the United States
has decreased, domestic oil production declined, and demand increased. By
2000 many experts predict that the United States will be importing 55 percent of its daily petroleum needs, of which two-thirds flows to the transportation sector. Given projected rates of economic growth and global
consumption, the world will one day—around the year 2075, say most
experts—come close to running out of petroleum.

One of the obvious reasons why Americans consume so much petroleum in the form of gasoline is that it is cheap compared to the price in other countries. In 1996 a gallon of gasoline in the United States cost $1.30 (with $.42 in tax), whereas in the Netherlands a gallon of gasoline cost $4.66 (with $3.32 in tax). This example shows that different governmental policies are used to discourage or tax certain kinds of energy usage.

6. Do you think U.S. citizens should pay a higher price for gasoline, as do Europeans? Explain.

The fastest growth in energy demand is in the developing countries. Throughout the developing world, there is a phenomenal increase in the demand for not only petroleum but electricity, produced principally by coal or nuclear power.

Energy use has enormous consequences in terms of economics, trade, capital flows, politics, international relations, and the environment. All nations therefore must be thoughtful about their energy resources (supplies, demand, cost) and their use of energy. As we move into the next century, the search will be on for ways to conserve and enhance the efficiency of energy, develop alternative renewable energy from the sun, and generate viable substitutes for nonrenewable fossil fuels like petroleum.

The Environment

Since the late 1960s, the industrial countries have been keenly aware of the progressive degradation of the earth's physical environment resulting from the kind of economic growth they have experienced since the 1940s. This economic growth has been characterized by rapid urbanization and industrialization on a global scale. It has been propelled by the availability of cheap energy, especially petroleum. The automobile industry has driven much of this growth.

From the 1940s to the present, industrialization has primarily involved large-scale energy-intensive industrial and agricultural production, modes of transportation, and development of synthetics, especially chemicals. These practices have increased the material wealth of industrialized nations but generated some negative consequences for the environment:

- Air pollution
- Water pollution
- Diminished soil quality
- Deterioration of the earth's ozone layer
- Warming of the earth caused largely by the burning of fossil fuels
- Extinction of species and the resulting loss of biological diversity
- Rapid depletion of nonrenewable resources
- Unsustainable rates of grazing, fishing, burning, and use of many of the earth's nonrenewable and renewable resources

These issues are controversial and experts disagree profoundly, but it is vital for responsible global citizens to be aware of these issues, to understand them, and to understand how they relate to the global economy. Most of these issues were on the agenda of the International Earth Summit held in Brazil in 1992. This conference produced a report that incorporated a strategy to save the planet from environmental degradation.

||| 7. Do you consider yourself an environmentalist? Explain. |

While environmental issues and problems seem at times overwhelming, many organizations and firms are acting to promote sustainable modes of production and life in various parts of the world. A rapid proliferation of nongovernmental organizations are educating people about these problems and trying to develop practical solutions. There is an undercurrent of optimism as global awareness is rising and the technical/scientific community is using its knowledge and technology to understand and solve these problems. Many multinational corporations are committing themselves to the goals of sustainable development and the process of **greening,** or adopting environmentally responsible production processes and programs.

Nevertheless, solving environmental problems is difficult. The world's population is growing at a rate of ninety million people a year. There are already almost six billion people on the planet, and the income per person is very uneven. About 80 percent of the new growth in population will occur in developing nations that are already poor and in some cases plagued by high levels of absolute poverty. Many of these developing countries are struggling with repaying large external debts that were accumulated in the 1980s.

▦ CONCLUSION

The new global economy is a complex entity. Modern production, communications, information systems, transportation, electronics, and finance technologies are ushering the global community into a new era. The new era will offer many opportunities and challenges for manufacturing workers, service employees, scientists, engineers, physicians, corporate managers, financial managers, environmentalists, economists, and educators. Innovation and risk taking will be the order of the day as opportunities are seized and difficult problems solved. The multinational firm will be at the center of this process, and nation-states will be challenged to perform their historic function of protecting and promoting national political and economic sovereignty. At the same time, the new global economy will require a redefinition of the role of the nation-state in the international arena. Many of the world's challenges—especially the environmental and natural resource issues—will require corporations and countries to transcend narrow self-interest to promote the collective well-being of the global community.

Review Questions

1. Make a list of all of the goods and services you consume or use in an average day that are from outside of the United States. How dependent is your lifestyle on international trade?
2. Take a major daily newspaper, like the *New York Times*, and list all the articles that have a title, topic, or theme directly related to the international economy (trade or finance). Summarize in a paragraph the essence of each article. How many did you find? What were the major topics?
3. What is the process of globalization? What is causing it to take place at such an accelerated pace?
4. Why do nations engage in international trade? How does the theory of comparative advantage contribute to an understanding of international trade? Can you think of any possible flaws in this simple theory?
5. What are the arguments that support the theory of free trade? What are the arguments that support protectionism? Which of these are you more inclined to support? Why?
6. The North American Free Trade Agreement, signed in 1993, generated a great deal of controversy. Why? Use your research skills to determine if the current consensus judges NAFTA to be a success or failure thus far. How is the argument made? What do you think?
7. What is an exchange rate? How is it determined? Why is it important?
8. If you have access to the Internet, look for data on the exchange rate of the U.S. dollar in terms of the Japanese yen from 1979 to 1998. Make a table of the data and then plot the data on a graph showing the movement of the annual exchange rate over this period of time. What do you think has caused the exchange rate to fluctuate in the manner that it has?
9. If the Japanese yen is strong relative to the U.S. dollar, what do you think the impact is on business performance in Japan?
10. How has the dynamic of technological change transformed the global economy? Give some examples.
11. What does it mean to call Toyota a world-class manufacturing firm? What was Toyota's role in setting into motion a management revolution?
12. Why is energy an important component of the global economy? What is the current level of petroleum consumption in the world? The United States? How dependent is the United States on imported oil? Where does U.S. imported oil come from? How much does the U.S. spend on imported oil?

THINKING CRITICALLY

ECONOMICS AND GLOBAL CHANGE

As we have seen in Chapters 1 and 2, economics is a social science that deals not only with the processes of production, distribution, consumption, and disposal of goods and services, but with people and institutions as well, all in a global context. Today's world is characterized by rapid and, at times, wrenching change driven by technological changes that occur in historically specific and unique societal contexts.

Chapter 2 presented an overview of the character and dynamics of the global economy. From the perspective of the United States, there clearly has been a fundamental transformation of the nature of competition in this new global economy. Many firms and institutions have had to adapt to the new competitive environment. Some firms relocate some or all of their business within the United States and/or outside of the United States in order to stay profitable and competitive. This mobility of capital—or restructuring of firms, as some have called it—has had a profound impact on labor and communities.

"The Year Downsizing Grew Up" appeared in the December 21, 1996, issue of *The Economist*.

Exercises

Read the article and answer the following questions.

1. What is meant by the term *downsizing?*
2. *The Economist* argues that corporations went from panic to planning in terms of their downsizing experience. What does this mean?
3. What are the lessons corporations should learn from the downsizing experience?
4. From reading this article, what questions still remain for you in terms of downsizing?
5. What additional information would you need to know to answer these questions?

6. Explain how downsizing might affect male and female employees differently at the organization's highest level, in middle management, and at the level of clerical workers.

THE YEAR DOWNSIZING GREW UP

Downsizing, it seems, has got itself downsized. At the start of 1996, mass sacking by American companies was causing a hullabaloo in the United States. Pat Buchanan, railing against "job-destroying" corporations, romped home in the Republicans' New Hampshire primary. Robert Reich, Bill Clinton's labour secretary, said that firms which devastated communities by moving jobs abroad might face punitive taxes. Magazines splashed stories about "killer bosses" who paid themselves millions while laying waste to their workforces. The *New York Times,* in a series of seven hefty articles, declared that "job apprehension has intruded everywhere, diluting self-worth, splintering families, fragmenting communities, altering the chemistry of workplaces . . . and rubbing salt on the very soul of the country."

In this mood of doom, AT&T's announcement last January that it was sacking 40,000 people came as a special shock. It was not just that the culprit was "cuddly old Ma Bell," rather than some fly-by-night sweat-shop in the South. Much worse, AT&T was prospering; the man who wielded the knife, Bob Allen, was prospering with it, having just seen his pay go up to $5m a year; and Wall Street greeted the dismal news by boosting the company's shares.

And yet, a few months later, the subject was almost forgotten. Bill Clinton and Bob Dole mentioned downsizing in the presidential fight about as frequently as Dubrovnik. Pat Buchanan's peasants returned to their six-packs and cheese whiz. The *New York Times's* series, repackaged into a book, drew little interest. "Downsizing" remained a reliable topic for comedians, but as a subject of economic analysis it had suddenly gone flat.

There are two reasons for the waning of interest. The first is that the people who made the loudest noise about the problem at the start of the year have now taken a closer look at the statistics.

The headlines may be full of household companies announcing gigantic lay-offs—50,000 at Sears, 10,000 at Xerox, 18,000 at Delta, 16,800 at Eastman Kodak, 35,000 at IBM, on top of AT&T's huge contribution. But the wider figures tell a different story. The unemployment rate came down from 7.1% of the workforce in January 1993 to 5.1% in mid-1996. The economy continued to create many more jobs than it destroyed, providing 8.5m new places for workers in 1993–96. And the employment growth was concentrated in jobs paying above the median wage rather than in a hamburger-flipping. In 1992–96 over half the employment growth was in jobs paying in the top third of wages (and the number of hamburger-flippers actually fell). For all its downsizing, America was far better at generating decent jobs than Europe with its loyalty to jobs for life.

The second reason is that many big firms have had enough of downsizing for the moment. Three enthusiastic downsizers over the past decade have been IBM, General Motors and Hughes Electronics, a division of General Electric. IBM slimmed itself down from 406,000 employees in 1987 to 202,000 in 1995, one of the most dramatic workforce reductions ever. Over the past year it has been recruiting 21,000 people, more than in the successful 1970s. General Motors cut its workforce from 800,000 in 1979 to 450,000 in the early 1990s. In the past year, it set out to recruit 11,000 people. Hughes Electronics has reduced its workforce by a quarter in the past decade—but in 1996 was set to add 8,000. After the downsizing, re-enter upsizing.

From Panic to Planning

For all that, it would be wrong to think the thing was over. Downsizing has spread from the private to the public sector and from workers to managers. Older white-collar workers were considerably more at risk of losing their jobs in 1991–92 than in the previous recession in the early 1980s. And the victims seldom have an easy time of it: two studies by Henry Farber of Princeton University and Ann Huff Stevens of Rutgers suggest that even people who get another full-time job earn on average 10% less than they did in their previous jobs.

The past decade has seen downsizing evolve from an act of desperation into a calculated choice. The first downsizers were failing companies; many of them had no choice but to go in for repeated bloodlettings as their businesses shrank and morale collapsed. But more recently a new sort of company has taken up the practice: successful firms that use job-cutting as a way to pursue a wider purpose.

General Electric led the way, removing 104,000 of its 402,000 workers in 1980–90 even though it faced no great crisis. Others have started to do the same. Compaq cut its workforce by 10% in 1992, despite healthy returns, because it thought the computer market was bound to stay intensely competitive. Goldman Sachs cut its workforce by 10% not once but twice, to increase productivity. Procter & Gamble sent away 13,000 workers even though it was the best-performing company in its business. AT&T sacrificed 40,000 not because it was desperate but because it wanted to divide itself into three smaller, sharper companies.

The transformation of downsizing is the result of two trends in management thinking. One is the realisation that size in itself is no longer a source of competitive advantage. The past decade has seen the humbling of a series of giants: Du Pont, Salomon Brothers and Westinghouse, as well as General Motors, IBM and Sears. Rather than celebrating their size, big companies have taken to hiding it; they try to imitate the agility of their smaller rivals by shrinking their headquarters, slashing away layers of management and breaking themselves up into smaller units. Some have gone the whole hog and broken themselves up into separate companies. In 1995 ITT, America's quintessential conglomerate, showed AT&T the way to do that.

The other new management fashion is to focus on your "core competences": the things that you—and you alone—can do better than anyone else. J.P. Morgan, an investment bank, has constructed an index measuring a company's focus on a scale of 1–100. American companies that decided to "clarify" their business (jargon breeds jargon) by focusing on the one thing they did best outperformed the market by 11% in the next two years; firms that diversified underperformed by about 4 %.

Naturally, the fashion for focus has led to an epidemic of "outsourcing." It is now routine for companies to have their catering, cleaning, building maintenance, security, computer systems and even their mail rooms run by outside contractors. Many are going even further. Nike designs and sells sports shoes without stitching a thread itself. Cirrus Logic, a semiconductor firm has all its manufacturing done by sub-contractors such as Taiwan's Semiconductor Manufacturing Corporation.

This explains one of the paradoxes at the heart of the downsizing debate: that the total number of jobs in the economy is growing at a time when big companies are laying people off in record numbers. Big companies have not so much been destroying jobs as handing them over to other people, often with a contract attached. The past decade has seen strong growth in two sorts of companies—small consultancies that provide specialist services to larger companies (of which they may previously have been a part) and large companies operating on a wider front, such as Electronic Data Systems, which manages information, and Pitney Bowes, which runs mail rooms. America's biggest employer is now Manpower, a temporary-help agency that hires out 767,000 substitute workers a year. . . .

The Gleam Ahead

So, is the worst over? Are most companies now so efficient that they can start growing again? Or will downsizing gather pace? Concerning America, opinion is divided.

Michael Jensen, of the Harvard Business School, thinks the worst is still to come. He sees the world in the middle of "a modern industrial revolution" it will take decades to adjust to. Lower trade barriers and the collapse of communism has brought more than a billion cheap workers into the global labour market. New technology has made it easier to send jobs abroad or to replace humans with machines at home. New management practices such as "total quality management" have made companies much more efficient. The result is a huge over-capacity in the rich world. Mr. Jensen predicts that millions of jobs will disappear, as western companies slim their operations or move into higher-value-added activities. Wages for manual work, he thinks, may fall by a half or more. . . .

Others take a less dramatic view. Nitin Nohria, a colleague at the Harvard Business School who has studied downsizing in *Fortune* 100 companies, argues that many firms shrank themselves in order to concentrate on their core businesses; now they have done this, they can start expanding again. And this time the growth is likely to be more enduring, partly because they are now doing what they are best at and partly because they will be increasingly free to invade the territories of more ramshackle companies in Europe and East Asia.

David Lewin, at the Anderson School of Management at the University of California, Los Angeles (UCLA), presents an even wider-ranging case for optimism. As newly efficient companies outperform their rivals, the demand for their products rises, and they have to hire new workers to keep up. Downsizing, properly done, is thus a self-eliminating process.

And downsizing, Mr. Lewin points out, has its downside, as companies are starting to discover. Having fired 12,000 people in recent years, Delta Airlines has found itself short of baggage handlers, maintenance workers and customer-service agents; none of which helps it to attract travellers. Downsizing can have a devastating impact on innovation, as skills and contacts that have been developed over the years are destroyed at a stroke.

Even the cult of contracting out, Mr. Lewin argues, can be carried too far. It is harder to draw the line between peripheral and essential than people once thought. Handing your computing system over to another company, for example, reduces your control over your information technology. Even if contracting out helps companies to control their costs when times are hard, it can put a break on growth when times are good. You have to take your turn in the queue along with all the contractor's other clients. And tight markets then lead to higher prices. This has been particularly worrisome for airlines, which have not always been able to get essential maintenance done in time to meet their flight schedules.

Companies, Mr. Lewin concludes, have begun to discover the virtues of stability. They can maintain their special efficiencies only if they can give their workers a unique set of skills and a feeling that they belong together. Teams work best if the team members get to know and trust each other—and if each team member masters a broad enough range of skills to be able to double up for absent colleagues. Profit-sharing makes sense only if the employees are around at the end of the year to enjoy their rewards. Mr. Lewin, profit-sharing is an anti-downsizing concept. In the past, companies resorted to downsizing because workers refused to take a pay cut. Now, for many firms, pay is on the way to becoming a variable rather than a fixed cost.

America's Lessons for the Laggards

It sounds like crossed fingers for America. About continental Europe and Japan, on the other hand, the management theorists are unanimous: downsizing is bound to get worse. These parts of the world still have hundreds of huge companies protected by the state against competition. Deregulation, when it inevitably comes, will make them shed jobs as savagely as AT&T and all those American companies already have done. Moreover, many European companies (think of Lagardère in France or Siemens in Germany) are still unfocused in comparison with their American competitors. Growing global competition will force these companies to choose between excelling in one business—cutting large numbers of jobs in the process—and becoming also-rans in dozens of them.

However, continental Europe and Japan have one big advantage: they have America's example to learn from. The Americans have made almost all the mistakes it is possible to make in downsizing. Europeans and Japanese can learn three lessons from America's experience.

The first is that there is a big difference between blind and thought-out downsizing. Most of America's early attempts were flops. A 1990 survey of downsizing by the American Management Association found that fewer than half the firms that cut jobs actually improved their performance. A 1991 study of stock-market reactions to downsizing found that, although companies at first increased their stock prices when they announced job cuts, they were performing below the market average three years later. But recent, better-planned downsizings have prospered. AT&T now looks better positioned to defend its market. Procter & Gamble is outperforming Kao in East Asia and Unilever in Europe. Goldman Sachs is arguably the world's most successful investment bank.

The second lesson is that there is an art—maybe a science—in deciding whom to sack. Many of the early downsizers let the victims select themselves, by offering early-retirement packages and generous severance pay. The result was that anybody who was capable of getting another job went off and got it, while the duds stayed behind. The point was taken, and companies started to do the choosing themselves.

Unfortunately, the criteria they used were often much too crude: last-in-first-out (which meant that they lost all their bright young people); or the removal of everybody below a certain level in the hierarchy (which meant that top-heavy firms became even top-heavier); or the weeding out of all middle managers (which meant that they lost a wealth of experience and connections). . . .

The third thing the American experience has taught is that there are good ways of getting rid of people and bad ones. Apple, a computer company, regularly announces that a certain number of people will be laid off in a few weeks' time, leaving its workers to wonder whose neck is for the axe. Some companies tell the victims by sending anonymous messages via e-mail or voice-mail. Others deliver the news simply by putting rubbish bags on the desks of those doomed to leave. This is not only brutal, but foolish. Workers waste their time worrying about the future. The survivors of each downsizing may spend less time working and more time in building their family life. Few have the energy or the commitment to engage in creative thinking.

Getting rid of people will never be nice, but some firms are doing it as unnastily as they can. They make it clear from the start that their employees need to keep their skills up to date and their options open: in short, that they cannot count on a permanent job. They use their own kindly people, or bring in professional "outplacement" companies, to give advice to employees who are being told to go. They try to keep work teams intact, so as to minimise disruption and demoralisation. And they try to ease the pain. Navcon, a Californian defence contractor, asks those who survive downsizing to make a point of helping those who leave. They also seek to tackle "survivors' guilt." Michigan National Bank encourages the survivors to get involved with local charities.

The language of downsizing is a nasty mix of pseudo-science and euphemism. These days you can be "rightsized," "displaced," even "put into the mobility pool." The reality is wrenching, even for those who have the luck to jump to another well-paid job. And some of the consultants who make a living from the business have all the moral dignity of ambulance-chasing lawyers. But European and Japanese managers will have to learn to live with downsizing over the next decade or so. Studying the American experience, however distasteful much of it sounds, makes better sense that flying by the seat of your pants.

Source: *The Economist*, December 21, 1996, pp. 97–98, 100. Copyright © 1996, The Economist, Ltd. Distributed by New York Times Special Features/Syndication Sales.

ECONOMIC HISTORY AND THE DEVELOPMENT OF MODERN ECONOMIC THOUGHT

Modern economic thinking has been influenced by many economists, among them Adam Smith, Thomas Malthus, David Ricardo, J. B. Say, John Stuart Mill, Alfred Marshall, John Maynard Keynes, Joan Robinson, Thorstein Veblen, and Karl Marx. Many of the economists who contributed to the growing body of economic knowledge were British. Britain's emergence as one of the first capitalist powers, through the spread of its colonial empire and the coming of the Industrial Revolution, accounts for this influence. We can trace many of our theories and ideas about the economy back to these early economists.

This book cannot examine all of the ideas of all of the economists who have made significant contributions to the history of modern economic thought; in this part, we will focus on the development of a few selected and persistent ways of thinking about an economy. Your own understanding of the economy may become clearer as you agree or disagree with some of the most important ideas formulated by past economists.

By examining some of the ideas of these economists as they developed and the historical context in which they emerged, we can gain insights into economic concepts and changing economic institutions, ideas, and theories. Some of this will help us directly in understanding our current economic reality. And it will give us perspective on how the thoughts of past economists have influenced the development of economic systems as well as our understanding of the economy today.

3

The Evolution of Economic Systems

INTRODUCTION

The first premise of all human history is, of course, the existence of living human individuals. Thus, the first fact to be established is the physical organization of these individuals and their consequent relation to the rest of nature. . . .

. . . The writing of history must always set out from these natural bases and their modification in the course of history through the action of men.

Men can be distinguished from animals by consciousness, by religion or anything else you like. They themselves begin to distinguish themselves from animals as soon as they begin to *produce* their means of subsistence, a step which is conditioned by their physical organization. By producing their means of subsistence men are indirectly producing their actual material life.

The way in which men produce their means of subsistence depends first of all on the nature of the actual means of subsistence they find in existence and have to reproduce. This mode of production must not be considered simply as being the reproduction of the physical existence of the individuals. Rather it is a definite form of activity of these individuals, a definite form of expressing their life, a definite *mode of life* on their part. As individuals express their life, so they are. What they are, *therefore*, coincides with their production, both with *what* they produce and with *how* they produce. The nature of individuals thus depends on the material conditions determining their production.

—Karl Marx, *The German Ideology* (1845–1846).

1. What does Marx mean by "the nature of the actual means of subsistence"? What is its relationship to the productive activity of human beings?

Every society is faced with the problem of providing for the day-to-day survival of its people. Production of goods and services on a systematic basis is necessary for the continuance and development of any society or nation. Institutions, traditions, rules, methods, and laws are developed to determine what goods and services will be produced, how they will be produced, and how they will be distributed among the people. According to Marx, the ways in which people organize themselves for the production and distribution of goods and services—the **economic system**—constitutes "the mode of life" of any society.

Individuals and organizations engage in economic activity for particular reasons and according to accepted procedures. This activity is a central and necessary aspect of all human life and societies. It provides us with food, shelter, clothing, and the other necessities of life. The production and distribution of goods and services transforms nature into human uses for survival and sustenance. People's actions in this process determine, to a large extent, their daily contacts and relationships with other people. The results of economic activity—what gets produced and how it gets produced—organized through an economic system, condition the nature, history, and development of a society and its people. Understanding the economic system, then, is fundamental to understanding that society.

To "know" the United States, it is necessary to acknowledge the importance of private production and consumption in providing for our day-to-day survival. Consequently, we would want to examine the roles of specialization, division of labor, and markets in the operation of our economic system. It is also important to realize that U.S. institutions, productive methods, and material conditions have changed over time. Corporations and labor unions have emerged and developed. Technology has progressed. The standard of living has advanced remarkably. Mass production has led to the assembly line and automation. The government has accepted more direct responsibility for the health of the economy. In other words, the economic system has evolved.

ECONOMIC DEVELOPMENT

Over time, all economic systems change. **Economic development** represents progressive changes in a society's ability to meet its economic tasks of production and distribution.

Economic development contains two key elements. One concerns the total amount of goods and services that are produced and available for consumption, and the other concerns institutions. Economic development occurs when a society is able to increase its total output; it experiences economic growth through the generation and usage of its economic **surplus** (more output than necessary for subsistence consumption). Very often a society's ability to produce such growth is a function of the second element of economic development. This concerns the changes in the economic institutions, relationships, and methods of the society. If the society experiences changes in its economic institutions, relationships, and methods that make it better prepared to produce a growing volume of goods and services for its people, then development will occur. The discovery of new resources will encourage economic development, as will technological improvements in the methods of production. The spread of education and attitudes toward work may facilitate a society's ability to produce goods and services. Economic development is obviously of crucial importance to any society and its continued survival.

The present U.S. economic system, its institutions, and its conditions developed out of previous methods of production and distribution. The historical background lies largely, but not exclusively, in U.S. and European experience. For example, the U.S. market system has its roots in the emergence of trade in the Middle Ages in Europe; the modern corporation has its roots in the development of earlier European and U.S. business enterprises. Yet the foundations of the U.S. labor force have been and are worldwide. An understanding of this background will provide some useful perspective on the current economic system in the United States and the global economy.

2. Do you agree with Marx that the "mode of production" of a society constitutes "a definite mode of life on [its] part"? How does the "mode of production" in the United States affect life in the United States? What is the "mode of production" at your college or university?
3. "The nature of individuals thus depends on the material conditions determining their production." What does this mean? Do you think it is true? How are people in the United States affected by "the material conditions" of production?

FROM FEUDALISM TO CAPITALISM

From time to time, economic change is so wrenching that major transformations occur and completely new economic systems emerge, with new institutions, rules, methods, and laws. Such was the transition from feudalism to capitalism in Western Europe from the twelfth to eighteenth centuries. The change occurred over several centuries but accelerated in the later periods. In the following discussion, we will concentrate on the highlights of this transition to illustrate economic change and to show the historical roots of modern capitalism.

As we have said, all societies must organize themselves for production, distribution, and consumption. If we are clear on what these economic activities are, we will be able to focus on the major differences among economic systems. **Production** refers to the activity that takes the **factors of production** (resources) and transforms them into goods and services. The factors of production are land, labor, and capital. **Land** includes raw materials and the land where productive activity takes place (i.e., farmland or the land on which a factory or office is located). **Labor** is the physical and mental effort of people that is necessary for all production. **Capital** includes the technology, buildings, machinery, and equipment that are used in production, as well as the financial resources necessary to organizing production. **Consumption** is the purchasing and using up of produced goods and services. **Distribution** refers to the manner in which goods and services are apportioned among the people of a society. As we will see, feudalism accomplished all of these with institutions and methods much different from those of capitalism.

> 4. All societies must be able to organize themselves for production, distribution, and consumption. What other economic goals should a society have? List at least five.

Precursors of Feudalism

The ancient empires of Egypt, Greece, and Rome were the precursors of modern Western societies. They were largely agricultural societies that struggled to produce enough food for continued subsistence. *Tradition* and *custom* were primarily responsible for organizing production and distribution. Things were done the way they always had been done. Sons followed their fathers into occupations and daughters assumed their mothers' roles as gatherers and homemakers. Slaves remained slaves. Peasants were agricultural producers tied to the land. The priests, kings, emperors, pharaohs, and lords continued in the role of the elite upper class removed from production. As economist Robert Heilbroner has described them in *The Making of Economic Society*, these societies had "a mode of social organization in which both production and distribution were based on procedures devised in the distant past, rigidified by a long process of historic trial and error, and maintained by heavy sanctions of law, custom, and belief."

Because these societies were unable to produce much more than was needed for subsistence, they could not support a large nonfarming population. Throughout history, the ability to produce an agricultural and economic surplus has been a source of growth and power. The existence of an agricultural surplus allows for a geographically separate urban population. Cities did exist in Egypt, Greece, and Rome, but they were not extensive enough to allow for a significant amount of nonagricultural production. Instead, the cities of ancient times were relatively parasitic and lived off the surplus of the rural area. What surplus the cities were able to produce themselves resulted from trade with other cities and from the institution of slavery, with its ability to exploit unpaid labor. With a largely rural population tied to tradition and an urban economy based on the unstable slave system, the ancient empires were economically stagnant—they were unable to amass economic surplus and to grow. Because of this base of internal weakness, each of these ancient empires eventually crumbled. They were replaced by feudalism during the Middle Ages.

Before we examine feudalism, it is worthwhile to pause and consider an additional aspect of economic surplus. If a society can produce more than it needs for consumption, it can use this excess to support an urban population that can pursue nonagricultural production, and it can devote resources to increasing further production. The surplus can be used to further a division of tasks within an economic system and thus to spur economic growth.

By forgoing current consumption, a society can use resources to increase its ability to produce goods and services in the future. A simple example would be using excess grain to feed oxen (instead of eating it) so that more grain could be produced in the future. Another example would be transporting food to an urban area where (fed) artisans would fashion simple tools for agricultural production.

Although the surplus can thus be a source of growth, how a society uses its surplus and who controls its use tell us a lot about that society. Egypt, Greece, and Rome did succeed in producing surplus, but very little was used in a direct attempt to further economic production. Religious and military elites controlled the surplus of these societies and used them to build temples, pyramids, sphinxes, magnificent roads, aqueducts, and buildings that are still with us today. Little of the surplus, however, went to the slaves, peasants, or artisans who were the producers of consumable goods and services, nor was the surplus directed toward improving the productive potential of these sectors of the economic systems. As a result, these societies were not able to generate significant economic growth.

5. What does the United States do with its economic surplus? Who determines how it is used?

Feudalism

The economic system that dominated Western Europe throughout the Middle Ages was **feudalism**. What exactly was feudalism? What were its major institutions, methods, and customs? The following selection by economic historian E. K. Hunt, from his book *Property and Prophets*, provides us with a concise description of feudalism.

FEUDALISM

E. K. Hunt

The decline of the western part of the old Roman Empire left Europe without the laws and protection the empire had provided. The vacuum was filled by the creation of a feudal hierarchy. In this hierarchy, the serf, or peasant, was protected by the lord of the manor, who, in turn, owed allegiance to and was protected by a higher overlord. And so the system went, ending eventually with the king. The strong protected the weak, but they did so at a high price. In return for payments of money, food, labor, or military allegiance, overlords granted the fief, or feudum—a hereditary right to use land—to their vassals. At the bottom was the serf, a peasant who tilled the land. The vast majority of the population raised crops for food or clothing or tended sheep for wool and clothing.

Custom and tradition are the key to understanding medieval relationships. In place of laws as we know them today, the *custom of the manor* governed. There was no strong central authority in the Middle Ages that could have enforced a system of laws. The entire medieval organization was based on a system of mutual obligations and services up and down the hierarchy. Possession or use of the land obligated one to certain customary services or payments in return for protection. The lord was as obligated to protect the serf as the serf was to turn over a portion of his crop or to perform extensive labor for the lord. . . .

The basic economic institution of medieval rural life was the **manor** [boldface added], which contained within it two separate and distinct classes: noblemen, or lords of the manors, and serfs (from the Latin word *servus*, "slave"). Serfs were not really slaves. Unlike a slave, who was simply property to be bought and sold at will, the serf could not be parted from either his family or his land. If his lord transferred possession of the manor to another nobleman, the serf simply had another lord. In varying degrees, however, obligations were placed upon the serfs that were sometimes very onerous and from which there was often no escape. Usually, they were far from being "free."

The lord lived off the labor of the serfs who farmed his fields and paid taxes in kind and money according to the custom of the manor. Similarly, the lord gave protection, supervision, and administration of justice according to the custom of the manor. It must be added that although the system did rest on reciprocal obligations, the concentration of economic and political power in the hands of the lord led to a system in which, by any standard, the serf was exploited in the extreme.

The Catholic church was by far the largest owner of land during the Middle Ages. . . . This was also an age during which the religious teaching of the church had a very strong and pervasive influence throughout western Europe. These factors combined to make the church the closest thing to a strong central government throughout this period.

Thus the manor might be secular or religious . . . but the essential relationships between lord and serfs were not significantly affected by this distinction. There is little evidence that serfs were treated any less harshly by religious lords than by secular ones. The religious lords and the secular nobility were the joint ruling classes; they controlled the land and the power that went with it. In return for very onerous appropriations of the serf's labor, produce, and money, the nobility provided military protection and the church provided spiritual aid.

In addition to manors, medieval Europe had many towns, which were important centers of manufacturing. Manufactured goods were sold to manors and, sometimes, traded in long-distance commerce. The dominant economic institutions in the towns were the **guilds** [boldface added]—craft, professional, and trade associations that had existed as far back as the Roman Empire. If anyone wanted to produce or sell any good or service, he had to join a guild.

The guilds were as involved with social and religious questions as with economic ones. They regulated their members' conduct in all their activities: personal, social, religious, and economic. Although the guilds did regulate very carefully the production and sale of commodities, they were less concerned with making profits than with saving their members' souls. Salvation demanded that the individual lead an orderly life based on church teachings and custom. Thus the guilds exerted a powerful influence as conservators of the status quo in the medieval towns.

Source: E. K. Hunt. *Property and Prophets,* 2nd edition. Abridged from pp. 5–8, 24, © 1972, 1975 E. K. Hunt. Reprinted by permission of Addison-Wesley Longman Inc.

6. What were the dominant institutions of feudalism? What classes existed in feudal society?
7. How does the feudal "custom of the manor" differ from our modern system of contracts?
8. What did the "religious lords and secular nobility" do with the economic surplus that they controlled?

The Breakdown of Feudalism

As feudalism developed, several new economic activities and trends emerged that eventually created the preconditions for a new economic order. Most notable were changes in technology, urbanization, medieval merchants, the Crusades and exploration, creation of the nation-state, decline of the manor, breakdown of the guilds, and the rise of Protestantism and individualism. These factors and others, as sources of change over centuries in Western Europe, eventually led to the destruction of feudal institutions and relationships. These were replaced by a new set of institutions and relationships that we have come to label capitalism.

Changes in Technology. In agriculture the widespread introduction, about the eleventh century, of the three-field system of crop rotation, replacing the two-field system, allowed for more productive use of agricultural land. In this system, all parcels of land would lie fallow every third year, preventing the land from becoming depleted by constant planting. This simple change increased the agricultural surplus and encouraged the use of more grain in supporting field animals. Agricultural production increased even further with greater use of oxen and horses, and later, with consolidation of agricultural lands. In addition, transportation of agricultural goods was facilitated by more horses and improvements in wagon technology.

Urbanization. The increasing agricultural surplus supported an expanding and more urbanized population. Larger urban centers fostered specialization

in economic production; the early medieval towns and cities began to concentrate on trade and manufacturing. This specialization led to further increases in production and stimulated trading among the cities and between the cities and the countryside.

Medieval Merchants. Given different specializations of agricultural and manufacturing production in different areas throughout Western Europe, individual merchants during the tenth to fourteenth centuries began traveling from place to place, buying, selling, and trading goods. These transient merchants exposed self-sufficient manors to the variety of products from the rest of Europe and Asia and created interdependencies that whittled away at the traditional patterns of feudal life. This very trade further encouraged the development of regional and urban-rural specialization—a source of increasing economic surplus. It also laid the roots for the later sophistication of European commerce. Traveling merchants were replaced by permanent markets in commercial cities by the fifteenth century.

The Crusades and Exploration. Between the eleventh and thirteenth centuries, the Crusades brought Europeans into contact with a civilization much more concerned with trading and moneymaking. It also exposed them to the wealth of Asia and its goods. This exposure encouraged an effort to expand the trading periphery of Europe. The nations of Europe began to explore Africa and Asia. These explorations ultimately led to the discovery of the New World. The example of moneymaking was not lost either. Merchants financed and profited from the Crusades, while European nations used their newfound exploring capability to establish colonies and reap from them raw materials and precious metals. These new forms of economic surplus financed further development and created fledgling capitalist institutions. In fact, the inflow of gold and silver produced such rapid growth that a great price inflation occurred during the sixteenth century in Europe.

Creation of the Nation-State. An additional factor that broke down feudalism and, in fact, supported exploration was the creation of the nation-state. The self-sufficient and decentralized nature of feudalism began to hamper trade as manors attempted to levy tariffs and tolls on merchants. However, as centralization of political power became the goal of certain nobles and lords, these forces were joined by the commercial merchants in the cities. This coalition of economic and political power ensured the emergence of nation-states. By the sixteenth century these newly unified nations within Europe were encouraging trade within and among their countries and exploration across the Atlantic and the Mediterranean. The new nation-states possessed the economic, political, and military power that formed the basis for a new economic order and increased economic growth.

Decline of the Manor. One of the most significant trends in the transition from feudalism to capitalism occurred on the manor. Increasingly, the feudal obligations between lords and serfs became monetized. As trade expanded, the need for money caused feudal lords to sell their crops for cash and to put their serfs on money payments for work. In turn, the serfs paid rents to the lords for the use of land. This conversion to a monetary system eventually destroyed the feudal manor as the lords were squeezed by market competition and the serfs were unable to pay their rents regularly. Eventually the serfs lost their feudal rights to the land.

The *enclosure movement* from the thirteenth through the eighteenth centuries sealed the fate of the manorial system. As monetization and trade progressed, lords began to use their manors for cash generation. Common pasture land on the manors, traditionally accessible to all, was "enclosed" for grazing sheep. The sheep, in turn, were the source of wool to supply the increasing demand throughout Europe for woolen cloth. The effects and methods of this process were widespread. Robert Heilbroner describes it in *The Making of Economic Society*:

> The enclosure process in England proceeded at an irregular pace over the long centuries; not until the late eighteenth and early nineteenth centuries did it reach its engulfing climax. By its end, some ten million acres, nearly *half* the arable land of England, had been "enclosed"—in its early Tudor days by the more or less high-handed conversion of the "commons" to sheep-raising; in the final period, by the forced consolidation of tenants' strips and plots into tracts suitable for large-scale commercial farming.

The enclosures contributed to growing output, trade, and incomes for some. The process also made it increasingly impossible for serfs/tenants to support themselves. In essence, they were forced off the land in search of work for wages. Most gravitated toward the cities.

9. What similarities and/or differences do you see between the enclosure movement in Europe and the modern replacement of family farms in the United States by agribusiness corporations?

Breakdown of the Guilds. Further accelerating the process of creating a laboring class of people and the extension of the market for labor service was the replacement of the guilds by the *putting-out system*. Under the guild system of production, independent craftspeople had used their own tools and shops to produce their products, then sold the products to merchants. Production and sales were overseen by the guilds. As trade expanded and the production of manufactured goods increased, the putting-out system began in the sixteenth century to replace the guilds. In this arrangement, a merchant-capitalist gained control of the tools, raw materials, and workplace and would hire, for wages, skilled individuals to produce the final product. Eventually this system led to the establishment of centralized industrial factories.

Two major elements of this new system differentiated it from the feudal guild system. First, production was controlled by the capitalist—the owner of tools, buildings, and other resources involved in production (i.e., the capital). This person would also arrange for the sale of product items. The goal was monetary profit. The guild no longer influenced the production and sale of the goods. Second, this new system created a labor force that depended on the capitalist for work. The craftspeople no longer owned capital; they had only their skills and labor power to sell to the capitalist.

As the putting-out system developed further, markets for goods and resources determined profits for capitalists. These market relationships, rather than the custom and tradition of feudal relations, governed decisions about who would work and for what wages, and how the work would be performed. Industrial production was organized on a capitalist, rather than feudalist, basis.

The combination of the enclosure movements and the putting-out system created a new class of individuals who controlled the productive land and resources of Western Europe and whose goal was profit. In both the countryside and the city, this centralization of control and ownership resulted in greater economic production. In addition, the changes created a new class of landless, propertyless individuals—people no longer tied to their hereditary lands or their crafts. This was a new kind of labor force: a "free" labor force in which work was not a guarantee and the individual was free to seek work for wages determined by emerging market forces. This labor force responded to the forces of change by attempting to sell their only resource, their labor power, at the best possible wage. They formed the emerging urban working class.

The Rise of Protestantism and Individualism. The final factor contributing to the decline of feudalism concerned a change in the philosophy of much of the European population as well as a decline in the power of one of feudalism's most powerful institutions, the Catholic church. The Catholic church emphasized in its teachings a concern with afterlife and deemphasized material life. In fact, the Church argued against lending money for interest (usury) and profit making; if people were poor, that was their station in this life (it was God's will). This philosophy elevated the role of the Church in the society and economic system, and downplayed the importance of the individual. The rise of the Protestant challenge to Catholicism weakened the controlling role of the Catholic church on feudal society.

In addition, Protestantism offered a philosophy more directed toward individual salvation. Calvinism, in fact, provided a justification of profit making as demonstrating service to God in one's "calling." Working hard, earning profits, and plowing those profits back into the business constituted circumstantial evidence that one was among God's chosen. This new religious idea and the Protestant churches as institutions, along with an increased emphasis on political freedom and liberty, supported the creation of a new *individualism*. This spirit, in turn, prompted much of the behavior necessary to the establishment of capitalist institutions.

10. From the preceding material, list the feudal relations and institutions that were destroyed by the centuries of change in Western Europe between 1000 and 1800.

11. List the new relationships and institutions that were emerging to form capitalism.

EMERGENT CAPITALISM

By the late fifteenth and early sixteenth centuries in England, France, Spain, Belgium, and Holland, modern nation-states involving a coalition of monarchs and merchant capitalists had effectively eliminated the decentralized power of the feudal system. In its place emerged a new type of economic system, whose key elements formed the historical roots of **capitalism**. Profits became the primary motivation for productive activity. The resources necessary for production and distribution—the raw materials, tools, shops, factories, machinery—were owned by a new class of capitalists. Capitalists used their ownership of capital to organize production, sell goods, and earn profits. The profits, in turn, could be used to enrich the capitalists and to develop more capital. More capital led to more output, more profits, and so on in an accumulation of economic growth.

The sources of this early **capital accumulation process** and the emergence of capitalism were rooted in the increase in trade, exploration (along with colonialism and slavery), the enclosure movement, and the putting-out system. The new class of capitalists developed as the leading force in the economic system, and a new labor force, dependent on wages for income, changed the character of society, as well as the distribution of income. Like feudalism, capitalism would also change and develop, although even today it retains its basic elements of private ownership, profit making, and markets. The following discussion briefly traces some of the most important periods in the development of Western capitalism.

Mercantilism

To build and consolidate their political, economic, and military power, the new nation-states adopted a policy of **mercantilism**. Underlying that policy was the assumption that the foundation of a nation's power and prestige was trading. The object of trading was to accumulate and retain gold and silver bullion, which could be used to finance further trade or to enhance the nation's political and military power. This concern led to exploration to discover and hoard more precious metals. It also led to policies designed to maximize the flow of money into the nation and minimize the flow of money out.

Consequently, mercantilism developed trade monopolies to minimize the prices of imports and maximize the prices of exports, controlled importing and exporting, levied tariffs on imports, subsidized exports, and controlled shipping extensively. The state thus took a large degree of responsibility in geographic expansion and in controlling economic activity. At first, this sponsorship aided some nascent capitalists, but the state's overriding control over the economy eventually began to burden increasing numbers of individualistic and profit-motivated businesspeople.

The Rise of Classical Liberalism and the Industrial Revolution

Mercantilist restrictions gave rise in the eighteenth and nineteenth centuries to an opposition that ultimately prevailed and drastically reduced the amount of direct state interference in economic affairs. The movement to end mercantilism was spearheaded by a new philosophical and economic body of thought—**classical liberalism**.

In 1776, the Scottish philosopher Adam Smith published *The Wealth of Nations*, in which he argued forcefully that mercantilist policies interfered with the ability of private individuals and markets to produce maximum social welfare. Smith maintained that, although everyone was basically out to maximize his or her own welfare, private *competition* in production and consumption would ensure the best possible outcome for all. Therefore Smith argued that the state should not be involved in economic activity, and that beyond providing for law and order, national defense, and some public goods like highways, the state should take a laissez-faire attitude toward the economic system. Individuals would guide production and consumption. The emerging capitalist class in Western Europe seized on this philosophy and used it eventually to legislate an end to most mercantilist restrictions on trade and other economic activity.

Left to their own devices and the profit motive, English capitalists took early advantage of the technological advances of the Industrial Revolution. The introduction of more sophisticated machinery in textiles, transportation, iron production, and other industries led to a fantastic increase in the productive capacity of the English economic system. The Industrial

■ Mills on the Androscoggin River, Maine. Water power was a crucial factor in the location of mills throughout New England during the Industrial Revolution. *(Photograph by Tom Riddell)*

Revolution, as well as the entrepreneurs who financed and led it, spread throughout Western Europe and to North America.

However, the increase in production was not the only outcome of the Industrial Revolution and emergent capitalism. The factory became the symbol of a new manufacturing society, alongside continuing agricultural and community life. In the factory, working conditions were often unsafe and oppressive. Child labor was a fact of early industrial life. Men, women, and children depended almost totally on factory work for their livelihood. Families flocked to the cities in search of work. Outside the factories, people were crammed into the adjacent slums. Friedrich Engels, in *The Condition of the Working Class in England in 1844*, quotes a government commissioner's description of a Glasgow slum, the "wynds":

> The wynds . . . house a fluctuating population between 15,000 and 30,000 persons. This district is composed of many narrow streets and square courts and in the middle of each court there is a dunghill. Although the outward appearance of these places was revolting, I was nevertheless quite unprepared for the filth and misery that were to be found inside. In some bedrooms we visited at night we found a whole mass of humanity stretched on the floor. There were often 15 to 20 men and women huddled together, some being clothed and others naked. There was hardly any furniture there and the only thing which gave these holes the appearance of a dwelling was fire burning on the hearth. Thieving and prostitution are the main sources of income of these people.

12. Why were capitalists and classical liberals opposed to mercantilism?
13. Why was early capitalism so unmindful of the social effects of industrialization brought on by the Industrial Revolution?

The emergence of capitalism and a free market for labor encouraged, as well as fed on, the Industrial Revolution. These forces produced rapid economic growth and the factory system, as well as urban slums and adverse working conditions. Central to these changes was the spread of markets for goods and services throughout Western Europe and the world. With the diminution of the roles of tradition, custom, and the state in the economic affairs of Western Europeans, capitalism relied increasingly on *markets* to organize production and distribution. As factors of production, land, labor, and capital all became commodities that were bought and sold on markets for prices. This required the emergence of a market system in which producers made calculations based on prices of resources and products and directed toward the accumulation of profits.

Economic activity was thus directed through the operation of these markets and the determination of prices in them. The treatment of land, labor, and capital as commodities contrasted with the feudal system, wherein land and labor were part of the social organization of communities (feudal manors and guilds) and were regulated by social custom, tradition, and institutions. With the emergence of capitalism, land and labor became subject to the market for their occupation and use. In this way, as the late historian Karl Polanyi has argued in *The*

Great Transformation, capitalism required the subordination of social considerations to the economic dictates of the private market system. Production and distribution were organized, for the society, through markets.

||| 14. What is the significance of markets to capitalism?

THE DEVELOPMENT OF CAPITALISM IN THE UNITED STATES

As capitalism was forming in Europe, many of its institutions and relationships were transplanted to the American colonies. When the colonists eventually removed the yoke of English political and economic control during the American Revolution, they cleared the way for the formation and development of the United States' own form of capitalism. However, the Americans retained their debt to Western civilization, thought, and institutions. This lineage was important to the establishment of emerging capitalist attitudes and institutions in the colonies and their continuance after the Revolution.

Most of the colonists were Protestants who emphasized individualism and hard work. Private ownership of rural and urban production was the dominant form of economic organization. International and domestic trade flourished with the goal of private gain and profit. Markets developed and guided production. In the early years of the new nation, the government utilized mercantilist policies of controlling international trade to foster economic development and to protect the emergence of the United States as a Western nation-state.

Sources of U.S. Development

Throughout its first hundred years as a nation, the United States was primarily an agricultural economy. Through the mid-1870s, agricultural output accounted for more than half of total U.S. production, but by the mid-1880s the value of manufactured goods surpassed the value of agricultural goods. At the same time, the nonagricultural portion of the labor force began to outnumber those who worked on farms. (Later, about 1920, the nation's urban population surpassed the rural population.) Despite the country's being primarily rural and agricultural, the development of industry began early in the nineteenth century. Industrial production accelerated during the middle years of the nineteenth century, stimulated in part by the demands of the Civil War. By the turn of the century, the United States was the world's leading producer of both manufactured and agricultural goods.

What accounted for this tremendous economic achievement? One important source of American economic development, which is often neglected, was the role of the government. In the formative years of the nation, the government played a crucial role in the construction of a federal system in which economic trade flowed freely from one state to another. Indeed, this concern with encouraging trade within the United States was one of the primary reasons behind the construction and ratification of the Constitution. In addition, the government passed tariffs to protect infant industries, established a national currency, and created a legal framework that governed economic transactions. In the nineteenth century, federal, state, and local governments financed and encouraged the development of different forms of transportation that facilitated trade within the expanding nation.

Another source of growth was the vast supply of land and resources available to the United States. The country expanded westward throughout the eighteenth century. This expansion was made possible by conquering one after another of the Native American tribes, by the purchase of land from France and Russia, and by military conquest over Mexico and several European countries that still controlled land in North America. Through what was called Manifest Destiny, the United States eventually controlled the middle part of the North American continent from coast to coast. This expanding geographical territory supplied space for expansion and raw materials for increasing agricultural and industrial production. It also supplied an expanding volume of cotton and wheat exports for sale to Europe. This international market encouraged further agricultural production and made possible imports that facilitated industrial production. At the end of the nineteenth and the beginning of the twentieth centuries, the United States joined Western European countries in the process of expansion beyond their borders. U.S. imperialism, as the nation pursued Manifest Destiny beyond the North American continent into the Pacific, Asia, and Latin America, provided raw materials, markets, and investments that fueled further economic expansion.

Technology played a crucial role in the growth and development of the U.S. economy. The adoption of European methods of manufacturing textiles spurred the use of factory production, and the Industrial Revolution in the United States eventually led to the American manufacturing system—relying on interchangeable parts and later the mass assembly line. In agriculture, tractors and combines spurred a tremendous increase in agricultural production.

The American people themselves, both the original colonists and the later immigrants, proved to be an important source of growth and development. Strongly individualistic and dedicated to hard work, they took risks, organized productive activities, educated themselves, invented, worked, and conquered. The United States became a thriving and growing economy through a primarily private economic system based on the efforts of individuals and groups of individuals tied together through an expanding system of national markets for goods and services.

Coincident with all of these sources of growth, many institutions emerged to stimulate development. The banking system, retail and wholesale organizations, and the transportation system facilitated the expansion of economic activity with improved organization and lower costs. Related to the development of these sectors of the economy was the emergence of one of the foremost institutions of U.S. capitalism and economic production, the corporation. A legal combination of individuals, the *corporation* was a successful device for amassing resources for production. And in several leading industries—oil, the railroads, banking, steel, automobiles, and so on—large corporations led the advance of U.S. growth. In a sense, the history of the corporation and its development is the history of modern U.S. capitalism.

By the middle of the twentieth century, the United States was the dominant economic, political, and military country in the world. It was the most advanced nation in terms of manufacturing and agricultural techniques and production. It had the highest standard of living, on the average, for its almost 200 million citizens. And its people still valued individual economic and political freedom. For the most part, its development had been a success story.

Negative Aspects of U.S. Development

Throughout its history, however, there have also been some negative aspects of U.S. economic development. The conquest and exploitation of the American Indians must be counted as—and remain as—a black mark in U.S. history (as well as the annexation of much of Mexico). Slavery throughout the colonial period and until the Civil War relied on the inhuman subjugation and exploitation of human beings as sources of increased production. As both economic and political power became more concentrated, scandals of political and economic corruption have been rife throughout U.S. history. Private economic power has led to political corruption ranging from the Crédit Mobilier affair of the 1870s to the Teapot Dome scandal of the 1920s to more recent instances of illegal corporate campaign contributions in the United States and bribery abroad.

The latter part of the nineteenth century was marked by the industrialization of the U.S. economy, but it also witnessed the abuses of the "robber barons," entrepreneurs who were generally successful as well as ruthless in their business practices. In the process of consolidating the leading industries of the economy, promoting technological developments, building giant corporations, and amassing great personal fortunes, such men as Jay Gould, Andrew Carnegie, J. P. Morgan, and John D. Rockefeller bilked their partners, eliminated their competitors, underpaid their workers, and/or overcharged many of their customers.

During the development of the U.S. economy through the present, the country has been plagued by a host of problems that are of an economic origin or at least have an economic dimension. These include poverty, commercialism, pollution, militarism, racism, and sexism. These problems continue to challenge our economic institutions, relationships, and methods.

An additional negative aspect of U.S. capitalist development has been its instability. Throughout the late nineteenth and early twentieth centuries, the United States suffered through repeated depressions in economic activity. Periods of prosperity and boom were regularly followed by periods of depression and bust. Figure 3.1 graphically depicts this pattern. In the midst of these depressions, unemployment and economic hardship for many people increased dramatically and tragically. The worst depression occurred in the 1930s, when the decrease in economic activity spread around the world. In 1933, almost one-third of the workforce in the United States was

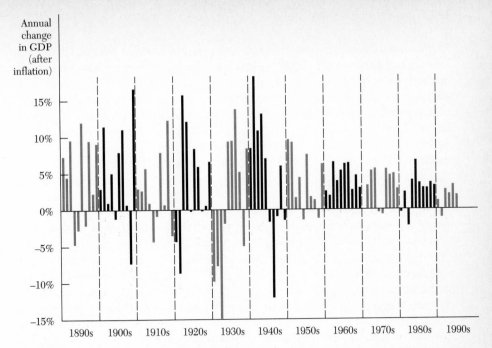

■ FIGURE 3.1 Economic instability in the U.S. economy (annual percent change in the U.S. gross domestic product)

Source: David Wyss, DRI/McGraw-Hill, for the *New York Times,* March 17, 1996.

without employment. The Great Depression was deep and lasted throughout the 1930s.

The Great Depression and the "escape" from it with the increased production and employment brought about by World War II, in fact, engendered one of the more recent alterations in the U.S. form of capitalism. Given the historical instability of capitalism's growth process, the federal government since the 1930s has taken a more direct responsibility for the overall health of the economy. It has attempted to prevent extremes in the cycles of boom and bust. Some would call this mixed capitalism; others might call it state capitalism. Still others, noting the role of the state and the role of large corporations in the economy, call it monopoly capitalism. At any rate, this expanded economic role of the state constitutes one more major change in the continuing development of U.S. capitalism.

15. On the basis of your conception of the U.S. economic system, list its five most important attributes. Are these positive or negative attributes? Are they results of the system? Or are they fundamental characteristics of it?

16. What is your name, or label, for our economic system? Why do you call it that?

The Post–World War II Experience

Following the demobilization of the economy after World War II, the United States experienced a quarter century of almost unprecedented economic growth and prosperity. During this time, there were periodic recessions, but the average standard of living increased at a rate of about 3 percent per year.

There were several bases for this era of prosperity. One was that the country emerged from the war as the world's leading military, economic, and political power, with its production base fully intact. From this position, it became the leader in establishing a new international economic trading and financial system that stimulated U.S. and western economies. Following the Great Depression and the war, the federal government, partly based on Keynesian economics (see Part 4), assumed increased responsibility for the general health of the economy and for maintaining prosperity. Building on the labor legislation of the New Deal, which granted labor unions the right to organize and collectively bargain, and the labor peace of the war period, big business and organized labor adopted a system of labor relations that minimized conflict and disruptions in production. Corporations themselves became larger and vigorously pursued profit-making possibilities at home and abroad. The result of these and other conditions was vigorous economic growth and the world's highest standard of living.

However, beginning in the late 1960s and early 1970s, the bases for the postwar prosperity began to break down, and specific events undermined the overall health of the U.S. economy. Consequently, at the beginning of the 1980s, the economy was plagued with stagflation—high unemployment (stagnation) and relatively high inflation—an energy crisis, and a general economic malaise.

The causes of this "crisis" in the economy were many, and they will be explored to some extent in the remainder of this book. But it is useful to mention a few of them briefly here. The United States lost some of its power in the world, partly as a result of its failure in Vietnam, but also because of the increased power of other countries, including Germany, France, Japan, and the Soviet Union. The United States encountered more effective competition in world markets. Third World countries assumed increased independence, nationalizing some U.S. corporations and adopting independent economic policies. Along these lines, the nations of the Organization of Petroleum Exporting Countries (OPEC) forced the United States to come to grips with expensive and scarce energy resources. The commitment to avoid depressions through the use of governmental economic policies had given the economy an inflationary bias. The relationship between big business and big labor also contributed to an inflationary spiral, with prices and wages moving ever upward. Inflationary expectations further fueled inflation. And there were many other problems as well, including declining productivity, a tax revolt, deregulation, racial and sexual discrimination, and continued poverty.

The Last Decades of the Twentieth Century

In evaluating the operation of the U.S. economy over more recent decades, economists can refer to many standard economic measures—such as the unemployment rate, the rate of inflation, gross domestic product, investment spending, and productivity—that are routinely compiled by government and other economists. By measuring economic activity over time, economists can develop a sense of how the economy is performing. Table 3.1 lists some important economic variables for the United States and shows how they have changed over the last half of the twentieth century.

As Table 3.1 indicates, the U.S. economy performed much less successfully in the 1970s than it did in the 1950s and 1960s. The unemployment rate and the rate of inflation were both higher, on average, than in the previous two decades. Average weekly earnings, after taking inflation into account, actually decreased during the 1970s. The rate of increase in total output per labor hour and the rate of increase in real total output both decreased. The economy was growing at a slower rate, although the rate of profit for corporations was higher than it had been in both the 1950s and the 1960s. In addi-

■ TABLE 3.1 Selected Measures of Economic Performance, 1950s–1990s

	1950s	1960s	1970s	1980s	1990s
Unemployment rate (annual average, percent)	4.5	4.8	6.2	7.3	6.3[a]
Rate of inflation (annual average increase in consumer prices, percent)	2.0	2.4	7.1	5.5	3.4[a]
Average weekly earnings (annual increase, in constant dollars, percent)	2.5	1.4	–0.3	–1.0	–0.5[a]
Output per labor hour (annual average increase, percent)	2.6	2.8	1.9	1.0	0.9[b]
Real output (annual average increase, percent)	4.0	4.3	3.2	2.8	1.8[b]
Rate of profit, after taxes (corporate profits as a percent of stockholders' equity, annual average)	11.3	11.1	12.8	12.2	9.9[b]
Rate of net investment (net private domestic investment as a percent of net national product, annual average)	8.2	7.7	7.6	5.1	3.4[b]

[a] Through 1996.
[b] Through 1995.
Source: *Economic Reports of the President,* various years.

tion, net investment, one of the most important sources of economic growth, was declining as a percentage of total output.

As the United States entered the 1980s, its economic system continued to be plagued with high unemployment and inflation and low rates of economic growth. For 1979 to 1981, real output grew by less than 2 percent per year. The unemployment rate was above 7 percent. Consumer prices were increasing at a rate of 12 to 13 percent a year. The real average weekly earnings for nonagricultural workers in 1980 were less than they had been in 1963. Interest rates were at historic highs. In 1981, the rate that banks charged their best corporate customers for loans was close to 20 percent. The federal deficit was beginning to increase and reached the $50 billion range in 1980 and 1981. And the value of the dollar in international exchange was at its lowest levels for the entire post–World War II period.

These various economic difficulties became a primary concern of economists and the centerpiece of Ronald Reagan's 1980 presidential campaign. The "Reagan Revolution" used the analysis of monetarist and supply-side economics to explain the slowdown in the economy and to develop a package of economic policies that came to be known as "Reaganomics." Very simply, Reagan argued that the country's economic difficulties were a result of too little economic growth. The source of the problem, he contended, was the excessive role of the government in the economy. There was too much regulation of business and too much government spending on social programs, taxes on corporations and individuals were too high, and the increase in the money supply was too rapid. All of this resulted in too much demand for output and not enough production to meet that demand—hence, slow growth and inflation. The solution was to increase the incentives and the rewards for the private sector. This would unleash corporations and individuals, and the nation would witness a massive surge in work and investment. The economy would grow more rapidly, providing economic prosperity with price stability once again.

The policies that President Reagan instituted and passed through Congress included a three-year package of cuts in individual and corporate income taxes, reductions in federal spending on a variety of social programs, deregulation in a variety of industries and business practices, a slowdown in the rate of growth of the money supply (actually the responsibility of the Federal Reserve System; see Chapter 17), and an increase in military spending to restore U.S. power in the world.

The immediate result of tighter money and cutbacks in federal spending was a severe recession in the early 1980s. Real output actually declined in 1982, and the unemployment rate rose above 10 percent. In 1983, however, the economy began to recover. Real output increased steadily throughout the mid-1980s, and the unemployment rate began to decline very slowly. Along with the recession, the rate of inflation dropped precipitously to just below 4 percent, but workers' average wages also continued to fall. With the recovery, the rate of productivity growth (output per hour) began to increase, as did investment spending. As a result of the recession, the tax cuts, and the massive increase in military spending, however, the federal deficit mushroomed to annual levels of close to $200 billion. All of these measurements suggest that there was some improvement in the economy but that significant problems remained at the end of the 1980s.

Table 3.1 provides some information on the overall performance of the U.S. economy during the 1980s. Real output continued to grow at a slower rate than in the 1950s and 1960s, at an average of 2.5 percent annually, although the economy grew continuously from 1982 without recession. The rate of productivity growth was less than half of what it was in the two decades immediately following World War II. With slower economic growth, the average unemployment rate actually increased during the 1980s, while the rate of inflation decreased somewhat. Average weekly earnings, adjusted for inflation, continued decreasing and by 1989 were no higher than they were in the early 1960s. Corporate profits, on the other hand, were as healthy as in the 1970s. Meanwhile, the rate of net investment decreased, suggesting continued slow growth in the economy. (Investment is a key determinant of economic growth. It represents spending on capital formation by businesses and expands the ability to produce.) Reaganomics and tight monetary policy by the Federal Reserve certainly led to a reduction in inflation, but they did not produce rampant economic growth, investment, and prosperity. The limited success was enough to form a basis for George Bush's winning 1988 presidential campaign.

A number of persistent and emerging problems accompanied these general economic trends. The federal budget deficit was reduced moderately by legislation (the Gramm-Rudman-Hollings Deficit Reduction Act of 1985), but remained in excess of $150 billion in the early 1990s, given Bush's reluctance to raise taxes and congressional resistance to reducing spending on federal social programs. The massive cost of bailing out the many savings and loan institutions that failed during this period compounded the difficulty of deficit reduction. The trade deficit showed some improvement as U.S. exports grew faster than U.S. imports during the late 1980s. But the U.S. economy was increasingly challenged in domestic and global markets by Japanese and European firms. The distribution of income in the United States became more unequal during the 1980s as a result of the 1981 tax cuts, restraints on government social spending programs, and the patterns of growth in the economy. Homelessness became an obvious national disgrace. At the same time, U.S. military spending was 50 percent higher in real terms than it was at the beginning of the decade. Global environmental problems received increasing public attention. The end of the Cold War held out the promise of reordered priorities.

In the early 1990s, there was a mild recession, just enough to cement George Bush's loss to Bill Clinton in the presidential election. As Table 3.1 shows, the economic news during Clinton's presidency indicated improvement. The unemployment rate continued to decline. The rate of inflation was reduced to half of what it was in the 1970s. The decline in average weekly earnings slowed somewhat. The increase in output per labor hour was the largest since the 1950s and 1960s. However, the growth rate for real output continued its long slowdown. Net investment also remained below the levels of the 1950s and 1960s. While a host of economic problems remain for the turn of the century, the early 1990s represented slow but stable growth—an adequate platform for Bill Clinton's reelection campaign.

The U.S. economy has come a long way in its 200-year history. It has largely been a history of successful development—not, however, without negative aspects and events. The United States has the world's largest and most industrialized economy. As we approach the end of the 1990s, some questions face the U.S. economy: Can the expansion (slow growth) be sustained? Can inflation be contained? Can the budget and trade deficits be reduced? Can the rate of productivity growth be increased?

CONCLUSION

In this chapter, we began with a description of what an economic system is and showed how economic systems change over time. In particular, we have explored the historical development of capitalism. In the remaining chapters of Part 2, we will examine how economic thought has changed as well over the years.

Review Questions

1. Discuss the distinguishing characteristics of ancient economic systems.
2. What must an economic system accomplish? Why?
3. Why is surplus a source of economic growth?
4. Explain the transition from feudalism to capitalism, and identify the main differences between the two systems.
5. What is the importance of markets to a capitalist economic system?
6. What accounts for the success of the U.S. economy?
7. Do you think the United States today has a capitalist economy? What are the major characteristics of capitalism?
8. Reread the passage by Karl Marx at the beginning of the chapter. Paraphrase his point in the last paragraph. Do you agree with his argument? Why or why not?
9. "The results of economic activity—what gets produced and how it gets produced—organized through an economic system, condition the nature, history and development of a society and its people." Give examples from the recent history of the United States. Give examples from your own experience.
10. "Economic development is obviously of crucial importance to any society and its continued survival." Why is this obvious? What would happen to a society if it didn't experience economic development? What are the advantages of economic development? Do you think that economic development has advantages for you? What are they?

4 Property, Adam Smith, and the Division of Labor

INTRODUCTION

All forms of life are sustained by the world, but much of the world is owned by only some of the people. What determines who owns the world and defines property rights? Who settles disputes over **ownership** (legal title to property)? Who disputes ownership? Individuals may evaluate identical economic situations in different ways because they have different perceptions of the situation and different personal interests. For example, slaves and slaveholders had a different relationship to and different ideas about slavery.

As population increases and requires increasing productivity from the land, the land becomes relatively scarce, and **property rights** (the rights to use owned property) become more important to owners. The distribution of property ownership is a significant determinant of the relative size of income received by the inhabitants of countries that stress the sanctity of **private property rights** (rights held by those who own their own, private, property).

Adam Smith was one of the first thinkers to develop a comprehensive description and analysis of this emerging economic system. Property and property rights contributed to the formation of new methods of production, including the division of labor, with specialization of tasks, which promoted an explosive expansion of output. The rise of capitalism also resulted in new ways of distributing income.

THE DEVELOPMENT OF PROPERTY IN ENGLAND

Great Britain is an island (comprising England, Wales, and Scotland) with a total area less than that of Pennsylvania and New York. Celts occupied early Britain, followed by the Romans, who arrived in 55 B.C. and departed about A.D. 410. Angles, Saxons, and Jutes arrived in the fifth century.

■ Property rights were established following the Norman Conquest of Britain by the building of a castle such as this one in York. Its vantage point, overlooking two rivers, assured the property holders that no invaders were sneaking up on them. *(Photograph by Tom Riddell)*

In 1066 William the Conqueror, with the approval of the pope, invaded England. With his Norman followers, he slew King Harold at the Battle of Hastings, burned houses, and destroyed crops and cattle. William and the Normans confiscated all the land, and William became the chief lord. He redistributed land titles to his favorite Norman subjects and reorganized the church. About 1085–1086 William ordered a detailed survey of every piece of land in England; it was to include information about the rights by which the land was held. This survey is the *Domesday Book*. William planned to use this information for tax purposes.

Almost two centuries later, in 1215, the barons (landholders), who felt threatened by the Crown, compelled King John to sign the Magna Carta, which would ensure the barons' rights from the encroaching authority of the king. This was a rebellion of feudal lords. The peasants and artisans were not rebelling, and the Magna Carta neither improved nor protected their rights.

A few centuries later, Henry VIII (1491–1547) established the Church of England. He closed the Catholic monasteries and abbeys, took all of their land, and appointed his own church officers. As British historian Maurice Keen notes in *The Outlaws of Medieval Legend*, "After that the way was clear for the biggest event in our agrarian history—the distribution of all monastery lands to the Tudor millionaires. These landowners—merchants now rather than barons or earls—built themselves . . . superb mansions."

1. In what ways might these events have helped shape the kind of economic system that developed in Britain?
2. What is a property right? What determines a property right?

Thus, private property emerged in England over the course of several centuries. Its roots lie in violent conquest by foreign armies under the leadership of individuals who became the medieval nobility. Later on, land was appropriated by kings and distributed to vassals, barons, and the church. This process was enforced by a combination of military power and monarchical or religious legal authority, and was often sanctioned by the church. As we saw in Chapter 3, the enclosure movement in the later Middle Ages accelerated this formal transfer of land to private owners.

THE SIGNIFICANCE OF PROPERTY

Through conquest, appropriation, and legislative act, land in England came to be privately owned. This was one of the bases for the private ownership of productive resources—one of the foundations of capitalism as an economic system. Under private ownership of property, an individual (or a group of individuals, as in a modern corporation) owns and controls a piece of land (or a factory, machine, or product). That ownership allows the owner to use the property, rent it to someone else, or even sell it. The decision about what to do with it rests with its owner.

If we assume that individuals are out to maximize their own self-interest, the property will be used in its most productive or profitable way. The property owner determines a use for the property based on his or her motivations, but also based on the operation of markets—for the property itself, either sold or rented, or for the outputs that it can produce. In other words, the property can be used to maximize the economic return to the owner. The owner has a right to the use and control of that property. And the existence of markets allows owners to seek out the most productive and profitable use for their property.

One necessary implication of property and property rights is that both must be defined within a particular society. Property implies possession and control. It has been, and can still be, determined by force and conquest. Property can be appropriated, willingly or unwillingly. In modern capitalist societies, we have legal documents that convey ownership—deeds, registrations, wills, and stock certificates. In addition, there are legislative, administrative, and judicial dimensions to the definition of property and property rights. Land is surveyed, counties record deeds of land and home ownership, communities pass zoning laws that regulate the use of property, and courts adjudicate disputes among property owners and enforce contracts. Property is an institution that is central to the functioning of markets in a capitalist economy, but it is also an institution that gets its essence from the social and political processes of the society.

Those without Property—The Peasants

During the early Middle Ages, the serfs on feudal manors seem to have accepted their lot in life. Their lives had security and certainty, if also hard work and poverty. What complaining there was seems to have been confined to individual peasants or manors. In the later centuries of the Middle Ages, however, as feudal institutions began to change and be replaced by emergent capitalist institutions, the peasants began actively and widely to oppose their rulers.

Beginning in the late fourteenth century and continuing through the sixteenth century, peasant revolts sprang up all over Western Europe. In most cases, the peasants were resisting change and attempting to secure their places in the feudal order. They opposed increasing mechanization of agricultural work, the consolidation of plots, the enclosure movement, the seizure of lands, and many of the other changes that signaled the rise of the landed gentry—and the demise of the peasants' rights to land and protection. All of these rebellions were brutally put down by the well-armed nobility. The peasants were leaderless, unorganized, and poorly armed. Their actions did, however, reflect a deep sense of outrage at the costs they bore as a result of fundamental changes in the economic, political, and social order of their day. Out of this history came the legends of Robin Hood and other outlaws of the Middle Ages.

During this period, British people in rural England were totally dependent on the productivity of the land. Those who lived in villages used common land to raise their crops, keep their bees, graze their livestock, and gather their firewood. Without access to land, they would have been without any means to sustain their lives. Over an extended period of time, a series of parliamentary acts converted many of the commons into private property. Whole villages were deserted; people who were independent when they could use the common lands became either vagrant or dependent on employment by those who owned the land.

3. What were the economic roots of the peasant rebellions?
4. What would you predict happened to the distribution of income in England as a result of these changes in property ownership?

Property and Economic Thought

The formation of truly private property, one of the fundamental prerequisites of capitalism, can be traced to the early history of England. As feudalism faded at the end of the Middle Ages, the notion of property in England was defined in legal terms. Laws conferred or acknowledged the right of ownership and protected the owner's control over the use of property. From the owner's perspective, such property rights and legal protection allowed for maximum earnings from the land and ensured their dominant position in society. From the perspective of the peasants, control of land was torn from them out of their own adversity and weakness through violent conquest and legal manipulation. This ensured their position at the bottom of society, forcing them into vagrancy or a dependence on wage labor for income. Out of frustration, peasants revolted against the emergence of private property throughout the late Middle Ages.

Control of the land was a dominant concern in England's emerging capitalist economy. Economic ideas were implicit in the struggle for control of the land, as well as in the organization of production. However, as capitalism moved into its adolescent stage with the coming of the Industrial Revolution in the eighteenth century, economic thinking became significantly more sophisticated.

The **division of labor** involves separating different parts of the production process of any good or service. Instead of one person making each computer, teams of workers make the casings, the chips, the boards, the connections, and the final assembly. **Specialization** results from workers' focusing on and developing expertise in one aspect of the entire process of producing computers.

ADAM SMITH AND THE DIVISION OF LABOR

Much of our current thinking about specialization and the division of labor has been influenced by the writings of Adam Smith (1723–1790). Smith was a Scottish scholar, primarily a moral philosopher, but also the real father of modern economics. His writing reflected changes he saw taking place, such as the introduction of modern productive methods, including the assembly line, which were derived from the early development of capitalism during the Industrial Revolution.

The year 1776 is significant because Adam Smith's great book *An Inquiry into the Nature and Causes of the Wealth of Nations* was published. It was the first comprehensive treatise about economics. However, there had been many books and essays about economic matters before Adam Smith, and he used ideas from them in his book. He brought them together and created a fairly complete picture of the way an economy behaves and why it behaved as it did in 1776. His observations coincided with the acceleration of the Industrial Revolution and the increasing importance of both domestic and international markets to British capitalists. He also argued for the replacement of mercantilism with competitive markets.

■ Adam Smith (1723–1790).
(*Corbis-Bettmann*)

Smith begins *The Wealth of Nations* with this classic description "Of the Division of Labour" in the context of emerging capitalist production:

> The greatest improvement in the productive powers of labour, and the greater part of the skill, dexterity, and judgment with which it is any where directed, or applied, seem to have been the effects of the division of labour.
>
> To take an example from a very trifling manufacturer: but one in which the division of labour has been very often taken notice of, the trade of the pin-maker; a workman not educated to this business (which the division of labour has rendered a distinct trade), not acquainted with the use of the machinery employed in it (to the invention of which the

same division of labour has probably given occasion), could scarce, perhaps, with his utmost industry, make one pin in a day, and certainly could not make twenty. But in the way in which this business is now carried on, not only the whole work is a peculiar trade, but it is divided into a number of branches, of which the greater part are likewise peculiar trades. One man draws out the wire, another straights it, a third cuts it, a fourth points it, a fifth grinds it at the top for receiving the head; to make the head requires two or three distinct operations; to put it on, is a peculiar business, to whiten the pins is another; it is even a trade by itself to put them into the paper; and the important business of making a pin is, in this manner, divided into about eighteen distinct operations, which, in some manufactories, are all performed by distinct hands, though in others the same man will sometimes perform two or three of them. I have seen a small manufactory of this kind where ten men only were employed, and where some of them consequently performed two or three distinct operations. But though they were very poor, and therefore but indifferently accommodated with the necessary machinery, they could, when they exerted themselves, make among them about twelve pounds of pins in a day. There are in a pound upwards of four thousand pins of a middling size. Those ten persons, therefore, could make among them upwards of forty-eight thousand pins in a day. Each person, therefore, making a tenth part of forty-eight thousand pins, might be considered as making four thousand eight hundred pins in a day.

||| 5. Were Adam Smith's perceptions influenced by historical time |
       when he wrote this part of the book? How so?

With this description of the division of labor, Adam Smith highlighted the role of specialization in significantly increasing productive potential. He attributed this great increase in productivity to three factors:

1. "The improvement of the dexterity of the workman necessarily increases the quantity of work he can perform; and the division of labor, by reducing every man's business to some one simple operation, and by making this operation the sole employment of his life, necessarily increases very much the dexterity of the workman."
2. The worker would gain time that used to be lost in moving from one type of work to another.
3. Labor would be made more productive by the application of machinery that would facilitate the division of labor.

Thus, specialization and the application of new technologies during the Industrial Revolution of the late eighteenth and early nineteenth centuries contributed to rapidly expanding output.

An important result of this increase in output accompanying the division of labor was that each worker "has a great quantity of his own work to dispose of beyond what he himself has occasion for." Since every worker is in the same position, **exchange** will take place. Smith puts it this way: "He supplies them abundantly with what they have occasion for, and they accommodate him as amply with what he has occasion for, and a general plenty diffuses itself through all the different ranks of the society." Through the division of labor, economic output will increase, and the existence of exchange will facilitate and further encourage this growth in output. The extension of **markets** (where goods and services are exchanged) throughout the world, the technological revolution, and the division of labor mutually reinforced one another.

> 6. "And the division of labor, by reducing every man's business to some one simple operation, and by making this operation the sole employment of his life, necessarily increases very much the dexterity of the workman."
>   a. How would you feel about having one simple operation made the sole employment of your life?
>   b. Would the people on an assembly line agree with your answer?

Smith traced the emergence of the division of labor in production to the fact that people do exchange goods and services: "It is the necessary, though very slow and gradual, consequence of a propensity in human nature which has in view no such extensive utility: *the propensity to truck, barter, and exchange* one thing for another" [italics added]. Because people have a tendency to exchange, they will begin to specialize in producing what they do best and to trade with others for the other things that they need. Through this process, the division of labor proceeds and economic output increases. Historically, the rapidly spreading and more sophisticated markets in Western Europe tremendously accelerated the development of the division of labor.

Adam Smith further argued that all of this great economic progress derived from the seeking of *self-interest* by individuals. Individuals enter markets for exchange to benefit themselves. But out of this quest for self-gain, a general good develops in the form of increasing prosperity for all:

> But man has almost constant occasion for the help of his brethren, and it is in vain for him to expect it from their benevolence only. He will be more likely to prevail if he can interest their self-love in his favour, and shew them that it is for their own advantage to do for him what he requires of them. Whoever offers to another a bargain of any kind, proposes to do this. Give me that which I want, and you shall have this which you want, is the meaning of every such offer; and it is in this manner that we obtain from one another the far greater part of those good offices which we stand in need of. It is not from the benevolence of the butcher, the brewer, or the baker, that we expect our dinner, but from their regard to their own interest. We address ourselves, not to their humanity but to their self-love, and never talk to them of our own necessities but of their advantages.

General prosperity and economic growth—the wealth of the nation—result from the pursuit of self-interest organized through the division of labor and markets. This is the essence of what Smith calls the "**invisible hand,**" the force whereby the operation of markets—unfettered by mercantilist regulations—produces general welfare for all, where resources are allocated efficiently.

7. Adam Smith thought the division of labor derived from people's "propensity to truck, barter, and exchange one thing for another." Do you agree with Smith's reasoning here? Why or why not?

8. "But man has almost constant occasion for the help of his brethren, and it is in vain for him to expect it from their benevolence only. He will be more likely to prevail if he can interest their self-love in his favour, and shew them that it is for their own advantage to do for him what he requires of them."
   a. Do you agree with Smith's assumption about the nature of people's behavior? How did Smith arrive at this conclusion?
   b. If it is an accurate assumption about present behavior, do people have any choice about behaving in any other way?

Side Effects of the Division of Labor

Adam Smith focused on the relation of the division of labor, specialization, exchange, and markets to the wealth of nations. He also showed sensitivity to some side effects of the division of labor. The first of these is a problem that we still experience today: the alienation and boredom of manual labor, the assembly line, and office work. These result from the division of labor and specialization within the workplace, motivated by the capitalist's search for profits and the need to manage labor. Smith wrote about this problem bluntly and graphically in this passage from *The Wealth of Nations:*

> In the progress of the division of labour, the employment of the far greater part of those who live by labour, that is, of the great body of the people, comes to be confined to a few very simple operations, frequently to one or two. But the understandings of the greater part of men are necessarily formed by their ordinary employments. The man whose whole life is spent in performing a few simple operations, of which the effects too are, perhaps, always the same, or very nearly the same, has no occasion to exert his understanding, or to exercise his invention in finding out expedients for removing difficulties which never occur. He naturally loses, therefore, the habit of such exertion, and generally becomes as stupid and ignorant as it is possible for a human creature to become. The torpor of his mind renders him not only incapable of relishing or bearing a part in any rational conversation, but of conceiving any generous, noble, or tender sentiment, and consequently of forming any just judgment concerning many even of the ordinary duties of private life.
>
> His dexterity at his own particular trade seems, in this manner, to be acquired at the expence of his intellectual, social, and martial virtues. But in every improved and civilized society this is the state into which the labouring poor, that is, the great body of the people, must necessarily fall, unless government takes some pains to prevent it.

An additional consequence of this tendency is that the guidance of society must fall to the few, the elite, who are not stupefied by the repetitiveness of their labors. In fact, the division of labor under capitalism not only increased efficiency, it also promoted the control of the capitalist over the work process and the workers. This can be seen in the emergence of the putting-out system and later the factory system (see Chapter 3). This process effectively splits society into classes—the educated elite and the "great body of the people"—which also have different claims on the income generated by production.

> 9. Does specialization normally result in workers who are "as stupid and ignorant as it is possible for a human creature to become"? How was this statement of Smith's conditioned by historical time? Do you agree with it? Why or why not?

THE DISTRIBUTION OF INCOME

Economic production creates value—goods and services for exchange on markets. Once this value has been produced, income determines how it will be divided among the people. Early economists, such as Adam Smith, who were beginning to think of economics as a social science, defined and classified income receivers as they appeared at that time. They classified the receivers of the shares of output into the following categories: (1) **laborers**, (2) **landowners**, and (3) **owners of capital**. Economists have also named the shares of income that each receives: labor receives **wages**, landowners receive **rent**, and owners of capital receive **profits**.

Each of these shares is received in money, but the money is only a claim for the real goods and services. It would have no value without those goods and services to claim as the money holder's share. Thus, income distribution determines the distribution of products.

> 10. Another way of thinking about money in relation to claims on the shares of production is to imagine each dollar in the hands of the income receivers (labor, landowners, and capital owners) as a draft on people's labor. Are there dollar drafts on your labor? Can you refuse to be drafted? Who might be exempt from the dollar draft? If drafted, when do you have to perform your service?

Adam Smith recognized that this division of the national product into shares must bring about some harsh conflicts among the three groups of share receivers:

Envy, malice, or resentment, are the only passions which can prompt one man to injure another in his person or reputation. . . . Men may live together in society with some tolerable degree of security, though there is no civil magistrate to protect them from the injustice of those passions. But avarice and ambition in the rich, in the poor the hatred of labour and the love of present ease and enjoyment, are the passions which prompt to invade property, passions much more steady in their operation, and much more universal in their influence. Wherever there is great property, there is great inequality. For one very rich man, there must be at least five hundred poor, and the affluence of the few supposes the indigence of the many. The affluence of the rich excites the indignation of the poor, who are often both driven by want, and prompted by envy, to invade his possessions. It is only under the shelter of the civil magistrate that the owner of that valuable property, which is acquired by the labour of many years, or perhaps of many successive generations, can sleep a single night in security. The acquisition of valuable and extensive property, therefore, necessarily requires the establishment of civil government.

The shares of the national product, then, are distributed unequally, primarily because of the unequal distribution of private property (land and capital). While this may lead to conflicts among the different groups of share receivers because each wants to maximize its own share, the government protects private property and, hence, its share of the output.

11. "The acquisition of valuable and extensive property, therefore, necessarily requires the establishment of civil government." Is the purpose of government to protect the rich from the poor? Explain.

In addition to the role played by the state, the operation of markets also resolves the conflict over the division of national output. Each group is out to maximize its position, its own share of production. However, all economic transactions take place in markets for goods and services and, as a result, are regulated by the operation of competition. A worker will not work for a lower wage if he or she can get a higher wage from another master. A person will not buy a product at a price greater than that of another seller. Smith explains this in the following passage on the "invisible hand":

Every individual is continually exerting himself to find out the most advantageous employment for whatever capital he can command. It is his own advantage, indeed, and not that of the society, which he has in view. But the study of his own advantage naturally, or rather necessarily leads him to prefer that employment which is most advantageous to the society.

But the annual revenue of every society is always precisely equal to the exchangeable value of the whole annual produce of its industry, or rather is precisely the same thing with that exchangeable value. As every individual, therefore, endeavours as much as he can both to employ his capital in the support of domestic industry, and so to direct that industry that its produce may be of the greatest value; every individual necessarily labours to render the annual revenue of the society as great as he can. He generally, indeed, neither intends to promote the public interest, nor knows how much he is promoting it. By preferring the support of domestic to that of foreign industry, he intends only his own security; and by directing that industry in such a manner as its produce may be of the greatest value, he intends only his own gain, and he is in this, as in many other cases, led by *an invisible hand* to promote an end which was no part of his intention. Nor is it always the worse for the society that it was no part of it. By pursuing his own interest he frequently promotes that of the society more effectually than when he really intends to promote it.

Despite the apparent conflict and the motivation of self-gain, the operation of the economic system produces the greatest good for the greatest number. According to Smith, social good results, even though "society . . . was no part" of directing the activity. Rather, it results from everyone's seeking his or her own advantage.

12. What does Smith mean when he says, "He is in this, as in many other cases, led by *an invisible hand*"? What is an "invisible hand"?
13. Do you agree with Smith when he says, "But the study of his own advantage naturally, or rather necessarily leads him to prefer that employment which is most advantageous to the society"? Can you think of any counterexamples?

CONCLUSION

Property, markets, exchange, division of labor, and specialization emerged in the development of capitalism. Along with these institutions and aspects of changing economic activity, economic theory began to develop to describe, explain, and promote capitalism. The next two chapters explore some of those theories.

Review Questions

1. What is property? Why is it important?
2. What is the origin of private property in the United States?
3. Who or what defines an outlaw? Was Robin Hood an outlaw?
4. Why is it important to know something about the history of economic thought?
5. Would production activity in the United States be as advanced as it is without assembly lines and the division of labor?
6. What is the relationship of private property (in the form of factories) to the division of labor? Are they necessary to each other?
7. Why is income in the United States distributed unequally?
8. Should income be distributed more equally? Why or why not?
9. "The extension of markets . . . throughout the world, the technological revolution, and the division of labor mutually reinforced one another." Use some examples to demonstrate that this process is still at work in the world.

5

The Rise of Laissez-Faire

INTRODUCTION

At the end of the eighteenth century, a new school of economists wished to transfer control of their national economies from the mercantilism of aristocratic ruling classes to the direction of a self-equilibrating free-market system. They called this system (from the Physiocrats in France) **laissez-faire**, meaning "let it happen," or "let it be." Such a policy, they argued, would produce rapid economic progress. As laissez-faire ideas were adopted, growth did take place, but it was accompanied by poverty and business cycles.

J. B. Say assured economists in 1803 that if markets were left free, there could be only temporary and minor problems of unemployment. This was because production always created its own demand, and demand created production. Known as **Say's law**, this doctrine was widely accepted by most economists throughout the nineteenth century.

However, some economists attempted to call attention to continuing unemployment problems and suggested various ideas for responding to the problems. These socialistic economists were either ignored or viewed as dangerous radicals by the dominant school of economists in the universities and the ruling classes. By 1926 John Maynard Keynes was convinced that laissez-faire was no longer an appropriate way of thinking about unemployment. Others had noticed this 50 to 100 years earlier, but it was Keynes's contribution that ultimately signaled the fall of laissez-faire.

THE FLOW OF ECONOMIC ACTIVITY

Some classical economists of the nineteenth century claimed that the demand for a product would always equal the supply. The reason, which seemed self-

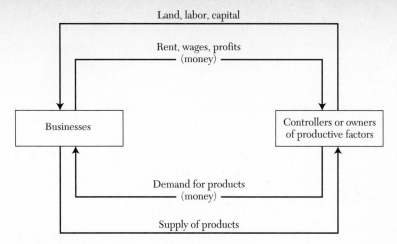

FIGURE 5.1 The Flow of Economic Activity

evident, was based on the flow of economic activity. As we have seen, three factors of production (land, labor, and capital) are combined to create the national product. Each controller of the three productive factors—landlords, laborers, and capitalists—receives a share of the total product transformed conveniently into money and uses it to claim output. Thus, the controllers of the factors of production receive claims on shares for everything they supply in the production process, and these claims become the demand for part of the total product. Demand for the product is therefore created in the process of supplying the product. Figure 5.1 illustrates this flow of economic activity.

J. B. SAY AND GLUTS

Jean Baptiste Say (1767–1832), a French economist who studied, modified, and amplified the ideas of Adam Smith, stated this idea in *A Treatise on Political Economy* (1803):

> It is worthwhile to remark that a product is no sooner created, than it, from that instant, affords a market for other products to the full extent of its own value. When the producer has put the finishing hand to his product, he is most anxious to sell it immediately, lest its value should vanish in his hands. Nor is he less anxious to dispose of the money he may get for it; for the value of money is also perishable. But the only way of getting rid of money is in the purchase of some product or other. Thus, the mere circumstance of the creation of one product immediately opens a vent for other products.

However, a few economists were concerned about unemployment resulting from more production than people might demand. What if some wrong products are produced, and they are not all purchased? Won't there be unemployment because of insufficient demand in those industries? What if there is more production generally than the people are able to purchase? Economists called this situation a **glut** in the market. Gluts create unemployment and poverty that lead to terrifying social conditions and great suffering. Wouldn't that concern economists?

Thomas Robert Malthus (1766–1834), a British economist, was one of the few economists concerned about these possible gluts. In his *Principles of Political Economy* (1820), he says:

> It has been thought by some very able writers, that although there may easily be a glut of particular commodities, there cannot possibly be a glut of commodities in general; because, according to their view of the subject, commodities being always exchanged for commodities, one half will furnish a market for the other half, and production being thus the sole source of demand, an excess in the supply of one article merely proves a deficiency in the supply of some other, and a general excess is impossible. M[onsieur] Say, in his distinguished work on political economy, has indeed gone so far as to state that the consumption of a commodity by taking it out of the market diminishes demand, and the production of a product proportionably increases it.
>
> This doctrine, however, as generally applied, appears to me to be utterly unfounded, and completely to contradict the great principles which regulate supply and demand.
>
> It is by no means true, as a matter of fact, that commodities are always exchanged for commodities. An immense mass of commodities is exchanged directly, either for productive labour, or personal services: and it is quite obvious, that this mass of commodities, compared with the labour with which it is to be exchanged, may fall in value from a glut just as any one commodity falls in value from an excess of supply, compared either with labour or money.
>
> In the case supposed there would evidently be an unusual quantity of commodities of all kinds in the market, owing to those who had been before engaged in personal services having been converted, by the accumulation of capital, into productive labourers; while the number of labourers altogether being the same, and the power and will to purchase for consumption among landlords and capitalists being by supposition diminished, commodities would necessarily fall in value compared with labour, so as very greatly to lower profits, and to check for a time further production.
>
> But this is precisely what is meant by the term glut, which, in this case, is evidently general not partial.

||| 1. Why has demand decreased, according to Malthus? |

Say and others countered the underconsumption argument set forth by Malthus by claiming that whenever a glut of any particular product emerged, markets would immediately adjust through price changes and the reallocation of resources. If one product was overproduced, its price would fall and resources would go elsewhere. Activity would shift to those products "most in request." Consequently, gluts would soon be eliminated through the operation of the market system. This reasoning supported the idea of laissez-faire.

J. B. Say won the argument with Thomas Malthus in the realm of economic theory. There were significant reasons for this victory, in spite of the prevalence of repeated gluts, unemployment, poverty, and economic depressions in capitalist nations.

Economists and businessmen were convinced that a self-adjusting economy, free from government controls, was the best system for generating profits and growth. This was Smith's concept of an "invisible hand" directing a free economy to prosperity at work. The idea of laissez-faire was similar to this "invisible hand." Businessmen wanted to run their own affairs without—well, almost without—government interference.

The laissez-faire idea is to permit market forces *under competitive conditions* to operate unhindered. Economists said that if the market were permitted to work on its own, it would be most efficient and most advantageous to society. People would demand the products they wanted as they spent their income. This would determine which products would be produced. Doesn't that seem better than having a powerful individual or group of people decide which products will be produced?

Laissez-faire, said the economists, has additional benefits: All of the owners of the factors of production will be directed into the most effective use of the factors of production by the market. It will be to their greatest advantage to produce the products for which there is a demand in the marketplace. If the owners of the productive factors use them to produce only what they themselves want, no one will purchase the products. There will be no shares given in the national pie of products to those productive-factor owners who don't follow market demand.

Therefore, the theory went, let the market be, *laissez-faire*; don't interfere with it. It is controlled by an "invisible hand." It will regulate itself. Furthermore, markets will eliminate any gluts and unemployment. Let it be.

All of this is based on the assumption that people will work for their own self-interest. Adam Smith had already asserted the validity of this assumption.

2. What is your evaluation of the laissez-faire idea?
3. What are your assumptions about people's behavior? Are they consistently selfish? Are they consistently altruistic (meaning their actions are based on regard for others)? Which are you? Were you born selfish or altruistic? Have you been educated to be selfish or altruistic? By whom or what?
4. Would Adam Smith think it is more patriotic to be selfish or altruistic? Why?

As mercantilist policies were abandoned and laissez-faire policies were adopted in England, the Industrial Revolution and the emergence of capitalist institutions proceeded. During this period, business sought freedom from intrusive state control, and prospered.

Adam Smith argued that it would be better to transfer control of the economy from the self-interest of the ruling class to individual self-interest as expressed in the marketplace. His preference for nontraditional direction led him to perceive the market as an impartial control of resource allocation and income distribution. He hoped the market was impartial, but was it? Smith was aware of the difficulties in his solution. He knew about the ability of combinations of employers to overwhelm the bargaining power of workers, but he continued to support markets free from government controls—laissez-faire.

What he may not have fully perceived was that the transfer of market controls from the self-interest of the ruling class to the self-interest of those who had the control of the largest quantities of productive resources was not necessarily the ideal solution for a sick economy. But it may have been an improvement in 1776. Smith thought it would be when he wrote in *The Wealth of Nations* about the allocation of capital by an individual:

> What is the species of domestic industry which his capital can employ, and of which the produce is likely to be of the greatest value, every individual, it is evident, can, in his local situation, judge much better than any statesman or lawgiver can do for him. The statesman, who should attempt to direct private people in what manner they ought to employ their capitals, would not only load himself with a most unnecessary attention, but assume an authority which could safely be trusted, not only to no single person, but to no council or senate whatever, and which would nowhere be so dangerous as in the hands of a man who had folly and presumption enough to fancy himself fit to exercise it.

THE SOCIALIST CRITIQUE OF LAISSEZ-FAIRE

The conditions of some members of the economy were improving with laissez-faire, but the fate of others was extreme poverty. Why weren't conditions for the poor improving as well? As markets and private property emerged in Western Europe, most people became dependent on wage labor for income. Work was not always available, and many peasants ended up in urban areas, where they inhabited emerging slums and, if possible, worked in the developing factories. Living and working conditions were extremely poor. And with so many competing for jobs, wages were very low. The growing working class during the Industrial Revolution paid the social cost of industrialization in the cities and the factories of Western Europe.

Pierre Joseph Proudhon (1809–1865), a French economist, came to a conclusion about the continuing situation of low income that he stated forcefully in his essay "What Is Property?" (1840):

> If I were asked to answer the following question: *What is slavery?* and I should answer in one word, *It is murder*, my meaning would be understood at once. No extended argument would be required to show that the power to take from a man his thought, his will, his personality, is a power of life and death; and that to enslave a man is to kill him. Why, then, to this other question: *What is property?* may I not likewise answer, *It is robbery*, without the certainty of being misunderstood; the second proposition being no other than a transformation of the first?

Reader, calm yourself: I am no agent of discord, no firebrand of sedition. I anticipate history by a few days; I disclose a truth whose development we may try in vain to arrest; I write the preamble of our future constitution. This proposition which seems to you blasphemous—*property is robbery*—would, if our prejudices allowed us to consider it, be recognized as the lightning-rod to shield us from the coming thunderbolt; but too many interests stand in the way! . . . Alas! philosophy will not change the course of events; destiny will fulfill itself regardless of prophecy. Besides, must not justice be done and our education be finished?

The proprietor, the robber, the hero, the sovereign—for all these titles are synonymous—imposes his will as law, and suffers neither contradiction nor control; that is, he pretends to be the legislative and executive power at once. Accordingly, the substitution of the scientific and true law for the royal will be accomplished only by a terrible struggle; and this constant substitution is, after property, the most potent element in history, the most prolific source of political disturbances. Examples are too numerous and too striking to require enumeration.

5. *"What is property? . . . It is robbery."* True or false? What does Proudhon mean by this? What historical developments in the emergence of private property would support this claim?

Proudhon is careful to differentiate **property** from **possessions**. He has no quarrel with people owning *personal* possessions—homes, farms, tools, livestock, furniture, or any of the things we might own and use. He protests the ownership of *impersonal* property that is not used by the owner except to collect rents on land and interest and profits on capital that are produced by others. The difference between property and possessions is an important distinction for many socialist authors. Here is Proudhon's statement about the difference:

> Individual possession is the condition of social life; five thousand years of property demonstrate it. Property is the suicide of society. Possession is a right; property is against right. Suppress property while maintaining possession, and, by this simple modification of the principle you will revolutionize law, government, economy, and institutions; you will drive evil from the face of the earth.

6. To demonstrate your understanding of Proudhon's definition, write five currently familiar examples of "possessions" and five of "property."

In fact, one of the great ironies of the concept of laissez-faire is that it requires the government to define and enforce its primary institution—private property. Karl Polanyi, in his history of the emergence of capitalism and laissez-faire, *The Great Transformation*, emphasizes the willful creation of a new economic order:

> There was nothing natural about laissez-faire; free markets could never come into being merely by allowing things to take their course. Just as cotton manufacturers—the leading free trade industry—were created by the help of protective tariffs, export bounties, and indirect wage subsidies, laissez-faire itself was enforced by the state.

Proudhon was only one of many who were sufficiently uncomfortable with economic conditions to want to try something entirely different. The United States seemed to be a country in which some of these dissatisfied people could experiment. A proliferation of various utopian communities developed in America. After all, wasn't it envisioned as a country for people with hopeful spirits? These people were seeking new forms of a social and political paradise. These communities practiced everything from communism to fascism, from celibacy to communal sexual intercourse and selective human breeding, and from anarchistic decentralization to dictatorial centralization. But what they had in common was a vision of a political and economic situation preferable to what they were experiencing.

Not all of the discontented people emigrated to the United States. Many participated in political action to change their home economies and governments. There were general strikes with all workers striking at the same time, revolutions, and political education activities working toward evolutionary change. John Stuart Mill (1806–1873) in his *Principles of Political Economy* envisioned a different kind of economy from the one of which he was writing in England in 1848:

> The form of association, however, which if mankind continue to improve, must be expected in the end to predominate, is not that which can exist between a capitalist as chief, and workpeople without a voice in the management, but the association of the labourers themselves on terms of equality, collectively owning the capital with which they carry on their operations, and working under managers elected and removable by themselves.

7. How would you evaluate these midnineteenth-century comments of John Stuart Mill?

The **socialist critique** of nineteenth-century capitalism was developed further in a piece also published in 1848. In this year Karl Marx (1818–1883) and Friedrich Engels (1820–1895) wrote *The Communist Manifesto* for the Communist League, an association of working people in Germany. Marx and Engels argued forcefully that the capitalist system itself was the source of the poverty and instability experienced by the growing working class. They urged workers to organize themselves for their own protection and to fight for socialism. We will explore Marx's ideas in more detail in the next chapter.

THE FLOWERING OF LAISSEZ-FAIRE

Despite the conditions of the poor and the socialist critique, laissez-faire capitalism flourished in nineteenth-century England and throughout Western Europe. Queen Victoria reigned from 1837 to 1901 and gave her name to the Victorian Age. This age witnessed increasing commercial dominance over formal and informal institutions that affected social values and behavior. Railway expansion and the telegraph revolutionized transportation and communication, thereby quickening the pace of life. People began to illuminate their homes with electricity. The first cars were on the roads. The

■ Brantwood, the elegant home of John Ruskin. *(Photograph by Tom Riddell)*

Carnegies, Vanderbilts, and Rockefellers were accumulating their enormous wealth. Coal and oil displaced animals and water power as sources of energy.

As the pace quickened, production increased, and more people attempted to succeed in business. A few individuals began to wonder about where all of this movement might lead. Among them was the English essayist John Ruskin (1819–1900), one of the great thinkers and writers in the Victorian Age, whose works about art, architecture, and political economy have continuing relevance today. In an 1864 essay named "Traffic," he questions the "ideal of human life" and describes the worshippers of the "Goddess of Getting-on":

> Your ideal of human life then is, I think, that it should be passed in a pleasant undulating world, with iron and coal everywhere underneath it. On each pleasant bank of this world is to be a beautiful mansion, with two wings; and stables, and coach-houses; a moderately-sized park; a large garden and hot-houses; and pleasant carriage drives through the shrubberies. In this mansion are to live the favoured votaries of the Goddess; the English gentleman, with his gracious wife, and his beautiful family; he always able to have the boudoir and the jewels for the wife, and the beautiful ball dresses for the daughters, and hunters for the sons, and a shooting in the Highlands for himself. At the bottom of the bank is to be the mill; not less than a quarter of a mile long, with one steam engine at each end, and two in the middle and a chimney three hundred feet high. In this mill are to be in constant employment from eight hundred to a thousand workers, who never drink, never strike, always go to church on Sunday, and always express themselves in respectful language.

8. Write a paragraph about your ideal of human life, discussing the same kinds of subjects mentioned by Ruskin: houses, environment, transportation, recreation, family, and industry.
9. Ruskin wrote, "There is no wealth but life." Do you agree? Explain.

The majority of people in England did not share the same vision. Their reality was one of poor housing, unemployment or low wages, and urban squalor. Poor people were still around throughout the Victorian Age, and the people in the mansions were uneasy about their presence. It was a time of general economic growth but also of continuing economic disparity. The implications of that disparity offered a potential threat to the existing social, political, and economic order. In *The Victorian Frame of Mind*, historian Walter E. Houghton explains this characteristic of the period:

> To think it strange that the great age of optimism was also an age of anxiety is to overlook the ambivalent reaction which the main social and intellectual tendencies of the period provoked. Expanding business, scientific development, the growth of democracy, and the decline of Christianity were sources of distress as well as of satisfaction. . . .
>
> For all its solid and imposing strength, Victorian society, particularly in the period before 1850, was shot through, from top to bottom, with the dread of some wild outbreak of the masses that would overthrow the established order and confiscate private property.

‖ 10. Are wealthy people in the United States today worried about revolution? Why or why not? Elsewhere?

THE SITUATION IN THE UNITED STATES AND VEBLEN'S CRITIQUE

In the United States, the Industrial Revolution occurred in the last half of the nineteenth century. By the beginning of the twentieth century, the United States was the world's leading producer of both agricultural and manufactured goods. U.S. capitalism and markets spread across the North American continent and began to reach out to the rest of the world. Economic output increased dramatically—but this success was not unchallenged. Poverty persisted, a militant labor movement emerged along with a growing working class, periodic financial crises and depressions disrupted the path of growth, and there were continuing problems associated with Native American tribes and the end of slavery. The development of the U.S. economic system was full of successes *and* difficulties.

Thorstein Veblen (1857–1929) was one of the first economists to develop a comprehensive critique of American capitalism. He wrote during a period marked by continuing industrialization and growth, but also by increasing business concentration and recurrent economic depressions. One of his first books, *The Theory of the Leisure Class* (1899), noted the rise of a new class of people in U.S. society, accompanying the economic progress of the Industrial Revolution. These propertied people were privileged to engage in "conspicuous consumption" as testimony to their success. Veblen, in a sarcastic but penetrating style, offered numerous examples of the new leisure class seeking status through the purchase of houses, clothing, and other goods. His tone and insight about "pecuniary emulation" also called attention to the fact that, as in Europe, the industrialization process did not enrich everyone, although it did subject the entire society to the influences of heightened materialism.

In later works, most notably *The Theory of Business Enterprise* (1904) and *Absentee Ownership* (1923), Veblen identified some trends that characterized U.S. economic experience with laissez-faire capitalism. These trends were part and parcel of the American economic success, but they also suggested some future difficulties. Veblen saw a distinction between business and industry. In *Absentee Ownership*, he wrote, "The industrial arts are a matter of tangible performance directed to work that is designed to be of material use to man. . . . [The] arts of business are arts of bargaining, effrontery, salesmanship, make-believe, and are directed to the gain of the business man at the cost of the community, at large and in detail."

This distinction was important to his interpretation of the primary trends in U.S. economic development: a tendency toward business concentration, rapid technological advance, and a constant difficulty with depression. Monopoly resulted from the business instinct to eliminate competition as one of the most effective ways to secure profits. But technological progress also was caused by the business drive for profits. The problem arose because technology constantly pushed the ability of the industrial arts to produce more, but monopoly held back production to get higher prices and profits. The consequence, according to Veblen, was a constant tendency toward depression. The depressions of the 1870s and 1890s in the United States provided real evidence that Say's law should be suspect, and that Veblen's concern with explaining the frequency of high levels of unemployment, if not exactly correct, was at least worth pursuing.

Veblen was an **institutionalist**. The institutionalists were critical of the neoclassical school of economics. They argued that the focus of such economists was too narrow and that their method was too abstract. The neoclassical economists paid too little attention to the influence of other factors in affecting economic behavior. Specifically, the institutionalists, and Veblen as one of their leading figures, argued that analysis of economic events must take account of history, institutions, the pursuit of power, and the complexity of human motivation. The following passage from Veblen's *The Place of Science in Modern Civilization* (1919) demonstrates the institutionalist critique of the neoclassical theory of markets and its assumptions about consumer behavior:

> The psychological and anthropological preconceptions of economists have been those which were accepted by the psychological and social sciences some generations ago. The hedonistic conception of man is that of a lightning calculator of pleasures and pains, who oscillates like a homogeneous globule of desire of happiness under the impulse of stimuli that shift him about the area, but leave him intact. He has neither antecedent nor consequent. He is an isolated, definitive human datum, in stable equilibrium except for the buffets of the impinging forces that displace him in one direction or another. Self-imposed in elemental space, he spins symmetrically about his own spiritual axis until the parallelogram of forces bears down upon him, whereupon he follows the line of the resultant. When the force of the impact is spent, he comes to rest, a self-contained globule of desire as before.

||| 11. Are you a "self-contained globule of desire"? Are you subject to "buffets of impinging forces"?

THE KEYNESIAN CRITIQUE OF LAISSEZ-FAIRE

The British economist John Maynard Keynes (1883–1946), followed the classical tradition, but in the early 1920s he began to write about his departure from the classical ideas held by most economists. By 1929 he was advising the British government to spend freely on public works programs to promote employment. A bit later, President Franklin Roosevelt, confronted by millions of families without any income because laissez-faire capitalism was unable to provide employment in the 1930s, increased the influence of government in the U.S. economy.

During the 1920s, Keynes wrote an essay, "The End of Laissez-Faire," in which he challenged the notion that the search for private interests always led to the greater good for the society as a whole. In particular, he was convinced that capitalism did not automatically produce full employment. He rejected Say's law and suggested that the state might have to assume some responsibility for the overall health of capitalist economies. Capitalism might be stronger, he argued, if some decisions were left in private hands; but some others, which were social in nature, ought to be the responsibility of the state.

Keynes thus began to explore the idea that laissez-faire did not always necessarily result in the greatest social good. He argued, in fact, that the state should take an active part in certain economic matters. This emerging argument and the Great Depression of the 1930s signaled the end of laissez-faire. Keynes, while accepting capitalism as an economic system, rejected the classical notion of laissez-faire. His primary argument in reaching this conclusion was that the laissez-faire capitalist economic system could easily result in chronic unemployment and instability. In Part 4 we will examine in more detail the Keynesian body of thought on instability and the proper role for the state in the economy.

12. What would Adam Smith think about Keynes's argument? Why?

CONCLUSION

In this chapter, we have examined the argument for laissez-faire capitalism as well as some of its criticisms. In the next chapter, we will explore in more detail Karl Marx's critiques of the development and operation of laissez-faire capitalism.

Review Questions

1. What are the strengths of laissez-faire capitalism both in theory and in practice?
2. What have been the major shortcomings in the operation of laissez-faire capitalism?
3. What reasons can you think of that would cast doubt on Say's law that supply always creates its own demand?

6

The Marxian Critique of Capitalism

As capitalism developed in Western Europe and the United States, a critique of some of its results began to emerge. As we have seen in Chapter 5, some economists and historians noted the spread of poverty and the recurrence of depressions. One of the first systematic analyses and critiques of capitalism was made by Karl Marx (1818–1883) in the mid- and late 1800s. Marx's system provides a comprehensive and consistent framework for understanding, evaluating, and criticizing the structure and development of capitalism. For that reason alone, it would be important to summarize Marx's system of thought concerning capitalism. In addition, Marxian economics has contributed to the development of economic thought, and Marxism as a political movement promoting socialism has been widespread in the modern era.

John Gurley of Stanford University in *Challengers to Capitalism* (1975) has said the following about why it is important to study Marxism:

> Many Americans . . . are unaware of Marxism as a philosophical world-outlook, a useful framework for understanding much of what is going on in the world. In a way, this is strange, inasmuch as hundreds of millions of people around the world know and use Marxism. . . . A study of Marxism is not only useful for understanding the robustness of the continuing attacks on capitalism and the Western way of life, but it is also helpful, almost indispensable, for understanding capitalism itself. Marxism offers new and surprising insights into this subject.

Even though the economic systems of socialism are undergoing dramatic change in the former Soviet Union, throughout Eastern Europe, and in China in the 1990s, Marxism as a system of analysis will continue to inform the goals and objectives of political and economic restructuring. It is extremely unlikely that these societies will completely adopt Western-style capitalism as they begin to rely more heavily on markets to guide economic activity. Rather, the new institutions they develop will be based on a combination of Marxian and orthodox economic theory. This chapter will provide a brief introduction to Marxist analysis.

KARL MARX: POLITICAL ECONOMIST AND REVOLUTIONARY

Marx was born in 1818 in Trier, Germany. His father was a successful lawyer, and Marx began his college career in legal studies. However, he soon switched to philosophy, in which he earned a Ph.D. at the age of twenty-three. Having already become a radical in his student days, he was unable to secure a teaching position. Instead he became the editor of the *Rheinische Zeitung*, in Cologne. However, this journal was suppressed by the Prussian government in 1843, and Marx, with his new wife, Jenny von Westphalen, moved to Paris. In Paris, Marx was active in left-wing journalism and in the workers' movement. It was there that he met Friedrich Engels and began to study political economy and capitalism.

Over the latter half of the 1840s, Marx's radicalism continually got him in trouble with governments. In 1845, he was expelled from France and moved to Brussels. There he wrote *The German Ideology* and *The Communist Manifesto* with Engels. In 1848 and 1849, several workers' revolutions occurred in Europe, and Belgium sent Marx packing. He first went to Paris and then to Germany. He was soon kicked out of Germany and then out of France again. Finally, in 1849, his family settled in London, where he was to remain for the rest of his life.

In London, Marx devoted himself to studying political economy and writing. His years there were spent in constant poverty, but he received substantial support from his friend Engels, who had a family interest in a manufacturing firm in Manchester. Marx developed into one of the most profound and widely known critics of capitalism in midnineteenth-century Europe. His work had two basic elements: one was his study and writing, and the other was his political activism. He was a correspondent for the *New York Daily Tribune* and published numerous books, the most famous of which is *Capital*. His political activism was as a socialist and communist in the workers' movement. He helped organize the International Working Men's Association—the First International—and was active in workers' struggles throughout the rest of his life.

MARX'S GENERAL SYSTEM OF THOUGHT

Marx's political activism and his analysis of capitalism were both based on his general theory of social development. This system amounted to a theory of history and of social change. As he put it in *The Communist Manifesto*, "The history of all hitherto existing society is the history of class struggles." This expressed his "materialist conception of history," which emphasized the role of the economic aspects of life in social development. This conception is central to Marx's system of thought and his analysis of capitalism, and we will explore it briefly here.

Dialectics

Marx's general system was based on two philosophical notions: dialectics and materialism. Marx borrowed dialectics from the German philosopher Hegel (1770–1831). **Dialectics** is the study of the contradictions within the essence of things. It emphasizes the idea that all things change and that all things contain not only themselves but their opposites. A rock is a rock, but it is also, at the same time, "not a rock" because it can become a million grains of sand. Consequently, development becomes the struggle of opposites—things becoming other things. Capitalists cannot be capitalists without their opposites, the workers (and vice versa), and capitalists and workers will develop as they interact with and influence each other. Out of this struggle of opposites comes change in which both elements, capitalists and workers, and the thing itself, capitalism, are transformed into something else. The source of change is internal to the social system. Ultimately, Marx thought that capitalism would develop into **socialism** (social ownership and social goals of production influenced by a strong state), and then into **communism** (communal control of the economy and a weak state).

By emphasizing change, contradiction, and the struggle of opposites, dialectics constitutes a challenge to formal logic that concentrates on things as they are and their interrelationships. Marx wrote the following in his Preface to *Capital* (1867):

> Dialectic . . . in its rational form is a scandal and abomination to bourgeoisdom and its doctrinaire professors, because it includes in its comprehension and affirmative recognition of the existing state of things, at the same time, also, the recognition of the negation of that state, of its inevitable breaking up; because it regards every historically developed social form as in fluid movement, and therefore takes into account its transient nature not less than its momentary existence; because it lets nothing impose upon it, and is in its essence critical and revolutionary.

1. Develop your own example that emphasizes the dialectical nature of some thing or process.
2. Why is the dialectic "critical and revolutionary"?

Materialism

The other philosophical notion underlying Marxian economics, **materialism**, concerns the principle that what is basic to the real life of human beings is their activity in the world. To understand the world, we must focus on real people and their day-to-day activities—especially those concerned with production for continued survival in this world. To Marx, materialism concerns "real, active men, and on the basis of their real life-process demonstrates the development of the ideological reflexes and echoes of this life-process."

To know the world, according to materialism, we must study things and their development. In addition, we must study the interrelationships of things: "Things come into being, change and pass out of being, not as separate individual units, but in essential relation and interconnection, so that they cannot be understood each separately and by itself but only in their relation and interconnection." To know the United States, we must study its productive process and how that relates to its laws, beliefs, social classes, patterns of consumption, and so on. Additionally, we must study the history of how all these elements have changed over time and developed.

Materialism contrasts with the notion that change takes place through the development of ideas. For Marx, the source of change rests, ultimately, in actual productive activity.

3. How else could we "know" our world other than through its material aspects?

The Materialist Conception of History: Historical Materialism

From these two philosophical bases, Marx developed his theory of history—the materialist conception of history, or **historical materialism**. All theory requires abstraction and oversimplification, and Marx's system of generalizations about social development is no exception. Historical materialism states that productive activity is fundamental to human beings and to their societies. Consequently, the organization of production, the economic structure, forms the basis of all societies. All other social institutions and ideas are derived from the economic structure of the society. If the economic structure changes, all other aspects of the society will also change.

Marx formalized his analysis in the following way. The economic structure, or base, is the **mode of production** and consists of the forces of production and the relations of production. The **forces of production** include all the things necessary to produce goods and services: tools, machines, factories, means of transportation, raw materials, human labor, science, technology, skills, and knowledge. Over time, obviously, the forces of production change. The **relations of production** are determined by the relationships among people in the productive process. When the forces of production are organized in a certain way, different classes of people will be defined by their relationship to each other in production. The relations of production, therefore, will be determined by patterns of ownership of productive resources, the nature of property relations, and the division of labor. These will determine a class structure of society. A certain mode of production, then, consists of specific forces of production and specific relations of production (that is, a specific **class structure**).

In addition, the mode of production is accompanied by the **superstructure** of society, which consists of the society's ideas, institutions, and ideologies, including laws, politics, culture, ethics, religion, morals, aesthetics, art, philosophy, and so on. The purpose of the superstructure is to support the economic base of society. For example, feudalism organized production with certain methods and institutions, and it had its own class structure and superstructure.

Within this framework is Marx's theory of historical change. Oversimplifying somewhat, when the forces of production change, the relations of production—social classes—also will change. This brings about a new mode of production that will, in turn, develop its own specific superstructure. It is in this context that class struggle takes place. Different classes have different interests and visions and thus will do battle over the organization of production and, hence, society. The "old" classes will fight to preserve the old mode of production, and the new will fight for change. One of the most fundamental aspects of this materialist conception of history is that people, by acting on the forces of production, create their own history and social change. Marx sums up his historical materialism in this passage from the *Critique of Political Economy* (1859):

> In the social production which men carry on they enter into definite relations that are indispensable and independent of their will; these relations of production correspond to a definite stage of development of their material powers of production. The sum total of these relations of production constitutes the economic structure of society—the real foundation on which rise legal and political superstructures and to which correspond definite forms of social consciousness. The mode of production in material life determines the general character of the social, political, and spiritual processes of life. It is not the consciousness of men that determines their existence, but, on the contrary, their social existence determines their consciousness. At a certain stage of their development, the material forces of production in society come into conflict with the existing relations of production, or—what is but a legal expression for the same thing—with the property relations within which they had been at work before. From forms of development of the

forces of production these relations turn into their fetters. Then comes the period of social revolution. With the change of economic foundation the entire immense superstructure is more or less rapidly transformed. In considering such transformations the distinction should always be made between the material transformation of the economic conditions or production which can be determined with the precision of natural science, and the legal, political, religious, aesthetic, or philosophic—in short, ideological forms in which men become conscious of this conflict and fight it out.

4. Apply the "materialist conception of history" (historical materialism) to the transition from feudalism to capitalism (see Chapter 3).
5. "It is not the consciousness of men that determines their existence, but, on the contrary, their social existence determines their consciousness." What does this mean? And how does it mean that human beings create their own history?
6. Can Marx's theory of historical materialism be used to explain the recent changes in the Soviet Union and Eastern Europe? How so?

Marx's model of social change thus focuses on the relationships and contradictions among the forces of production, social classes, and the general institutions and ideologies of society. This complex process, according to Marx, determines the development of societies. In that process, the forces of production are of initial importance, but class struggle and ideology in turn become extremely influential.

THE MARXIAN ANALYSIS OF CAPITALISM

From this view of social change and history, Marx proceeded to develop his analysis and critique of capitalism. His conclusion was a condemnation of capitalism and its results, as well as a scientific appraisal of its likely future development and eventual replacement by socialism. Here we will summarize Marx's theory of capitalist development.

Capitalism advances the methods of production, including factories, transportation, and technology, and, as it expands, has access to greater supplies of raw materials. Accompanying this mode of production are its own relations of production. Basically, according to Marx, with the advance of the division of labor and private property, there were two social classes in capitalism. They were defined by their relationship to each other in the productive process. First of all, there were the capitalists, or the bourgeoisie, who owned the means of production, controlled productive activity, and earned profits from the sale of produced goods in markets. Second, there were the workers, the proletariat, who had nothing to sell in markets but their own labor power and, as a result, had to work for wages to survive. The history of capitalism, then, can be seen as the history of the struggle between these two classes.

Marx condemned capitalism because it reduced social relations to impersonal market relations, or the "cash nexus." As he and Engels argued in *The Communist Manifesto* (1848):

> It has pitilessly torn asunder the motley feudal ties that bound man to his "natural superiors," and has left remaining no other nexus between man and man than naked self-interest, than callous "cash payment." It has drowned the most heavenly ecstasies of religious fervor, of chivalrous enthusiasm, of philistine sentimentalism, in the icy water of egotistical calculation. It has resolved personal worth into exchange value, and in place of the numberless indefeasible chartered freedoms, has set up that single, unconscionable freedom—Free Trade. In one word, for exploitation, veiled by religious and political illusions, it has substituted naked, shameless, direct, brutal exploitation.

Within that "nexus," workers and capitalists would struggle over wages, the length of the working day, the intensity of work, and working conditions.

Additionally, since workers were forced to work for capitalists for wages, and since the capitalists controlled production, capitalism produced **alienation**. In one of Marx's early critical works, *The Economic and Philosophic Manuscripts of 1844*, he described alienation as a consequence of capitalist production. The production of goods was external to the workers; they had no control over their labor or what they produced. Consequently, workers were alienated in their work; they felt dispossessed and their work was, in essence, forced labor. Alienation, thus, was one more contributor to labor's dissatisfaction with capitalism.

||| 7. Did Marx deplore the "cash nexus" because it destroyed feudal relationships?

From his early condemnation of capitalism, Marx went on to develop a detailed and lengthy analysis of capitalism in such works as *Wage Labour and Capital* (1849), *The Grundrisse* (1859), *Theories of Surplus Value* (1863), and *Capital* (1867).

Marx accepted the **labor theory of value** as it was developed by Adam Smith and others but turned it to his own purposes. For Marx it became a way of demonstrating the opposition of capitalists and workers and the exploitation of labor in capitalism. Marx contended that the value of all goods and services is a function of the labor (both direct and indirect) that went into them. Workers, in turn, are paid by capitalists to produce goods and services. However, since the capitalists control the productive process and the final output, they will earn **surplus value**. The trick is that the exchange value of goods and services, or what the capitalist sells, can be greater than the exchange value of labor power, or what the capitalist buys from the workers. The value created by labor at work is greater than the value of labor power, the ability to work, that the worker sells to the capitalist (based on market wages). The difference between these values is surplus value (the source of profit) which is appropriated by the capitalist (and which Marx called exploitation).

Because of the existence of a mass of unemployed workers (the *industrial reserve army* of the unemployed), the exchange value of labor power will always hover around "subsistence"—the value of goods and services necessary for continued survival and the reproduction of the working class. Workers can produce enough value in only part of the working day to cover their subsistence needs. The rest of the day they labor to produce surplus value for the capitalist. The more labor that capitalists can get out of the labor power they purchase from workers, the greater the surplus value for the capitalist. As a result, the very structure of capitalism and its social relations produce **exploitation of labor**. Labor accounts for the value of all goods and services, but it receives in return only a portion of that value because it does not own productive assets or control the production process.

Since capitalists derive surplus value and profits from production, and since they operate in a competitive environment in which other capitalists also attempt to earn profits from the same type of activity, they are forced to accumulate capital. **Capital accumulation** is the driving force of capitalism. Profit is used to increase the capital and hence the productive activity of capitalists. This capital accumulation results in additional profits, which, in turn, will be reinvested in more capital and the expansion of their markets. Capitalists, if they wish to stay in business, have no choice about this. If they do not reinvest their profits in new and better forms of capital, they will be driven out of business by their competitors. (For a more detailed treatment of the Marxian theory of profit, see the appendix to this chapter.) Marx also emphasized the role of technological development in stimulating capital accumulation.

This process of capital accumulation forms the basis of Marx's understanding of **capitalist instability**. Capital accumulation produces economic growth, but it does so in cycles, with periods of prosperity followed by depression. When production is expanding, capitalists buy more machines, raw materials, and other forms of capital. This also requires them to hire more workers. Doing so depletes the reserve army of the unemployed and consequently begins to drive up wages, which tends to reduce profits. Consequently, capitalists introduce new methods of production that save on the use of labor; more capital-intensive production allows them to produce more with less labor (substitution of capital for labor). In addition, workers lose jobs and the wage goes down as the reserve army is replenished.

This course of action is not without its own contradictions. With more workers out of jobs and with lower wages, it is more difficult to sell what is produced. This tends to reduce capitalists' profits. In addition, with more capital-intensive methods of production, the capitalists reduce relatively the source of profits in production, surplus value generated by labor. This also tends to produce a declining rate of profits. With profits reduced, capital accumulation slows down. All of these effects would combine to produce depressions in economic activity as goods went unsold, profits decreased, workers lost jobs, and capital accumulation slowed. In true dialectical fashion, the expansion, out of its own internal workings, turns into its opposite, a depression. With wage rates depressed, though, capitalists eventually rehire workers because they can once again produce surplus value and profits for the capitalists. And out of the depression comes an expansion of economic activity. Capitalism, Marx argued, grew in starts and spurts. The great mass of the people under capitalism, the working class, depends on this unstable process for its livelihood and subsistence.

In addition to this cyclical instability, Marx thought that there were long-run tendencies that would exacerbate the opposition between the capitalist class and the working class. Because of competition, **economic concentration** tended to occur as capitalists bought each other out or went bankrupt during depressions. The strong survived and came to dominate certain industries. As this occurred, the capitalist class became relatively smaller, as well as relatively more wealthy. Meanwhile, the working class became relatively larger and relatively poorer, as it remained near "subsistence." Marx called this the **immiserization** of the proletariat. And all the while, the capitalist class retained control and the workers were powerless. As a result of continuing instability and these secular tendencies, which reinforce the class structure of capitalist society, the workers would organize for their own class interests. Ultimately, Marx argued, the working-class organizations would overthrow the capitalist system.

The political requirement for workers in the socialist and communist movement was described by Marx and Engels as follows at the end of *The Communist Manifesto:*

> In short, the Communists everywhere support every revolutionary movement against the existing social and political order of things.
> In all these movements they bring to the front, as the leading question in each, the property question, no matter what its degree of development at the time.
> Finally, they labour everywhere for the union and agreement of the democratic parties of all countries.
> The Communists disdain to conceal their views and aims. They openly declare that their ends can be attained only by the forcible overthrow of all existing social conditions. Let the ruling class tremble at a Communistic revolution. The proletarians have nothing to lose but their chains. They have a world to win.

However, this social revolution would not be easy. As Marx emphasized from his general system of social development, capitalism supports itself with its superstructure. The institutions, ideologies, and beliefs of the society defend capitalist economic institutions and social relations. Perhaps most important in this connection is the state. The state, according to Marxian analysis, serves as the "executive committee of the ruling class." The state protects private property and property rights and thereby the class structure of the system. It is in the camp of the capitalists and will actively oppose the workers' movement with all the resources at its command.

8. Evaluate Marx's analysis of capitalism. Does it describe economic reality and the historical development of capitalism? Does it help you understand how capitalism works?
9. Why do you suppose Marx kept getting kicked out of European countries?

SOCIAL REVOLUTION

Marx argued that workers would be exploited, alienated, and condemned to subsistence standards of living under capitalism. He further argued that in their association at work and in their communities, they would be able to analyze objectively their reality and the reasons for this oppression. Consequently, they would organize themselves and transform the whole capitalist system. (Indeed, Marx spent much of his time in political activity with workers.) In *Capital*, he describes the process of **social revolution** as follows:

> Along with the constantly diminishing number of magnates of capital, who usurp and monopolize all advantages of this process of transformation, grows the mass of misery, oppression, slavery, degradation, exploitation; but with this too grows the revolt of the working class, a class always increasing in numbers, and disciplined, united, organized by the very mechanism of the process of capitalist production itself. The monopoly of capital becomes a fetter upon the mode of production, which has sprung up and flourished along with, and under it. Centralization of the means of production and socialization of labour at last reach a point where they become incompatible with their capitalist integument. This integument is burst asunder. The knell of capitalist private property sounds. The expropriators are expropriated.

Once the death knell of capitalism sounded, what would the socialists, communists, and workers create? What would they do? Although Marx never wrote extensively on this question, a hint at the answer is contained in *The Communist Manifesto*:

> The distinguishing feature of Communism is not the abolition of property generally, but the abolition of bourgeois property. But modern bourgeois private property is the final and most complete expression of the system of producing and appropriating products, that is based on class antagonisms, on the exploitation of the many by the few.
>
> In this sense, the theory of the Communists may be summed up in the single sentence: Abolition of private property.
>
> We Communists have been reproached with the desire of abolishing the right of personally acquiring property as the fruit of a man's own labour, which property is alleged to be the groundwork of all personal freedom, activity and independence.
>
> Hard-won, self-acquired, self-earned property! Do you mean the property of the petty artisan and of the small peasant, a form of property that preceded the bourgeois form? There is no need to abolish that: the development of industry has to a great extent already destroyed it, and is still destroying it daily.

Or do you mean modern bourgeois private property?

The proletariat will use its political supremacy to wrest, by degrees, all capital from the bourgeoisie, to centralise all instruments of production in the hands of the State, *i.e.*, of the proletariat organized as the ruling class; and to increase the total of productive forces as rapidly as possible. . . .

These measures will of course be different in different countries.

Nevertheless in the most advanced countries, the following will be . . . generally applicable.

1. Abolition of property in land and application of all rents of land to public purposes.
2. A heavy progressive or graduated income tax.
3. Abolition of all rights of inheritance.
4. Confiscation of the property of all emigrants and rebels.
5. Centralisation of credit in the hands of the State, by means of a national bank with State capital and an exclusive monopoly.
6. Centralisation of the means of communication and transport in the hands of the State.
7. Extension of factories and instruments of production owned by the State; the bringing into cultivation of wastelands, and the improvement of the soil generally in accordance with a common plan.
8. Equal liability of all to labour. Establishment of industrial armies, especially for agriculture.
9. Combination of agriculture and manufacturing industries; gradual abolition of the distinction between town and country, by a more equable distribution of the population over the country.
10. Free education for all children in public schools. Abolition of children's factory labour in its present form. Combination of education with industrial production, &c., &c.

10. Would the communists take your personal possessions away from you? What kinds of property would they "wrest" away?
11. In Marx and Engels's ten-point program, which measures are accepted in the United States? Which are partially accepted? Which are rejected?

AN ASSESSMENT OF MARXISM

Marx died over a century ago, in 1883. What can we say today about the relevance of his analysis of social change and capitalism? Most Americans either reject Marxism or never really study it. The rejection is often based on the fact that several of Marx's predictions have not transpired: the overthrow of advanced capitalism by socialism; the separation of society into only two classes, capitalists and workers; and the creation of a unified and political working class. In addition, Marxism is often associated with the repressive Soviet Union, and socialism as Marx described it has never really been put in place. Socialism and Marxism also offer a direct challenge to two of the basic economic foundations of U.S. society: private ownership of productive property and economic freedom for capital.

On the other hand, Marxian analysis is used by many economists in the United States and the rest of the world to understand economic events. Some aspects of Marxism offer continuing assistance in explaining the structure and development of capitalism. There remain conflicts between workers and capitalists over workplace health and safety, other working conditions, wages and fringe benefits, and the length of the workweek, not to mention downsizing and relocation. This conflict is built into the different interests that they have in the very structure of the economic system. Capitalists seek profits, and workers' demands often limit profits. Although the historical expansion of the middle class has mediated this structure, there are opposing class interests in the operation of the economy, and the classes do struggle over real economic issues in workplaces, bargaining, and public policy. Furthermore, while these struggles have not led to the collapse of capitalism, they have brought about significant changes in its institutions and operation. Marx's analysis of exploitation, surplus value, and class relations can help us to understand this dynamic of U.S. capitalism.

One of the most long-lived aspects of Marxian economic analysis is its theory of the process of capital accumulation. In this treatment, Marx explained capitalism's tendencies toward business cycles, economic concentration, and market expansion. By focusing on the importance of profits and the centrality of capital accumulation, Marx developed a framework that is still useful in understanding recessions and expansions, merger waves, and U.S. penetration of world markets.

Nevertheless, Marx's system retains some limitations and weaknesses. Marx's labor theory of value was supplanted by the development of economic theory that finds value reflected in the supply and demand for products and their resulting prices. Marx did not anticipate the tremendous increase in the average standard of living in the United States (and Western Europe) that went along with economic growth. A good portion of the increasing surplus was in fact apportioned to the middle class and some segments of the working class (although this varies depending on economic conditions and the strength of the working class). The social revolution in advanced capitalist countries anticipated by Marx required more than his prediction: It also necessitated political organization by the working class in the real world. (To his credit, although it is often not included in discussions of Marx, he did recognize this political fact; much of his life was spent in active political organizing among the working class.) Even though there have been communist and socialist parties in the West and in the United States, they have never been strong enough to organize a transition to socialism. Of course, they have not been unopposed. And throughout Western Europe, the social democracy movement reformed capitalism to take into account social issues, rather than eliminating it. Socialism, instead, has emerged where capitalism has been weaker, in the developing world.

Marx himself would probably be disappointed with the divergence of his ideal of socialism and its reality in much of the present world (particularly wherever it has taken anti-democratic forms). Even so, his ideas have definitely influenced the development and the progress of socialism and the pursuit of social goals in the Soviet Union, China, Cuba, Vietnam, Mozambique, South Africa, and other socialist nations (see Chapter 23). And Marxism as a method of analysis will continue to influence the transitions in the post–Cold War world.

CONCLUSION

In Part 2, we have reviewed the development of economic systems, focusing on capitalism. We have, at the same time, summarized the development of modern economic thought, both praising and critiquing capitalism. In Parts 3 and 4, we turn to the development of the modern economic theory about how capitalism and markets work—first, in terms of microeconomics, then macroeconomics.

Review Questions

1. Why do people in the United States tend to reject Marxism?
2. Why is it that some newly independent countries in the world have Marxian governments (i.e., politicians and leaders who rely on Marxian analysis)?
3. What do you feel is the weakest part of the Marxian argument?
4. What do you feel is the strongest part of the Marxian argument?
5. What is the purpose of Marxian economics?

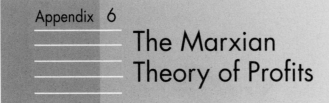

Appendix 6

The Marxian Theory of Profits

Adam Smith argued that competitive markets produce social welfare through the "invisible hand." In Chapter 9, we will examine the orthodox, neoclassical theory of the firm in a competitive market. In the long run, the results suggest that competition produces maximum social welfare (efficiency, consumer sovereignty, and the "invisible hand") and that firms earn only "normal" profits. From a Marxian perspective, the operation of competitive capitalism is shown to have results that are much less attractive. Marx concludes that there is inherent conflict between capital and labor, that the source of profits lies in the exploitation of labor, and, furthermore, that the orthodox analysis hides the source of profits and the social relationships in capitalist production.

Marx's analysis focuses on the process of production within the *capitalist mode of production*. According to Marx, the value of all goods and services is determined by their labor content (the labor theory of value)—both the direct labor of active labor power by workers and the embodied labor of past labor power in raw materials and capital goods. In addition, Marx assumes that firms are in business to earn profits through the process of capital accumulation (indeed, competition forces firms to seek profits). They do this by producing goods and services and selling them in markets as commodities. Finally, productive activity within capitalism inherently has certain *social relations of production*—essentially, there are two basic classes of people: capitalists, who own and control the means of production, and workers, who must sell their labor power to capitalists to earn a living.

Given this Marxian framework of analysis, we can examine the behavior of firms. Our analysis will concentrate on the source of capitalist profits, the determinants of the prices of products, and the relationships between capitalists and workers.

The capitalist owns the means of production and the capital necessary for the organization of production. This capital has two forms: constant capital and variable capital. **Constant capital** refers to factors of production that have embodied labor in them, that is, the factory itself, the machinery and equipment in it, and the raw materials used in production. Theoretically, it is possible to place a value on this constant capital. For example, to simplify the analysis, assume we can determine the value of 1 unit of labor power at $5. This assumes that we can value all labor in terms of some abstract unit of average labor. As a result, then, this $5 price for 1 unit of labor represents the value of the commodities necessary (at least) for the sustenance and the reproduction of this 1 unit of labor power. Assume that the constant capital (machines, raw materials, etc.) used up in production has embodied in it 6 units of abstract labor. Therefore, in our example, the constant capital is valued at $30 (that is, 6 units × $5/unit).

Variable capital refers to the capitalist's outlay of money for the purchase of the active labor power required, along with constant capital, to produce his or her product. It is variable in the sense that workers can work more or less time and more or less hard during the working day. The capitalist purchases labor power from the worker but wants labor, or work, and as much as possible. Assume that the capitalist hires 14 units of living labor to engage in production. Therefore, the variable capital (labor) is valued at $70, or 14 units × $5/unit.

What about the capitalist's share? This enters the picture via Marx's concept of **surplus value**. Capitalists hire labor to put into motion constant capital and the production process. Capitalists must pay both constant and variable capital according to the value of the labor embodied in them and required to enable them to work, respectively. However, in the process of production, additional value is created. The ultimate value of the product will depend upon the amount of labor contained in it. Capitalists must be able to organize production in such a way that the value of the final product *exceeds* the value of constant and variable capital.

This occurs as a natural result of the operation of capitalist production. The capitalist controls production and, specifically, the length of the working day. Let's assume that the working day is 10 hours long. During the working day, workers can produce value equivalent to the value of their abstract labor power in 6 hours. During the remaining 4 hours, the workers produce value over and above the value necessary for the purchase of their labor power. This is surplus value, which derives from surplus labor that is unpaid. Consequently, the 14 units of labor power are used to produce commodities embodying more than 14 units of labor power. Only 6 hours of labor are required to produce commodities necessary to cover the costs of the value of the labor power itself. The remaining 4 hours of labor produce surplus value. The proceeds from the surplus value go to the capitalists when they sell the products for the value contained in them. The 6 hours of labor produce commodities with a value of $70 (the value of variable capital). The 4 hours of surplus labor produce commodities with a value of $46 2/3 (that is, $70 × 4/6). This is the value of surplus value.

The 14 units of living labor power produce commodities embodying 14 units of labor power (the value of variable capital) *and* commodities embodying 9 1/3 units of labor power ($46 2/3 ÷ 5). The 6 units of labor embodied in the constant capital produce commodities with 6 units of labor embodied in them.

This analysis (which is quite simplified compared with Marx's original contribution) reveals that the source of profits for the capitalists—surplus value—results from the capitalists' control of the production process and their ability to pay living labor (variable capital) less than the full value of what it produces. Hence labor is exploited, since it has little control over the production process (the essence of which is human labor) and since it does not receive compensation commensurate with what it adds to the value of social production.

What's more, this mode of production inherently involves *conflict* between capitalists and workers. Workers prefer to work fewer hours, less hard, and for more money; capitalists prefer workers to work longer, harder, and for less money. Capitalists and workers will struggle with each other over the length of the working day, the intensity of work, working conditions, and the division of the fruits of variable capital (the return to variable capital versus surplus value). The operation of the capitalist system in Marx's view thus involves differing class interests. In fact, the source of capitalists' profits is the exploitation of labor. This is hardly Smith's picture of the "invisible hand" that leads to the greatest social welfare for all.

We can formalize this analysis in several ways. The objectives of capitalist production are to earn profits and to accumulate capital. The capitalist begins with money and purchases the commodities of constant and variable capital (machines, equipment, raw materials, labor power) in markets. These resources of production are then combined and organized in a production process that requires the application of human labor. The production process results in commodities (goods and services) to be sold in markets. These commodities are sold for money. The source of profits is the production process, wherein human labor produces enough value to cover constant and variable capital, as well as surplus value, which is appropriated by the capitalist.

We can characterize this process as follows:

$$M \to C \ldots P \ldots C' \to M',$$

where M = money, C = the value of commodities used in production, P = the production process, C' = produced commodities for sale, and M' = the money value of sales. If M' exceeds M, then the capitalist earns profits. In the next round, the capitalist can use profits to accumulate more capital and earn additional profits. Notice that there is no certainty that the capitalist will, in fact, earn profits. Capitalists are all in competition with one another. If resources cost too much, if workers do not work hard enough, if the production process is poorly organized, or if what gets produced is not sold, the capitalist might not make any profits at all.

In addition, from the Marxian perspective, we can express the total value of any product as being equal to the sum of the various forms of embodied labor in it:

total value = constant capital + variable capital + surplus value.

For example, from our previous analysis,

$29\frac{1}{3}$ units of labor = 6 units of labor + 14 units of labor + $9\frac{1}{3}$ units of labor.

If the value for 1 unit of labor power is $5, we can convert this value to dollars:

$146\frac{2}{3}$ = $30 + $70 + $46\frac{2}{3}$.

From an orthodox perspective, we can view this relationship as follows:

total sales = costs of fixed resources and variable resources (excluding labor) + costs of labor + profits.

So far, we have concentrated on the capitalist production process with the example of the single firm. However, because the same process of capital accumulation and the extraction of surplus value occurs in the economy as a whole, we can also develop an economy-wide example.* Let's say that the total output of the society in one year is valued at $500 billion (meaning that the output of goods and services multiplied by their prices equals $500 billion). Part of the money received for this output must be used to cover the costs of replacing the equipment and the raw materials used up in the production period. Assume this replacement cost is $100 billion. This sum of

---

*This section relies on the curriculum of the Summer Institute for Popular Economics prepared by the Center for Popular Economics, Box 785, Amherst, MA 01004.

Chapter 6 THE MARXIAN CRITIQUE OF CAPITALISM

money then allows for the purchasing of these resources for the next period of production. The total output minus the replacement cost equals the net output of the society:

$$\text{total output} - \text{replacement cost} = \text{net output},$$

$$\$500 \text{ billion} - \$100 \text{ billion} = \$400 \text{ billion}.$$

The net output of the society is divided into two parts. Workers get a portion of this output, which they purchase with their wages. Suppose labor's wages total $300 billion. Workers use their wages to buy goods and services so they can survive and continue to offer their labor power in the next round of production. The remainder of the net output goes to capital as profits—$100 billion, in this case:

$$\text{net output} = \text{wages} + \text{profits},$$

$$\$400 \text{ billion} = \$300 \text{ billion} + \$100 \text{ billion}.$$

We can rewrite the equation in terms of profits:

$$\text{profits} = \text{net output} - \text{wages}.$$

Profits, consequently, depend on the total value of net output and the wage bill. The higher the net output and the lower the wage bill, the higher capitalists' profits will be.

Perhaps an easier way to focus on Marx's insights about class relations and profits in capitalism is to identify the **rate of profit**. The rate of profit for capitalists depends on the profits they receive in comparison to the value of their investment in production. Their investment is the value of capital assets (the total monetary value of those assets—machines, equipment, buildings, etc.). In our example, if this capital is worth $300 billion, then the profit rate is computed as follows:

$$\text{profit rate} = \text{profits/capital assets},$$

$$33\tfrac{1}{3}\% = 100/300.$$

We can also put this in per-worker terms, by dividing the right side of the equation by the total number of workers:

$$\text{profit rate} = \frac{\text{net output} - \text{wages}}{\text{capital assets}}$$

$$\text{profit rate} = \frac{\text{net output per worker} - \text{average wage of each worker}}{\text{capital per worker}}.$$

We can use this formulation to see that a number of aspects of capitalism operate to keep profits and the profit rate positive. The average wage of the worker is determined by what is necessary to enable workers to purchase goods and services that provide them with an acceptable standard of living. This allows them to participate in production and to have enough income for food, shelter, and clothing for themselves and their families, allowing in turn for the reproduction of the working class. This wage is determined by historical experience and by the struggle between capital and labor over the level of wages. But the higher the wage, the lower the profit rate. Workers can organize to get higher wages, but capital has the power to hire and fire, as well as to organize and control the production process. Furthermore, the existence of unemployment (the reserve army) constantly puts downward pressure on wages. The dynamic relationship between wages and profits, in fact, accounts for much of the instability in capitalist growth. If wages get too high, profits are reduced and capitalists slow down the accumulation process. But when wages are low and profits are high, economic booms occur.

Net output per worker is analogous to productivity. If capitalists can increase output without raising wages, profits and the profit rate will go up. Ways to do this include increasing work intensity, increasing supervision over work, speeding up the work pace, or introducing technological innovations. On the other hand, because workers' demands to improve working conditions do not increase output for sale, such demands tend to reduce profits.

If nothing else changes, an increase in capital per worker would decrease the profit rate. This may result because capital replaces labor, and the exploitation of labor is the source of surplus value. But if net output per worker increases faster than capital per worker (i.e., productivity increases along with increased capital), then profits and the profit rate could go up.

Consequently, many factors influence the generation of profits and the rate of profit in capitalism. The pace of capital accumulation and the level of economic activity will be determined by changes in profits. Specifically, the higher (lower) profits, the greater (lower) the rate of economic growth will tend to be.

These relationships determining the rate of profit suggest, once again, from the Marxian perspective, the inherent instability of capitalist production. Over time, the rate of profit among enterprises will tend to be equalized through competition. (The rate of profit in this sense is comparable to the "normal" profits we will identify in Chapter 9.) However, Marx preferred to emphasize the tendency toward instability as profits rose and fell in the process of capitalist accumulation and production.

One additional aspect of Marx's analysis of the operation of the firm that is worth pointing out is the tendency toward **economic concentration** that results from long-term capital accumulation and the pursuit of profit. Firms become larger through capital accumulation, and the process of instability bankrupts some firms, so fewer firms remain in an industry. Historically, this theoretical tendency has accounted for the disappearance of competitive markets in capitalist systems.

Finally, one of the strengths of the Marxian analysis of capitalism is its integration of the micro and macro aspects of economic activity. Profits flow from the organization and control of the capitalist mode of production. The process of capital accumulation and the production of surplus value, in turn, provide the framework within which economic crises are engendered under capitalism.

Review Questions

1. Is the labor theory of value valid? Why or why not?
2. Marx's theories were originated over 100 years ago. Was labor exploited then? Is it now? Why or why not?
3. In the United States *most* people are not living on "subsistence" wages. What is the source of the increased wages for variable capital in many industries in the United States?
4. What is the *source* of profits, according to the Marxian interpretation? Criticize this explanation.
5. Given the production of surplus value in the production process, capitalists cannot realize profits unless they sell their products for more than the value of constant and variable capital (or for more than the value of replacement costs and wages). In fact, capitalists sometimes experience losses. What kinds of behavior will capitalists pursue in order to ensure the realization of profits?

THINKING CRITICALLY

ECONOMIC CHANGE MARCHES ON

As you have seen in Chapters 3–6, the emergence of the market system and capitalism has been an evolutionary process that has taken well over 400 years. The transition from feudalism to capitalism alone took a couple of hundred years. This transformation ushered a period of explosive scientific inquiry and innovation in the eighteenth century, which set the stage for the European Industrial Revolution of the nineteenth century. The twentieth century brought forward the rapid development of global capitalism and strong socialist economies up until the end of the century.

As the capitalist market economy evolved, the role of constant and, at times, rapid technological change has taken center stage. This change has continuously altered the relationship of labor to capital and the production process. You have seen the ways Adam Smith, Karl Marx, and others tried to describe this shifting relationship in an emerging capitalist market economy.

At the end of Part 1, we examined the issue of downsizing. Now, we turn to a more specific examination of the reality of labor in our emerging global economy. As a point of departure, read the following articles, "Economic Anxiety" and "Is All that Angst Misplaced?" which together served as the cover story for *Business Week* on March 11, 1996.

Exercises

1. How do you think Adam Smith would respond to these articles? Karl Marx?
2. Do you think there ought to be a new social contract in the United States to eliminate economic anxiety and job insecurity? Explain your answer.
3. In what way(s) could it be argued that economic anxiety (insecurity) is a good thing for a market economy? A bad thing?
4. To what extent does a competitive global economy make it difficult for a national economy to eliminate economic anxiety?
5. Do you think every able-bodied adult human being has a right to a job? Explain your answer.

Karen Pennar

You hear a rumor: A General Electric Co. plant in the Midwest is about to close its doors and move its operations south of the border. You talk to a friend: Her brother turned down AT&T's buyout offer, only to be faced with immediate dismissal. You consider your future: A career change might be nice, but not an involuntary one. So you rein in spending and ramp up savings, just to be safe.

This is not your father's economy.

Instead, it has turned into a high-wire act for everyone—from the blue-collar worker who's eking out $5 an hour plucking chickens to the bank teller whose job is being cut in a merger to the midlevel executive who's now working out of his home as a consultant. It is a story that can't be told by the numbers, because the numbers at times are misleading: 8 million jobs created in four years, the unemployment rate at 5.8%, inflation down to 2.7%, corporate profits on a four-year roll, and four years of economic recovery under our belts. "All the economic indicators are up . . . except mine," says Paul J. Szilagyi, 50, an unemployed North Miami Beach resident with a PhD in chemistry.

It's not just the unemployed like Szilagyi who are experiencing some cognitive dissonance these days. Real wages have been stagnant for most of the past two decades. The distribution of income among Americans has become more unequal . . . . During the past decade, Corporate America has restructured, downsized, right-sized, and reengineered millions of people out of their jobs while putting the squeeze on the wages of remaining workers. At the same time, top executives promised that the payoff would come—first in higher productivity and then, labor's due, in higher wages. . . .

There are economists who believe that robust economic growth would be a strong palliative for this angst—and its causes. James K. Galbraith, an economist at the University of Texas at Austin, argues that the unemployment rate—and by extension, economic growth—is the single most important factor affecting the distribution of income. Push the unemployment rate dramatically lower, he says, and income inequality will be far less of a problem.

Everybody agrees that economic growth stronger than last year's 2.1% would help. But macroeconomic policy is inadequate to address the powerful structural changes in the U.S. economy—the widespread diffusion of new technologies, the growth of trade's role, more rapid immigration.

Lost Contract

"People have a sense that these are changes radically different from anything they have seen before," says Claudia Goldin, an economic historian at Harvard University. Many workers lament the breakdown of the social contract between employees and employers—a contract that once made it possible to raise both a family and one's living standards. In a *Business Week*/Harris Poll of 1,004 adults conducted in late February, 77% of the respondents rated large corporations only fair or poor at providing job security for their workers, and 78% rated the companies similarly on their loyalty to employees.

The restructuring of Corporate America has carried enormous social costs. Nitin Nohria, a professor at the Harvard business school, tracked the changes that engulfed 100 of America's largest companies—"symbolic markers of our well-being"—from 1978 to the present. He found that on a net basis, 22% of the workforce of these companies, or 3 million workers, was laid off during the period, and 77% of all layoffs involved white-collar workers.

So perhaps it's no surprise that Corporate America gets its share of blame from alienated workers. Workers also believe that something should be done about imports to protect U.S. jobs: In the *Business Week*/Harris Poll, 50% of the respondents endorse import taxes or tariffs. Since the mid-1970s, the share of trade—imports plus exports—in the American economy has risen. But the perceived threat may be greater than the real threat. Economists believe that global trade explains perhaps 10% to 15%—at most 20%—of the increasing inequality of wages. By the same token, immigration is doing very little direct economic damage.

If trade and immigration don't play such a big role in determining people's economic well-being, what about that other bugaboo, technology? By and large, the *Business Week*/Harris Poll indicates, workers seem about evenly divided about technology's benefits and whether it's worth enduring the near-term pain for the long-term gain of higher productivity, better wages, and new jobs.

Speak to workers, though, and they know that there's no turning back and that they are going to have to make some adjustments. "It's not like the odd days when you graduated from high school and had the same job for 20 or 30 years," says Denis Velez, a 47-year-old commercial photographer. He has taken a job that pays $200 a week processing film at a Ritz camera shop in Deerfield Beach, Fla., so he can get health benefits for his family. "Technology, especially in the field I'm in, is changing so much. In a couple of years, film itself will be obsolete."

Although workers realize they have to retool, many hope for guidance. So far, notes Shoshana Zuboff, a Harvard business school professor and author of *The Age of the Smart Machine,* only a handful of companies have committed the resources to help their workforces develop new skills. Today, corporations essentially all have the same technology, the same networking systems, the same software, she says. The only way they can beat out their competitors is by enabling their biggest asset—their workforce—to be more innovative in using the technology to create new products and new services that sell well. Instead, throughout its decade-long restructuring, Corporate America has primarily viewed workers as liabilities rather than assets.

The Austrian-born economist Joseph Schumpeter observed that creative destruction was capitalism's hallmark, and today Americans are feeling its effects with a vengeance. If America wants the benefits of expanding trade and technological innovations, it needs to do more to ease the pain of transition. For corporations, that means better training programs, heightened sensitivity to the anguish of layoffs, and shared sacrifice by management. For policymakers, that means encouraging workers to gain new skills—by introducing training vouchers and expanded investment retirement-type accounts to pay for tuition.

Investing in human capital is not a new idea—but it needs to be pursued aggressively, not merely be given lip service. If America doesn't respond to this challenge, the antibusiness backlash already under way will worsen, and the tenets that have made the American economy so competitive and vibrant will be in danger of being undermined.

IS ALL THAT ANGST MISPLACED?

Michael J. Mandel

Ask Americans what worries them about the economy, and they'll tell you straight out: Almost everything. Slow growth. Unemployment. Inflation. Foreign competition. Somewhere along the way, they say, America has gotten off track. "I don't think you can say to your kids anymore, 'If you study hard and play by the rules, things are going to be O.K.,' says Stephen D. McGregor, 44 a public-relations executive at a Dallas technology company who in the past five years has been laid off by both American Airlines and MCI. "You can't promise that anymore."

The hard numbers, though, tell a much different story. The U.S. unemployment rate hovers at a low 5.8%. Real hourly wages are rising, for the first time in 10 years. Corporate America, flush with a string of record-busting quarters, is investing in new equipment at near-record levels. Productivity is rising. Exports are up more than 20% in just the past two years. And the soaring stock market is pumping up the retirement funds of much of the American workforce.

The problem, then? Job insecurity—and it's a big one. In January alone, U.S. corporations announced almost 100,000 job cuts, up sharply from a monthly rate of 37,000 during 1995. "In December, I was telling people [job cuts] were slowing down," says John A. Challenger, executive vice-president at Challenger, Gray & Christmas Inc., an outplacement firm. "But they're accelerating again."

The headlines are all too familiar. America's biggest companies are engaged in a brutal, wrenching transition toward a global, information-driven economy. And the price is being paid now by managers and professionals. A full 11% of male, college-educated workers lost their jobs from 1991 through 1993, according to a new study by Princeton University economist Henry S. Farber. By comparison, during the recession years of 1981 to 1983, 8% of this group experienced a job loss.

Big Blue Bounty

Look behind the headlines about massive corporate downsizings, though, and the news gets better. Of the 8 million new jobs created in the past four years, some 60% were managerial and professional positions. In 1995 alone, the U.S. economy created more than 1 million new managerial and professional jobs.

Even in industries where job-slashing is taking place at record levels, simultaneous hiring is compensating for the losses. Take communications. During the past two years, the seven regional telephone companies have slashed some 125,000 jobs, on top of the 40,000 latest cuts announced at AT&T. Nevertheless, the industry's total employment rose by 91,000 during the period, as companies beefed up employment in cellular and other fast-growing businesses.

Then there's IBM. Since 1987, it has cut about 180,000 workers. Now, IBM is handing out 8% pay increases to those who remain. More significantly, it is hiring again—for its computer-services arm. "We need roughly 10,000 people a year for that business," says IBM Chief Financial Officer G. Richard Thoman. "And our major constraint looking forward isn't demand. It is finding those 10,000 people."

For many communities, the downsizing or closing of major employers initially seems like an economic catastrophe. Yet new jobs often spring up to replace the old ones. That's true for Rochester, N.Y., which in recent years has absorbed big job cuts at Xerox, Eastman Kodak, and Bausch & Lomb. Nevertheless, the unemployment rate in the Rochester area has fallen from 4.4% to 3.8% during the past year, well below the national average.

But what about wages? Americans are gloomy because their paychecks seem to be growing more slowly than in the 1980s. But what they don't factor in is that inflation is much lower as well. Since 1993, consumer prices have risen at only a 2.6% annual rate, the slowest pace since the mid-1960s. As a result, real wages and salaries have posted about a 1% increase over the same stretch.

Compared with the huge jump in profits, those pay hikes are puny. Yet they are an improvement over the real-wage declines Americans experienced through most of the '80s and early '90s. And the trend remains positive. Based on DRI/McGraw-Hill forecasts, inflation should stay tame in 1996. So real wages and salaries could rise by another 0.6%. Surprisingly, the gains are filtering down to less-skilled workers. These are the people who saw their wages plummet even during the Reagan boom era. Yet during the past two years, real hourly wages for production and nonsupervisory workers have risen for the first time in 10 years.

Minimal Effect

Presidential candidate Pat Buchanan says U.S. jobs would be higher paying—and better protected—in a country with a closed border and though trade tariffs. Again, the numbers provide little evidence that either one has much of an effect on the wages of America's workers. A new analysis by economists George Borjas, Richard Freeman, and Lawrence Katz of Harvard University concludes that trade and immigration contributed only "modestly" to falling real wages for high school graduates in the 1980s.

The reason: Immigration and trade are simply not big enough, relative to the whole economy, to produce big effects on wages. Immigrants represent just 9% of the labor force, and merchandise imports account for only 10% of gross domestic product. Moreover, some 60% of U.S. non-oil imports come from countries with higher labor costs, like Japan and Germany, giving little incentive to cut wages in the U.S. to compete.

Indeed, trade may help explain why wages have risen during the past two years. Despite the $175 billion trade deficit in 1995, the largest on record, exports are far outpacing the growth of the overall economy. As exporting industries crank up output, they need more workers, helping push wages up. And these gains may be only a downpayment on the benefits of trade. In recent years, America's major trading partners—the European Community, Japan, and Canada—have been stuck in slow gear. As their economies stabilize, U.S. export growth should accelerate even further, pushing up wages in exporting industries.

Underlying all of these gains is a fundamental improvement in U.S. productivity growth. Right now, the official numbers show that output per worker is rising at a 1.1% annual rate, about the same as in the 1980s. But these statistics don't include data from the information economy—everything from the Internet to automated teller machines. Most economists agree that once the Commerce Dept. revises the statistics later in the decade, it will become clear that productivity is on the upswing.

Need more proof that productivity is on the rise? Look at Corporate America's profit performance. Since 1992, real corporate profits have risen by 34%, a bigger increase than they registered during the previous 15 years. And that's without significant price increases in their products. The higher profits have sent the stock market soaring by 68%—a big benefit for the approximately 20% of the workforce who own stocks or have 401(k)s. . . .

What about the payoffs? Is Corporate America's wrenching transition creating an economy that can successfully compete in a global economy? Future economic growth is fueled by investment in physical and human capital—and in both respects, the U.S. is in far better shape than it was during the 1980s. Business spending on new equipment, financed by strong profits, has climbed to a record 8% of national output. In 1995, the manufacturing capacity of the nation's factories rose by 4.3%, the biggest increase in 25 years.

Not only do workers have newer and more sophisticated equipment on their jobs, but they also are becoming better educated. In 1987, 57% of high school graduates went to college soon after graduation. That percentage now is 62% and climbing, despite rising college costs. By comparison, the percentage of high school graduates enrolling in college hardly rose from the late 1960s to the mid-1980s. . . .

Access to education is the key to success in a world where well-paid jobs for high-school grads are vanishing and being replaced by managerial and professional positions. The challenge for America: ensuring that everyone has the chance to get the education and training needed to succeed. "The data is very clear about the relationship between education levels and economic success," says IBM Chairman Louis V. Gerstner Jr. . . .

Can America stage a return to the 1960s, an era of wage increases and security for all? Not likely. But there is a payoff to America's transition: an economy that will benefit most Americans.

PART 3

MICROECONOMICS

Now that we are about to begin studying modern economic theory, we might pause to ask ourselves what economic theory should do. Ideally, it should have explanatory value to help us understand how economic forces work, predictive power to help us understand what might happen in the future, and relevance to help us solve the economic problems we face. Keep these criteria in mind as you learn economic theory in Parts 3, 4, and 5.

Markets have emerged in the Western world as a method of organizing society's production. Markets exist for all of the factors of production and for final consumption goods. Through the information transmitted by markets, producers decide what factors of production to use, and consumers decide what to consume. The information appears in the form of prices. On the basis of these decisions by various economic agents in the society, resources will be used in certain ways to produce certain goods and services. From their participation in production, people will earn certain incomes and will spend them, which will determine how goods are distributed in the society.

Early economists developed theories and concepts to explain these economic activities. The early development of economic thought provided a foundation for modern microeconomics. **Microeconomics** is concerned with describing how the economic system operates to allocate resources, determine incomes, and organize production. Consequently, it focuses on the decision makers—firms, consumers, the government—that determine how resources will be used.

Microeconomics is fundamentally concerned with the major problem of all economies: that not enough resources are available to satisfy all the desires of all the economic agents. **Scarcity** is the supreme economic fact of life. Given scarcity, microeconomics also concentrates on how the market system allocates resources by valuing them. Therefore it examines the operation of markets and price determination. Finally, microeconomics is concerned with evaluating how well society allocates and rations its scarce resources. Ideally, society should use resources efficiently. **Efficiency** means the minimal use of scarce resources to achieve the mix of output most highly valued by society.

7

Scarcity: "You Can't Always Get What You Want"

INTRODUCTION

Beginning in the 1970s, the United States became sensitive to the energy crisis. Prices for oil, natural gas, and gasoline increased dramatically. Shortages of petroleum-related products developed and, at times, were serious, driving prices up and forcing long lines at gas stations and even shutdowns of factories and schools. Some observers predicted the shortages would become even more serious (although by the mid-1990s, gas prices had fallen dramatically from their 1970s highs).

In 1975 the National Academy of Sciences issued a report warning of future shortages of important resources for advanced industrial societies. The report noted that the United States would continue to depend on oil imports for the next half century and that even the Middle East's oil reserves might be depleted. Other resources in possible short supply included asbestos, tin, copper, helium, and mercury. The academy went on to urge conservation coupled with efforts to increase supplies, substitution, and recycling:

> Because of the limits to natural resources as well as to means for alleviating these limits, it is recommended that the federal government proclaim and deliberately pursue a national policy of conservation of material, energy and environmental resources, informing the public and the private sectors fully about the needs and techniques for reducing energy consumption, the development of substitute materials, increasing the durability and maintainability of products, and reclamation and recycling.

In annual reports on worldwide energy, land, water, and environmental management, the Worldwatch Institute continually warns that the world cannot sustain the rate at which it is using up its resources. Every year billions of tons of topsoil are depleted, world population growth accelerates, forests are decimated in the Third World, and there is inadequate progress in the use of renewable energy and recycling.

As the world moves to the close of the twentieth century, resource problems continue to plague the global community. Resource shortages pose potential threats to energy-dependent economies, insufficient agricultural production threatens some countries with mass starvation, and soil depletion and deforestation endanger normally replenishable resources. Moreover, the environmental complications of these economic activities pose their own hazards, from oil spills to urban slums to global warming. These are profound challenges to human societies as the twenty-first century approaches.

Because there are constraints on the availability of resources, individuals, communities, and societies must make choices about the best uses of the resources available to them. Economists have developed concepts to highlight the consequences of these choices, and they have focused on understanding how societies allocate scarce resources.

1. Why are there shortages? What factors play a role in creating shortages?
2. What sorts of actions could be taken to alleviate these projected shortages?

SCARCITY: A FUNDAMENTAL ECONOMIC FACT OF MODERN LIFE

Scarcity is one of the fundamental economic facts of modern life. **Scarcity** refers to the limitations on the resources used in production. All societies must develop methods and institutions to produce goods and services and to distribute them to people for consumption. However difficult that task, it is further complicated by the overriding reality of scarce resources and unlimited human wants and needs. Human societies, and the individual people within them, have certain physical needs for short- and long-run survival. Food, shelter, and clothing must be provided. With the desire to live beyond subsistence and to experience a richer life, the wants of a society are subject to constant expansion.

But the physical and mental resources that can be used to provide for material needs are not subject to constant expansion. This constraint is especially true if we concentrate on the short run—the present and immediate future. The mental capabilities of humans are at a certain stage of development. Physical resources are at a fixed level. There are just so many people who can labor. There is just so much wheat, corn, coal, gas, bauxite, copper, and so forth. With more time, of course, science, technology, and exploration can expand the available resources. Even in the long run, though, the problem of scarcity governs the decisions that must be made; society must still concern itself with using its possibly expanding resource base in the best way possible to meet its needs.

3. Are human wants and needs unlimited? Why or why not? What determines human wants and needs?
4. If wants are not unlimited, does scarcity still exist?

The microeconomic problem for society is to allocate the available resources in the best way possible to meet as many of the needs and wants of its people as it can. This is **efficiency**. A society will be better off if it uses its resources efficiently. This is an incredibly difficult and complicated task. How much of our resources should be used to develop nuclear energy? Should we devote more or less to exploring the possibilities of solar energy? Should more resources go to housing or to transportation? Should we build automobiles for private transportation or buses for public transportation?

Because of scarcity, we must make choices. In addition to deciding how to organize for production and distribution, a society must develop mechanisms and institutions for making **economic decisions**—decisions about how best to use the resources that are available to it. How can we make sure that resources are allocated in the best way possible? Efficiency in the allocation of resources is an important economic objective. Different societies resolve and have resolved this task in different ways—for example, by tradition, by command, by markets. (Besides efficiency, of course, a society may favor other economic goals, such as economic growth and equity in income distribution.)

In the largely private U.S. economic system, many of these decisions are made through markets. Cars are produced because people demand them and are willing to buy them for the prices charged by producers. The prices reflect the costs to the producers for the resources that are used in production. Based on price information, income, and individual tastes and preferences, people decide what to spend money on. We will examine the workings of markets in Chapters 8 and 9 to see how they allocate resources.

Resource allocation also includes public choices about the use of resources. For example, every society desires to protect itself from foreign enemies. Some countries do this by establishing a military force; the threat of physical reaction is intended to forestall aggressive actions by others. In the event of attack or hostile action, the country can use military force to protect the society's interests and possessions. The construction of military force, however, requires the use of resources, which are then unavailable for other uses. This trade-off in the use of resources is what economists call **opportunity cost**—that is, the cost of the resources that are devoted to the production of one category of goods or services and therefore cannot be used in another activity. The opportunity cost of using resources to produce guns, tanks, planes, and so on is that those resources cannot be used for other purposes. Different societies have made different choices about the size of their military establishments, and thus over how to use their scarce resources.

As in this example, microeconomics is largely concerned with the allocation of resources in society. Are resources being used efficiently? What are the opportunity costs of alternative uses of resources?

THE PRODUCTION POSSIBILITIES CURVE

Economic choices, necessitated by scarcity, have costs. This fact applies to public choices about how to use tax revenues: Should we build more highways? Should we overhaul the railroad system? Should we expand space exploration? It also applies to analyzing the results of decisions usually made in the private sector: Should we produce more big cars? Or more little cars? Should we produce cigarettes? Or Fruit Roll-Ups? Or more housing? For these and other uses of resources, choices must be made; choosing to use resources in a specific way means that they cannot be used for other purposes.

> 5. What is the opportunity cost of not using resources for a particular purpose? For example, what's the opportunity cost of going to work right out of high school?

To illustrate this economic principle—that because the resources needed to produce goods and services are scarce, a society cannot have all of the goods and services it desires—economists have developed a graph called the **production possibilities curve**. The basic production possibilities curve makes the following assumptions:

- The economy is experiencing full employment of all its resources.
- The supplies of the factors of production are fixed at one point in time.
- Technology is constant (again, at one point in time).

We will apply this curve to the public choice between producing military and civilian goods. This requires one further assumption: The economy produces consumer goods and military goods (or "butter" and "guns"), and the resources can be used to produce both types of goods (although some resources will be better than others at producing one type of goods). With our resources (and our assumptions), we can make only limited amounts of both types of goods, so we must choose how much of each type of good to produce. Since our resources are fully employed and limited, we can produce more of one type of good only by producing less of the other. That is, if we decide to produce more military goods, we can do it only by taking resources away from the production of civilian goods and thus produce fewer consumer goods. The opportunity cost of producing more military goods is that we will have fewer civilian goods, and vice versa.

This production possibilities curve is graphed in Figure 7.1. If we produce only military goods (using all our resources to do so), we can have M_1 of them. On the other hand, if we produce only consumer goods, we can have C_1 of them. Assume that the economy is at A. Then we produce C_2 of consumer goods and M_2 of military goods. However, there is a whole range of different *combinations* of military goods and consumer goods that we could have. The locus of all those possible combinations gives us the production possibilities curve.

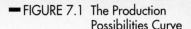

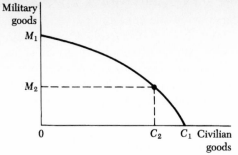

At a given moment in time, if a society chooses to have more of one type of good, it must sacrifice some of the other type of good. To have more military goods (moving toward M_1), the society will have fewer resources to devote to the production of civilian goods. This problem can be alleviated over time somewhat by the discovery of new resources or by the institution of new technology that allows us to get more production from our resources. In either case, the entire curve would move outward.

6. Can you graph and explain why the production possibilities curve will move outward with (a) an increase in resources available or (b) an improvement in technology that increases efficiency?

The production possibilities curve is shaped the way it is (concave to the origin) because resources are not completely adaptable to other uses. For example, the more consumer goods we sacrifice (moving toward M_1), the fewer and fewer military goods we will be able to *add* to military production for each marginal loss of consumer goods. (Can you show this on the graph?) The reason is that some resources (e.g., pacifists) are best suited for producing consumer goods and not suited for military production. As more of these resources are transferred to military production, the *addition* to military goods will decline. The reverse is true, too. If we disarmed, some generals might not excel at producing consumer goods.

▨ GRAPHS, EQUATIONS, AND WORDS

Economists like to use graphical representations. The production possibilities curve is one example of this pedagogical technique, and you will encounter many other graphs in this book. However, graphs are only one of three basic ways to present economic ideas.

Economic theory seeks to establish relationships among economic variables. To describe and explain these relationships, economists use words, graphical illustrations, and mathematical equations. To explain the production possibilities curve, we have discussed in words the notion of the opportunity costs between military goods and civilian goods. We have also illustrated this relationship on a graph. To show this relationship as an equation, we could write, $M_x = f(C_x)$. This means that the amount of military goods the society has (M_x) depends on the amount of civilian goods it has (C_x), given all of our assumptions.

On the graph in Figure 7.1, the amount of military goods is measured on the vertical axis, and the amount of civilian goods on the horizontal axis. Thus, any point on the graph represents a single combination of civilian goods and military goods. And every point represents a different combination.

> 7. What does it mean if society is at a point inside its production possibilities curve?

THE USE OF GRAPHS IN ECONOMICS

Economic theory identifies important economic variables and attempts to explain their relationships. Economists frequently rely on graphs to illustrate these relationships. This book contains numerous graphs, so it is important to be clear about how they are constructed and what they show.

Let's take a simple example of the relationship between the amount of oil a household uses and how much it costs. During a particular period of time—say, a month—a household can use different amounts of oil. Depending upon how much oil is used, the cost to the household will vary. Let's say oil (for heating and hot water) costs $1 per gallon. Table 7.1 gives information on the costs of using different amounts of oil.

We can illustrate this same information on a graph. In Figure 7.2 we measure increasing amounts of oil as we move out from the origin on the horizontal axis, and increasing costs of oil as we move up from the origin on the vertical axis. (Generally, the independent variable is placed on the horizontal, or x, axis, and the dependent variable is put on the vertical, or y, axis. Here, the amount of oil is the independent variable, and the cost is the dependent variable. The cost depends on the amount of oil used, given price.) Each combination of oil and its cost is represented by a point on the graph. When we connect all the different points, we have a graphical representation of the relationship between different amounts of oil used and the respective costs.

The graph provides a picture of the relationship between the amount of oil used and the cost to the household. It tells us that the cost goes up as the household uses more oil

TABLE 7.1 Monthly Cost of Oil for a Household

Point on Graph	Amount of Oil Used (Gallons per Month)	Cost ($)
origin	0	0
a	20	20
b	40	40
c	60	60
d	80	80
e	100	100

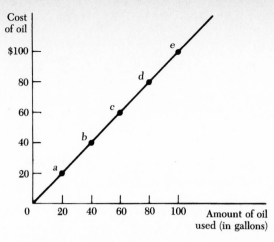

■ FIGURE 7.2 Relationship between Amount of Oil Used and Cost of Oil

per month. It represents exactly the same information contained in the table, but the graph presents the relationship in summary form. It is an efficient way to express the relationship between these two variables. Most people can more readily understand a visual comparison of relative size than they can see relationships in a table of numbers. Such illustrations are useful in developing economic theory about the more complicated relationships among economic variables.

The relationship between variables may be positive or negative. In Figure 7.2, the graph shows a positive relationship between oil used and cost—as oil use increases, so does cost. If there is a positive relationship between two variables, the graph will slope upward to the right. If there is a negative relationship between two variables—as one increases, the other decreases—the graph will have a negative slope (downward to the right). For example, if a household uses wood as well as oil for heat, its use of oil will decrease as its use of wood increases. We can represent this relationship in a table and in a graph (Table 7.2 and Figure 7.3).

The *slope* of a graph tells us precisely how one variable changes with another. The slope is the change in the dependent variable divided by the change in the independent variable between two points. (Other ways to say this are the height over the base of the line, or the rise over the run.) For example, the slope of the graph in Figure 7.2 equals

■ TABLE 7.2 Amounts of Oil and Wood Used for Heat per Month

Wood (in Cords)	Oil (in Gallons)
0	60
¼	50
½	40
¾	30
1	20

THE USE OF GRAPHS IN ECONOMICS

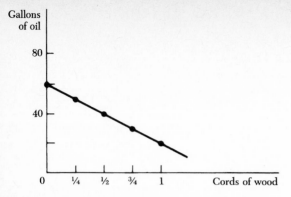

FIGURE 7.3 Relationship between Amount of Oil and Amount of Wood Used

the ratio of the change in the cost over the change in the amount of oil used. In moving along the line from point b to point c, the change in cost equals $20, and the change in the amount of oil used is 20 gallons:

$$\text{slope} = \frac{\text{change in cost}}{\text{change in oil used}} = \frac{\$20}{20 \text{ gal.}} = 1.$$

(Often the symbol Δ is used to denote the change in a variable.) In this case, the slope is equal to 1. (What is the slope of the graph in Figure 7.3?)

Graphs of the relationships between economic variables can also be curved lines, as in panels (a), (b), and (c) of Figure 7.4. In these cases, the slope changes as we move along each line. (The slope can be approximated by drawing a line tangent to each point on the curve.) For example, in Figure 7.4(a), the positive slope of the line becomes less steep as we move to the right. In Figure 7.4(b) from 0 to x_1, the slope is negative (y decreases as x increases); beyond x_1, the slope of the line is positive. At x_1, the slope of the line is 0, and y is at its minimum value. In Figure 7.4(c) the slope is positive to x_2 and negative beyond x_2. At x_2, the slope of the graph is 0, and y is at its maximum value. These graphs are similar to those of economic relationships we will encounter in Parts 3 and 4.

FIGURE 7.4 Examples of Relationships between Economic Variables

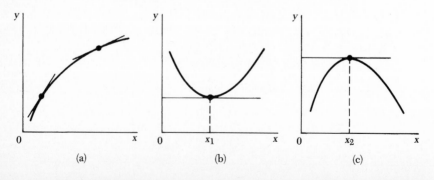

Chapter 7 SCARCITY: "YOU CAN'T ALWAYS GET WHAT YOU WANT"

MILITARY VERSUS CIVILIAN PRIORITIES

A controversial example of the problem of scarcity in recent years has been the debate about national priorities. Perhaps the sharpest focus of this debate has been on military spending versus spending on civilian priorities. Proponents of military spending want more resources for producing military goods. They argue that more is needed because of the potential military capabilities of the nation's enemies and because they believe military power is the best way to assure national security. Critics argue that too many resources are devoted to defense and that military spending deprives the nation of the use of resources for domestic purposes (e.g., education and health care).

The arguments on both sides have become more sophisticated and complex over the years, but at the heart of the matter is an economic choice about how best to use scarce resources. This public issue, though, is not simply an economic question. It is also concerned with philosophy (how best to resolve conflicts? what is social justice? what is security?) and with international and domestic politics.

> 8. What is national security? What determines whether a nation is secure?

Since World War II, the United States has devoted a substantial portion of its resources every year to military spending. Before the 1940s, with the exception of U.S. involvement in World War I, only about 1 percent of the nation's annual production of goods and services (measured by gross domestic product, or GDP) was devoted to armed forces. In the massive Allied war effort from 1941 to 1945, however, military production dominated the economy. In the period since then, the annual military budget has fluctuated between about 5 and 9 percent of GDP. In the mid-1990s, the national defense budget exceeded $250 billion annually. Worldwide military spending is almost $1 trillion and represents about 12 percent of the spending of national governments.

What does all this money buy? About 25 percent of the annual military budget pays for the personnel costs of past and present service people and civilian workers for the Pentagon. About 50 percent of it is used to purchase military supplies, equipment, and weapons: uniforms, food, planes, petroleum, ammunition, nuclear warheads, and so forth. The remainder provides for the general support costs (e.g., construction and maintenance) of the entire military establishment.

The history of this shift in the military policy of the United States is rooted in the two world wars, the Cold War, and subsequent "hot" wars and military interventions. For World Wars I and II, the United States mobilized production forces and military forces for the war efforts. U.S. peacetime military forces, its standing army and navy, were relatively modest and concerned primarily with defending the borders of the United States. After World War II, however, the United States decided to maintain relatively large and worldwide military forces. The arguments were that these forces were necessary to *prevent* aggression and that the Soviet Union, in the post–World War II period, represented a threat to U.S. interests and world peace. The U.S. arsenal consisted of the personnel in the Army, Navy, Air Force, and Marines, and sophisticated conventional and nuclear weapons.

From time to time, a perception of an increased Soviet threat or an active military engagement has caused increases in military spending. For example, the Korean (1950–1954) and Vietnam (1964–1975) wars led to increased budgets to finance U.S. participation in the conflicts. In the 1980s and 1990s, U.S. military forces were involved in invasions of Grenada and Panama and in the (Persian) Gulf War. During Ronald Reagan's presidency (1981–1989), the military budget increased significantly. Reagan argued that the Soviet threat had increased and that U.S. conventional and nuclear forces needed expansion and modernization.

The expansion in military spending under the Reagan administration accompanied reduced spending by the federal government on nondefense programs. Food stamps, job training, welfare, education, and other programs experienced significant budget cutbacks. The $100 billion in increased military spending from 1981 to 1985 was just about matched by the decreases in spending on social programs. In 1980 the national defense budget was almost 25 percent of federal spending, and social programs (other than Social Security, Medicare, and unemployment compensation) accounted for just over 30 percent of the budget. By 1985, the military budget's share was 30 percent, while the share of other social programs had shrunk to just over 20 percent.

What are the arguments for and against this use of the scarce material and labor resources of the United States? Ronald Reagan, George Bush, Bob Dole, and their supporters have argued that the United States must maintain clear military superiority to prevent nuclear war and to bargain for arms control. Moreover, they argue, larger military power will prevent political instability in the Third World and will enable the United States to protect its vital interests in the Persian Gulf and other regions of the world. The rest of the world must perceive that the United States is strong and willing to use its force. In this way, the United States can contribute to international stability and world peace.

The opponents of this view argue that the United States and other nuclear powers already have the capability to blow up the world. Even with the arms control agreements of the late 1980s and the promise of strategic arms reductions in the future, there are more than adequate forces for simple deterrence. In terms of foreign policy, they argue that military power is not the most powerful weapon in promoting peace or U.S. interests in the rest of the world. Rather, the United States should resign itself to the trend toward increased political and economic interdependence and recognize that it can no longer be the world's dominant power. Finally, they suggest that a country's national security is determined at least as much by internal health as by military might. Consequently, spending more money on the military and denying resources, as a result, for domestic priorities actually undermines the national security of the United States. What good is it to be first in military power when the country is eighteenth in infant mortality?

This debate over the use of society's scarce resources was sharpened in the 1980s and 1990s. Congress restrained the military budget's growth in response to mounting pressures to get the federal budget deficit under control, a proliferation of military contracting scandals about overpriced weapons and other forms of corruption, and exaggerations of Soviet military power and spending by the first Reagan administration. In real terms (adjusted for inflation), the national defense budget actually began to decrease in the late 1980s. Also, as the 1990s began, the United States and the Soviet Union agreed on substantial reductions in their strategic nuclear arsenals. Dramatic changes swept through all of Eastern Europe. The Soviet threat dissipated; many commentators proclaimed the end of the Cold War.

In this new environment, renewed pressure developed to further reduce the military budget. The possibility of a "peace dividend" was music to the ears of those who had alternative uses in mind for the savings in military spending. Some wanted to use it to reduce the deficit, others wanted to reduce taxes, and there was broad support for transferring federal spending to domestic priorities such as housing, health care, education, infrastructure, and research and development. On the other hand, the military and its supporters were quick to argue that the country should not wield the budget ax indiscriminately but rather go slowly to protect U.S. military capabilities. Presumably, this intense debate will continue throughout the rest of the 1990s—even as the military budget stabilizes at slightly lower levels.

9. What are the opportunity costs of increased military spending? What are the possible opportunity costs of not increasing military spending?
10. What is your opinion in this general debate concerning the use of our society's scarce resources? Focus your response on the economic ramifications of the various choices.
11. The Congressional Budget Office has estimated that the federal government could increase its spending on the nation's deteriorating infrastructure—highways, bridges, water and sewer systems, and so forth—by $10 billion a year. Would you support reducing the military budget to do so? Why or why not? Could the federal government spend more on both military and infrastructural programs? Explain.

APPLYING THE CONCEPT OF CHOICE TO PERSONAL DECISIONS

As is implicit in all of the foregoing, when making decisions about using society's resources, we compare the costs and the benefits of different uses of resources. Included in the costs are the opportunities forgone by not using resources for alternatives. This balancing of costs versus benefits also occurs in the economic decisions made by individuals, such as choices about work versus leisure, type of work, consumption, and so on.

Consumers weigh the benefits of buying a particular good (say, a used car) against its cost (that is, its price). They can also compare the benefits of purchasing a used car against the opportunity costs of not buying other goods (things they could have bought for the same price as the car, e.g., a fancy new personal computer and printer). On the basis of such judgments, consumers decide what goods to purchase in markets. (Furthermore, producers take consumers' decisions into account, and resources are allocated through markets to the production of particular goods and services.)

An example of a personal choice about resources is deciding whether to go to college. In making such a decision, an individual must weigh the benefits of going to college against the costs and opportunity costs of doing so. College costs money—for room and board, tuition, travel, books, and so on—and that money cannot be used for anything else. If you are in college, you are not working, getting experience, or earning income from a full-time job. On the other hand, a college education will develop your abilities, enrich your later life, and may qualify you for various types of employment. It is also a privileged period of time and space for growing and maturing in your experiences (curricular and extracurricular) and developing a philosophy of life.

A college education usually prepares people for white-collar, professional, higher-paying jobs. People with college educations, on the average, earn more than nongraduates. The earnings gap between college and high school graduates is substantial, with college graduates earning on the average at least 50 percent more in annual income. Over their lifetimes, college graduates earn in excess of $600,000 more than high school graduates. Typically, the unemployment rate of college graduates is half that of high school graduates. Such factors can influence an individual's choice about going to college.

12. What are the benefits of going to college?
13. What are the costs (and opportunity costs) of going to college?
14. Did you make the right decision about going to college? Why or why not?

CONCLUSION

Scarcity requires choices in both public and private matters. This fundamental economic fact requires societies and individuals to develop institutions and procedures for making hard decisions. Individuals rarely have enough income to buy everything they might want. Governments do not have enough tax money to do everything that their constituents would like them to do. In addition, decisions may result in benefits to someone or some group, while others suffer losses. Decision makers must weigh these costs and benefits in reaching decisions that maximize the use of scarce resources.

One of the most important institutions for facilitating such decisions in a private economy is the market. Markets determine prices for goods and resources. With this information, economic agents can compare alternative courses of action. Producers can decide what to produce and what resources to use. Consumers can decide what goods to purchase. In the next chapter, we will examine the economic theory of markets—how they operate and how prices are determined.

Review Questions

1. From your own experiences, do you think scarcity is really a problem for the United States? Is scarcity a problem in Ethiopia?
2. What is the difference between wants and needs?
3. Are wants and needs really unlimited? If they are, why?
4. How does the concept of opportunity cost help societies and individuals to make choices?
5. Why do economic choices have to be made?
6. Describe examples from your own life when the concepts of scarcity and opportunity cost have influenced your decisions.
7. Why don't the advances of science, technology, and exploration eliminate the problem of scarcity?
8. Why, at the beginning of World War II, could the United States increase its military output without sacrificing the production of civilian goods and services? Answer using a production possibilities curve.
9. The following table shows production possibilities for Brazil for consumption goods and investment goods:

Consumption Goods	Investment Goods
0	200
50	175
100	145
150	105
200	55
250	0

Graph the production possibilities curve. What are the opportunity costs of increasing the production of consumption goods by successive units of 50? Why might a country want to increase its production of investment goods?

8

The Theory of Markets

INTRODUCTION

Markets guide decisions about resource allocation—that is, how society decides to use its scarce resources. How exactly do markets accomplish this? This chapter will develop the economic analysis of markets to provide some insight into the relationship between markets and resource allocation.

As we saw in Part 2, markets emerged as one of the most fundamental institutions of capitalism. **Markets** are the institutions through which buyers and sellers exchange goods and services. They replaced tradition and feudal authority as the principal organizers of economic activity. Markets exist in capitalism for all consumer goods and productive resources.

Usually, goods and services are exchanged for money. All goods and services, then, must have prices that reflect their values and that govern their exchange. These prices end up guiding production and resource allocation. Producers and consumers use prices as basic information in deciding which resources to use and which products to purchase. Consequently, to see how markets allocate scarce resources, it is essential to understand how markets determine prices.

MARKETS AND PRICE DETERMINATION: SUPPLY-AND-DEMAND ANALYSIS

To highlight the economic analysis of markets, we will use as an example the market for college education in the United States. In Chapter 7, we referred to the decision about going to college as an example of a personal choice about the use of scarce resources. How much does it cost? What else could one do with the money? Why should (or shouldn't) one go to college? What

■ Examining snowboards in a sporting equipment store—a market in action. Markets exist whenever and wherever commodities are exchanged by buyers and sellers. (David Young-Wolff/PhotoEdit)

does one sacrifice by going to college for four years? Does it make more sense to enter the labor force right after high school? What are the benefits of a college education?

Obviously, one crucial element in making such an important decision is the dollar cost of going to college. In the following analysis, we will isolate the factors that determine the price of a college education. The analysis will help us to gain some insights into and understanding of how this market operates—how its price is determined and what implications there are for resource allocation. We will develop a method of analysis, the *theory of supply and demand*, that should assist us in understanding the general functioning of markets in a capitalist economy.

1. During the 1970s, the cost of a year at college for tuition, room and board, and fees almost doubled. However, the rise in costs was slightly less than the overall rate of inflation for the same period. In the 1980s, the costs for a year of college doubled and increased faster than the rate of inflation. In the 1990s, the costs for college have continued to increase but usually right around or just above the rate of inflation. Why do you think the price of a college education has been continually increasing? What can be done about this problem? Why is it a "problem"?

To conduct our supply-and-demand analysis, as in all economic theory, we will have to make some assumptions to simplify our model of the market. Despite these simplifying assumptions, our theory will provide us with some tools for understanding the functioning of real markets in the economy. It should also help us understand why market prices change over time. And it might also help us develop some possible solutions to economic problems.

We will begin with a fundamental assumption of microeconomics: that economic agents are rational calculators and are motivated by self-interest. We assume that consumers are rational with respect to their purchases and that they try to maximize their own welfare through consumption, given their available spending power (that, through calculations and trial and error, consumers seek to maximize their satisfaction). Generally, we assume that producers calculate costs and revenues and try to maximize their profits from production.

To analyze the market for a college education, we need some additional assumptions and qualifications. First, we will assume that there is, in some sense, a homogeneous product. In other words, we will concentrate on *a* college education as a good that is exchanged in a market of buyers and sellers, assuming away any differences between particular colleges or between private and public universities. Obviously, these differences do exist and account for price differences, but we wish to simplify and concentrate on *one* price for a college education. Once we have developed a model of supply and demand, we should be able to use it to account for cost differences at different institutions. We will also assume away the admissions problem (the product is not necessarily available to any buyer who might wish to purchase it), the financial aid dimension (not everyone pays the same price), and the graduation problem (actually getting the product in hand is not merely a matter of paying the costs to the cashier). Finally, although the producer of this product is not a profit-making institution, colleges and universities must take their costs and revenues into account, utilize scarce resources efficiently, and charge prices that reflect their costs (minus contributions from alumni, corporations, benefactors, etc.).

Higher education is a large market in the United States. In the mid-1990s, this "industry" spent almost $200 billion annually. Almost 13 million students are enrolled as undergraduates in more than 2,100 four-year institutions and almost 1,500 two-year schools. About 55 percent of the students are women, and about 25 percent are students of color.

U.S. higher education also has a very large comparative advantage in the global economy. The U.S. higher education system is one of the best in the world, and it attracts students from all areas of the globe. More than 450,000 international students are enrolled in U.S. institutions (about 225,000 as undergraduates), while 76,000 U.S. students study abroad. Of the international students in the United States, 57 percent came from Asia, 14 percent from Europe, 10 percent from Latin America, and 7 percent from the Middle East.

To see how the market price for a college education is determined, we will begin by examining each side of this market in isolation from the other. For the buyer's side of the market, we will focus on *demand;* for the seller's side of the market, we will focus on *supply.* Then we will put supply and demand together.

Demand

The buyer's side of the market involves the demand for the product. **Demand** is the amount of a particular good or service buyers want, given its price. More specifically, it represents the amounts of a particular good or service buyers are willing and able to purchase at various possible prices.

What determines the demand for any product? Many factors influence the demand for a college education. The essential factor behind the demand for any product obviously is that it is useful to the buyer; it satisfies some want or desire or need. Beyond this, we can list some other influences on the demand for a product: tastes and preferences, income, prices of related goods, number of demanders, and expectations of future prices, among other factors.

Tastes and Preferences. Consumers' tastes and preferences guide their demand for different goods. Tastes and preferences are influenced by social, political, and cultural forces, as well as by the physical, psychological, and mental requirements of daily survival in the world. Over time, in any given society, tastes and preferences will change and will, in turn, influence changing patterns of consumer demand for different goods and services. Tastes and preferences also differ among different countries.

Throughout the modern history of the United States, a college education has been a valued product. Presumably, it helps prepare people for coping with the world, broadens people's horizons and perspectives, prepares people for professional positions in society, and paves the way for further education. It also helps people gain entry to certain sectors of the labor force.

In recent years, the demand for a college education has been continually increasing (in 1960, there were 6 million students in higher education, half as many as in the mid-1990s). The primary reason for the increase is that people perceive a college degree to be necessary for obtaining specific types of employment. Indeed, the realities of the labor market suggest that a college education is extremely valuable in this regard. The President's Council of Economic Advisers has recently estimated that the annual rate of return on a college education is about 13 percent (significantly in excess of the return on most financial investments). Consumers' tastes and preferences thus influence the demand for a college education. Throughout the 1960s the percentage of high school graduates who went on to college steadily increased. In the 1970s the percentage leveled off, but in the 1980s and 1990s, it has continued to increase. In 1994, 62 percent of high school graduates enrolled in college.

2. Why do you suppose that tastes and preferences changed to cause a leveling off in the percentage of high school graduates who went to college? *Did* tastes and preferences change? Have they changed again in the 1980s and 1990s? Why?

Income. Demand depends not only on the desire to buy, but also on how much consumers have to spend. Spending power, in turn, depends largely on income. And who consumes what products depends on the distribution of income in the society.

Since we have assumed that consumers try to maximize their satisfaction and that they derive it from goods because the goods are useful, we conclude that with more money, consumers will purchase larger quantities of goods and services. During the 1960s, the United States experienced one of its longest periods of prosperity. The real income of the average family increased throughout this period. This increasing income certainly provided the resources for an increasing percentage of U.S. youth to attend college. In the 1970s and 1980s, however, the increase in average real incomes began to slow down. This probably accounts in part for some of the leveling off in college attendance in the 1970s.

Prices of Related Goods. The demand for a college education may be sensitive to (and influenced by) the prices of related products. Consumers are very sensitive to the prices of goods they consider to be *substitutes*—goods that satisfy the same need. For example, some substitutes for Coke are Pepsi, other soft drinks, fruit juices, and water; substitutes for plane transportation include train and automobile transportation to the same destination. In the case of the demand for a college education, if some nonprofessional training schools lowered their prices, the demand for college educations might fall, as some people substituted that educational experience for college.

Other goods may be *complementary*. Such goods go together or are consumed together. Examples of complements include computers and computer software, stereo components and CDs, and movies and popcorn. For would-be lawyers, college and law school are complements. An increase in the price of law school might dissuade some of these people from going to college.

Number of Demanders. The total demand for a product is affected by the number of people who desire to consume it. During the 1960s and 1970s, the number of college-age people in the United States was steadily expanding. In the 1960s, with an increasing percentage of youths attending college, the total number of "demanders" in the market increased dramatically. Recently, the increase in the numbers has been less dramatic, although older people are now increasing their attendance in college.

The number of eighteen-year-olds in the population actually declined by about 25 percent between 1979 and 1994. This had serious implications for the market for a college education in the United States. A number of colleges and universities developed vigorous efforts to recruit older students and international students to make up for this reduction in the number of demanders. Some private colleges began to accept part-time students. Many of these factors have already had an effect: Students over twenty-five now make up over one-third of the almost 13 million undergraduates enrolled in higher education, and over 40 percent of all students are part-time students. Beginning in 1995, the number of eighteen-year-olds began to increase again, which will have some impact on the composition of higher-education enrollments.

Expectations of Future Prices. If consumers expect the price of a product to change, this tends to affect their demand for that product. For example, if high school graduates expect that the price of attending college will continue to increase in the future, this may cause many of them to attend right away rather than wait, or they may decide not to go at all.

Notice that, as in the first sentence of this section, economists frequently use the words *tend to*. Their conclusions are often tentative because they are usually based on assumptions and expectations of normal behavior on the part of most economic agents and variables the economists are examining. But not everyone acts the same way! In your own thinking, try to replicate this word usage; the conclusions of economists are not carved in stone and should not be accepted as gospel. Economic theory deals with assumptions and tendencies; if "this" happens, probably "that" will happen.

Miscellaneous Factors. Other factors also may influence consumers' demands for products. One of these is government policies. In the 1960s the federal government and several state governments significantly increased their support of higher education in the United States. Increased interest in higher education's benefits to the country probably by itself influenced the demand for a college education. In addition, the government support made it easier for more high school graduates to attend college. By significantly expanding public universities and community colleges throughout the country, it also opened up the college experience to a class of people that historically had not had access to higher education in the United States. On the other hand, federal and state budget restraints in the 1980s reduced levels of assistance and increased students' reliance on loans and work to finance higher education. These factors, which have been reproduced in the 1990s, make the pursuit of higher education more difficult for many people in the society.

3. What other factor(s) would influence the number of students enrolling in college? (Consider only the demand side of the market.)

Ceteris Paribus and the Demand Curve

If you answered the previous question, "the *price* of a college education," you are on your way to becoming an economist. Economists attempt to isolate the effect of price on the quantity demanded for a product. In analyzing the demand for a product, they acknowledge that all of the factors just described do influence demand. But sometimes simplification helps analysis. Therefore, economists concentrate on the relationship between price and the quantity demanded of a good. To do this, they assume that at one moment of time, all of the other factors are given; then only price will affect the quantity demanded. The other factors (the determinants of demand) are considered to be in a *ceteris paribus* category—a Latin phrase meaning all other things being equal. *Demand is concerned with the relationship between price and quantity demanded, all other things constant.*

So let's make that rather large assumption and see what happens. What *is* the effect of price on the quantity demanded of a college education? At one moment in time, assuming (again) that there is some one average type of college education, there is only one annual price for this product. For 1996–1997, the College Board estimated that the average cost for tuition, room and board, and required fees at four-year private universities was $18,184. For public schools the average cost was $7,118. Since there were more students in public institutions, we will assume that $12,200 was about the average cost for the nation as a whole for a year of college. (For 1996–1997, tuition, room and board, and fees at a number of private colleges exceeded $26,000, prompting *Newsweek* magazine to proclaim that these institutions cost $1,000 a week!)

We can hypothesize about what would happen to the quantity demanded if the price were higher or lower. In fact, we would expect that *if* the price were lower, people would consume more—the quantity demanded would increase—and that *if* the price were higher, people would consume less—the quantity demanded would decrease. This is true for almost all goods and services: If the price is lowered, the quantity demanded will increase, and if the price is increased, the quantity demanded will decrease. In other words, price and quantity demanded are inversely related. When the price changes, there is a *change in the quantity demanded*—in the opposite direction.

We can state this relationship mathematically as well. A demand equation, generally, would show that the quantity of college education demanded, Q_d, is a function of the price of a college education, P_c, *given* all of the *ceteris paribus* conditions:

$$Q_d = f(P_c), \text{ ceteris paribus.}$$

To work with numbers, we can construct a hypothetical **demand schedule** (Table 8.1) showing different possible prices and the quantities demanded at those prices at one moment in time. Let's hypothesize about the national market for college educations for a year (again assuming that there is some average education). If the price were $12,200 (which was about the national average cost in 1996), then about 13 million people would be enrolled in the nation's colleges and universities as students. If, however, the price went up to $14,400 per year, then the quantity demanded would fall to 11 million. Table 8.1 shows several other possibilities as well.

We can also graph the relationship between price and quantity demanded. We call this a **demand curve**. The vertical scale measures price, and the

TABLE 8.1 Demand Schedule for College Education

P_c (Cost per Year, Tuition, Room and Board, and Fees)	Q_d (Number of Students, in Millions)
$18,800	7
16,600	9
14,400	11
12,200	13
10,000	15

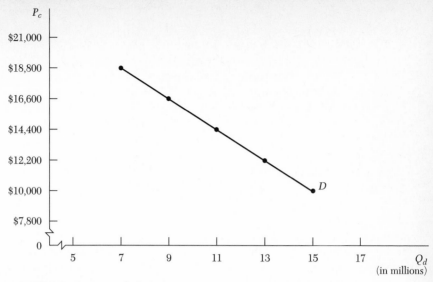

■ FIGURE 8.1 Demand Curve

horizontal scale measures quantity demanded. Any point on the graph represents a certain price–quantity demanded combination. Let's take the information from the demand schedule in Table 8.1 and transfer it to the graph. At a price of $10,000, the quantity demanded is 15 million; at $12,200, it is 13 million; and so on. Each combination corresponds to a point in Figure 8.1.

If we connect all the price–quantity demanded points, we get a demand curve for a college education during one year in the United States. It shows, hypothetically, all of the possible prices for a college education and the respective quantities demanded. It has a negative slope, reflecting the inverse relationship between price and quantity demanded. At lower prices, the quantity demanded is greater; at higher prices, the quantity demanded is lower. (For convenience, however, we normally draw demand curves as straight lines.)

The graphs of demand curves and supply curves are very important tools in economics. Make sure you understand how Figure 8.1 was constructed and what it shows.

The demand curve illustrates the buyers' side of the market. Now let's turn our attention to the sellers' side of the market and consider it in isolation. After that, we will put the two sides of the market together in our model and get a market price for a college education.

Supply

Now we will focus on the sellers' side of the market. This side involves **supply**—the amounts of a good that will be offered for sale at different possible prices. What influences the supply of a product? What factors deter-

■ Navigating homework in a computer lab. *(Tom Rosenthal/SuperStock, Inc.)*

mine the number of students that colleges and universities can allow to enroll? Obviously, the price that these institutions can get from students has a lot to do with it. But for the moment, let's discuss other influences. These include resource prices, technology, prices of related goods, sellers' expectations, and the number of sellers in the market.

Resource Prices. The costs of producing goods and services weigh heavily on the ability of sellers to supply the market. Thus, resource prices help determine the supply of any product offered for sale. In the supply of college educations, if the salaries of professors and other staff increase, the supply tends to shrink or college educations become more expensive. With the rapid inflation of the late 1960s and 1970s and the moderate inflation of the 1980s and 1990s, the labor resource costs of running universities have skyrocketed as employees have demanded commensurate increases in their incomes. Even though dollar labor costs have increased at colleges, in real terms faculty incomes dropped 20 percent during the 1970s due to inflation. This prompted many faculties to form labor unions; there are more than 200 at four-year colleges and almost 400 at two-year colleges. Physical plant workers, cafeteria personnel, and office workers also are often in unions on campuses around the country. Increasing costs for food, equipment, maintenance, paper, computers, construction, and energy also have increased total expenses significantly. As a result, the cost of supplying a college education has increased.

Technology. The techniques of production influence supply. If computers and television sets were used to teach students, to grade their work, and to write letters of recommendation for them, colleges and universities would probably be able to greatly increase the numbers of students to whom they could supply a college education. Other ways of changing the techniques of production involve the use of large lecture classes, sometimes even with video lectures, or computer-assisted learning. (Of course, these might make the process of getting an education a bit less attractive. But that is a *demand* factor.) For the time being, however, the technology of education still relies heavily on human beings and, in some places, on relatively small classes.

Prices of Related Goods

The ability of suppliers to supply any product to the market will also be affected by the prices of other products. If a college or a university could earn a better return on operating as a summer camp than offering summer sessions, then maybe it would decide to supply that product instead. Similarly, a college could display paintings and other artwork on its hallway walls, or it could sell wall space to corporate advertisers.

Sellers' Expectations. Sellers' expectations about the future will condition their supply of a product to the market. If colleges and universities expect lower enrollments in the future, they might be inclined to try to offer fewer students the chance to go to college now (that is, begin to decrease the supply of the product now). They might do this to prepare themselves for the foreseen lean days ahead. Given the likelihood of continuing high energy prices, some older dormitories might need to be retired, thus reducing the number of spaces available at some schools.

Numbers of Sellers in the Market. If the number of sellers in the market decreased, it would tend to decrease the supply of the product. And if the number of sellers increased, it would tend to increase the supply. In the late 1970s and early 1980s, a number of colleges and universities in the United States closed their doors. In 1981 there were 3,253 institutions of higher learning in the United States; in 1983 there were 3,111. Since then, the numbers have begun to increase, reaching more than 3,600 in 1995.

4. Of the five factors described as influencing supply, which, in your opinion, is the most influential in determining the supply of a product? Why?
5. What sorts of factors influence sellers' expectations about their markets?

Ceteris Paribus and the Supply Curve

As for the demand curve, we will hold the nonprice influences on supply constant when we create a supply curve. They constitute the *ceteris paribus* conditions for supply. As a result, we will concentrate on the effect of price on the quantity supplied of a product. At one moment in time, we assume that all of the *ceteris paribus* factors (the determinants of supply) are given and consider in isolation the effect of price. *Supply is concerned with the relationship between price and quantity supplied, all other things constant.*

At one moment, there is only one price in existence. But we can hypothesize different possible prices and examine the effects on quantity supplied. If the price were higher, we would expect sellers to increase the quantity supplied. If sellers were offered a lower price, we would expect them to reduce the quantity supplied. For supply, price and quantity supplied are directly related. When the price changes, there is a *change in quantity supplied* in the same direction.

TABLE 8.2 Supply Schedule for College Education	
P_c (Cost per Year)	Q_s (Number of Students, in Millions)
$18,800	19
16,600	17
14,400	15
12,200	13
10,000	11

We can state this as an equation as well. With all other determinants of supply held constant, the quantity supplied of a college education, Q_s, is a function of the price offered for a college education, P_c:

$$Q_s = f(P_c), \textit{ ceteris paribus.}$$

As for demand, we can construct a hypothetical **supply schedule** (Table 8.2), showing different possible prices and the quantities that would be supplied at those prices. Table 8.2 hypothesizes about the total national supply of a college education. *If* the price were only $10,000, then colleges and universities would offer places for only 11 million students. *If* the price were $18,800, then colleges and universities would be willing to offer places to 19 million students. The table includes other possibilities as well.

Again, we can show the supply relationship graphically. We measure price on the vertical scale and quantity supplied on the horizontal scale. Each point

■ FIGURE 8.2 Supply Curve

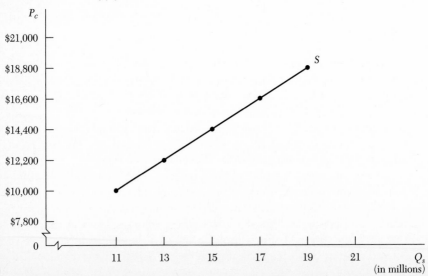

Chapter 8 THE THEORY OF MARKETS

TABLE 8.3 The Supply Schedule Combined
with the Demand Schedule

P_c ($)	Q_d (in Millions)	Q_s (in Millions)
18,800	7	19
16,600	9	17
14,400	11	15
12,200	13	13
10,000	15	11

in Figure 8.2 represents a certain price–quantity supplied combination. If we connect the five combinations from the schedule in Table 8.2, we get a supply curve for a college education. It shows, hypothetically, all the possible prices for a college education and the respective quantities supplied. It has a positive slope, showing the direct relationship between price and quantity supplied; at higher prices, greater quantities will be supplied, and at lower prices, lower quantities will be supplied. (For convenience, we usually draw supply curves as straight lines.)

The supply curve illustrates the sellers' side of the market. The demand curve shows the buyers' side. Let's see what happens when we put them together to look at both sides of the market.

The Market and the Equilibrium Price

Putting the supply and demand schedules together, as listed in Table 8.3 and graphed in Figure 8.3, gives us a hypothetical picture of the market. When

■ FIGURE 8.3 Market and Equilibrium Price

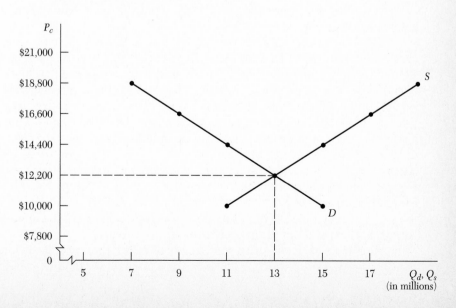

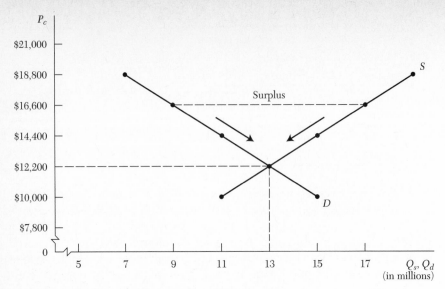

— FIGURE 8.4 Surplus Eliminated by Price Decreases

we put supply and demand together, the supply and the demand for the product determine a market price. It is an **equilibrium price.** Equilibrium connotes a situation in which the tendency is toward a certain state, and once that state is achieved it will be maintained, in the absence of outside disturbances.

In our example, a price of $12,200 is the equilibrium price. At this price, the desires of buyers and sellers are consistent. Buyers want to buy 13 million places at colleges and universities, and sellers are willing to offer 13 million places. The quantity demanded equals the quantity supplied. Stated mathematically, at P_c = $12,200, $Q_s = Q_d$. On the graph in Figure 8.3, the equilibrium price and quantity exchanged are the point at which the supply and demand curves intersect.

At any other price, Q_s does not equal Q_d, and the price will tend to change because buyers' and sellers' desires are not consistent. For example, at P_c = $16,600, Q_s = 17 million and Q_d = 9 million. If the price were $16,600, there would be an oversupply, or a **surplus.** That is, 17 million places would be available, but only 9 million students would want to go to college at that price. Sellers would lower their prices to eliminate the excess supply. This has a twofold effect. It reduces the quantity supplied and increases the quantity demanded. We can see this by examining what happens at a price of $14,400. At this price, the quantities supplied and demanded have moved closer together, but Q_s still exceeds Q_d (15 million > 11 million). Suppliers will then lower prices again. This process will continue until $Q_s = Q_d$. This occurs at a price of $12,200. Thus, as shown in Figure 8.4, price changes will eliminate a surplus in the market until the equilibrium price is reached.

In the same way, if the price were below $12,200, there would be a tendency to move toward the $12,200 price. At a price of $10,000, Q_d = 15 mil-

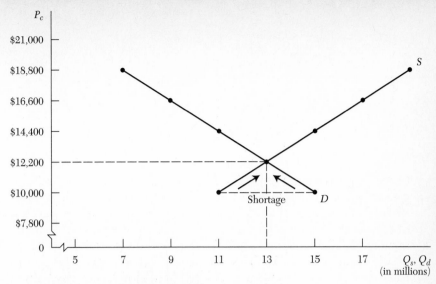

FIGURE 8.5 Shortage Eliminated by Price Increases

lion and Q_s = 11 million. In this case, the quantity demanded exceeds the quantity supplied (15 million > 11 million), and a **shortage** of places at colleges exists. Purchasers, facing a shortage, begin to bid up the price. Again, this has a twofold effect. It increases the quantity supplied but decreases the quantity demanded. This will continue until the desires of buyers and sellers are consistent at one price where $Q_s = Q_d$. (See Figure 8.5).

Supply-and-demand analysis has shown us how markets determine equilibrium prices. There is a tendency to establish, to move toward, the equilibrium price. And once buyers' and sellers' desires are consistent (when the quantity supplied equals the quantity demanded) and there are no outside disturbances, that price will tend to be maintained.

6. Why do sellers lower price when there is a surplus?
7. Why do buyers bid up the price when there is a shortage?

A Tinge of Reality: It's Not a *Ceteris Paribus* World

Our supply-and-demand model so far has included the rather strict and static assumptions involved in our *ceteris paribus* conditions on both sides of the market. However, one of the most useful aspects of this model is that we can use it to accommodate changes in the *ceteris paribus* conditions. In a changing world over time, these other determinants of supply and demand do change. A couple of examples will suffice to illustrate the richness of this approach and the ability of the supply-and-demand model to explain changes in market conditions and prices.

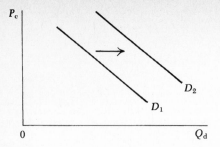

Changes in Demand. First, let's take a change in the demand conditions. We will call this a **change in demand**, and it will cause the whole demand curve to shift. Recall the various determinants of demand (or *ceteris paribus* conditions)—such as tastes and preferences, income, prices of related goods, number of demanders, and expectations about prices—and consider the complexity of factors that are behind a demand curve. Any of the determinants could change, or all of them could change. They could move in the same direction (causing an increase or a decrease in demand), or they could influence demand in opposite directions.

Let's examine just one possibility. Assume that in the 1990s, for whatever reasons, a college degree was perceived as being more attractive to students. This represents a change in tastes and preferences. What will it do to demand? What effect will it have on the market for a college education?

First of all, it will cause a shift in the demand curve. It causes an increase in demand; the demand curve will shift to the right. At every possible price, the quantity demanded will have increased, and we thus get a new demand curve. This is shown in Figure 8.6 as a shift in the demand curve from D_1 to D_2.

8. What other changes in demand might cause an increase in demand, a shift of the curve to the right?
9. What would cause a shift back to the left, a decrease in demand? Give some examples.

What happens in the market? Here we must look at supply and demand together, as shown in Fig. 8.7. With the new demand curve, D_2, we get a new

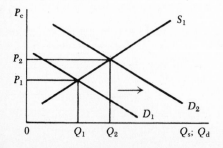

equilibrium price, P_2, and a new equilibrium quantity exchanged, Q_2, where $Q_s = Q_d$. With an increase in demand, we get a new higher price in the market. Also the amount exchanged by buyers and sellers has increased in our example (from Q_1 to Q_2). This analysis suggests that one place to look for an explanation of increasing prices in a market is in the dynamic changes in the determinants of demand. The market price of a college education tended to increase in the late 1980s and 1990s. Because enrollment (the quantity) also increased, we can conclude that the demand for the product increased. A possible cause was a change in the public's tastes and preferences. A word of caution, however, is in order. Tastes and preferences were not the only determinants of demand that changed during this period of time. For example, the increased number of international students also contributed to the shift in demand. Furthermore, the determinants of supply also were changing. We can conclude, though, that the change in preferences was partly responsible for the increase in demand and the increase in price.

Changes in Supply. The supply-and-demand model can also reflect a **change in supply**. Here we allow the determinants of supply to change. Remember the determinants of supply (the *ceteris paribus* conditions)—resource prices, technology, prices of related goods, sellers' expectations, and the number of sellers. Any or all could change, in the same direction or in opposite directions.

Assume that in the 1980s and 1990s the prices of the resources used in providing college educations were increasing. As a result, there would be a change in supply. Suppliers would tend to require higher prices for every different quantity supplied (or they would be willing to offer lower quantities supplied at every possible price). There would be a decrease in supply; the supply curve would shift to the left. The supply curve for a college education shifts from S_1 to S_2, as shown in Figure 8.8.

10. What other forces might cause the supply curve to shift to the left?
11. What factors might cause the supply curve to shift to the right?

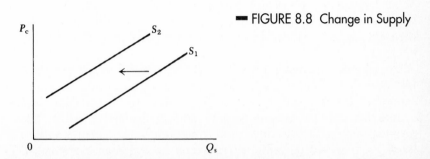

■ FIGURE 8.8 Change in Supply

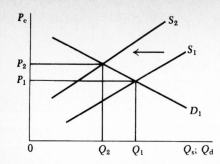

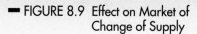

FIGURE 8.9 Effect on Market of Change of Supply

What will this do in the market? Assume that demand conditions are unaltered. Figure 8.9 puts supply and demand together. (We assume that D_1 remains unchanged.) With the new supply curve, S_2, we get a new equilibrium price, P_2, and a new equilibrium quantity exchanged, Q_2, where $Q_s = Q_d$. With this decrease in supply, we get a new higher market price and a lower quantity exchanged.

Again, this analysis may help us to explain price increases by examining what happens to the determinants of supply. If forces are creating decreases in supply for a particular product, that will help to explain the emergence of higher prices for it.

12. What happens if we combine our examples, an increase in demand and a decrease in supply? Show this result in your own graphical illustration.

A Word of Caution

One aspect of learning economics is identifying and defining economic concepts—and doing so precisely. This involves using words carefully. In some sense, it is like learning a foreign language. Some words that economists use have very specific meanings for particular concepts.

What happens on a demand curve if the price of the product changes? We get a *change in the quantity demanded.* If the price increases, the quantity demanded decreases. And if the price decreases, the quantity demanded increases. This represents a movement along a particular demand curve. What happens if one of the determinants of demand changes? We get a *change in demand.* If income increases, the whole demand curve shifts out to the right for most goods. Whenever there is a change in demand, the whole demand curve shifts.

For supply, a change in price causes a *change in the quantity supplied,* which is a movement along a supply curve. A change in one of the determinants of supply causes a *change in supply,* which causes the whole supply curve to shift.

A higher price causes a decrease in quantity demanded and an increase in quantity supplied. If the income of households decreases, the demand for most goods would decrease (there would be a change in demand). What would happen to the equilibrium price, then, if supply stays the same?

Chapter 8 THE THEORY OF MARKETS

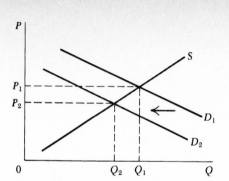

Right—price would decrease. And then what happens to quantity demanded and quantity supplied? Right—smaller quantities are demanded and supplied at the new equilibrium. Figure 8.10 shows this result graphically.

SUPPLY AND DEMAND AND THE VALUE OF THE DOLLAR

Since the early 1970s, the international financial system has operated on the basis of flexible exchange rates for currencies (see Chapter 21). This means there is an international market with buyers and sellers for all of the different currencies in the world. The prices of currencies are determined in these markets. Currencies are used for international economic activities. For example, people in the United States might want to buy products from Japan; to do so, they have to exchange dollars for yen. Or people in Japan might want to invest in U.S. government treasury bonds; to do so, they have to exchange yen for dollars. There are exchange markets because people all over the world want to buy goods and services, make bank deposits, travel, or invest in other countries. In addition, sometimes people want to protect the value of their assets by holding them in a currency whose value is increasing (and conversely getting out of currencies whose values are declining).

As a result of changing supply and demand conditions in the foreign exchange markets, the value of currencies is constantly changing. This can be seen in Figure 8.11, which shows the value of the dollar compared to the Japanese yen and the German mark during 1993–1995. This figure shows how many Japanese yen or German marks it took to buy a dollar at different times; the fluctuating exchange rates are then indexed to the rate at the end of 1993.

In early 1995, the value of the dollar declined dramatically against the yen. We can use supply-and-demand analysis to speculate as to why this might have happened (i.e., to explain the decrease in the value of the dollar). Figure 8.12 shows the market in its initial equilibrium at P_1 and Q_1. The supply curve, S_1, shows that people who hold dollars would be willing to supply more of them to the exchange market if the price for a dollar increased (i.e., if they could get more yen for each dollar). The demand curve, D_1, shows that people who want dollars would want fewer of them if the price for a dollar increased.

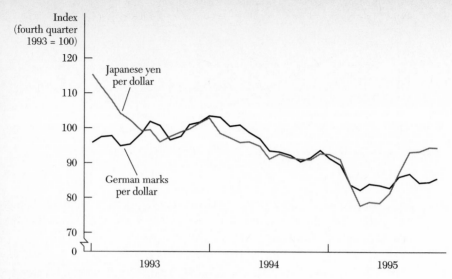

■ FIGURE 8.11 U.S. Dollar Exchange Rates

Source: *Economic Report of the President,* 1996, p. 256.

What seems to have happened in February 1995 is that investors began to lose confidence in the dollar; they expected its value would fall. Consequently, they wanted to exchange dollars for yen. In doing so, they drove the value of the dollar down (and the value of the yen up). These factors changed the conditions of demand in the foreign exchange market, causing a decrease in the demand for dollars. In Figure 8.13 the demand curve has shifted to D_2, causing the equilibrium price and quantity to decrease to P_2 and Q_2. This analysis is based on identifying some of the factors that caused a shift in demand and assuming that everything else is held constant. The conclusion is that, *ceteris paribus,* the change in expectations brought about a change in demand and a decrease in the value of the dollar.

But there's more to what happened. When the value of the dollar goes down, it decreases the purchasing power of the dollar in foreign countries. That is, it becomes harder for U.S. citizens to buy Japanese products (each

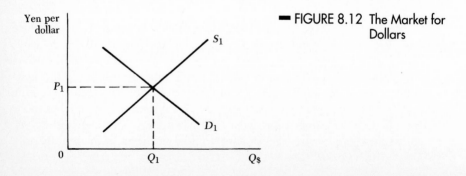

■ FIGURE 8.12 The Market for Dollars

Chapter 8 THE THEORY OF MARKETS

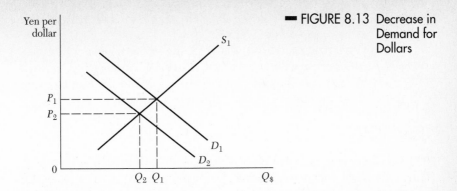

dollar is worth less yen; it takes more dollars to buy Japanese goods). Also, it becomes easier for U.S. firms to sell their products in foreign markets (it takes fewer yen to buy U.S. goods). The decrease in the value of the dollar thus tends to decrease U.S. imports and to increase U.S. exports. These effects also have adverse impacts on the Japanese economy—decreasing exports, increasing imports, and reducing overall economic activity in Japan. Given the precarious state of the Japanese economy at the time, international and U.S. monetary authorities were concerned about the decreased value of the dollar. To counteract the fall in the value of the dollar, they entered the foreign exchange markets and used yen that they held to purchase dollars. In other words, they decreased the supply of dollars. In Figure 8.14, the supply curve has shifted back to S_2. This produces a new equilibrium at P_3 and Q_3. The effect of the monetary officials' actions was to raise the price of the dollar. In fact, by late 1995, the value of the dollar was about what it had been at the beginning of 1995 (see Figure 8.11).

More than likely, after this episode, the value of the dollar changed again. With a flexible exchange rate system, the value of the dollar fluctuates daily. The lesson is that we can use the tools of supply-and-demand analysis to help us to understand and explain why the value of the dollar goes up and down. We can identify the factors on both sides of the market that might be responsible for such movements. We can also distinguish between movements along given supply and demand curves and shifts in those curves caused by changes in underlying market conditions other than price.

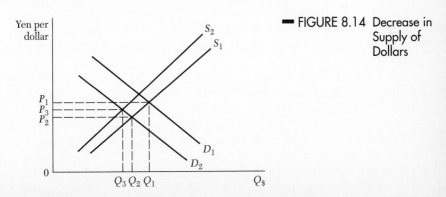

13. Would Japanese importers be in favor of a decrease in the value of the dollar? Why?
14. What other factors of demand, the *ceteris paribus* conditions, could cause a decrease in the demand for dollars?
15. What might happen, on either side of the market, to bring about an increase in the value of the dollar?

ELASTICITY

Thus far, we have concentrated on the relationship between prices and quantities supplied and demanded. But if a price changes, *how much* does the quantity demanded change? If the price goes up, *how much* does the quantity supplied increase?

The sensitivity of the demand for (supply of) a product to changes in its price is called **elasticity**. This concept is concerned with the relationship between the quantity demanded or supplied and the price of a particular good or service.

Price Elasticity of Demand

All other things given, if the price of a college education goes up, the quantity demanded will go down. But how much will the quantity demanded be reduced in comparison with the price increase? The **price elasticity of demand** is a measurement of the sensitivity of changes in quantity demanded to changes in price. It measures the responsiveness of the amount demanded to price changes. (Note that we are using terminology associated with movements along a single demand curve. With all the determinants of demand fixed at one point in time, we focus on the impact of a price change on the quantity demanded.)

The following equation measures the price elasticity of demand:

$$E_d = \frac{\text{percentage change in quantity demanded}}{\text{percentage change in price}} = \frac{\Delta Q_d / Q_d}{\Delta P / P}.$$

The percentage change in price is associated with a certain percentage change in the quantity demanded. In calculating elasticity, we ignore the direction of change of each variable and concentrate on the relative relationship between the percentage changes (that is, we take the absolute value of E_d).

If the percentage change in quantity demanded is larger than the percentage change in price, then $E_d > 1$, and we say that the demand for the good is *elastic* with respect to price. If the price of 35mm cameras is reduced by 20 percent and the quantity demanded increases by 30 percent, then $E_d = 1.5$. In this case, the demand for the cameras is elastic, or relatively sensitive to price change.

On the other hand, if the price of milk (or beer) increases by 10 percent but the quantity demanded decreases by only 5 percent, then elasticity is

0.5. In this case, we say that the demand for milk (or beer) is *inelastic*, since the percentage change in quantity demanded is less than the percentage change in price ($E_d < 1$).

For example, let's assume a computer store reduced the price of a personal computer model and printer from $3,000 to $2,500. The number of units it sold in a six-month period increased from 100 to 150. We can record these amounts in a table:

Price	Quantity Sold
$3,000	100
2,500	150

What is the elasticity of demand? The price decreased by $500, or $16\frac{2}{3}$ percent:

$$\frac{3,000 - 2,500}{3,000} = \frac{500}{3,000} = 16\frac{2}{3}\%$$

The quantity demanded increased by 50 units, or 50 percent:

$$\frac{150 - 100}{100} = \frac{50}{100} = 50\%$$

We can use those percentages to find the elasticity of demand:*

$$E_d = \frac{\text{percentage change in quantity demanded}}{\text{percentage change in price}}$$

$$= \frac{50}{16\frac{2}{3}} = 3.$$

Consequently, the demand for computers is fairly sensitive to price changes; the relative change in quantity demanded is much larger than the relative change in the price.

---

*Notice that there is another way we could have calculated the elasticity. We used the original price and quantity as the denominator in our calculations of the percentage changes in quantity and price. If we used the new price and quantity, we'd get the following results:

percentage change in price = 500/2,500 = 20%
percentage change in quantity demanded = 50/150 = $33\frac{1}{3}$%
$$\text{elasticity of demand} = \frac{33\frac{1}{3}}{20} = 1.67.$$

There is a way to resolve this difference in the calculated elasticity of demand by taking the average of the old and the new prices and quantities. This is called the midpoints formula:

$$E_d = \frac{\Delta Q / [(Q_1 + Q_2)/2]}{\Delta P / [(P_1 + P_2)/2]} = \frac{50/125}{500/2,750} = \frac{40\%}{18\%} = 2.22.$$

The important point, though, is that the elasticity of demand measures the *relative* change in quantity demanded due to the *relative* change in price, to see how sensitive quantity demanded is to price changes.

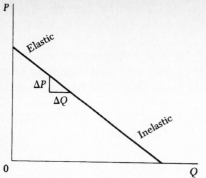

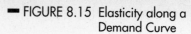 FIGURE 8.15 Elasticity along a Demand Curve

Elasticity Graphically. On the upper portion of the typical demand curve shown in Figure 8.15, the price elasticity of demand is elastic. On the lower portion, it is inelastic. Elasticity changes along the demand curve.

The elasticity of a demand curve does not equal its slope. The slope of the demand curve is the change in the price over the change in the quantity demanded between any two points (the height over the base, the rise over the run, etc.). The slope equals $\Delta P/\Delta Q$. To highlight the difference, we can rearrange the formula for elasticity as follows:

$$\frac{\text{percentage } \Delta \text{ in quantity demanded}}{\text{percentage } \Delta \text{ in price}} = \frac{\Delta Q/Q}{\Delta P/P} = \frac{\Delta Q}{\Delta P} \cdot \frac{P}{Q}.$$

This obviously makes elasticity unequal to the slope of the demand curve.

On the left portion of the demand curve, any percentage change in quantity demanded will be relatively large (since quantity is at low levels), and the percentage change in price will be relatively small. Consequently, elasticity will be greater than 1. On the right portion, percentage changes in quantity will be relatively small and percentage changes in price will be relatively large. Therefore, elasticity will be less than 1. Moving along the demand curve to the right will reduce elasticity or increase inelasticity.

The Determinants of Elasticity. What determines elasticity, or how sensitive to changes in its price is the demand for a product? Can you think of goods you demand regardless of price? Others to whose price you are very sensitive?

Generally, whenever there are substitutes for a good, your demand tends to be elastic. The more substitutes, the more elastic the demand. For example, if the price of green beans increases, most people will substitute other green vegetables. When the price goes up, people will reduce their consumption of green beans by relatively more—that is, we expect the price elasticity of demand for green beans to be greater than 1. On the other hand, if you heat your house with only oil and oil prices increase, you may decrease your use of oil, but not by much. The relative increase in price will outweigh the relative decline in the amount demanded; demand is relatively inelastic because there are no substitutes for oil to run your furnace.

Goods that are necessities tend to have inelastic demands. For example, in a household with young children, the demand for milk is likely to be relatively inelastic. As a student, you have a relatively inelastic demand for books. For these items, the demand is not very sensitive to price changes. The demand for luxuries, however, tends to be elastic. You, and others, are likely to be very sensitive to price changes for CDs, stereos, cameras, expensive clothes, automobiles, and so forth.

For the most part, the relative importance of an item in a household's budget also influences elasticity. High-priced items have elastic demands, and the demand for low-priced items is usually inelastic.

Finally, time influences elasticity. The more time consumers have to adjust to price changes, the more elastic their demand for certain products is likely to be. For example, many people in the United States have adjusted their usage of energy as a result of higher prices since the 1970s. Cars are smaller and more fuel efficient, people are burning more wood as a source of heat, bicycles are used for transportation, and solar energy is being developed. Taking another example, for many urban households, block ice may have been a necessity in the early 1900s, but it isn't anymore.

Elasticity and Revenue. Elasticity also holds implications for a firm's revenues or a household's expenditures when the price of a product changes. If the demand for a firm's product is elastic and its price decreases, then the percentage change in quantity demanded in the market will be relatively larger than the price change. The firm's revenues would then increase. (The firm's revenues equal the quantity sold times the price of the product. If the relative increase in quantity exceeds the relative decline in price, then revenues go up.) If a household's demand for a product is inelastic and its price increases, it will decrease its purchases by a relatively lower amount. Consequently, its total expenditures—quantity times price—will increase. Table 8.4 summarizes the possibilities (TR stands for total revenue and = P × Q). When demand is elastic, the quantity change is relatively larger. When the demand is inelastic, the price change is relatively larger.

TABLE 8.4 Elasticity and Total Revenue (TR)

$E_d < 1$			$E_d > 1$		
% Δ in Q_d < % Δ in P			% Δ in Q_d > % Δ in P		
P↑	Q_d ↓	TR ↑	P↑	Q_d ↓	TR ↓
P↓	Q_d ↑	TR ↓	P↓	Q_d ↑	TR ↑

Price Elasticity of Supply

We can also identify the **price elasticity of supply,** or the sensitivity of amounts supplied to price changes:

$$E_s = \frac{\text{percentage change in quantity supplied}}{\text{percentage change in price}}.$$

If the elasticity of supply, E_s, is less than 1, the supply of the product is inelastic—that is, the amount supplied is not very sensitive to price changes. If the elasticity of supply, E_s, is greater than 1, then the amount of the good supplied is sensitive to price changes.

Several factors can influence the elasticity of supply. If storage is not possible, then supply will be insensitive to price changes. If you have ten bunches of bananas in your store and the price goes up by 50 percent tomorrow, there is not much you can do to increase the amount of bananas that you have for sale. If you can put an item in inventory, the amount that you have available for sale will be sensitive to price. If the price of pencils goes down, for example, you can store them and reduce the amount you have out for sale. If the price goes up, you can increase the amount you have for sale by taking the pencils out of your inventory. The length of the production process matters as well. The longer the production period, the lower the elasticity of supply. Occasionally a new toy or game is popular (e.g., at holiday season) in the United States. In the short run, the supply is inelastic; consequently, there is a shortage. What happens to price? It rises; with higher prices, in the longer run, the supply becomes more elastic. If it is possible to substitute resources in production, then supply is likely to be more elastic. For example, in the fast-food industry, there are numerous sources of unskilled labor, many sources of hamburger meat, buns, and so forth, and consequently the supply of fast food is likely to be relatively sensitive to price changes.

Income Elasticity

We can also identify the **income elasticity of demand**. This measures how much the demand for a product changes when income changes. It is expressed by the following equation:

$$E_y = \frac{\text{percentage change in quantity demanded}}{\text{percentage change in income}}.$$

When income changes, we know that one of the determinants of demand has changed. Consequently, the entire demand curve will shift. For most goods, if income increases, the demand curve shifts out to the right. The income elasticity of demand, in essence, measures the relative change in the demand curve.

For most goods, the income elasticity is positive. Only inferior goods have a negative income elasticity of demand. For example, you might decrease your consumption of cheap meats if your income increased. For some goods we increase our consumption by only a little bit when our incomes go up. Food products in general fit into this category. The relative increase in the quantity demanded of food will be less than the relative increase in income. For goods like these, the income elasticity of demand is relatively low. For other goods, we increase our consumption a great deal when our incomes go up. The relative change in quantity demanded is larger than the percentage change in income, and the income elasticity of demand is greater than 1. The demand for "luxuries" is elastic with respect to income.

16. Do you think that the price elasticity of demand for a college education is greater or less than 1? Why?
17. For what kinds of goods and services will quantity demanded be relatively insensitive to price changes (i.e., inelastic)? Give some examples.
18. For what kinds of goods and services is the quantity demanded relatively sensitive to price changes (i.e., elastic)? Give some examples.
19. List some goods for which your income elasticity of demand is greater than 1.

CONCLUSION

In this chapter we have developed a theoretical model of markets to explain how markets determine prices. We have focused on demand and supply, how they are determined, and how they interact in markets. In the next chapter, we will explore the theoretical implications that this has for resource allocation.

Review Questions

1. Use supply-and-demand analysis to explain why your school's tuition and overall charges have been continually increasing the past few years. Address demand factors first and supply factors second; then put them together.
2. Some colleges have started to announce efforts to cut prices or to limit their price increases. Why would they do this?
3. How are tastes and preferences for goods and services determined in the United States?

4. Markets and prices for different products are interrelated. Why? Can you give some examples?
5. Examine recent issues of newspapers to see how prices of certain products are changing. Use supply-and-demand analysis to explain these changes.
6. *How* do prices influence resource allocation? Use examples.
7. Assume that the price elasticity of demand for gasoline in the United States is 0.3. If the president wanted to reduce gasoline consumption in the United States by 30 percent, by how much would prices have to be increased?

9

Perfect Competition and Efficiency

INTRODUCTION

Microeconomics assumes that consumers, in demanding goods, attempt to maximize their satisfaction. Furthermore, we assume that, in supplying goods, firms are concerned with profit maximization. In Chapter 8 we saw how supply and demand for a good determine a market price, given certain conditions (i.e., a supply curve and a demand curve). If either the demand curve or the supply curve shifts, or if both shift, we tend to get a new equilibrium price and quantity in that market.

This chapter uses supply-and-demand analysis and some new tools of economics to examine the decisions that individual firms make about what rate of output to produce—taking into account information from the market for their product and from the markets for the resources they use. We will develop a model of the firm in a competitive market. This model will demonstrate how profit maximization and competition theoretically produce Adam Smith's "invisible hand." That is, we will discover how competitive markets operate to allocate resources *efficiently* (to meet the most important demands of the society with the minimum amount of resources).

PROFIT MAXIMIZATION AND THE COMPETITIVE FIRM

In this section we will examine a particular market, concentrating our attention on the firm (developing a theory of the firm). This is a theoretical market, so we will state some definitions and make some assumptions about the behavior of the buyers and sellers in the market. As an example we will use the vast and expanding global market for personal computer software, such as programs for word processing, games, database management, and Internet navigation.

The **consumer** is the economic unit that demands goods and/or services because they serve some purpose and give the consumer some satisfaction. Consumers in this example include businesses, professionals, homes, elementary/secondary schools and students, colleges and college students, and so on who have a particular need for the host of tasks performed by computers. The invention and development of transistors, miniaturized circuitry, and silicon chips led to the development of computing technology and a boom in the market for personal computers during the last two decades. Along with this market, the market for complementary products, including software, has expanded.

The **firm** is the economic unit that brings goods to the market. It takes raw materials and other resources and transforms them into final consumer goods. Its motivation, or goal, is to maximize its profits. In our example, the firm would be any company that produces and sells personal computer software. The firm could produce this computer software in the United States or some other country. And its market is truly a global one. Basically, there are two markets for PC software—for Apple's Macintosh and for IBM PCs and their numerous clones (IBM compatibles).

If we put the firms and the consumers (the sellers and buyers) together, we have a market for personal computer software. We will assume that this is a competitive market, that is, one characterized by **perfect competition**. We define a perfectly competitive market as one having the following characteristics:

- The product is homogeneous.
- There is a large number of buyers and sellers in the market.
- No *one* buyer or seller can influence the price of the product. (A seller can't raise his or her price, because buyers can go to a competitor and buy.)
- There is free entry into the market. (Anyone can be a buyer or seller. There are no constraints on entry.)
- There is no need for advertising (since every seller has the same product and charges the same price).
- Firms have all the information they need on resource prices, markets, and technology to make rational, profit-generating decisions.

In a perfectly competitive market, there is a market equilibrium price. Can you illustrate this market graphically?

1. Are any of these theoretical characteristics absent from the actual market for personal computer software in the United States? Why?

Let's return to the firm. The firm's objective is to maximize its profits. Profits equal the revenues the firm earns by selling its products minus the costs it incurs to produce those products:

$$\text{profit} = TR - TC,$$

where TR equals total revenue and TC equals total cost. **Total revenue** is equal to the quantity sold times the price of the product:

$$TR = P \times Q.$$

The firm obtains revenues by selling its product. The greater the amount of personal computer software the firm sells, the more money it receives. In producing computer software and bringing it to market, the firm also has certain costs—labor, raw materials, depreciation, rent, interest payments on loans, and the firm's opportunity cost. **Total cost** is the sum of all the costs of purchasing the necessary resources for production.

As in Chapter 7, we define the firm's *opportunity cost* as the amount of money the firm could earn by using its facilities and its resources to produce something else profitably (such as computer programming services, business consulting, etc.). It would be the "next best use" of its resources. The firm has some expectation of a "normal profit" from doing business. The producer of personal computer software must earn at least its opportunity cost (a normal profit) to stay in the business of making computer software. Anything above that is **economic profit**.

If the firm's revenues are just sufficient to cover all of its costs for raw materials, labor, and so on, *and* its opportunity cost, then the firm will earn no economic profits. For example, if the firm's revenues were $100,000, its opportunity cost were $20,000, and the costs of all other resources were $80,000, it would earn zero economic profits. Its opportunity costs would be covered by the $20,000 of "normal" profits. If revenues exceed costs, then there will be economic profits; that is, the firm will earn a return over and above its opportunity cost.

Profits, revenues, and costs for the firm will vary with the amounts of computer software produced and sold. For a firm in a competitive market, the price is determined by the market and will not vary with the number of units that the firm sells (see the third characteristic of a competitive market in the list given earlier). Consequently, total revenue increases at a constant rate as the firm sells more personal computer software. Total cost also increases as more computer software is produced. It costs more to produce more. (We will explore the shape of the total cost curve in the next section.) In Figure 9.1, profit (the shaded area) is the difference between TR and TC at different rates of output and sales. We measure amounts of computer software on the horizontal axis and money (costs and revenues) on the vertical axis. Profit is at a maximum at the rate of output where the difference between TR and TC is greatest.

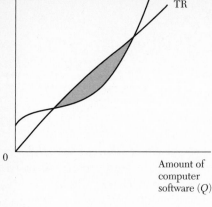

FIGURE 9.1 Total Revenue and Total Cost

TC

TR

$

0

Amount of
computer
software (Q)

2. A small firm's "normal profit" is $75,000 for one year. All of its other costs are $200,000. The firm's revenue in one year is $300,000. What are its economic profits?

TOTAL COST AND THE LAW OF DIMINISHING RETURNS

As additional background for our analysis, it is useful to pause for a bit to explain the shape of the total cost curve (see Figure 9.1). The total cost curve increases slowly at first with increasing output; but then, beyond some point, total costs increase by greater and greater amounts. The reason for this is the **law of diminishing returns**. This economic law, a fundamental aspect of production and its related costs, holds that with continuing use of some resources, eventually the contributions to output begin to decrease.

Output requires the use of inputs. In production, there are certain physical relationships between these inputs and the output. To construct a simplified example, assume that a farmer has one acre of land on which to grow peaches. We will hold constant the land used as an input, the amount of trees planted, and the level of technology available. The only variable resource, then, will be the amount of labor that the farmer uses as an input to produce peaches. At first, with increasing amounts of labor, the farmer adds larger and larger amounts of peaches. The marginal contribution of each added worker is the amount of peaches that worker adds to total output. Each worker adds more to total output than the last worker. However, beyond some point, although more workers may continue to add to output, the marginal contributions of the last workers are less than the contributions of the previously added workers. The problem is essentially that there is not enough space for all the workers to work together well. They get in each other's way, they spend time talking to each other, and so on. In fact, the farmer might add so many workers to the land that the marginal contributions of the last added worker to total output might be negative; that is, the last worker added might cause total output to decrease.

THE LAW OF DIMINISHING RETURNS

What happens to the output of the peach orchard as workers are added? The addition of the second worker causes total output to increase from 100 to 110. The marginal contribution is thus 10. For the third worker, the marginal addition to output is 20; for the fourth, it is 30. With the fifth worker, though, the marginal contribution begins to decrease; only 20 units of output are added to total output. The pattern continues with the sixth worker; the marginal contribution falls to 10. With the addition of the seventh worker, total output actually declines; the marginal contribution is negative.

Input of Land (in acres)	Input of Labor (in workers)	Total Output (in peaches)	Marginal Contribution of Last Unit of Labor (in peaches)
1	1	100	
1	2	110	10
1	3	130	20
1	4	160	30
1	5	180	20
1	6	190	10
1	7	185	–5

This simplified example describes what happens in any productive activity in which there are fixed and variable resources. In the case of a computer software producer, the fixed resources would be the plant and the equipment used in production, and the variable resources would be the raw materials and the labor utilized.

So now that we know what the law of diminishing returns is, how does it influence the shape of the total cost curve? The cost curve compares total costs with increasing output. If we assume that the law of diminishing returns holds for all variable resources, there will be some point in increasing output at which costs will begin to increase at an increasing rate. If resources have diminishing returns, then more and more resources must be used to get additional units of output. But to use more resources costs more. And when diminishing returns set in, the total costs will increase at an increasing rate. To produce an additional unit of output will cost more than the last additional unit of output because more additional resources will be required. Because of the law of diminishing returns, the total cost curve, beyond some level of output, will increase at an increasing rate.

3. Why does the total cost curve increase at a *decreasing* rate at relatively low levels of output?

PROFIT MAXIMIZATION IN THE SHORT RUN

Figure 9.1 shows us a very important relationship between total costs and total revenue. As the firm brings more personal computer software to the market and sells it, its costs and revenues also increase. Stated mathematically, costs and revenues are each a function of output:

$$TC = f(Q), \text{ and } TR = f(Q).$$

This is true both in the **short run**, where some resources are fixed and others are variable, and in the **long run**, where all resources are variable. Furthermore, profits are determined by the relationship between costs and revenues (TR – TC) in both time horizons.

In our model of the firm, we will explore the costs and revenues of the firm in more detail. This analysis of costs and revenues will lead to the theory of profit maximization in the short run. Then we will turn to what happens to the firm in the long run.

The Firm's Costs

The costs of production result from the very act of production. To produce any good or service, firms must use resources—raw materials, mental and physical labor, machinery, energy, and so forth. To secure the various factors of production, firms must purchase resources in markets; the resources must be paid their opportunity costs. Hence the costs of production are determined by the prices of resources in resource markets.

In the short run, a firm has a fixed-size plant or operation. The scale of its productive activities has been determined by decisions it has made about its physical location, the buildings it will use, the machinery and equipment it has purchased, and its management team. Let's take a simple example of a small firm engaged in the production of computer software. It is run by a group of individuals, leases a building outside of Chicago, and owns all of the furniture and equipment in its office. It has borrowed money from the First Chicago NBD Corporation (a bank) to finance its business. In this sense, then, it has a certain size of operation for its short-run production expectations. Within this fixed plant size, it can expand its output of software by using more variable resources—that is, more raw materials and more labor. These variable resources can use the fixed plant more or less intensively to produce more or less output. (In the long run, as we will see shortly, all of the resources that the firm uses in production can be expanded or contracted. That is, the firm can change the size of its operation.)

In the short run, the firm incurs two types of costs—fixed and variable costs. **Total fixed costs** are the costs that the firm must pay for the fixed resources of production involved in the firm's particular short-run plant size.

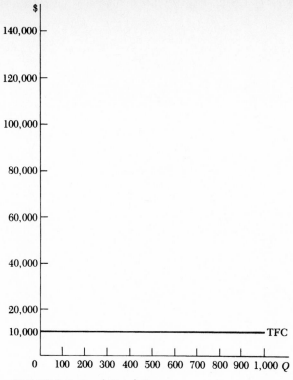

— FIGURE 9.2 Total Fixed Costs

These costs do not vary with the rate of output that the firm produces. The firm has a monthly mortgage payment that it gives to the bank to repay the loan it used to purchase its equipment for producing software. The owners of the firm also have an opportunity cost for their participation in the firm's activities. In other words, the owners will get salaries based on what they could earn in some other activity. If these salaries weren't paid, the owners would seek some other job in which they could earn their opportunity cost (e.g., as computer programmers). All of these costs are fixed costs; they are incurred by the firm regardless of the level of output in any particular month. Even if output is zero in the short run, fixed costs are still positive.

Let's assume that the monthly fixed costs of a software firm are $10,000. Figure 9.2 illustrates total fixed costs (TFC). It shows that as output (measured on the horizontal axis) increases, total fixed costs remain constant.

Total variable costs are the firm's expenses for using varying amounts of raw materials and labor to expand output within a fixed-size plant (in the short run). To get greater amounts of output, the firm uses more and more variable resources; consequently, total variable costs increase as output increases. However, given the law of diminishing returns, we know that at first, relatively few added resources will achieve expanded output, and that later, the firm will have to add greater amounts of resources to get equivalent

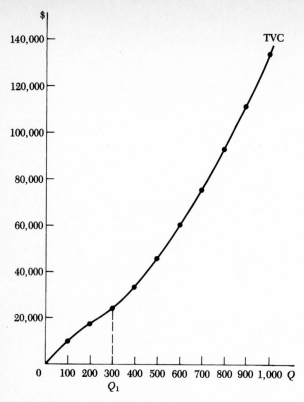

— FIGURE 9.3 Total Variable Costs

additions to output. Therefore, total variable costs will normally increase first at a decreasing rate and then, when diminishing returns set in, at an increasing rate. Figure 9.3 illustrates what happens to total variable costs (TVC), measured on the vertical axis, as output increases. At rates of output below Q_1, total variable costs increase at a decreasing rate, and at rates of output greater than Q_1, diminishing returns to the use of variable resources set in, and total variable costs increase at an increasing rate. At a rate of output of zero, total variable costs are zero.

If we add total fixed costs and total variable costs together, we get the total costs (TC) of production:

$$TC = TFC + TVC.$$

Table 9.1 presents different possible levels of output during a one-month period for our software firm and the total fixed costs, total variable costs, and total costs of each level of output. Figure 9.4 illustrates total costs, with costs measured on the vertical axis and output measured on the horizontal axis. Notice that when output is 0, total costs equal total fixed costs.

Level of Output	Total Fixed Costs	Total Variable Costs	Total Costs
0	$10,000	0	$10,000
100	10,000	$10,000	20,000
200	10,000	18,000	28,000
300	10,000	24,000	34,000
400	10,000	34,000	44,000
500	10,000	46,000	56,000
600	10,000	60,000	70,000
700	10,000	76,000	86,000
800	10,000	94,000	104,000
900	10,000	114,000	124,000
1,000	10,000	136,000	146,000

We can also use this cost information to derive average and marginal costs. These cost measures will prove useful in analyzing the firm's profit maximization decisions. Average cost takes the various total costs of production and averages them over each unit of output. For example, at 100 units of output, total fixed costs are $10,000. The average fixed cost for each unit of

■ FIGURE 9.4 Total Costs

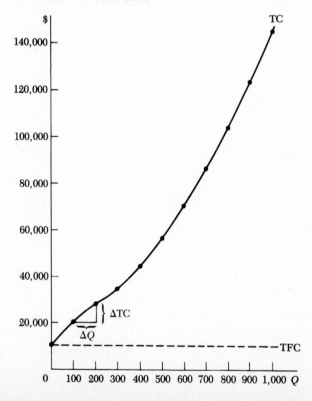

output is \$100. For each different level of output, then, **average fixed cost** is defined as follows:

$$AFC = \frac{TFC}{Q}.$$

In the same way, **average variable cost** is

$$AVC = \frac{TVC}{Q},$$

and **average cost** is

$$AC = \frac{TC}{Q}.$$

Since TC = TFC + TVC, then AC = AFC + AVC.

Marginal cost is the additional cost of producing one additional unit of output. It indicates the amount of change in total costs as a result of additional output:

$$MC = \frac{\text{change in TC}}{\text{change in } Q} \text{ or } \frac{\Delta TC}{\Delta Q}.$$

Since fixed costs do not change with the level of output, marginal costs can also be defined as the change in total variable costs as output changes. For example, when the firm moves from producing 100 units of output to 200 units of output, total costs increase from \$20,000 to \$28,000 (and total variable costs increase from \$10,000 to \$18,000). Consequently,

$$MC = \frac{28,000 - 20,000}{200 - 100} = \frac{8,000}{100} = 80.$$

▰ TABLE 9.2 Software Firm's Average and Marginal Costs

Output	$AFC = \dfrac{TFC}{Q}$	$AVC = \dfrac{TVC}{Q}$	$AC = \dfrac{TC}{Q}$	$MC = \dfrac{\Delta TC}{\Delta Q}$
0	—	—	—	—
100	\$100	\$100	\$200	\$100
200	50	90	140	80
300	33	80	113	60
400	25	85	110	100
500	20	92	112	120
600	17	100	117	140
700	14	109	123	160
800	12	117	129	180
900	11	127	138	200
1,000	10	146	156	220

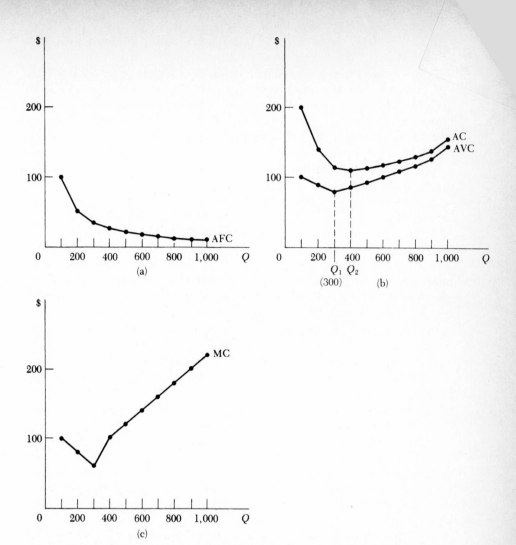

■ FIGURE 9.5 Average Fixed Costs (a), Average Variable Costs (b), Average
Costs (b), and Marginal Costs (c)

The marginal cost of producing 100 more units of software (expanding to
200 from 100) is $8,000, or $80 for each unit. In essence, marginal cost
equals the slope of the total costs (or total variable costs) curve (see Figure
9.4). Since total costs first increase at a decreasing rate and then begin
increasing at an increasing rate, MC will first decrease and then begin
increasing.

As shown in Table 9.2, we can use the information in Table 9.1 to derive
data on average fixed costs, average variable costs, average costs, and marginal
costs. Figure 9.5 graphs the resulting data. AFC, AVC, AC, and MC all vary
with the rate of output. In each case, costs are measured in per-unit or marginal terms. The horizontal axis always measures output, and the vertical

axis measures average or marginal costs. Average fixed cost in Figure 9.5(a) constantly decreases, since it is total fixed cost divided by increasing rates of output. Average variable cost, shown in Figure 9.5(b), is generally U-shaped, reflecting the law of diminishing returns. Over a range of output, AVC decreases at first, reaches a minimum at Q_1, and then begins to increase for greater levels of output. At first, when there are increasing returns to the use of variable resources, the per-unit cost of production decreases as output increases. The per-unit amount of resources needed to produce increasing amounts of output decreases. However, beyond Q_1, AVC begins to increase as each unit of output requires the use of increasing amounts of variable resources. This, again, is the result of diminishing returns to the use of variable resources.

Average cost, also shown in Figure 9.5(b), is also U-shaped because of the law of diminishing returns. Since AC is the sum of AFC and AVC, and AFC is positive and constantly decreasing, AC is above AVC, but the difference between them is constantly decreasing. AC reaches a minimum at the rate of output of Q_2. This is a slightly higher rate of output than Q_1. AVC is increasing, but because AFC is constantly decreasing, it takes a higher level of output for AC to begin increasing (where the effects of increasing AVC begin to outweigh the effects of decreasing AFC).

In Figure 9.5(c), marginal cost is also U-shaped due to the law of diminishing returns. Since marginal costs register the *additional* costs of producing greater rates of output, rather than the per-unit costs, marginal costs will more dramatically illustrate the effects first of increasing returns and then of decreasing returns to the use of variable resources.

It is also useful to know the exact relationship of the MC curve to the AVC and AC curves. Figure 9.6 relates marginal cost to both average variable cost and average cost. Marginal cost, average variable cost, and average cost curves are usually represented by smooth, curved lines; in Fig. 9.6 we have smoothed the curves of Figure 9.5(b) and (c). The MC curve cuts through the minimum point of both the AVC and AC curves. We will not go into a lengthy proof of these relationships. Suffice it to say that if MC is below AVC or AC, then AVC or AC must be decreasing. If the cost of producing the last unit of added output is below the per-unit cost, then per-unit cost has to decrease. From output levels 0 to Q_1, MC is below AVC, and AVC is decreasing. From output levels 0 to Q_2, MC is below AC, and AC is decreasing. If, on the other hand, MC is above AVC or AC, then AVC or AC must be increasing. (Why?) Beyond Q_1, AVC is increasing, and beyond Q_2, AC is increasing. Then, at output Q_1, where AVC is at a minimum, MC = AVC. And, at output Q_2, where AC is at a minimum, MC = AC.

The significance (for the society as a whole) of the point where average cost is at a minimum is worth further comment. The level of output that minimizes the average cost of output is the *most efficient rate of output* because it means that society is minimizing the cost of using its resources with respect to the production of a good. Q_2 in Figure 9.6 represents an *optimum level of output* because it minimizes the per-unit cost of producing that good. Raising or lowering output would increase average cost.

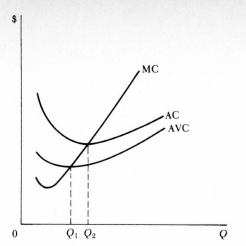

■ FIGURE 9.6 Relationship of Marginal Costs to Average Costs and Average Variable Costs

4. Explain how the law of diminishing returns causes the MC curve to be increasing beyond some rate of output.
5. Why is marginal cost equal to the slope of the total cost curve? What *is* the slope of the total cost curve?
6. If the Los Angeles Dodgers have a team batting average of .275 (that is, on the average they get 275 hits every 1,000 times they come to bat) and they acquire a new outfielder whose batting average is .298, what happens to the team batting average? What if they trade away two players with averages of .260 and .274 for one player with an average of .278?
7. Explain why the minimum point on the AC curve represents an optimum rate of output.

The Firm's Revenues

The revenues of the software firm in our example come from selling the PC software it produces. *Total revenue*, you'll recall, equals the price of the software multiplied by the number of units sold (TR = $P \times Q$). We can also define average revenues and marginal revenues for the firm. **Average revenue** is revenue per unit:

$$AR = \frac{TR}{Q}.$$

Marginal revenue is the change in total revenues from producing and selling an additional unit of output:

$$MR = \frac{\text{change in TR}}{\text{change in } Q} = \frac{\Delta TR}{\Delta Q}.$$

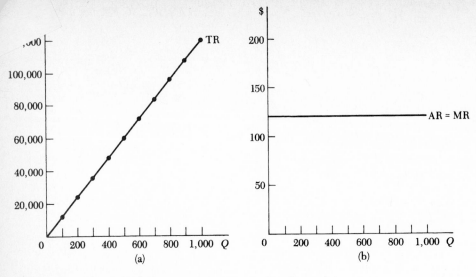

FIGURE 9.7 Total Revenues (a), Average Revenues (b), and Marginal Revenues (c)

For a firm in a perfectly competitive market, the price is determined in the market by the forces of supply and demand. The firm gets the price of the product for every unit that it sells, so $P = MR = AR$. If the price of a software program is $120, then the firm's revenues per unit are $120, and its marginal revenues also are $120. Figure 9.7(a) illustrates total revenues, and Figure 9.7(b) shows marginal and average revenues. These graphs show what happens to revenues, measured on the vertical axis, as output expands.

Profit Maximization

We are now ready to put the cost information and the revenue information together to describe the profit maximization decision of the PC software firm. Table 9.3 and Figure 9.8 provide information and an illustration of the firm's profit maximization decision. Recall that we have assumed that the firm's objective is to maximize its profits, that in the short run it has a fixed-size plant, that it has access to certain production techniques and technical knowledge, and that it can buy resources in markets for certain prices. What level of output could the firm produce to get the maximum level of profits? The answer is that the software firm will produce that rate of output at which the difference between TR and TC is greatest. This also happens to be the rate of output at which MC and MR are equal. *When the marginal cost of producing one more unit of output is equal to the marginal revenue from selling one more unit, the firm maximizes its profits.* This occurs at Q_e in Figure 9.8.

Table 9.3 and Figure 9.8 demonstrate why this level of output maximizes profits (or TR – TC). If the producer brings Q_1 to market, the marginal revenue of the last unit sold is above the marginal cost of producing it. In this

TABLE 9.3 Data for a Firm's Profit Maximization Decision

Output	TC	AC	MC	TR	MR (and AR)	Profit (or Loss)
0	$10,000	—	—	0	0	$(–10,000)
100	20,000	$200	$100	$12,000	$120	(–8,000)
200	28,000	140	80	24,000	120	(–4,000)
300	34,000	113	60	36,000	120	2,000
400	44,000	110	100	48,000	120	4,000
500	56,000	112	120	60,000	120	4,000
600	70,000	117	140	72,000	120	2,000
700	86,000	123	160	84,000	120	(–2,000)
800	104,000	129	180	96,000	120	(–8,000)
900	124,000	138	200	108,000	120	(–16,000)
1,000	146,000	156	220	120,000	120	(–26,000)

case, the addition to revenues from selling the last unit of software is greater than the addition to costs, on the margin. As a result, total revenue increases more than total costs (since MR > MC); thus profits will go up. The addition to revenue was greater than the addition to cost from producing and selling the last unit of software, so profits increase. In fact, as long as MR > MC, the producer increases profits by bringing additional amounts to market (the marginal revenues from doing so exceed the marginal costs). These marginal additions to profit stop when the producer reaches that level of output Q_e at which MC = MR. If additional amounts of software are brought to market, the marginal cost of doing so exceeds the corresponding marginal revenue. As a result, additional costs exceed additional revenues, and profits decrease. For example, at Q_2 marginal cost is greater than marginal revenue; the addition to total costs from producing the last unit of output to get to Q_2 is greater than the added revenue from doing so. As a result, profits will decrease. The firm can increase profits by moving to lower levels of production. Profits are at a maximum at Q_e, where MC = MR.

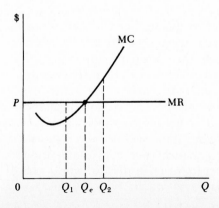

■ FIGURE 9.8 Marginal Revenues, Marginal Costs, and Profit Maximization

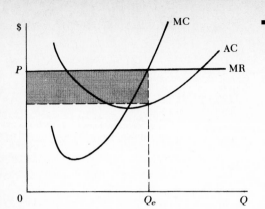

As you can see from Table 9.3, MC = MR at 500 units of output. It is also at this rate of output that total profits are at a maximum. (In this numerical example, because we are increasing output in increments of 100, the marginal cost figure is actually an *average* of the marginal cost of producing each added 100 units of software. As a result, profits are maximized at both 400 and 500 units of output. The firm could pick either rate of output and maximize its profits—at $4,000. But, since MR > MC at 400 units of output, the firm will expand to 500.) At higher rates of output, marginal costs are larger than marginal revenues, and profits decrease. At lower rates of output, marginal revenues exceed marginal costs, and the firm can increase its profits by producing and selling larger levels of output.

Figure 9.9 adds average cost to the picture. At a rate of output of Q_e, where MC = MR and profits are maximized, notice that the price of the software is greater than the average cost of producing each unit. That is, for each unit, the revenue that the firm earns exceeds its cost. This is, in fact, profit per unit, since profit = TR – TC:

$$\frac{\text{profit}}{Q} = \frac{\text{TR}}{Q} - \frac{\text{TC}}{Q}$$

profit per unit = $P - \text{AC}$.

As long as price exceeds average cost, the firm earns economic profits of $Q(P - \text{AC})$. Total profits are equal to the area of the shaded rectangle in Figure 9.9. If the price is below the average cost, however, the firm experiences losses. Does this conclusion fit the information in Table 9.3?

What we have just shown summarizes one of the most important results of the economic theory of the firm. A firm will maximize its profits when it produces a rate of output at which its marginal revenues equal its marginal costs. This is its equilibrium rate of output. If a firm expands its output to a point at which MC > MR, its profits decrease. What will it do in response? It will probably reduce its rate of output. The theoretical conclusion would seem to be borne out by what we would expect firms in the real world to do. They will tend to produce that rate of output at which MC = MR.

8. For our software firm, what happens to its profits if it reduces output from 500 to 300? What is the relationship between *P* and AC at this rate of output? What is the relationship between MC and MR?
9. For Figure 9.8, explain why profits increase by moving from Q_2 to lower levels of output.
10. Construct an AC curve with its own MC curve. What would the firm do if the price of its product passed through the point at which MC = AC? What level of output would it produce? What would its profits be? Would this firm be earning its opportunity costs?
11. From Table 9.3, if the firm produces 800 units of output, what are its profits? What is the relationship between *P* and AC? Between MR and MC?

THE FIRM IN THE LONG RUN

In the long run, the firm always has more options than in the short run. It can alter the size of its plant. It can change the technology it uses to produce its good or service. For PC software firms, if the market for the product expands or the firm thinks that it will, it can seek a larger factory to buy or rent, borrow more money so that it can purchase more machinery and equipment, hire more programmers, take on partners to expand the size of its operation, or relocate its operations to Mexico or elsewhere in the world.

▬ Interior of a computer software store. *(PhotoEdit)*

In the long run, the firm can vary all of its production resources; there are no fixed resources.

The long run is no specific period of time; rather, it is that time frame in which people make decisions based on the future. If a PC software firm expects its market to expand in the future, it will adjust for the long run. Or if it expects the market to begin to contract, it can make a different long-run adjustment. In addition, in the long run, firms can enter or leave the industry. The decision to enter or leave is a long-run investment decision for individuals and firms.

In essence, the firm can pick an infinite number of different possible short-run plant sizes in the long run. At any moment in time, the firm is in the short run; it has a fixed-size plant with fixed resources, and it has a corresponding short-run average cost curve. Given the long-run option of different possible plant sizes, the firm will obviously pick the plant size that minimizes the average cost of producing every different possible level of output. For example, in Figure 9.10, there are three different short-run average cost curves representing different possible plant sizes for different ranges of output. AC_1 represents the first size plant, AC_2 the second size plant, and AC_3 the third size plant. For Q_1, AC_1 minimizes the average cost of production. So if the firm wanted to produce Q_1, it would pick plant size 1. But if the firm wanted to produce Q_2, it would pick plant size 2, since this minimizes the average cost of that rate of output. Similarly, if it wanted to produce an even larger rate of output, say Q_3 it would pick plant size 3. Notice that this represents a long-run decision. The firm makes a choice of a plant size based on its expectations of or experiences with the market. The decision requires time to make arrangements for physical facilities, new and larger equipment, borrowing, and so forth. The firm generates its long-run average cost curve by picking the plant size that minimizes the cost of producing every possible rate of output. It is the heavy line in Figure 9.10.

When we assume that there is an infinite number of possible plant sizes for the firm to choose from, the firm's typical long-run AC curve looks like the one in Figure 9.11. It is U-shaped just like the short-run AC curve (and has its own long-run marginal cost curve, LMC), but for different reasons. The short-run curve was U-shaped because of the law of diminishing returns,

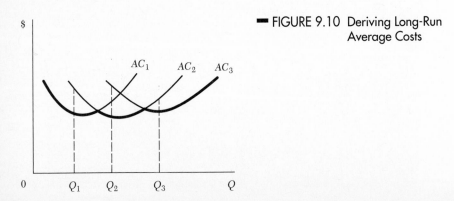

■ FIGURE 9.10 Deriving Long-Run Average Costs

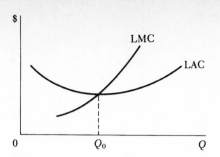

which assumed that a firm increased output by applying variable resources to fixed resources. In the long run, however, there are no fixed resources; a firm expands output by using more of all resources. If that is the case, then why would long-run average costs (LAC) decrease over a range of output, reach a minimum at Q_0, and then begin to increase?

Economists attribute the shape of the LAC curve to economies and diseconomies of scale. As the firm adjusts its plant size, it alters the scale of its operations. At first, as the firm expands at relatively low levels of output, by building a larger plant, it can take advantage of specialization, division of labor, and more advanced technology. The result is lower average costs. The firm experiences **economies of scale**. However, beyond some rate of output (Q_0 in Figure 9.11), the firm encounters difficulties in organizing the now larger operation—coordination and communication make efficient production more difficult. Average costs begin to increase; it costs more to produce each unit of output. **Diseconomies of scale** have set in. As in the short run, the long-run marginal cost curve (LMC) in Figure 9.11 is below LAC while it is decreasing and above it while it is increasing.

The shape of the long-run average cost curve defines an optimum plant size. At the rate of output at which LAC is at a minimum, the firm picks the plant size that produces the rate of output at lowest average cost. The firm expands output and plant size throughout the range of economies of scale. At higher rates of output, LAC begins to increase because of diseconomies of scale. At Q_0, the firm produces a rate of output that minimizes the per-unit cost of production.

In fact, in the long run, in competitive industries, firms tend to produce a rate of output that minimizes long-run average costs. Competition forces them to do so.

12. If a firm experienced economies of scale over some range of output and then LAC was constant, what would its LAC curve look like? Does it seem reasonable to you that a firm could keep expanding and not encounter diseconomies of scale? If this happened, what would the optimum size plant be?

13. In Figure 9.11, Q_0 represents the optimum rate of output and the optimum size plant. Does the firm earn its opportunity costs if it gets a price equal to this level of average costs?

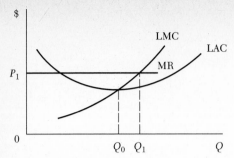

COMPETITIVE MARKETS IN THE LONG RUN

In this section, using the model that we developed for the individual firm, we will develop a general model of the behavior of a competitive market. The analysis focuses on the long-run equilibrium for the firms in the industry and for the entire industry. Although we have concentrated on a single example, the model of a competitive market is intended to be generalizable to all competitive markets or to an entire economy that is competitive. We will also interpret the results of the long-run equilibrium for competitive markets.

In Figure 9.12, with a price of P_1, the firm will produce Q_1, since it is at this rate of output that MR = MC. The price is determined in the competitive market for the firm's product. This price is constant, and the firm has no effect on it. Hence, P = MR = AR, and the firm can produce as much as it wants at that price. The firm, of course, will produce Q_1, since that is where its profits are maximized. At Q_1, price exceeds AC, so we know that the firm is earning economic profits.

But in the long run, if resources can earn above their opportunity costs, new firms will enter the industry in pursuit of economic profits. In other words, the existence of economic profits provides an incentive for other firms to enter the industry. If economic profits can be made, given the price in the market for PC software and the average costs of production, new firms will enter that market and begin to produce and market their own products.

As new firms enter the market, however, the market supply curve shifts out to the right. There is an increase in supply because one of the determinants of supply has changed. This increase in supply, assuming the demand does not change, produces a lower price for software, say P_2 (see Figure 9.13). At P_2, the firm will pick a new rate of output, Q_2, at which MR = MC. But P still exceeds AC, firms will make economic profits, and other new firms will enter the market. This further drives down the price of the product.

This process will continue until economic profits no longer exist to provide an incentive for new firms to enter the industry. This occurs at a price of P_3 in Fig. 9.14. At this price, the firm picks Q_3, since that is where MR = MC. At this rate of output P = AC, so there are no economic profits. The firm is in equilibrium because it is producing the rate of output that maximizes its

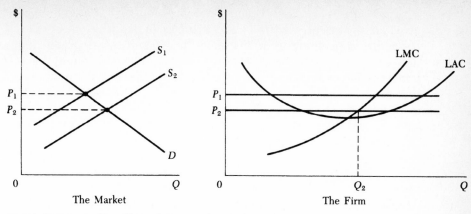

■ FIGURE 9.13 The Effect of Entry in the Long Run

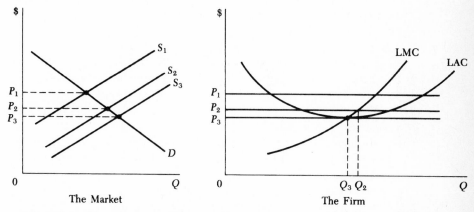

■ FIGURE 9.14 Long-Run Equilibrium in Competition

profits—even though this means zero economic profits. But the firm does earn what we called, at the beginning of this chapter, normal profits—that is, it covers all of its opportunity costs. The firm collects enough revenues to pay opportunity costs to all of its variable and fixed resources, including a return to the owners of the business equivalent to their opportunity costs. The firm earns as much from its involvement in this activity as it could earn doing anything else. If a firm cannot earn normal profits in the long run, it will exit from the market.

Competition and Efficiency

The existence of economic profits encourages new firms to enter the industry until economic profits are eliminated. Firms choose a rate of output that maximizes their profits, which in long-run equilibrium equals zero economic profits, or normal profits. The industry is in equilibrium because there is no incentive for firms to enter or exit from the industry. What are the consequences of this result in terms of a society's use of its scarce resources?

Efficiency in production occurs when the per-unit cost of production is minimized. The firm produces at that rate of output that minimizes AC. This means that the amount of resources used to produce each unit of output is minimized. Given resource scarcity, this is an attractive result of the operation of competitive markets. But note how this has happened. Because of competition and free entry, the firm has been forced to produce at the level of output that minimizes average cost! Competition, through the forces that we have analyzed, tends over time to result in efficient production. Firms tend to produce at the optimum level of output, minimizing the per-unit cost of production. So competition tends to produce efficiency.

What assumptions have we made? We assumed that D stayed constant and that the cost curves did not change. With these simplifying assumptions, our analysis showed the tendency toward efficiency. Obviously, changes in the real world would make our analysis a bit more complicated, but the essential conclusion remains: Competitive markets tend to result in efficiency in the use of scarce resources.

14. Explain and show in an illustration what happens in our competitive market when the market price goes below P_3. What happens to profits? What do the firms in the industry do? What happens to market supply? To market price? What is the new equilibrium?

15. Do you think that the model of long-run equilibrium—wherein profits attract entry, prices fluctuate, exit of firms is possible, and there is a tendency toward efficiency in production—applies to the example we have been using, the market for PC software? Why or why not? Can you think of some other markets that have demonstrated some of these same characteristics in recent years?

16. In the PC market itself, IBM has faced increasing competition from the producers of "clones" or IBM-compatible computers. Why? Why hasn't Apple experienced similar competition for its Macintosh computers (very popular among college students)?

Another type of efficiency results from long-run equilibrium in competitive markets: **efficiency in resource allocation**. At the long-run equilibrium in Figure 9.14, P_3 equals minimum AC. But P_3 also equals MC at the equilibrium rate of output, Q_3. This is an important result. The price of a product measures the amount of money that people are just willing to spend to purchase one more unit of that good. In other words, the price provides a measure of the marginal benefit that people derive from purchasing a unit of the good or service. The MC of the good (shown by the LMC curve) measures the cost to society of getting additional units of the good. To get one more unit, resources must be paid their opportunity costs. A rate of output that equalizes the marginal cost to society of getting one more unit of a good with the marginal benefit that people get from consuming one more unit maximizes social welfare (with respect to the production of that good). It also implies that resources have been allocated efficiently, given the opportunity costs of resources and given consumers' valuations of goods as shown by their prices.

To demonstrate this, let's consider different rates of output in Figure 9.14. First, take any rate of output lower than Q_3. At all rates of output lower than Q_3, the price of the product exceeds LMC. As output expands, the marginal benefit from getting one more unit of the good is larger than the marginal cost to society of producing it. Expanding output, then, makes a positive contribution to the society's welfare. The additional benefit exceeds the additional cost, so social welfare increases. More resources should be allocated to producing the good.

On the other hand, any rate of output greater than Q_3 results in MC exceeding P. The additional cost of producing one more unit is larger than the extra benefit from getting one more unit for consumers. Consequently, at rates of output above Q_3, social welfare decreases. To increase social welfare requires reducing the rate of output and allocating fewer resources to its production. Therefore, social welfare is maximized at a rate of output of Q_3 at which P = MC. This represents efficiency in resource allocation.

The long-run equilibrium tendency of competitive markets is to produce exactly this result! Competitive markets tend to produce efficiency in resource allocation.

Zero economic profits, production at lowest AC, and efficiency in resource allocation are all theoretical results of competitive markets. These results are brought about by the pursuit of profit by firms within the market and by the force of competition itself—the free entry and exit of firms to and from the market and in competition with one another for consumers.

Notice that we have again been using the phrase *tends to* in our analysis of the long-run equilibrium for a competitive market. We have been constructing a model of competition, a theory about how competitive markets work. Given the assumptions that we have made and the concepts that we have defined, we have determined the equilibrium result for competition. This does not mean that such equilibrium exists all the time for every competitive market, or that there won't ever be any economic profits in competitive markets. What it does suggest, though, is that without disturbances (given our assumptions), there are some general tendencies in the operation of competition. The system tends toward equilibrium. And even if it is disturbed—for example, by a change in consumers' incomes or tastes and preferences, by a change in resource prices, or by technological advances—the model that we have developed will allow us to follow through the effects to determine what the new equilibrium will be. In fact, competition encourages adaptability and responsiveness to changes in consumers' behavior.

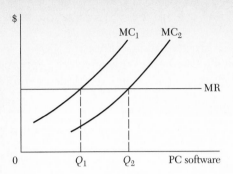

The "Invisible Hand" and Consumer Sovereignty

What does all this have to do with the "invisible hand" and consumer sovereignty? Remember, Adam Smith's notion of the invisible hand was that the market tends to promote social welfare. **Consumer sovereignty** means that the market follows the "dictates" of consumers, in terms of their tastes and preferences.

Markets and prices indicate to potential producers where profits can be made in the economy. If producers can produce a product at a lower average cost than the price at which they can sell it, then they can earn a profit. In addition, producers will attempt to maximize their profits. We can see immediately, then, that producers will probably try to lower their costs, because that increases their profits. Consumers also benefit from this because the price of the product will eventually be lowered due to the cost reduction.

The price reduction following a cost reduction may not be intuitively obvious, so let's examine this theoretical conclusion in more detail. Suppose we have a software producer with an MC and MR graph that looks like Figure 9.15. MC_1 represents the firm's costs, and MR is determined by the market price for software. This firm then discovers a new and cheaper method of making its products. As a result, MC falls from MC_1 to MC_2 (each successive unit can now be brought to market for a lower marginal cost).

With the change in costs, the firm makes a new decision about the level of output to produce. Originally, profits were maximized at Q_1; with the new marginal cost curve, the profit-maximizing level of production increases to Q_2. (Since average costs also decrease, the firm also will make larger profits, since price is still the same and the firm is now producing more.) At first, the price stays the same; the firm is so small in relation to the market that the additional amount brought to market is not noticeable and has no effect on market price. However, the firm does have larger profits.

Eventually, other participants in the market notice the improvement this firm made and the extra profits it is earning as a result. These other suppliers begin to use the same or similar cost-reducing methods of production. In addition, the lure of economic profits (a return to the firm over and above opportunity costs) may induce some new firms to enter the market as sellers. (Again, a characteristic of a competitive market is free entry.) What does

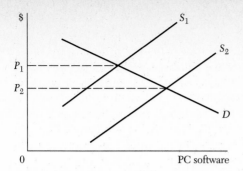

this do to market supply? It increases it; more software will be brought to market. Graphically, in Figure 9.16, we get a new supply curve, S_2; more units of software are brought to market at each possible price.

Consequently (note we have assumed that D stays the same), the market price will decrease from P_1 to P_2. The cost reduction ended up also reducing the market price! This was brought about through the market and by competition. The market showed that profits could be made, and competition allowed new firms to enter the market. (Note that each producer's profits are lowered because of the price decrease, although each producer will still bring to market the amount that maximizes its profits. Show this using MR, MC, and AC curves.)

Although each producer (firm) is out to maximize its own profits, the market and competition have brought about a situation in which there is an incentive to lower costs and whereby prices are reduced when costs are. Consumers benefit as a result; they get their product for a lower price. The "invisible hand" lives (at least theoretically)! (Go back to Chapter 4 and review what Adam Smith had to say about the "invisible hand.")

In addition, the market responds to consumers' demands. This response is referred to as consumer sovereignty. For example, let's assume that consumers come to regard PCs and software as necessities. This change in tastes and preferences (and the increase in the number of consumers in the market) tends to increase the demand for software. What effect do these changes have on the market price for software? Figure 9.17 shows that the price of

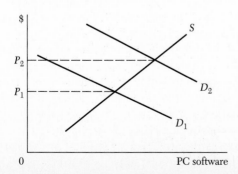

■ FIGURE 9.17 Change in Demand

software tends to increase. What assumption have we made in this illustration? (And is this a realistic assumption? What has happened in recent years in the software market on both sides of the market?)

With this increased price, the profits of software producers should increase, and they will produce increasing amounts of software. Consequently, the desires of consumers show up in the market and indicate to producers what to do with respect to production. If consumers want more software, the market will indicate that, and the producers will respond by producing more. This is consumer sovereignty. By extension, this process also has implications for resource use in the economy. When production of any good or service is expanded or contracted, the use of resources for that purpose will also increase or decrease.

17. Using Figure 9.17, if a reduction in resource costs allowed a software firm to lower its long-run average costs, show what the new long-run equilibrium would be for the firm and for the industry.

CONCLUSION

The competitive market model has some attractive results. Firms earn normal profits. There is a tendency toward an equilibrium at which entry and exit cease. The firms in the market produce a rate of output that minimizes average costs; there is efficiency in production. Output takes place at a rate that maximizes social welfare; when $P = MC$, there is efficiency in resource allocation. If products are homogeneous, then there is no need to allocate resources to advertising. Competitive markets are adaptable. Whenever costs change, or supply and demand conditions change, these changes are registered and are taken into account in the decisions firms make in pursuit of maximizing their own profits. Since technological change can lower the firm's costs, there is always an incentive for the firm to try to lower costs, because profits will increase (at least for a while). Competitive markets register the desires of consumers, and those desires guide production and the allocation of resources. The "invisible hand" will bring about cost and price reductions for consumers.

The competitive market system also links the interdependence of all economic agents in the whole economy. Markets for resources and products provide prices that people use as information in all of the decisions they make about what work they will do, what goods and services they will consume, what business activities they will pursue, and what resources firms will use. As a result of all of these decisions linked by the operation of markets, the scarce resources of society are allocated to meet the needs of people in that society. The competitive market system thus operates to solve the questions of what to produce, how to produce it, and how to distribute it. All of this occurs because of the existence of markets and of competition. Competition and markets guide resource allocation.

If every market were competitive (remember our definition of what that means), then the whole economy would be characterized by efficiency, the "invisible hand," and consumer sovereignty in the long run. Stated different-ly, the competitive market model in *theory* produces efficiency, consumer sovereignty, and the "invisible hand." As a result, there is no need for the gov-ernment to be involved in the economy. If the competitive markets are allowed to operate freely and individuals are allowed to follow their maxi-mizing opportunities, the best economic results are achieved. The competi-tive model, then, justifies a policy of laissez-faire.

Unfortunately, however, the model of competitive markets is not the same thing as the real economy. The theoretical results of the model of competi-tion we have developed are certainly attractive. In fact, this theory is the basis of the argument that the capitalist system is the best economic system possible. It can be seen in innumerable advertisements from corporate America as well as the ideas of chambers of commerce and the National Association of Manufacturers. Many politicians use the argument to demon-strate their version of patriotism in search of support and votes. But the real world doesn't always duplicate theory, and the results of the model cannot uncritically or without qualification be ascribed to the real world.

It is important to recognize the various ways in which the operation of the real economy departs from the model of competitive markets. Not all mar-kets are, in fact, competitive. Corporations and labor unions, for example, have market power, can influence prices, and have been able to limit the effects of competition. Sometimes markets do not work at all; no one can make profits putting up street signs, for example. The calculation of profits by the firm does not take into account the external costs of production (such as pollution), an omission that can interfere with efficient resource allocation. The operation of resource markets can result in an unfair distribution of income. All of these results of the operation of the real economy limit the extent to which it produces the attractive results of the theoretical model of competition.

In the next four chapters, we will develop some economic theory that analyzes these problems in the operation of the real market system. We will also explore the response of public policy to the existence of these problems connected with the operation of the economy.

Review Questions

1. How accurate is this competitive model with respect to the current U.S. economy? Are its conclusions generally applicable to our economy? Why or why not?
2. Why are profits maximized when MR = MC? Can you explain this log-ically?
3. Do you think firms really do try to maximize their profits? Do they have other goals? Which are most important?
4. Give some examples of the law of diminishing returns in production. Specify which resources are variable and which ones are fixed.

5. Explain why economic profits cease to exist in competition in the long run (as a tendency). What is the implication of this? Why do firms stay in a market in which there are no profits?
6. In Table 9.3, show what happens if the price of software increases to $180. Fill in new MR, TR, and Profit columns. What rate of output will the firm choose? Why?
7. Illustrate (with cost and revenue curves) a firm making economic profits in the long run. Show the corresponding market-determined price.
   a. Assume (show) an increase in demand for the product (e.g., rugs imported from India). What happens to market price? What adjustments do the firms in the industry make?
   b. How will long-run equilibrium develop? Illustrate long-run equilibrium for the firm and the industry.

10

Noncompetitive Markets and Inefficiency

INTRODUCTION

According to neoclassical theory, competitive markets tend to produce consumer sovereignty, provide for the operation of the "invisible hand," and lead to economic efficiency. However, if markets are *not* competitive—that is, if they do not have all of the characteristics of competition—these results are less likely. In fact, in noncompetitive markets there is likely to be some amount of *producer sovereignty*, "monopoly" profits (i.e., economic profits not eliminated by competition), and inefficiency. In this chapter, we will define some other models of market structure and examine their results.

NONCOMPETITIVE MARKET STRUCTURES

The competitive market model gives us a standard by which to judge *real* economic markets and other models of market structures. Chapter 9 defined a competitive market and examined its workings and results. In what follows, we will examine some other market structures. With these additional models we will have a more complete theoretical system for understanding the behavior of firms in the economy and for evaluating their performance.

Before we examine monopoly, oligopoly, and monopolistic competition, we must emphasize that the competitive model is a *model*, and that it roughly describes about 10 percent or so of the total private economic activity in the United States. The best examples of competitive markets are those for raw agricultural products—which are homogeneous, are not advertised, have large numbers of buyers and sellers, and can be entered by almost anyone. In the rest of the economy, there are firms and markets from which some or all of these characteristics are missing. The industry may include very few firms, and they may have the market power to control their prices. Products may be differentiated rather than homogeneous. Advertising occurs beyond the simple level of informing consumers about products. And entry into markets isn't always "free" or easy.

The existence and emergence of noncompetitive market structures should not be too surprising. As we demonstrated in Chapter 9, the long-run tendency of competition is to eliminate economic profits. One effective way for a firm to ensure long-run economic profits is to limit the effects of competition, which may involve the elimination of competition.

MONOPOLY

A **monopoly** market structure is one in which there is only one seller of a good or service. The firm is the industry. Some monopolies have developed because of the large initial investment required, and only one firm occupies the market. Some monopolies have been established and protected by governments. Many monopolies are legalized because of the confusion that competition would create. At the same time, their prices are usually regulated by public authority. The characteristics of monopoly markets include the following:

- There is one seller of a good or service.
- The product is unique, and there are no close substitutes; buyers must buy the good or service from the monopolist.
- The monopoly has **market power**, meaning it can exercise control over the price of the good or service, since it supplies the total quantity. (In contrast, for the competitive firm, price is determined by the market; the competitor has no influence on the price of its product.)
- Monopolies usually exist because there are absolute **barriers to entry** into the market; no other firm can supply the product because of legal, technological, or geographical factors limiting provision of the good or service.
- The monopoly may or may not advertise.

Examples of legal monopolies are local gas, electric, telephone, cable, and water companies. Professional sports teams in the United States have regional monopolies. Network Solutions, Inc., as a result of a contract with the National Science Foundation, had a virtual monopoly on the business of assigning Internet addresses. F. M. Scherer, an industrial economist, has esti-

TABLE 10.1 Monopoly Price and Marginal Revenue

Output	Price	Total Revenue	Marginal Revenue
1	10	10	—
2	9	18	8
3	8	24	6
4	7	28	4

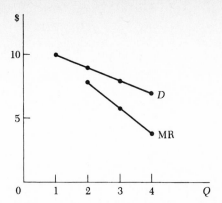

mated that about 6 to 7 percent of private economic output originates in monopolies.

The theoretical results of monopoly markets are that producers tend to restrict output and charge higher prices than they could if there were competition in the market for that monopoly's product. As a result, monopoly markets are less beneficial to consumers, who would prefer to have more of the product at a lower price. Monopolies also interfere with efficient resource allocation. Monopoly power allows a firm to remain immune from competition and to retain monopoly profits. (For these reasons, most monopolies in the United States are regulated.) Monopoly thus is less desirable than competition.

We can demonstrate these results with a theoretical analysis. The monopolist faces the entire demand curve for a product, since there are no competitors. Thus, to sell more, the monopolist must lower price. Or if the monopolist raises prices, less will be demanded. As a result, the monopolist's marginal revenue curve will be below the demand curve. Since price must be lowered to sell more, the marginal addition to revenue will always be below the price. This is demonstrated in Table 10.1 and illustrated in Figure 10.1. This information shows the revenue situation for a typical monopoly firm, with a downward-sloping demand curve and a marginal revenue curve below it. If we assume that the monopoly buys its resources in competitive markets, its MC and AC curves will look like the ones we derived in Chapter 9. Figure 10.2 illustrates the cost situation for the monopolist.

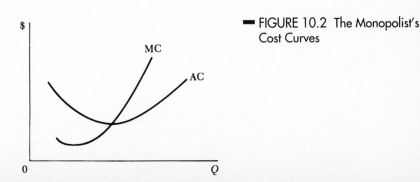

■ FIGURE 10.2 The Monopolist's Cost Curves

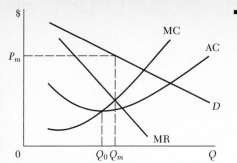

FIGURE 10.3 Equilibrium for the Monopoly Firm

Figure 10.3 combines the revenue and cost information to demonstrate the equilibrium result for a typical monopoly firm. What level of output will the monopoly choose to produce? It will produce Q_m, where MC = MR, because that level of output maximizes its profits. It will charge a price of P_m for that amount of output, because that is the price the market is willing to pay for that quantity. The monopoly is earning profits, since P is well above AC. And the monopoly is producing at a rate of output that does not minimize average costs. (Q_0 is where AC is at a minimum.)

This illustrates the short-run equilibrium for a monopoly. In this case, the monopolist earns economic profits. However, there is no assurance that even monopolies will always earn profits. If costs are too high or there is no demand for the monopolist's product, a monopoly could suffer economic losses. For example, there is no major-league baseball team in Washington, D.C., because several teams in the past have failed there.

What happens in a monopoly in the long run? Figure 10.4 shows the long-run cost and revenue curves for a monopolist (assuming economies and diseconomies of scale). In the long run, the monopolist has the option of building different size plants, and the demand curve for the product could change. Given the cost and revenue curves in Figure 10.4, the monopolist produces at Q_{mlr}, the rate of output at which MC = MR, and charges a price of P_{mlr} (from the demand curve). P is above AC, so the monopolist earns economic profits. The monopolist is in long-run equilibrium. But in a pure monopoly, even with economic profits, there is no entry into the market; this firm has a monopoly. Therefore, Figure 10.4 shows the long-run equilibrium

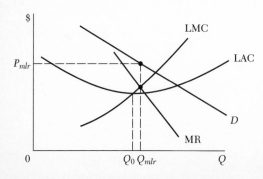

FIGURE 10.4 Long-Run Equilibrium for the Monopolist

result for a typical monopoly market. As long as cost and demand conditions remain the same, the monopoly firm produces Q_{mlr}, charges a price of P_{mlr}, and earns economic profits.

What conclusions can we draw about the theoretical results of monopoly? Economic profits may exist, but because of the monopoly, no entry occurs to seek those extra returns above opportunity costs. The monopolist will not produce at a rate of output that minimizes average cost (Q_0); nothing forces the monopolist to produce at the most efficient rate of output. In monopoly, then, there tends to be **inefficiency in production** (at least from the perspective of the society, since output is not at minimum average cost). The monopoly firm produces the rate of output that maximizes its profits—that is its goal. Moreover, at that rate of output, price exceeds marginal costs. Society values an additional unit of the good or service more than the cost to produce an additional unit. From a social perspective, then, it would be preferable if more resources were allocated to increased production of the commodity. Monopoly thus tends to result in **inefficiency in resource allocation** (since price does not equal marginal cost). Because monopolies get economic profits, some resources earn more than their opportunity costs. Finally, some monopolists may engage in advertising, which, although some may be informative or entertaining, requires the use of scarce resources. Consequently, we can see that the long-run equilibrium result of monopoly is significantly inferior to the long-run result of competition. The pursuit of profit, in this case, does not maximize social welfare.

We can also examine the theoretical results of monopoly by focusing on the market, shown in Figure 10.5. *If* there were competition in the market, new firms would enter, market supply would increase to S_c, and market price would decrease to P_c. Thus, monopoly restricts output, since $Q_m < Q_c$. And monopoly charges higher prices, since $P_m > P_c$. Finally, monopolies earn monopoly profits.

An important conclusion that can be drawn from the monopoly model is that the existence of market power (ability to control supply and price) tends to prevent consumer sovereignty, the attainment of economic efficiency, and the operation of the "invisible hand." The monopoly benefits at the expense of society. This says nothing at all about the further problem of the relation-

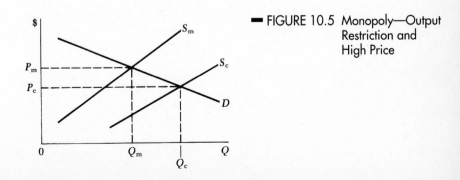

■ FIGURE 10.5 Monopoly—Output Restriction and High Price

ship of economic power to political power. Monopolies, through their economic power and resources, may come to wield undue political power. As a result, monopolies may also tend to disrupt democracy. In the words of Henry Simons, an economist who taught at the University of Chicago, "Political liberty can survive only within the effectively competitive economic system. Thus, the great enemy of democracy is monopoly." Any economic unit tending toward monopoly power, consequently, tends toward these same results.

As a result of these adverse effects of monopoly, the public sector has frequently been involved in regulating the operations and/or prices of monopolies. Many times, the public regulation is in return for governmental granting of a legal monopoly, as is the case with local telephone service. The usual goal of the public oversight is to increase monopoly output, lower monopoly prices, or reduce monopoly profits. (In Chapter 13, we will explore the regulation of monopoly in more detail.)

Occasionally the profit motive itself can limit the existence of a continuing monopoly. For example, a monopoly might produce a good or service for which a close substitute could be developed. Or the monopolist might have some technical advantage that can be duplicated. The very existence of monopoly profits gives other firms an incentive to try to "break" the monopoly. For example, Xerox developed the technique and the machinery for instant photocopying. Given the lucrative results from the monopoly on the technique, other firms developed substitutes and entered the market. Similarly, Apple once had a virtual monopoly on personal computers, but that was "broken" by IBM and numerous IBM-clone producers. The extent to which other firms challenge a monopoly may reduce the adverse theoretical consequences of monopoly.

1. What is so bad about monopolies? What can we do if they exist? What are some possible benefits of monopolies?
2. Analyze Henry Simons' comment above. Do you agree or disagree? Why?
3. Local phone companies often have a monopoly but advertise. Why?
4. In Figure 10.3, explain what would happen to the firm's profits if it produced at Q_0.
5. "Some resources [in monopoly] earn more than their opportunity costs." Can you think of any examples?

MONOPOLY ON THE INTERNET—AND DISRUPTING REGULATED MONOPOLIES

Network Solutions, Inc., of Herndon, Virginia, under an agreement with the National Science Foundation (NSF), has been responsible for assigning "domains," or addresses, for electronic mail and the World Wide Web. The firm maintains a registry of addresses on the Internet, e.g., those ending in .com for commercial enterprises, .edu for educational institutions, .gov for governmental entities, and .org for organizations. Since 1995, Network Solutions has been allowed to charge fees for registering and renewing addresses. The fees are regulated by the NSF.

However, the monopoly thus far is no guarantee of profits. For 1995 and 1996, the firm posted losses. As a result of rapid expansion of the Internet and proliferating addresses, the firm's billing system was overtaxed and behind. Over 20 percent of fees were past due, and over 10 percent of addresses were disconnected due to nonpayment. On the other hand, almost all addresses are activated the same day the registrations arrive. Also, the company must deposit 30 percent of its revenues in a fund for improving the Internet.

Other firms have cried foul. They think there should be no monopoly and that the business should be open to competition. The future will tell if Network Solutions catches up with the demand for addresses and can effectively capture the revenues that go along with its "monopoly" in this expanding market. Moreover, a group of experts, the Internet International Ad Hoc Committee, is likely to recommend a vast expansion of Internet addresses, which would effectively eliminate Network Solutions' monopoly.

Recently, there has been a similar trend toward competition in markets that were previously regulated monopolies. Long-distance phone service originating in the United States, for example, used to be a monopoly of AT&T, which owned all of the long-distance transmission lines for phone calls. Changes in technology—fiber optics and satellite transmission—have made it possible to open this market to more competition. Hence, consumers have many options for long-distance telephone service—witness the TV ads and the telephone soliciting campaigns. Do you think that the end of AT&T's monopoly has been good for consumers?

Several states, including Massachusetts, are permitting similar experiments in the provision of electricity and natural gas. Traditionally, electric and gas utilities have been monopolies, usually regulated by state utility commissions. The state grants firms exclusive rights to sell electricity and gas, delivered by electric and gas distribution systems, and regulates their prices. The experiments involve letting consumers choose who their supplier will be from among several firms authorized by the state to supply electricity and gas. These firms all use the same distribution system, so there is no duplication of gas transmission pipes or electric lines all over the countryside, but they can offer different prices and services. Again, time will tell if the experiments work and whether consumers will see competition in the provision of these monopolized services.

MONOPOLISTIC COMPETITION AND OLIGOPOLY

The other two major models of market structure that economists have developed to approximate economic reality are monopolistic competition and oligopoly. Around 80 percent of private economic production comes from firms with monopolistic competition or oligopoly elements. In *Economics and the Public Purpose*, Harvard economist John Kenneth Galbraith estimates that about 50 percent of private production originates in industries that are competitive or monopolistically competitive, and the remainder comes from firms that are monopolies or oligopolies.

Monopolistic Competition

The model of **monopolistic competition**, developed in the 1930s by E. H. Chamberlin and Joan Robinson, is used to describe industries that are close to competitive but have some elements of monopoly. Monopolistic competition has the following major characteristics:

- There are large numbers of buyers and sellers in the market. The firms are all relatively small with respect to the total size of the industry.
- The products are **differentiated**, or distinguished from competitors' offerings by quality and design differences, advertising, and psychological appeal. The products are close substitutes for one another, but each firm tries to create a "monopoly" for its product. A strong stimulus for this behavior is the tendency toward the elimination of profits in competitive industries with homogeneous products.
- Firms have limited control over the prices of their products. Although the firms are small in relation to the market, they sell a differentiated product. Some consumers are loyal to the unique brands of individual firms, even though there are close substitutes. This "monopoly" element gives firms some control over prices.
- Entry into the market is relatively easy, although the costs of differentiation (e.g., for advertising) can be large. Since firms are small, relatively small initial investments make entry feasible.
- Unlike competition, monopolistic competition has an abundance of advertising. The products are not homogeneous, and advertising exists to persuade consumers about the differences. (In the mid-1990s, U.S. businesses spent over $150 billion annually on advertising.)

Some examples of monopolistically competitive industries are retail sales in urban communities, fast-food establishments in any particular area, personal computer and printer stores, processed chicken for retail sales, and clothing.

> 6. Review the characteristics of monopolistic competition. Does the market for a college education in the United States demonstrate any of these characteristics? Why might this market move toward monopolistic competition?

To develop the model of what happens in this type of market structure, let's begin by examining the firm's output and pricing decision in the short run. The objective of a firm in monopolistic competition is the same as that of any other firm, so this decision will be a function of the firm's cost and revenue conditions.

Because the firm has some control over the price it charges for its differentiated product, it will face a downward-sloping demand curve. It can raise its price and not lose all of its sales, which is what would happen in perfect competition because consumers would just go to the firm's competitors if it raises its prices. In monopolistic competition, some consumers will remain

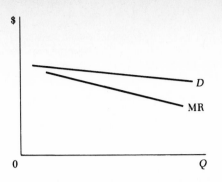

■ FIGURE 10.6 Demand and Marginal Revenue for a Firm in Monopolistic Competition

loyal to the firm's product and continue to purchase it even though the price has gone up and there are close substitutes. Even so, when the firm raises its price, it will experience a decrease in its sales because there are substitutes. The firm can also lower its price and expect to get a significant increase in its sales because its loyal customers will consume more and because it may also steal business from its competitors (and because the demand for its product is elastic). In other words, the demand curve for a monopolistic competitor is downward sloping and relatively elastic. Because the demand curve is downward sloping, the firm's marginal revenue curve is also downward sloping and below the demand curve. Figure 10.6 shows typical demand and marginal revenue curves for a firm in monopolistic competition.

Since monopolistically competitive firms buy their resources in the same markets as do all other firms, their cost curves will be the same. The typical short-run average cost and marginal cost curves, reflecting the law of diminishing returns, are shown in Figure 10.7. Figure 10.7 gives us the information we need to describe the output and price decision of the monopolistic competitor in the short run. Given these cost and demand conditions, the firm produces at Q_{mc}, since that is the rate of output at which MC = MR. The firm will charge a price of P_{mc}, since the market will be willing to pay that price for the amount produced and offered for sale. The firm is earning economic profits because P is greater than AC. This is the firm's short-run equilibrium position.

What happens in the long run in a monopolistically competitive industry? In Figure 10.7, the firm is earning economic profits. Since entry is relatively easy, other firms will enter the market in search of returns above opportuni-

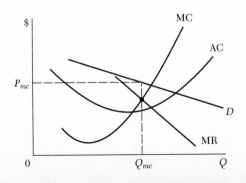

■ FIGURE 10.7 Short-Run Equilibrium for a Firm in Monopolistic Competition

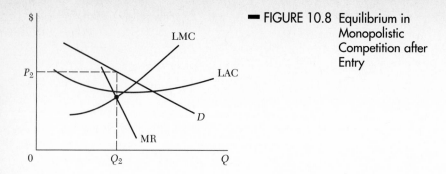

■ FIGURE 10.8 Equilibrium in Monopolistic Competition after Entry

ty costs. The entry of new firms will tend to reduce the share of every firm already in the industry. (Here, we are assuming that the size of the market is "constant.") This will have the effect of shifting every firm's individual demand curve to the left. For example, let's say that entry has occurred; Figure 10.8 illustrates the effect of this on the firm's demand curve. It also reflects the firm's long-run plant-size choices with an LAC curve. What is the new output-price decision by our typical firm?

The firm will pick Q_2 as its rate of output and charge a price of P_2. P is still above AC, however, so the firm earns economic profits. The continued existence of economic profits still offers an incentive for firms to enter the market. As long as profits exist, entry will continue. Entry will cease and the industry will achieve long-run equilibrium when economic profits no longer exist. This result is shown in Figure 10.9. The firm produces at Q_{mcl} and charges a price of P_{mcl}. Since $P = AC$, the firm does not earn any economic profits. New firms will stop entering the market. *The firm* is in equilibrium as well, earning zero economic profits.

What are the implications of this long-run equilibrium result for monopolistic competition? $P = AC$, so there are no economic profits. However, P does not equal minimum average cost (at Q_0). The long-run equilibrium in monopolistic competition therefore does not result in efficiency of production. In addition, P exceeds MC, which means that there is inefficiency in resource allocation. From the perspective of social welfare, monopolistic competition results in an underallocation of resources to the production of its

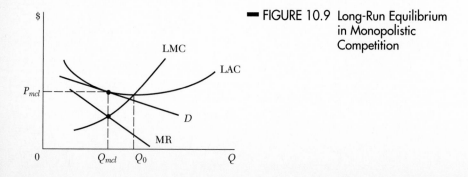

■ FIGURE 10.9 Long-Run Equilibrium in Monopolistic Competition

goods and services. Since one of the primary characteristics of this market structure is product differentiation, resources also get used up in the advertising and promotion of one product over another. From the perspective of the society's use of resources, this represents a waste. Compared with the model of competition, then, monopolistic competition falls short of maximizing social welfare.

On the other hand, the functioning of monopolistically competitive markets has some positive attributes. Relatively free entry by firms when economic profits exist promotes adaptability; resources are reallocated in response to market conditions. Entry also puts downward pressure on prices, as it does in competitive markets. Product differentiation contributes to one of the wonders of the U.S. economy—variety and choice. When efforts to differentiate products lead to quality improvements, consumers benefit, and firms must be sensitive to consumers' desires. There is also a possibility, however, that product differentiation may not lead to real improvements or that too much choice will only confuse consumers' informed decisions. Finally, in monopolistic competition, entry and limited competition do force firms to produce as efficiently as possible. If firms do not match the costs of other firms, they are in danger of being eliminated from the market by economic losses.

Given the tendency of monopolistic competition to eliminate economic profits in the long run, occasionally the firms in such an industry will engage in efforts to prevent the disappearance of long-run economic profits. A favorite tactic is to stay ahead of the effects of entry by continued differentiation and advertising. By improving the quality, design, or even advertising of a product, a firm may be able to continue earning economic profits in the long run. In addition, monopolistically competitive firms might be able to get legislative protection that controls the entry of firms into the industry. For example, beauty parlors and barber shops must have licenses from the state in order to operate. The licensing requirement restricts entry into the market, and it preserves some economic profits for existing firms.

7. In Figure 10.9, show and explain what would happen if the demand for the firm's product (and its close substitutes) increased (e.g., from a change in consumers' tastes and preferences).

8. In Figure 10.9, show and explain what would happen if the costs of production decreased as a result of a technological breakthrough.

9. For the long-run equilibrium result of monopolistic competition, show the effect of an improvement in quality, design, or advertising on the part of one firm attempting to maintain long-run economic profits.

10. Why is the market for processed chicken sold in grocery stores an example of monopolistic competition?

■ Lunch in a familiar setting. *(Mary Kate Denny/PhotoEdit)*

MONOPOLISTIC COMPETITION IN FAST FOODS

It used to offer hamburgers, french fries, milk shakes, and soft drinks—and that was it. Now you can get all of that plus breakfasts, chicken nuggets, salad bars, stuffed potatoes, and more—including occasional "new" products. The fast-food industry in the United States is a good example of a monopolistically competitive industry.

Although McDonald's, Burger King, and Wendy's account for about 67 percent of the national hamburger fast-food market, the market is broader than that. The fast-food market consists of hamburger, pizza, chicken, taco, sandwich, and other establishments. And, while McDonald's and "friends" dominate the national markets for fast foods, area markets experience stiffer competition, with local and regional firms competing for customers' stomachs and dollars. Also, the fast-food firms must compete in the broader category of commercial dining, a $200 billion industry in the 1990s.

The market itself has expanded tremendously in the post–World War II period, with mobility and changing lifestyles. The late Ray Kroc took over two hamburger stands run by the McDonald brothers in 1955, and McDonald's hasn't stopped expanding since then. There are now well over 8,000 McDonald's establishments—mostly in the United States but also all over the world. Burger King has about half as many outlets.

What characteristics of monopolistic competition are demonstrated by the fast-food industry? Regional markets have a large number of competitors, and entry is relatively easy. You don't have to rival the size or sophistication of McDonald's in order to start a hamburger or pizza joint. The rate of failure also is high, with thousands of restaurants going bankrupt every year. There is obvious and substantial product differentiation. Pizza is not chicken, and hamburgers are not salad. Some hamburgers are frozen, and some aren't. Some are fried, while others are grilled. French fries are notoriously non-standardized. You can't get a hot dog everywhere. Pizza comes in infinite styles and qualities. The decors of different places distinguish them from one another. Quality is an issue among the various choices. And, recently, the fast-food industry has become concerned about its junk-food image, and some firms have begun to offer more nutritional and low-fat food items. Finally, since McDonald's first started advertising in 1966, television advertising has become a necessary aspect of the competition for the national fast-food industry. The name of the game is diversification, differentiation, aggressive advertising and marketing, and broad appeal. So, where's the fast food?

Oligopoly

An **oligopoly** is an industry dominated by a few large firms. They are not like small competitive firms, but they are also not monopolists. There is great variety in oligopolistic industries, so economists have developed a number of different models of oligopoly to describe their behavior and results. Oligopoly has the following major characteristics:

- A few firms produce most of the output in an industry. These firms are thus usually large with respect to the market, and dominate its activities. Examples include automobiles, computers, steel, aluminum, cigarettes, and chewing gum. In some cases, there may be fewer than ten firms in the entire industry. In others, there may be hundreds of companies, but four or five firms dominate.
- The product of an oligopoly may be homogeneous or differentiated. If it is a consumer good, it is usually differentiated to gain consumers' attention and loyalty (e.g., automobiles). And, if it is a raw material sold to other firms, it is usually homogeneous (e.g., steel, copper, or aluminum).
- There may be technological reasons for domination of an industry by a few firms. Large-scale operations may enjoy lower costs. Economies of scale may allow only a few firms to constitute the entire industry, given the size of the market. Firms may also have grown large due to mergers. As a result, entry into such markets is difficult. Because of the substantial initial investment, a firm must be large to enter.
- The firms in an oligopolistic industry are *interdependent;* their pricing and output decisions affect the other firms in the industry. Each firm must pay close attention to the actions of its rivals. This creates a constant possibility for **price wars** (progressive price cutting to increase sales) among oligopolists or collusion to avoid those price wars. It can also lead to price leadership or a reluctance to alter price. Despite this interdependence, oligopoly firms do have some control over their prices.
- Oligopolies usually have a significant amount of nonprice competition, such as product differentiation and advertising.

Because oligopoly firms are independent, it is difficult to develop one model of what happens in an oligopolistic industry. Depending on how rivals react to price and output decisions, a variety of models are possible, including price wars, collusion, stable prices, and price leadership. We will briefly develop some of these models.

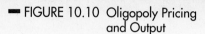
FIGURE 10.10 Oligopoly Pricing and Output

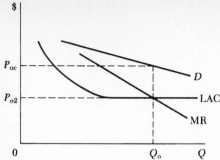

Figure 10.10 illustrates a general possibility for an oligopolist. Because the firm has some control over the price of its product, it has a downward-sloping demand curve and a marginal revenue curve that lies below it. Many oligopolies experience economies of scale. The long-run average cost curve in Figure 10.10 reflects economies of scale that are reached at relatively low rates of output; thereafter average costs remain constant. That is, the firm does not encounter diseconomies of scale, so there is no limit to the firm's expansion. If long-run average costs are constant, then, for that range of output, AC = MC. Given these demand and cost conditions, the firm will pick Q_o as the rate of output that maximizes its profits (since that is where MC = MR). The price will come from the firm's demand curve, at P_{oc}. At this price-output combination, the firm earns economic profits, since P is above AC. Since entry is very difficult in oligopoly, these long-run profits are relatively secure.

Price Wars. However, in oligopoly there is always a possibility of price cutting by rivals. Other firms might try to steal away customers by lowering their prices; this action could spark retaliation. Theoretically, firms could lower prices all the way down to P_{o2} before encountering losses. As prices decreased, the oligopolists' profits would shrink.

Collusion. In response to this threat of price wars and the possibility of losing all of their economic profits, oligopolists might collude to avoid price competition among themselves. **Collusion**, or agreements to avoid competition and/or to set prices, is illegal in the United States. However, light bulb manufacturers, paperboard companies, and others have been found guilty of price fixing. And oligopolists might avoid price wars through indirect ways of setting prices, such as trade associations, industry meetings, governmental standardization of technical materials, or informal tacit agreements. Given the illustration in Figure 10.10, the firms could simply attempt to set prices as close to P_{oc} as possible. This would maximize their economic profits.

In international markets and some European countries, **cartels** are legal and may set prices for their products. One example of a cartel is the Organization of Petroleum Exporting Countries. OPEC consists of thirteen oil-producing countries that operate government-owned petroleum indus-

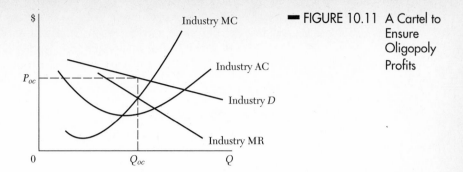

FIGURE 10.11 A Cartel to Ensure Oligopoly Profits

tries and sell oil in international markets. OPEC functions as a cartel that sets production quotas and prices for its members. The intention of the cartel is to control the world's supply of oil, avoid price wars among the members, and, consequently, maximize members' joint profits. The members of OPEC in the 1970s and early 1980s dominated the international oil market, and they used this position and their cooperation to control the international price of oil. Later, with the development of non-OPEC oil sources (e.g., Mexico and Great Britain), OPEC's ability to maintain high prices diminished.

In essence, a cartel can accomplish a result similar to that of monopoly. For example, Figure 10.11 shows the combined cost and revenue conditions for a cartel as a whole. The cartel decides to produce a combined output of Q_{oc} and to charge a price of P_{oc}. As is the case in monopoly, output is restricted, and the price is higher than it would be if there were competition. Economic profits exist for the cartel as a whole. The members of the cartel then agree among themselves how to split up the production goal and profits based on their different cost functions, reserves, and negotiating skills.

Whether collusion is formal, as in a cartel, or informal, its members often have difficulty maintaining it, even though the reward for doing so is the avoidance of price wars and the accumulation of continued long-run economic profits. If the cartel consists of a large number of countries or firms, it has more difficulty reaching and maintaining agreement on production quotas and price levels. If the products of the cartel are differentiated (e.g., by quality of oil), the cartel has more difficulty establishing consistent price schedules for the varieties of the commodity. If the members of a cartel have different cost conditions in their productive operations, they will have more difficulty agreeing on price levels. Those with relatively high costs will want higher prices, or they will experience lower profits. In the same way, the size of the firm or country in the market will influence its bargaining power in the cartel—that is, different members will have different negotiating power when it comes to setting production quotas and prices. Additionally, an external force, e.g., the United States, might attempt to disrupt the unity among cartel members through its pursuit of foreign policy objectives.

The characteristic of cartels that most demonstrates their fragility is their tendency toward price breaks. Given the controlled price of the cartel, which will always be higher than the price that might prevail without the cartel, there is always a temptation for an individual member to offer lower prices to attract its rivals' customers. If it can get away with secret price breaks, it can increase its sales and profits. The problem is that once one member does so, others are likely to do the same, and then the cartel is faced with a price war and reduced profits for all its members. The other difficulty with cartels in the United States is that they are illegal. For all these reasons, collusive behavior and its ultimate form—the cartel—are difficult to establish and maintain.

11. When OPEC raised its oil prices in 1974, many U.S. analysts argued that OPEC would have difficulty maintaining its cartel. With the passage of time, they suggested, oil prices would fall as OPEC dissolved. What was the basis of this argument? Why has OPEC recently lost its ability to control world oil prices?

Price Stability. Another tactic that oligopolistic industries use to avoid price wars involves simply keeping prices stable. If all of the firms in the industry maintain their prices over some period of time, they will avoid the tendency of interdependent firms to engage in self-destructive price competition.

Price Leadership. When oligopolists do change their prices occasionally, they may use one other tactic they have developed to avoid price wars. It is called **price leadership**—the practice of a single firm in an industry announcing a price change, which most if not all of the other firms follow. In some industries, the same firm is consistently the leader. In other industries, the leader may change; it may be one of the giants in the field, or it could be one of the smaller firms. The leader of changes in the prime rate, the rate that banks charge their best borrowers, is not always one of the big New York City banks. In addition to this form of price leadership, uniformity in prices that avoids the danger of price wars can also be achieved through the sharing of information in informal contacts (at lunch, golfing, etc.) among the firms in an industry or through more formal meetings in conferences and trade associations. The primary goal is the same, though—the protection of oligopoly profits.

Outcomes of Oligopoly. What are the theoretical results of oligopoly? There is no one model of oligopoly, as we have seen. But, in general, difficulty in entering the market protects oligopolies from the results of competition. Oligopolies have market power over their output and prices, they tend to earn oligopoly profits, and they are somewhat insulated from the dictates of market forces. The force of competition does not require them to produce at the most efficient rate of output. And because they, like other noncompetitive firms, face a downward-sloping demand curve, P will always exceed MC; consequently, oligopolies result in inefficiency in resource allocation. Oligopolies that sell differentiated products also engage in advertising and use scarce resources to convince consumers that their products are better than those of their rivals. Because oligopolies do not face the competition of new entrants into their markets and have market power, some critics suggest that such firms can resist technological change. For example, it might be possible for an automobile company to introduce production and product improvements that would benefit consumers, but because the firm has money tied up in current production techniques and product lines, it puts off introducing changes.

Large oligopolistic firms have enormous resources at their command. They have economic power over plant location, the pace of investment spending in the economy, and the advance of technology. This concentrated economic power can also be translated into concentrated political power, which can pose some difficulties for the operation of democratic institutions.

On the other hand, the defenders of oligopoly and large firms have argued that the pursuit of profit by such firms has spurred technological advancement and economies of scale in many oligopolistic industries. The history of some of the dominant heavy industries in the United States offers proof that economic concentration has accompanied increased output and efficiency. The steel and automobile industries pioneered large factories and the assembly line. The aircraft industry stimulated other industries and transportation in the post–World War II period. More recently, photocopying and computers have revolutionized information processing. With their economic profits, large firms can also afford to establish research and development labs to discover new processes and products. Finally, the persistence of large corporations may lend a certain stability to the operation of the entire economy. Without the rapid entry and exit of competitive markets, oligopolists can plan for the long run and serve the society.

12. Can you think of examples of firms in oligopolistic industries that have not been very sensitive to the wishes of U.S. consumers in recent years? Do you think the increase of global competition, even among very large firms, minimizes the market power of oligopolies (i.e., forces them to be more attentive to change and the preferences of consumers)?

13. Do you think large corporations tend to provide a certain dynamism to the economy, or do you think they obstruct progress?

▰ VIDEO OLIGOPOLY

At the local level, most communities have a host of video stores, with a good bit of competition among them in terms of inventory, pricing, membership fees, parking convenience, etc. However, the national market has one clear, emerging giant, Blockbuster. Will Blockbuster, with its vast supply of recent titles, global distribution system, and healthy complement of older movies, drive out the smaller, local video stores? Will local firms be able to find their own niche in the market and discover methods of staying in business? Or will TV cable companies saturate the public's demand for movies with direct provision of numerous movie channels, as well as the possibility of access to video libraries? What difference will these trends make for consumers?

THE IMPORTANCE OF NONCOMPETITIVE MARKETS IN THE U.S. ECONOMY

The models of noncompetitive market structures are helpful in building a theory of how the U.S. economy operates, because product differentiation and economic concentration are present throughout the real economy. The following data on economic concentration demonstrate the pervasiveness and importance of concentrated markets in the United States.

TABLE 10.2 Share of Value of Shipments Accounted for by the Largest Companies in Selected High-Concentration Industries, 1982

Industry	Four Largest Firms	Eight Largest Firms	Twenty Largest Firms
Chewing gum	95%	withheld	withheld
Household refrigerators and freezers	94	98%	99%
Motor vehicles and car bodies	92	97	99[†]
Electric lamps (bulbs)	91	96	98
Cigarettes	90*	100*	—
Primary copper	87[†]	100[†]	—
Cereal breakfast foods	86	withheld	withheld
Flat glass	85	withheld	withheld
Tanks and tank components	85	95	99
Malt beverages	77	94	99
Photographic equipment and supplies	74	86	91
Carbon black	73	100	—
Aircraft engines and parts	72	83	91
Sewing machines	72	82	93
Guided missiles and space vehicles	71	96	100
Tires and inner tubes	66	86	98
Roasted coffee	65	76	90
Primary aluminum	64	88	100
Phonograph records and prerecorded tapes	61	71	81
Soap and other detergents	60	73	83
Cookies and crackers	59	71	85
Metal cans	50	68	89
Radio and TV receiving sets	49	70	86
Elevators and moving stairways	47	65	82
Distilled liquor	46	68	89
Petroleum refining	28	48	76

[†]1977

*1989

Source: Bureau of the Census, 1982 *Census of Manufacturers*, and *Busines Week*, February 19, 1990.

In 1963, the 100 largest manufacturing corporations accounted for

- 25 percent of all domestic manufacturing employees,
- 32 percent of domestic manufacturing payrolls,
- 33 percent of value added in manufacturing,
- 43 percent of after-tax profits in manufacturing,
- 34 percent of domestic manufacturing sales, and
- 36 percent of domestic manufacturing assets.

In 1950, the top 200 corporations in the United States controlled 48 percent of all corporate assets. In 1960, they controlled 56 percent; in 1965, it was 57 percent; in 1975, it increased to 58 percent; and it had reached 60 percent by 1981.

In the post–World War II period, the top 50 industrial corporations have accounted for 25 percent annually of value added in manufacturing; the top 100 have accounted for 33 percent. The share of the top 200 has increased from 30 percent in 1947 to 40 percent in 1962, 43 percent in 1970, and 44 percent in 1977.

In 1993, the 500 largest industrial corporations accounted for

- over 75 percent of final sales in the manufacturing sector of the economy,
- about 20 percent of total profits in the economy, and
- about 11 percent of employment in the whole economy.

Given the shift to service production during the 1980s and 1990s, corporate power in the economy has recently shifted away from the industrial sector. In Chapter 12, we will explore the dimensions and implications of the corporate sector of the economy in more detail.

Tables 10.2 and 10.3 show the concentration ratios in various U.S. industries. The **concentration ratio** is the percentage of total sales in an industry that is accounted for by a specific number of firms. Usually, if the ratio is above 50 percent for the four largest firms in an industry, we say that the industry is an oligopoly. By this standard, most of the industries in Table 10.2 are oligopolistic. If one firm had 100 percent of a national market, it would be a monopoly. If the eight largest firms had less than 10 percent of industry sales and there were many other firms in the industry, we would say that the market was close to being competitive. Table 10.3 lists some markets with relatively low concentration ratios; these have some of the characteristics of monopolistic competition. These two tables demonstrate the importance of concentration in the American economy. Most of the leading sectors of the U.S. economy are heavily concentrated—hence the relevance of models of noncompetitive market structures.

TABLE 10.3 Share of Value of Shipments Accounted for by the Largest Companies in Selected Low-Concentration Industries, 1982

Industry	Four Largest Firms	Eight Largest Firms	Twenty Largest Firms
Wood pallets and skids	5	8	15
Ready-mixed concrete	6	9	16
Commercial printing, lithographic	6	10	17
Women's and misses' dresses	6	10	17
Signs and advertising displays	6	10	18
Typesetting	7	10	16
Miscellaneous plastic products	7	10	17
Plating and polishing	7	11	18
Concrete blocks and bricks	8	12	19
Women's and misses' blouses	8	14	27
Metal doors, sash and trim	11	17	30
Wood kitchen cabinets	12	19	29
Fur goods	12	19	33
Boat building and repairing	14	22	35
Bottled and canned soft drinks	14	23	39
Brass, bronze, and copper foundries	16	23	38
Fluid milk	16	27	48
Sawmills and planing mills	17	23	34
Sporting and athletic goods	17	28	44
Women's and misses' suits and coats	19	28	40
Men's and boys' dress shirts and nightwear	19	29	48
Newspapers	22	34	49
Men's and boys' suits and coats	25	37	57

Source: Bureau of the Census, 1982 *Census of Manufacturers.*

Table 10.4 presents some more recent information in a slightly different format. For the industries listed, it indicates the number of firms in the industry with more than 100 employees, the percentage of those firms compared to the total number of firms in the industry, and the share of the value of total industry shipments accounted for by the firms with more than 100 employees. The most concentrated industries are at the top of the table, with the largest firms accounting for more than 90 percent of the industries' shipments; the least concentrated industries are at the bottom of the table.

14. Examine Tables 10.2, 10.3, and 10.4. Are you surprised by the high or low concentration ratios of any industries in these tables? Do the industries exhibit the characteristics of monopolistic competition and/or oligopoly? Explain.

15. Can you offer explanations for why some of the industries in Table 10.2 (and 10.4) are oligopolies, and why some of the industries in Table 10.3 (and 10.4) are less concentrated?

TABLE 10.4 Selected Industries, Indicative of Concentration

Industry	Number of Establishments with 100+ Employees	% of Establishments with 100+ Employees	% of Industry Shipment Values by Establishments with 100+ Employees
Guided missiles and space vehicles	34	85.0%	99.5%
Vehicles and bodies	108	26.2	99.4
Primary aluminum	24	49.1	99.1
Breakfast cereal	26	49.1	98.8
Malt beverages	45	33.6	98.7
Home refrigerators	19	38.8	98.6
Tires and inner tubes	70	42.9	97.9
Sanitary paper	72	54.1	96.9
Woven cotton	106	35.2	96.9
Aircraft engine parts	149	34.3	96.6
Light bulbs	46	36.2	96.6
Navigation equipment	245	22.6	96.6
Flat glass	23	27.4	96.3
Cheese	81	12.8	96.1
Paper mills	217	77.0	94.3
Pharmaceuticals	181	24.7	93.9
Vehicle parts	595	21.2	93.0
Greeting cards	28	17.3	92.8
Photo equipment and supplies	74	9.4	92.0
Chewing tobacco	11	37.9	91.6
Batteries	74	38.9	91.5
Cookies and crackers	88	23.2	91.5
Women's blouses	194	13.0%	44.7%
Dolls and toys	9	4.6	43.5
Jewelry	58	2.5	40.6
Soft drinks	320	26.9	33.1
Signs and displays	112	3.0	32.4
Women's dresses	168	3.1	31.7
Metal heat treating	21	2.9	29.6
Marking devices	9	1.4	28.1
Plating and polishing	91	2.6	26.2
Typesetting	45	1.3	23.6
Ready-mixed concrete	87	1.6	14.0
Prepared feeds	29	1.7	11.4
Industrial gases	7	1.2	11.0
Wood pallets and skids	17	1.0	9.1
Concrete blocks and bricks	7	0.6	4.3

Source: Bureau of the Census, 1987 *Census of Manufacturers.*

SOURCES OF CONCENTRATION IN THE ECONOMY

Several factors have contributed to increasing concentration and centralization in the economy over the last century. First, legislation and government policy have promoted both competition and monopoly. Governments have granted legal monopolies. In addition, the government has provided support and assistance to several industries with a high degree of concentration—for example, railroads, airlines, defense, and automobiles. On the other hand, antitrust legislation and some regulatory legislation are designed to promote competition. The goal is to control the adverse results of market power by splitting up companies, preventing mergers, prosecuting price setting and other noncompetitive activities, and regulating monopolies. These laws are based on economic arguments; our theory has demonstrated that competitive markets tend to produce efficiency, consumer sovereignty, and the "invisible hand," and that noncompetitive markets, with market power and economic concentration, do not operate as well. One could argue over how well the antitrust laws have been enforced and whether they have prevented the accumulation of economic power by many industries and large firms.

16. Articulate why the government ought to promote competition and prevent extreme economic concentration and market power.

Business policies and practices, including trusts, pools, holding companies, and mergers, also have tended to create monopolies and oligopolies. If competition tends to eliminate economic profits, then one way to ensure long-run profits is to eliminate competition. Many firms have amassed substantial economic power in their markets and in the economy at large. The elimination of cutthroat competition through bankruptcy, mergers, and so on has decreased the number of competitors in many industries. The auto industry comprised more than 100 companies in the late 1920s. Several merger waves in U.S. economic history have produced increased economic concentration. Corporate America experienced a wave of "unfriendly" mergers in the 1980s, in which a company was merged with another against its will. The merger continues to be a strategy of firms to increase market share and economic power.

Technology has developed in some industries to the extent that large-scale operations are necessary for efficiency. This trend promotes large firms and oligopoly. Technology allows some firms to take advantage of economies of scale and outpace their competitors, which then fall by the wayside. An argument in favor of oligopoly, in fact, is that it can use some of its oligopoly profits to finance research to further advance technology (and presumably its own oligopoly power!).

Capitalism's economic freedom of enterprise is permissive of the growth of private corporations. With a motive of profit making and a laissez-faire attitude by government, the creation of economic power has been tolerated (and even lauded by some) in U.S. economic history.

CONCLUSION

Whatever the reasons for noncompetitive markets, we can still conclude that they are theoretically inferior to competitive markets in terms of consumers' and society's preferences. Resources *are* allocated throughout the noncompetitive sectors of the U.S. economy, but noncompetitive markets and prices do not produce the ideals of the "invisible hand," consumer sovereignty, and efficiency, as do competitive markets (theoretically). Adam Smith, where are you, and what would you think?

In the next chapter, we will shift our attention to the operation of resource markets and examine the factors that influence resource prices. One important result of resource markets is that they determine the incomes of resource owners. We will also take a look at the distribution of income in the United States.

Review Questions

1. What are the theoretically adverse results of monopoly markets?
2. What benefits might be derived from oligopoly to offset its inefficiencies and higher prices? Can you give some examples?
3. Why do you think the automobile industry is not competitive, according to our model of competition? What evidence can you cite to show its noncompetitiveness and inefficiency?
4. Why is local phone service a monopoly? What would happen if it weren't?
5. What would happen to the marijuana "industry" if it were legalized in the United States? What kind of market is it now?
6. If you were the adviser for an OPEC country that had relatively low levels of petroleum reserves, would you advise the setting of high or low prices? Why? What if you were advising a country with extensive reserves?
7. In the mid-1990s, the Walt Disney movie *Pocahontas* premiered. It was accompanied by a new line of toys. What kind of market is this? Can you think of other examples of this kind of phenomenon?

11

Resource Markets and the Distribution of Income

INTRODUCTION

In the last two chapters, we developed models of competitive and noncompetitive markets for produced goods and services. As we mentioned previously, there are also markets for the resources used by firms in production. (It's a bit more complicated than that, since some firms produce raw materials used by other firms as factors of production.) The basic resources of the society are mental and/or physical labor, land and its raw materials, and capital.

Resource markets are important for two primary reasons. First of all, resource prices determine costs for firms. Second, since individuals own resources, the operation of resource markets forms the basis of the distribution of income in the society.

In this chapter, we will explore the operation and significance of resource markets—including the determination of resource prices and the allocation of resources throughout the economy. We will also examine the distribution of income in the United States and attempt to explain why it is relatively unequal.

THE ECONOMICS OF RESOURCE MARKETS

There are markets for all resources because they are productive; they are used to produce goods and services sold in markets. The demand for resources is thus a **derived demand**, meaning these resources are demanded for the production of the final product.

In the following discussion, for the sake of simplicity, we will concentrate on one resource to illustrate the general operation of resource markets. While we could develop models of the markets for raw materials, land, and

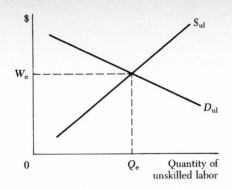

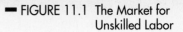
■ FIGURE 11.1 The Market for Unskilled Labor

capital, we will present a model of the market for unskilled labor as an example. It is one of the broadest of labor markets. The number of people who could work in a McDonald's restaurant or do unskilled work in a factory is about equal to the size of the labor force in the United States—now over 120 million people. And there are many businesses that hire unskilled workers.

Like all markets, this one has a demand side and a supply side. Figure 11.1 illustrates the market for unskilled labor. On the supply side of the market, there is a positive relationship between wages offered and the amount of unskilled labor supplied by workers. The higher the wage, the greater the amount of labor supplied. On the demand side, there is an inverse relationship between wages and the amount of unskilled labor demanded by employers. The higher the wage, the lower the amount of unskilled labor that employers will want to use.

This market, with large numbers of suppliers and demanders, will determine an equilibrium wage and quantity for unskilled workers. That wage influences a firm's potential costs and its decisions about how much of this resource to use (compared with other resources). The wage also determines the decisions that workers make about offering their labor to employers (or not) and influences their incomes.

In a general way, this model applies to other resource markets. To see how resource markets work, let's explore both sides of this market in a little more depth.

Demand for a Resource

The demand for any resource is derived from consumers' demands for goods and services and from producers' "demands" for profitable enterprise. But we can be much more specific about the nature of the firm's demand for a resource.

Remember, the firm's objective is to maximize profits, the difference between total revenues and total costs. Whenever a firm uses a resource, the firm's costs and revenues are both affected. If a firm uses one unit of a resource, how much will its costs increase? If a McDonald's restaurant hires one more unskilled worker to be a cook, its costs will go up by the worker's wage times the number of hours worked. The firm's costs increase by the price of the resource, and that price is determined in a market. The added cost of the resource, or its **marginal factor cost** (MFC), equals its price:

$$\text{MFC} = \text{price of the resource.}$$

In this case, we find the marginal factor cost of unskilled labor:

$$\text{MFC}_{ul} = P_{ul}$$

where P_{ul} is the wage of unskilled labor. Since the market is competitive, the firm will be able to use as much of that resource as it wants at that price.

The second effect of using more of a resource is that it adds to the firm's revenues if demand is elastic. Why? Because it adds to the firm's output, and that output presumably gets sold in a product market. In fact, the addition to the firm's revenues, which we will call the **marginal revenue product** (MRP) of unskilled labor, equals the **marginal physical product** of unskilled labor (MPP_{ul}) times the marginal revenue of the product (MR_x):

$$\text{MRP}_{ul} = \text{MPP}_{ul} \times \text{MR}_x$$

The marginal physical product is the extra output from adding one more unit of a variable resource. For unskilled labor, MPP_{ul} is the additional output from adding one additional worker to the production process (with other factors held constant). Table 11.1 shows the marginal physical product in terms of the number of Big Macs produced in one hour as McDonald's hires additional cooks. For example, the MPP of the sixth worker is three Big Macs. Notice that the output from this variable resource follows the law of diminishing returns.

What happens to the extra output in the example? It will be sold for the market price of Big Macs. If we assume, for ease of analysis, that McDonald's is in a competitive market, then the marginal revenue of a Big Mac equals the price of a Big Mac (that is, they are both constant). The firm's additional rev-

TABLE 11.1 The Marginal Physical Product of Unskilled Labor

Number of Workers	Total Output of Big Macs	Marginal Physical Product of Unskilled Labor
1	20	—
2	27	7
3	34	7
4	40	6
5	44	4
6	47	3
7	49	2

enue from hiring one more unit of unskilled labor comes from the extra output produced and then sold.

Given that using more of the resource has a marginal effect on the firm's costs and revenues, it should not surprise you that a firm maximizes its profits by choosing the amount of a resource for which the marginal contribution to the firm's revenues equals the marginal contribution to the firm's costs:

$$\text{MFC}_{ul} = \text{MRP}_{ul}.$$

This is illustrated in Figure 11.2. Since MPP_{ul} is decreasing due to the law of diminishing returns and MR_x is constant if the firm sells its product in a competitive market, MRP_{ul} decreases as we add more unskilled labor (along the horizontal axis). MFC_{ul} is equal to the prevailing wage in the market for unskilled labor.

To maximize profits, this firm would use L_1 of unskilled labor, since that is where $\text{MFC}_{ul} = \text{MRP}_{ul}$. If the firm uses less unskilled labor, the firm's revenues from using one more worker exceed the extra cost of using an additional unit (e.g., at L_2). Therefore, expanding the use of the resource would add to the firm's profits. At levels above L_1, the cost of adding the resource exceeds what it adds to the firm's revenues. If the firm uses unskilled labor beyond L_1, the firm's profits will decrease. (Notice that we are assuming the demand for the product is constant; this is reflected in the marginal revenue the firm receives for selling additional units of output.)

1. Assume that the minimum wage for unskilled workers is $4 an hour and that the price of a Big Mac is $1. Given the information in Table 11.1, how many workers would McDonald's hire? Why?

Profit maximization leads a firm to choose a specific amount of a resource to use in its productive activities. In addition, the marginal revenue product curve in Figure 11.2 represents the firm's demand curve for this resource. Remember, a demand curve shows the amounts of a good or service that will be demanded at different possible prices. If the price of unskilled labor were

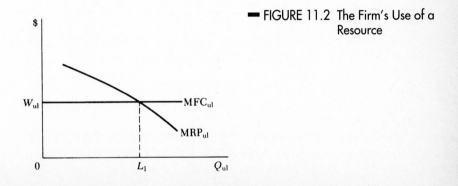

■ FIGURE 11.2 The Firm's Use of a Resource

lower, with everything else the same, the firm would hire additional workers; if the price were higher, the firm would hire fewer workers. The MRP_{ul} curve, then, gives us the firm's demand for unskilled labor.

The firm's demand for a resource is thus determined by the productivity of the resource, the importance of that resource in producing the good, and the price of the good itself.

> 2. Using Figure 11.2, explain why a firm would hire fewer work-ers if the price of the resource were higher.
> 3. Show what would happen to the demand for unskilled labor if there were an increase in the demand for Big Macs.

Supply of a Resource

As we pointed out earlier in this chapter, in general the amount supplied of a resource increases as its price increases. If the wage for unskilled work increased, for example, we would expect the amount of unskilled labor offered to increase. From the workers' perspective, the wage for labor indi-cates the opportunity cost of time. An increase in a wage or a salary makes time more valuable and, in most cases, encourages people to work more. From the perspective of an employer, the wage indicates the opportunity cost for the resource; it is what the firm must pay to get that resource to work for it. In a similar manner, buildings and land earn rent, raw materials have prices, capital or money earns interest, and professional workers get salaries.

The sensitivity of a resource to the price offered for its productive services varies over time. That is, the elasticity of supply of a resource can differ in the short run and long run. In the short run, the amount of a resource supplied depends on the mobility of the resource to different possible uses. For exam-ple, for unskilled workers, raising the wage at McDonald's would most likely lead to a significant increase in the number of people willing to work there. (Remember, a supply curve is a hypothetical construction; it shows the amounts supplied at different possible prices.) Many individuals are available to work for the relatively low wages in fast foods and would be attracted by a higher wage. This means that the supply of unskilled labor is relatively elas-tic. On the other hand, if wages increased for computer programmers, some time is necessary for the amount of programmers supplied in the United States to increase, because of the training necessary. For computer program-mers, then, the supply is somewhat inelastic in the short run. For buildings and machinery, supply is relatively inelastic in the short run because time is required to construct them or to free existing ones for other uses.

In the short run, the supply of a resource can be elastic or inelastic, depending on the type of resource. Price increases (or decreases) will produce large or small responses in the quantity supplied, depending on the nature and qualities of the resource.

In the long run, the supply of most resources is more elastic. The long-run supply of any resource depends on decisions about the development of resources, which are in turn determined by expected rates of return. People decide to go to college depending on the expected payoff from graduating. That decision consequently influences the supply of professional employees. Decisions about graduate, law, or medical school involve the same calculation, which eventually affects the supply of Ph.D.s, lawyers, and doctors.

These factors determine the supply curves for resources. And, as we suggested at the beginning of this chapter, the supply-and-demand conditions for resources, taken together, produce resource prices. Markets for resources establish resource prices.

What other factors influence resource prices? Legislation may affect the wage paid to certain types of workers, as in the case of the minimum wage. Licensing requirements affect the supply of hair stylists, real estate agents, and many professional workers. Unions can control the supply of certain types of workers through apprenticeship programs, seniority systems, and membership dues. Cartels and trade associations can influence some resource prices. Finally, the general state of the economy and the level of unemployment profoundly affect wages and salaries. The higher the level of unemployment, in general, the lower the wages of unskilled and semiskilled workers.

4. Why would higher rates of unemployment put downward pressure on wages?
5. Wages in Alaska are relatively high. Why would the elasticity of supply for labor partially explain this?

THE ECONOMICS OF THE MINIMUM WAGE

Our assumption that the wage for unskilled labor is determined by the supply and demand for that resource (see Figure 11.1) is a slight oversimplification. In fact, whenever interstate commerce is involved, employers must pay workers at least the minimum wage. This wage is mandated by congressional legislation, and it has progressively increased throughout the post–World War II period. During the 1980s it was constant at $3.35 an hour. In 1990 it increased to $3.80, and in 1991 it increased to $4.20. By early 1996 the minimum wage had increased a nickel, to $4.25. In mid-1996 Congress passed legislation that increased the minimum wage to $5.15. (States may set their own minimum wage higher than this level.)

The intent of this legislated minimum wage is to require employers to pay a wage higher than the rate determined by the market for unskilled labor. It is meant to support the incomes of people who work in low-wage jobs, and it was motivated by a concern for fairness. The people who hold low-wage jobs usually have little experience or few skills. In other words, their marginal productivities are relatively low. Also, the products they produce may have low market values. Dishwashers get low wages; doctors, lawyers, and engineers earn much more. In addition, with any amount of unemployment, there is ample supply of unskilled workers.

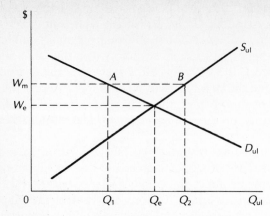

■ FIGURE 11.3 Effect of Minimum-Wage Laws on Unskilled-Labor Market

These factors produce a market that can be illustrated with the supply and demand curves shown in Figure 11.3. The equilibrium wage would be at W_e, but legislation mandates a wage above that, at W_m.

What are the results of the minimum wage? At W_m, employers hire Q_1 of unskilled workers. But Q_2 workers are willing to work at W_m. Hence, there is a surplus of unskilled workers—unemployment of unskilled workers equal to AB. Those who have jobs have higher incomes than they would have at a wage of W_e. But Figure 11.3 shows that the minimum wage has increased unemployment among unskilled workers.

Some economists and politicians have argued that lowering the minimum wage would decrease unemployment. The Reagan administration several times suggested a lower minimum wage for teenage workers. Along with the increase in the minimum wage in 1990, Congress created a "training wage" for teenage workers for six months of initial employment. The basis of the argument lies in Figure 11.3. If the wage were reduced to W_e, there would be an increase in the amount of unskilled labor demanded and a decrease in the amount of unskilled labor supplied. At Q_e, an equilibrium amount would be supplied and demanded—no unemployment in this market! Employers would tend to use more unskilled workers.

But several critical questions can be raised about this analysis. Seven of every ten workers earning a minimum wage are over twenty years of age. Sixty percent of all women workers work in minimum-wage jobs. Employers might replace older, higher-paid workers with younger, lower-paid workers, which would only shift the incidence of unemployment and would not necessarily reduce the overall amount of unemployment. And what about the difference between Q_2 and Q_e in terms of the amount of unskilled labor supplied? One effect of lowering the minimum wage would be that some teenagers would prefer to spend their summers doing something other than working for a "subminimum wage." Does that mean they are not unemployed?

The minimum wage does not create unemployment. To some extent, it may exacerbate unemployment because it tends to reduce the amount of unskilled labor demanded and increase the amount supplied. But the reasons for unemployment among low-wage, inexperienced, and unskilled workers have more to do with the overall level of economic activity than with the minimum wage.

In addition, even though the minimum wage increased from $2.10 in 1975 to $4.25 by 1996 (which led some people to argue that it has increased unemployment), in real terms (after taking inflation into account) the minimum wage has continually decreased throughout that period. By 1996, the purchasing power of the minimum wage was the lowest it had been in forty years. A family of three supported by a single minimum-wage worker would earn an income that would place the family 27 percent below the 1996 poverty level of income. Since the "real" minimum wage has decreased, it ought to have produced an increase in the amount of unskilled labor demanded by employers (ceteris paribus).

At any rate, over time, numerous other factors have changed that have also affected the supply and demand for unskilled labor. Thus, the claim that reducing the minimum wage would relieve unemployment is oversimplified. One recent study by David Card and Alan Krueger indicated that raising the minimum wage would not exacerbate unemployment.

6. Over 3.5 million people work in the fast-food industry in the United States. Some 70 percent of them are seventeen to twenty years old. Given the analysis that we have developed about a firm's demand for a resource, show how lowering the minimum wage should increase the amount of unskilled labor that McDonald's, for example, might hire.
7. Do you think there should be a lower minimum wage for teenage workers? Explain.

THE DISTRIBUTION OF INCOME

In Chapter 4 we examined the division of income among the different factors of production in a private, market economy: Labor gets wages, landowners get rent, and owners of capital get profits. Adam Smith concluded that any conflict over the distribution of income would be resolved, to the benefit of all, by the operation of the competitive market system. However, there are some other ways of looking at income distribution. A society may decide that the way markets distribute income is undesirable.

In a market system, the distribution of income tends to be fairly unequal. Why? As we have suggested, income is derived from the participation of resources in productive activity. Income is paid to the factors of production for their involvement in the production process. The incomes that individuals earn therefore depend on the resources they own and the prices they command in resource markets. Some individuals have only their unskilled labor power to sell; consequently, they tend to have low incomes. People who possess professional skills, work experience, or capital resources will have higher incomes.

Quintile	Percentage of Total Income	Income Range ($)
Lowest 20%	4.4	0–19,070
Second 20%	10.1	19,071–32,985
Third 20%	15.8	32,986–48,985
Fourth 20%	23.2	48,986–72,260
Highest 20%	46.5	Above 72,260
Top 5%	20.0	Above 123,656

Source: *Current Population Reports,* Series P60, Tables F1 and F2, U.S. Census Bureau, 1997.

The Size Distribution of Income

What is the actual distribution of income in the United States? A convenient and instructive method of examining the distribution of income is to group people in families and then rank them by income. The result is called the **size distribution of income**. Table 11.2 shows the size distribution of income for the United States in 1995. It covers all before-tax income—including governmental transfer payments such as Social Security and veterans' benefits, unemployment compensation, and welfare—for the 69.5 million American families. When all of the families are ranked by income from the highest to the lowest, we take each successive 20 percent (13.9 million) of the families, add up all of their incomes, and take that income as a percentage of total income. For example, the bottom 20 percent of the families received 4.4 percent of total family income in 1995, the middle 20 percent got 15.8 percent of total income, and the top 20 percent got 46.5 percent.

Table 11.2 also shows the ranges of income for each successive 20 percent. For example, families with incomes below $19,070 found themselves in the bottom 20 percent. If a family's income was $50,000 in 1995, it was in the fourth quintile. To get into the top 5 percent of family income required at least $123,656.

These statistics indicate a relatively unequal distribution of income. The 13.9 million families at the bottom of the income ladder got only 4.4 percent of total family income, while the same number of families at the top got 46.5 percent. The top 5 percent (more than 3.5 million families with incomes over $123,656) got more than six times as much income as the poorest 20 percent. If income were distributed equally, each 20 percent would get 20 percent of total income.

No society has a totally equal distribution of income. Table 11.3 shows that many of the Western and Northern European countries have distributions of income that are significantly less unequal than that in the United States. Many poor countries in Latin America, Africa, and Asia have very unequal income distributions.

A **Lorenz curve** illustrates the degree of inequality in the distribution of income. Figure 11.4 shows a Lorenz curve based on the distribution of income in the United States in 1995. The horizontal axis measures each 20

Country	Year	Lowest 20%	Second 20%	Third 20%	Fourth 20%	Highest 20%	Highest 10%
United States	1985	4.7	11.0	17.4	25.0	41.9	25.0
United Kingdom	1979	5.8	11.5	18.2	25.0	39.5	23.3
Netherlands	1983	6.0	13.2	17.9	23.7	38.3	23.0
France	1979	6.3	12.1	17.2	23.5	40.8	25.5
Canada	1987	5.7	11.8	17.7	24.6	40.2	24.1
Sweden	1981	8.0	13.2	17.4	24.5	36.9	20.8
Japan	1979	8.7	13.3	17.5	23.1	37.5	22.4
Brazil	1983	2.4	5.7	10.7	18.6	62.6	46.2
Malaysia	1987	2.6	9.3	13.9	21.2	51.2	34.8
Botswana	1985	2.5	6.5	11.8	20.2	59.0	42.8
Colombia	1988	4.0	8.7	13.5	20.8	53.0	37.1
Guatemala	1984	9.8	13.0	16.4	21.4	39.4	25.4
Sri Lanka	1985	4.8	8.5	12.1	18.4	56.1	43.0

Source: OECD, 1992.

percent of the families, and the vertical axis measures their cumulative shares of total income. The bottom 20 percent got 4.4 percent of total income, the lowest 40 percent got 14.4 percent, and so on. If income were distributed equally, we would get a straight Lorenz curve at a 45° angle. Instead we get the curved line in Figure 11.4.

The degree of inequality can be measured by taking the area between the straight line and the Lorenz curve (area *A*) and comparing it to the area below the 45° line (area *A* plus area *B*). The technical name for this ratio is the **Gini coefficient**. The lower this ratio, the lower the degree of inequality; the higher the ratio, the greater the degree of inequality. In 1960, the Gini coefficient for the distribution of income in the United States was 0.364; in 1970, it was 0.390; and in 1995, it was 0.445.

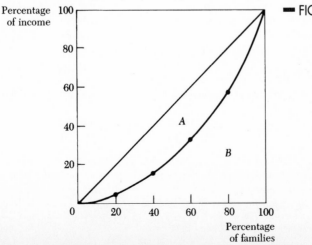

FIGURE 11.4 Lorenz Curve and Gini Coefficient Measurement

8. Should income distribution be more equal than it is? Explain.
9. According to the Gini coefficient, the distribution of income in the United States became less unequal from 1960 to 1970 and then more unequal from 1970 through 1993. There was a slight move toward more equality in 1995. Can you suggest some reasons why this may have happened? What do you suppose has happened to the degree of inequality in income distribution since 1995?

Why is income distributed so unequally in the United States? Fundamentally, it is a function of the ownership of resources and the prices of those resources. Individuals possess different labor and nonlabor resources, and different resources get different prices. Furthermore, the private market system relies on those very differences to allocate and motivate resources.

The Influence of Property

The U.S. economy is basically a capitalist system with private property as one of its most fundamental characteristics. The ownership of land, money, and capital resources is even more unequally distributed than income. Wealth statistics for the United States are not readily available, but studies done in the early and mid-1980s show that the poorest families have very little in financial and personal assets.

Tables 11.4 and 11.5 both show that income-producing forms of wealth are even more unequally distributed than general forms of wealth. According to Table 11.4, the median financial assets of families in 1995 totaled $13,000, with the median for white families reaching $16,900 and the median for "nonwhite" and Hispanic families at $5,200. Table 11.5 shows the shares of different forms of personal wealth (other than personal assets such as private homes)—real estate, savings accounts, corporate stocks, bonds, and so on—owned by the richest 10 percent and the richest 1 or 2 percent of all persons. For example, the richest 1 percent (about 650,000 families) held 37 percent of all net worth, 45 percent of all stock, 43 percent of all non-owner-occupied residential real estate, and 65 percent of bonds. Other financial assets, including individual checking account deposits, automobiles, owner-occupied residential real estate, are more evenly distributed among the population.

▬ TABLE 11.4 Distribution of Financial Wealth in the United States, 1995

Family Income	Median Financial Assets
Under $10,000	$ 1,200
$10,000–$24,999	5,400
$25,000–$49,999	12,100
$50,000–$99,000	40,700
$100,000 and more	214,500

Source: *Federal Reserve Bulletin*, January 1997.

TABLE 11.5 Distribution of Wealth

| | Percent of Total Assets Held by Families | | | |
| | Richest 10% | | Richest 2% | Richest 1% |
Asset	1983	1989	1983	1989
Total net worth	64%	68.0%	54%	37.0%
Stock	72	82.1	50	44.8
Bonds	70	93.5	39	65.2
Business equity		90.0		
Real estate*	50	82.1	20	43.0
Life Insurance		38.0		12.0
Cars		5.0		22.0

*Excludes owner-occupied homes.

Sources: *New York Times,* April 21, 1992; *Federal Reserve Bulletin,* January 1992.

Note: In the Federal Reserve survey, families were asked the total value of their financial assets, including cash, checking and savings accounts, certificates of deposit, savings bonds, money market funds, stocks, bonds, and trusts.

The unequal distribution of wealth contributes to the unequal distribution of income in the United States. Households with the highest 20 percent of income earned close to 70 percent of the property income generated in 1993. Households in the lowest quintile of the income distribution earned only about 1 percent of the property income generated.

   10. Do you or your family members own any income-producing wealth?

The Influence of Labor Incomes

Approximately 60 percent of personal income in the United States comes from wages and salaries. This percentage is higher for families in the middle of the income distribution. Like property income, income from mental and physical labor is unequally distributed. There are a variety of reasons for the differences in wages and salaries that individuals receive for their contributions to economic activity. The labor that people perform is not homogeneous, and there are differences in the jobs that people hold.

The capabilities, training, and intelligence of individuals have a great deal to do with their respective incomes. Consequently, the distribution of these attributes contributes to an unequal distribution of income. Some people are more productive in certain tasks than others are. For example, someone with physical strength probably can lift and stack more bales of hay in an hour than someone with less strength; someone with mathematical aptitude can balance a firm's books more quickly and accurately than someone without such aptitude. Some people, because of their concentration and motivation, produce more than other people in specific activities over a given period of time. In general, the greater an individual's productivity or contribution to economic output, the higher her or his wages will be. (However, despite overall growth in productivity during the 1990s, wage growth stalled for other reasons.)

Different people also have different skills. A large number of people are available for jobs that require minimal skills (e.g., clerks, sales personnel, custodians). As a result, they usually command low wages in labor markets. Others, who make up a smaller segment of the population, have professional skills (doctors, lawyers, economists) or possess unique qualities (athletes, entertainers) that earn them higher incomes. The more specialized the skill or the longer the period of training or education necessary to develop a skill, the higher the wages of people with those skills tend to be. For example, people with college educations, on the average, earn more than people with only high school diplomas.

Age and experience also contribute to the unequal distribution of income. People who are older and have accumulated work experience tend to be paid more than younger, less experienced workers. An English professor who has taught for twenty years in a university earns more than a colleague who has taught for only two years.

Individuals also have different attitudes and preferences about work and income. Some people have a strong preference for work over leisure. Some people have very strong desires to earn high incomes. In fact, capitalism relies on monetary incentives for productive activity, so it has developed a hierarchy of jobs with different levels of pay. People are motivated to work hard in order to move up the job ladder and to get higher incomes.

Racial and sex differences also have an impact on the unequal distribution of income. As we shall see in some detail in the next section, white males in the United States tend to earn higher incomes than nonwhite males, and males tend to earn more than females.

In addition, differences in the kinds of jobs that people perform contribute to inequality in income distribution. The type of work performed and the conditions surrounding it influence compensation. Dangerous or unpleasant work (e.g., coal mining or garbage collection) is often rewarded with premium wages. Some people, on the other hand, may be willing to give up higher wages in return for significant control over the work that they do. Teachers or people who work for small businesses tend to be paid less than people whose work is more directly controlled by supervisors or institutional demands. The organizational structure of employment also influences wages and salaries. People who work for large corporations tend to earn more. Workers who are members of labor unions usually have higher wages than nonunion workers (see Chapter 12). Finally, the location of a job may influence an individual's remuneration. Someone who works in Idaho tends to be paid less than a person who works in Los Angeles with exactly the same job, skills, and experience.

||| 11. Why is the payoff for a college degree higher for men than for women?

Many factors account for the differences in the wages and salaries people earn for the work that they do, and these factors help to explain the inequality of income distribution in the United States. Most of the explanations just given imply that market forces play an important role in determining the different wages and salaries individuals receive in our society. The necessity of a medical education, for example, limits the supply of doctors and hence tends to increase their incomes. The widespread demand of moviegoers and video purchasers for films starring Will Smith, Denzel Washington, Mel Gibson, or Julia Roberts accounts for their astronomical incomes.

On the other hand, many nonmarket conditions also influence people's wages and salaries. In the United States, women do most of the work related to household management and child care, and their work is often unpaid. People's class backgrounds have an impact on the development of their skills and attitudes toward work. Luck—being in the right place at the right time— can influence the jobs and incomes people have.

Income from wages and salaries is somewhat more equally distributed among households than overall income. However, labor incomes tend to be positively related to property income; that is, those with high labor incomes are also likely to have property income. This further contributes to the unequal distribution of income.

Transfer Income

As we noted earlier, in measuring income distribution, we calculate household income before taxes and include governmental transfer payments such as Social Security and veterans' benefits, unemployment compensation, and welfare payments. While property income is positively related to wage and salary income, transfer income largely goes to those at the lower end of the income distribution spectrum.

Some transfer payments are non-means-tested government programs, including such programs as Social Security, unemployment compensation, and some veterans' benefits. Other programs, including Aid to Families with Dependent Children (AFDC), Supplemental Security Income (SSI), and some veterans' benefits are means-tested, so recipients must meet minimum income and/or other requirements before the transfer is awarded. While the means-tested transfer payments are allocated to low-income individuals and families, Social Security—by far the largest transfer program—is not.

How much do transfer payments influence income distribution in the United States? Table 11.6 shows the impact on income distribution in 1994. The first column shows the distribution of income as it is commonly defined. Column 2 shows what the distribution would have looked like without transfer income. Column 3 shows the effect of including only non-means-tested transfer income such as Social Security.

When both means- and non-means-tested transfer income is subtracted from the official definition of household income in Table 11.6, income is distributed even more unequally. Without transfer income, the highest 20 percent of income earners would receive about 50.3 percent of the income, and the

TABLE 11.6 Percentage of Aggregate Income Received by Income Quintiles, 1994

Quintile	Percentage of Income	Percentage of Total Income MINUS All Government Transfers & Taxes	Column 2 PLUS Income Value of Non-Means-Tested Transfers
Lowest 20%	3.6	1.0	3.7
Second 20%	9.1	8.1	10.4
Third 20%	15.1	15.7	16.2
Fourth 20%	23.1	24.9	23.7
Highest 20%	49.1	50.3	46.0

Source: Bureau of the Census, *Current Population Reports: Consumer Income*, Series P60-186, Table J, p. xxii.

lowest 20 percent would receive 1 percent of the income. If we add back only the non-means-tested transfers, the largest of which is Social Security, income distribution approaches the actual 1994 levels. This shows that non-means-tested transfers are more significant contributions to households in lower income brackets than means-tested programs. Transfer programs do indeed change the distribution of income; in 1994, they accounted for a 1.2 percent decrease in the percentage of income received by those in the highest quintile and a 4.2 increase in the percentage received by the lowest three quintiles.

In the mid-1990s many of the means-tested transfer programs came under attack in an attempt to significantly alter the U.S. welfare system. AFDC was one of those programs. While we see that means-tested transfer programs do contribute income to families in the lower quintiles, they are less significant contributions than non-means-tested programs. Means-tested transfers are often received by women who head low-income households where children are present.

The Influence of Race and Gender

Another characteristic of income inequality in the United States is that women often earn lower incomes than men and that blacks earn lower incomes than whites. The existence of racism and sexism in our society contributes to income inequality in a number of ways. Racism and sexism are systems of social, political, cultural, ideological, and economic domination, whereby one group has less power and control over decisions and resources than another group. Instances of both racism and sexism are manifested in numerous noneconomic ways in the day-to-day life of our society. In addition, racial minorities and women in the United States are systematically less well off in economic terms than white males.

The racial and ethnic composition of the U.S. population is quite diverse and will change dramatically in the near future. Approximately 83 percent of all Americans are white, while 12.5 percent are black, 4.5 percent are Asian or Native American, and 10 percent are of Hispanic origin (and may be of any race). Blacks, Native Americans, and those of Hispanic origin are more likely to be unemployed than whites. In 1995 the unemployment rate for all white persons over sixteen was 4.9 percent; for blacks, it was 10.4 percent; and for Hispanics, it was 9.3 percent. Members of racial minority populations in the United States are less likely to work in professional and white-collar occupations than whites and are more likely to work in the lower-paying blue-collar and service sector jobs. Over 50 percent of whites work in white-collar jobs, while around 60 percent of blacks and Latinos work in blue-collar and service jobs.

As a consequence of these factors as well as outright racial discrimination, nonwhites in the United States, on the average, earn less than whites do. The data in Table 11.7 compare the median income of black families with that of white families for various years from 1955 to 1994. The median income of black families has consistently been significantly below that of white families. Some of the decline since 1975 reflects an increase in black families headed by women, and some of it reflects the impact of the recessions of the early 1980s and 1990s. Similarly, in 1993, the median income of Hispanic families was 69 percent of the median income of white families.

The incidence of poverty also differs among racial groups. In 1994, the federal government classified 12.2 percent of whites in the United States as being in poverty. The figure for blacks was 33 percent; for Native Americans, 31 percent; for Asians, 15 percent; and for Hispanics, 29 percent.

These data suggest that racial factors have an important impact on the unequal distribution of income in the United States. In a 1982 report to President Reagan, the U.S. Commission on Civil Rights concluded that, despite a generation of civil rights and affirmative-action legislation, discrimination persists "virtually everywhere, at every age level, at every educational level, at every skill level." This statement continues to reflect the reality of poverty data as we approach 2000.

Similarly, women are concentrated in low-paying jobs, tend to work for low-paying concerns, and are "systematically underpaid." A study in 1981, prepared for the Equal Employment Opportunity Commission by the National Research Council (a branch of the National Academy of Sciences) and focusing on the

TABLE 11.7 Median Black Family Income as a Percent of White Family Income

Year	Percentage
1955	55.0
1960	55.0
1965	55.0
1970	61.0
1975	61.5
1980	58.0
1985	58.0
1990	58.0
1994	60.4

Source: *Statistical Abstract of the United States*, 1996, No. 718.

Nicole Hollander, *My Weight Is Always Perfect for My Height—Which Varies*. Reprinted by permission of St. Martin's Press, Inc. © 1982 by Nicole Hollander.

economic position of women, found that "despite the tremendous changes that have occurred in the labor market over the past 20 years, there has been no change in the relative earnings of men and women." When that study was published well over a decade ago (as the cartoon illustrates), women workers earned sixty cents for every dollar earned by a male worker. Today women earn more— moving the ratio of women's earnings to 74 cents for each dollar earned by male workers. Table 11.8 presents information on the incomes of year-round, full-time female workers compared to the incomes of year-round, full-time male workers for various years from 1955 to 1994.

Over the past three decades the participation of women in the paid labor force increased substantially. In 1960, about 40 percent of women over sixteen were in the labor force (working for wages or looking for paid work). By 1980, women's labor force participation rate was up to 52 percent. In 1995, it had increased further, to 59 percent.

Men and women remain segregated into different occupations, and usually women are concentrated in the lower-paying occupations. To eliminate occupational segregation in the workplace, 55 percent of the nation's working men and women would have to switch jobs. A majority of the nation's working women are in occupations that are at least 70 percent female, and one-fourth of

TABLE 11.8 Female Worker Income as a
Percent of Male Worker Income

Year	Percentage
1955	64
1960	60
1965	60
1970	59
1975	59
1980	60
1985	65
1990	71
1994	74

Source: *Statistical Abstract of the United States*, 1996, No. 725.

working women are in occupations that are at least 95 percent female. In the early 1990s, women constituted 82 percent of health services workers, 95 percent of nurses, 99 percent of dental hygienists, 80 percent of clerical workers, 99 percent of secretaries, 86 percent of elementary teachers, and 76 percent of eating, apparel, and accessory store workers. Men constituted 93 percent of engineers, 99 percent of auto mechanics, 99 percent of carpenters, 96 percent of machinists, over 90 percent of upper-level corporate managers, 74 percent of doctors, 70 percent of lawyers and judges, 66 percent of college teachers, 88 percent of guards, police, and firefighters—and 85 percent of economists. For many jobs that require equal educational levels and comparable skills, women are systematically paid less than men. The influence of occupation-linked gender differences and sex discrimination thus also contributes to inequality in the distribution of income in the United States.

12. Why do economic differences based on race and sex persist in the United States?
13. In recent years, the civil rights and women's movements have challenged racism and sexism. These struggles have led to legislation regarding equal opportunity and affirmative-action programs, as well as to some court cases. In a case in Colorado in the late 1970s, a group of nurses sued the city and county of Denver for sex discrimination. Tree trimmers, sign painters, and repairmen were all paid more than nurses. U.S. District Judge Fred Winner decided against the nurses' claim and concluded, "This is a case pregnant with the possibility of disrupting the entire economic system of the United States of America. . . . I'm not going to restructure the entire economy of the U.S." What was Winner worried about? Does the operation of the U.S. economy require that women be paid less than men (even for comparable work)? Why or why not?

Income Distribution and Child Poverty

As some U.S. households have received increasingly lower shares of income, greater numbers of children are living in poverty. In 1994, some 14.6 million

TABLE 11.9 Percentage of Children under Nineteen below the Poverty Line

Year	Total	White	African-American
1959	26.1	18.1	63.1
1969	15.6	10.4	41.1
1979	17.1	11.7	36.1
1990	20.6	15.9	44.8

Source: Haveman and Wolfe, "Children's Prospects and Children's Policy," *Journal of Economic Perspectives*, vol. 7, no. 4, p. 158.

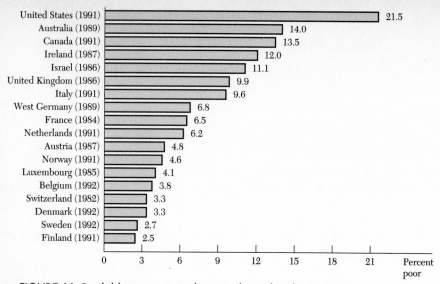

━ FIGURE 11.5 Child Poverty in Eighteen Industrialized Countries

Source: Children's Defense Fund, *The State of America's Children Yearbook,* 1996. © All rights reserved.

children under the age of eighteen, including 5.9 million children under the age of six, were poor. This represents 21.2 percent of all children under eighteen, 24.5 percent of all children under six years of age, and 50 percent of all black children under six. Table 11.9 shows the distribution of child poverty among white and African-American children under nineteen. The risk of an African-American child living in poverty is nearly three times as great as it is for a white child.

Child poverty is dramatically higher in the United States than in other industrial nations. Figure 11.5 shows the results of the Luxembourg Income Study, published in 1995, showing that the percentage of poor young people in the United States was the highest of eighteen industrialized nations. The researchers could not fully determine the causes, but attributed the possible cause to several factors, including the widest gap between the rich and poor among all of the other countries studied.

The past few decades have seen rapid growth in the number of children in poverty who live in homes where a single female is the head of the household. In 1960, 20 percent of all families below the poverty line were headed by women with no husband present. By 1986, this figure had increased to 46 percent. In 1994, 38.6 percent of all female-headed families with children were living in poverty (50.2 percent for black families with female heads). The lower incomes received by women have a detrimental effect on these families. Just over half of all poor children live in female-headed households. Table 11.10 shows that poverty is at least partly due to women household heads working full-time for wages that return less than a poverty level of income.

TABLE 11.10 Labor Market Problems among Women Who Maintain Families

Labor Market Problem	Percentage Having Problem	
	Women at or above Poverty	Women below Poverty
Low earnings	8.5	73.9
Unemployment	9.0	43.3
Involuntary part-time work	5.3	25.0

Source: Bureau of Labor Statistics, "Working and Poor in 1990," *Monthly Labor Review*, December 1992, Table 5.

14. What impact does the federal government have on the distribution of income? How does it affect the distribution of income?

CONCLUSION

In this chapter we have briefly considered the operation of resource markets and the distribution of income in the United States. Resource markets, through the forces of supply and demand, determine the costs of production for firms and the incomes of households. Many factors account for the relatively unequal distribution of income in the United States. People own different resources, the jobs they do are different, and race and sex both influence wages and salaries. Unequal income distribution in turn affects the well-being of families and of the children who live in them.

Review Questions

1. Why is the market for unskilled labor relatively competitive?
2. What influences a firm's demand for a particular resource?
3. A firm tends to use the amount of a resource at which its MRP equals its MFC. Explain why.
4. In the September 17, 1984, issue of *Business Week*, there was an article titled, "The U.S. May Finally Have Too Many Lawyers." Using the economic analysis of resource markets, explain how a surplus of lawyers could happen.
5. Money is a resource; it can be used to finance capital projects. What influences the demand for credit? What influences the supply of credit? What is the price of credit?
6. Polls have reported that a significant majority of people in the United States believe that star athletes, entertainers, and corporate executives are overpaid. In 1995, Val Kilmer was paid $2 million to play Batman in *Batman Forever*, and he was later expected to receive $6 million for his film *The Saint*. In the mid-1990s, the annual salary for superstar baseball players increased to over $6 million. What drives these high salaries? What are the economic effects?

7. Do you think the federal government should develop explicit policies to redistribute income to reduce the inequality of income distribution? Why or why not?
8. What are the sources of inequality in the distribution of income? Which ones might be reformed to reduce income inequality? What political and/or systemic limits are there on the redistribution of income?

12

Corporations and Labor Unions

INTRODUCTION

Now that we have examined the economic theory of competitive and noncompetitive market structures and explored the results of different types of firms, it is worthwhile to take a more "realistic" approach to the firm. The corporation, as a productive unit in the U.S. economic system, has become a dominant institution. In Chapter 10 we saw statistics that showed the impact of the largest U.S. industrial corporations on several economic categories—manufacturing employment, manufacturing assets, and so on. U.S. corporations stand out for consideration in any discussion of production and resource allocation in the United States. Therefore, this chapter will concentrate on U.S. corporations, describing what they are and the economic power they have, and analyzing what that power implies.

In Chapter 11 we surveyed the operation of resource markets. We suggested that in addition to the forces of supply and demand, labor unions have an impact on labor markets. Labor unions have also emerged as important institutions in the structure of the U.S. economy. The chapter will conclude with a brief examination of the history and the effects of labor unions in the economy and how each of these relate to the behavior of corporations.

KINDS OF FIRMS

There are about 25 million businesses in the United States and two-thirds are small businesses. Each year about one million new firms are started—many of which fail. Profit-driven businesses fit into one of three major classifications: (1) sole proprietorships, (2) partnerships, or (3) corporations.

A **sole proprietorship** has a single owner, who has the right to all profits and who bears the unlimited liability for the firm's debts. This kind of busi-

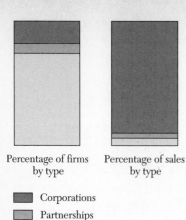

■ FIGURE 12.1 Number and Sales of Each Type of Firm

Source: *The American Almanac: Statistical Abstract of the United States, 1995–1996*, U.S. Bureau of the Census, 1996.

Percentage of firms by type   Percentage of sales by type

- ▮ Corporations
- ▮ Partnerships
- ▯ Sole Proprietorships

ness is simple and easy to organize. The owner is in complete control but must be responsible for investing the money necessary to establish the business. In 1995, sole proprietorships represented 74 percent of all firms in the U.S. economy, yet because they are generally small, they represent only 6 percent of all business sales.

A **partnership** has two or more owners, who share the firm's profits and who bear unlimited liability for the firm's debts. It is often easier to raise the financial resources required to go into business. Partnerships are common in the fields of law, medicine, and accounting. This is the least common form of business organization, making up only 8 percent of all firms and accounting for around 4 percent of all business sales.

Figure 12.1 shows the types of business organization in terms of their number and sales.

THE CORPORATION

A corporation is a legal entity that engages in the provision of goods and services for the public. Corporations have legal authority to enter into contracts with other parties. The characteristic of corporations that distinguishes them from other productive units—such as partnerships or proprietorships—is that the individuals who own the corporations, the stockholders, have limited liability. Stockholders are liable to the corporation's creditors only to the extent of the value of their stock. They cannot be sued by creditors. This differs from other forms of business, in which the individuals who operate the business are personally liable to creditors.

This gives the corporation a great advantage in amassing financial resources to underwrite production. Issues of corporate stock can raise capital, and this capital base can be used to raise further capital through bank loans and so forth. Corporations have used this ability to form large productive operations—large plants, nationwide production and distribution facilities, and even worldwide networks. The technological advances of the Industrial Revolution spurred the development of larger and larger corporations, and modern technology continues to do the same. Through these legal advantages and historical developments, many U.S. corporations have grown to be quite large in terms of assets, profits, employees, and economic (and political) power.

How many corporations are there in the United States? And just how large have they grown? In 1990, there were more than 3.6 million corporations in the United States; they constituted less than 18 percent of businesses but had 90 percent of all business receipts. So corporations handle the vast majority of business transactions in the United States. They also earn most of the profits in the economy.

Which corporations are the biggest, and how big are they? The largest firms, less than 1 percent of the corporations in the United States, earned more than two-thirds of corporate receipts. Some U.S. corporations have grown very large indeed and dominate certain sectors of the economy. So what? The question is a good one, and the answers to it will differ among those of us in the United States who are affected by corporations. Some will argue that the large size and dominance of corporations are necessary to organize production, provide employment, and produce goods and services efficiently. Others might use economic arguments, pointing out that almost all large corporations are in concentrated industries and are thus theoretically likely to be deficient because of their economic power. (If the economy were perfectly competitive, there would be many more companies, and none would be so dominant.) Others might be less theoretical and say that corporations are only out to make a buck, have too much economic power, and sometimes do things to the detriment of society.

1. How do you feel about corporations?
2. Why do you think corporations can become so big?

THE ROLE OF PROFITS IN THE CORPORATE SYSTEM

In 1974, the chairman of General Motors, Richard C. Gerstenberg, argued in the *New York Times*, "There is no conflict between corporate profits and social progress. Not one of our grand national goals can be accomplished unless business prospers. Profits fuel the growth of our nation, and our future depends on the profitability of free enterprise." Many would argue that he is correct. We depend on corporate success and profitability for jobs, products, economic growth, technological change, innovation, research and development, and so on. Corporations are in business to earn profits, and in the process of doing so, they provide jobs, investment, goods and services, and economic growth. If they are profitable, they pay taxes that help to finance social programs, and they often contribute to civic and educational endeavors.

However, over the years, a set of counterarguments have informed public sentiments about corporations and led to public opinion polls that at times have concluded that corporate profits are too high. The following list of complaints of corporate wrongdoing and questionable behavior is long and not exhaustive: pollution for decades without cost to the corporation;

exploitation of workers (minorities, women, children, illegal immigrants, etc.); three-martini lunches charged off as business expenses; corporate bribery of foreign officials; illegal corporate political campaign contributions; high oil company profits in the midst of gas lines; food additives that destroy our health; disproportionate economic and political power; misleading advertising; and so on—all to make a buck.

Corporations have tended to respond to these criticisms defensively. Gerstenberg charged, "Most [Americans] are ill-equipped to recognize the economics in these issues, much less to recommend the economic remedies. This lack of public understanding," he suggested, "seriously threatens the continuation of our competitive private enterprise system."

Early in the 1980s, the *Wall Street Journal* and the Gallup Organization polled about eight hundred chief executives of small, medium, and large companies on their perceptions of the public's opinion of business. Almost two-thirds of the executives from medium and large businesses thought the public's opinion was unfavorable, whereas only 36 percent of the small-business executives thought so. "The public thinks when business reports a profit, it goes right into our pockets. They have to be told the truth," said one business leader.

Businesspeople had plenty of ideas about how to improve the image of business in the country. Small-business leaders suggested the importance of product quality and ethical standards. Many of the executives of the large companies emphasized communication and education, based on the conclusion that the low regard for business comes from a lack of knowledge. Suggested remedies ranged from getting the "media and press on the side of business," increasing corporate involvement in community issues, teaching more courses about free enterprise in high schools and colleges, and making advertising better. "We need to start in the elementary schools, with teachers and students both," said one respondent. An energy executive said, "We need to make people realize that it is business and not the government that provides over 100 million jobs in this country." And a transportation company official added, "We need to make it clear that business profits are not just arbitrarily squirreled away, but reinvested for the benefit of the company, its workers and the public. If we can get this across, we may be able to change the adverse to at least normal."

3. Do you have a positive, negative, neutral, indifferent, or balanced view of the corporation's role in the U.S. economy? Explain.

U.S. CORPORATIONS GO GLOBAL

No treatment of the modern U.S. corporation would be complete without reference to one of the dominant corporate trends in the post–World War II period—the increasing multinationalization of U.S. corporations. We explore this issue in more detail in Part V, on international economics. The multinational corporation has already been introduced in Chapter 2.

Multinational corporations have productive facilities, offices, and operations in more than one country. Some U.S. multinational companies date back to the end of the 19th century. At that time, international activities of most companies involved trade. In the post–World War II period, U.S. corporations began increasingly to invest in productive facilities in other parts of the world. At first, foreign direct investment was directed toward getting around tariff barriers and other impediments to U.S. exports. Much of this investment took place in Western Europe and Canada. In addition, multinationalization could also cut transportation costs for international markets, take advantage of various tax incentives offered by many countries, and cut production costs with cheaper foreign labor. In the 1950s and 1960s, much of this investment by U.S. corporations took place in the underdeveloped countries of Latin America, Asia, and Africa.

In the 1970s the pace of U.S. multinational investment in the rest of the world slowed down somewhat for a variety of reasons. The dollar was devalued during the 1970s, making foreign investment more expensive for U.S. corporations. Many Third World nations had become more critical about unconditional multinational investment in their countries. Political instability and the expropriation of corporate assets in some Third World countries also led to a deterioration of the investment climate, as perceived by U.S. multinationals.

The primary motivation for multinationalization, as with virtually all corporate activity, has always been profitability—from cutting transportation and labor costs to access to raw materials and foreign markets. As the potential profitability of foreign investment was reduced or threatened, U.S. corporations slowed down their overseas expansion. In the 1980s this trend was reversed, and U.S. multinational investments began to increase again, by over $100 billion from 1980 to 1988. By 1995, the book value of U.S. direct investment in foreign countries was over $500 billion. The income from these and other foreign investments amounted to almost $100 billion in 1995.

The existence and operation of U.S. multinationals raise a multitude of issues. In some sense, multinational facilities are of crucial importance to the corporations in their search for profits. By the end of the 1970s, one-third of the profits of the 100 largest industrial companies and banks came from their overseas operations. In 1976, about one-third of U.S. imports came from majority-owned U.S. corporations in foreign countries. Without these activities, U.S. corporations would be less profitable than they are.

On the other hand, multinational corporate activities place constraints on the development of U.S. foreign policy. For example, multinationals tend to operate in countries that limit organized labor unions, and often these countries are dictatorial and oppressive in other ways as well. Consequently, U.S. foreign policy may support these regimes and oppose national independence movements as it "protects" U.S. investments. Similarly, policies of the United States toward the Middle East have always been at least partly formed by its importance to U.S. oil companies. In Operation Desert Storm in 1990, the U.S. military defended Kuwait against Iraq's invasion because of the strategic importance of oil. This war alone cost over $50 billion, as well as the lives of U.S. and Iraqi soldiers (the European press estimated Iraqi casualties at well over 200,000).

The relationship between multinationals and Third World countries has created a debate about the effects of these corporations on economic development. Some argue that the multinationals bring jobs and technology and stimulate growth. Others suggest that they cause economic dependence and unequal growth where some individuals prosper while others remain mired in poverty and exploitation, and that corporations take advantage of cheap labor and raw materials but export their profits.

There is no question that a primary motivation for corporations to become global producers in developing countries is the wage factor. When labor is $.25 an hour in China and $.60 an hour in Mexico, a company that must pay its U.S. labor anywhere from $6 to $35 will seriously consider moving production abroad.

The incentive to set up production operations in foreign locations (**outsource** production) is incredible at these low wage rates. Geography is less important when corporations have the advantage of mobile capital resources; easily transferred technology, communications, transportation, computer information and production system technologies; and access to raw materials and other markets. Becoming a global entity is an imperative to remain competitive. Even smaller companies are discovering opportunities for growth and expansion in overseas production of goods and services.

A particularly controversial domestic consequence of U.S. multinationals is the movement of productive facilities out of the Northeast and the Midwest, as well as other parts of the country. Corporations often choose to close down old factories and to relocate new facilities, in other parts of the United States or the world. This is a fundamental aspect of the free enterprise system. Capital is mobile and corporations make decisions about what to do with their capital based on profitability. "Capital flight" may occur in the search for lower taxes, lower wages, less regulation and unionization, or closer proximity to expanding markets. Unfortunately, along with these "runaway shops" go the jobs and, in some cases, the economic health of local communities. Labor unions and communities react to threats of corporate capital flight with wage and tax concessions, because when corporations close down operations, people lose their jobs, communities lose income and business, and governments lose tax revenues. Occasionally, workers or communities have attempted to take over the legal ownership and operation of corporate facilities rather than let them leave.

4. What effect does capital flight have on workers and communities? What would Adam Smith say about this?
5. In the late 1980s federal legislation was passed that requires prenotification of shutdowns. Additional legislation has been proposed to grant assistance to workers who want to restart businesses. Does this seem like a good idea to you? What do you think U.S. multinationals feel about these proposals?

■ TABLE 12.1 The World's Largest Multinationals, Ranked by Foreign Assets

Corporation/Country	Foreign Jobs	Total Jobs
Royal Dutch/Shell (U.K./Netherlands)	79,000	106,000
Ford (U.S.)	96,726	337,778
Exxon (U.S.)	55,000	86,000
General Motors (U.S.)	117,730	692,800
IBM (U.S.)	115,555	219,839
Volkswagen (Germany)	96,545	242,318
General Electric (U.S.)	36,169	216,000
Toyota (Japan)	27,567	172,675
Daimler-Benz (Germany)	79,297	330,551
Elf-Aquitaine (France)	43,950	89,500

Source: The United Nations Conference on Trade and Development.

A look at the Top 100 companies in the world in 1996 finds General Electric, a U.S. firm, at the top with a market value of $137 billion. Twelve U.S. firms made the Top 20 list as shown in Table 2.1 in Chapter 2. Table 12.1 shows the number of foreign jobs and total jobs for the world's largest multinationals, including Royal Dutch/Shell, Ford, Exxon, General Motors, IBM, Volkswagen, General Electric, Toyota, Daimler-Benz, and Elf-Aquitaine. For example, General Motors (U.S.) had 692,800 total jobs, of which 117,730 were foreign. In terms of sales and profits, Table 12.2 shows General Motors first in sales worldwide with $168 billion, yet Royal Dutch/Shell Group was first in profits with $6.78 billion.

■ TABLE 12.2 Sales and Profits of the Largest Corporations

Rank	Corporation	Sales (Billions of U.S. Dollars)	Rank	Corporation	Profits (Billions of U.S. Dollars)
1	General Motors	$168.8	1	Royal Dutch/Shell Corp.	$6.78
2	Mitsubishi Corp.	164.6	2	General Motors	6.72
3	Mitsui & Co.	162.1	3	General Electric	6.57
4	Itochu	151.1	4	Exxon	6.47
5	Sumitomo Corp.	149.6	5	IBM	6.02
6	Marubeni	143.8	6	AT&T	5.52
7	Ford Motor	137.1	7	Philip Morris	5.48
8	Exxon	107.9	8	Ford Motor	4.14
9	Royal Dutch/Shell Corp.	107.8	9	HSBC Holdings	3.82
10	Toyota Motor	99.2	10	Glaxo Wellcome	3.79

Source: *Business Week*, July 8, 1996, p. 46.

A perennial issue surrounding corporate power is the relationship between corporations and the federal government. Corporate officials constantly complain of governmental regulation and interference with business, such as occupational health and safety legislation and environmental protection legislation. They argue that restriction on business hampers their initiative and independence in bringing goods to the U.S. consumer. Sometimes they even imply that continued regulation will dry up their profits and hence their corporations. These officials see corporations and government as adversaries. Others argue that if regulation and other governmental controls over business increase the costs of business, corporations then simply pass on these costs to consumers.

Beyond these two perspectives, a more fundamental criticism sees governmental regulation as protecting corporations from competition—government is an ally of business. An oft-cited example is the protection the railroad and trucking industries receive from the Interstate Commerce Commission. The government has also provided direct assistance in the form of loans to troubled corporations, such as the massive bailout of the savings and loan industry in the late 1980s and early 1990s. This symbiotic relationship has its roots in common goals shared by business and government, such as economic growth, profits, employment, technological advance, and defense. Furthermore, corporations have substantial political power in the government through lobbying, direct campaign contributions, and corporate representatives in all branches of the government.

6. What are your views with respect to government regulation of corporation?

Corporate Challenges and Responses: The 1980s

The debate about the relationship between corporations and the government is relevant to recent discussions concerning the source of modern economic difficulties of the United States. As we learned in Chapter 2, the U.S. economy in the 1980s experienced "waning competitiveness," with lower rates of productivity growth than its trading rivals in the other advanced countries and with several of its leading industries (such as steel, auto, rubber, and machine tools) experiencing hard times and retrenchment. Some conservative critics charged that the federal government's involvement in the economy—its claim on resources for its programs and its regulation of the private sector—was the principal source of the problem. Others pointed to labor union demands, the 1970s oil crisis, or the decline of the work ethic to explain these economic problems, while yet others pointed the finger of responsibility at the corporations themselves.

They argued that the very approach of corporate managers to their businesses accounted for lower productivity growth and decreased competitiveness in international markets. U.S. managers, they charged, took a technocratic view of production, emphasizing technology, internal planning, and computer analysis. But technology and plans do not always work in practice. With more attention to hands-on experience and what is actually happening with the production process on the factory floor, Japanese and European firms made faster advances in production techniques and quality. In addition, U.S. managers have tended to focus on short-run profits through portfolio management, financial oversight, and market control. In contrast to this stress on short-run financial performance, the long-run vision would ensure the maintenance of competitiveness and technological development.

To some corporate critics, a perfect example of this shortsightedness was the merger wave of the 1980s. A **merger** is the legal financial action of one corporation acquiring another corporation. Many corporations took advantage of undervalued corporate stocks to mount takeover campaigns of other corporations. They accomplished these mergers by offering to pay more than market value for the stock of the target corporation. Oftentimes, these takeovers were "hostile" because they were opposed by the managers or directors of the target. In addition, a lot of the financing of these mergers came from borrowing from banks or the issuance of "junk" bonds (bonds with very low ratings that are judged to be high risk). Junk bonds are simply a means for corporations to borrow large sums of money outside the normal channels of borrowing, that is, loans from banks and bonds issued to finance capital expansion. In other words, they are a high-risk investment for anyone who buys them (and thus lends the borrowing corporation money). The problem with this flurry of merger activity was that it did not generally result in any new economic activity by financing new factories or equipment. All it did was allow one company to claim the assets and profits of another company. In some instances, these mergers may have led to improvements in operations and efficiency and, consequently, to increased competitiveness. But critics argued that the mergers primarily shifted around the pattern of ownership without contributing to long-run U.S. competitiveness.

Corporate critics in the 1980s argued for a changed outlook, approach, and strategy on the part of U.S. corporations. These critics advocated the development of an industrial policy to resolve the competitive difficulties and production dilemmas of U.S. corporations. Such a policy would generally call for increased cooperation between the government and the corporate sector over future plans for economic growth and technological development. The intention of the policy would be more coordinated and effective efforts to compete with the Japanese and Europeans.

The Corporate Response in the 1990s

By the late 1990s, U.S. global firms had started to reestablish their global competitiveness. Faced with the new global competition that began in the 1970s with the economic emergence of Japan and West Germany, and newly emerging industrial countries (NICs) like Mexico, Brazil, Taiwan, Singapore, Malaysia, South Korea, and Hong Kong, U.S. global corporations charted a strategy for increasing their competitiveness. This strategy involved the following:

- Moving some operations overseas
- Reducing the wage level and the amount of labor used
- Increasing the use and quality of technology
- Reorganizing the structure and management of the corporation
- Devoting more resources to the training and education of the labor force
- Becoming more flexible and lean.

The past decade has been a period of rapid change for global corporations, including the controversial process of downsizing or restructuring that we examined in Chapter 2. The management revolution that took place forced global firms to reexamine every aspect of their behavior.

Global firms accepted the challenge of focusing on total quality management and continuous improvement. They placed the goals of customer satisfaction and value-added production at the top of their performance objectives. Global competition gave them no choice. These firms also accepted the challenge of entering into new relationships with other firms, many of which had been their traditional rivals. It is not uncommon today for firms to form alliances in activities ranging from research and development to the full production of a good or service.

Of all of the forces driving the competitive character of the global economy, none has been as significant as the **information system revolution**. The use of computer technology in all activities of the firm—design, production, finance, accounting, services, information, sales, and planning—has changed everything. Rapid advances in computer technology and software have pushed the firm into the virtual world of the internet.

Many firms successfully adapted to the changing global reality, but others did not. Each firm had to find ways to become more efficient and productive, and it needed a stable and healthy domestic economic context to support its efforts.

By the mid-1990s, several things were evident. Many firms survived the transition. Figure 12.2 identifies the number of employees at the top ten Fortune 500 companies for 1984 and 1994. Except for Wal-Mart and Philip Morris, all had fewer employees. The United States had also moved ahead of its global competition in terms of productivity—i.e., growth in output per hour in manufacturing. It moved ahead of Japan, Germany, and France in the period from 1990–1994, with a 3 percent annual increase.

The context of the U.S. economy in the last decade is a big part of this story. The driving force of this productivity push came from several factors:

1. Inflation was under control.
2. High-tech equipment prices were falling.
3. High-tech investment spending was robust.
4. Workers were more efficient.

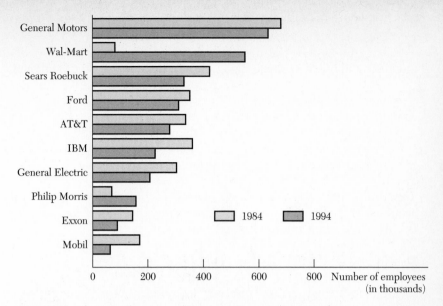

FIGURE 12.2 Change in Employee Numbers in the Ten Largest U.S. Firms, In Thousands of Employees

Source: *Fortune*

The economic payoffs were healthy economic growth, swelling corporate profits, and a booming stock market, yet there was a downside. The trade deficit was large, wages were stagnant, and layoffs were rampant.

LABOR UNIONS IN THE UNITED STATES

The role of labor in corporate decision making and growth is crucial. We have noted the influence of labor unions on wage rates and on the decisions that firms make about plant location. In the remainder of this chapter, we will briefly explore the history of labor unions in the United States and the effects they have on the economy.

In 1996, labor unions and employee associations represented almost 18 million workers, or 15 percent of the 120 million people in the public and private sectors of the labor force. There are over 200 labor unions across the United States, representing industrial workers, secretaries, teachers, and many other employees. Some of the largest and most powerful unions are well known; for example, the United Auto Workers, the Teamsters, and the United Steel Workers. Others are less well known but are growing rapidly, such as the United Food and Commercial Workers, the American Federation of State, County, and Municipal Employees, the Service Employees International Union, and the United Farmworkers.

Labor unions were formed and exist to promote the interests of their members and other workers. Early unions attempted to do the following:

- Get better pay and benefits for their members
- Provide job security for their members
- Improve the health and safety of their members
- Provide for legitimate representation of their members in the decision-making process of the firms they work for.

Today, however, unions are often blamed for inflation and for disrupting economic and community life with strikes and other acts of conflict. How has the impact of labor unions changed over time?

The History of U.S. Labor Unions

Labor unions emerged as a response to the lack of bargaining power that individual workers in a capitalist economy had with their employers over such things as wages, control of work, and working conditions. The employer owned the factory and offered employment paying the lowest wages possible. If there were a large pool of unemployed people, an individual

■ Child labor in a Carolina cotton mill, 1908; photograph by Lewis Hine.
(Corbis-Bettmann)

employee would not be very successful in demanding higher wages or better working conditions.

In response to this structural reality of capital–labor relations, employees formed associations of working people. Only through such unity could they have the power to protect their interests. In the early part of the 19th century, courts held such worker organizations to be illegal restraints of trade, and thus labor unions were legally powerless to bargain with employers or to **strike**—to refuse to work. However, in 1842 the Supreme Court ruled that attempts to organize workers into labor unions were not criminal conspiracies. After this ruling labor unions began to have a national presence. It was also during this period that the economy became increasingly industrialized—a precondition for effective labor organization.

Following the Civil War, the National Labor Union attempted to build a social and political movement around a loose federation of trade unions. However, the craft unions left the organization because they were more interested in union recognition by employers, bargaining with employers over wages, and increasing their wages. In the 1870s and the 1880s, the Knights of Labor attempted to unite all workers against monopolies and to promote the interests of working people. The Knights of Labor organized some successful nationwide strikes against the railroads, but the organization was eventually disbanded because of a lack of internal cohesiveness and as a result of Jay Gould's use of strikebreakers in the 1886 railroad strike.

The modern labor movement can be traced back to the formation of the American Federation of Labor in 1886. The **American Federation of Labor** (AFL), under the leadership of Samuel Gompers, organized in the crafts, accepted capitalism as an economic system, and focused on obtaining higher wages, better working conditions, and shorter hours through collective bargaining, trade agreements, and strikes. The AFL was a confederation of craft unions, each powerful in its own area, that united in conventions and cooperated in strikes, picketing, and boycotts. The AFL believed firmly in the **union shop**, requiring all employees in a factory or shop to belong to the union (and this requirement was included in labor contracts with employers). The AFL also supported the strike as the ultimate weapon of organized labor in disputes with employers.

The AFL shunned direct political activity and also avoided organizing the emerging industrial sectors of the U.S. economy in the late 19th and early 20th century. Many of these industrial workers were unskilled, and many were immigrants. Other labor organizers throughout the 1920s and 1930s actively began industrial organizing and eventually formed the **Committee for Industrial Organization** (CIO). In the 1930s these forces were successful in forming labor organizations that won the right to represent and collectively bargain for the automobile and steel workers. Also in the 1930s, the Wagner Act was passed. This important piece of labor legislation gave all labor unions the legal right to organize and to collectively bargain for their members with employers. Since 1935, labor relations have been overseen by the National Labor Relations Board, which has the authority to spell out the rules of labor organizing for both employers and labor unions.

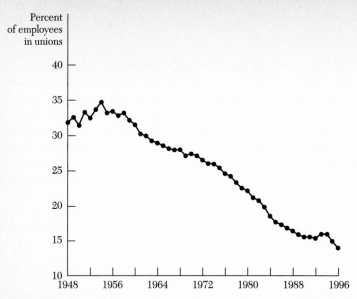

FIGURE 12.3 The Decline in Nonfarm Unionization, 1948–1996
Source: Bureau of Labor Statistics.

Since World War II, industrywide contracts have been negotiated by industry representatives and national labor unions in some cases. In other cases, large corporations and large labor unions have reached settlements that establish a pattern for the rest of an industry. During this period there has also been a tremendous increase in public employees' unions for police, firefighters, teachers, and so forth. The **Taft-Hartley Act**, in 1947, allowed states to pass "right-to-work" laws that forbid union shops. Most of the right-to-work states are in the South. The act also allowed the president to order a 90-day injunction against any strike deemed to threaten "national security." The 1950s saw the merger of the AFL and CIO as a national labor organization—the AFL-CIO—to support workers' interests.

Figure 12.3 shows the growth in the organized labor force in the United States. There has been a clear decline in union membership since 1958. Some analysts suggest that the 1980–1992 drop was a result of the Reagan administration's critical stance toward unions. In 1981 President Ronald Reagan fired federal air traffic controllers who went on strike over working conditions. The hostility toward labor unions was also apparent in a National Labor Relations Board that was less hospitable to labor union organizers' disputes with employers. Higher unemployment rates than in the 1960s and 1970s made it more difficult for labor unions to organize, because people were worried simply about getting and holding jobs. Also, much of the job loss during the 1980s was in industries with heavy union membership. With reduced output and employment in auto and steel, for example, labor unions lost members. While the service sector has been expanding, it has traditionally had fewer workers organized into labor unions.

Labor organization in this country has also been characterized by conflict and occasionally by violence. Capital owners and corporations have always had the power of ownership, and labor has had the power of numbers, unity, and strikes. There have been clear and opposing interests over such issues as the rights of employees to form labor unions, the level of wages, the length of the working day, and working conditions. The interests have clashed and tempers have flared. Labor organizers were often branded as revolutionaries and Communists. The police force of the state has often been used to break strikes, and working people have often responded with their own weapons. To some extent, the conflict is inherent in the structure of the economy, with private ownership and workers both dependent on labor for their incomes. However, one of the great achievements of modern labor legislation has been to mute this conflict and reduce it to legal and institutional forms that are much less likely to break out into violence.

7. Do any members of your family belong to labor unions? What are their opinions of their unions? What do you think of labor unions? Would you want to be in one? Why or why not?

THE ECONOMIC EFFECTS OF LABOR UNIONS

Labor unions are an important force in the economy and in U.S. society. They affect wages, working conditions, and the lives of union members. They also affect the business decisions about location, numbers of employees, and so on. Unions affect communities through civic work, political action, and sometimes strikes. In the following discussion we concentrate on two of the most significant effects of labor unions on economic conditions: wages and workplace environment.

First of all, what is the general effect of labor unions on wages and employment? Here it will be useful to refer to the supply-and-demand model for a labor market, as shown in Figure 12.4. Assume that there is an organized work force negotiating with an employer over a new contract. The workers are willing to supply their labor power for wages. The higher the wage, the greater the quantity of labor power they will tend to supply, as shown in the supply curve, S_L. The employer has a demand for labor; the

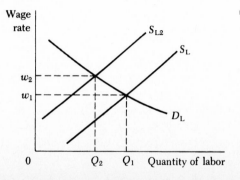

■ FIGURE 12.4 The Effect of Unions on Wages and Unemployment

higher the wage, the lower the quantity of labor the employer will demand, which is shown in the demand curve, D_L. At the point where the two curves, S_L and D_L, intersect are the equilibrium wage rate and the equilibrium quantity of labor that will be supplied and demanded.

The labor union is presumably interested in obtaining higher wages for its workers and achieves this goal with the threat of its ultimate weapon, the strike. The workers can shift their supply curve for labor upward to get higher wages. What this means is that they will supply every different possible quantity of labor power in return for higher wages. If the employer is unwilling to meet this request for higher wages, the workers may go on strike. Shifting the supply curve upward, S_{L2}, increases the equilibrium wage rate. It also tends to reduce the equilibrium quantity if the demand curve for labor does not change. Consequently, we can conclude that labor unions tend to increase wages for their members. It has been historically true that labor union members do get higher wages and higher wage increases than nonunion workers.

On the other hand, the rapid transformation of the global economy has brought increased competitive pressures on U.S.–based companies and concurrent pressures on labor unions to maintain their members and successfully represent their interests. Since the late 1970s, U.S. workers have received a smaller share of national income, and their real wages have stagnated. In the late 1970s labor compensation was 84 percent of national income. In 1996, it had declined to about 80 percent. The growth rate in real compensation per hour has been flat since the early 1980s. This is particularly interesting in the context of the fact that wages (real hourly compensation) in the United States for manufacturing employees are considerably less than in many other advanced indus-

TABLE 12.3 Average Real Hourly Compensation of Manufacturing Employees, 1994

Country	Hourly Wage
Belgium	$22.97
Canada	15.65
Denmark	20.44
France	17.04
Germany	27.31
Italy	16.16
Japan	21.42
Netherlands	20.91
Norway	20.91
Sweden	18.81
United Kingdom	13.62
United States	17.10

Source: U.S. Bureau of Labor Statistics data.

trial countries. In 1996, average U.S. wages were $17.10 per hour, compared to the high of $27.31 in Germany and a low of $13.62 in the United Kingdom. Most European countries had average wages above the United States, as did Japan. Table 12.3 shows real hourly compensation for several countries.

> 8. What has happened to labor compensation as a share of national income and real wages? What explains these trends? What are some of the consequences of these trends for U.S. labor? The U.S. economy? The global economy?

The second significant effect that labor unions have had on the economy is reforming the institutions and the conditions that surround work in the United States. In negotiations with employers, labor unions have focused on their own members' wages and conditions of employment, but the labor movement has been at the forefront of political efforts to improve the wages and the working conditions for all workers in the country. Legislation at the state and federal level includes workers' compensation, minimum-wage laws, the eight-hour day and overtime, the right of workers to form labor organizations and collectively bargain with employers, improved working conditions, and occupational health and safety regulations. Unions have also supported broad social legislation to improve the lot of working and poor people, including public education, maternity and paternity leave, Social Security, Medicare and Medicaid, environmental protection, civil rights laws, and the government's income-support programs.

> 9. Using Internet and library resources, research the General Motors Corp.–United Auto Workers strike that took place in March 1996 in Dayton, Ohio. Why did the strike take place? What were the respective positions of GM and the UAW? What was the settlement? What were the economic consequences of the strike?

Labor unions have been successful in gaining legitimacy in our society, winning improved wages and working conditions for members, and promoting general labor and social legislation. However, they are not without internal problems and potentially adverse effects on the economy. Some unions have become tremendous bureaucracies that have lost touch with the rank-and-file workers. Some union officials have been found guilty of corruption and illegal activities. And finally, it has been argued that unions contribute to the wage-price spiral that fuels inflation. (With inflation under control in recent years and real wages stagnant, this has not been an issue recently, nor would it seem to be in the near future).

One of the most contentious issues between labor and management is the level of compensation received by top management, particularly in recent years when wages for workers are stagnant, layoffs are large and frequent, and corporate profits are soaring. In 1995, the average salary and bonus for a chief executive officer (CEO) rose by 18 percent, to $1,653,670. Including gains from long-term compensation, such as stock options, the average CEO's pay actually climbed to $3,746,392. The highest paid CEO in 1995 was Lawrence Coss from Green Tree Financial, who made $65 million.*

||| 10. Do you think that the compensation of the nation's top execu-
tives is excessive? Explain your answer.

The Future of Labor Unions

The economy of the 1980s and 1990s weakened organized labor's position somewhat. Many unions are now developing new strategies and approaches for this new economic and global context. Many are becoming more aggressive and assertive in terms of seeking new members and performing their historic functions with more diligence. The new head of the AFL-CIO, John Sweeney, has made expanding labor union membership one of his top priorities. Some labor advocates like the late David Gordon, a professor of economics at the New School for Social Research, have also argued that the corporation's rationale for downsizing is flawed. Gordon, in his last book, *Fat and Mean: The Corporate Squeeze of Working Americans and the Myth of Managerial Downsizing*, argues that corporate managers and executives made up 14 percent of the corporate workforce in 1996, compared to 12.7 percent in 1989. The increase in supervisors has been part of the corporation's strategy to use a "stick" rather than the "carrot" when dealing with workers: Workers are motivated by threats from supervisors rather than by better wages and job security. Gordon argues corporations need to pay these extra supervisors, thus taking money away from labor, and partially explains the stagnant real wages of labor—too many supervisors weigh down the economy and hold down productivity growth.

Gordon offers a five-step plan for labor in response to the "wage squeeze" by corporate America.

▮▬▬ CAN WE TAKE THE HIGH ROAD?

In July 1995 *Business Week* ran a cover story on "The Wage Squeeze." Profits were at record-high levels, four years into the expansion, but workers' earnings were stagnating. Should business worry?

To *Business Week*, ever mindful of corporate interests, the "wage squeeze" seemed to pose two threats:

- One problem involved consumer demand. Since working households spend more of their money on consumption than affluent households—which are typically able to put away a little for a rainy day—a squeeze on wages was bound to crimp consumer expenditures as well. "The risk for Corporate America in all

---

* "How High Can CEO Pay Go?," *Business Week*, April 22, 1996.

this," the article warned, "lies in the prospect of chronically weak demand." "This is weakest consumption cycle of the postwar period," one Wall Street economist explained, "which is largely a reflection of the wage slowdown."

- More speculatively, the magazine worried about the prospect of mounting anger and, ultimately, class-based political rebellion. The story concluded as follows: "The sight of bulging corporate coffers co-existing with a continuous stagnation in Americans' living standards could become politically untenable. . . . In the past few years, . . . all but the most elite employees have landed in the same leaky boat. If they all come to stress their common fate more than their differences, it could spell trouble for corporations and politicians alike."

Thus we have the World According to Business, a vivid etching of corporate self-interest. For the rest of us, traveling the "low road" raises substantially different concerns. Millions of workers and households have been directly clubbed by the Stick. Millions more of us are feeling the ripple effects in our schools and communities and government institutions. All of us must endure the bumpy macroeconomic consequences of travels on the low road. These costs are huge.

Some conservatives and business analysts have finally begun to appreciate the magnitude of these costs and the threats they pose. "The emergence of codes of corporate ethics and the emphasis on fashioning a defensible corporate culture," political scientist James Q. Wilson writes, "are not, I think, merely public relations (though they are sometimes just that). They are, at their best, a recognition that people want to believe that they live and work in a reasonably just and decent world." "When people feel like valued assets of their companies," Harvard Business School's Rosabeth Moss Kanter reports, "they express satisfaction with their lives and more willingness to help others." It is not enough for conservatives and corporations, Wilson continues, to express blind faith in the invisible hand:

> The problem for capitalists is to recognize that, while free markets will ruthlessly eliminate inefficient firms, the moral sentiments of man will only gradually and uncertainly penalize immoral ones. But, while the quick destruction of inefficient corporations threatens only individual firms, the slow anger at immoral ones threatens capitalism—and freedom—itself.

William J. McDonough is president of the Federal Reserve Bank of New York, a pillar of the establishment. But he too is concerned. At a conference he convened in 1994 to consider the wage squeeze and rising inequality, he expressed his fears:

> These dramatic wage developments raise profound issues for the United States, issues of equity and social cohesion, issues that affect the very temperament of the country. We are forced to face the question of whether we will be able to go forward together as a unified society with a confident outlook or as a society of diverse economic groups suspicious of both the future and each other.

Left to their own devices, however, U.S. corporations show little sign of letting up, of heeding the broader social and moral consequences of their addiction to the low road. *Business Week* characterizes their current views: "To ease up now, many executives feel, would be to snatch defeat from the jaws of victory." "There's a very intense determination in executive suites across America," Mobil's vice-president for administration reports, "not to give away hard-fought improvements. It may be a long time before this shakes through and wages rise." The rest of us cannot afford to wait that long.

A Five-Step Program

This section considers *only* policy reforms whose primary purpose is to affect the organization of production and the structures of labor management in U.S. corporations.

This inclusion principle neglects many economic policy reforms that would make sense in the United States in confronting other problems—such as reducing the political independence of the Federal Reserve Board so that, at the least, monetary and fiscal policies could be better coordinated. More important for the purposes of this book, it also leaves out policy reforms that could significantly moderate corporate reliance on the Stick but whose primary rationale lies elsewhere.

For example, among the most important sources of the emergence of the "disposable" worker have been our archaic and misguided systems of health insurance and payroll taxation. Alone among the advanced countries, we do not provide some form of universal health coverage. This has meant, especially during the era of skyrocketing health care costs, that employers have had a strong incentive to treat their employees as "disposable" in order to avoid incurring the costs of health insurance. Virtually alone among the advanced countries, further, we finance social security out of a special trust fund rather than out of general revenue. Faced with that separate payroll tax, employers have also been tempted to hire relatively fewer employees on regular lines and rely increasingly on temps for who they do not incur payroll tax obligations. Pushing for single-payer universal health insurance and for social security financed through general taxation would make sense for many reasons in the United States. Not the least would be a reduced temptation for employers to shortchange their employees through various kinds of "contingent" employment relations.

Raising the Wage Floor

The first and perhaps most important source of the wage squeeze has been the dramatic decline in the real value of the minimum wage. The remedy to this problem seems obvious: *increase the minimum wage and ensure that its real value does not fall in the future.*

Once there, the federal minimum wage should be tied to the consumer price index so that erosions of its real value will not recur. Some economists worry that an indexed minimum wage would put "excessive" pressure on wages above the minimum wage. But that's precisely the point. In order to push U.S. employers toward the high road, I have argued, their labor costs need to rise. They need to begin modernizing or get out of the kitchen.

More Effective Worker Voice

A second critical source of the wage squeeze has been the decline in union reach and power. This points to an equally obvious potential remedy: *legislation to enhance workers' abilities to achieve effective workplace representation.* I propose three specific pieces of such legislative reform. These do not include all the elements of a comprehensive approach to labor law reform, but merely those elements that could contribute most to encouraging the Carrot approach.

Flexible, Not "Disposable" Work

Part of the problem with the emergence of the "disposable" worker is that the potential advantages of true "flexibility" at work have been compromised. Employers can benefit from some leeway in how they schedule their workforce. And many employees, especially those with children, can benefit from choice and discretion in scheduling their own working time. But disposability is not flexibility. As a result of recent trends, part-time and more contingent work is becoming a sentence, not an opportunity. Workers are losing rights, choice, and benefits.

As already noted, changing our systems of health insurance and payroll taxation would help break down the artificial distinction between regular and contingent employees. What else can be done to enhance the benefits of flexibility and reduce the penalties of disposability?

"Part of the worktime problem," Juliet Schor writes, "is that we are still operating with a 'male' model of employment—full-time hours and full-time dedication to the job." She continues:

> [This is] a take-it-or-leave-it option. As women have entered the workforce in large numbers, they have had to conform to this model to succeed. But this causes serious problems, because women still retain primary responsibility for and attachment to child care and household work. And increasingly, men want time off the job too, often to be with their children.

When employers seek to avoid paying benefits for new employees, for example, they force present employees to work overtime rather than opening up jobs for others who need them. To avoid benefit costs for new workers, a *New York Times* reporter concluded, "employers have been stretching the workweek, not cutting it back." Compulsion, not choice.

In our current system, employers have discretion to shift their employees around virtually any way they would like. We should reduce their temptation to do this exploitatively by altering the environment affecting worktime decisions. Proposal: *Amend the Fair Labor Standards Act to prohibit mandatory overtime; to substitute compensatory time as an optional alternative to voluntary overtime premia; to include salaried (in addition to hourly) workers within its coverage; and to mandate three-weeks vacation, rising to four weeks after an interim period of (say) 5–10 years, for all wage-and-salary employees.*

A Carrot for Cooperative Workplaces

Not only do we need to pressure corporations to abandon the Stick but we should also provide them with incentives for it. In the current U.S. context, firms are provided virtually no material encouragement to make the commitments and investments that adopting the Carrot Strategy involves. Some economists refer to this as a "market failure": for many firms it would be profitable to adopt the Carrot Strategy, but they either cannot afford or cannot gain access to the funds that would be necessary to move in that direction. Proposal: *establish a National Cooperative Investment Bank that would provide investment credits and subsidies to firms with cooperative and democratic organizational structures.*

Governments in the United States at the federal, state, and local levels have long subsidized certain kinds of economic activities they have wanted to encourage—think of the vast subsidies provided for private home ownership in the postwar period. But we have never sought to provide direct incentives for firms that practice cooperative work relations. We can and should begin to do so.

There are many precedents for specific trusts or investment banks aimed at encouraging targeted investment projects. For example, the Community Development Financial Institutions (CDFI) Fund, enacted by Congress and signed into law by President Clinton in 1994, has been established to provide financial assistance for community-based banks and organizations in community development projects. The Southern Finance Project has called for a complementary fund, a National Reinvestment Fund constructed with assessments on nonbank lenders, to help capitalize the growth of the CDFIs supported by the federal government.

We need to apply these kinds of instruments to direct support for more cooperative enterprises. Firms that can establish that they provide worker ownership or substantial and effective worker participation or control in organizing production could receive low-interest loans to help finance reorganization and expansion. As with any investment support, from banks or from the government, the firms would need to be monitored periodically to ensure that their claims of "cooperative" practices were not mere window dressing. U.C.–Berkeley economist David I. Levine suggests, for example, that firms might receive special government support if they could show that they had allotted employees at least one seat on the board of directors; featured an elected employee relations committee in each establishment; also featured a health and safety committee at each establishment; maintained some kind of profit-sharing plan; and sustained some kind of formal procedure for dispute resolution. One can imagine other practicable variations on the same basic theme. The essential point is that this kind of federal subsidy involves an opportunity, not a constraint. Firms would be free to seek the incentive or to eschew it. If we would all benefit from taking the "high road," surely we can afford to provide some carrots for firms that are trying to move in that direction.

Training and Assistance for Cooperation

Two additional barriers impede movement to the high road. Neither managers nor workers are in the habit of relating cooperatively in production. And it's expensive to provide the training and assistance to help them shake their established habits. Proposal: *establish a National Cooperative Training and Assistance Agency to help workers and managers acquire the skills and habits necessary for more cooperative labor relations.*

Many have noted that U.S. firms provide remarkably little training for their employees—especially when compared to leading competitors such as Germany. More important, U.S. firms tend to concentrate their training on higher-level employees, leaving less-skilled production workers to fend for themselves in an increasingly turbulent marketplace. This practice neglects precisely those employees whose contributions to more productive and cooperative enterprises can prove most crucial. One clear finding from surveys of participation experiments in the United States is that they lead to increased investment in education and training of the workforce. We need to establish training instruments and funds that will help ensure that thousands of U.S. firms engage in intensive retraining. Managers and workers can't just stumble toward the high road; they need to be carefully taught.

Bucking Business

[The table] pulls together this five-step program. Taken on its own terms, the proposals are tangible, practicable, easily legislated.

But that doesn't mean, of course, that these proposals will be enacted as soon as the 105th Congress convenes in January 1997. Most of these proposals don't sit well with the political agenda of either established political party or with most business leadership in this country.

Steps	Provisions
1. Raising the wage floor	Increasing minimum wage to $6.50 by year 2000
	Indexing minimum wage to consumer price index
2. More effective worker voice	Automatic union certification with 55% signature cards
	Extend NLRA protection to most nonproduction and supervisory employees
	Mandate employee participation councils in most workplaces
3. Flexible, not disposable work	Amend Fair Labor Standards Act to
	— prohibit mandatory overtime
	— substitute comp time for overtime premia
	— extend working time regulation to salaried employees
	— mandate universal 3-weeks vacation, rising to 4 weeks
4. Carrots for cooperative firms	Investment subsidies for cooperative and democratic firms
5. Training, assistance for cooperation	National Cooperative Training and Assistance Agency

And so we face a fairly stark political choice in the United States as we confront the wage squeeze and corporate bloat: Do we continue to allow U.S. corporations to exercise an effective veto over public policy, condemning us to continued travels along the low road? Or do we seek to challenge and overcome business opposition? "Absent a sudden upsurge from below," Ferguson and Rogers write, "the new, more conservative party system will be maintained. Democrats and Republicans will squabble and maneuver. The costs to the population will rise. But the basic structure of the party system will remain unchanged. America will continue its right turn."

Most of the U.S. citizenry understands the starkness of this choice better than established elites. In an August 1995 *New York Times*/CBS poll, four-fifths—"the highest figure in several decades"—said that "the Government is run by a few big interests looking out for themselves" and three-fifths that "people like themselves don't have much say in what the Government does." Logical conclusion? As other recent polls have also revealed, people are ready for a new party. More than half agreed that "the country needs a new political party to compete with the Republicans and Democrats."

This kind of political movement requires more than a figurehead, a charismatic independent leader like Ross Perot or Colin Powell or Jess Jackson to articulate popular discontent. It requires persistent, clear-headed continuing mobilization in support of specific policies and priorities—all of which take time.

This endurance test should hardly surprise us. The cooperative economies did not acquire their labor-management systems overnight. Business interests initially bristled at some of the proposals for cooperation, codetermination, and power-sharing. Partly through union mobilization, partly through independent citizens' initiatives, the German, Japanese, and Swedish systems were constructed over decades. Roy J. Adams reviews this experience: "In Sweden, Germany, and Japan, agreements that in retrospect had very positive effects were initially entered into only grudgingly. . . . The experience of these countries also suggests that agreements once reached cannot be considered safely done. Agreements have to be worked out continually and fundamental understandings must be respected or the overall structure can collapse."

U.S. corporations are fat and mean. We all bear the costs of their commitment to the low road. We cannot expect those corporations to change their ways either easily or willingly. We need to change the environment in which they operate and to push and pull them, no matter how deeply they dig in their heels, in order to overcome the wage squeeze and corporate bloat. It will take time and it will take power. "So [said the good doctor at the end of *Portnoy's Complaint*]. Now vee may perhaps to begin. Yes?"

Source: David Gordon, "Can We Take the High Road?" *Fat and Mean: The Corporate Squeeze of Working Americans and the Myth of Managerial Downsizing* (New York: The Free Press, 1997), pp. 239–253. Reprinted by permission of the publisher.

11. What are Gordon's five steps for reform? Which of these do you support? Which of these do you disagree with? Why? Do you think this strategy can and will work over time? Why?

CORPORATIONS AND LABOR: TOWARD THE 21ST CENTURY

As the 1990s come to a close, U.S. corporations have firmly reestablished their economic and financial dominance in the global economy. This transition, which began in the mid-1970s, has left the U.S. economic landscape radically altered. New relationships exist between corporations and government, corporations and labor, and corporations and communities.

TABLE 12.4 Total U.S. Corporate Profits, 1980–1995

Year	Profit in Billions of Dollars
1980	$167
1981	183
1982	159
1983	212
1984	268
1985	282
1986	271
1987	309
1988	357
1989	356
1990	369
1991	382
1992	401
1993	464
1994	529
1995	586

Note: With inventory valuation and capital depreciation adjustments.

Source: *Economic Report of the President,* February 1997, p. 401.

While the issues and arguments put forward by critics of corporations are just as legitimate today as they were decades ago, there is also the reality that for most of the citizens in mainstream America and the larger global economic community, the corporation is the dynamic organizational engine that drives the growth and prosperity of the global economy. The U.S. economy has been without a recession since 1990, and its sustained economic growth and performance, highlighted by the phenomenal growth of the stock market and corporate profits (see Table 12.4), is largely attributed to the success of global corporations in the U.S. economy. With the government's policy of deregulation, corporations can do whatever they feel necessary to grow and compete in world markets. The recent character of mergers and acquisitions in the telecommunications, financial, and manufacturing sectors illustrate this fact. Yet, organized labor and community members demand social responsibility from corporations; they insist that corporations be held publicly accountable for their decisions and actions that impact domestic politics, the health and safety of individual workers, the economic viability of individual communities, and the natural environment. It is unlikely that these conflicts will ever disappear.

CONCLUSION

This chapter focuses on two of the most important economic institutions in the United States: corporations and labor unions. Having stepped outside the realm of pure microeconomic theory, we examined the development, behavior, and importance of corporations and labor unions.

Review Questions

1. Why is the corporation a dominant institution in the U.S. economic system?
2. Why have corporations gone global? What are some of the implications of this trend?
3. Why are labor unions a dominant institution in the U.S. economy?
4. Is the relationship between big corporations and big labor unions adversarial or symbiotic?
5. Do you think CEOs are worth the large compensation they receive?
6. Corporations have gone global. Will labor unions? Why or why not?
7. What is Gordon's strategy for labor? Do you agree or disagree with his proposals? Explain.
8. What do you think will be the relationship between corporations, labor, and the government in the early part of the 21st century? What do you think it should be?

13

The Economic Role of Government

INTRODUCTION

In the previous chapters of Part 3, we concentrated on the operation of markets and their role in allocating resources. We also introduced the importance of corporations and labor unions as economic factors in the private sector. But the United States has a **mixed economy**—one in which business firms and markets in the private sector exist alongside economic institutions in the public sector. (In fact, all the world's economies are "mixed," with varying levels of public sector involvement.)

The **public sector**, in the form of local, state, and federal governmental offices, organizations, and institutions, performs many important economic functions. Think about your local community. What goods and services are provided by governmental units? The list is actually quite long, and the activities are fundamentally important to the day-to-day economic (as well as noneconomic) operation of a community. Public services also provide capabilities for the long-run survival of a society. Postal service, police and fire protection, road construction and maintenance, street signs, sewers, parks and recreation services, a court system, schools, traffic signals, welfare services, and so on are all provided by local, state, and federal governmental units.

In general, the economic role of government in capitalism results from the failure of markets to allocate resources to certain tasks or from a public conclusion that the results of markets are unacceptable. Consequently, governments have taken responsibility for limiting the practice and the results of economic concentration, correcting the inequality of the distribution of market-determined incomes, providing public goods when markets fail to supply them, and regulating activities of the private sector that produce external costs to the rest of society. In this chapter, we will explore each of these aspects of governmental economic activity in more detail.

THE ROLE OF GOVERNMENT IN THE ECONOMY

In response to the various failures of the market system, government has developed many different programs. Public regulation of monopolies and antitrust legislation are intended to control economic concentration. The progressive income tax system and income support, job training, equal opportunity, and affirmative-action programs exist for the purpose of reducing economic inequality. The public use of resources to provide such socially desirable goods and services as education, parks, police and fire protection, and roads results from the failure of the private sector to adequately supply them. Zoning laws, pollution controls, environmental protection legislation, restrictions on child labor, occupational health and safety regulations, and food and drug inspections are meant to correct some of the abuses resulting from the operation of private markets. These public activities have all been developed throughout the history of U.S. capitalism, as well as in other economic systems.

In addition, governments provide an economic framework within which private economic activity takes place. The justice and legal systems, public infrastructure (e.g., transportation and national defense), the monetary and banking systems, and, frequently, public subsidies for private businesses all create an environment in which short-run and long-run economic activity can proceed. Seen in this light, the public sector complements the private sector. Furthermore, local, state, and federal governments have created taxation and revenue systems to finance their activities. Through raising money, governments can make a claim on the resources of the society by purchasing them in markets. (The federal government also uses its spending and taxing power, as well as its influence over the money supply, to limit economic instability. We will explore this function of government in Part 4.)

All these governmental activities are intensely political and controversial. The decisions about which programs to pursue, how much money to spend on them, and how to raise the revenues to finance them involve public discussion and debate, legislative resolution, administrative direction, and judicial oversight. People, organizations, politicians, political parties, and even ideas are joined in the political process to decide what governments will do and how they will do it.

> 1. Do you think governments should reduce their spending? On which programs? Why or why not?

Throughout the history of U.S. capitalism, there has been debate about the economic role of the government. At times the debate has been lively and heated. Two hundred years ago, Alexander Hamilton and Thomas Jefferson argued about whether the country should be an agrarian or industrial society and about what role the federal government ought to play in promoting one or the other. Before the Civil War, the South and the North disagreed about the imposition of tariffs by the federal government as well as slavery. Later in the nineteenth century, a controversial issue was the role of the government in giving land to the railroads and then in regulating their rates. During the

Depression, there was vociferous debate about the growing role of the government in regulation, relief, public employment, social spending, labor legislation, and even public ownership.

Since that time, along with the growth of government, the debate has continued. During Ronald Reagan's presidency, the discussion was revitalized with a renewed attack on the general role of the government in the economy. One of Reagan's primary campaign themes was that the government was interfering too much in the private sector and that its size and its rules were preventing economic growth. In the 1990s, Congressman Newt Gingrich's "Contract with America" echoed these themes. Only time will tell if this challenge will succeed in permanently reducing the role of the government in the economy.

Going back to the writings of Adam Smith, we can see that there has always been a case for some necessary tasks on the part of the state in support of the operation of the economy. Smith suggested that the government needed to protect private property, enforce contracts, provide for a monetary system, supply a defense capability, and provide some public goods, such as education and transportation. Beyond that, the role of the government should be circumscribed. Note, however, that what Smith has delineated is of fundamental importance to the economy and requires a large and powerful government. Smith said that its powers should be limited—never that it should be weak or small.

Since Smith's time, the general discussion about the role of the government has been partly about the scope of its activities and partly about its limitations within the kind of economic system that we have. To review the debate, it is useful to use the conservative, liberal, and radical perspectives.

Conservatives argue that the state's involvement in the economy limits personal freedoms, and that markets, if left alone, will produce economic growth and social welfare. This follows the lines of Smith's arguments in *The Wealth of Nations*. Individuals, pursuing their own interests in business, will provide jobs, technological development, and growth in the economy. Conservatives, consequently, tend to oppose efforts to break up big corporations, redistribute income, and regulate directly the externalities of the private sector. Such governmental activities interfere with the operation of the "invisible hand." It is largely the conservatives who have mounted the New Right attack on the government's role in the economy. (Part of their critique also deals with Keynesian fiscal and monetary policy, which we will discuss in Part 4.)

The liberal position suggests that the operation of the market economy in capitalism tends to produce economic growth and efficiency, along with an emphasis on individual economic freedom. However, liberals acknowledge some of the problems that the development of the economy produces, such as economic concentration, income inequality, and externalities. Consequently, they think it is entirely appropriate for the government to attempt to correct and address some of those problems. They also argue that such government intervention can, in fact, improve the allocation of resources in society. This position has largely won out in twentieth-century public debate concerning the role of government.

The radical position begins with the assertion that the government plays a particularly important role in the operation and maintenance of capitalism as an economic system. For example, the state protects private property and the rights of owners to pursue their economic freedom. However, it does not offer the same kind of freedom or protection to poor people. Another way of saying this is that the state's role is constrained by its relationship to capitalism as a particular type of economic system. This point is the basis of the radical critique of liberal policies of government involvement in the economy. There is a limit on the extent of government involvement in the private sector as to redistributing income, regulating externalities, or enforcing antitrust laws. The limit is the requirement of capital accumulation for the growth of capitalism. Without capital accumulation, the economy will stagnate. If state policies interfere with corporate profits or profit expectations, capital accumulation can become endangered. In other words, if state intervention proceeds too far, it may interfere with capital accumulation, and government policies will have to retreat somewhat. On the other hand, radicals recognize that the political response to the abuses and inequities of capitalism has required and led to governmental programs that address these problems.

2. What programs are included in "welfare spending"? Does welfare spending hinder the operation of capitalism? How would you find out if you are right (or if you don't know)? Why does welfare spending take place? What would a conservative say? A liberal? A radical?
3. Which position best describes your attitudes toward government spending in general? Why? How do you feel about government spending for military purposes?

THE GROWTH OF GOVERNMENT'S ROLE

The public sector has significantly expanded its role in the economy during the twentieth century. Through the political process, governmental institutions make decisions about pursuing particular programs. Table 13.1 presents information on the range of spending programs and the relative priorities of state, local, and federal governments in the 1990s. Education is by far the most important category for state and local governments; it accounted for 33 percent of state and local government spending in 1992–1993. In the federal government's budget for fiscal year 1996 (October 1, 1995 to September 30, 1996), national defense, income security, Social Security, and interest on the debt were the four largest spending categories; they accounted for about 70 percent of $1.5 trillion in total federal spending.

Table 13.2 presents information on public sector taxes and receipts for various years from 1929 to 1995. The table includes data on the total amount of governmental revenues as well as their percentage share of gross domestic product (GDP), the total value of output for each year. For example, in 1929, total governmental revenues were $11.3 billion, which amounted to 10.9

percent of total output. From even a quick look at this table, we can see that the relative importance of government in the economy has increased significantly over the past sixty years. Revenues in 1994 amounted to more than $2.1 trillion and have increased by almost two-hundredfold since 1929! However, the most useful way to gauge the relative position of any economic variable is to compare it to GDP. Revenues in 1994 were 30.7 percent of GDP. This threefold increase in government's share since 1929 represents a shift in the role of government in the economy.

From 1929 to 1940, total revenues increased from 10.9 percent to 17.7 percent of output. Most of this increase occurred in the federal sector in

▇ TABLE 13.1 State-Local and Federal Government Spending

State and Local Government Spending, 1992–1993

Program	Spending Level ($ Billions)
Education	342.6
Highways	68.1
Public welfare	170.7
All other*	446.1
Total	1,027.5

Federal Budget Outlays, Fiscal Year 1996

Program	Spending Level ($ Billions)
National defense	265.7
International affairs	13.5
General science, space, and technology	16.7
Energy	2.8
Natural resources and environment	21.6
Agriculture	9.2
Commerce and housing credit	−10.6
Transportation	39.6
Community and regional development	10.7
Education, training, employment, and social services	52.1
Health	119.4
Medicare	174.2
Income security	226.0
Social Security	349.7
Veterans' benefits and services	37.0
Administration of justice	17.5
General government	11.9
Net interest	241.0
Offsetting receipts	−37.6
Total	1,560.3

*Includes health and hospitals, police and fire protection, corrections, interest on debt, parks and recreation, sanitation, administration, housing and urban renewal, protective inspection and regulation, etc.

Source: *Economic Report of the President, 1997.*

	Total Government		State-Local Governments		Federal Government	
Year	$ Billions	Percentage of GDP	$ Billions	Percentage of GDP	$ Billions	Percentage of GDP
1929	11.3	10.9	7.5	7.3	3.8	3.6
1940	17.8	17.7	9.1	9.1	8.7	8.6
1950	69.4	24.1	19.0	6.6	50.4	17.5
1960	138.8	26.3	41.8	7.9	97.0	18.4
1970	299.6	28.9	104.6	10.1	195.1	18.8
1980	834.2	30.0	272.7	9.8	561.5	20.2
1990	1,726.4	30.0	596.5	10.4	1,129.8	19.7
1995	2,268.4	31.3	790.0	10.9	1,478.4	20.4

Source: *Economic Report of the President, 1990, 1997.*

response to the Great Depression. The increase in the share of total revenues from 1940 to 1950 from 17.7 to 24.1 percent resulted from the expansion of the federal government and the retrenchment of state and local governments during World War II. From 1950 to 1970, the public sector continued expanding, and revenues increased to almost 30 percent of GDP. During this period, federal revenues increased their share by less than 10 percent while the share of state-local revenues expanded by just over 50 percent. More recently, the relative share of governmental revenues in GDP has stabilized. Total revenues have remained at slightly over 30 percent of GDP, federal revenues are about 20 percent, and state-local revenues have been about 10 percent of GDP since 1970.

4. Look at the figures for 1970 and 1980 federal revenues in Table 13.2. When Ronald Reagan ran for the presidency in 1980, he argued that the growth of government was a primary reason for the economic difficulties of the 1970s. Was this an exaggerated claim? What happened to the growth of government from 1980 to 1990?

For comparative purposes, Table 13.3 shows the relative importance of government in several economically advanced countries. Government spending as a percentage of gross domestic product is higher in all these countries, except Turkey and Mexico, than it is in the United States.

We can also measure the size of the government in terms of what it spends. Table 13.4 contains data on governmental expenditures in the United States from 1929 to 1995. In 1929, all levels of government spent $10.3 billion, which was 9.9 percent of output. By 1995, total governmental spending surpassed $2.3 trillion, or 32.2 percent of GDP. In this period, there has been a more than threefold increase in the relative importance of the governmental sector in the economy. The relative share of state and local government spending has almost doubled, while the share of the federal government has increased almost ten times. From 1929 to 1940, most of the growth was in the federal sector as a result of New Deal programs to cope with the effects of the Great Depression. From 1940 to 1970, the federal share grew as a result of defense spending and expanding social spending. There was also an expansion of federal grants to state and local governments, which contributed to their increasing share. From 1970 to 1980, the share of state and local spending stabilized, and the share of the federal government increased slightly, reflecting continued growth of social spending in the 1970s. From 1980 to 1995, the share of state-local governments stayed about the same. Despite the efforts of the Reagan team to reduce the federal government's

TABLE 13.3 Total Tax Revenue as a Percentage of Gross Domestic Product at Market Prices (1994)

Country	Percent of GDP
Denmark	51.6
Sweden	51.0
Czech Republic	47.3
Finland	47.3
Belgium	46.6
Netherlands	45.9
Luxembourg	45.0
France	44.1
Poland	43.2
Austria	42.8
Greece	42.5
Italy	41.7
Norway	41.2
Hungary	41.0
Germany	39.3
Ireland	37.5
New Zealand	37.0
Canada	36.1
Spain	35.8
United Kingdom	34.1
Switzerland	33.9
Portugal	33.0
Iceland	30.9
Australia	29.9
Japan	27.8
United States	27.6
Turkey	22.2
Mexico	18.8

Source: *Revenue Statistics of OECD Member Countries,* 1996 ed.

TABLE 13.4 U.S. Governmental Expenditures

	Total Government		State-Local Governments		Federal Government	
Year	$ Billions	Percentage of GDP	$ Billions	Percentage of GDP	$ Billions	Percentage of GDP
1929	10.3	9.9	7.8	7.5	2.5	2.4
1940	18.5	18.4	9.3	9.3	9.2	9.1
1950	61.4	21.3	22.5	7.8	38.9	13.5
1960	121.5	23.1	38.4	7.3	83.1	15.8
1970	292.4	28.3	108.2	10.5	184.7	17.8
1980	840.8	30.2	307.0	11.0	533.8	19.2
1990	1,800.4	31.4	648.8	11.3	1,152.1	20.1
1995	2,335.1	32.2	901.1	12.4	1,434.0	19.8

Note: Intergovernmental grants are counted by the spending source.

Source: *Economic Report of the President, 1990, 1997.*

role in the economy, the federal share increased from 19.2 percent in 1980 to 20.1 percent in 1990. This resulted from increased spending on the military, Social Security, and interest payments on the federal debt. From 1990 to 1995, federal spending decreased slightly to 19.8 percent of GDP, mostly due to efforts to reduce the federal budget deficit.

The government spending in Table 13.4 includes transfer payments. **Transfer payments** are governmental programs that transfer spending power from one group to another group. Examples include veterans' benefits, unemployment compensation, Medicaid, food stamps, Social Security and Medicare benefits, and Aid to Families with Dependent Children. Consequently, total government spending overestimates the claim of government programs on the society's resources. When the government collects Social Security and Medicare taxes from people's wages and salaries (and from their employers), it pays benefits to people who are retired and eligible for Social Security and Medicare. The claim on the society's resources is transferred through this program from one set of people (those working now) to another (those retired). People who pay taxes have their spending power reduced, and people who receive benefits have their spending power increased. The money flows through the Social Security Administration, but the federal government makes no direct claim on resources in this transfer program (except for the costs of administering the program). Much of the growth in federal government expenditures as a percentage of output since 1929 has come as a result of the expansion of federal transfer programs.

This conclusion is reinforced by an examination of the information in Table 13.5, which shows governmental purchases of goods and services. In contrast to transfer payments, governmental purchases of goods and services represent **exhaustive spending**. With this type of spending, governments are making claims on society's resources in the pursuit of their priorities. Exhaustive spending includes the purchase of weapons, pencils, government employees' labor, road construction materials, computers, police and fire

TABLE 13.5 Governmental Purchases of Goods and Services

	Total Government		State-Local Governments		Federal Government (Defense)			
Year	$ Billions	Percentage of GDP	$ Billions	Percentage of GDP	$ Billions		Percentage of GDP	
1929	8.8	8.5	7.4	7.1	1.5		1.4	
1940	14.2	14.2	8.1	8.1	6.1	(2.3)	6.1	(2.3)
1950	38.8	13.5	19.8	6.9	19.1	(14.3)	6.6	(5.0)
1960	113.2	21.5	47.6	9.0	65.6	(54.9)	12.4	(10.4)
1970	236.1	22.8	120.2	11.6	115.9	(90.6)	11.2	(8.7)
1980	572.8	20.6	324.4	11.6	248.4	(174.2)	8.9	(6.3)
1990	1,176.1	20.5	672.6	11.7	503.6	(373.1)	8.8	(6.5)
1995	1,358.3	18.7	841.7	11.6	516.6	(345.5)	7.1	(4.8)

Source: *Economic Report of the President, 1990, 1997.*

vehicles, and so forth. By spending on public programs, governments demand the use of resources. This is different from a governmental program that transfers spending power from one group to another.

From 1929 to 1940, total governmental purchases almost doubled their share of output, with almost all of the growth in spending coming from the federal government. From 1940 to 1960, total purchases increased their share from 14.2 percent to 21.5 percent. Most of this growth occurred in the federal government sector, with the lion's share being accounted for by purchases of goods and services for national defense. However, from 1950 to 1960, there was also a significant postwar expansion in state and local spending, especially for roads and schools. Since 1960, the overall level of government purchases has stabilized at about 20 percent of GDP. Government consequently makes a direct claim on about one-fifth of the society's output every year.

Figure 13.1 illustrates the growth of the government in the economy from 1929 to 1994. It also contrasts the growth of total government spending with purchases of goods and services. As we saw in the tables, total governmental exhaustive spending has stabilized as a proportion of GDP since 1960. During the same time, transfer programs have continued to expand, thereby increasing governmental spending as a percentage of GDP.

Public sector employment also demonstrates the growth of government in the twentieth century in the United States. Figure 13.2 illustrates the increase in public sector employment since 1929. In 1929, public sector employees were about 6 percent of the total U.S. labor force; by 1994 this figure had increased to almost 17 percent. In 1994, over 19 million people were employed by the federal, state, and local governments, with over 16.5 million working for local and state governments and 2.8 million civilians employed by the federal government. The vast majority of the growth in public sector employment since 1950 has come in state and local governments. These workers are employed in education, hospitals, law enforcement, highway work, and general governmental administration.

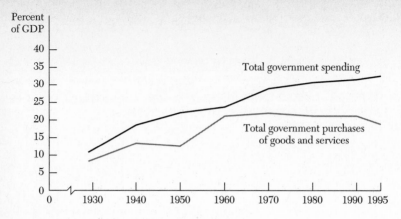

FIGURE 13.1 The Expansion of Government

||| 5. Why has the relative importance of government increased over
the past fifty years?

MARKET FAILURE, PUBLIC GOODS, AND EXTERNALITIES

In Chapter 9, we demonstrated that competitive markets operate in a manner
that produces efficiency in resource allocation and a maximization of social
welfare. The theoretical model of perfect competition proves Adam Smith's
contention about the "invisible hand" in a private market economy—it promotes growth, efficiency, and consumer sovereignty. However, some aspects

FIGURE 13.2 Public Sector Employment

Sources: Advisory Commission on Intergovernmental Relations, *Significant Features of Fiscal Federalism* (1984
ed.), Washington, D.C., 1985; U.S. Department of Commerce, Bureau of the Census, *Statistical Abstract of
the United States,* 1989; and *Economic Report of the President,* 1996.

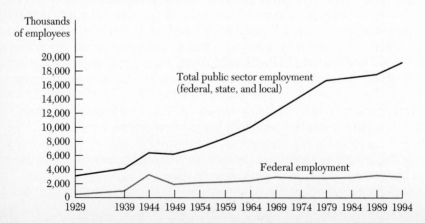

of economic reality interfere with the attractive theoretical results of competitive markets.

We have already examined one instance when markets fail to produce an efficient allocation of resources. In Chapter 10, we showed that whenever there is imperfect competition in a market, there is also inefficiency in resource allocation. In perfect competition, allocative efficiency occurs because firms in the long run produce at the rate of output where $P = MC$. In oligopoly, monopoly, and monopolistic competition, firms tend to produce a rate of output in the long run at which P is greater than MC. Because P indicates the extra benefit that consumers derive from one more unit of a good and MC indicates the extra cost of one more unit of the good, society would prefer to have more of that good produced. That is, there is a restriction of output, or an underallocation of resources to the production of that good. Whenever markets are imperfectly competitive, the operation of markets fails to maximize social welfare.

In Chapter 11, we also learned that the distribution of market-determined incomes might fail to satisfy society's concerns with fairness. Consequently, the public sector might decide to redistribute income through taxing and spending programs.

But there are other instances in which markets fail. Private markets organize the exchanges of goods and services between suppliers and purchasers. These exchanges between willing participants are based on the costs to producers and the benefits to consumers of the relevant commodities. The price indicates how much money someone is willing to give up in order to possess something, and it also registers the amount of money a seller must get to turn that something over to someone else. However, this exchange can miss a proper evaluation of the true social benefits and costs of the production and consumption of some goods and services.

Social benefits or costs that occur outside the sale of a good or service are called **externalities**. For example, when someone buys a pack of cigarettes based on that person's demand for them and the producer's costs, there are external effects outside of this exchange. These externalities include the effects of cigarette smoke on other people and smoking-related medical problems the buyers may develop (which may not have been part of the original demand, regardless of required warnings!). These are *external costs* connected with this one good. In a similar fashion, if someone who lives next to you purchases a CD and plays it so loud that you can hear it, and you like it, then you derive an *external benefit* from that exchange. In both cases, the external results are not taken into account in the transaction between the buyer and the seller of the commodity. Whenever externalities are present, the operation of markets does not assure an efficient allocation of resources.

In all of these instances of **market failure** (where the market fails to register all of the costs or benefits of a transaction, or to produce an efficient result), the public sector may attempt to improve the allocation of resources. That is, governmental programs to limit the effects of economic concentration and to account for external benefits and costs may improve the allocation of resources and increase social welfare.

6. Identify at least one other example of an external cost of a specific exchange. Also, identify one other example of an external benefit.
7. What external costs might be associated with a cigarette smoker's eventual medical bills?

Public Goods

If a society relied only on markets to allocate resources to important activities, there would be inefficiency in resource allocation. That is, in some cases, the operation of markets either fails to provide any of a good or underallocates resources to it. Street signs are a good example. Without street signs, businesses would be unable to deliver products, people could not find each other's homes, and general confusion would reign. But street signs are not provided by markets.

The reason is that private markets require suppliers to be able to charge people for the right to possess or consume a commodity. There is property ownership in a private exchange. Someone who owns a bicycle can prevent other people from using it. With street signs, however, there is no ownership, and people cannot be excluded from using them. In this case, no private firm would provide them because there would be no way to force people to pay for using them. Some people might be willing to pay, but not everyone would. Consequently, communities have used governmental institutions to create public provision of street signs, and citizens are compelled to pay for them through taxation. Services or activities provided or subsidized by the public sector are called **public goods**.

In the same way, even when private markets do work to provide a certain good or service, if external benefits aren't taken into account, resources could be underallocated to that activity. A good example is education. Figure 13.3 shows the demand for education based on the collected individual preferences

■ FIGURE 13.3 The Supply and Demand for Education

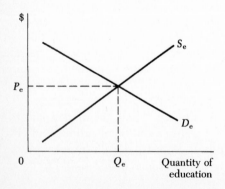

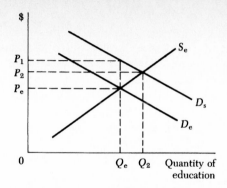

■ FIGURE 13.4 External Benefits from Education

of people for their own education and the supply of education based on the resources necessary and their costs. The market equilibrium is at P_e and Q_e.

But there are external benefits to education that accrue to the whole society. Literacy, the advance of science and technology, culture, and economic intercourse require and benefit from having an educated population. The total social benefits from education, then, include the private benefits to individuals plus the external benefits to society. In Figure 13.4, D_e shows the private demand for education, the marginal private benefit of additional amounts of education. D_s, however, is a "social demand curve" that includes both the private and the external benefits of education. That is, it shows the marginal social benefit of education:

$$MSB = MPB + MEB,$$

where MSB = marginal social benefit, MPB = marginal private benefit, and MEB = marginal external benefit. The marginal external benefit of education is the difference between D_e and D_s.

If the external benefits are not taken into account, there will be an underallocation of resources to education. At Q_e, the social benefit of education, at P_1, exceeds its MC at P_e (off the supply curve). Society would benefit from increased output of education. In fact, maximal social welfare would occur at Q_2, where the marginal social benefit of additional education equals the marginal cost of education (where the supply and demand curves intersect). The public sector in the United States, for more than a century, has responded to this situation by providing various forms of assistance to education—the provision of public schools, scholarship assistance, tax exemptions to private educational institutions, funds for teacher training and educational development, and others. In this way, when external benefits are present and markets tend to underallocate resources, public sector provision of the good or service or subsidization can improve social welfare by encouraging increased allocation of resources to the activity.

8. In an interview in the October 1984 *Redbook*, Dr. Benjamin Spock, the famous pediatrician, argued that "the family is the most important thing in life" and that "fathers have just as much responsibility as mothers for caring for their children or deciding who will care for them." Spock went on to suggest that the United States needs more quality day care centers and that there should be subsidies for parents who prefer to stay home with young children. What are the external benefits from good parenting that might justify the use of public resources for child care or home-parenting subsidies? Would you favor such programs? Why or why not?

Externalities (External Costs)

In Chapter 9 we developed the cost curves that the firm faces in making decisions about what level of output to produce (the one that maximizes profits). We also saw how the competitive market encourages firms to produce at the lowest average cost—that is, the rate of output that minimizes the per-unit use of scarce resources. However, this characterization of the competitive firm's behavior poses one large problem.

When firms make decisions about the use of resources and the rate of output, the cost information they take into account concerns their own out-of-pocket, internal costs. But there may be some other costs of production that are external to the firm. These externalities are costs of productive activity that the firm is not forced to bear. For example, in the process of making paper, a paper company may produce air and water pollution. The costs are borne by people who must breathe and smell the befouled air and by the potential downstream users of the dirtied water. These are social costs of production. The firm does not have to pay a price for the use of these resources.

Because these costs do not enter into the firm's calculations, these resources will tend to be overused, and there will be an inefficient use of resources. Therefore, the conclusion that competitive markets tend to produce resource efficiency is true only if there are no externalities in the production process.

9. What other social costs of production, besides pollution, can you identify?

We can illustrate this point graphically. In Figure 13.5, we assume a constant price, at MR = *P*. MC represents the marginal private costs that face the firm at different levels of output, and MSC represents the marginal social costs of production at different levels of output (including both MC and the social costs that are external to the firm). That is, MSC = MPC + MEC, where MSC = marginal social cost, MPC = marginal private cost, and MEC = marginal external cost. In attempting to maximize its profits, the firm will produce output Q_p. However, from a social perspective, at Q_p, MSC > *P*, so

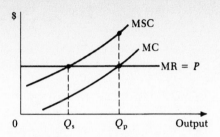

FIGURE 13.5 Marginal Social Costs

resources are overallocated to output of this product. Social welfare would be maximized where MSC = P at output Q_s. With social costs taken into consideration, there would be a tendency toward lower rates of output. Alternatively, if the external costs were considered and the firm were to maintain its rate of output at Q_p, the product's price would have to be higher.

10. Would an individual firm be willing to take any or all of the social, external costs of production into account? Why or why not?

The existence of externalities in capitalist production has made it necessary for federal, state, and local governments to intervene by requiring firms to consider externalities. Eliminating such externalities as pollution involves costs, so firms will avoid incurring them—because they reduce profits and because the firm faces competition. Consequently, government control forces firms to take the externalities into account. Areas where governmental regulation has emerged include occupational health and safety, noise pollution, hazardous wastes, strip-mined land reclamation, air and water pollution, and the operation of nuclear power plants and disposal of their wastes. In each of these cases, the government has made private firms accountable for the external costs.

For example, each year industries in the United States generate billions of pounds of hazardous wastes—acids, strong bases, and chlorinated hydrocarbons. In the past, most hazardous wastes found their way to illegal waste dumps, where they pose severe potential health problems for local communities. Douglas Costle, administrator of the Environmental Protection Agency, noted the dangers in 1980: "These sites with their contents of long-lasting chemicals now represent time capsules releasing their toxic contents into the surface waters, into our groundwaters and seriously degrading our landscapes and our water supply." Some experts have estimated that there are more than 55,000 illegal waste dumps in the United States; the Hooker Chemical Company dump at Love Canal in Niagara Falls, New York, was one of the most widely publicized of these.

Toxic chemicals are linked to higher incidences of cancer among workers and residents of areas where such chemicals were produced. Toxic wastes are considered to be the third largest environmental cause of cancer. The

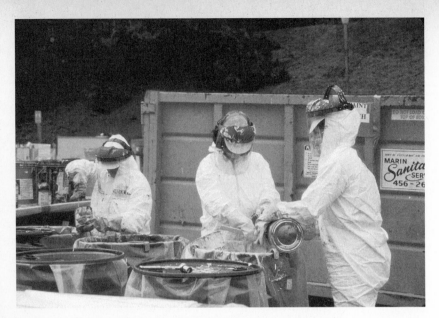

■ Sanitation workers disposing of hazardous paints and chemicals.
(Bonnie Kamen/PhotoEdit)

high-tech industry, one of the most rapidly expanding sectors of the U.S. economy, relies heavily on the use of many chemicals (arsenic, strong acids, and solvents) that are poisonous or carcinogenic. Thus, as we near the end of the twentieth century, workers and communities across the United States are faced with a major, continuing environmental hazard in coping with the production, usage, and storage of toxic chemicals. Jonathan Harr's Pulitzer Prize–winning book *A Civil Action* focuses on the intense community, corporate, legal, and political conflict in Woburn, Massachusetts, as a result of the alleged effects of hazardous wastes on groundwater supplies and public health. Robert Redford has bought the movie rights to this dramatic story of externalities and what to do about them.

As a result of rules established by the Environmental Protection Agency in 1980, companies are now responsible for keeping track of their hazardous wastes and ensuring that they are properly disposed of. Firms must take some of the cost into consideration and may not pass all of it along to the public at large.

How much of our resources should we devote to dealing with this problem? Environmentalists want increased funding for the cleanup of hazardous-waste sites, but the Congress is concerned about budget deficits and overregulating businesses. Who is responsible for the dangerous waste sites already in existence? Who should have to pay for their cleanup? How long will it take? Who will be liable for the health effects of toxic wastes, which may not appear for over two decades? The externalities associated with one of the most dynamic and important sectors of our economy in the post–World War II period obviously raise some fundamental economic and political questions.

11. Explain why no one firm would be likely, *on its own*, to reduce the air pollution or to keep track of and clean up the toxic wastes from its production process.
12. In recent years, there has been intense controversy over acid rain. Many residents of Canada and the northeastern United States, as well as scientific studies, blame pollution from coal-burning electricity-generating plants and other factories in the Midwest for higher acidity in lakes and rivers. The higher acidity, in turn, has threatened the ecology; in fact, many lakes no longer can support fish life. The Reagan administration resisted efforts to institute stricter controls on sulfur dioxide emissions on the grounds that not enough information existed to place the blame for acid rain on air pollution.
    a. Explain why acid rain is or is not an externality. What should be done about it? By whom? What difference does it make?
    b. The 1990 Clean Air Act required utilities in the Midwest to use more expensive, low-sulfur coal to reduce acid rain. What should be the effects of this legislation be?

THE REGULATION OF ECONOMIC CONCENTRATION

In Chapters 9 and 10, we demonstrated that the theoretical results of competitive markets are superior to those of all forms of imperfect competition. This conclusion suggests that an appropriate response by the public sector would involve attempting to control the effects of imperfect competition and to encourage competition. The regulation of monopoly prices and antitrust policy are both informed by this approach.

Regulating Monopolies

If a monopoly exists, the government has several options. The monopoly can be left alone, with the notion that in the long run monopoly profits will provide an incentive for some competition. The government can take over the operation of the activity itself, as in the case of the postal service. It can break up the monopoly so that it has less economic power, as in the reorganization of AT&T in the 1980s. On the other hand, oftentimes governmental units acknowledge the existence of a monopoly, give it legal sanction, and then regulate its prices.

To see how this works in theory, consider Figure 13.6, which illustrates the demand and cost conditions for a monopolist. With the goal of profit maximization and its monopoly, the firm would produce at Q_m and charge a price of P_m. Since $P > MC$ at Q_m, we know that output is restricted. Society would

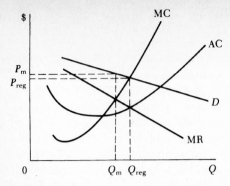

■ FIGURE 13.6 Monopoly Price Regulation

be better off if the monopolist could be forced to produce a greater rate of output and charge a lower price. *Price regulation* can accomplish this goal. If the government regulates the price of the monopolist at P_{reg}, the monopolist may not charge a higher price. From rates of output 0 to Q_{reg}, the firm's demand curve becomes P_{reg}, and MR equals P_{reg}. Profit maximization then would require the firm to produce Q_{reg} and to charge a price of P_{reg}. The effect of price regulation is to force the firm to charge a lower price and produce at a higher rate of output. At Q_{reg}, P equals MC, and there is efficiency in resource allocation, *ceteris paribus*. At Q_{reg}, P is still above AC, so the monopolist still earns economic profits, but they are less than at Q_m.

Governmental price regulation therefore can improve the economic results of monopoly. However, the actual process of price regulation is not quite as easy as Figure 13.6 suggests. Governmental regulators need to have information on the monopoly's costs, its capital assets, and the demand for its products. They cannot regulate the quality of the service provided. Other problems involve the relationships between regulators and the regulated.

The Federal Communications Commission's regulation of AT&T's long-distance phone service offers some examples. The FCC begins with a decision to provide AT&T with a certain rate of return based on the value of its capital assets. Prices are then set so that the excess of revenues over costs produces the determined rate of return. AT&T then has an incentive to exaggerate its capital base as well as its costs so as to increase its profits. Not only must the FCC collect a great deal of information, it needs to keep tabs on AT&T's capital and cost estimates. Given the specialized knowledge required to regulate AT&T's business, the regulators are often people familiar with the industry, perhaps through past involvement in it. (To some extent, the purpose of opening long-distance phone service to other companies was to reduce the regulatory effort, since prices would be influenced by some competition.)

Despite these potential difficulties, price regulation of utility rates throughout the United States does succeed in limiting monopoly pricing power and in requiring monopolies to submit to some degree of public accountability.

Antitrust and Economic Concentration

Based on the economic theory that competition produces a maximization of social welfare and that imperfect competition, in the form of economic concentration, interferes with an efficient allocation of resources, the U.S. government has developed antitrust policies. In general, **antitrust policy** consists of laws intended to limit monopoly and promote competition. Antitrust policy in the United States has always been controversial.

The first national antitrust legislation was the **Sherman Antitrust Act,** passed by Congress in 1890. Political support for the act was based on a reaction to and antipathy toward large and rapacious corporations at the end of the nineteenth century. Farmers, workers, consumers, and small businesses all were, or felt they were, victimized by the railroad, steel, sugar, and other trusts. The act prohibited combinations in "restraint of trade" and price-fixing. Most national corporations and the trusts themselves, however, were not enthusiastic about the new legislation. In fact, the Sherman Antitrust Act was first applied to labor unions as conspiracies in restraint of trade! Since that time, the act has been used to break up some large companies (e.g., the Standard Oil Company), and it has been supplemented by other legislation aimed at preventing mergers that would limit competition or move industries toward "too much" concentration.

In recent years, the antitrust debate has shifted ground to some extent. During the 1980s, a merger wave swept the U.S. economy. Mergers occur when one company purchases the stock of another company. In a **horizontal merger**, companies in the same industry are merged—for example, Texaco Oil's purchase of Getty Oil in 1984. In a **vertical merger**, the merged companies are in different production stages of a particular product, as in the case of the large oil companies that have merged the production, refining, and distribution systems of petroleum products. A **conglomerate merger** takes place when the merging companies do not have similar or related businesses, as is the case with ITT, which comprises a large number of previously independent companies producing many different goods and services. Antitrust policy has historically been concerned with mergers because they tend to limit competition and to increase economic concentration—with the possible consequences of higher prices, monopolization, and economic inefficiency. In addition, increased economic concentration has always been accompanied by a fear that individual firms will wield increased economic and political power.

Some economists have charged that the merger wave of the 1980s increased corporate borrowing and contributed to higher interest rates in the 1980s. Others are concerned about the implications for the concentration of economic and political power if this trend is not checked. Many liberal economists would like to see the antitrust laws enforced more vigorously, and many anticorporate radicals would even like to see some of the larger corporations broken up.

On the other hand, some liberal economists and most conservative economists would prefer to follow a policy of "benign neglect" toward merger activity and large corporations. They do not see bigness per se as a problem.

Even large firms must be sensitive to the market, they argue; if the demand for a product shifts, the firms will respond. Even large firms have an incentive to innovate, because it might increase their profits. Large firms can take advantage of economies of scale, thereby increasing the efficiency of production. Antitrust enforcement, charge these economists, can limit the ability of U.S. firms to compete with overseas companies, or it can prevent a healthy company from swallowing up an unhealthy one, which might improve the overall operation of the merged entity. Furthermore, antitrust litigation costs corporations, and ultimately consumers, billions of dollars in court and legal fees. During the 1980s, the Reagan administration adopted a policy of very lax enforcement of the antitrust laws. The Clinton administration did not adopt a very different stance toward preventing corporate mergers.

13. Is there a difference between a "bad" merger and a "good" merger? Are the mergers between Gulf and Standard Oil, between Texaco and Getty, and between General Electric and NBC good or bad?

14. Do you think antitrust policy should be vigorously enforced? Why?

15. In 1984, a Supreme Court case upheld a law that involved an example of the public (and political) definition of property in Hawaii, where the state took land to reduce economic concentration. In the mid-1960s, eighteen landowners held over 40 percent of the private land in Hawaii. In writing the majority opinion for the Supreme Court, Justice Sandra Day O'Connor concluded, "Regulating oligopoly and the evils associated with it is a classic example of a state's police powers. We cannot disapprove of Hawaii's exercise of that power. . . . [It is] a comprehensive and rational approach to identifying and correcting market failure." What is the "market failure"? Is it appropriate for the state to correct it?

POVERTY AND INCOME REDISTRIBUTION

In Chapter 11 we examined the size distribution of income in the United States and explored why it is distributed relatively unequally. One aspect of income inequality is the existence of poverty. Poverty can be both an absolute and a relative concept. In an absolute sense, poverty might refer to a society or individuals within it that cannot easily meet the day-to-day requirements for continued survival. For example, street beggars in an underdeveloped country or homeless people in the United States are poor. But poverty can also have a relative meaning. Even the families in the United States with the lowest incomes are probably better off materially than many families were in the latter half of the nineteenth century. Nevertheless, given the standard of living and the operation of markets in the U.S. economy, it is clear that some people and some families are demonstrably much less well off than most and that survival and development are very difficult for them.

TABLE 13.6 Persons Below the Poverty Line

Year	Number of Persons (in Millions)	Percentage of Population
1960	39.9	22.2
1965	33.2	17.3
1970	25.4	12.6
1975	25.9	12.3
1980	29.3	13.0
1982	34.4	15.0
1983	35.5	15.3
1984	33.7	14.4
1987	32.5	13.5
1990	33.6	13.5
1993	39.3	15.1
1994	38.0	14.5
1995	36.4	13.8

Source: *Statistical Abstract of the United States*, 1989, 1995, 1997.

The federal government estimates a level of income called the **poverty line**. For different family sizes and locations in the country, the poverty line is meant to measure the amount of income required to purchase the basic necessities of life—food, clothing, and shelter. For an urban family of four in 1993, the poverty line was $14,763. All urban families of four with incomes less than this for 1993 are classified as being poor. (Only cash income from work or from assistance is counted.) Given this standard, the federal government estimates the number and percentage of people below the poverty line every year. Table 13.6 shows the number of persons below the poverty line and their percentage of the total population for various years from 1960 to 1995.

In the early 1960s, almost 40 million Americans, more than one-fifth of the nation's citizens, were classified as being poor. In 1973, the number and the percentage reached their lowest levels—23 million people and 11.1 percent of the population. Since then, both the number and the percentage in poverty increased until 1983 and decreased moderately through 1990. In part, the general health of the economy in the 1960s and early 1970s and the crisis in the economy since the mid-1970s accounted for this movement in the country's poverty population. In the late 1980s, moderate growth ameliorated poverty slightly. In the early 1990s, however, with slow growth, the poverty rate increased fairly dramatically, but decreased somewhat in the mid-1990s.

Over the past thirty years, the response of the public sector has also had an impact on the incidence of poverty. The case for income redistribution to correct for the inequality of market-determined incomes is at its strongest when directed toward attempts to limit poverty. At the height of its postwar prosperity in the early 1960s, the United States recognized the extent of the poverty in its midst and developed public policies to try to eradicate it. A former Catholic lay worker, Michael Harrington, wrote *The*

Other America, identifying the extent and incidence of poverty in the country; another Catholic, John F. Kennedy, took up the political challenge of persuading the country to develop federal programs to give relief and promise to its poor. In 1980, the National Advisory Council on Economic Opportunity in its twelfth annual report on poverty concluded that the progress in reducing the ranks of the poor between the mid-1960s and 1980 almost totally resulted from federal income assistance and antipoverty programs. During the 1970s, they noted that the number of poor people stayed fairly constant, at about 25 million, and that the growth of the economy did not contribute much to the access of poor people as a whole to adequate jobs and earnings. And, while the total number of poor remained stable, the composition of the poverty population became increasingly concentrated among women, the very young, and minorities. They also predicted that if federal programs for the poor were cut back, the poverty rate would increase.

Their prediction has been borne out. The Reagan administration, as part of its overall economic program, cut back on the growth of many federal programs directed toward the poor, including cash transfer programs such as Aid to Families with Dependent Children and noncash programs such as food stamps, housing assistance, Medicaid, and school lunch subsidies. As a result of these cutbacks and the worst recession since the Depression (in 1981–1983), the poverty rate increased. In 1983, more than 35 million people were classified as poor—15.3 percent of the U.S. population. With continued budget constraint, significant progress in reducing poverty seems unlikely in the 1990s. Indeed, in 1993, the poverty rate was close to its level during the severe recession of the early 1980s.

16. Do you think the federal government should contribute income to poor families? Noncash assistance such as food stamps? Training programs for disadvantaged youth? Why or why not? Does society have a public responsibility to eliminate poverty? What external costs does poverty have? What is the chance that you will be poor in the future?

17. In 1984 the Census Bureau reported that 29.6 percent of all nonfarm citizens received at least one form of federal assistance ranging from Social Security to unemployment compensation to Medicare. Further, 18.8 percent of the population received benefits based on need, such as Medicaid, food stamps, public housing, or Aid to Families with Dependent Children. Why is the impact of the federal government on people's incomes and economic status so widespread? Is it too widespread?

THE LIMITS OF GOVERNMENT'S ROLE

In this chapter, we have focused on the expanding role of government in the economy and the economic arguments that can be and have been made to justify that expansion. During the twentieth century, the liberal view of the state has largely won the debate and informed public choices about antitrust policy, the provision of public goods, the regulation of externalities in the private sector, and income redistribution programs. However, some criticisms can be made of government's economic role, and its ability to pursue its objectives efficiently has some inherent limitations.

As conservatives point out, governmental programs often limit the pursuit of individual freedom in a democratic society. Public provision of goods and services, taxation to finance governmental activities, and regulation all require compulsion. Children must go to school, property owners must pay taxes, factories must clean up their pollution, and so on. Political decisions in a democracy by nature place some limitations on individuals in the interests of the general welfare. The trade-off, which is often only implicit, is a collective good for individual sacrifice. In return for paying taxes, we get schools, parks, national defense, roads, welfare, and so on. As individuals, we might not choose all of the things we get, but as members of local, state, and national communities, we participate in the political decision-making process (to a greater or a lesser extent) and must live with the results. Freedom is not an unqualified right. Nevertheless, there is a fervent debate about the appropriate degree of limitation on individual freedom.

To facilitate the legislative process and to administer public programs, public institutions have been created. Office buildings, legislatures, and other public edifices are physical evidence of the public sector, and the bureaucracies that they contain are living and continuing proof of its vitality. To accomplish public objectives, bureaucracies are necessary, but their operation can produce some problems. If there is no measurable output sold in markets (as there is in the private sector), there is no way to calculate success in economic terms. Without profits as an indicator, bureaucracies may have difficulty maintaining efficiency. Roads obviously provide an important public service, but how do we know whether construction companies or road crews are performing at top efficiency? In the private sector, the market theoretically weeds out inefficiency. In the public sector, patronage and/or a civil service system might limit the ability of supervisors to fire employees (justly or unjustly). Finally, bureaucracies develop vested interests in their own programs. Consequently, inertia may affect decisions about the allocation of resources to public programs—rather than having the decision based on the maximization of social benefit compared with the social costs incurred in the use of scarce resources.

The decision-making process in the public sector is imperfect. When we suggest that public involvement in the economy might improve the overall allocation of resources or correct some of the problems of the private sector, we are implicitly assuming that the decision-making process is rational. Through reasoned debate, research on the effects of different programs, cost-benefit analysis, a free press, and democratic procedures and institutions, we may approach rationality. However, the practice of democracy may also veer off from the ideal. Voters and the voting process often emphasize the people, personalities, and parties involved rather than an unemotional, reasoned consideration of the issues. Modern media certainly reinforce the tendency toward superficiality. Special interests have the edge in the political process. Their issues are well defined, their numbers are organizable, and they often have access to significant amounts of money. They lobby, advertise, and persuade, and they are effective in influencing the course of legislating and administering public policies.

As we emphasized at the beginning of this chapter, the government's role in the economy is an issue rich with controversy. In addition, the interpretations of its actual operations and institutions are varied, depending in part on the ideological predispositions of the analysts.

CONCLUSION

Much of the analysis in Part 3 on microeconomics is directly derived from classical and neoclassical economics. In the realm of the market and the firm, the analysis is helpful, although qualified by the historical emergence of non-competitive market structures and the corporation. We are no longer in the ideal and competitive world of Adam Smith. However, supply-and-demand analysis can still help us understand how markets work to determine prices and allocate resources. And the focus of microeconomics on the firm has caused economists to pay increasing attention to the modern corporation and labor unions. The existence of various market failures, ranging from external costs and benefits to the distribution of income to economic concentration, has also led to the continued development of the role of the public sector in the economy.

In the realm of the operation of the total economy, classical theory has had more severe problems. It contends that the market system will produce growth and full employment. However, this theoretical result conflicts with historical experience. As a result, Keynesian theory emerged to provide an alternative understanding of the macroeconomy. We will explore this theory in Part 4.

Review Questions

1. What is the appropriate role of the government in the economy? What functions should it be responsible for performing?
2. Is it proper for the government to regulate the prices of monopolies? Why or why not?
3. The federal government, in particular, has a number of programs intended to reduce poverty in the United States. Should the government be responsible for this effort? What other possible solutions are there to the problem of poverty? Or is there nothing that can be done about it?
4. Traffic accidents as a result of intoxication are an external cost of the consumption of alcohol. Is this true? Why or why not? If yes, specify what the external costs are. If not, explain. What private and public efforts might contribute to a reduction of this problem?

5. The postal service provides a public good, for example, in the delivery of first-class mail anywhere in the country for the same price. (Before you start thinking of all kinds of nasty jokes and comments about the post office, consider what has to happen in order for a letter that you put in a box somewhere to get to its recipient, say, all the way across the country.) What is the *external* benefit from postal service? Could the same service be provided by the private sector? Who would object to the private provision of postal service?

6. In March 1990, an Exxon supertanker, the Exxon *Valdez*, crashed into a reef and spewed 11 million gallons of crude oil into Alaska's Prince William Sound.

   a. What were the external costs of this event? Who bore the costs?

   b. Later, fishing firms, tour operators, and the state of Alaska sued Exxon for damages. Why? How could damages be valued?

   c. In 1990 a federal grand jury indicted Alaska for violating federal pollution and marine safety laws. What was the purpose of those laws? What is the current status of these efforts to make Exxon account for the external costs of this oil spill? What will the effects be on Exxon?

7. In 1988, RJR Nabisco, a tobacco company that merged with a food company, proposed a $17 billion deal to make the company privately held, and Philip Morris offered to buy out Kraft Foods for $11 billion. Why are tobacco firms interested in food companies? Philip Morris also owns the Miller Brewing Company. What kinds of mergers are these? Do you think antitrust policy should be concerned about such mergers?

8. Many states have laws requiring that children under twelve wear seat belts in automobiles.

   a. Using concepts from this chapter, what is the logic of these laws?

   b. School buses are not required to have seat belts. Why not? Should they be?

9. In the mid-1990s, welfare reform was summarized by the slogan "workfare, not welfare." From 1996 to 1997, along with a growing economy, millions of welfare recipients moved from welfare to work. Is this success likely to be maintained if the economy stops growing? What might happen then?

EXPLORATIONS IN MICROECONOMICS— AFFIRMATIVE ACTION

D uring the 1996 presidential campaign, the issue of reforming or abolishing the nation's affirmative-action policies gained prominence when attacked by California's Republican governor Pete Wilson. Others immediately joined the debate. Wilson supported initiatives to roll back affirmative-action policies, and the University of California's Board of Regents voted to discontinue considering race in giving preference in admission to one candidate over another.

Issues present in the current debate over affirmative action reflect not only different assumptions held by conservatives, liberals, and democratic socialists, but also incorporate many microeconomic concepts we have studied, including opportunity costs, resource markets, cost, revenue, income distribution, poverty and discrimination, equality of opportunity versus equality of condition, and access to markets.

HISTORY OF AFFIRMATIVE ACTION

Initially affirmative-action policies were aimed at increasing employment opportunities for black workers. Executive orders in 1941 and 1961 barred race discrimination in employment, and in 1967 President Lyndon Johnson signed an executive order extending nondiscrimination to include women. At the same time, Johnson emphasized the need for companies to go further to ensure that women and minorities would be actively recruited, hired, and promoted. In 1972, the Equal Employment Act mandated that federal contractors with more than fifty employees take "affirmative action to ensure that applicants are employed and that employees are treated during employment without regard to their race, color, religion, sex, or national origin." These contractors are to have an affirmative-action plan with timetables and goals to correct any shortcomings, which might include an obvious underrepresentation of women or minorities on the company payroll. As a result of suits brought under Title VII of the Civil Rights Act, courts ordered that employers must take steps to ensure nondiscrimination. Complaints are heard by the Equal Employment Opportunity Commission for private employers and the Department of Justice for state and local governments. (In 1994 the EEOC litigated 0.5 percent of the complaints filed.)

These affirmative-action programs—executive orders mandating nondiscrimination and the Equal Employment Act—came under attack during the early 1990s.

THE CRITICS

In a 1994 essay titled "Discrimination and Income Differences," economist June O'Neill noted the mounting concerns about affirmative-action policies:

> Generally speaking, I believe that the civil rights movement of the 1960s played a positive role. During the 1970s, however, antidiscrimination policy took a more militant and, in my opinion, a destructive turn as the policy known as affirmative action took center stage. At the federal level, the policy requires that firms holding federal contracts set numerical hiring goals for women and minorities with the threat of loss of their federal contracts if they fail to meet these targets. The setting of hiring goals requires the estimation of available pools of qualified minorities and women that in practice cannot be done with any precision. In consequence, the original standard of the Civil Rights Act, which made discriminatory behavior by employers illegal, has given way to a new standard based almost entirely on numerical results. A firm that does not have the proper composition of women and minorities can be found in violation, even if it has not engaged in any discriminatory act.
>
> There are several things wrong with this new direction. One is that it is a serious departure from the principle of equal treatment under the law, which requires that a person's race, religion, national origin, or gender should not be the basis for preferential treatment. Affirmative action is intended to help disadvantaged groups overcome the effects of past oppression. But in violating principles of justice and individual freedom to enforce equality, it employs tactics that become reminiscent of a Maoist "cultural revolution." . . . Moreover, it is not likely to be genuinely helpful. Some who obtain a job through affirmative action may be pleased. But if the job is viewed as undeserved, the process will generate ill will and divisiveness, and perhaps a loss of self-image on the part of the protected minority. Finally, affirmative action has misplaced the emphasis on what is really needed to improve economic status, and in so doing it has given young people the wrong message. In the long run, it is hard work and the acquisition of job skills that ensure success, not jumping ahead in the queue. A better direction for public policy is to provide the resources that are needed to acquire these skills.
>
> —June Elenoff O'Neill, "Discrimination and Income Differences,"
> in *Race and Gender in the American Economy: Views from across the Spectrum,*
> Susan F. Feiner, ed. (Upper Saddle River, N.J.: Prentice-Hall, 1994).
> Reprinted by permission of Prentice-Hall.

THE DEFENDERS

Defenders of affirmative action argue that despite very limited federal enforcement of affirmative-action policies, they nonetheless have led to small increases in the number of women and minorities in traditionally white male workplaces. One limited, but successful example of this is found in a 1989 class-action suit filed against the Shoney's restaurant chain for alleged racial discrimination. After settling the suit out of court for $134.5 million, the company initiated a "turnaround" and began to actively pursue workplace diversity. (For more information on the Shoney's case, see *The Wall Street Journal*, April 16, 1996.)

In her 1996 book *In Defense of Affirmative Action*, economist Barbara Bergmann notes that affirmative action seldom comes into question when a black or woman candidate is clearly superior to other job applicants. Nor do critics complain about "casting a wide net" to obtain the best applicant pool (thus also casting the net to white males who would otherwise be excluded). The difficult decisions come on the close calls, when there is no clearly superior candidate, when white male, white female, and minority candidates have comparable skill levels and strengths—but they are clearly *not* alike in what they bring to the workplace. Bergmann makes the following observations about such circumstances:

> Some might say that in those hard cases fairness and justice are best served by putting an immediate end to segregation by giving a chance to a highly acceptable black candidate. Others would say that fairness to the "best" candidate overrides all other considerations, and requires that the employer put off ending the segregation for as long as it takes to find that black candidate who will be judged to be the "best." In deciding which side to come down on in these hard cases, we have to balance the value of bringing segregation to a quick end with the value of avoiding violations of a (perhaps imperfect) merit system. . . .
>
> That violations of the merit system occur regularly for purposes other than bringing race segregation to an end—purposes such as helping a nephew or a friend, or taking on someone who will help the sports team—also needs to be taken into account when thinking about the hard cases. When such violations occur, fairness to the displaced "best" candidate is seldom an issue. As we have already noted, geographic balance is routinely shown when political appointments are made, and religious balance is considered as well. When a university gives preference in admission to an applicant who might strengthen the tennis team or is the child of an alumnus, grades and test scores are given less than usual weight in the decision. However, little resentment seems to be stirred by such decisions, even among those directly affected in a negative way. . . .
>
> It causes no adverse comment when large and important businesses such as the W. R. Grace Company, the Washington Post Corporation, and the New York Times Company place at their head the son or son-in-law of the majority stockholder or the previous head. No protest is made that the company is acting unfairly to a better-qualified non-relative who might otherwise have gotten the position. Nor is there any complaint, even from the stockholders that the company's performance will be degraded by its failure to find the most qualified person. But if the *New York Times* attempts to ensure that it has blacks among its reporters and editors, then resentments arise. That some departures from choosing the "best" are accepted with no complaint at all, while departures made for the purpose of reducing the exclusion of African Americans or women are complained of bitterly, is something that bears thinking about. . . .
>
> The fact is, of course, that in the labor market white males retain largely intact the highly favored position that they had in 1964, the year employment discrimination by race and sex was made illegal. In 1994, among those working full-time,

pay for white non-Hispanic males was 49 percent higher than pay for other labor force participants. Differences in skill levels account for some of this pay difference, but nowhere near all of it. Segregation on the job by race and sex remains a common pattern. Opening access for all to the job enclaves that are now the preserves of white males would take a far more rigorous application of affirmative action techniques than has yet occurred. It would take the introduction of vigorous affirmative action programs into the many workplaces where they have been absent or ignored.

—From *In Defense of Affirmative Action* by Barbara R. Bergmann. Copyright © 1996 by Basic Books, a division of HarperCollins Publishers, Inc.

Many of the concepts discussed in the chapters on microeconomics as well as earlier chapters are at issue in discussion of affirmative action. Answer the questions below to more carefully think about some of these concepts and relate them to another. Also, examine the following case Bergmann presents involving possible questions of affirmative action through the eyes of an outside observer giving employment advice to the company in question.

ACME AND AFFIRMATIVE ACTION

The Acme Company employs 310 machine operators, who operate large machines used in construction, such as bulldozers and cranes. Acme pays them $525 a week, which is good pay for a person without a college education. The personnel manager is concerned that the company has never hired a black in this job. The law says the company has to treat blacks and whites fairly, and he wants to make sure the company is hiring in a fair way.

A machine operator for Acme needs the kind of ability and judgment that an excellent car driver has. The person also needs a sense of responsibility, since careless mistakes could be costly and dangerous. All special training can be given on the job.

Acme had twenty-three vacancies last year, about two a month. Each time there is a vacancy, the employees are asked to spread the word, and an ad is put in the newspapers. Those who apply are given an aptitude test and an interview. The personnel department is then supposed to pick the best applicant.

The company, which is in a city that is half black, got applications last year for the machine operator vacancies from 440 whites and 45 blacks.

Acme's personnel manager reviewed what had happened to the black applicants. He found that they had done about as well as the white applicants on the aptitude test, However, most of the black applicants did not make a good impression on the interviewers. No black had been selected as the best candidate for any of the twenty-three vacancies, although for one of the vacancies a black had been rated third best.

Given this scenario, which of the following actions would you endorse? Briefly explain why.

1. The personnel manager should remind the interviewers to be careful to be fair to blacks. He should tell them that black and white applicants have an equal right to be considered for machine operator jobs.

2. The personnel manager should try to find ways to encourage more black candidates to apply, with a goal of doubling the number of black applicants.
3. The personnel manager should encourage the interviewers to hire at least a few of the blacks who have been judged competent to perform the job.
4. For the next few years, the personnel manager should try to fill at least 10 percent of the vacancies with blacks who have been judged competent to perform the job.
5. To break the pattern of an all-white work force, the personnel manager should ask the interviewers to find competent blacks and hire them for the next five vacancies.

Source: Excerpts from *In Defense of Affirmative Action: The Case for Colorblind Justice* by Barbara R. Bergmann © 1996 by Basic Books, a division of HarperCollins Publishers, Inc.

Exercises

1. What are the opportunity costs of affirmative-action policies to each of the following groups?
   a. qualified women and minority workers
   b. employers
   c. consumers
   d. other employees of the company
   e. society
2. What are the opportunity costs of not using affirmative-action policies to each of the following groups?
   a. qualified women and minority workers
   b. employers
   c. consumers
   d. other employees of the company
   e. society
3. How might Shoney's cost analysis have been affected by its alleged race discrimination? Its revenue stream?
4. Is Bergmann correct in her assessment that few are concerned when sons of corporate leaders (or even coaches) are hired? Why or why not? Does merit have different meanings in different circumstances? Explain.
5. John Bates Clark, one of the early contributors to microeconomic theory, wrote, "The distribution of the income of society is controlled by a natural law, and . . . this law, if worked without friction, would give to every agent of production the amount of wealth which that agent creates." What does this mean? (Use MRP = MFC to explain your answer.) Does this explain why college-educated women and black men earn lower incomes than college-educated white men?
6. Watch newspapers and other media for current affirmative-action cases. In 1996 several visible affirmative-action cases captured headlines as women and minority workers charged major corporations with discrimination. In November 1996, Texaco settled out of court in a race discrimination suit, paying $176.9 million. In January 1997, Publix, a large southern grocery chain, also settled a discrimination case out of court, paying $81.5 million to 150,000 current and former women employees.

Women workers had charged Publix with denying them access to higher-paying management jobs and promotions. (See *The Wall Street Journal*, January 27, 1997, p. B4.) A federal sexual-harassment case against Mitsubishi's U.S. unit began in mid-1996.

    a. How was the Mitsubishi case resolved? (See Rochelle Sharp, "A Mitsubishi U.S. Unit Is Taking a Hard Line in Harassment Battle," *The Wall Street Journal*, April 22, 1996.)

    b. What are the major issues in current affirmative-action cases? Have any gone to trial? Were any settled out of court? What are the circumstances?

9. In the mid-1990s, welfare reform was summarized by the slogan "workfare, not welfare." From 1996 to 1997, along with a growing economy, millions of welfare recipients moved from welfare to work. Is this success likely to be maintained if the economy stops growing? What might happen then?

MACROECONOMICS

In Part 3, we examined how microeconomics analyzes the behavior of consumers and firms in the U.S. economic system. We focused on the behavior of markets, the different types of market structures, efficiency, scarcity, the nature of the modern corporation and labor unions, and the role of the government.

We will now supplement this microeconomic theory with macroeconomic theory and policy. **Macroeconomics** is the body of economic theory that attempts to analyze the behavior and performance of the whole economy. It describes and explains the dynamics of the institutional and governmental framework of our economic system by focusing on *the total or aggregate performance* of the economy. We begin our discussion of macroeconomics with an exposition of income-expenditures theory, which explains the performance of the economy in terms of employment, income, output, and price levels. A macroeconomic perspective further requires that we explore the relationship between the monetary system and the economy's aggregate performance. We can then use our understanding of monetary theory and policy and the role of governmental fiscal policy (government spending and taxation) to focus on how best to achieve the major macroeconomic goals of full employment, economic growth, and price stability.

While microeconomics focuses on the decisions of individual actors in the economic system, macroeconomics studies the more aggregate behavior of consumers, businesses, and the government, as well as the market for imports and exports. Although we are shifting to the macroeconomic viewpoint of the aggregate, our examination of the markets for goods and services, money, and even labor will use many of the tools of microeconomics. Such microeconomic concepts and methods as markets, supply, demand, equilibrium, and marginal analysis can help us describe and explain aggregate economic behavior. Thus, while the focus of the discussion will clearly be different, macroeconomic theory relies heavily on microeconomic foundations.

Chapter 14 identifies and describes some of the most important goals and problems of macroeconomics. It also introduces the measuring tools of the National Income and Product Accounts (NIPA). Chapter 15 explores the theoretical roots of modern macroeconomics and describes the Keynesian model, using graphical analysis and simple algebraic formulas. Chapter 16 focuses on the role of government in making fiscal policy. Chapter 17 introduces money, financial intermediaries, and monetary policy. Chapter 18 combines elements of monetary theory and aggregate expenditures theory in examining aggregate supply and aggregate demand. Finally, Chapter 19 explores the major macroeconomic problems we face today—unemployment, inflation, and slower economic growth. It also integrates, summarizes, and critically reflects on the past and present efficacy of contemporary macroeconomic policy in the United States.

14

Macroeconomics: Issues and Problems

INTRODUCTION

This chapter begins our focus on **macroeconomics**, which examines the economy as a whole. Instead of studying individual parts of the economy, such as firms or labor unions, or concepts such as property and value, we turn our attention to entire sectors that make up our national and international economic system and to aggregate concepts and problems, such as unemployment, inflation, interest rates, deficits, and taxation. These are topics that affect every one of us.

In this chapter we will examine the goals of macroeconomics, review postwar U.S. macroeconomic trends, develop several tools that will aid our understanding of macroeconomic theory and macroeconomic policy, and define aggregate measures for economic activity in the National Income Accounts. We will begin by considering the importance of macroeconomic theory and some of the ways macroeconomic policy might help to alleviate economic problems.

MACROECONOMIC GOALS

In the early 1950s, the U.S. government accepted as its responsibility three basic macroeconomic goals: (1) economic growth, (2) full employment, and (3) price stability. Government policies should help the economy attain these goals. However, as we will see later, these goals are not necessarily compatible. Despite conflicts among these goals, many would agree that economic growth, full employment, and price stability are rational goals. We want people employed. Stable prices are good for most of us. And economic growth has become synonymous with a higher standard of living and economic progress.

Economic Growth

Simply put, **economic growth** is the increased output of goods and services over time. Not only is growth assumed to be necessary and good, but more growth is assumed to be better than less. Economic growth, after all, creates employment and income.

To measure economic growth, economists have developed sophisticated tools that measure the performance of the economy and its annual rate of real growth. By using a method known as national income accounting (explained later in this chapter), they calculate the **gross domestic product (GDP)—** the total dollar value of all goods and services produced in a given year—and monitor its rate of growth. The obsession with economic growth is symbolized by a "GDP clock," built during the Nixon administration in the early 1970s at a cost of $1 million. It ticked off a $2 trillion GDP in 1978 and $4 trillion in 1985; 1995 brought the $7 trillion GDP figure into view. Each tick officially registers the fact that the United States continues to have the world's largest GDP. Once we have measured GDP, we can find the percentage change to calculate its growth rate from year to year. Table 14.1 shows recent average growth rate.

During the 1960s and early 1970s, critics challenged the basic assumptions concerning economic growth, arguing that more growth does not necessarily mean an improved standard of living. Others now charge that the GDP merely quantifies the performance of the economy but does not reflect the qualitative dimension addressed by the question, What is the real societal value or cost of increased GDP growth?

Much of this critique stems from a consideration of the environmental aspects of increasing economic growth. Human health and well-being are endangered by toxic wastes and air and water pollution, while acid rain threatens the quality of our food supply. Issues including the demise of the rain forests, global warming, and population growth have reminded us that these are worldwide concerns. Growing ecological awareness in the context of energy and environmental crises has made us examine our values, attitudes, goals, and economic assumptions more intensely.

The economic growth controversy also focuses on issues of income distribution in the United States. Annual increases in economic growth do not lead to more equitable distribution of the increased output. Empirical data support the claim that despite the tremendous increases in GDP since World

■■■ TABLE 14.1 Average Annual Rates of Growth, Unemployment, and Inflation

	1950s	1960s	1970s	1980s	1990s
Real growth rate[a]	4.0%	4.1%	2.8%	2.7%	2.0%
Unemployment	4.4	4.8	6.2	7.3	6.4
Inflation	2.4	2.0	7.1	6.7	3.5

[a] In constant dollars.

Source: *Economic Report of the President,* 1984, 1990, 1997.

War II, the distribution of income in the United States did not change significantly until the 1980s, when it became *less* equal.

Another concern is that economic growth may be too rapid, causing labor and input shortages, which in turn increase prices. In addition, economic growth has not evolved in a stable pattern. The United States has experienced nine major recessions since World War II. The instability characterized by the fluctuations of the business cycle has been a primary feature of the postwar era.

Full Employment

The attainment of high levels of employment has been a goal of the U.S. government since the passage of the Employment Act of 1946 following the Great Depression of the 1930s. Congress reaffirmed that goal in passing the Full Employment and Balanced Growth Act of 1978, which set targets of 3 percent inflation and 4 percent unemployment and directed the president to take steps consistent with these goals. These steps might include creating a more favorable business climate and direct federal expenditure policies, among others. The country has come closest to full employment mostly during times of war.

Unemployment refers to people who would like to have jobs but don't. The Department of Labor defines people as unemployed when they are over age sixteen, are actively seeking work, do not have a job, and have made

TABLE 14.2 Selected Unemployment Rates 1950–1995

Year	All Workers	By Sex and Age			By Color		Experienced Wage Earners	Household Heads	By Selected Group			
		Both Sexes 16–19	Males— 20 and Over	Females— 20 and Over	White	Black and Other Races			Married Men— Spouse Present	Women Who Maintain Families	Full-Time Workers	Blue-Collar Workers
1950	5.3	12.2	4.7	5.1	4.9	9.0	6.0	—	4.6	—	5.0	7.2
1955	4.4	11.0	3.8	4.4	3.9	8.7	4.8	—	2.8	—	3.8	5.8
1960	5.5	14.7	4.7	5.1	4.9	10.2	5.7	—	3.7	—	—	7.8
1965	4.5	14.8	3.2	4.5	4.1	8.1	4.3	2.7	2.4	—	4.2	5.3
1970	4.9	15.3	3.5	4.8	4.5	8.2	4.8	2.9	2.6	5.4	4.5	6.2
1975	8.5	19.9	6.7	8.0	7.8	13.9	8.2	5.8	5.1	10.0	8.1	11.7
1980	7.1	17.8	5.9	6.4	6.3	13.1	6.9	—	4.2	9.2	—	—
1985	7.2	18.6	6.2	6.6	6.2	13.7	6.8	—	4.3	10.4	—	—
1990	5.6	15.5	5.0	4.9	4.8	10.1	5.3	—	3.4	8.2	—	—
1991	6.8	18.7	6.4	5.7	6.1	11.1	6.6	—	4.4	9.3	—	—
1992	7.5	20.1	7.1	6.3	6.6	12.7	7.2	—	5.0	10.0	—	—
1993	6.9	19.0	6.4	5.9	6.1	11.7	6.6	—	4.4	9.7	—	—
1994	6.1	17.6	5.4	5.4	5.3	10.5	5.9	—	3.7	8.9	—	—
1995	5.6	17.3	4.8	4.9	4.9	9.6	5.4	—	3.3	8.0	—	—
1996	5.4	16.7	4.6	4.8	4.7	9.3	5.2	—	3.0	8.2	—	—

Source: *Economic Report of the President*, 1990, pp. 338–339; 1996, p. 324; February 1997, p. 346.

some effort to find work during the last four weeks. The unemployment rate is the percent of people without jobs relative to the total number of people in the labor force (those with jobs or looking for jobs). About half of the U.S. population is in the labor force, and this base is used for the unemployment estimates. By 1995 almost 132 million of the 263 million people in the United States were in the civilian labor force. Table 14.2 shows unemployment rates for selected groups of workers from 1950 to 1995.

> 1. Does it surprise you that married men typically have lower unemployment rates than other groups of men (see Table 14.2)? Why or why not?

Economists have defined five basic types of unemployment:

1. **Frictional unemployment** is caused by the temporary mismatching of people with jobs because workers change jobs, employers seek new workers, and new people enter the labor market. All labor markets have frictional unemployment; even during the severe labor shortage of World War II, unemployment persisted at about 2 percent.
2. **Seasonal unemployment**, as the name implies, results from changing seasonal demand and supply for labor. Ski instructors seeking jobs in the summer and farmworkers laid off in the winter contribute to seasonal unemployment.
3. **Structural unemployment** presents a more serious problem. It results from permanent displacement of workers due to shifting product demand or technological changes that require new skills. The shift in demand from natural to synthetic fibers created problems of structural unemployment for places such as Fall River, Massachusetts. The mechanical picking of tomatoes caused many migrant farmworkers to become structurally unemployed. Such unemployment is a function of geographic, as well as skill-level, mobility.
4. **Cyclical unemployment** is due to the decreased demand for labor during a downturn in the business cycle. The high unemployment of the 1930s was basically a problem of cyclical unemployment. More recently, the high unemployment rates of the early 1990s were also cyclical.
5. **Hidden unemployment** is not included in the official unemployment rate and is probably the hardest concept to define and measure. Growing evidence suggests that many people would like a job if they thought one was available, but many have become so discouraged by their past failures to find employment that they have literally given up trying. Technically, such people are outside the labor force, but as a practical matter, they are unemployed. One sign that hidden unemployment exists is the rise in the labor force participation rate (the proportion of the total population seeking jobs) during the early stages of economic recovery. If more people seek jobs as the number of jobs increases, why weren't they part of the labor force when the unemployment rate was higher? In addition, many people work part-time but would prefer to work full-time. These people

are counted as being employed. (We might also add people who work but earn incomes below the poverty level.)

More than 10 million people (on the average) were unemployed during the recession of 1980–1982. (Princeton economist Alan Blinder calls them "cannon fodder in the assault on inflation.") Although the number of unemployed fell to 6.5 million in 1989, it quickly rose to 9.4 million in 1992 as the result of the recession that began in 1990. Unemployment rates then trended downward to 5.4 percent in the recovery that continued through 1997. Unemployment has direct social consequences for unemployed individuals, their families, and communities facing closed factories, unemployment lines, and discouraged workers.

Counting the Unemployed. Beyond the real costs to those unemployed and to lost output, there are also problems in simply counting and defining the unemployed in our economy. Critics claim that the national measures of unemployment actually understate the real rate of unemployment. They argue that a different definition and measurement technique would reveal a national "underemployment" rate of 9 to 16 percent.

David Gordon, who taught at the New School of Social Research, called attention to the problem of *underemployment* and suggested that it was a more appropriate measure than the traditional notion of unemployment. As a more meaningful statistic, it would give economists better information and be more instructive to policy makers. Gordon defined underemployment as the number of people who fall into the following four categories:

1. *Unemployed people*—those who are actively looking for work but unable to find a job
2. *Discouraged workers*—those who are unemployed and want work but have given up in frustration because they believe no jobs are available
3. *Involuntary part-time workers*—those employed part-time who want full-time work but are unable to find it
4. *Underemployed people*—those who are working full-time but earning less than the poverty level of income as specified by the Bureau of Labor Statistics (in 1994 for an urban family of four, $15,141 per year, compared to approximately $7,900 per year paid to a person working full-time at the 1994 minimum wage).

We can use these categories to adjust the traditional measure of unemployment. During the first quarter of 1990, the Bureau of Labor Statistics reported just over 4.0 million workers who were involuntary part-time employees and 6.6 million who were underemployed. Discouraged workers are estimated at 1.2 million. When combined with the unemployed, these 20.4 million discouraged, involuntary part-time, and underemployed workers generate an "expanded unemployment rate" of 19.5 percent in 1990. Some critics argue for counting only part of the involuntary part-time employees (since they are employed part of the time) and only part of the underemployed (since they too are employed). Using half of these two categories, we arrive at a rate of 14.2 percent.

2. Do you anticipate unemployment in your future? Why or why not? What are your "odds"?
3. Does it make any difference how we count the unemployed? Explain.

Costs of Unemployment and Underemployment. Unemployment is an economic (opportunity) cost. Every 1 percent of the labor force that is unemployed represents several billion dollars of potential GDP.

In addition, unemployment has social and psychological costs—crime, family disintegration, and increasing mental health problems, to name a few. An examination of the nature of unemployment in the United States also reveals an identifiable institutionalized process of discrimination according to race, sex, and age. This became increasingly evident as unprecedented numbers of minorities, women, and teenagers entered the labor force in the 1980s. In 1994, when the national unemployment rate averaged 6.1 percent, the unemployment rate for minorities averaged 11.5 percent—and over 35 percent for black male teenagers.

A last consideration related to unemployment involves poverty and welfare. Almost 7.6 million Americans who work full-time or part-time are earning less than the U.S. government's 1994 poverty level of $15,141 for an urban family of four. For U.S. citizens who are neither employed nor receiving any form of income from unemployment compensation, Social Security, or disability, welfare is the only way to meet survival needs. Welfare became a costly, cumbersome, degrading, inefficient, and unmanageable government program. During the next few years, we will see the effects of welfare reform measures undertaken in 1996. Nevertheless, the absence of full employment makes welfare programs necessary.

Price Stability

One thing that many people have in common is an aversion to **inflation**, which is an upward movement in the general price level. Deflation, on the other hand, indicates a downward movement of the general price level. Price stability occurs when there is relatively little movement in the general price level.

The price level is measured by some sort of price index, such as the **Consumer Price Index (CPI)**. A typical price index measures the average level of prices in one year or period as a percentage of the average price level in some base period. The Consumer Price Index is computed by the Bureau of Labor Statistics (BLS). Each month the BLS surveys markets in some fifty urban areas for the prices of 400 "typical" consumer goods and services. The bureau then computes the CPI by measuring the present cost of this "basket" of items as a percentage of the cost in some base period:

$$\text{CPI} = \frac{\text{current cost of basket}}{\text{cost of basket in base year}} \times 100.$$

The inflation or deflation rate then measures the percentage change in the price level:

$$\text{current inflation or deflation rate} = \frac{\text{current CPI} - \text{last year's CPI}}{\text{last year's CPI}} \times 100.$$

In the 1970s the U.S. economy experienced frequent periods of inflation. During the 1980s and 1990s, annual rates of price increase remained low overall. Still, price increases have been greater than the overall inflation rate in some selected markets. For example, college students have experienced rapid rises in the cost of tuition each year, as well as higher than average prices for textbooks. In the 1980s potential home buyers were confronted by high housing prices.

Because rapidly increasing prices often affect our consumption and saving decisions, we tend to have a greater sense of well-being when prices are stable. We don't have to worry (as much) about whether our savings will suffice to send us to college or help maintain our standard of living after we retire. We do know, however, that inflation is not a problem for those who correctly anticipate it and take appropriate precautions. For example, if prices rise by 7 percent and workers are aware of these economic developments, they expect a 7 percent inflation rate. To keep real (inflation-adjusted) wages at the same level, workers will demand at least a 7 percent wage increase. They will also put their savings into assets that will yield at least 7 percent. With these adjustments, workers correctly anticipate inflation and insulate themselves from it. But, if wages rise by only 4 percent with a 7 percent increase in prices, workers' income will lose 3 percent in purchasing power.

Those hurt by inflation include people on fixed incomes, usually the elderly; those working under fixed-cost or fixed-wage contracts; and individuals or institutions who have lent money at an interest rate less than the current rate of inflation. Many contracts now allow for price fluctuations, and many pensions are adjusted for inflation. Financial institutions react to inflationary pressures by charging higher interest rates, or even variable rates pegged to bonds that reflect price or inflationary changes. Still, people prefer price stability as a way to avoid the necessity of forecasting correctly and adjusting behavior to that forecast.

During the 1970s, the United States experienced record levels of inflation caused by factors related to demand, supply, and expectations. Owing to the same factors, the 1980s brought an ebbing of inflationary pressures. Several unexpected forces entered into the scenario during the 1970s, all of which heightened the problem of inflation. In 1973 an embargo imposed by the then-powerful Organization of Petroleum Exporting Countries (OPEC) nations sent energy prices soaring. The reduced supply of oil caused the general price level to rise and output to fall. Shortages and price increases were also felt in the markets for food, metals, and other primary materials.

The 1970s also ushered in a period of increased government regulation. This time, instead of antitrust legislation, the government regulated various aspects of our living and working environments and promoted equal opportunity. While the social benefits of these regulations were widespread, they were also expensive, and these costs initially came on board during the 1970s. Accelerated government expenditures resulting from the Vietnam War added an estimated 3.25 percent to the underlying inflation rate, while the surge in oil prices, first in 1973 and again in 1979, added 4.75 percent. These factors alone explain an inflation rate of 8 percent during the 1970s.

At the beginning of the 1980s, events eased inflationary pressures. Oil prices began to drop as production increased and demand fell. The prices of other raw materials declined as well, due to overproduction in many of the developing nations. Deregulation, or the rollback of government regulations, in a number of industries increased competition and lowered prices. The value of the dollar restrained prices of imported goods, helping to lower inflation in the United States by providing a supply of cheaper imports and by keeping domestic prices in check as U.S. producers struggled to remain price-competitive. Labor made many concessions during the recession of 1980 to 1982, and these "givebacks" kept wages from rising. More importantly, the Federal Reserve cut the growth rate of the money supply to halt the inflationary trends, and lower inflation rates were gained at the cost of high rates of unemployment.

With the Federal Reserve policy continuing to target low inflation rates, the late 1980s to late 1990s saw relatively stable prices, averaging growth rates between 2 and 4 percent. This period was accompanied by stable oil and resource prices, and slow wage growth.

The goal of price stability is sometimes achieved due to good economic policy, good luck, or some combination of the two, particularly when factors outside the realm of domestic economic policy tools are operating.

4. Which of the three macroeconomic goals—growth, full employment, or price stability—is the most important to you? Why?
5. If you could add another goal to this list, what would it be? Explain.

MACROECONOMIC TOOLS

To achieve the three macroeconomic goals of growth, full employment, and price stability, economists and the government use economic theory to analyze the economy and to formulate macroeconomic policy. The primary macroeconomic tools are monetary and fiscal policy. Let's briefly define each of these and see how they are used.

The Federal Reserve System manages, coordinates, and controls the monetary system of the U.S. economy. Proper management of this system makes available the quantity of money necessary for desired economic growth at interest rates capable of inducing the desired levels of investment and spending. **Monetary policy** consists of tools that can change the amount of money and credit available in the economy. It is administered by the Federal Reserve

System to achieve and promote economic growth, maximum employment, and price stability.

Through **fiscal policy**, the government manipulates its expenditures and taxation to attain the basic macroeconomic objectives. Fiscal policy is administered by the executive and legislative branches of the federal government and is coordinated with monetary policy. (See Chapters 16 and 17 for more on fiscal and monetary policy.)

Fiscal and monetary tools have both been part of contemporary macroeconomic policy as it has developed over the last fifty years. Several important issues and problems are associated with this policy. We shall examine a few of these in the context of the economic history of the post–World War II period, when monetary and fiscal policy became mainstays in a U.S. economy aiming to achieve the goals of growth, high employment, and price stability.

The Rise of Pax Americana: 1946–1960s

Just as the Victorian period in the late nineteenth century was dubbed "Pax Britannia," the period after World War II until the middle to late 1960s has been called "Pax Americana." The world seemed ripe for economic quests and successes by the United States. In the last three decades, however, we have become acutely aware of the reduction in U.S. power in the international economic arena and are often uncomfortable with this loss of prestige. The U.S. position continued to worsen until conditions taking advantage of economic growth, improvements in levels of employment, and deficit reductions arose in the mid-1990s.

At the beginning of this period, however, many important institutions characteristic of the U.S. economy were already in place. Monopolies and large corporations had been present since the turn of the century, and the 1930s brought increasing levels of government intervention in the economy. After the prolonged recession and depression of the 1930s and the wartime economy of the 1940s, the setting was ripe for the United States to push ahead and prosper. The 1950s arrived with abundant potential and opportunity; Europe and Japan lay in ruin, and the United States possessed the only productive industrial capacity not debilitated by the war. These industries were immediately called on in the effort to rebuild Europe and Japan, as well as to meet the increased demands for consumer goods and services that had developed in the United States during the war. In the decade following the war, economic growth skyrocketed. Real weekly earnings increased at an average of 2.3 percent per year. Productivity increases held steady at 3.2 percent, and real GDP growth was about 4 percent. Unemployment averaged only 4 percent. When unemployment rose to 5.5 percent in the recessions of 1949, 1954, 1958, and 1960, inflation slowed to the astonishingly low level of 2 percent.

As the prosperity of the 1950s passed into the 1960s, the government began to actively participate in the growth that had earlier been dominated by the private sector. The new federal interstate highway system was the highlight of federal expenditures of the 1950s. These expenditures continued into the 1960s and were joined by a federal Model Cities program that contributed to the U.S. urban infrastructure. In 1964 Congress passed a tax cut specifically designed to increase income—the first planned policy action of its type. Later in the 1960s, the Great Society program was put into place to reduce poverty. Only now are we realizing the successes of these programs—as well as some of their shortcomings. The 1960s also brought the war in Vietnam and a demand for more federal expenditures to finance it.

Also by the 1960s, Japan and the industrial nations of Western Europe had rebuilt their plants, and their economies were strengthened. Increased foreign production challenged U.S. goods in world markets, and U.S. economic growth slowed. In the international sphere, the dollar, which served as the "key currency" in all international transactions, was coming under economic attack as other nations regained their prewar economic positions. This pressure eventually led to a devaluation of the dollar and a new system for determining international exchange rates.

The Decline of Pax Americana: 1970s–mid-1980s

The decade of the 1970s was to bring even more distressing news on the economic front. U.S. economic growth and strength were challenged from several sides. The oil embargo of 1973, coupled with agricultural shortages, showed the vulnerability of the U.S. economy (and others as well) to supply shocks on a world level. A severe recession in the midseventies sent unemployment to 9 percent. As the economy began to recover in 1977 and 1978, inflation skyrocketed to 13.3 percent. In the last half of 1979, the Federal Reserve put in motion a series of credit restraints that sent the economy plummeting into yet another recession. Economic growth slowed, and throughout the decade, growth was due almost entirely to rising employment and not greater productivity. The service sector dominated the employment growth of the seventies, with many dead-end, low-paying jobs providing entry for an expanding labor force.

While the 1970s were marked by record levels of inflation in the United States, the early 1980s witnessed both the highest levels of unemployment since the 1930s and the lowest levels of inflation since the 1960s. In 1981 the economy experienced a recession and modest recovery, then plunged into the deepest recession since the Great Depression. This recession can largely be explained by actions of the Federal Reserve, which was using monetary policy to actively restrict the supply of money between late 1979 and 1982. (Chapter 17 explains these concepts in more detail.)

Monetary ease and historically high government expenditures and tax cuts combined to generate the recovery of 1983–1984, which, despite very slow economic growth, persisted until 1989. Unemployment fell as some workers headed back to the factories and many others moved into the service sector. Inflation remained stable at 3 percent, but increases in real weekly earnings averaged only 0.3 percent. The economy, however, had been left with very high real rates of interest, resulting at least partially from large government expenditures and tax cuts creating deficits. Throughout the 1980s, the federal government incurred large and persistent budget deficits. High interest rates hurt the economy by hindering job creation and investment in new plants, equipment, and housing. In addition, these high rates of return attracted foreign money to the United States and kept the value of the dollar high through 1985. This promoted the importation of relatively cheap foreign goods, hurting U.S. producers, who lost out in two ways: not only were more foreign goods purchased in the United States, but fewer U.S. products were exported to the rest of the world. In the early 1980s, high interest rates also affected debt-plagued developing nations, whose debt payments mounted with each rise in the U.S. interest rate.

6. Why do you think inflation is usually high when unemployment is low? Explain.
7. What is debt? How does it arise? Do you worry about going into debt? Why?

The U.S. Economy of the late 1980s and early 1990s

During the 1980s, the Federal Reserve continued to increase the money supply, resulting in lower interest rates. During this period of sustained growth and low inflation, a stock market crash in the United States wiped out some $500 billion of wealth, signaling that all was not well with the U.S. economy. By the end of the week of October 19, 1987, nearly $1 trillion of wealth* had vanished.

The repercussions of the crash were felt throughout the world. Quick intervention by the Federal Reserve assured both confidence and sufficient liquidity to underwrite any instability that might spread to the banking and credit industries. Indicators showed the economy to be in reasonable health; the 6 percent unemployment level was the lowest in a decade, prices were stable, and economic growth had been led by a massive consumer spending boom. There were, however, economic as well as structural problems that prompted the dramatic decline in the New York Stock Exchange on that day, referred to as Black Monday.

After the 1987 crash, the underlying debt, low saving rate, and institutional problems persisted. The economic recovery of the early eighties continued, with economic growth averaging just over 3.7 percent between 1987 and 1989. In 1989 unemployment reached its lowest point since 1973, when it fell to 5.3 percent. After this, growth stagnated and an economic slowdown continued through 1991.

---

*This wealth is referred to a "paper wealth" by some. It accumulates due to the changing value of stock prices.

The U.S. Economy into the 1990s

The recovery that followed the recession of the late 1980s and early 1990s has lasted through 1997 and has been characterized by increased investment, strong productivity growth, and steady economic growth without inflation.

These six years of continued growth were accompanied by corporate downsizing and sluggish wage growth. Budget and trade deficits continued despite the attention by the president and Congress. The income gap between the haves and have-nots continued to widen, with women and children bearing the brunt of the effects of income redistribution. Although an impressive number of jobs were created between 1982–1988 and 1992–1997, the large number of less-educated workers vying for those jobs has reduced the real earnings of high school graduates and dropouts alike. Rank-and-file workers have experienced an inflation-adjusted 18 percent decrease in real wages since 1973, while corporate chief executive officers have seen their pay increase by an average of 19 percent (66 percent after taxes). Homelessness has become a national problem. The U.S. infrastructure, comprising the stock of highways, bridges, water and sewer lines, that contributed to the growth of the 1950s and 1960s is rapidly deteriorating. Environmental problems confront the United States and the world. Corporate downsizing and reengineering have cost middle managers and skilled and unskilled workers their jobs. And there is little agreement on how best to solve these problems, or which should have priority.

Has the focus on macroeconomic national goals been effective in the post-war years? Certainly the United States has approached desired levels of price stability, lower unemployment, and steady economic growth, but at what cost to the economic future of its citizens?

8. Since 1997, what has happened to economic growth? What has stimulated the rapid or slow growth? Has unemployment increased? Inflation? Why or why not?
9. List five macroeconomic goals you think are important for the next millennium. Briefly explain your choices.

NATIONAL ACCOUNTING MEASURES

As we chart macroeconomic goals through the next few years, it is important to understand what these concepts mean and how we measure them. The scheme of National Income and Product Accounting was developed to put economic growth measures into perspective. These measures give quantifiable definitions to the activities of the major macroeconomic actors (consumers, businesses, governments, and the international sector) and show how they interact to generate production, consumption, and investment.

To help understand the ways in which the economy continues to change over time, economists collect and analyze data that measure economic variables. Economic measurement is usually designed to aid forecasting and explanation of economic events, or it may be used to compare the size or the value of things. When economists speak of the value of the annual output of a nation, they refer to gross domestic product (GDP), published in quarterly reports issued by the Department of Commerce. The media, politicians, and others who regularly comment on economic affairs await the Commerce Department reports in order to assess whether GDP and its accompanying growth rate are up or down. Economists then assess these results and often qualify them—for example, GDP was up 2.5 percent over last quarter, but prices have been increasing by 3 percent at the same time.

In December 1991, the Bureau of Economic Analysis began to emphasize GDP in place of gross national product (GNP). The distinction between the two accounting measures is that GDP includes the income earned by foreign residents and companies in the United States, but not the income earned by U.S. citizens and corporations abroad. The main reasons for the switch are that GDP more closely follows the short-term economic performance of the economy and that most other countries use GDP as their primary accounting measure. The difference for the United States is minimal compared to that of smaller countries, which have many foreign companies setting up shop. In 1995, for example, the percentage difference between GNP and GDP for the United States was only 0.13%. The reason for this small percentage is that the income earned by international firms and citizens in the United States was very close to the income earned by U.S. citizens abroad.

Many decisions and judgments are made on the basis of these accounts. We therefore will spend some time looking at the components of the GDP and other measures of income accounting, or, as they are called, the *National Income and Product Accounts*.

There are two basic ways of arriving at final figures for the various accounting measures:

1. The *goods- or product-flow approach* focuses on the prices and quantities of goods and services sold.
2. The *income-flow approach* focuses on income paid to those producing goods and services.

These approaches appear in the circular flow diagram in Figure 14.1. We can measure either the top part of the circular flow (the income flow) or the bottom part of the circular flow (the goods or product flow) to arrive at equal measures of national income.

The definitions, relations, and data in Tables 14.3 and 14.4 show the derivation of GDP with the goods-flow approach. GDP consists of the total expenditures of the four sectors that purchase goods and services:

$$GDP = C + I + G + (X - M),$$

Chapter 14 MACROECONOMICS: ISSUES AND PROBLEMS

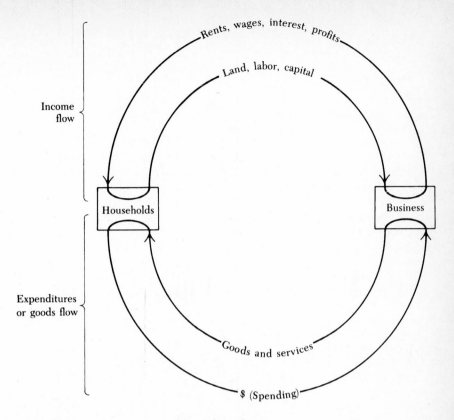

FIGURE 14.1 The Income and Spending Flows

where C represents the expenditures made by consumers, I is investment expenditures made by the business community, G is expenditures on goods and services by government, and $(X - M)$ represents net exports, or exports (X) minus imports (M). The income-flow approach entails summing the various forms of income received from the production process.

POTENTIAL PROBLEMS WITH THE NATIONAL INCOME ACCOUNTS

The measures in the National Income Accounts are corrected for inflation with the use of a price index. Also, use of a value-added approach in the measurement process avoids possible double-counting. There are, however, criticisms of the accounts that have not been addressed. Particularly troublesome are issues of what is and what is not included in the National Income Accounts. Let us see how some potential problems have been avoided and discuss some that remain.

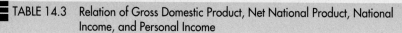

The sum of	Billions of Dollars		
	1992	1994	1996
Personal consumption expenditures (C)	4,219.80	4,698.70	5,151.40
Gross private domestic investment (I)	790.40	1,014.40	1,117.00
Government consumption expenditures and gross investment (G)	1,263.80	1,314.70	1,406.40
Net exports of goods and services (X – M)	–29.50	–96.40	–98.70
EQUALS: Gross domestic product (GDP)	6,244.40	6,931.40	7,576.10
PLUS: Receipts of factor income from the rest of the world	137.90	159.20	228.40
LESS: Payments of factor income to the rest of the world	126.80	168.10	237.30
EQUALS: Gross national product (GNP)	6,255.50	6,922.40	7,567.10
LESS: Consumption of fixed capital	754.20	818.80	858.30
EQUALS: Net national product (NNP)	5,501.30	6,103.70	6,708.80
LESS: Indirect business tax and nontax liability	505.60	572.50	617.90
Business transfer payments	28.40	29.90	32.20
Statistical discrepancy	43.70	31.30	-74.60
PLUS: Subsidies less current surplus of government enterprises	27.10	25.10	17.50
EQUALS: National income (NI)	4,950.80	5,495.10	6,150.90
LESS: Corporate profits with inventory valuation and capital consumption adjustments	401.40	526.50	654.70
Net interest	414.30	392.80	403.30
Contributions for social insurance	571.40	628.30	689.70
Wage accruals less disbursements	–15.80	14.80	0.00
PLUS: Government transfer payments to persons	835.70	933.80	1,056.70
Personal interest income	667.20	661.60	738.20
Personal dividend income	159.40	199.60	230.60
Business transfer payments to persons	22.50	22.60	23.00
EQUALS: Personal income (PI)	5,364.20	5,750.20	6,452.30
LESS: Personal tax payments	627.30	742.10	863.80
EQUALS: Disposable personal income (DPI)	4,430.80	4,959.60	5,588.50
LESS: Personal outlays	4,218.10	4,756.50	5,314.00
Personal consumption expenditures (C)	4,095.80	4,628.40	5,151.40
Interest paid by consumers	112.10	117.60	146.30
Personal transfer payments to rest of world	10.30	10.50	16.30
EQUALS: Personal savings (S)	212.60	203.10	214.60

Note: Dollars are not constant dollars.

Note: Numbers do not add up to the totals shown because of adjustments or inclusion of minor categories.

Source: *Survey of Current Business*, April 1992; April 1997.

The sum of
1. *Personal consumption expenditures (C)* consist of the market value of purchases of goods and services by individuals and nonprofit institutions and the value of food, clothing, housing, and financial services received by them as income in kind.
2. *Gross private domestic investment (I)* consists of acquisitions of newly produced capital goods by private business and nonprofit institutions and of the value of the change in the volume of inventories held by business. It covers all private new dwellings.
3. *Government purchases of goods and services (G)* consist of government expenditures for compensation of employees, purchases from business, net foreign purchases and contributions, and the gross investment of government enterprises. This measure excludes transfer payments, government interest, and subsidies.
4. *Net exports of goods and services (X – M)* measures the excess of (1) domestic output sold abroad over purchases of foreign output, (2) production abroad credited to U.S.-owned resources over production at home credited to foreign-owned resources, and (3) cash gifts and contributions received from abroad over cash gifts and contributions to foreigners.
5. The *residual (r)* —in real GDP only;see item 6—is the amount created by chain-weighted measurement of GDP. (See footnote in the section titled "Real versus Nominal GDP.")

Equals
6. *Gross domestic product (GDP)* is the market value of the newly produced goods and services that are not resold in any form during the accounting period (usually one year).

Plus
7. *Receipts of factor income* from the rest of the world are the moneys received from foreign affiliates of U.S. corporations. The moneys take the form of interest, dividends, and reinvested earnings.

Less
8. *Payments of factor income* to the rest of the world are the payments to foreign residents of interest, dividends, and reinvested earnings of U.S. affiliates of foreign companies.

Equals
9. *Gross national product* (GNP) is the market value of the newly produced goods and services that are not resold in any form during the accounting period (usually one year).

Less
10. *Capital consumption allowance* is an allowance for capital goods that have been consumed in the process of producing this year's GDP. It consists of depreciation, capital outlays charged to current expense, and accidental damage.
11. **Net national product (NNP)** is the net creation of new wealth resulting from the productive activity of the economy during the accounting period.

Less
12. **Indirect business tax** consists primarily of sales and excise taxes, customs duties on imported goods, and business property taxes. These taxes are collected from business and are chargeable to their current costs.

Equals
13. **National income (NI)** is the total income of factors from participation in the current productive process.

Less
14. Contributions for *Social Insurance* consist of payments by employees and the self-employed.
15. *After-tax corporate profits with* inventory and capital consumption adjustments subtracts federal and state taxes levied on corporate earnings and depreciation allowances from corporate profits.
16. *Net interest* is interest earnings minus interest liabilities and part of national income.

continued

POTENTIAL PROBLEMS WITH THE NATIONAL INCOME ACCOUNTS

Plus

17. *Personal dividend income* includes that part of corporate profits returned to stockholders.

18. *Transfer payments* (government and business) consist of monetary income received by individuals from government and business (other than government interest) for which no services are currently rendered.

19. *Personal interest income* includes all interest payments made to persons.

Equals

20. *Personal income (PI)* is income received by households, as opposed to income earned by households.

Less

21. *Personal taxes* consist of the taxes levied against individuals, their income, and their property that are not deductible as expenses of business operations.

Equals

22. **Disposable personal income (DPI)** is the income remaining to persons after deduction of personal tax and nontax payments to general government.

Less

23. *Personal consumption expenditures (C)*—same as item 1.

Equals

24. *Personal savings (S)* may be in such forms as changes in cash and deposits, security holdings, and private pension, health, welfare, and trust funds.

Real versus Nominal GDP

These definitional relationships ignore many difficult and rather perplexing problems. First, there is the problem of the yardstick, money. This is a very flexible yardstick, since dollars are most often worth more or less as time passes (usually less). To solve the flexibility dilemma, economists use index numbers, meaning they compare a "market basket" of selected goods and services from one accounting period with a similar "basket" from some previous accounting period, or base year.* Thus, they can avoid the perils of price instability by inflating or deflating the dollar value accordingly. For example, if prices increase at a rate of 5 percent during a year, a good that cost $100 at the beginning of the first year would be priced at $105 at the beginning of the next. Using a price index, this item would be valued at $100 in constant dollars. This device allows us to remove the effects of price changes from GDP, so that we can measure the changes in *real* output and better assess the actual physical volume of production in the two periods.

---

*In January 1996, the Bureau of Economic Analysis (BEA) released new estimates for the national income and product accounts, moving to a system that uses chain weights instead of fixed weights in the adjustment of real GDP, to remove biases caused by the fixed-weight price system of the past. This formula for this adjustment is no longer as simple as the common market basket example using fixed weights. By adopting the chain-weighting system, the BEA hopes to provide more accurate measures of real GDP. For additional information on these changes, see the 1996 *Economic Report of the President*, pp. 48, 50, and 59.

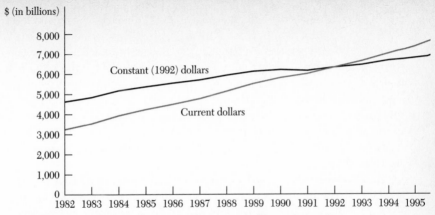

FIGURE 14.2 GDP in Current and Constant Dollars 1982–1996

Source: U.S. Department of Commerce, 1994, p. 446.
Economic Indicators, May 1997, p. 1.0

The GDP deflator is a systematized equation that has been shown to be a reasonable indicator of how much the national product has gained or lost due to recession or inflation. For example, in 1979 GDP went up by 12 percent, but prices went up by 11.3 percent, so real GDP increased by only 0.7 percent. Figure 14.2 shows the variation between real and nominal GDP since 1982.

Value-Added Counting

A second problem encountered in the national income accounting framework is the actual counting process. We can either count the final products produced or sum the amount of value added by each stage of the production process. For example, to enter a loaf of bread into the accounting scheme, we could use the final sale price of the loaf of bread, or we could sum the value added to the loaf of bread by the wheat farmer, miller, baker, grocer, and so on. Both methods should yield the same result, but in the final-product method, there is often a chance of double-counting the components of production. Therefore, the value-added approach is preferred.

What Is Counted in GDP?

The significance of the accounts has also been called into question. These accounts are primarily derived from market transactions with known prices and quantities, and some market transactions are excluded. Excluded transactions include capital gains and losses as well as all illegal transactions. (What would the illegal drug market add to the GDP?) Also excluded is the economic activity of the underground economy—individuals who earn but do not report income on services they render or goods they produce, e.g., cash paid for babysitting. Barter exchange also is part of the underground economy. The size of the underground economy has been estimated at 5 to 30 percent of GDP. Other industrial nations are estimated to have underground economies comparable to that of the United States.

The accounts also include some imputed values for nonmarket transactions. For example, imputed values are added for owner-occupied homes (room and board services exchanged for). But imagine what would happen to the accounts if we made yet another nonmarket inclusion, the value of homemakers' production. If homemakers simply exchanged homes with their neighbors each day and paid one another $50 or more a day (the estimated market worth of homemakers' services), their production would be included in the accounts. These activities are productive; they are services. Currently, however, they are neither measured nor included in the National Income Accounts.

Marilyn Waring, a political economist and former member of the New Zealand Parliament, has suggested in her book *If Women Counted: A New Feminist Economics*, that throughout the world, accounting systems that define productive activity, as well as the economic analysis and teaching that sustain them, automatically exclude the non-market activities of women. To this point she quotes retired Harvard economist John Kenneth Galbraith:

> That many women are coming to sense that they are instruments in the economic system is not in doubt. But their feeling finds no support in economic writing and teaching. On the contrary, it is concealed and on the whole with great success, by modern neo-classical economics—the everyday economics of the textbook and classroom. This concealment is neither conspiratorial nor deliberate. It reflects the natural and very strong instincts of economics for what is convenient to influence economic interest—for what I have called the conventional social virtue. It is sufficiently successful that it allows many hundreds of thousands of women to study economics each year without their developing any serious suspicion as to how they will be used.
>
> —Marilyn J. Waring, *If Women Counted*. Copyright 1989 by Marilyn J. Waring. Reprinted by permission of HarperCollins Publishers.

10. How will you be used by the economic system? Does it matter? Why?
11. What are "natural" instincts? Do you trust them?

The National Income Accounts are often misrepresented as an indicator of social well-being. In 1995, Clifford Cobb, Ted Halstead, and Jonathan Rowe published an article in the *Atlantic Monthly* entitled "If the GDP Is Up, Why Is America Down?" The article noted that the U.S. economy was performing in textbook fashion, with productivity and employment increasing and inflation remaining at low levels, but people didn't "feel" better. Indeed, President Clinton later called it a malaise. These authors argue for new measures for economic progress that would "change the social and political landscape":

> The GDP is simply a gross measure of market activity, of money changing hands. It makes no distinction whatsoever between the desirable and the undesirable, or costs and gain. On top of that, it looks only at the portion of reality that economists choose to acknowledge—the part involved in monetary transactions. The crucial economic functions performed in the household and volunteer sectors go entirely unrecognized. As a result the GDP not only masks the breakdown of the

social structure and the natural habitat upon which the economy—and life itself—ultimately depend; worse, it actually portrays such breakdown as economic gain.

Economic "bads," such as pollution and deaths due to lung cancer attributed to smoking cigarettes, actually increase the GDP. These social costs are not subtracted from, but added to the GDP. As we spend more and more to clean up the environment, the spending *adds* to our national product. As cigarette sales increase, GDP increases. As hospital costs for increased numbers of cases of lung cancer and emphysema occur, GDP increases. GDP, in other words, is not a measure of overall welfare.

12. Can you give other examples in which individual or societal welfare is diminished but GDP is increased?

Social scientists are attempting to construct a qualitative index that measures social welfare. Thus far, the index is quite crude, but it shows that nations with the highest GDP do not necessarily have the highest social welfare ratings, while a few countries with extremely low GDP have *relatively* high standings on the social welfare index.

While GDP and GNP do not measure social welfare, we often look at per capital GNP to show potential effects of a nation's income on its citizens. Table 14.5 shows that while the U.S. GNP is the largest of any nation in the

TABLE 14.5 Per Capita GNP for Selected Countries, 1993	
Country	U.S. Dollars
Switzerland	36,410
Japan	31,450
Denmark	26,510
Norway	26,340
Sweden	24,830
United States	24,750
Germany	23,560
France	22,360
Canada	20,670
Finland	18,970
United Kingdom	17,970
Australia	17,510
Spain	13,650
Mexico	3,750
Chile	3,070
Turkey	2,120
Jamaica	1,290
Philippines	830
Mozambique	80

world, in the United States the per capita GNP is lower than for some other industrial countries. The per capita GNP for less developed countries is only a fraction of the income in the industrial economies.

13. Why is it important to collect data on all of these different macroeconomic variables?

CONCLUSION

This brief overview of macroeconomic problems and issues and summary of aggregate economic measurements provides a conceptual framework for describing relationships among important economic variables. While it is clear that recent trends in the U.S. economy have left us with many questions concerning future directions, we need to ask ourselves, to what extent does contemporary macroeconomic theory adequately explain our current economic reality? We will attempt to provide satisfactory answers for this question and develop an understanding of macroeconomic theory and policy in the following chapters. So let us continue this voyage through macroeconomics by first learning about aggregate measures and then interpreting the theory in the context of its historical roots.

Review Questions

1. Why were full employment, economic growth, and price stability selected as the basic macroeconomic goals in the United States? Should there be others? Explain.
2. The three goals are often at odds with one another. Has the relative emphasis of these different goals changed over time? Why?
3. What do you see as some of the costs associated with unemployment? Inflation?
4. Do events elsewhere in the world affect the U.S. economy? Give some examples.
5. Is it possible to establish an effective body of macroeconomic policy using only fiscal tools or only monetary tools? Why or why not?
6. Do policy measures aimed at alleviating one set of economic problems sometimes make others worse? Should a policy action be undertaken to aid one aspect of the macroeconomy to the detriment of another? Explain.
7. Examine a daily newspaper (e.g., the *New York Times*) for a few days and see how many articles address macroeconomic issues and problems. Make a list of the macroeconomic terms, concepts, and issues that you find.
8. Why should reports of current levels of GDP be received with care?
9. What do the National Income Accounts measure?
10. Increasing numbers of women have entered the paid labor market during the past three decades. What impact would you expect this to have on GDP? Explain.

15

The Classical and Keynesian Models of the Macroeconomy

INTRODUCTION

The tenets of classical macroeconomic theory, formed by Adam Smith, David Ricardo, John Stuart Mill, and others, which focused on growth were carried pretty much intact through the nineteenth century. Economists in the latter part of that era concentrated more on the microeconomic concepts of utility and production than on the total economy. This chapter will sort out four major parts of the classical doctrine, illustrate their use, and then examine the Keynesian critique of classical macroeconomic theory and its inability to deal with high unemployment in the depression-plagued world of the 1930s. We will then formulate the Keynesian model.

Keynes's theory challenged the long-standing economic traditions. Some view the Keynesian contribution as a new paradigm, while others view it as simply a major revision of classical theory. The classical model we discuss in this chapter was never formally set up as such by any of the classical economists. Rather, Keynes drew together the foundations from the writings of the classical economists and constructed the model primarily as a foil against which he could contrast his model in *The General Theory of Employment, Interest, and Money*.

THE CLASSICAL MODEL

We will discuss four elements of the classical model that show how economists analyzed unemployment, inflation, and growth, particularly when the economy suffered during the Great Depression. We will begin by examining the quantity theory of money and the equation of exchange, which was used to show the relationship between money and prices. Next we will briefly examine the goods and labor market, Say's law, and the credit market in the classical model.

The Quantity Theory of Money

A major tenet of classical economic theory is the **quantity theory of money**. Most often this is expressed by the **equation of exchange**:

$$MV = PQ,$$

where M is the money stock in the economy, V is the income velocity of money (the rate of turnover of money), P is the price level, and Q is the level of real national income (real GDP). This equation appears simple enough—perhaps too simple, for when it is examined carefully, it becomes an identity. It is true because it is by definition true. This is because of the definition of velocity—the rate at which money moves through the economy during a given period, or the number of times a piece of money gets spent:

$$V = \frac{PQ}{M}$$

Since national income is a measure of all output (Q) in a country for a year multiplied by the price (P) of each good or service, V is equal, in effect, to national income in a given year divided by the total amount of money available (on the average) during that year.

The classical economists elaborated further on each of the variables in the equation of exchange. They proposed that each of the variables in the equation is affected by both external and internal forces. Q, or national output, is determined primarily by real factors that change slowly over time, such as capital, technology, resource availability, and labor. The quantity of money (M) would not influence these variables in any significant way. The classical economists argued that the income velocity of money (V), on the other hand, is determined by institutional factors that are also independent of any change in the money stock (M). Some of these institutional factors are population density, custom, transportation factors, the state of the art of banking, and wage payments and practices. With Q and V unaffected by changes in the supply of money, the level of prices (P) is directly related to changes in the quantity of money (M).

Since Q and V were defined as relatively constant, this means changes in the quantity of money produce nearly proportional changes in the price level. Thus, if the quantity of money in the economy doubles, the price level is likely to double as well. In terms of output and employment in the economy, money, therefore, does not matter very much; in terms of wages and prices, however, it matters a great deal. The following equations show this:

$$M\overline{V} = P\overline{Q} \qquad\qquad \Delta M = \Delta P$$

Assuming that $\overline{V}$ and $\overline{Q}$ are constant at a point in time, any changes in the quantity of money (ΔM) must lead to changes in prices (ΔP).

The classical economists viewed money as neutral in that it satisfies no direct utility or want. It merely reflects real activity in the economy. It serves as a veil behind which the *real* action of economic forces, such as the growth of the national product and employment, are concealed. Yet money was viewed as a lubricant for the economy, keeping it well oiled and enabling it to run smoothly and effectively. In the classical model, money does not affect the level of output. The labor market plays a role in determining output.

The Goods and Labor Markets in Classical Economics

A second part of the classical model centers on the production of goods, or real output. Equilibrium output is determined by the demand for and supply of labor. Increases in the demand for labor increase output (Q), and decreases in the supply of labor decrease output. In the classical system, the level of output is determined by full employment. The equilibrium real wage defines the level of full employment in the labor force. Anyone willing to work at the prevailing equilibrium wage will be employed—the quantity supplied of labor equals the quantity demanded of labor. Anyone unwilling to work at that wage is regarded as not desiring to work, and therefore not classified as unemployed. As long as wages are flexible (both upward and downward) in the classical world, no conflict will arise. Full employment, as they defined it, is the norm. This fully employed labor force will produce an equilibrium level of goods and services (Q) for the economy.

Say's Law

A third part of classical macroeconomic theory is Say's law, named for the French economist Jean Baptiste Say (1767–1832). In its oversimplified form, the "law" is often expressed as supply creating its own demand. Businesses in the process of producing or supplying goods and services for the market will pay wages or rents to employees, landlords, and others engaged in producing the product. That income may be used to purchase goods supplied by the firm or goods supplied by other firms. The act of production, which supplies goods to the market, at the same time generates income to workers and others, who in turn demand goods and services in the market and spend the dollars they earn on those products. For every dollar of product produced, a dollar of income is created and spent.

Say's law is the basis of the circular flow diagram, in Figure 14.1 on page 307, which is very important in both the Keynesian and classical models. The crude circular flow of the classical economists shows the flow of goods and the flow of income. The lower part of the loop shows the movement of goods from the business sector of the economy to the household sector in return for income spent (expenditures). The upper loop shows the transfer of land, labor, and capital from households to business for use in the production of goods and services in exchange for rents, wages, and interest (income).

The supply, or output, that "creates its own demand" consists of the goods and services produced by the firms or businesses. The factors of production (land, labor, and capital) receive returns of rents, wages and salaries, and interest and profits for their part in the production process. Over time, with expanding population, higher income levels in the household sector create more demand for goods and services. The household sector then spends this income on the goods and services that have been produced, thereby creating an income stream for the business sector. As a result, the aggregate expenditures on goods and services by the household sector will equal the aggregate supply of those goods and services produced by the business sector. Equilibrium occurs when aggregate income or output equals aggregate expenditures.

The Classical Credit Market

Thus far we have assumed that Say's law means all income received during the production process will be spent on goods supplied by producers. But what if some of that income is saved? The classical model accounts for both saving and investment in its analysis of the credit or loanable funds market. Any income saved by consumers will flow into the business sector as investment, through the credit or loanable funds market. In this market, a flexible interest rate adjusts to yield an equilibrium between saving and investment.

The classical model assumes that both saving (S) and investment (I) are functions of the rate of interest (r):

$$S = f(r), \text{ and } I = f(r)$$

The supply of credit comes from people who save. Some of their income is not spent and may be saved in the credit market. The classical economists assumed that higher interest rates cause people to save more because of the higher return on any money they save. Therefore, interest rates are directly related to saving. As Figure 15.1 shows, this gives us an upward-sloping line that represents saving or the supply of credit or loanable funds.

■ FIGURE 15.1 The Classical Credit Market

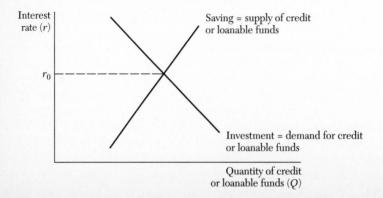

Investment is inversely related to the interest rate. If businesses must borrow funds at high interest rates to finance investments, they will be less willing to borrow and invest. So, at higher interest rates investment will be low; at lower interest rates, investment will be higher. Investors, like savers, make decisions based on the interest rate. In Figure 15.1 the downward-sloping line represents investment or the demand for credit or loanable funds. At r_0 the amount saved is motivated by the amount invested; what isn't spent by some is borrowed and spent by others.

FLAWS IN THE CLASSICAL MODEL

Between 1860 and 1929, the U.S. economy generally displayed rapid economic growth. The phases of growth tended to be cyclical, with upswings in economic activity accompanied by downswings, but with an overall upward trend in economic activity averaging about 2 percent per year. We call these recurrent swings in business activity **business cycles**. Figure 15.2 shows a hypothetical series of business cycles. Note that periods of growth and peaks are followed by periods of slump and troughs.

Economists have offered many explanations to account for business cycles. While few classical economists fully explained these fluctuations, economists who followed them offered explanations ranging from increases in sunspot activity to theories suggesting problems in overconsumption and underinvestment, monetary expansion and contraction, and innovation trends. Indeed, compelling arguments have been made for most of these in explaining cycles of growth.

1. If you were to extend Figure 15.2 to include this year, where would the economy be? In an upswing? A downswing? A peak or a trough? Why?

When economic conditions were in the downswing or trough of the cycle, as in the 1930s, classical economic theory explained the resulting levels of unemployment by insisting that those out of work were voluntarily or temporarily unemployed. They believed that businesses could make more employment opportunities by reducing the prevailing wage rate. As wages fell, the amount of labor demanded by businesses would increase. According to classical theory, these unemployed workers would be more than happy to

▬ FIGURE 15.2 Business Cycles

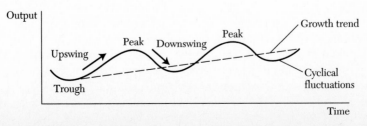

work as long as their wages were above zero. However, during the Great Depression, as wages dropped lower, the number of people out of work actually rose. The classical system failed to explain this.

THE GREAT DEPRESSION

The Great Depression lasted for ten years, from 1929–1939, and left enduring imprints on millions of Americans. It resulted from many different phenomena that seemed to culminate all at once. Some people who are interested in business cycles believe that short-, medium-, and long-run cycles all reached bottom at the same time. Certainly, more than just the 1929 stock market crash sustained the Depression for such a long period. Despite the robustness of the stock market before its fall, several industries in the economy were essentially weak.

Agriculture and manufacturing were perhaps the most important sectors contributing to the duration of the Depression. As the United States grew in the first few decades of this century, the number of agricultural workers fell. Hurt by the exploitation of the rail and storage bosses, and burned by their own speculative activities in land, more and more farmers were leaving or selling out to join the urban migration or to become tenants. The number of independent farms dropped by 40 percent during the 1920s. Output, however, was increasing, and the inelastic demand for farm production did little to help farmers. Unlike the other industries, in which greater supplies meant lower prices and increased demand, demand did not increase for the lower-priced agricultural products. In addition, the European export market declined, as European agricultural production was restored following World War I.

In manufacturing, conditions were mixed. Many people in business foresaw a time of weakness, and although sales, prices, and output were at all-time highs, employers cut back their work forces substantially, especially in the mines and mills. Only in the service and construction industries did employment levels hold their own, for these were areas in which men and women could not yet be displaced by technology. Growth increased throughout the 1920s, but workers were no better off than before. Wages and employment levels simply did not increase. Profits, on the other hand, swelled rapidly, as did the concentration of economic power in the hands of a few wealthy individuals. Profits in 1929 were three times those of 1920. But firms were not reinvesting. This was partially because firms had no incentive to invest; supply was already greater than demand.

The weaknesses in these two industries are directly linked to other causes of the Depression: the lopsided distribution of income, with 5 percent of the population receiving about 30 percent of all income, and the lack of new investment by the business sector. In addition, the existing banking system was troubled. A series of unexpected and urgent demands by customers on some poorly managed banks created fear among all bank depositors, so that even economically sound banks were subjected to "runs" (when large numbers of depositors withdrew their money) and potential failure. Some 5,000 of the nation's banks failed during the Great Depression. Other factors added to the instability: several European governments defaulted on U.S. loans, and in the United States, Congress adopted a balanced-budget philosophy that, by increasing taxes and reducing government expenditures, helped to worsen an already bad situation.

From this description you can see that the U.S. economy had fundamental problems at the time of the stock market crash. From the widespread prosperity of the early 1920s, the late 1920s saw a lack of capital formation, overproduction of goods and services, and an agricultural glut, in addition to international disequilibrium and deep-seated psychological effects of the crash. All these led to prolonged instability, which caused many businesses, organizations, and institutions to collapse and brought havoc to the lives of unemployed workers, the heads of failed businesses, and their families and friends. The Depression of the 1930s was a time of severe unemployment and poverty for the men, women, and children who endured it. Over one-third of the nation was unemployed or living in poverty. Conditions were abysmal for all but a few of the well-to-do.

As conditions worsened worldwide, the U.S. Congress passed the Smoot-Hawley Act imposing a 45 percent tariff on a third of U.S. imports. Other nations retaliated with high tariff barriers to protect their domestic industries from U.S. imports. Retaliation led to even higher tariffs and very high prices on all imported goods. World trade slowed dramatically. During this same period there was a severe contraction in the supply of money, which worsened financial conditions. Between 1929 and 1932, in the United States, 85,000 businesses failed, and stock values decreased from $87 billion to $19 billion. Manufacturing and farm income decreased by 50 percent. By 1933, the GDP had declined from $104 billion in 1929 to $56 billion, and unemployment stood firmly at 25 percent, with 12 million people unemployed. Despite the human misery that swept the nation, Secretary of the Treasury Andrew Mellon advised, "Liquidate labor, liquidate stocks, liquidate the farmers, liquidate real estate."

ENTER JOHN MAYNARD KEYNES

The most important work of John Maynard Keynes (1883–1946) came at a time when the classical model was most under fire because of its inability to account for continued and worldwide depression and the masses of unemployed in the 1930s. Keynes, who was born into a prosperous Victorian family, watched the economic importance of his native Britain wane after World War I, with the rapid growth of the United States and continental Western Europe. He developed his ideas and critique of the classical model slowly over a long period of time. Much of his writing was highly critical of the British authorities. Keynes was one of the first to recognize the implausibility of the British attachment to the gold standard for international payments and to object to the Versailles Peace Treaty after World War I. (He believed correctly that it would be impossible for Germany to meet the reparations called for by the treaty.)

John Maynard Keynes (1883–1946).
(UPI/Corbis-Bettmann)

During the 1930s, the major question being asked in each world capital was what to do about the depression. According to the classical doctrine, the simple remedy was to reduce wages to eliminate the excess supply of workers. But wages were falling, and more unemployment resulted, not less, violating Say's law. Supply was not creating its own demand. The circular flow was not working as it should. Markets were not adjusting to an equilibrium position as laissez-faire predicted. Classical theory and classical economists were in a quandary.

Keynes focused on unemployment and argued, "The postulates of the classical theory are applicable only to a special case and not the general case . . . and not . . . those [conditions] of the economic society in which we actually live." In so doing, he illustrated the futility of the classical scheme, particularly Say's law and the limited circular flow.

The Keynesian Solution

Keynes and some contemporary economists recognized that there are leakages or transfers of funds out of the income and spending flows as well as injections or additions of funds to them. Leakages include saving, taxes, and purchases of goods and services in international markets (imports). With each of these actions, income flows out of the circle in the circular flow diagram of the classical economists. Saving and hoarding remove money from the spending stream and occur when households, deciding that future consumption is better than present consumption, put their money into savings accounts at banks, into the stock market, or under their mattresses. Taxes leave the spending stream of the household and business sectors and are turned over to the government. Imported goods and services from other nations increase the goods and services received by households but reduce the total domestic spending, since these dollars go abroad to pay for the goods and services received.

On the other hand, Keynes noted that injections can be and are made to the income and spending stream. Government spending, investment, and the sale of goods in international markets (exports) add to the flow. Government spending, like consumer spending, increases the income received by the business sector, since government and consumer purchases are made of business products. Government spending may also go directly to the household sector in the form of wages, transfer payments, or income supplements, which in turn will increase spending as well. **Investment** occurs when the business sector creates new capital in the form of new plants, additions to equipment, and the buildup of inventories, or existing stocks of goods and services. Investment is, in effect, business spending. Exports create

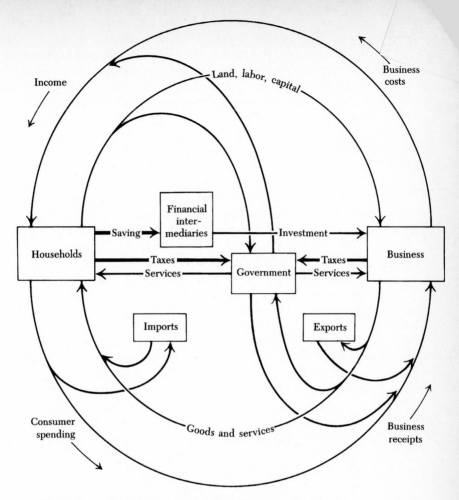

Income

Business costs

Land, labor, capital

Financial inter-mediaries

Households — Saving → — Investment — Business

Taxes — Services — Government — Taxes — Services →

Imports

Exports

Consumer spending

Goods and services

Business receipts

■ FIGURE 15.3 The Circular Flow with Leakages and Injections

an injection into the income stream, since businesses have a new market for their products and receive income. Figure 15.3 illustrates the dynamics of these flows.

For the economy to be in equilibrium, the injections must equal the leakages. As a result, aggregate expenditures for goods and services in the economy will equal the aggregate output or income. This establishes an equilibrium level of income and output that may or may not be at full employment. According to Keynes, an economy can have an infinite number of equilibrium positions, one of which is at full employment. The equilibrium depends on the level of spending in the economy. The classical economists, however, saw one and only one equilibrium—the one that exists at full employment.

Keynes recommended that governments use spending policies to counter cyclical upswings and downswings. These policies could cure a full range of economic maladies. In a depression, increased government spending would increase the levels of income, employment, and output.

The Keynesian model has remained a prevailing economic paradigm for the past half century. It has not always been successful, and economists have continued to add to and revise its core. Despite the conservative challenges of the 1980s, however, it still solidly forms the basis for much of macroeconomic theory. Monetarist Milton Friedman perhaps stated it best when he said, "We are all Keynesians now."

THE KEYNESIAN ECONOMIC MODEL

In the discussion that follows, we will describe the assumptions, methods, and implications of the full Keynesian model, exploring the sources of spending and how they affect aggregate output or GDP in any period.

Consumption

To begin our construction of a simple Keynesian model, we will first examine the assumptions and hypotheses for the consumption function. The importance of consumption on economic activity is fairly straightforward. In 1995 the U.S. population spent 97 percent of personal income on goods and services. Consumption is simply purchasing of goods and services, spending of income for necessities and luxuries. The level of consumption depends on many things, including income, interest rates, price levels, and expectations, along with the other financial assets the consumer might possess. But, as one might well expect, consumption is primarily a function of income. In our simplified version of the Keynesian model, we will express consumption as

$$C = f(Y_y),$$

where C is the consumption of individuals over some period of time, Y_y is income (the subscript in Y_y indicates income associated with output or GDP), and f is a functional notation.* In what Keynes called a "fundamental psychological law," he states, "As a rule and on the average, [people] are disposed to increase their consumption as their income increases." In other words, as your income increases (perhaps after graduation and upon securing a better job), your consumption spending will rise as well—but, says Keynes, not by as much. This relationship can be expressed graphically with consumption (C) measured on the vertical axis and income (Y_y) on the horizontal axis. Since

---

*Studies have shown consumption to be a linear function of income, or $C = a + bY_y$, where C is the consumption of individuals over time, a is the intercept of the consumption function (or C where $Y_y = 0$), b is the slope of the function, and Y_y is disposable income (that is, GDP – depreciation – taxes – undistributed corporate profits + transfer payments). Y_y, then, is income that a household has available for consumption spending. Since a is positive, individuals must consume some amount of food, clothing, and shelter even if they have no income.

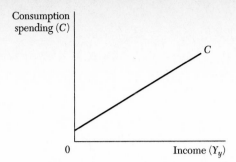

FIGURE 15.4 The Consumption Function

consumption is an increasing function of income, as Y_y increases, C will also increase (see Figure 15.4).

What happens to the income *not* spent on consumption? People save it. *Saving* is any part of income that is not spent on consumption. There is nothing left to do with it. (Burning it isn't rational, and Keynes assumes that we are all rational.) We can express the relationship between income, consumption, and saving as follows:

$$Y_y = C + S,$$

where Y_y is income, C is personal consumption expenditures, and S is personal saving. Saving is, in effect, a residual of consumption.

Saving occurs when individuals defer present consumption and keep the funds for future use. People save for many different reasons: precaution or fear of what might lie ahead, financial independence, or pride or avarice. In contrast to the classical model, which assumes that saving is a function of the rate of interest, Keynes assumed that consumption expenditures are a priority, and we save whatever funds are left after we make these consumption expenditures. No matter how much a high interest rate might make us want to increase our saving, we pay for food, housing, and other necessary consumption expenditures first. Whatever is left can be saved. So in the Keynesian model, saving, like consumption, is also a function of income:

$$S = f(Y_y)$$

2. Do you or your family behave as though $S = f(Y_y)$ or $S = f(r)$? Which comes first, the mortgage or rent payment, grocery and clothing expenditures—or saving?

Before we proceed further in the analysis of consumption and saving, it is important to establish a reference position (or helping line) to make it easier to discuss the relation of the level of consumption spending to the level of income. This helping line is a 45° line from the origin of the consumption-income axis (see Figure 15.5). The 45° line represents the locus of equilibri-

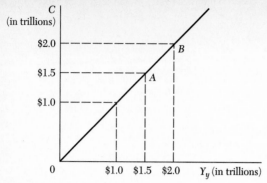

FIGURE 15.5 The 45° Line

um points where total spending equals total output or income (Y_y). If firms produce $1.5 trillion worth of goods and services and spending in the economy equals $1.5 trillion, we will be at point *A* on the 45° line. Each of these points is on the 45° line, which bisects the origin and represents a level of spending just equal to a corresponding level of income (Y_y). Here and throughout the Keynesian analysis, we assume that *prices are constant.*

We can now use the relationship between expenditures and income in examining consumption. Since the 45° line bisects the 90° angle, at any point on the 45° line, income (Y_y) will equal consumption. For example, at point *A*, $Y_y = C = \$1.5$ trillion; at point *B*, $Y_y = C = \$2.0$ trillion. If we superimpose the consumption curve on this 45° line, we can compare the relationship of consumption spending to the actual level of income in the economy.

In Figure 15.6, at point *A*, consumption and income are equal, since the consumption curve passes through the 45° line at that point. Point *A* is called the **breakeven level of income.** Saving equals 0 (since $S = Y_y - C$, and $1.5

FIGURE 15.6 The Consumption Function and the 45° Line

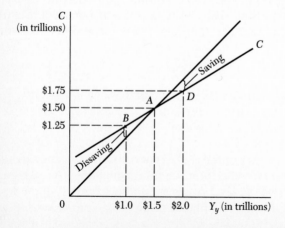

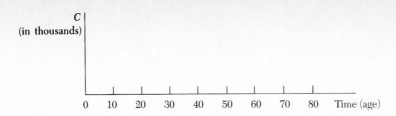

C
(in thousands)

0 10 20 30 40 50 60 70 80   Time (age)

■ FIGURE 15.7 Your Consumption Function

trillion – $1.5 trillion = 0). At point D, however, consumption (C) is less than income, indicating that saving occurs. Since income is $2.0 trillion and consumption is only $1.75 trillion, $0.25 trillion must be saved. At point B, consumption is greater than income; income is $1.0 trillion, but consumption spending is $1.25 trillion. Dissaving is taking place to allow the desired level of consumption. Dissaving consists of borrowing or drawing down other financial assets in order to purchase products for current consumption. Individuals on low fixed incomes frequently dissave, as do young people starting families or households. (Note that even when income is 0, there is some amount of consumption spending.)

3. Do you dissave now? Do you expect to dissave in the next year or two? Draw a curve on the graph in Figure 15.7 indicating what you expect your consumption pattern to look like for the rest of your life. At what periods do you think you might be dissaving?

Marginal Propensity to Consume

From the information given thus far, we can determine two ratios: the average propensity to consume (APC) and the **marginal propensity to consume (MPC)**. APC is simply C/Y_y. MPC is the ratio between the *change* that occurs in consumption with some given change in income:

$$MPC = \Delta C/\Delta Y_y$$

where Δ is a symbol for change, C is consumption, and Y_y is income. In the previous example, if income increases from $1.5 trillion to $2.0 trillion, consumption increases from $1.50 trillion to $1.75 trillion. The change in income is $2.0 trillion – $1.5 trillion, or $0.5 trillion; the change in consumption is $1.75 trillion – $1.50 trillion, or $0.25 trillion. The MPC, then, is $\Delta C/\Delta Y_y$ = $0.25 trillion/$0.5 trillion, or 0.5 (see Table 15.1). For every additional dollar of income, consumers use $0.50 for consumption and save the remaining $0.50 (see Table 15.1 and Figure 15.8).

Y_y (in Trillions)	C (in Trillions)	MPC = $\Delta C/\Delta Y_y$
$1.0	$1.25	
		0.5
1.5	1.50	
		0.5
2.0	1.75	

4. What is MPC when we move from point B to point A in Figure 15.8?

The relationship MPC = $\Delta C/\Delta Y_y$ is also the slope of the consumption function* (see Figure 15.8). Note that the consumption function is a straight line only when MPC is constant at all levels of income. This will seldom occur in practice, since each individual as well as each income-earning group reacts differently to changes in income. However, to simplify the analysis, in most cases we will assume a constant MPC (and thus a straight-line consumption function).

5. How might your reaction to a change in income be different from that of Michael Jordan, Madonna, or Tom Cruise? From that of a poor person?

Saving

Given that saving is a residual of consumption ($Y_y = C + S$, so $S = Y_y - C$), we can analyze the saving function as we did the consumption function. Data for a saving function are derived in Table 15.2 and graphed in Figure 15.9.

■ FIGURE 15.8 Marginal Propensity to Consume

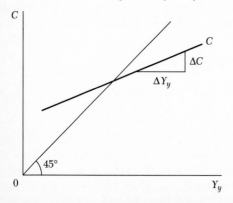

*MPC is the slope of the consumption function, or b in $C = a + b \cdot Y_y$.

TABLE 15.2 Derivation of Saving Function from Consumption Data

Y_y (in Trillions)	C (in Trillions)	$S = Y_y - C$ (in Trillions)
$1.0	$1.25	$-0.25
1.5	1.50	0.00
2.0	1.75	0.25

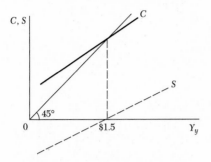
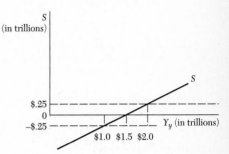

FIGURE 15.9 The Saving Function

Marginal Propensity to Save

We can also express the average propensity to save (APS) and the **marginal propensity to save (MPS)**. APS is the ratio of saving to income, S/Y_y. MPS is the ratio of the change in saving to any change in income:

$$\Delta S/\Delta Y_y.$$

In Table 15.3, we find MPS using the data for S we derived earlier.

Note that MPS + MPC = 1. This must be true, since the change in C and the change in S must add to the whole of every new dollar of income.[*]

TABLE 15.3 Data for Hypothetical Saving Example

Y_y	S (in Trillions)	MPS $= \Delta S/\Delta Y_y$
$1.0	$0.25	
		0.5
1.5	0.00	
		0.5
2.0	0.25	

---

[*] $Y_y = C + S$
   $\Delta Y_y = \Delta C + \Delta S$
$\Delta Y_y/\Delta Y_y = \Delta C/\Delta Y_y + \Delta S/\Delta Y_y,$
      $1 = $ MPC + MPS

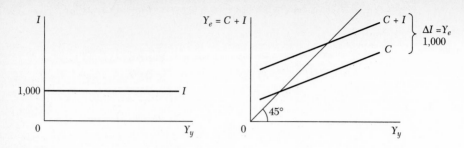

FIGURE 15.10 The Investment Function

Investment and the Two-Sector Model

The simplest Keynesian model describes the behavior of two sectors in the economy: the household and business sectors. This model ignores the government and foreign sectors. We represent total spending by individuals and businesses as follows:

$$Y_e = C + I,$$

where Y_e is income, C is consumption, and I is investment. (The subscript in Y_e stands for expenditures—in this case, expenditures of households and businesses.) This relationship is derived from expenditures flow in the circular flow diagram in the National Income Accounts examined in Chapter 14. Consumption represents spending by households, and **investment** consists of business spending on additions to plants, equipment, inventories, and newly constructed housing. Inventories may be goods of any type, from raw material inputs to intermediate and finished products. Together, consumption and investment make up the aggregate expenditures for goods and services produced. From the preceding section, we know that $C = f(Y_y)$. But we know little about investment.

In this simple two-sector model, we assume that investment is determined outside the model itself.* For example, if General Motors decides to invest $1,000, it makes the decision without considering the variables included in this model. Expected profits, interest costs, or business confidence might be more important to investment decisions than income and consumption levels.

---

*Investment in a more sophisticated model is a function of changes in income, since as income in the economy increases, businesses will likely increase their level of investment. Investment decisions also depend on interest rates, expected inflation, expected profits, depreciation, and other factors. Investment fluctuates over time and plays a major role in accounting for business cycles. With a more sophisticated model, our analysis can include investment decisions more typical of businesses. For simplicity, however, we use the less complex model and assume that investment decisions are given and constant.

Graphically, then, investment would be constant at all levels of income, as shown in Figure 15.10.

In the two-sector model, we know that expenditures (Y_e) equal consumption plus investment $(Y_e = C + I)$, and that the resulting income (Y_y) can be spent or saved $(Y_y = C + S)$. For an equilibrium in the macroeconomy, income Y_y and expenditures (Y_e) must be equal $(Y_y = Y_e)$. A level of spending produces a level of income, which, in turn, generates the same level of spending, and so on (as in the circular flow of activity). Putting these two equations together tells us that in the two-sector Keynesian model, the only leakage, saving, must equal the only injection, investment. This describes the equilibrium condition for the model: when aggregate income $(Y_y = C + S)$ equals aggregate expenditures $(Y_e = C + I)$, then $S = I$.

$$Y_y = Y_e$$
$$C + S = C + I$$
$$S = I$$

Several factors are important in the $S = I$ relationship. First, saving and investment are done by two different groups of people for totally different reasons. Second, realized (or actual) saving must equal realized (or actual) investment. There is no guarantee that the dollar amount of investment *planned* by the business sector will be the same as the saving planned in the household sector.

Using the data in Table 15.4, which assumes planned investment spending of $0.25 trillion, we can illustrate this with an example. I_p equals planned investment, and I_a equals actual investment. Figure 15.11 shows that the equilibrium income level in this simple model is at point A, where the $C + I$ line intersects the 45° reference line. This graph is sometimes referred to as the *Keynesian cross*. Here, $Y_e = C + I = \$2.0$ trillion, $C = \$1.75$ trillion, and $I = \$0.25$ trillion. All higher and lower levels of income are not at equilibrium; planned $S \neq$ planned I and planned aggregate expenditures do not equal planned aggregate income. At $Y_y = \$2.0$ trillion, $C + I = C + S$, and aggregate expenditures equal aggregate income. Only when income and output are at $2.0 trillion does planned investment equal actual investment $(I_p = I_a)$.

At disequilibrium position B, $C = \$2.0$ trillion, $S = \$0.5$ trillion, and $Y = \$2.5$ trillion. Here, intended saving is greater than intended investment, since saving is $0.50 trillion and investment is only $0.25 trillion. With I_p at $0.25 trillion, there will be an unplanned increase in inventories, since some of the goods produced will not be sold, because consumers desire to increase their

TABLE 15.4 Data for Hypothetical Investment Function

Y_y	C	S	I_p	I_a
$2.0 T	$1.75 T	$0.25 T	$0.25 T	$0.25 T
2.5	1.50	0.50	0.25	0.50

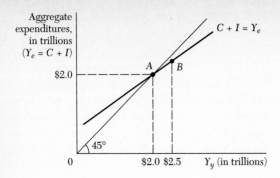

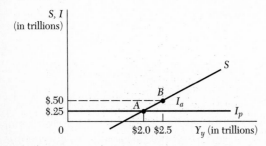

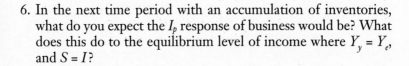

FIGURE 15.11 Equilibrium Level of Income

saving balances. At $Y_y = \$2.50$ trillion, $C + I =$ (only) $\$2.25$ trillion (and $C + S = \$2.50$ trillion). Aggregate output is greater than aggregate expenditures. Total output is $\$2.50$ trillion, but total spending is only $\$2.25$ trillion. Therefore, inventories increase by $\$0.25$ trillion. Since the increase in inventories is counted as investment, I_a will increase to $\$0.50$ trillion. Actual saving equals actual investment.

> 6. In the next time period with an accumulation of inventories, what do you expect the I_p response of business would be? What does this do to the equilibrium level of income where $Y_y = Y_e$, and $S = I$?

Since planned S is greater than planned I, however, this is not an equilibrium position. With increased inventories, which were unplanned, producers will cut back production and lay off workers. As output is cut, income will also be reduced. This movement will continue until an equilibrium is reached where aggregate expenditures equal aggregate output or income. This new equilibrium occurs at point A, where $C + S = C + I$, and where planned S of $\$0.25$ trillion equals planned I of $\$0.25$ trillion. This equilibrium may be or may not be at full employment. Unlike the classical model, the Keynesian model may have equilibrium conditions at greater than full, less than full, or full employment.

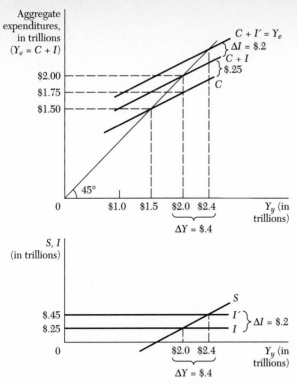

■ FIGURE 15.12 An Increase in Investment Spending

Changes in Investment and the Keynesian Multiplier

Once the economy is in equilibrium, it tends to remain unchanged until some disturbance occurs, such as a change in the level of investment. Suppose investment increases from $0.25 trillion to $0.45 trillion, a change of $0.20 trillion. This change is graphed in Figure 15.12.

How much does income increase as a result of this $0.20 trillion increase in investment? What is the new equilibrium level of income? Here, the **Keynesian multiplier** (k) has its effect. When additional investment enters the model, the equilibrium level of income (Y_y) increases by some multiple of the change in investment. This multiple (called the Keynesian multiplier) equals $1/(1 - MPC)$ or the ratio between the change in income and the change in investment ($\Delta Y_y/\Delta I$).

To demonstrate how the multiplier works, consider a nursery that decides to expand by adding a greenhouse costing $200,000. The first round of spending is $200,000, which is added to the income stream. The contractor and workers who built the greenhouse now have the $200,000 (as income) and will respend it according to the MPC. If the MPC is 0.5, the contractor and her workers will spend $100,000 and save the remaining $100,000. The $100,000 then enters the income stream (as other people's income); half of that will be spent and half saved in the third round. Table 15.5 illustrates this process.

TABLE 15.5 Keynesian Respending Effect

Expenditure for Greenhouse $\Delta I = \$200,000$	ΔY_y	$\Delta C = 0.5\Delta Y_y$	$\Delta S - 0.5\Delta Y_y$
Round 1	$200,000	$100,000	$100,000
Round 2	100,000	50,000	50,000
Round 3	50,000	25,000	25,000
Round 4	25,000	12,500	12,500
Round 5	12,500	6,250	6,250
Round 6	6,250	3,125	3,125
Etc.			
Total*	$400,000	$200,000	$200,000

*Until $200,000 {1/(1 − 0.5)} = $200,000 × 2 = $400,000 is generated in new income. The initial increase in spending is multiplied through the economy.

A SIMPLE DERIVATION OF THE MULTIPLIER

We know that at equilibrium in the Keynesian model $\Delta I = \Delta S$. If both sides of this identity are divided by ΔY_y, the right side of the equation becomes MPS:

$$\frac{\Delta I}{\Delta Y_y} = \frac{\Delta S}{\Delta Y_y} = \text{MPS} = \frac{1}{\text{the multiplier}}.$$

To get the multiplier (k), we invert the equation:

$$k = \frac{\Delta Y_y}{\Delta I} = \frac{\Delta Y_y}{\Delta S} = \frac{1}{\text{MPS}}.$$

Since MPC + MPS = 1, we can restake this in terms of MPC:

$$\frac{\Delta Y_y}{\Delta I} = \frac{1}{1 - \text{MPC}} = k.$$

Example: Given MPC = 0.75,

$$k = \frac{\Delta Y_y}{\Delta I} = \frac{1}{1 - 0.75} = \frac{1}{0.25}.$$

In this example, for each ΔI, income (Y_y) will increase by 4 times ΔI.

FIGURE 15.13 The Government Spending Function

The MPS of 0.5 yields a multiplier of 2. Thus, the $200,000 increase in investment will generate $400,000 of new income. In Figure 15.12, an increase in I of $0.2 trillion will produce a new equilibrium level of Y_y = $2.4 trillion (representing a "multiplied" increase in Y_y of $0.4 trillion).

> 7. What is the new level of consumption in Figure 15.12 at Y_y = $2.4 trillion? What is the level of saving?

The Three-Sector Model

To add a bit more realism, we can add the government sector to the simple two-sector Keynesian model. *Government expenditures* (*G*) are purchases of goods and services by the government during a given period. Like investment, we will assume in this extension of our simple model that government spending is determined outside of the Keynesian model. For example, Congress decides to spend $G = G_0$. This means there is a given level of government spending for goods and services at all levels of income, as shown in Figure 15.13.

Once we add government spending to the model, aggregate expenditures become $Y_e = C + I + G$, as shown in Figure 15.14. The 45° line again represents equilibrium points where aggregate spending equals aggregate output or income. Expenditures for goods and services are now made by consumers, investors, *and* the government, creating the aggregate expenditures graph for the three-sector economy. The equilibrium level of income is Y_a where $Y_y = Y_e = C + I + G$. At any other level of income, $Y_y \neq C + I + G$.

Government expenditures include expenditures by state and local governments as well as by the federal government. Currently, about 19 percent of the GDP is made up of purchases by the government. The government buys a wide range of goods and services, from paper to computers to M16 rifles. The government makes such purchases to support its normal operations or as part of programs designed to stimulate the economy when the business cycle is declining, as Keynes suggested in his *General Theory*. Transfer payments from the government are not included as part of these

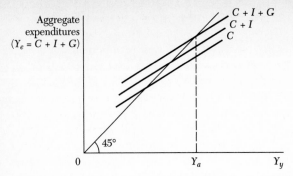

■ FIGURE 15.14 The Keynesian Model with *C, I,* and *G* Spending

government purchases. (We will examine the effect of transfers in Chapter 16.)

The size of *G* may change. Indeed, the government may make decisions that will affect the level of income in the economy. These expenditures are often aimed at *directly* changing the level of income—perhaps from a level not at full employment to a new equilibrium level at full employment. Government expenditures for goods and services are subject to the Keynesian multiplier just as investments are. Government spending becomes income that enters the spending flow as recipients consume and save at levels increased by their MPC and MPS. Any increase in *G* will increase Y_y by an amount equal to $\Delta G/(1 - \text{MPC})$.

We can analyze the results of government spending by looking at a purchase of 150,000 reams of printer paper by the Government Services Administration at a total cost of $500,000. Figure 15.15 shows that aggregate

■ FIGURE 15.15 Effects of Increased Government Spending on the Equilibrium Level of Income

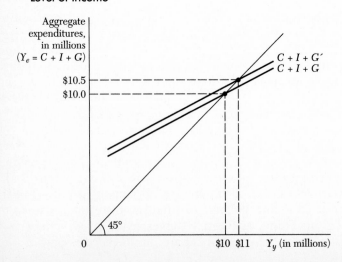

expenditures have increased from the equilibrium position at $10 million (where $Y_e = C + I + G$). If the marginal propensity to consume remains at 0.5, the multiplier is 2. The increase in income that results from the purchase of printer paper is $k \times \Delta G = 2 \times \$500,000 = \$1$ million. The new equilibrium level of income is therefore $11 million ($10 million + $1 million).

An increase in government allocations for research for the space program will boost the economies of Huntsville, Alabama; Houston, Texas; and Cape Canaveral, Florida; as well as increasing the enrollments in aerospace engineering courses. Cuts in government expenditures reverse the Keynesian multiplier effect. A decrease in defense spending, such as military base closures, will have the effect of contracting the economies of Alameda, California, and Charleston, South Carolina. Entire communities will be affected by the decreasing income and increasing unemployment levels.

> 8. What kinds of government spending programs would stimulate growth in your area? What are a few government spending programs that would help us all?

The Four-Sector Model

Thus far, we have extended our economic model by adding *injections* of investment expenditures and government purchases of goods and services into the spending flow and observing how the Keynesian multiplier affects each of them. There is, of course, one more injection into the spending stream, and that comes from the foreign sector through foreign trade. Whenever U.S. goods and services are exported to other nations, dollars flow into the U.S. economy in payment for these exported goods. These dollars then enter the spending stream as injections. On the other hand, imports take money out of the income flow, since goods and services come into the country in return for dollars that flow out of the U.S. income stream and into the income stream of the exporting nation.

In dealing with both of these flows, we will use the quantity *net exports*, which is simply $X - M$, where X represents exports and M accounts for goods and services imported into the nation. If $X - M$ is positive, then money is flowing into the U.S. income stream. If $X - M$ is negative, then money is flowing out of the U.S. income stream as imported goods and services flow in. A positive net export figure $(X - M > 0)$ will mean additional income, as Y expands. If net exports are negative $(X - M < 0)$, Y will fall.

The equilibrium level of income is at the point where the total for expanded aggregate expenditures intersects the 45° line. When the imports to the United States exceed exports, more goods and services are coming into the country and more income (money) is going out of the country. Net exports are negative. The equilibrium level of income will be lower.

Domestic and foreign economic policies may directly affect import or export expenditures or both. We will direct our attention to some of these policy effects in Chapter 16.

CONCLUSION

We have examined the impact of the Keynesian multiplier on several sectors of the economy and noted that income (output) expands by the value of the multiplier times the value of the injection. Prices do not change in the Keynesian model as a result of changes in aggregate expenditures. In this chapter we have examined *only* the effect of changes in injections on income. We will explore the effect of changes in leakages, including saving and transfers, in the next chapter, and will explore the complications that arise from price changes in Chapter 18. We have made many assumptions about investment and spending decisions; the economy is somewhat more complex than our model. Nevertheless, the model helps us begin to understand how the macroeconomy functions.

The Keynesian model gives us a theoretical framework within which to analyze how the aggregate economy operates and to examine the sorts of macroeconomic problems one might expect to encounter and how we might develop stabilization policies to try to correct them. If aggregate output or income exceeds aggregate expenditures, we can expect a lower level of national income. On the other hand, if aggregate expenditures exceed aggregate income or output, we would expect an expansion of economic activity and a higher equilibrium level of national income. An equilibrium level is where aggregate income (Y_y) equals aggregate expenditures $(Y_e = C + I + G)$.

Review Questions

1. What phenomena caused the Great Depression? Why did it continue for so long? Why did it affect so many sectors of the economy?
2. What did your grandparents and their families do during the Great Depression? How were they affected by the economic conditions of the time?
3. Why would the classical economists distinguish between real factors and monetary ones as influences of the variables in the equation of exchange? What is the implication of prices increasing as the quantity of money increases?
4. Why might Keynes's theory be called a "depression theory"? Can you make a few arguments as to why it might command a more general use?
5. What were Keynes's major criticisms of the classical theory?
6. What are leakages? Why are they called leakages? How do leakages differ from injections?
7. Why must leakages equal injections in the Keynesian world for an equilibrium level of income to exist?
8. In the Keynesian circular flow diagram (Figure 15.4), do leakages and injections ever leave the economy permanently? How are they fed back into the economy?
9. If depressions become self-fulfilling prophecy, can inflationary periods also be self-fulfilling? What would you expect the Keynesian prescription to be in such a case?

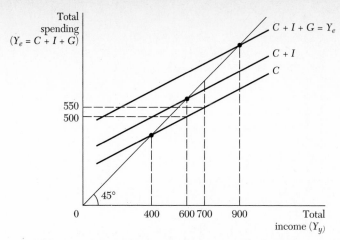

FIGURE 15.16 A Problem on the Keynesian Model

The intersection of income or output (Y_y) and aggregate expenditures (Y_e) = $900.

Use the information in Figure 15.16 to answer questions 10–17.

10. Explain in words why the equilibrium level of income would be $400 if there were no saving or investment. What would be the level of output at this income level?
11. Why would the consumption function (if extended) intersect the spending axis at a positive value? What does this mean? Is it realistic?
12. The slope of the consumption function tells us that as income increases, consumption (increases/decreases) but at a (slower/faster) rate. Is this realistic?
13. What assumptions are required to draw an investment function parallel to the consumption function? How realistic are these assumptions? What is the amount of desired investment in Figure 15.16?
14. What is the level of saving at an income of $600? What is the level of desired investment at an income of $600? Why is income of $600 an equilibrium level of income (with $C + I$)?
15. What would be the level of saving if the income were at $700? What is the level of desired investment at this income level? What forces are at work at an income of $700? What will be the equilibrium level of income?
16. What is MPC in Figure 15.16?
17. Assume that income is at $600, but that an income of $900 is needed to generate enough jobs for full employment. What level of government spending will be necessary to achieve full employment?
18. Why is there a multiplier effect for injections into the U.S. economy? Are there different multipliers for different economies? What determines the multiplier?
19. How do net exports affect national income? Can income be reduced by net exports? How?

16

Fiscal Policy: Government Spending and Taxation

INTRODUCTION

For the past fifty years, the federal government has been officially committed to maintaining employment, price stability, and output. The **Employment Act of 1946** states,

> The Congress hereby declares that it is the continuing policy and responsibility of the Federal Government to use all practicable means consistent with its needs and obligations and other essential considerations of national policy, with assistance and cooperation of industry, agriculture, labor, and state and local governments, to coordinate and utilize all its plans, functions, and resources for the purpose of creating and maintaining, in a manner calculated to foster and promote free competitive enterprise and the general welfare, conditions under which there will be afforded useful employment opportunities, including self-employment, for those able, willing, and seeking to work and to promote maximum employment, production, and purchasing power.

Within the framework of these economic objectives, the government establishes and implements its **fiscal policy**—actions of taxation or government spending that are designed to change the level of income.

According to Keynesian theory, when poverty, unemployment, or inflation rises, the government has tools to try to fix each problem. The existence of unemployment and poverty suggests a need for government spending and/or transfers. These may take the form of unemployment and welfare benefits, food stamps, Medicaid, or a variety of other payments, or they may be purchases of goods and services. Other possible remedies are increases in employment opportunities and decreased tax levels. The government may try to stimulate employment by directly adding programs that put people back to work—for example, through a series of tax credits or advantages for those firms increasing employment and investment. To combat inflation, fiscal policy requires spending reductions or tax increases. Cutbacks of all types and tax increases restrict household and business spending. Fiscal policy can also be used to affect aggregate supply; for example, a tax cut might be designed to stimulate investment.

While normally we think of the federal government as the major spending and taxing authority, state and local governments are very active in the process as well. In some cases, however, state and local governments exacerbate economic problems (pursuing *procyclical* rather than *countercyclical* measures—for example, spending during times of economic expansion rather than during times of contraction).

Fiscal policy is also subject to the constraints of the political process. At the federal level, the president receives advice on fiscal policy from his Council of Economic Advisors (CEA) and the National Economic Council created in the 1990s to coordinate policy making. Some of the advice is accepted and successfully makes its way through the bureaucratic channels, but other advice does not. In addition, the president receives advice from the Office of Management and Budget. Meanwhile, in addition to its own committees Congress has the Joint Economic Committee and Congressional Budget Office to assist in legislative decisions on government spending and taxation. Policy studies in all these bodies are constantly ongoing. Often the dynamics of these public offices, plus the host of private organizations engaged in economic research, lead to a profusion of mixed analysis and advice. Since each advisory body has its own priorities and operates under its own assumptions about economic growth, policy recommendations vary widely.

This chapter will explore how each type of fiscal action works. Some fiscal policies may directly affect the level of imports and/or exports as well as the domestic economy. We will explore these implications and deal with the shortcomings and advantages of using fiscal policy to address economic problems. We will also explore the budget process of fiscal policy's major player, the federal government. The discussion of the federal budget includes the impact of the federal debt on the economy, balanced budgets, and the difference between structural and cyclical deficits.

FISCAL POLICY

The tools of fiscal policy may be selected to resolve a particular problem, or they may occur automatically with a given change in economic conditions. The former uses constitute **discretionary fiscal policy**. The automatic, nondiscretionary forms of fiscal policy are called **built-in stabilizers**. Examples of built-in stabilizers include the progressive income tax system, unemployment insurance, and all other compensatory programs that come into effect when income levels are low and that are shut off when income levels are high. As economic activity decreases during a recession, income is lost. This threatens additional decreases in economic activity. However, as unemployment increases, unemployment compensation *automatically* increases income and spending to slow a cumulative decrease in economic activity. Additionally, during a recession, people find themselves in lower tax brackets, which reduces the tax bite on individuals as their incomes fall.

||| 1. If income is increasing at a highly inflationary rate, how do progressive income taxes help to stabilize the economy automatically?

Government Spending

The government often adopts a fiscal policy position when politicians and public opinion consider employment levels to be inadequate—for example, if the full employment level of income is thought to be at $5.7 trillion and income is currently $5.1 trillion. In this situation, a substantial amount of unemployment is likely, and the government can opt for fiscal action that will increase employment and boost the level of income by $0.6 trillion ($5.7 trillion – $5.1 trillion).* In its arsenal of policies are spending, taxing authority, and the ability to issue transfer payments (income supplements such as Social Security and welfare paid to individuals). Since transfer payments are not for current productive services, they are not included in the yearly national product accounts but enter the income-spending flow as part of the personal income tally.

Government spending on goods and services like defense, the space program, buildings, etc. will have the largest expansionary impact on income in the economy, since the full amount of spending enters the economy in the first round. In the case of transfer payments and tax reductions, some of the impact in the first round is "leaked" into savings. Table 16.1 provides an example of the difference.

In the example, MPC in the economy is 2/3. From the formula $k = 1/(1 - MPC)$,[†] we can determine that the multiplier is 3. To discover the amount of government spending necessary to increase the level of income by $0.6 trillion, we need only know these two variables, since $\Delta Y_y = k \times \Delta G$. We know the desired ΔY_y to be $0.6 trillion and k to be 3, so we can find ΔG:

$$\Delta Y_y = k \times \Delta G$$
$$\Delta G = \Delta Y_y / k = \$0.6 \text{ trillion}/3 = \$0.2 \text{ trillion.}$$

---

*Conversely, we could establish an example in which inflation was the primary problem, with income being above the full employment level. For example, income could be at $5.7 trillion, with the full employment level at $5.1 trillion. In that case, the policy measures would be the opposite of those we discuss in the following sections.

$$^†k = \frac{1}{1 - \text{MPC}} = \frac{1}{1 - \frac{2}{3}} = \frac{1}{\frac{1}{3}} = 3$$

TABLE 16.1 Multiplier Effect of Government Expenditures and Tax Cuts

ΔG = \$.2 Trillion		ΔTx = \$.3 Trillion	
Spending Sequence			
Round 1 (direct expenditure)	$\Delta G = \Delta Y = \$.200$ T	(indirect expenditure; $\Delta Tx \times MPC = \Delta Y$	$\$.3$ T $\times$ $^2/_3$ = $\$.200$ T
Round 2 ($\Delta Y \times MPC$)	$\$.200$ T $\times$ $^2/_3$ = $\$.133$ T	($\Delta Y \times MPC$)	$\$.200$ T $\times$ $^2/_3$ = $\$.133$ T
Round 3	.133 T $\times$ $^2/_3$ = $\$.090$ T		$\$.133$ T $\times$ $^2/_3$ = $\$.090$ T
Round 4	.090 T $\times$ $^2/_3$ = $\$.060$ T		.090 T $\times$ $^2/_3$ = $\$.060$ T
Round 5	.060 T $\times$ $^2/_3$ = $\$.040$ T		.060 T $\times$ $^2/_3$ = $\$.040$ T
Round 6	.040 T $\times$ $^2/_3$ = $\$.027$ T		.040 T $\times$ $^2/_3$ = $\$.027$ T
Round 7	.027 T $\times$ $^2/_3$ = $\$.018$ T		.027 T $\times$ $^2/_3$ = $\$.018$ T
Round 8	.018 T $\times$ $^2/_3$ = $\$.012$ T		.018 T $\times$ $^2/_3$ = $\$.012$ T
Round 9	.012 T $\times$ $^2/_3$ = $\$.008$ T		.012 T $\times$ $^2/_3$ = $\$.008$
etc.			
	Total $\$.600$ T		Total $\$.600$ T

Our policy recommendation, then, is that the government build a (big) dam at a price of $0.2 trillion to increase income by $0.6 trillion to the full employment income level of $5.7 trillion. This is graphed in Figure 16.1.

Although the example shows that the needed increase in income is $0.6 trillion, policy decisions certainly are not made by such quick calculations. Partisan politics and economic philosophies play a crucial role in these decisions. We might recommend the construction of a dam, but each of the 435 representatives and 100 senators has his or her own plan, which often involves a particular congressional district or state. This and the following examples describe fast technical economic "solutions" to extremely complex economic, political, and social problems—what theoretically needs to happen to achieve economic goals.

2. What do you suspect really goes on in economic policy debates? As illustration, clip a recent newspaper article on some federal, state, or local economic issue.
3. In the example you found, are the various positions based on ideology, theory, or rhetoric?

Tax Policy and Income Effects

If the government decides it wants to accomplish the desired income increase of $0.6 trillion through a cut in taxes, it must decide how much of a tax reduction is needed to generate new increases in income equal to the $0.6 trillion. The answer is more difficult to determine, since tax cuts are initiated through a different channel for their progression through the economy. Earlier we examined the effect of injections to spending flows; now we must address the behavior of leakages. The crucial difference between the effect of leakages and that of injections occurs during the first round of spending.

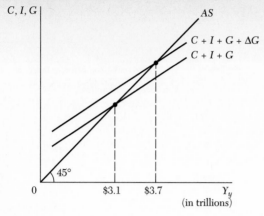

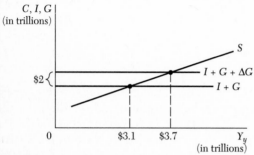

■ FIGURE 16.1 Effect of Increased Government Spending

Instead of $0.2 trillion being directly spent on a dam, the $0.2 trillion in tax cuts goes into the pockets and bank accounts of the taxpayers. According to the marginal propensities given, taxpayers will save part of the $0.2 trillion and spend the remainder. With an MPC of 2/3 and a tax cut equal to $0.2 trillion (or $200 billion), the first action is to consume 2/3 of $200 billion, or $133 billion, and save $67 billion. In the initial round of spending, only $133 billion enters the total income stream, instead of the $200 billion that would enter in the case of government spending.

The *tax multiplier* is therefore less than the spending multiplier—in fact, 1 less:*

$$k - 1 = k_{tx}$$

$$k_{tx} = -\text{MPC}/(1 - \text{MPC}).$$

---

*This can be derived as follows:

$-k_{tx} = 1/(1 - \text{MPC}) - 1$

$$= \frac{1}{(1 - \text{MPC})} - \frac{(1 - \text{MPC})}{(1 - \text{MPC})} = \frac{\text{MPC}}{(1 - \text{MPC})}$$

$k_{tx} = -\text{MPC}/1(1 - \text{MPC}).$

(Note the negative sign, since a tax *cut* will increase income.) Using our previous example, to get a $0.6 trillion increase in income with a tax multiplier of 2 (because 3 − 1 = 2), the following decrease in taxes must occur:

$$\Delta Y = k_{tx} \times \Delta Tx$$

$$\$0.6 \text{ trillion} = 2 \times \Delta Tx$$

$$\Delta Tx = \$0.3 \text{ trillion}$$

In other words, taxes must be reduced by $0.3 trillion to increase income by $0.6 trillion.

Impact of a Tax Leakage on Equilibrium Income

Thus far, we have dealt only with the effect of injections (government spending, investment, and net exports) on equilibrium income. Now we turn to the effect of leakages or withdrawals in the Keynesian model. We will focus specifically on taxation, although the analysis is similar for other withdrawals, including transfers. In the two-sector model, the only leakage we encountered was saving. When saving increases (*S* to *S'*) and consumption decreases (*C* to *C'*), the saving schedule shifts up and to the left, while the

■ FIGURE 16.2 Decrease in Consumption; Increase in Saving

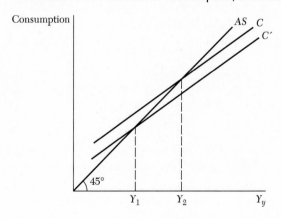

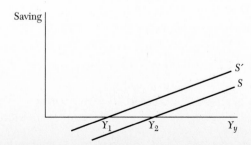

consumption schedule shifts down and to the right, and equilibrium income moves to Y_1 in Figure 16.2.

Just as all injections—C, I, G, and $(X - M)$—are components of aggregate expenditures and are graphically represented as part of the aggregate expenditures function, all leakages or withdrawals are represented on an aggregate leakage curve. To illustrate our aggregate leakage curve, we again expand the model from two to three sectors by adding the taxation leakage to the saving schedule. We add the exogenous tax leakage to the savings function, which in this analysis gives the leakage function its slope (MPS), just as the consumption function gives the injection function or aggregate expenditures curve its slope (MPC). The leakage curve represents positive and negative tax and saving changes. (A tax increase would represent a positive leakage; a tax decrease would represent a negative leakage.) An increase in saving or taxes will shift the leakage curve up and to the left. A decrease in saving or taxes will shift the curve down and to the right; thus, at every level of income, leakages are lower.

Continuing our example of a $0.3 trillion tax cut, we arrive at the new equilibrium income after a series of three steps (see Figure 16.3). (These three steps occur simultaneously but are shown as a series to clearly demonstrate each part of the adjustment process.) The steps describe how people respond to a cut in taxes. (Note that this is not a cut in the tax rate.) The cut brings an increase in income, but how is that increase allocated? Our answer conforms to what we learned in Chapter 15. Part of the $0.3 trillion will be consumed, and part will be saved; the MPC and MPS tell us how consumption and saving are allocated. In the first step, Figure 16.3(a), the saving-tax leakage curve shifts down by $0.3 trillion, as taxes are cut by the $0.3 trillion. Second, since income initially rises by the amount of the tax cut, individuals will boost their consumption by MPC times the tax reduction (2/3 × $0.3 trillion = $0.2 trillion). In Figure 16.3(b), we see the effect of this increase in consumption as the aggregate expenditures curve shifts up by $0.2 trillion. At this point there is an equilibrium level of income in the upper or aggregate expenditures graph, but not in the lower, leakage graph. To arrive at equilibrium in both the upper and lower graphs, we must complete the final step. Just as individuals increase consumption by MPC times the tax reduction, they will increase their saving by MPS times the tax reduction (1/3 × $0.3 trillion = $0.1 trillion). Thus, the saving-tax leakage curve shifts up and to the left by $0.1 trillion, as shown in Figure 16.3(c). In the final analysis, we find that income increases from Y_0 to Y_1, or by $0.6 trillion. To arrive at this result more directly, we can multiply the tax multiplier by the change in taxes:

$$k_{tx} \times \Delta Tx = \Delta Y$$
$$2 \times \$0.3 \text{ trillion} = \$0.6 \text{ trillion}$$

4. Create a set of graphs for a $0.3 trillion tax *increase*. Trace through the steps in Figure 16.3. How much will income decrease?

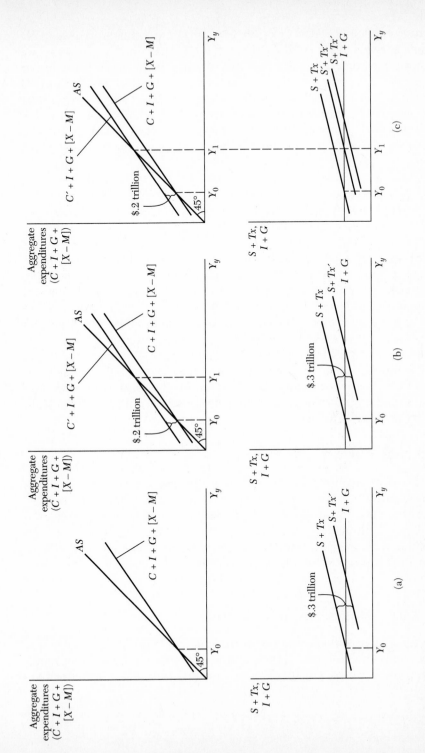

■ FIGURE 16.3 Impact of a Tax Cut

(a) Tax decrease of $0.3 trillion is shown as a negative leakage.
(b) Consumption increases as a result of the addition to income from the tax cut (ΔC = 2/3 × $0.3 trillion = $0.2 trillion).
(c) Saving increases as a result of the addition to income from the tax cut (ΔS = 1/3 × $0.3 trillion = $0.1 trillion).

Transfer Payments

The macroeconomic effects of increases in transfer payments are essentially the same as those of tax cuts.[*] Looking at their impact on the economy, we find that the income of households will increase in the first round. In our example, the change in spending during the first round will be two-thirds of $0.3 trillion, since part of the transfer will be consumed and the remainder will be saved. The **transfer multiplier**, like the tax multiplier, is $k - 1 = k_{tr}$ (only it is positive, since an increase in transfers increases income). Transfer expenditures worth $0.3 trillion would be necessary to raise income by $0.6 trillion.

> 5. If Social Security transfers were to increase by $4 billion and if MPC were 0.9, how much of an impact would this transfer package have on the economy?

The government, of course, might choose one or any combination of tax, spending, or transfer alternatives. It also might decide to pass legislation to encourage new consumer or investment spending. Tax credits and incentives have been used in recent years to stimulate certain industries that might be suffering more than others. During a housing slump in 1974, a 5 percent income tax credit was given to purchasers of newly constructed homes. The measure was designed to pick up a depressed housing industry, as well as to stimulate economic activity in general. More recently, unemployment benefits were extended during the 1990–1993 recession so that those who were unable to find jobs during the normal benefit period could receive an additional six weeks of benefits.

PROBLEMS WITH FISCAL POLICY

With these "mechanical" fiscal fixes firmly in mind, it is well to remember that problems are likely to arise in the determination of fiscal policy. The political machinery involved in fiscal decisions is often slow, the product of many lags. Additionally, policies of state and local governments offer their own brand of fiscal effects, which more often than not is ill timed for national objectives because of interest costs, spending capacity, and political considerations.

Lags and Lumps in Fiscal Measures

From the discussion thus far, it seems that full employment in the economy requires only a mighty snap of the government purse strings. Several rather sticky problems emerge in the deployment of these strings, however. One

---

[*]Transfer payments, however, redistribute income, while tax cuts may not.

problem encountered early on is the time it takes simply to recognize that a problem exists—in other words, a *recognition lag*. Another is trying to estimate MPC and thus the multiplier effect that each expenditure might have on the economy. Additionally, government spending tends to be lumpy. Projects are normally large and are generally confined to a reasonably small geographical area. Constructing a flood wall in Lewisburg, Pennsylvania, will probably not help alleviate unemployment in Dubuque or Detroit.

Legislation also tends to move slowly through Congress. By the time funds are allocated, new and different problems might emerge. During this time, higher resource prices might increase the inflation rate, and the expenditure of government funds would only add to the problem of rising prices. The enactment of tax policies takes time. For example, the 1964 tax cut was proposed in 1963 and approved after more than a year of hearings. This particular tax cut was an example of Keynesian economics well thought out and proposed, but legislative reluctance delayed the cut for over twelve months. Oftentimes a conflict between the president and the Congress leads to bitter policy debates. We refer to the undue passage of time before a proposed policy measure is signed into law as the *legislative lag*.

Execution presents another delay in transferring the legislation into action. Tax policies tend to be faster and more efficient after passage, but spending packages may be hung up in a bidding and allocation process for months. This has been called the *implementation lag*.

Finally, once the legislation for government spending is enacted and executed, time passes before the policy becomes effective. Results from empirical econometric models show that this *reaction lag* can be as long as one or more years before even part of the policy has affected GDP.

Procyclical Tax and Spending Policy

In the introduction to this chapter, we mentioned that policies of state and local governments have their own fiscal effects. They are active in spending and taxing as well as in issuing transfers. Often, however, these tools are used at the "wrong" time. Federal fiscal policy is designed to counter inflationary and recessionary trends in economic activity. Yet local government spending often occurs when fiscal "good times" prevail. Voters more readily approve bond issues for schools, libraries, or parks during boom periods, so these construction projects add to the boom. In the same vein, when times are hard, state and local governments often have difficulty financing new spending projects that might stimulate the economy, thus reinforcing a recession.

6. What does Keynesian theory tell you about this kind of spending? What would be the economic effects?
7. Is there any salvation to the procyclical spending of state and local governments? (What happens when bond issues to finance libraries and schools are passed?)

FISCAL POLICY IN AN OPEN ECONOMY

Thus far, we have examined the effects of fiscal policy in our three-sector closed economy of domestic households, businesses, and government. Since international economic activity is becoming increasingly important, we need to examine how the foreign sector or net exports (as we are representing the foreign sector) responds to fiscal policy. We can examine two specific effects on net exports: responses to changes in interest rates and responses to changes in currency value. Both affect national income.

Fiscal policy, such as an increase in government expenditures or a tax cut financed by an increase in government borrowing, may cause interest rates to rise in the short run as the government increases its demand for credit. Higher interest rates on government bonds will make U.S. government securities more attractive to both domestic and foreign investors than foreign security offerings with lower interest rates. An increase in the demand for U.S. bonds by foreign investors will create an increased demand for dollars by foreign individuals and institutions and a decrease in the supply of dollars offered by U.S. investors in foreign security markets. As we learned in Chapter 8, this will cause the value of the dollar to increase with respect to other currencies. Each dollar will purchase a larger volume of foreign goods, so imports should increase. On the other hand, U.S. products (exports) will cost more to those desiring U.S. goods, so the demand for U.S. exports should fall because of their relatively higher prices on international markets. When we account for this effect of fiscal policy actions in an open economy, we see that it acts in opposition to the initial fiscal policy designed to increase levels of income and output. With imports rising and exports falling, net exports $(X - M)$ will fall. In our aggregate expenditure analysis, where $Y = C + I + G + (X - M)$, the increase in G may, through a higher interest rate, cause an appreciation of the U.S. dollar and thus a decrease in net exports. The expenditures multiplier will be less effective due to the presence of an international market.

We should observe the second effect of fiscal policy in an open economy when we look at the effect of output on exchange rates. Here, however, the effects on imports and exports are offsetting, so the total effect is assumed to be zero. As increased government expenditures or tax cuts increase income, those who receive this additional income will be inclined to increase their expenditures on goods and services. Some of this increased demand will be for international products. The demand for imports should increase as incomes rise. This increased demand for imports will yield a greater supply of dollars in the currency markets as U.S. customers exchange dollars for imported goods. The increased supply of U.S. dollars will have the effect of decreasing or depreciating the value of the dollar in the international market. A lower-valued dollar will increase the demand for U.S. exports and decrease the demand for imports in the United States. In this case, fiscal policy in an open economy has essentially a neutral effect. An initial increase in import demand will be followed by a rise in exports and a fall in imports as the dollar depreciates in value, so the original fiscal policy stimulus will not be weakened.

THE FEDERAL BUDGET

The federal government's fiscal policy is directly related to the federal budget. During the past decade, the public and politicians have objected to the size of the federal government, the size of the budget deficit, and its effects. As illustrated in Figure 16.4, the level of the federal budget deficit increased sharply in the 1980s, with annual deficits of over $150 billion and the total accumulated debt of around $1 trillion in 1980 increasing to over $5 trillion by 1996. The United States is not the only industrialized country with a large debt. Figure 16.5 illustrates the deficits of the Group of Seven (a group of major industrial countries) in 1994.

In the United States, a few deficit watchers have always been alarmed at prospects of deficits and their implications, but as large deficits were projected to continue throughout the decade, it became an important political and economic issue. Indeed, much of the 1992 presidential campaign focused on the issue of deficit reduction, with third-party candidate Ross Perot entering the race under a banner of deficit reduction. In 1993, Congress enacted a deficit reduction measure (OBRA93) that lowered the growth of projected future deficits. The Republican Party's Contract with America highlighted deficit reduction as a central issue in the 1994 elections, and in 1995 the Congress and President Clinton agreed to balancing the budget during the next seven years.

■ FIGURE 16.4 The Federal Budget Surplus or Deficit, 1935–1996

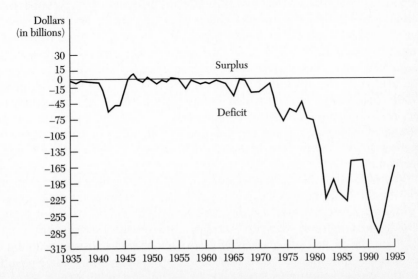

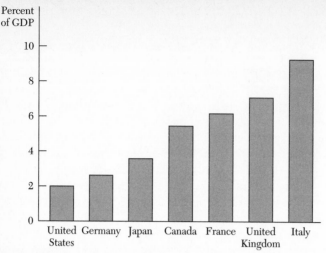

FIGURE 16.5 General Government Deficits of Major Industrialized Countries

Source: *Economic Report of the President*, 1996, p. 21.

The Federal Budget and the Economy

Just as the budget of a family or business determines the direction, priorities, and obligations of that unit, the federal budget determines the direction, priorities, and obligations assumed by the nation. The federal budget is made up of expenditures (such as direct purchases of goods and services) and receipts (such as taxes). Elements of fiscal policy are directly reflected in the annual federal budget, which not only indicates a president's view about fiscal and social policy, but also reflects electoral policies and the process of government. The budget that the president proposes and Congress passes, in what is now a yearlong process, reflects what will happen and what priorities are to be set. As is the case with household budgets, receipts are balanced against expenditures. If receipts are greater than expenditures, a surplus results; if expenditures exceed receipts, there is a deficit.

The most obvious source of federal government revenue is tax receipts. Individual income taxes provided 44.5 percent of the $1.25 trillion collected in 1994. As shown in Figure 16.6, the importance of individual income taxes has steadily grown since the 1940s. Social Security taxes now provide the next largest single receipt, having increased from only 11 percent in 1950 to 35 percent in 1996.

Corporate income taxes provided a substantial portion of federal receipts during the 1950s and 1960s, but as a result of the Reagan tax cut package of 1981, the corporate share of the total tax burden shrank to 6.2 percent in 1983. The Economic Recovery Tax Act, as it was called, cut personal income tax rates by 23 percent over three years. The measure also accelerated the rate at which businesses could take depreciation deductions, and gave other deductions and additional loopholes to individuals and businesses alike. The

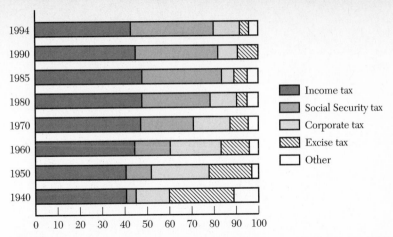

FIGURE 16.6 Tax Type as a Percentage of Government Revenue, 1950–1996

Source: *Economic Report of the President,* 1997, p. 392.

much-heralded Tax Reform Act of 1986 reduced corporate tax rates, eliminated the investment tax credit (which had saved corporations billions in taxes), and made depreciation allowances stricter. Still, while the corporate share of taxes increased to 11.4 percent in 1988, the promised $120 billion shift of the personal income tax burden to corporations did not fully materialize. Since this tax package was "revenue neutral," the revenue losses from earlier tax reductions have continued, so that in 1996 corporate taxes contributed 11 percent to total revenues.

The other side of the federal government's budget is expenditures. Table 16.2 shows federal expenditures both as the proportion of the budget going to selected areas and as a percentage of GDP for selected years. Military expenditures, while not changing dramatically as a percentage of the federal budget, increased dramatically as a percentage of GDP during the 1980s. In 1988 total defense expenditures were $290 billion, or 6.0 percent of GDP. Thanks to the end of the Cold War and the breakup of the former Soviet Union, U.S. defense expenditures were reduced to $272 billion, or 4.1 percent of GDP in 1995. Substantial increases have occurred in Social Security and interest payments on the federal debt.

Most budgeted programs have, in fact, been cut as part of the Reagan and Bush programs to enhance the role of the private sector while reducing the role of government. However, since military, agriculture, Social Security, and interest expenditures increased so significantly in the 1980s, Reagan was unable to keep his campaign promise of reducing government's role. Under his administration, expenditures rose to a record 23.7 percent of GDP in 1983. Clinton continued to reduce the size of government during his first term. Figure 16.7 illustrates how the major categories of government expenditures have changed since 1975.

▌▌ TABLE 16.2 Government Expenditures as a Percentage of Budget Outlays and GDP, 1975–1996 (Selected Categories)

Expenditure	1975 % Budget Outlay	% GDP	1980 % Budget Outlay	% GDP	1985 % Budget Outlay	% GDP	1990 % Budget Outlay	% GDP	1995 % Budget Outlay	% GDP	1996 % Budget Outlay	% GDP
National defense	26.5	5.3	23.2	4.8	26.7	6.0	23.9	5.2	17.97	3.7	17.03	3.5
Education/ health	13.2	2.6	9.2	1.9	6.6	1.5	7.7	1.7	11.2	2.3	11.0	2.2
Social Security (includes Medicare)			26.1	5.4	26.9	6.1	27.7	6.0	29.8	6.8	33.6	6.9
Income security	33.3	6.7	15.0	3.1	13.5	3.0	11.76	2.6	14.5	3.0	14.5	3.0
Net interest	9.5	1.9	9.1	1.9	13.7	3.1	14.7	3.2	15.3	3.2	15.5	3.2
Agriculture	0.51	0.1	0.84	0.17	2.7	0.6	0.95	0.2	0.64	0.13	0.5	0.12
Total budget	20.0		20.7		22.6		21.7		20.9		20.6	
Deficit	2.76		2.14		5.0		3.8		2.2		1.4	

Source: Economic Report of the President: 1989, pp. 316, 398, 399; February 3996, p. 369; February 1997, p. 397.

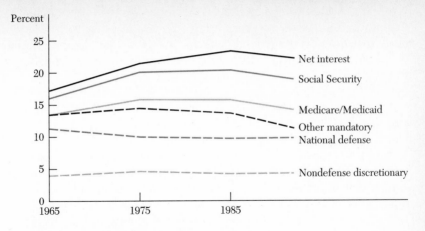

▬ FIGURE 16.7 Outlays as a Percent of GDP
Source: Office of Management and Budget, 1996.

By grouping these outlays another way, we can see why policy makers are having such a difficult time reducing the deficit. Figure 16.8 shows the discretionary and nondiscretionary spending as a percentage of the total budget. Discretionary spending—expenditures that are voted on annually—accounts for about 36 percent of spending. The remaining 64 percent of the expenditures are nondiscretionary, or mandatory, meaning the government automatically spends money on these programs. The largest of these entitlements is Social Security, which grows as increasingly large numbers of the population reach retirement age.

The combination of tax reductions and expenditure increases has led to record **budget deficits**. And although the federal budget deficit has been larger when measured as a percentage of GDP, deficits of the present size have seldom been recorded during a time of peace or economic growth. In

▬ FIGURE 16.8 Discretionary vs. Nondiscretionary Spending
Source: Office of Management and Budget, 1996.

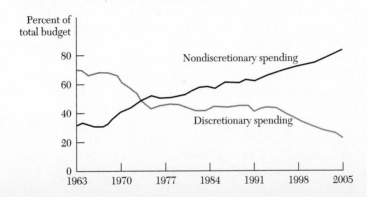

Chapter 14 we noted that the GDP clock registers each change in the nation's output. Now, however, Times Square in New York City boasts a clock that ticks off the federal debt. In mid-1997 that clock registered $5.3 trillion, noting unofficially that the United States is the largest debtor nation in the world and is increasing that debt at a rate of more than $694 million per day (For an update, contact http://www.brillig.com/debt_clock/).

In an attempt to deal with large actual and projected deficits, Congress passed the Balanced Budget and Emergency Deficit Control Act (better known as Gramm-Rudman-Hollings, which mandated a balanced budget first by 1991, then by 1993, and required automatic spending cuts in military and nonmilitary expenditures if Congress and the president failed to meet annual deficit reduction targets in the federal budget. Those targets were never achieved, in part due to the cost of the savings and loan bailout in the late 1980s (see Chapter 17). In 1990 spending cuts and tax increases were enacted to cut the deficit. The Budget Enforcement Act limited discretionary spending and ensured that new entitlement programs would not worsen the deficit. Unfortunately, these were enacted at the same time the 1990 recession began, so tax receipts did not rise as they were expected to and government spending increased to offset the higher unemployment levels generated by the recession. In 1993 Congress passed a five-year deficit reduction plan designed to cut spending and increase revenue. Deficits fell from $290 billion in 1992 to $164 billion in 1995. After much political posturing, Congress in 1996 passed a seven-year plan to balance the budget. Still, deficits are projected to increase as the baby boom generation begins retiring.

8. Which categories of federal government expenditures have grown most rapidly over the past two decades? Which revenues have seen the greatest growth?
9. Can the federal deficit be reduced? If so, how? With your solution, which groups will be most affected?

The Federal Deficit

Continued deficits in the federal budget give rise to the **national debt**. The national debt is the debt or obligation of the federal government, and is the accumulation of annual budget deficits. When expenditures are greater than revenues, the government must borrow the difference to finance its spending. The government finances its deficits by borrowing from the public through the sale of treasury bills and bonds. Treasury bonds are debt issues of the government that guarantee the repayment of the original investment plus a specified rate or amount of interest. The Treasury Department sells them to the public, to government agencies, and to institutional investors.

The national debt has always been, and now is even more so, one of the great conversation topics of Americans concerned with the growth and size of the national debt. The historical record indicates that all forms of debt have increased dramatically since World War II. In the 1960s the total federal debt was $300 billion, while in 1997 it reached $5.3 trillion, almost $5 trillion more than it was at the end of 1965. It more than tripled during the 1980s.

We might ask why the debt is so worrisome to citizens, as well as to economists and policy makers. The government could eliminate it quite simply by assessing every man, woman, and child in the country an additional $19,930 (in 1997), their per capita share of the national debt. But more important facets of the debt need to be examined. The federal debt did not overly concern the majority of U.S. economists until the 1980s. To understand why such an issue is being made of the debt, we need to examine how debt that accumulated before the 1980s differs from debt that accumulated during the 1980s and after.

The Budget Deficit through Leakages and Injections. One way to examine the federal deficit as a way of understanding the problems deficits bring to our economy is to analyze aggregate expenditures. In Chapter 15 we noted that in equilibrium, all leakages out of the economy must equal all injections into the economy:

$$\text{injections} = \text{leakages}$$

$$G + I + X = S + Tx + M.$$

We can also restate this by subtracting M from both sides of the equation:

$$G + I + (X - M) = S + Tx,$$

where G represents government expenditures, I is investment expenditures, $(X - M)$ is net exports, S is saving, and Tx is taxes.* We can rearrange the terms in this equation to show the federal budget deficit (or surplus):

$$G - Tx = S - I - (X - M)$$

We know that the deficit (or surplus) is represented by government expenditures less receipts, or $G - Tx$. If taxes (receipts) are less than government expenditures, there is a deficit.

Reviewing this budget equation clarifies the government's options. If tax receipts are chronically less than government expenditures, the deficit must

---

*We can also express this in our national accounting framework, since

$$Y = C + I + G + (X - M)$$

where

$$Y = C + S + Tx$$

Now substitute and simplify:

$$C + S + Tx = C + I + G + (X - M)$$
$$S + Tx = I + G + (X - M)$$

be offset by one or a combination of factors represented on the right side of the equation just given. The government can fund its expenditures by borrowing savings balances from the private and public sectors. This leaves fewer funds for private investment. Or it can increase borrowing from abroad, thus increasing its obligations to foreign citizens and institutions.

What's the Problem with Deficits? Before the 1980s, most of the national debt accumulated during war years, especially during World War II and the Vietnam War. Until early 1982, the debt as a percentage of national income continued to fall. As long as GDP was rising faster than the debt each year, there were only three major concerns:

1. Does the debt compete with other uses of credit?
2. Who pays the interest?
3. Who owns the debt and receives the interest?

The question of alternative financing sources is particularly cause for concern when the economy is operating at close to full employment. The government can increase taxes or borrow. Either action reduce the spending potential of another sector. Tax increases reduce the spending power of consumers and businesses. Borrowing, or enlarging the debt, may force interest rates up because government bond issues will have to be offered at a higher yield to attract enough investors. Most of these bond issues will be sold to financial intermediaries, corporations, and others, so government spending will tend to take place at the expense of investment (instead of consumption); the financial intermediaries would otherwise lend to corporations for investment purposes rather than buying bonds. This crowding out of private investment may occur when the economy is expanding. If there were severe levels of unemployment and excess capacity, interest rates would probably not have to rise with the new bond issues, and businesses would be reluctant to invest anyway, no matter how low the interest rate may fall.

Recently, the large budget deficits have caused concern for future levels of economic growth. While there are many uses for funds made available by businesses and household saving, there is a limit to that saving. National saving consists of private saving and government saving. Government saving is the budget surplus, or the part of its revenues the government does not spend. If the government must borrow from private saving to finance its deficit, it may divert funds from domestic investment. This is a particular problem today because there has been a marked decrease in the savings rates. Table 16.3 shows that the national saving rate fell from 8.0 percent of NNP in the 1950s through the 1970s to 3.1 percent in the first half of the 1980s and to 2.4 percent in the last half. Private saving dropped from 9.2 percent to 6.3 percent. Current government deficits are thus consuming many of the resources that must be parceled out among a variety of credit demands. If interest costs rise, the higher costs will have detrimental effects on housing and other investment markets. Many economists believe that deficits must be lowered if the nation is to achieve long-term prosperity.

Saving Type	Percentage of Net National Product		
	1951–1980	1982–1986	1987–1988
Private saving	9.2%	8.1%	6.3%
Government deficit	−1.2	−5.0	−4.0
National saving	8.0	3.1	2.4

private saving – government deficit = net national saving

Source: Thomas E. Mann and Charles L. Schultze, "Getting Rid of the Budget Deficit." *The Brookings Review,* Winter 1988–89, p.9. Reprinted with permission.

The second, more obvious, concern over who owns the debt arises with regard to repayment. It is one thing to pay the interest to ourselves and quite another to owe it to someone else. In 1985, about 11.5 percent of the debt was owned by foreign individuals and governments. By the early 1990s, this figure was almost 20 percent. Table 16.4 shows that borrowing from international sources has allowed the government to continue accumulating debt. The increased borrowing bid up interest rates, and foreign investors responded by purchasing U.S. bonds. This increased the demand for dollars, thereby raising the dollar's exchange value with respect to other currencies, depressing U.S. exports, and expanding imports.

10. Why has the foreign-held debt increased? Do you think it will continue to do so? Why or why not?

It would be naive to assume that all of us own some of the debt (government bonds) held by the U.S. public. Some of us own much more of the debt than others, and the richer we are, the more debt (or bonds) we are likely to own. The poorer among us hold few if any bonds. Institutions and middle- and upper-income individuals use government bonds as a safe and profitable way to hold their savings. Lower-income groups tend not to have substantial savings, since they consume most if not all of their income.

This brings us to the final problem of the interest payments on the debt. In 1980 the $900 billion debt cost $52 billion in interest payments. By 1985 the government spent $129 billion on interest payments. And in 1995, the $5 tril-

■ TABLE 16.4 Financing U.S. Domestic Investment

Domestic Investment Source	Percentage of Net National Product		
	1951–1980	1984–1986	1987–1988
National saving	8.0%	3.1%	2.7%
Domestic investment	7.6	6.2	5.9
U.S. investment abroad	0.4	—	—
Overseas borrowing	—	3.2	3.7

Source: Thomas E. Mann and Charles L. Schultze, "Getting Rid of the Budget Deficit." *The Brookings Review,* Winter 1988–89, p.9. Reprinted with permission.

lion debt cost taxpayers over $200 billion in interest payments. Since the interest payments come from budget receipts, and budget receipts come from taxation, this interest payment/ownership phenomenon leads to a redistribution of income in the economy, from bottom to top. Almost everyone pays taxes, some of which are used to pay the interest on the debt. But only individuals with higher incomes—the ones who own government bonds—receive these interest payments. This is a concern for some economists and politicians.

11. Does the ownership of the debt concern you? Why or why not?
12. Do the redistributive effects of the debt concern you? Why or why not?

Historically, the debt has financed wars, higher levels of employment and income, and inflation. In the 1980s, it financed additional military and Social Security expenditures and lower taxes. Some argue that the results are a bargain at $19,438 per person. While many economists believe that deficits are an urgent problem, Robert Eisner, former president of the American Economic Association and a professor at Northwestern University, has a more positive perspective on the federal budget deficit.

GROWTH AND THE MYTH OF THE DEFICIT

Hobart Rowen

Most of the nation's establishment economists think the federal budget deficit is the root cause of all of the economy's troubles. But they haven't convinced one of their colleagues, Robert Eisner, professor of economics at Northwestern University.

To the contrary, Eisner—a past president of the American Economic Association— says, deficit spending is what keeps the economy going—especially now, when business and consumer demand is lagging.

Eisner's philosophy—that there are bigger things to worry about than budget deficits—may prove a heady rationale for whoever sits in the White House next Jan. 20.

Despite the Perot-led budget-balancing bandwagon, it now seems probable that the next president will be forced to postpone deficit-cutting for at least a year and turn attention instead to pump-priming a weak economy.

In an interview after Perot got back in the presidential race, Eisner said that anxiety about the budget deficit is misplaced. Instead, he argues, we should be worried about the deficits in jobs, health care, adequate housing and our educational system:

"My point essentially is that the [budget] deficit is completely misunderstood. Most people literally don't know what they're talking about."

On the matter of definition of the deficit, Eisner is not alone. Two former Johnson administration budget officials, Charles J. Zwick and Peter A. Lewis, were quoted in last Sunday's *New York Times* as saying that "not one person in 10,000—including most members of Congress and professors of economics—has the foggiest idea how the deficit is, or should be, defined."

Recently, the figure of $400 billion has been bandied about to represent the deficit, even though the Congressional Budget Office puts the total for fiscal 1993 at $331 billion.

Bob Eisner finds that the deficit that has most meaning for the economy is even smaller, around $220 billion. Here's how he gets that figure: The CBO's $331 billion becomes $300 billion when government loans are excluded. Then, he subtracts $80 billion, directly attributed to the recession (lost revenue, higher unemployment benefits). He believes that this $80 billion distorts the true deficit picture.

That brings him to the $220 billion. The optimum deficit in today's economy, Eisner said, would be almost exactly that—$210 billion, which means "the budget is not that far out of balance right now."

How does he arrive at $210 billion? Eisner argues that "one rule of thumb in a growing economy, as with a growing firm, is that the deficit should be such that the debt does not grow faster than income."

Currently, he puts national debt owed to the public at $3 trillion. (There's another $1 trillion in debt held by the Social Security and other government trust funds.) Since the gross national product, now $6 trillion, grows about 7 percent annually (in money terms), Eisner would allow the debt to grow annually by the same percentage—7 percent of $3 trillion or $210 billion, maintaining the 1 to 2 ratio of debt to GNP.

Anything less, he contends, would throw the economy into a tailspin. In fact, he sees "an awful lot of room for stimulus at this point."

Even $220 billion exaggerates the real extent of the problem, Eisner insists, because much of that goes to pay for physical assets—roads, buildings, schools, the defense system—which ought to be separated, as is done by corporations, into a capital budget. That's reasonable.

But Eisner goes further. He argues that budget deficits not only do not inhibit real growth but also that deficit spending is what promotes national growth, prosperity and savings.

Eisner credits only "one real argument against the deficit," one he says is made best by Brookings economist Charles L. Schultze and others—and he takes issue with Schultze.

Schultze complains, according to Eisner, that "the deficit over the long run is reducing national savings, and because we have [only] so much savings, if we use it not to finance private investment, but to finance the budget deficit, that means there's less for private investment." Eisner contends that Schultze "presumes the deficit has no effect on income, which is hardly true."

He admits that bigger deficits in boom times add to inflation, not to additional production. But during the past 30 years, Eisner contends, the record shows that when deficits go up, the GNP rises in the following year.

Eisner is right that talking about deficits in the abstract is meaningless. He's right, also, that deficits can at times be too small as well as too large and that federal expenditures for capital assets should not be lumped with operating expenses.

But for the long term, the nation can't ignore the pile-up of debt, as Eisner would. Interest has to be paid not only on the $3 trillion owed to the public, but on the $1 trillion owed to trust funds. That money could be invested in the real economy; as of now, it represents a transfer in excess of $200 billion a year from lower income groups (who tend to be borrowers) to the rich (who are the main lenders).

Source: *The Washington Post*, October 8, 1992. © *The Washington Post*.

13. Talk of a "peace dividend" resulting from military reductions in Europe and reduced tensions with the Soviets has revolved around deficit reduction. What happened to the "peace dividend"?

The Deficit Reduction Budgets of 1993 and 1995

After a 51–50 Senate vote on August 6, 1993, President Clinton hailed the victory of his first budget package, billed as a deficit reduction plan. The budget package was a combination of tax increases and spending cuts designed to reduce continued projected budget deficits. A variety of tax increases were forecast to raise revenue, and budget cuts would reduce expenditures. At the same time, administration officials argued that such resolve to deal with future projected deficits would stabilize or lower long-term interest rates believed necessary to stimulate investment.

In 1995 the deficit had in fact decreased as a percent of GDP, and it decreased in dollar terms between 1993 and 1995. With the recovery that began in 1993, slow but steady economic growth continued through 1997. This gave the deficit reduction plan of 1993 a sound revenue base from which to reduce expenditures. When the measure was first introduced, some economists predicted that the contractionary nature of the tax increases and spending cuts would slightly dampen economic performance in the short run and promote modest growth in the longer run. In 1995, after a contentious budget battle, the president and Congress agreed to balance the budget over the next seven years.

14. Now that the deficit reduction budget package has been in place for a while, what have been its longer-run effects?
15. Given the prolonged 1990–1993 recession, would you have seen deficit reduction as important if you were a presidential adviser? What would the Keynesian model predict from such a program?

Cyclical and Structural Budget Deficits

The Keynesian philosophy toward budgets was that deficits should accumulate during recessions, when additional government expenditures were necessary to boost the economy by stimulating aggregate expenditures. He believed that governments should accumulate surpluses during times of prosperity. There would then be a cyclically balanced budget. Granted, the amounts spent during the recessions might not equal the amounts accumulated during prosperity, but on the whole they would more or less even out. In the United States, however, during the eighty-eight quarters between 1960 and 1981, only four surpluses were recorded. And since then, there have been none.

When deficits accumulate as a result of economic downturns, they are called **cyclical deficits**, measured by the economic cost of the recession in

TABLE 16.5 Unadjusted Structural and Cyclical Deficit, 1992–1995

	Billions of Dollars			
	1992	1993	1994	1995
Unadjusted deficit	290.4	255.1	203.2	163.9
Less: Cyclical component	63.6	51.1	19.2	–3.2
Structural deficit	226.8	204.0	184.0	167.1

Source: Office of Management and Budget, 1996.

terms of added expenditures due to unemployment and lost tax receipts. During the recession of the early 1990s, higher levels of unemployment and lower incomes meant that cyclical factors were acting with structural factors to create a much larger than projected federal budget deficit.

Deficits that accrue during times of prosperity or high employment are called **structural deficits**. They result from the structure of federal receipts and expenditures, regardless of the level of economic activity. Over the past two decades, structural deficits averaged less than 2 percent of GDP until 1983, when they reached 2.9 percent of GDP. Estimates are for structural deficits to rise as a percentage of GDP unless the government increases revenues or cuts expenditures. With economic growth between 1993 and 1995, the cyclical component of the deficit shrank, and in 1995 there was a negative cyclical component, since unemployment was below 5.7 percent (the unemployment rate used to calculate "full employment"). Table 16.5 illustrates that much of the improvement in the total deficit between 1993 and 1995 was due to the smaller cyclical deficits.

16. Do you believe further cuts in federal expenditures are possible? Why or why not?
17. Have any tax increases been passed since 1997? Have new or different types of taxes been proposed? What are they?
18. How large was the federal deficit last year? How large is the federal debt?
19. What would be the effect on income of a decrease in government spending of $0.3 trillion and a tax cut of $0.3 trillion? Is this a balanced budget?
20. Given the $155 billion deficit of 1988, what could have been done to balance the budget? What would the macroeconomic effect have been?

CONCLUSION

This chapter has highlighted the process and ways in which fiscal policy works through the tax, transfer, and spending multipliers. For a wide variety of reasons, fiscal policy is not always efficient, but it is most often effective—at least when estimated by Keynesian models. We have also seen the growing concern with budget deficits and the desire to balance receipts against expenditures in periods of economic growth. Chapter 17 will introduce money into the Keynesian model of the economy; this provides yet another set of tools for achieving policy objectives.

Review Questions

1. What fiscal policy recommendations would you make to combat unemployment and recession? (a) What fiscal measures would you recommend if the economy was in the middle of a prolonged period of inflation? (b) Would you favor a taxing policy over a curb in government spending? Why or why not? (c) What might be the end result of your policy? (d) How long do you expect the lags to last before your policy would be enacted?
2. What are the differences between automatic stabilizers and discretionary fiscal policy?
3. Would you ever recommend a balanced budget for the federal government? Why or why not? If so, when?
4. Can federal budget deficits be beneficial to the economy?
5. Why does Robert Eisner think the deficit is not a big problem for the economy?
6. How do deficits limit the productive potential of the economy?
7. Are structural deficits more cause for concern than cyclical deficits? Explain.
8. Would you make any recommendations to alleviate some of the lags involved with fiscal actions? Are these delays "healthy"? Explain.
9. If MPC = 0.8, what would be the effect of a $10 million tax cut and a $6 million increase in government purchases?

17

Financial Markets, Money, and Monetary Policy

INTRODUCTION

Money is an asset accepted in exchange for the goods and services we wish to purchase. Economists have long debated about money and its role in the economy, a debate that persists today. The role of money and the operation of the markets for money and other financial instruments are important in economic decision making and policy making.

Key players in the market for money and other financial instruments are institutions called **financial intermediaries**, which hold the funds of depositors and make those funds available to borrowers. Financial intermediaries include banks, savings and loan institutions, credit unions, life insurance companies, mutual funds, and pension funds. They provide financial services demanded by consumers in a changing society.

To begin examining money and financial intermediaries, we will first look at the uses of and demands for money. Next, we will examine the money supply, including the ways the Fed can increase and decrease the money supply and the role of money in the Keynesian model. Finally, we examine monetary policy and the school of economics known as monetarism.

THE USES OF MONEY

Money is important to economics because of its uses. Some say that money is as money does. Few individuals hold dollars for the sheer joy of counting or stacking them.

Money is valued for the goods and services that it buys—for its use as a **medium of exchange**. It is commonly accepted in payment for goods and services. Before money was institutionalized, barter economies prevailed; people simply exchanged goods and services. Of course, problems arose when two parties could not agree upon objects to trade, or when there was no double coincidence of wants. For example, barter fails if one trader desires shoes and has only nuts to offer in exchange, while the shoemaker wants only leather in exchange for shoes. Larger problems would arise if one had only assets that could not be divided, such as a horse to trade for less valuable objects.

Because it is an accepted medium of exchange, money can also be used as a measuring rod for the value of each good or service—in other words, as a **unit of account**. In our economy, goods are measured by a dollar amount. In shopping we observe that a pound of nuts is priced at $3.69, a pair of shoes at $65.98, and a horse and buggy at $5,753. In Chapter 14, we used money as our unit of account in measuring the National Income Accounts of GDP and NNP. Firms use money to account for the flow of goods and services produced and sold.

Besides its unique role as a medium of exchange and unit of account, money has two functions that it shares with other assets (things of value that are owned). Money may serve as a **store of value**. To be a store of value, an asset must hold its value into the future. Some other assets that serve this function are stocks and bonds, precious metals and gems, and property. Money may also be a **standard of deferred payment**. Standards of deferred payments are assets that are accepted by others for future payment.

||| 1. What assets would you accept as payment for your work? |

DEMAND FOR MONEY

The four uses of money are associated with the three categories of demand for money. The **transactions demand**—the only category recognized by the classical economists—indicates the amount of money balances that individuals desire for transaction (purchasing) purposes. This demand corresponds to money's function as a medium of exchange and is often constant with a given level of income and pattern of consumption expenditures.

People also have a **precautionary demand** for money, or a demand for money to hold to meet unforeseen expenses. John Maynard Keynes wrote about this demand as a separate category in *The General Theory*. We observe this precautionary demand as we try to hedge our risks by saving, perhaps for the proverbial "rainy day" or for some other reason. We have, as Keynes said, a propensity to save.

||| 2. Divide your demands for money into transactions and precautionary balances. What percentage of your money balances do you hold for each? |

The precautionary demand, like the transactions demand, is generally constant; people at certain income levels will tend to save or keep a relatively fixed proportion of their income for precautionary purposes. Figure 17.1 shows a demand curve for the transactions and precautionary balances plotted on a price-quantity axis. (This adds money to the array of goods and services for

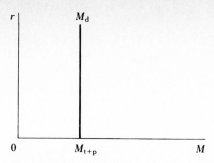

FIGURE 17.1 Precautionary and Transactions Demand for Money

which there is a demand—and later, of course, a supply.) The quantity of money (M) is measured along the horizontal axis, and the price of money, represented by the interest rate (r),* is measured along the vertical axis. The vertical line M_d indicates that at all rates of interest, the precautionary and transactions demand will be constant for a given individual at a given income level.

The third demand for money (or, as he called it, **liquidity preference**†) recognized by Keynes is the **speculative demand.** This demand arises from people's desire to maximize their returns on the funds left over after satisfying their transactions and precautionary demands. The speculative demand for funds is inversely related to the interest rate. If the interest rate is high, people will hold relatively few speculative or liquid balances. Instead, they will hold stocks and bonds or goods. If the interest rate is low, individuals may decide to wait and see what happens to interest rates in the future. If interest rates rise, people want to avoid being locked into low-yielding assets, so they prefer to hold (speculative) cash or money balances. One can plot the speculative demand for money with respect to interest and the quantity of money, since $M_{spec} = f(r)$, as shown in Figure 17.2.

At extremely high interest rates, the speculative demand for money balances approaches 0, whereas at very low rates of interest, people will desire to hold only money balances. This low-interest range in which the demand for money is perfectly elastic is called the Keynesian **liquidity trap.** Keynes pointed out that at extremely low rates of interest, people believe interest rates can go no lower and can only rise. To buy bonds would be courting disaster, so people hold on to their cash. This liquidity trap area becomes important when discussing various aspects of monetary policy, a topic we will return to later in the chapter.

---

*The price of money is the rate of interest, since a person who buys or borrows money pays for it at the prevailing rate of interest. Although there is a wide array of interest rates in the economy at any one time, depending on such factors as risk and time until the asset matures, we will focus on *an* interest rate—assuming that all of them behave similarly.

†Liquidity is the degree of "moneyness." One hundred percent liquid suggests that all of one's assets are in cash and/or demand deposits. Stocks and bonds and property are assets of somewhat lesser levels of liquidity since they cannot immediately be converted into cash.

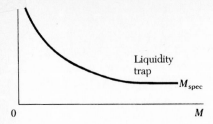

— FIGURE 17.2 Speculative Demand for Money

If we combine all three demands for money, we obtain the total demand for money, which is plotted in Figure 17.3. This demand curve for money, like all demand curves, indicates that the quantity demanded varies inversely with price. As the interest rate rises, people will hold smaller money balances, down to the amount needed to satisfy transactions and precautionary demands.

Changes in the Demand for Money

Like other demand curves, the demand for money may not remain constant over time. Shifts, or changes in demand, are often caused by a change in the level of income. For example, if an individual's income increases from $30,000 a year to $40,000 a year, that person's demand for money will more than likely increase. The reason is that the demand for precautionary and transactions balances increases as income increases. Figure 17.4 shows how changes in income affect the demand for money.

SUPPLY OF MONEY

Unlike the supply of most goods and services, the total supply of money is controlled not by individual firms, but by the Federal Reserve System, more commonly known as the Fed.

— FIGURE 17.3 Total Demand for Money

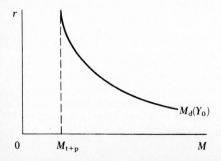

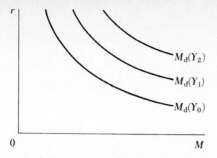

$M_d(Y_2)$

$M_d(Y_1)$

$M_d(Y_0)$

0   M

■ FIGURE 17.4 The Effect of Income Changes on the Demand for Money

The Fed

To mend an ailing national banking system by promoting stability in the banking system, the Federal Reserve Act of 1913 established the **Federal Reserve System (the Fed)** as the central bank in the United States. The Fed is an independent agency of the government, established by Congress to centralize control over the banking system and the money supply. Figure 17.5 shows the basic organizational structure of the Federal Reserve System.

Members of the Board of Governors of the Federal Reserve System, appointed to fourteen-year terms by the president with congressional

■ FIGURE 17.5 Elements of the Federal Reserve System

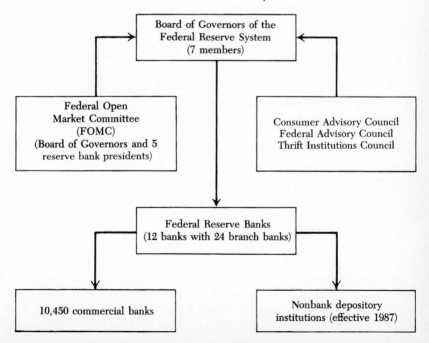

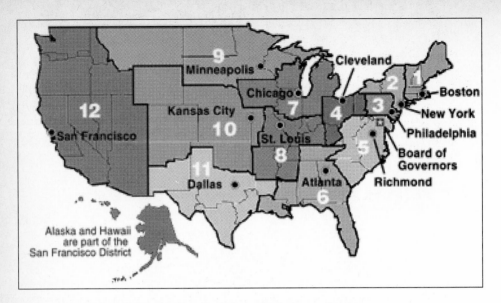

■ FIGURE 17.6 Boundaries of Federal Reserve Districts and Their
Branch Territories *(Source: Federal Reserve Bank Internet Web page.)*

approval, coordinate and regulate money policy in the United States. The
chair of the Board of Governors acts as spokesperson for the entire system.
The Federal Open Market Committee directs Fed sales and purchases of
U.S. Treasury bonds, and the other councils advise. The twelve regional
Federal Reserve Banks and their twenty-four branches throughout the coun-
try oversee operations of the member commercial banks in their districts.
Figure 17.6 shows the locations of these regional banks.

The Monetary Control Act of 1980 stipulates that the Federal Reserve can
require that *all* banks and depository institutions in the country hold reserves
(or a percentage of deposits). The passage of this act gave the Fed control
over the reserves placed on money held in commercial banks, savings banks,
savings and loan associations, and credit unions.

3. Why do you suppose Congress established the Federal Reserve
   as an independent agency of the federal government (that is,
   outside the operational control of Congress or the president)?
4. Who is the current chair of the Fed?

Regulation of Financial Markets

There are many institutional players in the U.S. financial markets, all of
them subject to some degree of regulation. Commercial banks are the oldest
financial intermediaries. Savings banks and insurance companies emerged in
the late nineteenth century, while credit unions, real estate trusts, investment banks, bank holding companies, and finance companies developed in

the twentieth century. A number of innovations in existing financial institutions occurred in the 1980s, and we can expect to see continuing changes resulting from new regulation and deregulation legislation in the 1990s.

The history of financial market regulation has been interesting. Financial institutions have seen periods of total control and regulation, as well as periods that might be called banking anarchy. The current period of regulation resulted from controls instituted after the Great Depression, as Congress enacted legislation to avoid the recurrence of widespread banking failures. Investors as well as depositors wanted protection from financial market failures, and state as well as federal governments responded with laws and regulations designed to assure the safety of the financial system. Federal deposit insurance agencies began insuring a variety of deposits, and agencies began to regulate the activities of financial institutions.

Regulations limited the kinds of loans and assets each type of financial institution could issue and possess. As a result, the financial industry was segmented into largely different types of institutions with little competition among them. Commercial banks, for example, specialized in commercial loans to businesses, while savings and loan institutions generated home mortgages. Started by builders in the 1870s, savings banks made money available to people wanting to buy the builders' products.

Perhaps the most onerous of the regulations was **Regulation Q**, which placed ceilings on the interest rate financial institutions could pay for time and savings deposits. The purpose of interest ceilings was to "restrain excessive price competition," which was thought to be a cause of the 1933 banking collapse. The interest ceiling was above the market rate of interest through the mid-1960s, so until then it caused no concern. After 1966, market rates rose above the interest ceiling on several occasions. This effectively prevented financial intermediaries from attracting money and then lending it. Instead of depositing their funds in financial intermediaries, people withdrew their dollars and put them into stocks or other assets to get higher returns. Instead of **financial intermediation**, there was **disintermediation**. To avoid interest ceilings, financial intermediaries began creating new financial instruments, since only time and savings deposit accounts were then subject to Regulation Q. But the Federal Reserve was not to be caught short. While Regulation Q covered only two types of accounts in 1965, twenty-four types were covered by 1979.

Because of these rapid financial innovations, Congress came under pressure to deregulate financial markets. The regulation of the 1930s had limited competition and the ability to work within the market system to bid for funds. By the end of the 1970s, the mood toward regulation had substantially changed as described in the 1984 *Economic Report of the President*:

> In the 1930s, financial instability was attributed to the natural operation of competitive markets, and this view supported a very substantial extension of regulatory controls over financial markets. More recently, however, a renewed respect for the efficiency of competitive markets has developed, as well as increased recognition of the costs of regulation. Regulation tends to spread in unproductive direc-

tions and often causes industries to evolve less efficiently than they otherwise would. For these reasons, the promotion of efficiency by furthering competition is also an important regulatory goal. The purpose of regulation should not be to protect poorly managed individual firms from failure, but rather to prevent such failures from shaking the stability of the financial system as a whole. Regulation should be designed to achieve stability of the system, while individual firms are afforded the maximum possible freedom to compete and innovate.

In the early 1980s, financial deregulation significantly changed the rules of the game in the financial markets. Between 1980 and 1984, most interest rates on federally insured deposits were deregulated, allowing banks and thrift institutions (savings and loan institutions, savings banks, and credit unions) to freely determine the rate of interest they paid on most types of deposits. This added both competition and uncertainty to a vast financial system. The deregulatory activity was started by the Monetary Control Act of 1980 and extended by the Garn–St Germain Depository Institutions Act of 1982. The Monetary Control Act set lower reserve requirements for all nonmember banks, established the Fed as the lender of the last resort for depository institutions, and eliminated Regulation Q. The Garn–St Germain Act authorized all financial institutions to offer interest-bearing checking accounts and extended the power of regulators to promote mergers for depository institutions that were failing. It also expanded the lending

TOLES © 1992 *The Buffalo News.* Reprinted with permission of UNIVERSAL PRESS SYNDICATE. All rights reserved.

and deposit powers of thrifts. This permitted some new lending and investing powers, including commercial and real estate loans by savings and loan institutions.

Following deregulation, the rate of bank failures and instability increased, and the savings and loan industry nearly collapsed. Continental Illinois, a major U.S. national bank, paved the way for bank failures in the late 1980s and early 1990s. Unable to arrange a merger for this ailing giant, the Federal Deposit Insurance Corporation (FDIC), which insures deposits of most banks, took over operations. Other failing banks and thrifts were either merged with institutions believed to be more stable or liquidated. Many have therefore questioned the wisdom of financial deregulation.

BANKING AND THRIFT INSTABILITY, 1980S- AND 1990S-STYLE

Deregulation posed enormous problems for the nation's commercial banks and savings institutions. Nearly eight times as many banks closed between 1980 and 1990 as closed during the 1970s. Some 1,570 savings institutions closed their doors or merged with other depository institutions during this period. The government's response to the turmoil in the thrift industry cost U.S. taxpayers an estimated $500 billion or more.

A number of thrifts were in financial difficulty prior to deregulation. Initially chartered to provide mortgage funds to the housing market, savings and loan institutions were legally restricted to holding only mortgages as assets. After World War II, amidst a large upswing in purchases of single-family homes, the demand for mortgages rose, and savings institutions prospered despite the long-term, low-interest nature of these mortgages. Thanks to Regulation Q limiting the interest rate that could be paid to depositors, tax benefits to the industry, and federal insurance guarantees to depositors, savings institutions could thrive as long as interest rates remained low. However, interest rates rose markedly in the 1970s, and savings institutions had to pay higher interest rates to attract deposits. Their profits were squeezed, since the long-run returns on the mortgages already in their portfolios remained fixed at low rates, even though new mortgages reflected the higher rates. Furthermore, the institutions faced geographic restrictions on their customer base, so institutions in agriculture and oil-producing states were especially fragile. Energy and agricultural prices plunged in the 1980s, and increasing numbers of firms in the Midwest and Southwest failed, rendering many loans worthless. Deregulation freed these institutions to engage in potentially more lucrative but riskier areas of investment. Thrifts diversified into office buildings, commercial loans, and some direct purchases of franchises. At the same time, federal depository insurance was increased from $40,000 per account to $100,000 per account, so thrifts sought out larger deposits by offering more attractive rates of return. They hoped the new channels of investment open to them would more than offset the higher interest rates they were paying for funds. The risk for bankers (and depositors) was limited, since most deposits were insured.

During this same period, federal budget cuts, combined with a spirit of deregulation, reduced the number of bank examiners hired to oversee these more risky (and sometimes fraudulent) activities. The reduction in regulation and inspection, along with an overextension of risky loans, left many institutions with deposit liabilities in excess of the value of their assets. These ingredients completed a recipe for widespread thrift failure.

With the mounting failures draining federal deposit insurance funds, Congress in 1989 enacted the Financial Institutions Reform, Recovery and Enforcement Act (FIRREA). This law provided funds to merge or liquidate failing thrift institutions and prevent the thrift failures of the eighties from recurring. FIRREA created the Resolution Trust Corporation (RTC) to manage a bailout of the savings and loan industry through the early 1990s. Among its charges, the RTC was to sell houses, apartment buildings, golf resorts, office buildings, and other assets of failed thrifts. Much of the real estate sold at bargain basement prices, recouping only a small fraction of the moneys lost. These massive sales depressed real estate markets and new construction in communities with the highest levels of RTC sales.

FIRREA also eliminated other thrift regulatory agencies and established several new agencies in their place. The law established more stringent capital standards, requiring thrifts to meet the higher capital requirements of banks. Regulators continued to examine bank and thrift capital requirements through the 1990s.

Economists estimated that in the early 1990s, closing or selling insolvent thrifts cost taxpayers some $10 million for each day the S&Ls stayed open.

Source: Statistical Abstract of the United States: 1992, p. 499; 1996, p. 513.

5. What are current estimates of the total cost to bail out the failed S&Ls? How much will it cost your family?
6. What are some of the opportunity costs of the thrift bailout? (What could have been purchased with these amounts?)
7. Some economists argue that markets function more efficiently without regulation. Why did deregulation of the S&L industry work so poorly?

Measures of the Money Supply

Besides controlling the amount of credit in the system of depository institutions (which is often referred to as the banking system), the Fed also regulates the money supply. Because a number of financial assets are "used" as money, economists measure the money supply in broader terms than currency used for exchange. They use measures of the money supply called **monetary aggregates**, which include measures for M_1, M_2, M_3, and L. Figure 17.7 illustrates the growth in these money measures.

The most narrowly defined monetary aggregate includes most of the "money" that we use for our day-to-day transactions and is called M_1. M_1 includes coins and currency plus demand deposits (checking accounts), traveler's checks, and other checkable deposits (including NOW and ATS accounts*) held by the public. In 1996, currency and coins accounted for

---

*Negotiable order of withdrawal (NOW) accounts are interest-bearing checking accounts. They became legal throughout the United States on November 1, 1980, with an initial maximum interest rate of 5¼ percent. NOW accounts may be issued by all depository institutions. ATS accounts are automatic transfer service accounts.

M_1 = Currency	
+ Traveler's checks	
+ Demand deposits	
+ Other checkable deposits	
Total M_1	1,
M_2 = M_1	
+ Small denomination time deposits	782.9
+ Savings deposits and money market deposit accounts	1,215.5
+ Money market mutual fund shares (noninstitutional)	348.8
+ Overnight repurchase agreements	72.5
+ Overnight Eurodollars	17.0
+ Consolidation adjustment*	−2.0
Total M_2	3,563.1
M_3 = M_2	
+ Large-denomination time deposits	338.9
+ Money market mutual fund shares (institutional)	197.0
+ Term repurchase agreements	95.4
+ Term Eurodollars	45.7
+ Consolidation adjustment*	−15.3
Total M_3	4,224.8
L = M_3	
+ Short-term Treasury securities	323.4
+ Commercial paper	386.8
+ Savings bonds	171.7
+ Banker's acceptances	16.3
Total L	5,123.0

*An adjustment to avoid double counting. For example, the M_2 consolidation adjustment subtracts short-term repurchase agreements and Eurodollars held by money market mutual funds (which are already included in money market mutual fund balances).

Source: Board of Governors of the Federal Reserve System, Statistical Release H.6, April 1994.

■ FIGURE 17.7 Measures of the Monetary Aggregates, 1960–1995.

Source: *Economic Report of the President,* February 1996, Table B-65.

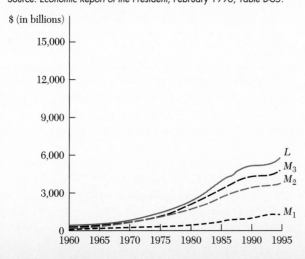

bout 33 percent of M_1, demand deposits for 35 percent, other checkable deposits for 30.6 percent, and traveler's checks for 0.8 percent. The total money supply measured as M_1 stood at \$1.12 trillion in early 1996. M_1 has historically grown at an annual rate of around 5 or 6 percent. In 1990, the growth rate of M_1 was only 4 percent, but it increased to 14 percent in 1992, as the economy slowed. During the economic recovery in 1995, the annual change in M_1 fell by 5 percent.

An expanded monetary aggregate M_2 includes M_1 and adds other short-term accounts that are easily converted into money. M_2 equals M_1 plus short-term time and savings accounts and other interest-bearing accounts, including money market deposit accounts and noninstitutional money market mutual funds and some other very liquid assets.* In early 1996, M_2 was \$3.7 trillion—over three times the value of M_1.

Some economists believe that the use of the M_2 definition better explains consumption and other decisions made in the economy. At one point, the Fed used M_2 targets for implementation of monetary policy. Recently, however, M_2 has not been as effective as the Fed would like, leading the Fed's current chairman, Alan Greenspan, to look to alternative targets. Broader concepts of money and liquid assets measured by the federal government and often used by economists in analyzing the economy include M_3 and L. Other econo-mists, however, believe that the Federal Reserve—when reflecting on policy actions that will result in changes in the money supply—really looks at the availability of credit in the economy rather than any precise M_1, M_2, or M_3 definition. For example, if the Fed concludes that credit is too tight, it will take measures to increase credit availability by increasing the money supply.

Although the Fed is responsible for initiating changes in policies to alter the money supply, individual depository institutions allocate the money to the public, and to a large extent their allocation reflects the interest rates in the economy. If interest rates are low, depository institutions are reluctant to lend large quantities of money and risk being locked into low-yielding assets. On the other hand, if interest rates are high, the depository institutions will be more willing to lend money *if it is available to them* (or if the Fed has allo-cated additional money by implementing policies which increase the money supply). We can illustrate this by constructing a money supply curve. The interest rate is on the vertical axis, and the quantity of money is on the hori-zontal axis, as in Figure 17.8.

When we combine the supply and demand curves for money, the inter-section of the two curves signifies equilibrium in the money market, as shown in Figure 17.9. At point E the quantity of money demanded equals the quan-tity supplied at an interest rate of r_0. In equilibrium, there is no excess demand or supply. If the Fed allows the money supply to increase, then the

---

*Money market mutual funds (MMMFs) and money market deposit accounts (MMDAs) are funds issued to savers and backed by holdings of high-quality short-term assets. MMDAs are fed-erally insured bank deposit accounts.

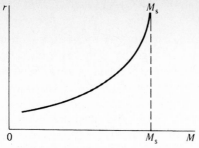

■ FIGURE 17.8 The Money Supply

M_{s0} curve will shift to the right (M_{s1}), usually resulting in a lower interest rate (r_1), as in Figure 17.10. A decrease in the money supply will shift M_{s0} to the left (M_{s2}) and increase the interest rate (r_2). Later in this chapter, we will look at the tools with which the Fed changes the money supply. First we will examine the process by which commercial banks "create" money and how this money works within the Keynesian model.

■ FIGURE 17.9 Equilibrium in the Money Market

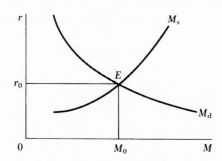

■ FIGURE 17.10 A Change in the Money Supply

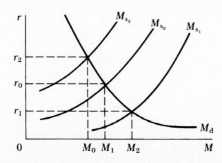

Suppliers of Money

All financial intermediaries facilitate the exchange of money, but commercial banks and other depository institutions also have the power to "create" money. They create money on the basis of a **fractional reserve system** of deposit balances. The Fed requires that every depository institution hold reserves, setting aside a certain percentage of its total deposits in its vault or in the nearest Federal Reserve Bank to ensure safety and the ability to meet deposit withdrawals. The **reserve requirements** (the percentage of reserves that must be held) varies according to the asset size of the depository and the type of account. Table 17.1 lists the most recent reserve requirements mandated by the Fed.

||| 8. Why isn't there a 100 percent reserve requirement? |

An example of the money creation process should help clarify what happens to a deposit in a commercial bank or other depository institution. For simplicity's sake, we shall use a 10 percent reserve requirement for demand deposits and begin with a newly created $1,000 deposit. With this deposit, new deposits in the depository or banking system increase by $1,000, and required reserves increase by $100. This leaves the commercial bank with $1,000 minus $100, or $900. The prudent (profit-maximizing) banker would use the $900 to generate loans and investments of an equal amount.

Perhaps you are in the market for a $900 loan. If our friendly neighborhood banker decides you are creditworthy, you may receive the "extra" $900. If you spend the $900 on new stereo components, there is a good chance that the full $900 will enter the banking system when the Stereo Shack deposits its daily balances. The banking system then has another deposit, this time one of $900. It must hold 10 percent of $900, or $90, as the reserve requirement on the *new* $900 deposit. Total new deposits are now $1,900, and total new reserves are $190 in the banking system. And what will happen to the $900 minus $90, or $810, left in the bank? Of course, it becomes a potential source

---

▌▌▌ TABLE 17.1 Reserve Requirements of Depository Institutions

Type of Deposit	Requirements	
(Net Transaction Accounts)	% of Deposits	Date Effective
Up to $49.3 million	3	1/2/97
More than $49.3 million	10	1/2/97
Nonpersonal time deposits	0	12/27/90
Eurocurrency liabilities	0	12/27/90

Source: *Federal Reserve Bulletin*, June 1997.

TABLE 17.2 Money Creation: Example

Position of Depository Institution	New Deposits	New Loans and Investments	New Reserves
Original depository institution	$1,000.00	$900.00	$100.00
2nd depository institution	900.00	810.00	90.00
3rd depository institution	810.00	729.00	81.00
4th depository institution	729.00	656.10	72.90
5th depository institution	656.10	590.49	65.60
6th depository institution	590.49	531.44	59.05
7th depository institution	531.44	478.30	53.14
8th depository institution	478.30	430.47	47.83
9th depository institution	430.47	387.42	43.05
10th depository institution	387.42	348.68	38.74
11th depository institution	348.68	313.81	34.87
12th depository institution	+ 313.81	+ 282.43	31.38
Sum of 12 depository institutions	$7,175.71	$6,458.14	$717.61
Sum of remaining depository institutions	+ 2,824.29	+2,541.86	+232.39
Total for system as a whole	$10,000.00	$9,000.00	$1,000.00

Note: Totals may not be accurate due to rounding.

for increases in loans and investments. Table 17.2 shows the final result of the initial $1,000 demand deposit.

Rather than carrying this process to its final result, we can more easily find the total amount of money "created" by using the following formula:

$$\Delta R \times 1/r_{dd} = \Delta DD,$$

where ΔR is the original change in reserves, r_{dd} is the reserve requirement on demand deposits, and ΔDD is the total change in demand deposits. We can substitute numbers from our example:

$$\$1,000 \times 1/(1/10) = \Delta DD$$

$$\$1,000 \times 10 = \Delta DD$$

$$\$10,000 = \Delta DD$$

From $1,000 with the stroke of a pen—depository institutions can "make" $10,000, or $9,000 of *new* money.

Before we accept this fountain pen magic, however, we must take note of several things. The first is that an individual bank or depository institution acting alone cannot create money. The process must operate throughout the whole system. To more easily understand this, imagine that a single depository institution tried to expand or create money on its own. Based on the

$1,000 increase in its reserves with the $1,000 deposit, the institution loaned $9,000. What happens to that depository institution when someone comes to withdraw or use the funds the depository institution has just lent? As you might imagine, many problems can result, one being that the bank cannot maintain its reserve requirement.

||| 9. What other difficulties might this depository institution run into?

A second point to remember is that the simplified money creation process as described works only if there are no leakages in the system. Leakages can occur in several places. Individuals may decide to place their funds elsewhere, either outside the depository institutions or in hoards. If they do not deposit the funds, then there are no reserves to expand upon. Consumers may place some funds in time accounts. These funds have a lower reserve requirement, so the money multiplier is larger. Consequently, such deposits will lead to an even greater expansion of the money supply.

Another leakage may appear within the financial system itself. Bankers and other deposit managers may decide that they can earn greater profits by holding assets other than loans or investments. Perhaps they believe their liquidity is too low and desire to place their remaining funds (or excess reserves) in more short-term assets (such as government bonds). In either case, there is a leakage of funds that do not reenter the demand deposit flow for an indefinite period of time. Indeed, the amount of assets that depository institutions hold in loans or investments is approximately 60 percent of their total portfolio.

Caution should therefore be the byword when examining the money creation process. Nevertheless, the process does suggest that commercial banks and other depository institutions can expand the money supply by "creating" demand deposits. In addition, the simple formula $\Delta R \times r_{dd} = \Delta DD$ approximates the amount of money that the system can create from a new deposit.

||| 10. What happens to the money supply when people take $1,000 out of their depository institution deposits?

The Myth and Mystique of Money

In the following excerpt from "Commercial Banks as Creators of Money," Yale economist James Tobin tries to steal our thunder in explaining the multiple money creation process in a principles text:

> Perhaps the greatest moment of triumph for the elementary economics teacher is his [her] exposition of the multiple creation of bank credit and bank deposits. Before the admiring eyes of freshmen [s]he puts to rout the practical banker who is so sure that [s]he "lends only the money depositors entrust to him [her]." The banker is shown to have a worm's-eye view, and his [her] error stands as an introductory object lesson in the fallacy of composition. From the Olympian vantage of the teacher and the textbook it appears that the banker's dictum must be reversed: depositors entrust to bankers whatever amounts the bankers lend. To be sure, this

is not true of a single bank; one bank's loan may wind up as another bank's deposit. But it is, as the arithmetic of successive rounds of deposit creation makes clear, true of the banking system as a whole. Whatever their other errors, a long line of financial heretics have been right in speaking of "fountain pen money"—money created by the stroke of the bank president's pen when he approves a loan and credits the proceeds to the borrower's checking account.

In this time-honored exposition two characteristics of commercial banks are intertwined. One is that their liabilities—well, at least their demand deposit liabilities—serve as widely acceptable means of payment. Thus, they count, along with coin and currency in public circulation, as "money." The other is that the preferences of the public normally play no role in determining the total volume of deposits or the total quantity of money. For it is the beginning of wisdom in monetary economics to observe that money is like the "hot potato" of a children's game: one individual may pass it to another, but the group as a whole cannot get rid of it. If the economy and the supply of money are out of adjustment, it is the economy that must do the adjusting. This is as true, evidently, of the money created by bankers' fountain pens as of money created by public printing presses.

The commercial banks possess the *widow's curse* [an expression implying unending supply; emphasis added]. And because they possess this key to unlimited expansion, they have to be restrained by reserve requirements.

—J. Tobin, "Commercial Banks as Creators of Money," in *Banking and Monetary Studies*, D. Carson, ed. Richard D. Irwin, 1963. Reprinted by permission of the publisher.

MONEY AND THE KEYNESIAN SYSTEM

Money can be an integral part of the Keynesian system. In Chapters 15 and 16, we saw that the gist of the Keynesian system is that changes in consumption, investment, and government spending can effectively be used to expand or lower the level of income in the economy. Money can and most often does work within the Keynesian sphere to allow income changes as well. Changes in the money supply often directly influence both the business and household sectors in their investment and consumption decisions.

An increase in the supply of money will lower the interest rate (Figure 17.11), just as (*ceteris paribus*) any increase in supply will decrease the price of

■ FIGURE 17.11 The Interest-Investment Relationship

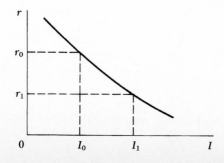

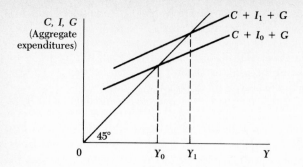

■ FIGURE 17.12 Income Response to a Change in Investment

a product. As Figure 17.10 shows, an increase in M_s from M_{s0} to M_{s1} lowers interest rates from r_0 to r_1. These interest rates along with investment demand are shown in Figure 17.11. As money becomes "cheaper," investors reconsider their present levels of investment. Low interest rates will encourage businesses to borrow from commercial banks and to spend these funds on new plants and equipment (i.e., investment); high rates, on the other hand, deter investment decisions. This is expressed graphically in Figure 17.11 as an inverse relationship between the rate of interest (r) and the level of investment (I), or $I = f(r)$. As the interest rate falls from r_0 to r_1, investment (in housing, equipment, or plants) will expand from I_0 to I_1.

Returning to the Keynesian model developed in the last two chapters, we can again examine the effect of an increase in investment. This time, however, the investment increase is stimulated by a reduction in the interest rate, generated by an increase in the money supply (see Figure 17.10). As the money supply increases from M_{s0} to M_{s1} in Figure 17.10, the interest rate decreases from r_0 to r_1. As this occurs, investment increases from I_0 to I_1 (Figure 17.11). Finally, this increased investment, working through the multiplier, generates a new higher income level, Y_1, as in Figure 17.12. (Remember, $I_1 - I_0 = \Delta I$, $Y_1 - Y_0 = \Delta Y$, and $\Delta Y = k \times \Delta I$.)

11. When the Fed decreases the money supply, what happens to interest rates? The level of investment? The level of income? Employment?

Keynes relied more on fiscal policy for the stimulation of aggregate expenditures because he expected that during times of depression the economy would operate in the area of the liquidity trap. In this area, no matter how much the money supply increased, the rate of interest would fall no lower. And the business community's grim expectations of the future would discourage any further investment activity, even with low rates of interest. As we can see in Figure 17.13, changes in the money supply within the range of the liquidity trap will have no effect on interest rates. And if interest rates are

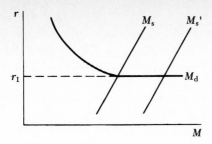

■ FIGURE 17.13 Money Supply Increase in the Liquidity Trap

unchanged, the levels of investment and income also will remain the same, yielding no effect on aggregate expenditures.

Keynes also believed that business and consumer expectations could change during depressions, thereby thwarting the effect of monetary policy. For these reasons, economists often say that increasing the money stock to increase investment is much like pushing on a string. In *The General Theory*, Keynes expressed substantial doubt about the ability of monetary policy—a policy that changes the money supply—to rescue the economy from a severe depression. Yet, during the past three decades, we have seen the power of monetary policy to affect the levels of aggregate expenditures in the economy. During this period, the Fed has played an active role in determining aggregate expenditures, a practice that has drawn frequent criticism. Still, monetary policy has continued to be an important tool for economic stabilization.

MONETARY POLICY

Some critics have argued that the Fed is too powerful, too independent, and too business oriented. Others believe that the money supply is much too important to be left to the discretion of mere mortals. In this section, we shall examine the tools that enable the Federal Reserve to control the supply of money and credit in the economy and outline the philosophy and principles of the school of economists known as the monetarists. Then we shall examine recent Federal Reserve policy and the interaction between monetary and fiscal policy.

Tools of the Trade

To affect the level of income in the economy, the Fed has at hand several primary tools: (1) reserve requirement changes, (2) open-market operations, and (3) discount rate changes. On occasion—for example, during World War II—the Fed has implemented several selective credit controls on home mortgages and consumer credit. The only credit control regularly used is the margin requirement for stocks, which stipulates the percentages of payment that must be in cash on any security purchase. In

March 1980, the Fed responded to President Carter's request for tighter credit to help quell the inflationary trends by announcing new controls on consumer and business credit. These controls were quickly withdrawn when it became evident that they were dramatically worsening the recession of 1980. The Fed can also use moral suasion in pursuit of its economic goals; that is, it can attempt to persuade relevant economic actors to engage in or refrain from certain activities. During the recession of the early 1990s, President Bush called on Fed chairman Alan Greenspan to continue increasing the supply of money to bring interest rates down. Since inflation was relatively low and stable at that time, the Fed continued pumping money into the economy and lowering rates.

Reserve Requirements. As we saw earlier in Table 17.1, each depository institution must keep a reserve requirement at the Federal Reserve or as cash in vault. The Board of Governors of the Federal Reserve can change the levels of reserves required at any time. In general, the central bank views its ability to change reserve requirements as its most powerful tool and uses this tool with utmost discretion. Since only a 1 percent change in reserve requirements alters the monetary situation geometrically, changes in reserve requirements have been infrequent since 1935, when this tool became available.

Critics claim that this tool works like an ax rather than a scalpel. An example shows why. Assume the Fed wishes to restrict economic activity by reducing the money supply (e.g., to fight inflation). If banking assets are at $400 billion with 10 percent reserve requirements, some $40 billion is being held as reserves. If reserve requirements are increased by 1 percent, to 11 percent, some $44 billion must be held. This takes $4 billion out of the money supply immediately, as loans and investments are called in to increase reserves to the new level. More would be taken out of the system later through multiple deposit contraction—the reverse of the multiple deposit expansion explained previously.

12. In the example just given, what might happen to interest rates? Why?
13. What would happen if reserve requirements were lowered by 1 percent? How much would member banks be required to hold? What would happen to the "extra" money (or excess reserves)?

An increase in reserve requirements can absorb large changes in *excess reserves*, or additional moneys held by depository institutions, such as those that occurred during the 1930s when substantial amounts of gold flowed into the country. A reduction in the reserve requirement may offset a large loss in reserves. In either case, a change in reserve requirements announces a change in Fed policy to the public as well as to the banks and other depository institutions. Critics of the Fed suggest that other means are more appropriate for the announcement of policy changes.

Open-Market Operations. The Fed is engaged daily in **open-market operations** through the activities of the Federal Reserve Open Market Committee. Activities in the open market involve purchases and sales of government bonds, bills, and notes at the New York Fed. These actions affect the money supply as well as interest rates. To increase the money supply and economic activity (e.g., to combat recession), the Fed actively buys bonds (Treasury issues). Buying bonds takes them out of the hands of the banks and other depository institutions, and increases the money supply by exchanging the bonds for money (in the form of a check or cash from the Fed). If, on the other hand, the Fed wants to reduce the money stock, it will step up bond *sales* to commercial banks and other depository institutions, this time increasing the stock of bonds at banks and decreasing their stock of reserves.

As we will see in the box titled "Interest Rates, Bond Prices, and the Money Supply," the effect on interest rates of these bond sales and purchases is inversely related to the money supply. When bond sales reduce the money stock, interest rates must increase in order to attract businesses as well as households to purchase the bond offerings. Otherwise, investors would place their funds elsewhere. Bond sales, then, encourage interest rates upward as they compete with other assets for the public's cash balances. Once the sales have been made, the interest rate will also rise because of the shortage of money.

Open-market operations are the Fed's most important tool. They take place on a day-to-day basis, and the Fed's Open Market Committee meets regularly to decide how open-market operations should affect the money supply and interest rates.

14. How do bond purchases by the Fed affect interest rates in the economy? Why?

INTEREST RATES, BOND PRICES, AND THE MONEY SUPPLY

We can use an example to illustrate how the interest rate is related to the price of bonds and to the purchase of a bond by the Federal Reserve. First, assume you receive a $100 government bond for your birthday. In the fine print on this bond, the U.S. government promises to pay you $100 at the end of ten years. Obviously, the people who gave you the bond did not pay $100 for something that is worth $100 at the end of ten years; they paid less.

To find the price they paid, we can examine a present-value table such as Table 17.3. The *present value* of your $100 bond payable in ten years is the amount it is worth today; more generally, present value is what a dollar at the end of a specified future year is worth today. Examining the abbreviated present-value table in Table 17.3, we find that the present value depends on the interest rate. At an interest rate of 10 percent, the present value is $38.50; if the interest rate were 15 percent, the price of the bond would be $24.70. As the interest rate rises (from 10 to 15 percent), the price of

TABLE 17.3 Present Value of $100.00

	Interest Rate		
Year	7%	10%	15%
1	93.50	90.90	87.00
2	87.30	82.60	75.60
3	81.60	75.10	65.80
4	76.30	68.30	57.20
5	71.30	62.00	49.70
6	66.66	56.40	43.20
7	62.30	51.30	37.60
8	58.20	46.60	32.60
9	54.40	42.40	28.40
10	50.80	38.50	24.70

*The formulate for finding the present value entries in the table is $P = R/(1 + r)^t$. The present value, P, equals the future return, R (in this case, $100), divided by $(1 + \text{rate of interest})^t$, where t is the number of years to maturity. (In our example, $t = 10$ years.)

the $100 bond falls (from $38.50 to $24.70). There is an inverse relation between the rate of return (interest rate) and the price of the bond. In essence, the bondholder earns interest on the bond every year it is held.

When the Federal Reserve purchases bonds (not $100 savings bonds, but $100,000 and larger denominations of U.S. Treasury bonds, notes, and bills) in the open market in order to increase the money supply, the demand for bonds increases, so the price of bonds rises (see Figure 17.14). The interest rate is inversely related to price, so the interest rate falls. Thus, as the Fed buys bonds, increasing the money supply, interest rates fall.

FIGURE 17.14 Increased Demand for Bonds

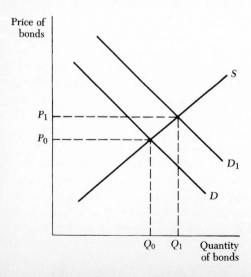

The Discount Rate. The Federal Reserve also establishes the **discount rate**—the rate at which a bank or depository institution can borrow from the Fed. Often, institutions borrow from the Fed to protect their reserve position. They typically present collateral consisting of bonds, which the Fed discounts for short-term borrowing purposes. To increase the money supply (and economic activity), the Fed would lower the discount rate, making borrowing more attractive for the banks and other depository institutions. They can then pass the funds along to households and businesses by increasing the availability of loans. When the Fed desires tight money, it can increase the discount rate, making borrowing from the discount window available only when absolutely essential. The Fed lowered the discount rate several times between 1980 and 1992, both to increase the money supply and to signal concern about economic activity.

In "emergency" situations, the Fed may serve as "the lender of last resort." The Fed stood ready in this capacity immediately after the stock market crash of October 1987. Alan Greenspan, then chairman of the Fed's Board of Governors, issued the following statement on the day following the crash: "The Federal Reserve, consistent with its responsibilities as the nation's central bank, affirmed today its readiness to serve as a source of liquidity to support the economic and financial system." This brief statement seemed to reassure financial markets, particularly as the Fed took necessary actions to ensure adequate liquidity to the financial system.

Lags in Monetary Policy

As is true with fiscal policy, lags or delays are inherent in monetary actions. Economists have classified these lags into two major types, the *inside lag* and the *outside lag*. The inside lag comprises a *recognition lag* (the time it takes for the Federal Reserve authorities to recognize there is a problem in the economy) and an *action lag* (the time of recognition until the time some policy is implemented). These lags are usually a function of measurement and forecasting. After the action takes place, there is an outside lag before the impact of the policy (either partial or total) is felt in the economy. The length of impact lags is a subject of dispute among economists and economic models. Monetarists—economists who favor monetary policies over fiscal policies—argue that the impact lag with monetary actions is much shorter than the one estimated by their Keynesian counterparts.

Monetary Policy in an Open Economy

Monetary policy has two types of effects on international markets in an open economy. One is an interest effect, similar but not the same as that experienced in fiscal policy in an international environment. The second is an effect on prices due to monetary changes.

If the Fed takes some policy action to increase the money supply (to expand the economy), interest rates will fall. In international financial markets, demand for U.S. assets, which yield a return attached to this lower

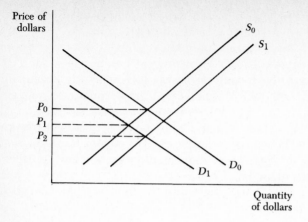

■ FIGURE 17.15 Demand and Supply of Dollars in the International Market

interest rate, will decline. This will decrease the demand for dollars, shifting the dollar demand curve to the left, as in Figure 17.15. At the same time, because of the lower interest rates, U.S. investors will seek higher-yielding securities in the international arena. As U.S. citizens trade their dollars or dollar-denominated securities for higher-yielding foreign securities, the supply of dollars in the international market will increase, shifting the dollar supply curve to the right (also shown in Figure 17.15). These changes in the demand for and supply of dollars in the international financial markets will depreciate the value of the dollar (bid the value of the dollar down with respect to other currencies currently in demand).

This lower-valued dollar will create a demand for U.S. exports, since they are now cheaper to foreign citizens. At the same time, imports into the United States will decline, since imports now cost more of the lower-valued dollar. Net exports $(X - M)$ will rise. This increases aggregate expenditures and income, thus reinforcing the monetary expansion also designed to increase aggregate expenditures.

Monetary policy will also produce a long-run price effect in the international financial markets. To the extent to which increases in the money supply lead to increases in domestic prices, foreign exchange markets of U.S. trading partners will be affected. If the increase in the money supply brings about a 5 percent increase in prices of domestic products, this price increase will be felt in both domestic and international markets.

Let's look at the effect of this on trade between the United States and Japan. A 5 percent increase in the price of U.S. products will decrease the demand for or purchase of U.S. products by the Japanese (assuming an elastic demand for U.S. exports). This will cause a decrease in the demand for dollars, since the Japanese are purchasing fewer U.S. goods. This decrease causes the demand curve for dollars to shift to the left (from D_0 to D_1 in Figure 17.15). At the same time, a 5 percent increase in domestic prices makes Japanese products relatively less expensive in the United States. As U.S. consumers increase their demand for Japanese products, they supply more dollars to the international market, thus shifting the supply curve for dollars to the right, as in Figure 17.15.

Both of these actions serve to lower the value of the dollar and appreciate the value of the yen. From here on out, consumer reactions are reversed. The Japanese will resume purchasing U.S. products. Although prices did increase, the yen appreciation offsets this price increase. Likewise, demand for Japanese products will fall back to previous levels. Despite the price effects produced by monetary policy, after currency adjustments, the level of exports and imports should remain about the same.

In Chapter 21, we will see another example: interest rate increases initiated by monetary restriction can instantly increase the interest payments a Third World country must pay to international creditors. For nations struggling with insurmountable debt, a small increase can easily create an ever larger crisis.

||| 15. After income has increased due to the monetary expansion, what will be the reaction in international markets?

U.S. monetary policy does not operate on a one-way street with respect to the world economy. Actions of other industrial countries might hinder the functioning of U.S. economic policy as well. The Fed usually succeeds in its bid to reduce short-term interest rates, but the international community may make its task a bit more difficult. In late 1989, for example, the Fed attempted to decrease interest rates but failed. While the Fed was actively working to lower rates, buyers of bonds in the international community were actively purchasing U.S. bonds, believing that U.S. financial markets were preferable to a German market facing reunification.

||| 16. Can you think of ways the Fed might regain control of interest rates?

MONETARISM

The role and behavior of money on economic activity is the focus of *monetarism*. Monetarism is a way to analyze macroeconomics using the equation of exchange from the quantity theory of money. This relationship, which we discussed in Chapter 15, is the identity $MV = PQ$, where M is the quantity of money, V is the velocity, P is the price level, and Q is the volume of physical output. In the equation of exchange, the relationship between M and P was of primary concern.

Unlike the Keynesians, the monetarists see the money stock as the major stimulus for economic activity. Although their model is more sophisticated than the one used by the classical economists, today's monetarists still use the velocity of money as the major link between money and the GDP (or output). Monetarists argue that short-run economic growth (or decline) can be gained by altering the money supply. Monetarists believe that the transmission mechanism through which monetary policy works is velocity, not the rate of interest as in the Keynesian system. Velocity had a predictable growth rate through the 1960s and 1970s. In the 1980s, however, velocity of M_1 fell and has behaved erratically since.

According to the monetarists, money is the most important stimulus to economic activity, but it is often misused by the Federal Reserve. Monetarists essentially believe that inflation as well as recession can be and must be controlled through monetary policy. Monetarists argue that the only fiscal actions that have any impact at all on the economy are those financed by new money or by Treasury borrowing from the Federal Reserve. These actions will increase income and output in the short run. In the long run monetarists see only price effects from increases or decreases in the money supply. Any other means of financing fiscal expenditures, such as borrowing from the public through deficit financing, merely takes money from one sector and gives it to another. By borrowing from the private sector, the government crowds out expenditures. Monetarists such as Milton Friedman, who have studied the historical trends of the U.S. economy, believe that fiscal policy per se can shape the trends and paths of the economy, but that it has no predictable effect on inflation or unemployment. For example, monetarists argue that the fiscal policy of the 1964 tax cut was effective not because of the tax cut itself but because of the expansion in the money supply that accompanied the tax cut.

Friedman, the leading monetarist, has severely criticized the Fed's "erratic" policy toward money creation. Friedman argues that more problems have been created by the discretionary actions of the monetary authorities—pumping money into and pulling money out of the economy—than a monetary rule would have created. Friedman's *monetary rule* would allow the money supply to grow at a constant annual rate to facilitate investment and real economic growth. It would also eliminate the need for the Federal Reserve. According to Friedman, periods of inflation would be eliminated since the money supply would not be permitted to grow at a rate that would fuel inflation. Recession would be averted because a guaranteed supply of money would be available for investment purposes at all times, and businesses could be confident that the economy would not be tightened intentionally.

The Monetarist Experiment

The Fed has powerful tools, and its independence gives it the authority to carry out the monetary policy it views as best. During the 1950s and 1960s, the Fed followed its collective instinct in managing money matters. After economists severely criticized this policy in the mid-1960s, the Fed began to target interest rate levels in adjusting the nation's money supply. This type of policy, despite outcries from monetarists, continued until the fall of 1979. Monetarists believe that control of the nation's money supply is far more

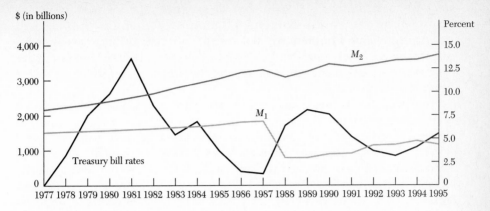

■ FIGURE 17.16 The Money Supply and Treasury Bill Interest Rate

important than control of interest rates. In contrast, the Keynesians rely heavily on interest rates to transmit the effects of monetary policy to the economy.

Monetarists had argued since the 1950s that the Federal Reserve should stabilize the growth rate of the money stock to ensure economic growth without inflation. The lesson fell on deaf ears until the fall of 1979, when Paul Volcker, newly appointed chairman of the Federal Reserve, called on the Fed to institute an essentially monetarist policy to bring down the 12-plus percent inflation that prevailed at the time. The Fed slashed monetary growth rates from 8 percent in 1979 to 5 percent by 1981. The results were spectacular. Inflation dropped to 6.2 percent, and the unemployment rate rose to 9.7 percent. The Fed and monetarists had predicted a decline in the interest rate, but rates remained high throughout the recession, as financial markets demanded high interest rates to hedge their bet that inflation would not fall despite monetarist policies of decreased growth in the money supply (see Figure 17.16). In fact, real interest rates (the nominal rate minus inflation) increased dramatically. Inflation fell much faster than interest rates until 1984. The Fed began increasing the growth rate of the money supply in June 1981, but again, monetarist and Fed predictions failed as the nation lingered in deep economic recession. After two years of higher monetary growth rates, of up to 13 percent, the economy began to recover. Efforts to sharply reduce interest rates were thwarted by increasingly large federal deficits.

After the short period of monetarist experimentation, few retained confidence in the monetarists' predictions of the forecasted results. Democrats and Republicans alike began calling for continued monetary growth to sustain current levels of economic growth. The monetarist experiment of the early 1980s was not a pleasant one. Admittedly, inflation slowed, but the policy took a heavy toll. At a call by monetarists to continue strict monetary growth, chairman of the House Banking Committee Fernand J. St. Germain responded, "This Congress will not tolerate a return to flinty-eyed monetarism, high interest rates, and recession. Our citizens have suffered under three years of miscreant monetarism, and the time to stay with the recovery is upon us."

In 1982, amidst low inflation and economic recession, the Volcker-led Fed began increasing the monetary growth rate and paid more attention to interest rate targets. Low inflation continued and, coupled with economic growth, left the recession of the early 1980s behind. By 1987, when Alan Greenspan assumed the chairmanship of the Fed's Board of Governors, the economic recovery was into its fifth year. Greenspan, however, was forced to reassure financial markets when the stock market crash in October shook the confidence of investors and governments throughout the world. Greenspan has played a more activist role in fine-tuning the economy, carefully watching leading indicators that might suggest greater levels of inflation. Indeed, the Bush administration was quick to criticize his tolerance of higher interest rates at the expense of slower economic growth and continued to argue that the Fed had not worked to lower interest rates enough to ward off the recession of the early 1990s. Still watchful of inflationary pressures that might threaten the economy, Greenspan's Fed did see both short- and long-term interest levels at their lowest level in two decades by 1993. As the economy recovered into 1994, the Fed increased the discount rate, tightening the money supply to avert possible inflationary activity. The Fed has continued to monitor any potential for inflationary activity through 1997.

17. Why can't the Fed target both the money supply and interest rates?
18. Plot what has happened to the general level of interest rates and to M_1 and M_2 since this book has been published. (This information is published monthly in the *Federal Reserve Bulletin*.) What does the Fed appear to have been targeting?
19. Are you convinced that there is a relationship between the money supply and prices? Why or why not?
20. Have inflation rates increased in recent years? What is the inflation rate?

THE FUTURE OF MONETARY POLICY

Recent changes in both supply and demand factors for money, caused by financial deregulation and innovation, and increased international interdependence have caused concern about the effectiveness of monetary policy. Macroeconomists have debated the effects of these changes on monetary policy. Not only is the institutional framework that facilitates financial transactions changing rapidly, but money itself has been changing with the advent of money market accounts and the rapid movement into cyberspace transactions. These financial innovations might bring about changes in the responsiveness of expenditures to variations in interest rates and/or the amount of money demanded at various levels of income. John Weinninger, an economist at the Federal Reserve Bank of New York, stated the problem clearly: "If relationships between key variables are changing then it simply is not practical for policy to focus in some mechanical way on any single variable, whether it be M_1, GDP, interest rates, or even reserves themselves."

During the past few years, the Fed has been unable to target effectively, with M_1 exceeding the targets on many occasions. More recently, M_2 has proved an unreliable target, causing Alan Greenspan to begin searching for a new target in mid-1990. If the predictability and stability of these known relationships continue to deteriorate because of these changes and innovations in the financial sector, monetary policy cannot be as reliable or as predictable as it has been in the past. This will impose additional problems on policy makers as problems of recession and inflation arise.

The effectiveness of monetary policy was questioned during the recession of the early 1990s as well. Economic turnaround was not forthcoming despite lower interest rates in the late 1980s and early 1990, in part because of a credit slowdown or "credit crunch." While the Fed made more money available, financial intermediaries did not lend large sums to businesses and consumers—thus thwarting any chance at economic growth. Borrowers and lenders both apparently shared in responsibility for the credit crunch. Several hypotheses put forward to explain this lack of lending included fallout from the deregulation of the 1980s, hangovers from debt that financed the 1980s, an overinvestment in real estate, and the thrift crisis. Whatever the cause, credit flows slowed. In 1993 low interest rates sent funds into the stock market in search of higher returns.

Furthermore, the role of depository institutions in the economy seems to have shrunk, thus potentially weakening the Federal Reserve's policies. In the third of a series of articles titled "The End of Banking as We Know It," *Wall Street Journal* writer Kenneth H. Bacon focuses on banks' declining role in the economy. Some call for regulation of all financial intermediaries; others call for deregulation of the depository institutions so that they might more effectively compete with brokerage firms, insurance companies, and mutual funds.

BANKS' DECLINING ROLE IN ECONOMY WORRIES FED, MAY HURT FIRMS

Kenneth H. Bacon

The Federal Reserve, which began curing the banking industry's immediate ills two years ago with low interest rates, now is worrying about the patient's long-term health.

In the past 20 years, commercial banks' share of U.S. financial assets has declined to 24.5% from nearly 40%. "The banking industry is becoming irrelevant economically, and it's almost irrelevant politically," says William Isaac, a former chairman of the

Federal Deposit Insurance Corp. who now heads Secura Group, a Washington consulting firm.

Fed Chairman Alan Greenspan is sounding alarms as bank's best customers are being stolen away by less-regulated brokerage firms, mutual funds, finance companies and industrial giants such as General Electric Co. "Public policy should be concerned with the decline in the importance of banking," he has said recently. "The issues are too important for the future growth of our economy and the welfare of our citizens."

Analysts in government and out worry that the bank's slide could:

- Weaken the Fed's ability to influence the economy through monetary policy.
- Increase the size and complexity of risks the Fed must get under control in a stock-market crash or similar crisis.
- Hurt small and medium-sized businesses that depend primarily on banks for loans and financial advice.
- Reduce access to traditional banking offices by spurring consolidation among the nation's 11,300 commercial banks.

A Shift in the Risk

With interest rates at the lowest levels in decades, banks' profits are soaring because their cost of funds has declined far more than their returns on loans and investments and because the low rates have bailed out some troubled borrowers. But those rates are also aggravating a long-term problem: Investors are seeking higher yields by moving money out of federally insured deposits at banks and thrifts and into uninsured mutual funds. Some experts worry that this trade of security for higher yields could expose depositors to potentially severe losses.

"I think that banks play a fundamentally important role in society that is less well filled by others," says Comptroller of the Currency Eugene Ludwig. "I see a decline in the banking system as shifting of risk—rather than an elimination of risk—to the public from the government."

At current trends, total investments in mutual funds soon will eclipse the $2 trillion in savings and time deposits at banks and thrift institutions.

Andrew Hove, the FDIC's acting chairman, says this shift of funds raises a crucial question for Washington policy makers and credit-seeking entrepreneurs: "Will banks be able to attract the money back as loan demand increases? I think they will, but you wonder." Ironically, he adds, the government is spending $200 billion to insure deposits in failed S&Ls just when "the importance of insured deposits isn't as great as it was" to savers.

The Clinton administration has begun an ambitious review of the nation's financial system. Doing preliminary work are Mr. Ludwig, Treasury Under Secretary Frank Newman and Ellen Seidman, a staffer on President Clinton's National Economic Council. The starting point is Mr. Clinton's belief that banks and other financial companies can do more to meet the credit needs of small firms and capital-starved rural and inner-city areas.

So, the review, officials say, will look beyond such traditional "bank reform" issues as: How much regulation is needed to keep banks safe and sound? Should banks be allowed to diversify their risks by, as many have long desired, branching nationwide or offering a broader range of insurance and securities?

Mr. Newman has said the administration may ask whether mutual funds and other financial companies should be required to meet community-investment standards like those imposed on banks. Ms. Seidman has begun discussing ways to encourage pension funds and insurance companies to invest in long-term urban-renewal and community-development programs. Another issue is whether to seek federal regulation of insurance, which is currently supervised at the state level.

White House officials have read a tightly reasoned but controversial study from the Economic Policy Institute, a liberal think tank. The paper by Jane D'Arista and Tom Schlesinger contends that all financial institutions should operate under the same regulations, including capital and reserve requirements and fair-lending standards. At a time when banks say regulation should be relaxed so they can operate more like securities firms, the paper seeks the opposite: the imposition of bank-type regulation over the "parallel" financial system of mutual funds, investment banks and insurers that are performing banking functions.

The administration isn't expected to go nearly so far, and, at any rate, no decisions are likely until next spring at the earliest. If Mr. Clinton does seek basic regulatory changes, the administration and Congress will get embroiled in "the mother of all turf wars" as financial companies and their regulators fight for advantage, says Bert Ely, a bank consultant.

Two forces—innovation and regulation—explain banking's decline. Many of the innovations started in the late 1970s, when an inflation-driven surge in interest rates and federal limits on rates banks could pay on deposits drove borrowers and depositors alike away from banks. Money-market mutual funds, banks' sales of home mortgages to the secondary market to collateralize securities and blue-chip corporations' tendency to meet short-term cash needs by selling commercial paper rather than bank loans all took off.

As banks lost their most credit-worthy customers, they began to chase higher returns by lending to riskier borrowers—real-estate developers, Third World nations and corporations scrambling to finance multibillion-dollar buyouts. Charge-offs of bad loans rose steadily throughout the 1980s, and so did bank failures. Meanwhile, mismanaged deregulation nearly destroyed the S&L industry.

The Restrictive 1991 Law

After a decade of deregulation, Congress began to impose new safety rules on depository institutions. Fearing that skyrocketing bank failures were about to drain the Bank Insurance Fund. Congress passed in 1991 a law sharply increasing the scope—and cost—of bank regulation.

When making loans, bankers face capital, documentation and collateralization rules that don't apply to nonbank lenders. In addition, the Fed requires banks to hold noninterest-earning reserves of 10% against checking accounts and other transaction balances. The FDIC imposes at a deposit-insurance premium averaging 24.8 cents (up threefold over four years) on each $100 of domestic deposits. One reason money-market mutual funds can pay depositors higher returns than banks can is that they don't face such expenses.

The diversion of money from banks to mutual funds is complicating monetary policy. "The relationship between money and the economy may be undergoing a significant transformation," Mr. Greenspan says. "If this is true, the liabilities of depository institutions will not be as good a gauge of financial conditions as they once were." So, the Fed is trying to devise new, more-useful money-supply gauges.

A broader problem is that "there are so many ways to create credit outside of the banking system that monetary policy is of declining relevance," Mr. Ely says. When the Fed launched its war against inflation by sharply slowing growth of the money supply 14 years ago, it found it couldn't choke off credit to willing borrowers; it could only force them to pay more. The Economic Policy Institute paper also contends that the surge of financial assets outside of the banking system "affects the primary role of banks in transmitting monetary policy and deploying central-bank liquidity to smooth volatility, prevent disruptions and manage crises."

Lender of Last Resort

Fed officials deny that the central bank is losing its leverage over the economy. As long as the Fed retains unfettered power to act as lender of last resort, it can provide the liquidity necessary to quell a financial crisis, just as it responded to the 1987 stock-market crash. In 1991, Wall Street firms fought for and won legislation strengthening the Fed's ability to lend directly to troubled brokerage firms.

But officials agree that the flow of assets and deposits from the banking system poses a wider range of risks. The Federal Reserve Board is devoting more energy to policing the $7 trillion market in derivatives—the new financial products that link banks, investment firms and corporations in efforts to hedge against changes in interest rates, stock prices, commodity prices and currencies.

One of the fundamental changes that increased saving and investment outside of insured deposits has wrought is the spreading of risk. "Millions of people have branched out from passively holding deposits in banks and thrifts and indirectly owning securities through such intermediaries as private and public pension funds to becoming direct participants, primarily through mutual funds." says Henry Kaufman, a Wall Street economist known for gloomy predictions. He warns that "the household sector may not appreciate all the risks it's taking on, with the result that it may act quite unpredictably if there is a sudden upheaval in the financial markets" that threatens to inflict huge losses in its savings. If this were to happen, he adds, politicians might face pressure to force the Fed to support stock and bond prices.

In fact, however, huge amounts of money didn't flee mutual funds for bank deposits after the Dow Jones Industrial Average plunged 500 points in October 1987. Fidelity Investments and other fund groups found that customers moved money from stock funds to money-market funds within the same family. But it's worth noting that in 1987, mutual-fund holdings totaled just $752 billion, compared with $1.8 trillion today.

A Basic Fed Goal

The Fed's goal is to manage and limit risk, not to eliminate it. Mr. Greenspan believes that Congress went too far with its 1991 law tightening regulation. "If minimizing risks to taxpayers is interpreted as minimizing bank failures, then we are very likely to deter banks to an excessive degree from accepting the kinds of risk that create the value of their franchises," he says. "The optimal degree of bank failure is not zero, and, in all likelihood, not even close to zero."

The banking industry is pushing regulatory-relief bills in Congress, arguing that lower costs enable them to make more loans. However, the chairmen of both the House and Senate banking committees oppose weakening the safety and soundness measures that they helped craft in 1991. In addition, the Clinton administration isn't ready to support broad banking legislation this year.

Instead, Mr. Ludwig has launched an effort to weed out unnecessary regulations. "Government has layered on banking a mountain of regulations that are often duplicative, superfluous or otherwise wasteful," he says. He notes, for example, that the Office of the Comptroller of the Currency uses seven different definitions of bank capital. "We can maintain safety and soundness while lowering regulatory cost," he says.

Basically, he is studying ways to move away from one-size-fits-all regulation. Strongly capitalized banks and small banks—those that pose the least risk to the financial system—would get more freedom to make loans with reduced paperwork and administrative costs and to offer insurance and other new products. Some of the changes would require legislation.

Besides less regulation, banks want to be unshackled from rules that prevent them from expanding their activities as investment bankers, insurance agents, stockbrokers and mutual-fund salesmen. Expansion into these businesses would enable them to earn more income from commissions and fees, reduce their reliance on volatile interest-rate spreads and help diversify their risks.

But two powerful House Democrats—Banking Committee Chairman Henry Gonzalez of Texas and Energy and Commerce Chairman John Dingell of Michigan—stand in the way. They worry that the heavy movement of banks into mutual-fund sales may be confusing consumers about which bank products are insured and which aren't. And nationwide branch banking has been a nonstarter for years.

Bankers are frustrated by their lack of success in winning relief from Congress. The nation "has got a vested interest in keeping the banking industry alive and competitive," says Robert Gillespie, the chairman of Society Corp., a Cleveland bank holding company. "It really isn't in anybody's interest to kill the goose that used to lay the golden egg."

Source: Kenneth H. Bacon, "Losing Ground: Bank's Declining Role in Economy Worries Fed, May Hurt Firms," *The Wall Street Journal*, July 9, 1993. Reprinted by permission of the Wall Street Journal, © 1993 Dow Jones & Company, Inc. All Rights Reserved Worldwide.

21. List three reasons why economists are concerned that monetary policy is becoming less effective due to the declining importance of banks and other depository institutions directly affected by Federal Reserve actions.

22. Should the public be concerned with the declining importance of banks? Why or why not?

23. After reading the arguments, do you tend to agree with the economists at the Economic Policy Institute that all intermediaries need to operate under the same type of regulation, or with those who argue that fewer restraints should be placed on banks, freeing them to compete with other financial intermediaries? Explain. What are the opportunity costs of each proposal?

Still another concern has been the growth of foreign banks in the United States. In 1991 the Foreign Bank Supervision Enhancement Act (FBSEA) strengthened the Fed's control over foreign banks and their branches operating in the United States. The Bank of Credit and Commerce International (BCCI) scandal in 1991 illustrated how foreign-owned banks and their branches could underwrite illegal activities here and abroad.

MONETARY AND FISCAL POLICY

Models constructed to measure the effectiveness of monetary and fiscal policy yield different results if underlying assumptions used in the models differ. Monetarists emphasize velocity as the mode of transmission, and the Keynesians stress the rate of interest.

Monetarists assume that there can be no effective expansion of fiscal policy unless it is accompanied by an increase in the money supply. Why? The government *must* finance its expenditures with increases in taxes or by debt issue. In either case, money is being transferred from one sector of the economy to another. As government spending proceeds and GDP increases, if the money supply has not grown, consumers and investors will find themselves short of cash and will begin to try to increase their liquidity by selling their financial holdings. This will increase bond sales even further, driving the price of bonds down and the interest rate up. As the interest rate rises, business investors are crowded out of financial markets by the government so that GDP doesn't change. Spending is just transferred from one sector to another.

For Keynesians, however, the reason for government spending is to stimulate an economy in which neither business *nor* households are spending, so that the government would at least get the process started. Expansionary fiscal policy increases economic activity. This would encourage spending by consumers and businesses in the future.

In practice, monetary policy is very effective at slowing the economy, but not very effective when used to stimulate economic activity. The presence of an international sector tends to reinforce the income and output effects of monetary policy.

Shortcomings of Monetary Policy

Several factors can prevent monetary policy from being totally successful in its efforts to regulate and stimulate the economy. The following list reviews five of these factors and the ways in which each has thwarted monetary policy at one time or another:

1. *Institutional offsets*—Banks, specialized financial institutions, and private corporations can outwit Fed policy by developing new monetary instruments or new institutional relations or by moving their operations off-

shore. Creating and then borrowing from the Eurodollar market (dollar deposits in non-U.S. bank accounts) allowed banks to successfully avoid Regulation Q in the 1970s. U.S. depository institutions chartered in other countries and operating under perhaps more liberal restrictions continue these time-honored offsets.

2. *Cyclical asymmetry*—Policy can be victimized by changing economic conditions. This is a problem of timing. A policy designed to treat a particular set of circumstances may be implemented after conditions have changed; when the policy does take effect, the problem may be totally different. This is a problem of lags and policy backfiring.

3. *Velocity*—Monetary policy is often frustrated by the tendency of changes in velocity to jeopardize targeted goals of the money supply, as we have seen in the past few years.

4. *Cost-push inflation*—Monetary policy does not effectively attack the causes of inflation that lie on the cost or supply side of the market.

5. *Investment impact*—Some argue that the Fed's policies have a marginal impact upon consumer spending. Others argue that the impact of the Fed policy on the investment process is overstated, since many corporations finance their investments internally.

Coordination of Monetary and Fiscal Policy

Monetary and fiscal policy may provide a rather powerful punch when used together to fight inflation or stimulate economic recovery. However, coordinating the two policies may be problematic. Since the Fed determines monetary policy, and fiscal expenditures are in the hands of Congress and the president, policy decisions sometimes offset one another or are not complementary. For example, the Fed reacted to the high inflation rates of 1980 by attempting to reduce the money supply in order to decrease aggregate expenditures. On the other hand, Congress decreased taxes, which increased aggregate expenditures. High interest rates created by the tight money supply tended to counteract the desired investment effects from lower tax rates.

The chairman of the Federal Reserve Board now regularly informs Congress of impending Fed action so that there are no surprises, but policies may still offset one another. Currently, high budget deficits caused by an expansionary fiscal policy tend to raise interest rates in the economy. This could prove problematic to a Fed interested in achieving greater price stability without plunging the economy into recession.

Some people have called for a reduction in the Fed's independence in order to achieve greater coordination of monetary and fiscal policies. Critics of this suggestion argue that to have either the legislative or the executive branch of the government control the Fed would make the money supply a political tool—as surely as many fiscal expenditures and taxing decisions already are. They argue that we could expect regular increases in the money supply in election years and decreases after elections. Whatever the solution, it is clear that monetary and fiscal policy must at least be aimed in the same direction in order to have effective economic policy.

24. What is the Fed doing today to defeat the forces of inflation? Is policy being coordinated with the executive branch?
25. What kinds of "political mischief" might occur if the monetary authority were controlled by the executive branch?

CONCLUSION

By examining the institution of money and the institutions that extend and regulate monetary instruments in the economy, we have discovered rather powerful tools by which the economy has been regulated over the past several decades. This regulation has focused on monetary ease during economic downturns and monetary restraint during periods of inflation. In the following chapter, we will see how changes in the money supply and demand coupled with fiscal changes affect aggregate expenditures in the economy and the importance of aggregate supply.

Review Questions

1. Explain the differences among the transactions, precautionary, and speculative demands for money. List five factors that influence your demands for money.
2. Why is a barter economy unsuitable for today's world?
3. What is the difference between M_1 and M_2? Is it important to distinguish between them? Does it really matter what the money supply is? Discuss.
4. Suppose you discovered $50,000 of old dollars stuffed in a mattress in your dorm.
   a. What would be the effect of the $50,000 of "new money" on the banking system? Explain.
   b. What would be the effect if you spent the money on a new BMW?
   c. What if you stuffed the money back into the mattress?
5. How do the demands for money relate to Keynesian income and employment theory?
6. Which of the monetary policy tools is used most actively by the Fed? Under what situations would the Fed use its other tools?
7. What are the basic differences between a monetarist and a Keynesian?
8. Why do monetarists argue that fiscal policy is ineffective in adjusting the economy?
9. Of the basic monetary policy tools the Federal Reserve can use, which do you think is the most effective? Why?
10. What are some of the factors that inhibit the successful implementation of monetary policy?

11. In what kinds of situations is fiscal policy more effective than monetary policy? In what kinds of situations is monetary policy more effective than fiscal policy?
12. What would be some of the complications of finding the proper mix of monetary and fiscal policy?
13. If the economy were experiencing high unemployment and moderate inflation, what would be the appropriate monetary policy? Why?
14. Some economists argue that eliminating the federal budget deficit would allow for an easier monetary policy.
    a. What would be the macroeconomic effects of balancing the budget?
    b. What would be the macroeconomic effects of an easier monetary policy?

18

Aggregate Demand and Aggregate Supply

INTRODUCTION

Although Keynes himself pointed out limitations to his theory of aggregate expenditures, the shortcoming of the Keynesian analysis that has most bothered modern economists is the lack of an analysis of prices. In the "real world" economy, since the 1960s, we have experienced regular price changes, not just on certain goods and services, but across the whole economy. In this chapter, we will develop an analysis of aggregate demand and aggregate supply that allows us to illustrate how changes in economic policy or changes in other economic variables affect aggregate prices and output. From this analysis, we will be better able to examine the potential stabilizing effects of price changes, an issue central to the ongoing debate over stabilization policy.

Aggregate demand is the total quantity of goods and services demanded by households, businesses, government, and the international sector at various prices. The aggregate demand curve illustrates aggregate demand, showing the negative relationship between aggregate output of goods and services, or real GDP demanded, and the overall price level. **Aggregate supply** is the total quantity of goods and services firms are willing to supply at varying price levels. The aggregate supply curve illustrates the relationship between the aggregate output supplied by all firms and the overall price level. The aggregate demand curve for the economy is downward sloping, while the aggregate supply curve generally illustrates a positive relationship between the price level and GDP, depending mostly on the time frame we choose to examine. Figure 18.1 shows the relationship between aggregate demand and aggregate supply. Equilibrium is the point where aggregate demand equals aggregate supply.

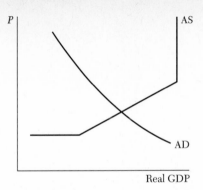

FIGURE 18.1 Aggregate Demand and Aggregate Supply

We will save derivation of the aggregate demand curve for a more advanced course in macroeconomic theory, but we will show logically why the curve is downward sloping and examine factors that induce shifts in it. Recognizing that in macroeconomic theory, an analysis of supply has historically accompanied one of demand, we will then turn our attention to factors important to aggregate supply. We will also attempt to understand why supply policies are often precarious in their outcome. We will discuss how supply-side economists of the 1980s viewed the economic situation and the results of supply-side policies during the Reagan administration.

Aggregate demand has served as the center of economic theory and policy for the past four decades, and Keynesian solutions have remained at the helm of economic thought and have often been preferred by policy makers. Our analysis of aggregate demand and aggregate supply will allow us to understand the role of economic policy variables as well as of supply shocks and productivity changes on real income and prices.

AGGREGATE DEMAND

The aggregate demand curve relates the price level to real output (or real GDP) in the overall economy. It shows how the demand for goods and services varies with the price level. This is possible since all points on the aggregate demand curve are equilibrium points in both the money (financial) and goods (and services) markets. Exogenous changes in both the money and goods markets affect the aggregate demand curve and thus prices and real GDP.

Although this particular aggregate demand curve looks like demand curves we saw in Part 3 on microeconomics, it is very different. A price rise is not analogous to a jump in the price of butter that prompts us to switch to margarine or some other substitute. All domestic prices are rising, including the prices of domestically produced substitutes.

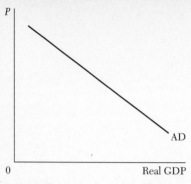

FIGURE 18.2 Aggregate Demand

Conditions for Goods and Money Market Equilibrium: A Review

Equilibrium positions in the goods market are found at every point on the aggregate demand curve. Recall from Chapter 14 that the components of the goods and services market are

$$C + I + G + (X - M) = \text{aggregate expenditures,}$$

where C is consumption expenditures, I is investment expenditures, G is government expenditures, and $X - M$ is net foreign expenditures (net exports). This market is at equilibrium when aggregate expenditures equal aggregate output of goods and services.

In the money market, equilibrium is achieved when money supply equals money demand. The aggregate demand curve is derived from equilibrium conditions in both markets. Therefore, at any point on the aggregate demand curve, aggregate expenditures are equal to aggregate output, and money supply equals money demand.

Prices are measured by some weighted price index such as the GDP deflator, and are represented by P on the vertical axis in Figure 18.2. Real income and output changes are represented by real GDP on the horizontal axis. We have assumed that the aggregate demand curve is downward sloping, showing an inverse relation between prices and real GDP. While we do not have all the tools necessary to derive this relationship here, we can intuitively show that this relationship is plausible by asking ourselves what happens to aggregate demand when there is a general rise in prices. If we aren't careful, however, we are likely to arrive at an answer that would yield a downward sloping aggregate demand curve, but for the wrong reasons. Since our experience has been more as consumers rather than as economists, we are likely to conclude that a general rise in prices will decrease the real income of consumers, thus reducing consumption expenditures. Aggregate expenditures for goods and services would decline, leading to a decrease in GDP. But price increases yield additional revenues for producers, which they may share with the household sector

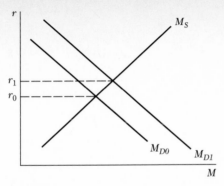

■ FIGURE 18.3 Money Demand with a Price Increase

through wage increases or higher dividends. If production is unchanged, then income would stay the same, so our assumption about the effect of an increase in the general price level on the goods market is a bit premature.

If, however, we look to the money or financial market, we will arrive at a better answer to our question about the slope of the aggregate demand curve. If there is a rise in prices, and if the Federal Reserve does not increase the money supply, the demand for money will increase, since consumers will need more money to keep their levels of consumption if velocity is constant. (With M constant and P rising, the demand for money increases.) As the demand for money rises, interest rates will rise. (Figure 18.3 shows that in response to an increase in the overall price level, money demand increases from M_{D0} to M_{D1}, and with M constant, interest rates rise from r_0 to r_1.) This means that less money is available at every interest rate for investment by the business sector (see Figure 18.4) and for expenditures by consumers. So, with everything else remaining the same, a rise in prices means that the same amount of (nominal) money balances must be used to purchase goods and services at higher prices. Interest rates will be bid up, demand for funds for investment and consumption purposes will fall, and thus aggregate expenditures will fall. This analysis logically gives us the downward-sloping aggregate

■ FIGURE 18.4 Demand for Investment Funds

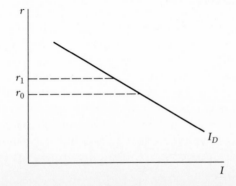

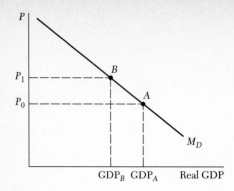

FIGURE 18.5 Movement along the Aggregate Demand Curve

demand curve and the inverse relation between prices and real GDP. On the graph in Figure 18.5, we can see that a price increase from P_0 to P_1 decreases real GDP from GDP_A to GDP_B, a movement from point A to point B on the aggregate demand curve.

Two other relationships explain the inverse relationship between prices and real GDP. As prices rise, the real wealth of people holding money balances declines. Those who are holding money balances cannot purchase the same quantity of goods and services as they did at lower prices, so the demand for goods and services falls, as does real GDP. Secondly, when prices increase in the United States, we can expect net exports $(X - M)$ to decline, since the prices of domestic goods have increased relative to foreign goods. U.S. exports are relatively more expensive, so the international market will demand fewer U.S. exports. Again, price increases will lower GDP; hence, the movement from point A to point B in Figure 18.5.

Conversely, a decrease in the price level will raise the aggregate quantity of goods and services demanded. Three reasons account for this: The real interest rate falls due to a greater availability of money balances, since the real money supply increases as prices fall. The real wealth of persons holding money balances increases when prices fall. Net exports increase as prices of domestic goods fall relative to prices of foreign goods.

Shifts in the Aggregate Demand Curve

The analysis of aggregate demand allows us to observe how exogenous changes affect aggregate demand and thus the overall price level *and* the level of real GDP. The aggregate demand curve describes the economy in equilibrium in both the goods (and services) market and the money market. Any exogenous or induced change that results in a shift in the aggregate expenditures curve or in the demand or supply curve of money will by definition cause a shift in the aggregate demand curve. As we saw in Chapters 14 and 15, with prices remaining constant, increases in government expenditures (G), investment expenditures (I), exogenous consumption expenditures (C),

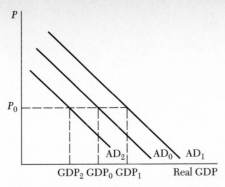

FIGURE 18.6 Shifts in the Aggregate Demand Curve

and net exports $(X - M)$ as well as tax cuts and an increase in the money supply will increase income in the goods market and will cause the aggregate demand curve to shift outward to the right. In Figure 18.6, the aggregate demand curve AD_0 shifts to the right to AD_1. At every price level, real GDP is higher on AD_1. Tax cuts or increases in G, C, I, net exports $(X - M)$, and the money supply cause the aggregate demand curve to shift to the right, away from the axis, as shown by AD_1 in Figure 18.6. With this shift, at every price level, GDP is higher.

We can now envision the effects of monetary policy and fiscal policy and changes in autonomous spending on price levels as well as on real income and output. Table 18.1 summarizes the effects of policy changes on aggregate demand.

1. In 1993 Congress passed and President Clinton signed a so-called "deficit reduction" budget. This budget called for income tax increases on the "more wealthy" and government spending cuts. Using the preceding aggregate demand curve analysis, illustrate and explain what these curves predict will happen to aggregate demand.

TABLE 18.1 Effects of Monetary and Fiscal Policy on Aggregate Demand Curve

Policy	Effect on Aggregate Demand (AD)
Monetary Policy	
Increase in money supply	AD curve shifts to the right.
Decrease in money supply	AD curve shifts to the left.
Fiscal Policy	
Increase in G	AD curve shifts to the right.
Decrease in Tx	AD curve shifts to the right.
Decrease in G	AD curve shifts to the left.
Increase in Tx	AD curve shifts to the left.

While we are primarily interested in policy changes that can shift the aggregate demand curve, several non-policy-related factors can cause a shift in the aggregate demand curve. An increase in real wealth will cause an outward shift. If stock market prices rise dramatically, holders of stock have increased their wealth and thus may increase their demand for goods and services. An increase in housing prices may produce the same result. The increased equity in the homes they own may cause homeowners to increase their borrowing and thus increase their demand for goods and services.

Expectations also influence shifts in the aggregate demand curve. If consumers and investors become increasingly optimistic about the economy, aggregate demand may shift to the right. An expectation that the inflation rate will rise will produce the same result, as consumers and investors purchase durable goods now while prices are lower than those they predict in the future. On the international front, if real income rises abroad so that foreign citizens have more to spend, we can expect an increased demand for domestic goods and services. Again, the aggregate demand curve will shift to the right. All of these shifts indicate that real GDP is higher at every level of prices, as shown in Figure 18.6.

> 2. List the conditions unrelated to economic policy that would cause the aggregate demand curve to shift to the left, indicating lower real GDP at all price levels.

SHORT-RUN AGGREGATE SUPPLY

The short-run aggregate supply shows the relationship between the output that is hypothetically supplied by the nation's producers of goods and services in response to changes in the price level. In the short run, producer responses will be restrained by the level of plant capacity available for producing additional output and by the speed at which the prices of inputs or factors of production respond to the increase in the overall price level. Many economists believe that there is a delay between a rise in the general price level and resulting increases in prices for raw materials and labor. We will assume that in the short run, input prices do not change. Our examination of long run aggregate supply will account for increases in resource prices in response to increases in overall prices.

Producers respond to increases in demand by increasing production, since increases in demand tend to bid prices up and, with factor costs stable, to increase producer profits. Thus, we must examine the level of plant capacity available in the economy to trace the level of real output (GDP) that can be supplied at various price levels, given increases in demand. Tracing these responses will give us a curve that represents short-run aggregate supply.

If the economy is in a severe recession or depression, plenty of plant capacity will be available for producing additional products. Excess labor and capital will be available for the production process, since by definition, high levels of unemployment and low levels of output mean that greater increases in output (GDP) can be made available without producers incur-

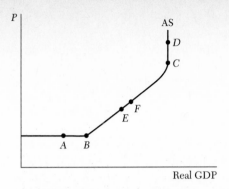

— FIGURE 18.7 Short-Run Aggregate Supply

ring large costs. Thus, if the economy were operating at a point such as point *A* in Figure 18.7, a small increase in demand—to point *B*—would increase real GDP without an overall price increase or with only a very small increase.

At the other extreme, if the economy is operating near or at full capacity, large quantities of output are already being produced. By definition, at full capacity, no new output can be produced. Producers are literally using every available machine, worker, and plant as much as is possible. At point *C* in Figure 18.7, an increase in demand—to point *D*—can only bid up the level of prices. Little or no additional output will be forthcoming.

Most often the economy is operating somewhere between these two extreme possibilities of short-run aggregate supply responses. More normally the economy might be at point *E*. At this point, if demand is increased—to point *F*—there will be increased GDP in the form of goods and services, and there will be a modest increase in the overall price level.

The upward slope of the aggregate supply curve is partly due to diminishing returns and partly due to resource and factor costs (particularly fixed wages) rising less rapidly than prices when demand for additional output increases. Moving along the aggregate supply curve illustrates the effect of increased aggregate demand at different levels of output and different price levels. Thus, the aggregate supply curve shows us the price level associated with each level of output, where firms will produce a profit-maximizing output at a fixed wage rate and a given level of productivity.

Causes of Shifts in the Short-Run Aggregate Supply Curve

The short-run aggregate supply curve may shift for many reasons, including changes in the labor market, supply shocks, and government policies that affect supply. Positive factors that cut costs, such as technological innovations, will cause the aggregate supply curve to shift to the right. Negative factors, such as rising costs, will cause a shift to the left. Let's examine some conditions that will cause such shifts.

Labor market forces have had and continue to have effects on the aggregate supply curve. Increases and decreases in the labor force are obvious causes of a shift. Over the past two decades, men and women have entered the labor force in record numbers. Increases in the labor supply will, of course, increase aggregate supply and shift the curve to the right. Any factor that makes people want to work less—such as attending school, avoiding higher taxes, or pursuing more leisure activities—will cause a shift to the left.

Expectations also cause the short-run aggregate supply curve to shift. If producers expect higher inflation in the future, they will adjust short-run production levels to reflect the expected price hikes. Expected crop failure or surplus will also be reflected in the short-run aggregate supply curve as drought or perhaps freezing weather affects the production level of various crops.

3. If most producers expected prices to rise in the near future, which way would the short-run aggregate supply curve shift? Why? Illustrate with an example.

Most of us are familiar with price changes for domestic and imported resources, another factor affecting the aggregate supply curve. The oil price increases of the 1970s created supply shocks throughout the world, causing a leftward shift in the short-run aggregate supply curve. **Supply shocks** are unexpected events that cause increases in prices. They occur when the cost of producing a wide variety of products increases dramatically, causing the aggregate supply curve to shift to the left and thus push prices upward. During the 1970s, the United States and the world economy experienced a variety of supply shocks, which sent prices soaring. The most noteworthy supply shock occurred in 1973 and 1974, when the then powerful OPEC nations placed an embargo (restriction on the import or export of a good) on oil exports. The reduced supply of oil products to many nations of the world severely curtailed production and increased prices, as shown by the shift from AS_0 to AS_1 in Figure 18.8. The price level on AS_1 is raised for each level of real output.

Other, less noteworthy supply shocks have affected the prices and output of many goods and services throughout the world. Price increases of raw materials and/or agricultural products have often been the cause of these shocks. The price increases may be caused by weather—from drought to floods—and by wars, both of which are beyond the control of policy makers. Large, rapid, and perhaps unexpected currency depreciations may also result in dramatic price increases or a supply shock for a nation heavily reliant on imported goods.

4. List other possible shocks to a nation's aggregate supply.
5. List some factors that would be the reverse of shocks and that would increase the nation's supply.

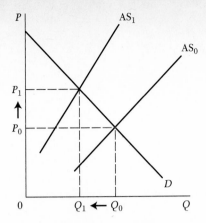

— FIGURE 18.8 A Supply Shock

6. List five ways that the government might increase production of the supply of goods and services to the public (i.e., shift the AS curve to the right).

LONG-RUN AGGREGATE SUPPLY

Many economists believe that in the long run, the aggregate supply is a vertical line at the full-employment level of output; as new resources and technologies develop, this vertical line shifts to the right. According to this view, in the long run, economic policy will have only price effects unless productivity or technology improves. Before we examine these factors that cause shifts in long-run aggregate supply, we will illustrate how equilibrium is reached using the short- and long-run aggregate supply curves with the aggregate demand curve.

ARRIVING AT EQUILIBRIUM

Now that we have introduced the concept of aggregate supply, let's see how changes in aggregate demand will lead first to equilibrium with short-run aggregate supply and then move to an equilibrium on a long-run aggregate supply curve. In our previous analysis in Chapter 14, we assumed that any increase in aggregate expenditures increased real output or real GDP but left prices unchanged. (In Figure 18.9 the entire multiplier effect is seen on the horizontal part of the short-run aggregate supply curve AS.) However, under normal economic conditions, the short-run aggregate supply curve slopes upward. As aggregate demand increases from AD_0 to AD_1, perhaps due to increased government expenditures or decreased taxes, the effect of the expenditure increase is shown as increased real income, GDP, or output; GDP rises from GDP_0 to GDP_1. On the short-run aggregate supply curve AS_1, real GDP increases (from GDP_0 to GDP_1) as do prices (from P_0 to P_1).

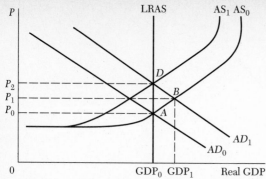

■ FIGURE 18.9 Equilibrium with Aggregate Demand and Long-Run and Short-Run Aggregate Supply

Equilibrium is found where $AS_0 = AD_1$ at point B. Equilibrium moves from point A to point B. As the economy reaches its capacity to produce additional goods and services, further increases in aggregate demand push up prices.

Is this a stable equilibrium? No. Firms may be happy with this adjustment, but workers will not be. Prices have increased from P_0 to P_1, so workers' real wages have fallen. Workers will not be satisfied with a reduction in their real wages and will insist on a nominal wage increase during the next round of wage negotiations. Since the short-run aggregate supply curve was derived within the context of a model that assumed nominal wages were set and unchanged, any increase in the nominal wage, which increases producers' cost of production, will cause the short-run aggregate supply curve to shift. Responding to the increase in nominal wages, the short-run aggregate supply curve shifts from AS_0 to AS_1 in Figure 18.9. Now we find our short-run equilibrium position at D, where GDP has fallen from GDP_1 to GDP_0 and P has increased from P_1 to P_2.

If there are no additional exogenous changes, there will be no more tendency for movement in the economy. We can see that the long-run aggregate supply curve (LRAS) is vertical at GDP_0. (If, as we will see later, technology improves in the long run, LRAS would shift to the right, and so would real GDP.)

We examine the short-run aggregate supply curve to see the effect immediately after some fiscal, monetary, or other stimulus to aggregate demand has been introduced, before the economy has time to adjust to these changes in the long run. Firms will adjust their production levels based on the changes in aggregate demand. They will try to increase output to meet the increased demand at a higher price level, since, as we learned in Chapter 8, supply is a function of price. Short-run effects are particularly important to economists who see stabilization policy as important to fine-tuning the economy, and to an understanding of the economy that we face from day to day. Perhaps Keynes expressed the concerns of those economists interested in the short run best when he remarked, "In the long run, we are all dead."

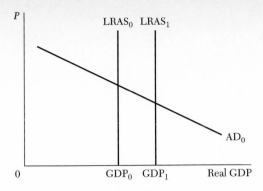

■ FIGURE 18.10 Impact of Productivity Increases on Long-Run Aggregate Supply

Shifts in the Long-Run Aggregate Supply Curve

Since the long-run aggregate supply curve is not responsive to price changes, it is vertical. Any shift in the long-run aggregate supply curve will reflect a change in the quantity of resources available, a change in the productivity of resources, a change in technology, or perhaps some institutional change that affects resource efficiency or productivity. Each of these will increase or decrease output at all price levels and thus cause the LRAS curve to shift. These factors are mostly insensitive to price changes and are not *immediately* affected by short-term macroeconomic policy.

Productivity

An important source of shifts in the long-run aggregate supply curve comes from increases and decreases in labor **productivity**, or the amount of output produced by a unit of input, in this case, a laborer. Increased productivity shifts the LRAS curve to the right, indicating more output at each price level. The importance of productivity growth is that it allows for noninflationary increases in real GDP, as shown in Figure 18.10.

Productivity is difficult to measure. One problem is the measurement of actual output. As the nation's labor force has shifted from industrial production to service activities, physical output is more difficult to measure. Only 18 percent of the nation's nonagricultural workers produce a tangible product. The rest produce services that can be measured in dollars only by examining the number of hours worked. Furthermore, the lack of accounting for quality improvements in manufactured goods understates U.S. productivity figures.

During the past two decades, economists and politicians have become increasingly concerned with the apparent decline in the growth rate of U.S. productivity. Gains in labor productivity, measured as output per person-hour worked, appear to have been sluggish until the 1990s. While the average annual growth of output per worker averaged 1.9 percent between 1950 and 1973, Table 18.2 shows it grew 0.6 percent annually between 1973 and 1980, and it averaged less than 1 percent until the 1990s. In contrast, between

TABLE 18.2 Growth of U.S. Output, 1973–1995

Period	Average Annual Growth*
1973–1980	0.6%
1980–1981	0.7%
1981–1990	0.9%
1990–1995	2.2%

*Output is defined as net domestic product.

Source: Robert Litan et al., "Improving American Living Standards," *The Brookings Review*, Winter 1988/89. Reprinted with permission. *Statistical Abstract of the United States*, 1992, p. 409; 1995, p. 423.

1960 and 1973, productivity increased by more than 4 percent annually in Germany and by more than 5 percent in Japan. Since 1979, productivity increases have averaged between 2 and 3 percent in Germany and 3 and 4 percent in Japan (see Figure 18.11).

More recent trends in the United States show productivity to be increasing at 2.2 percent annually between 1990 and 1995. (Productivity normally increases during a recession, so this increase would be expected in the early 1990s.) Despite faster growth rates in output per worker in Japan and Germany, U.S. workers remain the most productive in the world, with the average worker producing some $28 worth of goods and services per hour and $49,000 worth of goods and services annually.

Economists often attribute slowdowns in worker productivity to a slowdown in innovation and technological change. Other culprits that have been cited as contributors to the slowdown in productivity growth include slower growth of private and public investment expenditures, flagging funding for research and development efforts, increased costs of health and safety regulations, and high energy prices during the 1970s.

7. Why would slower growth of investment expenditures contribute to decreases in productivity growth rates? How would increased energy costs contribute?

■ FIGURE 18.11 Output per Employee in Selected Countries

Source: Bureau of Labor Statistics; *Business Week*, October 9, 1995, p. 140.

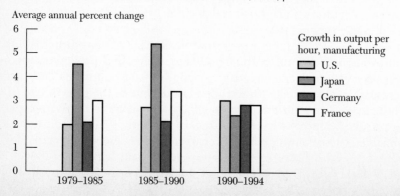

Labor and capitalists, however, sometimes view policies to increase productivity differently. Corporations would suggest tax cuts for business to stimulate capital investment and other incentives for research and development, and thus shift the aggregate supply curve to the right, providing lower prices at each level of output. Labor, on the other hand, would argue for training programs and higher wages to improve productivity growth. That approach requires that output increase faster than the costs of training and pay increases.

Princeton economist William Baumol and his associates have argued that while productivity is a concern, it should be viewed in a long-run rather than a short-run context, and that recent increases in U.S. and U.K. productivity growth must be sustained to have a long-run impact:

> It is only in the long run that productivity growth makes a big difference to the welfare of the populace, and it is only in the long run that productivity growth is subject to fundamental changes. . . . Since the beginning of the nineteenth century average labor productivity growth in the United States probably was a bit more than 1½ percent per year, yet that was sufficient to produce an estimated twenty fold increase in total productivity and living standards, a figure so large that it is difficult to comprehend. A point lag in productivity growth for one century was sufficient to transform the United Kingdom from the world's undisputed industrial leader into the third-rate economy that it is today. It was sufficient to cut real wages in the United Kingdom from about 1½ times that in other leading European economies to about two-thirds of the real wages in those countries today. All of this shows that now is the time to worry about America's standing in productivity growth and that, in particular, it is the time to worry about that standing half a century hence. Fifty years from now the deed may have been done. It may then simply be too late to do much about it.
>
> —William J. Baumol, Sue Anne Baley Blackman, and Edward N. Wolff,
> *Productivity and American Leadership: The Long View*, MIT Press, 1989, pp. 2–3.

Productivity, along with increases in the labor force, increases in capital, and changes in technology, has a powerful effect on aggregate supply and on the nation's standard of living. Therefore, now that we have developed the theory of aggregate supply and understand how various factors influence it, we must examine how our theory of supply relates to economic policy.

SUPPLY-SIDE ECONOMIC POLICY

In 1975, a handful of academic economists, together with politicians and journalists, began to reexamine the problems of the U.S. economy from a different perspective than mainstream Keynesian economics. The focus of the reexamination was on the "supply side." As we have seen previously, the orthodox Keynesian approach to the problems of inflation and unemployment focused on the demand side of the economy. If the economy showed signs of recession or depression, the verdict was that the economy was suffering from insufficient aggregate demand. If there were inflationary trends, then aggregate demand was too robust. Supply-side economists argued that those policies tended to be inflationary; once the government had initiated spending for particular programs, spending was hard to reduce.

Rationale for Supply-Side Economics

Neither Keynes nor the classical economists totally ignored the supply side of the market in their economic analysis, but the policies they designed were predominantly aimed at either shoring up a weak aggregate demand or calming one that was excessive. To them, income or output was a function of aggregate demand.

Proponents of the supply-side approach argued that federal, state, and local governments had stifled production and incentive in the United States with their emphasis on liberal and Keynesian policies, which led to increased spending, taxation, and regulation. They argued that higher tax rates (particularly progressive taxes) and increased government regulation reduced incentives, while spending fueled inflation.

Supply-side advocates argued that increased tax rates inhibited production and reduced output as people substituted leisure activities for productive activity and did more work in which they had less skill. This would reduce the time spent in more productive economic activities, which because of higher taxes were less financially rewarding, and lead to an inefficient allocation of economic resources. Further inefficiencies would occur if tax-deductible goods became less desirable than those that were nondeductible. Finally, advocates of a supply-side approach pointed to the declining productivity in the United States and argued that lower corporate tax rates would generate more business investment and thus increase productivity.

This theory also predicted increased saving and perhaps increases in the rate of saving. Supply-side economists argued that lower tax rates would induce more saving in the private sector; the tax reductions would leave people more income from which to consume and save. If the government also reduced its spending, additional investment funds would become available. Greater investment should lead to lower interest rates and economic growth.

In summary, advocates of the supply-side approach to economic policy saw tax rates as extremely important in determining total output in the economy. They believed that decreases in tax rates caused individuals and businesses to substitute such productive activity as work, investment, and specialization for nonproductive activities. This would result in a more efficient allocation of resources. Total economic output would rise with lower tax rates.

8. How do taxes directly affect supply? Illustrate on a graph of supply and demand how a tax cut works.

Supply-Side Critics

Some economists sympathized with the notions put forth by advocates of the supply-side approach but agreed with the following statement by Herbert

Stein, chair of the Council of Economic Advisors under Presidents Nixon and Ford:

> What we can do on the supply side is not big enough to solve the problem. We have demand growing by about 12 percent a year and supply growing by about 2 percent per year, which yields 10 percent inflation. To increase the rate of growth of supply by 50 percent, from 2 percent a year to 3 percent a year, which is a difficult task, would still leave an enormous inflation, especially if the increase of supply is accomplished by means of cutting taxes, which at the same time increases demand.
>
> —Herbert Stein, "Some Supply Side Propositions," *Wall Street Journal*, March 19, 1980. Copyright © 1980 Dow Jones and Company, Inc. All rights reserved.

Another supply-side argument that came under fire was the assertion that lower tax rates would provide incentives for people to work more, since they could "keep" more of their income. Critics of this notion argued instead that higher tax rates had forced some people to work more than they would like to simply to maintain their standard of living. These people already had two jobs or worked overtime to keep the same level of income in the face of high tax rates. It was hard to conceive of them working more, yet easy to envision their working less if the tax rate fell.

Tax cuts for businesses had critics as well. Although in theory the cuts should stimulate investment, the critics questioned whether these funds would in fact be spent on new, productive activities. They cited the growing number of corporate mergers, such as the purchase of Montgomery Ward by Mobil Oil, and Nabisco by R. J. Reynolds, as examples of corporate spending that created no new jobs or productive output for the nation.

Finally, the supply-side approach tended to shift the distribution of income. Wealthy individuals benefited far more than middle- and lower-middle-income groups. In absolute dollar amounts, the benefit to those earning less than $10,000 a year was minimal, if not negative.

The Federal Reserve set the recovery of 1983–1984 in motion by pumping up the growth rate of the money supply in 1982, at the same time Congress increased military spending and tax cuts. This stimulated a *demand-led*, rather than a supply-led, recovery, although business tax cuts did kick in somewhat higher levels of investment as the recovery mounted. The effects of supply-side policies of the early 1980s had decreased economic growth rates while increasing unemployment and budget deficits. Tax incentives to individuals and businesses had unexpected outcomes: decreases in the personal saving rate and investment expenditures as a percentage of national income.

CONCLUSION

The aggregate demand and aggregate supply model allows us to analyze and show the effect of prices when economic policies are implemented. Since price stability is one of the three macroeconomic goals, we need to be aware of price changes that may result from monetary and fiscal decisions as well as from supply shocks and productivity changes. With this model in mind, we move to Chapter 19, where we examine stabilization policy and the trade-off between inflation and unemployment.

Review Questions

1. How is monetary policy related to aggregate demand?
2. What is the difference between the Keynesian fixed-wage model and the classical model of aggregate supply? What is the result of the differences in explaining aggregate supply?
3. What incentives do supply-side policies attempt to improve? Are incentives important in economic analysis?
4. Explain the relationship between supply-side tax policies and "demand-side" policies. Are the two interrelated? Explain.
5. Why is it so difficult to increase output and thus expand economic growth through supply-side policies?
6. What was the last supply shock to occur in the United States? Explain its significance.
7. What are some of the reasons for the slowdown in productivity in the late 1970s and early 1980s?
8. Why are wages fixed or "sticky" in the short run? Are prices fixed as well? Why?
9. Does it matter whether productivity is viewed in the short or long run? How does one increase productivity?

19

Unemployment, Inflation, and Stabilization Policy in a Global Economy

INTRODUCTION

The previous chapters dealing with macroeconomic theory and policy have touched only slightly on the controversy that surrounds most policy decisions. We have hinted that there is some conflict between the monetarists and the Keynesians about solving these problems or that there might be other contending opinions. Conservatives, liberals, and radicals see different sorts of problems and different sets of solutions. One of the most heavily debated issues, which we shall focus on in the first part of the chapter, is the trade-off between the macroeconomic goals of unemployment and inflation. An even more troublesome situation results when inflation and unemployment occur at the same time, resulting in what economists call **stagflation**.

We will begin by examining unemployment and inflation, the trade-off between the two, and the implications for stabilization policy. From there we will outline the views of several competing schools of economic thought to see how (or, in some cases, if) we can effectively use macroeconomic policy to reach societal goals.

THE TRADE-OFF: UNEMPLOYMENT AND INFLATION

Given the economic goals of price stability, full employment, and growth, Keynesian macroeconomic policy prescriptions advise us that increased spending and/or increases in the money supply may be necessary to attain full employment, with price increases as a side effect. On the other hand, if policy makers attempt to curb inflation through monetary and fiscal measures, income will fall—and so will employment. We seem to be between a rock and a hard place. But an even more difficult problem emerges when the economy develops high inflation as well as high unemployment rates.

The Phillips Curve

At one time, economists believed they had a rather simple answer to questions dealing with the trade-off between full employment and price stability. Economist A. W. Phillips studied the British economy over the past century and found a rather stable relationship between increases in the wage rate and the rate of unemployment. High rates of unemployment were associated with low wage increases, and wage increases appeared to be related to the general rate of inflation. In the 1960s U.S. economists Paul Samuelson and Robert Solow related rates of price increase to rates of unemployment and found that inflation and unemployment were inversely related. High inflation rates were associated with low unemployment rates and vice versa. When plotted, this downward-sloping relationship between the inflation rate and the unemployment rate came to be known as the **Phillips curve**.

If the Phillips curve is valid, then the matter of priorities seems to be rather straightforward. Economists could present a menu of the various trade-offs that were possible—perhaps a 4 percent inflation rate with 5 percent unemployment rate, or a 2 percent inflation rate with a 6 percent unemployment rate. Through the democratic process, the electorate would establish which combination it desired, and the policy makers would fine-tune the economy to obtain this trade-off. If the economy had 5 percent inflation and 4 percent unemployment but the electorate and policy makers desired 4 and 4.5 percent rates, then economic policy should be ever so slightly more restrictive.

During the 1960s, the United States had one of its longest periods of uninterrupted economic growth, inflation averaged around 2 percent (although it accelerated to over 5 percent by the late 1960s), and the unemployment rate declined from 6.7 percent in 1961 to 3.5 percent in 1969 (see Table 19.1 and Figure 19.1). But the 1970s and early 1980s presented a vastly different picture. In 1971, the unemployment rate climbed above 5.9 percent while the inflation rate rose to nearly 5 percent. By 1981 the unemployment rate reached 7.6 percent, and inflation was 10.3 percent. As inflation dropped to between 3 and 4 percent, unemployment peaked at 9.6 percent in 1983 and declined somewhat to 7.5 percent in 1984. The idea of a simple trade-off between inflation and unemployment had broken down. It took increasingly higher levels of unemployment to reduce inflation by increasingly smaller amounts.

Despite the generally inverse relationship between unemployment and price pressures, the trade-off appeared to worsen, leading some economists to suggest that the Phillips curve had shifted. By "connecting the dots," between the annual points plotted between 1960 and 1968 and between 1969 and 1974 on Figure 19.1, we show a shifting Phillips curve. After that time, connecting the dots creates an upward and then a downward spiral, indicating a longer upward movement in the 1970s and early 1980s, followed by a more recent downward trend, renewing the idea of a trade-off.

Some economists attributed shifts in the Phillips curve to supply shocks the economy had received during the 1970s. These included the very high increases in oil prices caused by the OPEC embargo, increased prices of agricultural products, and finally the increased prices of foreign goods brought about by the fall in the dollar's value in 1973.

TABLE 19.1 The Short-Run Phillips Curve and the U.S. Economy, 1960–1996

Year	Percent Change in Consumer Price Index	Percent Official Unemployment (Civilian Workers)
1960	1.7	5.5
1961	1.0	6.7
1962	1.0	5.5
1963	1.3	5.7
1964	1.3	5.2
1965	1.6	4.5
1966	2.9	3.8
1967	3.1	3.8
1968	4.2	3.6
1969	5.5	3.5
1970	5.7	4.9
1971	4.4	5.9
1972	3.2	5.6
1973	6.2	4.9
1974	1.1	5.6
1975	9.1	8.5
1976	5.8	7.7
1977	6.5	7.1
1978	7.6	6.1
1979	11.3	5.8
1980	13.5	7.1
1981	10.3	7.6
1982	6.2	9.7
1983	3.2	9.6
1984	4.3	7.5
1985	3.6	7.2
1986	1.9	7.0
1987	3.6	6.2
1988	4.1	5.5
1989	4.8	5.3
1990	5.4	5.5
1991	4.2	6.7
1992	3.0	7.4
1993	3.0	6.8
1994	2.6	6.1
1995	2.8	5.6
1996	3.3	5.4

Source: *Economic Report of the President*, 1997, pp. 347, 369.

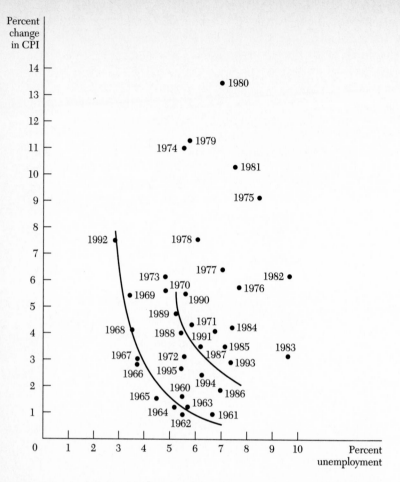

FIGURE 19.1 The Phillips Curve and the U.S. Economy, 1960–1995

The 1990s brought the U.S. economy relatively low levels of unemployment and inflation accompanying a record number of months of sustained economic growth. Even so, significant concerns remained about budget deficits and trade deficits, S&L bailouts, and the stability of financial institutions. Other structural problems appeared troublesome as well. In a nation with one of the world's highest standards of living, homelessness increased, and the infant mortality rate remained among the highest of the industrial nations. Continuing increases in poverty levels, particularly among the young, were particularly troublesome.

Recent attention to these problems has focused on corporate downsizing and on the inability of the U.S. and other industrial economies to create enough good jobs for workers. In the Thinking Critically section following this chapter, we shall examine the critics and those who argue the importance of downsizing and restructuring of workplaces.

INFLATION

We have defined inflation as a rise in the general price level. We can expect price increases to accompany a growing, viable economy, but if these price increases are larger than increases in productivity or real output would dictate, they are inflationary. Table 19.2 indicates what has happened to prices in the past quarter century. Note the rates of inflation in recent years.

1. On the average, how much would something that cost $200 in 1967 cost in 1997? How much inflation has there been since you were born? Current data for the CPI is available from the *Economic Report of the President* (or at http://www. whitehouse.gov/fsbr/esbr.html).
2. Does any information in the table surprise you?

TABLE 19.2 Consumer Price Index and Percentage Changes for Urban Wage Earners and Clerical Workers (1982–1984 = 100)

Year	CPI	Year-to-Year Change	Year	CPI	Year-to-Year Change
1948	24.1	8.1%	1972	41.8	3.2%
1949	23.8	-1.2	1973	44.4	6.2
1950	24.1	1.3	1974	49.3	11.0
1951	26.0	7.9	1975	53.8	9.1
1952	26.5	1.9	1976	56.9	5.8
1953	26.7	0.8	1977	60.6	6.5
1954	26.9	0.7	1978	65.2	7.6
1955	26.8	-0.4	1979	72.6	11.3
1956	27.2	1.5	1980	82.4	13.5
1957	28.1	3.3	1981	90.9	10.3
1958	28.9	2.8	1982	96.5	6.2
1959	29.1	0.7	1983	99.6	3.2
1960	29.6	1.7	1984	103.9	4.3
1961	29.9	1.0	1985	107.6	3.6
1962	30.2	1.0	1986	109.6	1.9
1963	30.6	1.3	1987	113.6	3.6
1964	31.0	1.3	1988	118.3	4.1
1965	31.5	1.6	1989	124.0	4.8
1966	32.4	2.9	1990	130.7	5.4
1967	33.4	3.1	1991	136.2	4.2
1968	34.7	3.7	1992	140.3	3.0
1969	36.7	5.5	1993	144.5	3.0
1970	38.8	5.7	1994	148.2	2.6
1971	40.5	4.4	1995	152.4	2.8
			1996	156.9	3.3

The Consumer Price Index (CPI) measures changes in the "cost of living."

Source: *Economic Report of the President,* 1997, pp. 365, 369.

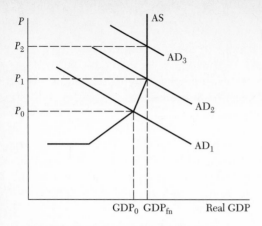

■ FIGURE 19.2 Demand-Pull Inflation

From our analysis of aggregate demand and aggregate supply in Chapter 18, we can see that any action that shifts the aggregate demand curve to the right or the aggregate supply curve to the left causes price increases and possibly inflation. We can classify the prevailing types of inflation according to the possible cause of each: demand-pull inflation, cost-push inflation, and expectations-generated inflation. These types of inflation can occur simultaneously or independently.

Demand-pull inflation is a rise in the price level attributed to excessive aggregate demand. Aggregate demand can increase for a number of reasons, including increases in autonomous consumption, investment, government spending, net exports, and the money supply or decreases in taxes or saving. We can view this graphically in Figure 19.2, where AS represents the aggregate supply curve, and AD represents aggregate demand. All are plotted with respect to real output (real GDP) and the general price level (P). A rightward shift of the aggregate demand curve from AD_1 to AD_2 increases both prices and real output in the short run as real GDP increases from GDP_0 to GDP_{fn} and prices increase from P_0 to P_1. As income levels increase, the demand for goods and services will rise. Initially, as demand increases, prices are bid up, output increases, and more laborers are hired to produce products. If resources are fully employed and aggregate demand continues to rise, as illustrated by a shift from AD_2 to AD_3, there is no increase in GDP, only an increase in prices. From our analysis in Chapter 18, we know that the higher aggregate demand in the face of limited supply will cause shortages of goods and services and the need for additional labor to increase production. The increased demand for goods and services, raw materials, and labor may even exceed the capacity to generate new output.

A simple remedy for aggregate demand inflation is to cut back on spending and the money supply. The same technique can thwart inflationary expectations. Reductions in the growth rate of the money supply are particularly effective (and painful).

Cost-push (or supply) **inflation** puts the responsibility for price increases on rising costs of production. From the analysis of demand and supply in

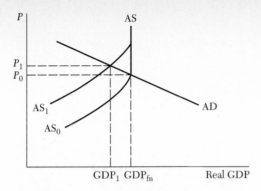

FIGURE 19.3 Cost-Push Inflation

Chapter 8, we found that as production costs increased, the supply curve shifted to the left, leading to higher prices. A few of the cost factors that might cause a shift in the supply function are wages, raw material prices, interest rates, and profits. In Figure 19.3 higher costs bring about increases in price as well as a reduction in output. In the long run, producers will be able to reduce wages because of higher levels of unemployment, and output will return to the original level (GDP_0).

Cost increases can come from many places, including increases in raw material prices, labor costs, and higher profits. As market structures have become more concentrated, large corporations have gained more ability to administer prices for their own benefit—which in most cases means to increase prices and profits. During the 1970s, resource shortages pushed the prices of some goods upward. The lack of supply created a bottleneck in the production process, with limited amounts of raw materials forthcoming, even at higher costs.

Unlike aggregate demand inflation, cost-push or supply inflation has no simple remedy. Resource shortages are difficult to prevent. Cartels that withhold raw materials are hard to bargain with. Controls placed on wages and prices, and other types of income policies, do not seem to work very well, when viewed in a historical context. Indeed, controls often lead to contrived shortages, as suppliers hesitate to continue production when they cannot recoup rising costs.

This analysis of supply-led inflation explains shifts in the Phillips curve. As aggregate supply falls, shifting to the left, prices increase and output falls. Higher unemployment results. With a decrease in aggregate supply, higher rates of inflation and unemployment are accompanied by lower output and higher prices. Sustained price shocks cause the Phillips curve to shift outward.

As businesses respond to higher output and profits by hiring additional workers, more jobs become available, and unemployment falls. If the current rates of inflation are expected to continue, *Expectations-generated inflation* may occur. Workers, trying to restore the purchasing power of their wages, press for increases based on inflationary expectations. Once workers attain higher wages, the aggregate supply will shift from AS_1 to reflect the increased costs to firms. With these higher costs, profits fall, and firms cut back on output. Real GDP falls back to its original level at GDP_{fn}, but prices are now at a higher level (P_2).

While expectations may seem an unlikely candidate for economic analysis, inflationary expectations are at times important in explaining inflation. Each time we expect inflation, we tend to incur its generation. Yale economist William Nordhaus stated this well:

> Inflation is a highly inertial process. It will go along to whatever rate it has been going at until it is shocked to a different level. . . . From 1973 to 1980 we had 6 to 9 percent inflation built into the wage and price system. It [higher inflation] was built into contracts. It was built into expectations. The recession [1980–1982] beat it down to 5 percent and now we have lower inertial rates.

Inflationary expectations directly affect aggregate supply. As wages increase because workers expect inflation, costs to firms increase. Firms then pass on these increased costs to consumers in the form of higher prices. On the demand side, expectations of higher interest rates generate consumer and business borrowing and expenditures. These activities increase aggregate demand and drive up prices.

When inflationary expectations are low, inflation is easier to moderate with monetary and fiscal policy. In the 1970s, when inflationary expectations were high, the fiscal policies employed were largely ineffective. They resulted in increased unemployment without significantly lower inflation. The late 1980s through the late 1990s have seen inflation rates averaging a relatively low 2½ to 4 percent.

IMPACT OF UNEMPLOYMENT AND INFLATION

Although policy makers and politicians would prefer to have low inflation *and* low unemployment, the trade-offs shown by the Phillips curve require decisions about which goal, full employment or price stability, is preferable. Economists studying this question have found that higher unemployment and higher inflation affect different groups in different ways.

According to a study by Princeton economist Alan Blinder, former member of the Federal Reserve Board and Council of Economic Advisors, and Northwestern University economist Rebecca Blank, the unemployment rate for teens increases at two times the base rate and unemployment for the elderly increases at about half the rate. Blinder and Blank also made the following observations:

> The burden of unemployment is distributed unequally across age, race, and sex groups. In particular, nonwhite and young workers are more severely affected. On the other hand, female and older workers—who are also typically low-wage workers—are not as sensitive to changes in general unemployment levels.

They conclude, "The business cycle is not neutral in spreading the burden of unemployment. Certain workers experience much larger increases in

■ Thousands of employees from five European countries demonstrate in the streets of Paris against expected job cuts, May 1996. *(Agency France Presse/Corbis-Bettmann)*

unemployment when the general economy turns down than others." Blank and Blinder also found that whites, males, and the middle-aged receive a larger share of unemployment compensation than do unemployed workers in other categories.*

Inflation particularly hurts creditors and those on fixed incomes, while borrowers in general are helped. The poor seem to be hurt less by inflation than the rich are. Prices generally rise for consumers at all income levels, but so do wages and salaries. However, the income from and worth of wealthy people's assets are more readily eroded by inflation.

3. What effect will supply shortages have on the trade-off between inflation and unemployment, for example—when unemployment is increasing?
4. How is a person who borrows money helped by inflation? Is this always so?

*Rebecca M. Blank and Alan S. Blinder, "Macroeconomics, Income Distribution and Poverty," in Sheldon H. Danziger and Daniel Weinberg, eds., *Fighting Poverty: What Works and What Doesn't.* Cambridge, Mass.: Harvard University Press, 1986, p. 191.

TABLE 19.3 Unemployment and Inflation Rates in Selected Countries, 1994

Country	Unemployment Rate	Change in Consumer Price Index
United States	6.1%	3.0%
Australia	9.7	2.0
Canada	10.4	2.0
France	12.7	2.0
Germany	6.5	3.0
Italy	11.3	4.0
Japan	2.9	1.0
Sweden	9.6	2.0
United Kingdom	9.6	3.0

Source: *Statistical Abstract of the United States*, 1996, pp. 842–843.

STABILIZATION POLICY: AN INTERNATIONAL PERSPECTIVE

Unemployment and inflation concern policy makers throughout the world's industrial and developing nations. The 1990s have brought generally low rates of unemployment and inflation in the United States, Germany, and Japan, but several other industrial nations have experienced substantially higher unemployment. Table 19.3 shows recent unemployment and inflation rates in some of the nations that actively compete with the United States in international markets.

Many of the European nations listed in the table have chosen more aggressive social programs than those in the United States for dealing with the effects of unemployment. These more generous programs have at least partially resulted in higher taxes. As Figure 19.4 illustrates, the United States has a relatively lower tax burden than the other industrialized nations. At the same time, many of these nations have also experienced higher government

FIGURE 19.4 Total Tax Revenues of Selected Countries, 1993

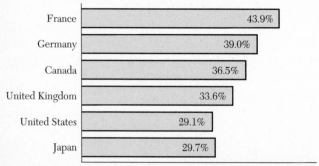

Tax revenues as a % of GDP

Source: Organization for Economic Cooperation and Development, 1996, pp. 46–47.

deficits (see Figure 16.5). In 1996, government officials in France and Germany proposed cuts in social programs to reduce the level of current deficits. (In the 1997 elections, French voters rejected these plans.) In the United States, Republicans and Democrats have agreed on a seven-year deficit reduction package.

MACROECONOMIC SOLUTIONS: THE ALTERNATIVES

While the Keynesian aggregate expenditures model we have explored commends the use of monetary and fiscal policy in stabilization efforts, other economic models and theories question the effectiveness of intervention. The dilemma of the 1990s is therefore what to do—not so much about inflation and unemployment but about government budget and trade deficits, slow rates of economic and productivity growth, and the myriad of other economic problems that surround us in the context of a complex and increasingly interdependent world economy. Traditional Keynesian remedies, declared deficient during the stagflation of the 1970s, returned with renewed vitality to the **New Keynesians** by the end of the decade. Ever an evolutionary theory, Keynesianism is becoming more eclectic, encompassing some of the better ideas presented by other schools of macroeconomic thought in the 1980s. These include a larger framework on which consumers base their expectations of the future and a reaffirmation that, along with fiscal policy, monetary policy is important to stabilization efforts. As Keynesians are returning to the limelight, popular movements of the 1970s and 1980s have rapidly lost favor. To better understand the status of stabilization policy, we will briefly summarize some of the theories and policies of contending schools of thought and review their standing in the 1990s.

Monetarist Solutions

Monetarists believe that growth rates of money control inflation and business cycle activity. Monetary policy, therefore, is the most effective way to stabilize the economy, although most monetarists prefer a nondiscretionary rule rather than small changes in policy that aim to fine-tune the economy. Monetarists contend that only money matters, since increases in money allow fiscal policy to be effective in the long run. (Actually, it is monetary policy that is effective.) The monetarists focus on the long run and avoid short-run solutions.

Boosted by the failures of Keynesian theory and policy to explain and counter the stagflation of the 1970s, the monetarists entered the 1980s at the top of the hit parade. But even the 1970s and certainly the 1980s dealt monetarists a cruel blow. Predictions fell by the wayside. Velocity was unstable, as was the demand for money. The money supply proved hard to target. Inflation of the 1970s proved not to be a monetary phenomenon, and inflation predicted in the 1980s failed to materialize. The monetarists fell from favor. Keynesians, however, accepted the need to use monetary policy with fiscal policy to achieve stabilization targets.

Supply-Side Solutions

Supply-siders have also fallen from favor. Wishful thinking proved no match for the economy that resulted from supply-side policies. Marginal tax rate policies designed to stimulate investment and incentives brought about increased unemployment, decreased saving and investment, large budget deficits, and increased income and wealth inequality. We discussed supply-side economics at length in Chapter 18 and will not repeat those arguments here. While economists still believe that marginal tax rates can help to increase incentives and investment, they see them having a rather small effect on overall economic activity. Supply-side stabilization policies should not be disregarded, but their stabilization effect is small.

New Classical Solutions

The New Classical or Rational Expectations school of macroeconomic thought gained support and prestige during the 1970s and early 1980s. Its abstract theoretical and mathematical model, based on classical assumptions of pure and perfect competition, appealed to a number of academic economists. New Classical economists argue that firms and workers acquire, assess, and utilize information very quickly and rationally. For example, in our prior discussion of inflation, economists subscribing to the New Classical view would argue that as soon as laborers realized policy makers were trying to stimulate demand, they would adjust their consumption and wage demands, making the "short-run" Phillips curve trade-off even shorter and making the long-run aggregate supply and vertical Phillips curves the only appropriate ones for examining policy actions. Short-run stabilization policy would be useless, since rational people would react immediately and "outguess" the policy. Only policy "surprises" would be effective. Rational individuals would use all information, not just past data about prices or income. Inflationary expectations could be introduced or curbed simply by the appointment of a new Federal Reserve chair known to be easy or tough on inflation. New Classical economists would rely on perfectly competitive markets—ones without collusion, price fixing, or monopoly—to chart the best course for the economy.

When economists examined the evidence from the late 1970s and 1980s, New Classical theories fell short. According to the theories, inflation could be reduced without an increase in unemployment. With the Federal Reserve decreasing the growth rate of the money supply, economic actors should have adjusted their inflationary expectations downward, avoiding high levels of unemployment. But recent history has shown the short-run Phillips curve to be alive and well, and Rational Expectations remains a theory without an accompanying reality.

Post-Keynesian Solutions

Post-Keynesians, distrustful of market solutions and the long-run timing of such solutions, and relying heavily on the role of demand in the economy, recommend adoption of an incomes policy to determine an annual noninflationary rise in all types of income. This would involve controls over the rates of increase in personal and business income. Tax incentives would assure compliance. The post-Keynesians believe that government and business should jointly make decisions for long-run public and private investment, and that employment and growth policies are central to a recovery and economic restructuring.

Post-Keynesian alternatives such as wage and price controls faded from sight as means to combat inflation or reduce unemployment in the 1980s. Yet every president except Reagan and Bush in the postwar era at some point flirted with controls or guidelines. Outside of the political machismo derived from controls, there has been little evidence that the particular types of controls instituted have been effective.

Feminist Economists Solutions

Feminist economics notes the failure of present economic models to predict and address real-world concerns of women and men. It seeks to go beyond formal economic models based on what it sees as oversimplified assumptions about human behavior. Policies based on these improved analyses will follow.

Radical Solutions

Radical economists argued that the stagflation of the 1970s was symptomatic not only of a failure of Keynesian theory and policy but also of a fundamental breakdown of U.S. capitalism. Radicals viewed U.S. capitalism as experiencing a long-term structural crisis, explained not by factors external to the economy but by the business cycle. A radical critique of Keynesian theory and policy challenges the "theory of the state," with the state as the legitimate arbiter of societal conflicts resulting from interest group political behavior and lobbying. Arguing that the state consciously guides the economy and cyclical instability in order to serve the needs of the dominant economic class, Raford Boddy and James Crotty summarize the functional analysis of a recession in the business cycle:

> It is the economic function of the recession to correct the imbalances of the previous expansion and thereby create the preconditions for a new one. By robbing millions of people of their jobs, and threatening the jobs of millions of others, recessions reduce worker demands and end the rise of labor costs. They eventually rebuild profit margins and stabilize prices. During recessions inventories are cut, loans are repaid, corporate liquidity position is reversed. All the statements of Keynesian economists to the contrary notwithstanding, recessions are inevitable in the unplanned economy of the United States because they perform an essential function for which no adequate substitute has thus far been available.
>
> —Raford Boddy and James R. Crotty, "Who Will Plan the Planned Economy?" *The Progressive*, February 1975.

Radicals see increases in concentration and specialization of production by domestic and multinational corporations as expanding both their political and their economic power. An increasingly symbiotic relationship between government and business explains the structural transformation of U.S. capitalism since World War II, prohibits the possibility of genuine democracy in the United States, and clearly depicts an underlying class character of government functions and policies. Radicals view stabilization policies as outside the interests of workers and the democratic process.

CONCLUSION

We must increasingly adapt our theory and policy within the context of the existing U.S. and world economies, finding solutions that are effective within this context. The U.S. economy is far different from what it was in the era of Pax Americana. The workforce is changing, and the economic base, which was continually regenerated through economic growth, is no longer solely industrial. Additionally, policy decisions must reflect the fact that the U.S. economy in the 1990s is greatly dependent on the other nations of the world. As government leaders plan for economic growth in the United States in the 1990s, they must do so within a world context. Today more than 10 percent of the products made in the United States are exported to other nations. Exports plus imports made up about 25 percent of the U.S. GDP in 1992, compared with 12.4 percent of GDP in 1970 and less than 10 percent in the 1960s. If the economies of U.S. trading partners are unhealthy, we cannot expect the U.S. economy to remain vigorous.

This chapter completes our discussion of macroeconomics. We have seen that the Keynesian approach to economic policy has carried us a long way from the classical approach. Yet problems still exist, and new approaches may be needed to deal with future problems. Many of these issues are increasing our attention toward macroeconomics and the functioning of specific markets. Before we look further at policy, however, we need to broaden our perspective and see what is happening in international economics. An understanding of the global arena is necessary to appreciate the full complexity of macroeconomic problems.

Review Questions

1. What is the basis for the trade-off between inflation and unemployment? Why can't there be zero unemployment and zero inflation?
2. Do you think fighting inflation is more important than fighting unemployment? Why or why not?
3. What competing theories explain inflation in the economy?
4. What structural elements in the economy limit the effectiveness of fiscal and monetary policies?
5. How does avoiding a boom avoid a recession? What is the resulting impact on inflation?

EXPLORATIONS IN MACROECONOMICS —JOBS IN THE WORLD ECONOMY

D uring the mid-1990s, newspaper headlines reported corporate downsizing, slow growth of wages, and the resulting stress on families. The *New York Times* ran a seven-part series, "The Downsizing of America," between March 3 and 9, 1996. Among other topics, the series examined the "Battlefields of Business, Millions of Casualties," reporting that "corporate cost cutting has helped make American businesses more profitable, but has taken a heavy toll in job layoffs." American workers began to face the results of corporate decisions to increase profits or to ensure the survival of the company into the future. As international competition grows more intense, as Marx predicted, there is little room for sympathies.

The decisions of these firms affect such macroeconomic outcomes as unemployment rates, the economic base of communities, income distribution, job security, standards of living, and economic growth. Should the government use macroeconomic stabilization policies to offset the effects of corporate downsizing and corporate flight? Can monetary and fiscal policies be used to increase employment, stimulate economic growth, and alter the trends in income distribution? These questions are complicated by the increasing globalization of economic activity. Unemployment of unskilled workers in the United States is overshadowed by staggering unemployment in developing countries.

In this section we present two arguments: one highly critical of corporate decisions and policies, and one defending them. Richard J. Barnet, a senior fellow at the Institute of Policy Studies in Washington, contends that "employment is one thing the global economy is not creating" and that the "worldwide job crisis threatens not only global economic growth but the capitalist system itself." He argues that both national and international interests are at stake. Barnet's view of downsizing and corporate flight contrasts markedly with the perspective taken by Harvard researchers Michael Jensen and Perry Fagan. In the *Wall Street Journal*, Jensen and Fagan argue that "Capitalism Isn't Broken," citing the necessity for industries worldwide to adjust to new technology and workplaces. According to Jensen and Fagan, this prolonged period of corporate restructuring, the so-called Third Industrial Revolution, promises even more riches in the future.

THE END OF JOBS

Richard Barnet

In 1914, Henry Ford raised the pay of his workers enough so that they could buy Fords. The *Wall Street Journal* immediately denounced the cranky automaker for committing an "economic crime," but Ford understood that, as he once put it, "if you cut wages, you just cut the number of your customers." Now, however, the social system based on high-volume assembly-line production employing well-paid workers who can afford to purchase what they make is fast disappearing. Since 1989, the United States has lost 1.6 million manufacturing jobs, and such losses will continue to mount. . .

Thanks to automation, the increasing use of subcontractors, suppliers, and temporary workers . . . and the reorganization of the workplace in order to provide greater output per worker, steady jobs for good pay are becoming poignant memories or just dreams for more and more people. This is true not only in factories but in banks, stores, insurance companies, brokerage houses, law firms, hospitals, and all sorts of other places where services are rendered. . . .

As factories moved out of the United States in the 1970s and 1980s, the Panglosses of the day called it progress and celebrated the transition to a "service economy" that would provide an ever-expanding source of jobs at every level of society. The dirty factories would move abroad and the nasty work would be done in the poor countries. The United States would invent the software on which the new global system would run, and highly paid lawyers, accountants, deal makers, and other servants of corporations and rich investors would somehow generate enough economic activity to keep armies of fast-food handlers, health-care aides, and clerks gainfully employed. . . . The mushrooming service sector, however, turned out to be vulnerable to the same fierce competition that has shriveled factory payrolls in the United States and caused real wages in manufacturing to drop 9 percent since 1973.

. . . Job insecurity, however, is no respecter of class. In 1991, overall unemployment in the United States jumped 15 percent as companies "downsized" in the name of efficiency and an increase in productivity. But the unemployment rate for managers rose 55 percent. As the organization of the world's work shifts, more and more of us, from the wastebasket emptiers to CEOs of multinational corporations, are waking up to the fact that we are swimming in a global labor pool.

It turns out that just because we have lived and worked in Connecticut all our professional lives is no guarantee that our Connecticut-based employer will not hire a Malaysian or a Russian do our job. . . .

The dimensions of what Marx called the reserve army of the unemployed are now staggering. According to the International Labour Organization, an estimated 47 million additional job seekers enter the already overcrowded labor market each year. Approximately 38 million of them are in Asia, Africa, and Latin America. With the exception of Japan, of two industrializing nations in Asia (South Korea and Taiwan) that have been highly successful in creating jobs and building a middle class, of two commercial city-states in the same part of the world (Hong Kong and Singapore) that are free from typical Third World population pressures, and of China, where the majority of people still farm and the industrial economy is growing at an incredibly fast rate, Asia is struggling with chronic unemployment problems. And Africa and Latin America face an employment crisis on a scale far beyond anything Americans and Europeans encountered during the Great Depression. This includes a number of nations that are aggressively pursuing strategies of industrialization.

Within the next twenty years throughout the underdeveloped world, more than 750 million men and women will reach the legal working age and will enter the labor market, adding to the 700 million currently unemployed or underemployed in poor countries. (These are United Nations figures and represent extremely rough estimates, but it can be safely assumed that the national and international officials involved in compiling these figures have no interest in inflating them.) . . .

A problem with any jobs strategy [to educate and train workers] tied to increased productivity is the perverse consequence of such gains. Workers who raise their hourly output eliminate jobs for other workers and in the long run may endanger their own jobs. Ultimately there is a conflict between, on the one hand, the profitability of individual corporations and the pressures of global competition and, on the other, human needs everywhere for high employment levels, decent pay, healthy working conditions, and job security. It was precisely this contradiction that gave rise to the socialist movement, and it was the failure of authoritarian command economies to resolve it that led to the demise of state socialism.

A recent study by Steven M. Fazzari for the Economic Policy Institute (based on data from firms that account for between 40 and 50 percent of all plant and equipment spending in the United States) lends support to this argument [that government tinkering with the economy is less effective than it used to be]. Fazzari notes that "interest rates and the cost of capital play a very uncertain role" in investment decisions; these have much more to do with financial conditions and prospects of the companies than with interest rates. Fazzari's study suggests that cutting the deficit, a worthy objective under the right conditions, is not the way to put the country back to work.

According to the prevailing credo, however, the way to get more jobs is to enable entrepreneurs to keep more of their earnings so that they can invest them in job-creating technologies and expansion. In the Alice in Wonderland world of the 1980s and 1990s, it is ideologically sound to spend millions of dollars in taxpayers' money on "incentive packages" to lure corporations and the jobs they promise into a city or state, but it is politically incorrect for the government to act as employer of last resort, hiring unemployed young people to clean up cities, rehabilitate houses, visit the elderly, and the like.

Subsidizing corporations to make jobs is no answer. Unless long-term obligations are written into the deal, private companies are free to take the money and run once the benefits run out, and they do. Enforcing obligations on global companies is hardly easy. As global competition becomes fiercer, the odds are increasingly stacked against governments that try to buy jobs. Once the corporation has received the land, money, and tax breaks, company executives have every incentive to keep payrolls down. Flexibility, downsizing, outsourcing (hiring temporaries or subcontractors), automation, and relocation are the buzzwords of the day.

What remains? There are a number of sensible ideas for attacking aspects of the job crisis. None is a quick fix.

For example, shortening the workweek could encourage job sharing. This, in turn, would create more jobs, accommodate more working mothers, and perhaps encourage the healthy notion that a job is not the whole of life.

Government programs that target poor neighborhoods, where unemployment may reach 40 percent, can help create some jobs if the goal is local self-reliance and the support is designed to enable people to make maximum use of the considerable skills, relationships, and savings that exist even in inner-city blocks from which drugstores and supermarkets have fled. There are now operating in the United States more than a hundred programs to furnish start-up capital for neighborhood businesses along the innovative model of the Grameen Bank in Bangladesh.

And small businesses begun with small amounts of capital, usually from relatives, make up much of the informal economy that is all that stands between millions of people across the world and starvation. This mix of off-the-books activities, ranging from sidewalk barbershops to global drug cartels, eases personal financial problems around the world. The drug trade aside, much informal-sector activity is legitimate, meets important human needs, and should be encouraged rather than repressed by governments.

The suggestions that Walter Russell Mead and other analysts have made to apply Keynesian full-employment policies on a global level are theoretically sound. There are no national solutions to the job crisis. Coordinated strategies at the global level are needed to promote the sort of world economic growth that avoids flooding the planet with goods and services far in excess of what people want or the planet can afford. The government of every industrial power, however, faces such acute problems that cooperation of this sort seems improbable at this time. Clinton's call for an international jobs summit at least makes the global dimension of the crisis more visible. Yet a concerted look at the job-destroying incentives built into the global industrial system and a cooperative strategy to alter this system may well be the only means for dealing with the very domestic political and economic problems that threaten world leaders with early retirement.

The lack of decently compensated jobs under decent working conditions is a global deficit so vast as to require fundamental rethinking about the global economic system itself. The global machine for producing goods and services in ever greater quantities depends upon a growing population of consumers with enough money in their pockets to keep the system going. Even the super-rich buy only a limited number of refrigerators and computers. Yet the pressures on the production system are pushing income distribution in precisely the opposite direction. While millions in the workforce dropped out or dropped down, the average CEO of a large U.S. based corporation in 1992 was taking home $3,842,247, a 56 percent increase from the previous year. Between 1960 and 1992, the average worker's pay rose from $4,665 to $24,411. The recent trend toward greater inequality in the United States, and throughout much of the rest of the world, means that the vast majority of the 8 billion human beings expected to be living on the earth in the first quarter of the next century will be neither producers nor consumers in the new global economy.

The global job crisis is the product of a value system that prizes the efficient production of goods and services more than the human spirit and of an economic strategy riddled with contradictions. Contemporary society is built on a social system in which the individual's livelihood, place, worth, and sense of self are increasingly defined by his or her job. At the same time, jobs are disappearing. The global economic system is fragile because it depends on growth fueled by the expansion of consumption, but the fierce drive to eliminate work and cut wages is clearly not the way to bring spenders to the car lots and shopping malls. Except for cigarettes, Coke, and a few other products, most of what the global production system disgorges is consumed by fewer than 2 billion of the more than 5 billion people who now live on the planet.

In the end, the job crisis raises the most fundamental question of human existence: What are we doing here? There is a colossal amount of work waiting to be done by human beings—building decent places to live, exploring the universe, making cities less dangerous, teaching one another, raising our children, visiting, comforting, healing, feeding one another, dancing, making music, telling stories, inventing things, and governing ourselves. But much of the essential activity people have always undertaken to raise and educate their families, to enjoy themselves, to give pleasure to others, and to advance the general welfare is not packaged as jobs. Until we rethink work and decide what human beings are meant to do in the age of robots and what basic economic claims on society human beings have by virtue of being here, there will never be enough jobs.

Some of the elements of a global strategy for reorganizing work are beginning to take shape, but politicians everywhere continue to promise prosperity without confronting the international dimensions of the problem. We have yet to summon the courage and the imagination to face the human assault on human beings that we call the "job problem."

CAPITALISM ISN'T BROKEN

Michael C. Jensen and Perry Fagan

AT&T is a sick company, and CEO Robert Allen is a courageous man for trying to fix it. AT&T's announced breakup into three companies and the layoff of 40,000 people is the beginning, not the end, of a difficult, painful process. If the company is not fixed, most of its current 300,000 employees will be out of a job over the next decade or so. AT&T is not alone in this challenge.

Yet AT&T and other "downsizing" corporations are the targets of vicious attacks from special interests, misled pundits and politicians angling for votes. This political frenzy threatens grave damage to our country's economic engine.

Restructuring a company is a dirty, distasteful, tough, yet necessary job. No one likes to fire friends, close plants, or become the object of name-calling and personal attacks. *Newsweek*'s characterizations of such courageous leaders as "corporate killers" and "greedheads" is both wrong and irresponsible. Like the Second Industrial Revolution of the last century, today's economic dislocations are wreaking havoc on the national psyche. But they are also the source of a wonderfully optimistic future. If past experience is a guide, this industrial revolution will likely take another 30 years to deliver all of its benefits. Yet the current reaction, triggered by Pat Buchanan's call for a return to the "secure" days of our economic past, threatens to make the situation more painful, not less.

Requiring Changes

The Third Industrial Revolution that began in 1973 promises increased productivity, large reductions in the world-wide inequality of wealth, and substantial increases in world-wide living standards. At the same time, it is disturbing the status quo and requiring changes that people do not want to make—even though in the long run we will be better off for having made them. The immediate sources of the changes are large increases in capacity and productivity resulting from major political and technological progress.

The political dynamic behind the Third Industrial Revolution is the spread of capitalism in response to the world-wide failure of communism, socialism and other central planning systems. This move to market-oriented, open economic systems has initiated a process that is putting 1.2 billion Third World workers into world-wide product and labor markets over the next generation. Over a billion of these workers currently earn less than $3 a day, while the approximately 250 million workers in the U.S. and the European Union currently earn roughly $85 a day.

With relatively modern technology, experience indicates that these Third World workers can produce from 85% to 100% of the output of their Western compatriots. The major shifts in the world product markets brought about by the 90 million workers in Hong Kong, Japan, Korea, Malaysia, Singapore and Taiwan in the past 30 years provide some insight into the even greater changes that are yet to take place in the West.

One can confidently forecast that the transition to open capitalist economies will generate great conflict over international trade as special interests try to insulate themselves from competition. The transition of established industrial economies will require a major redirection of Western labor and capital to activities where it has a comparative advantage.

The upshot of all this for Western workers is that their real wages are likely to continue their sluggish growth and some will fall dramatically over the coming two or three decades, perhaps as much as 50% in some sectors. Wages will, however, reach a trough and recover as the cycle works its way through the system. Remember, these 1.2 billion Third World workers and their families represent huge new markets as well as competitors.

In addition to political revolutions, major changes in technology are dramatically increasing productivity, and this is reflected in re-engineering and downsizing programs. By instituting such programs, companies regularly find that current output can be produced by a labor force that is 20% to 30% smaller. These workers have been "unemployed" on the job, producing little of social value. Thus, paradoxically, their release from such old-line companies as AT&T, IBM, Kodak, Chase Manhattan, and many others increases, rather than reduces, social welfare.

As these "freed up" employees are put to work producing goods and services that people value, our total standard of living rises. And the resulting increased efficiency is reflected in the increased profits and stock prices of enterprises that stop wasting society's most valuable resource—human labor hours.

In the short term, however, the workers who must find alternative skills and employment bear the pain of uncertainty, cutbacks, moves, and even failed families. This pain is something all reasonable people would like to relieve. But we cannot stop it. Indeed, if we do, we reduce or eliminate the transfer of these underemployed resources and we continue the waste. There is no way to completely eliminate the private pain that comes from this adjustment. We all wish it were different, but without the private pain, most people will not change. The waste will continue, and in a generation or two this will result in a nation crippled by poverty. (Witness the effects of such efforts in Eastern and Central Europe over the past 60 years.)

World-wide excess capacity in industry after industry requires the release of resources from traditional areas of production so they can be rechanneled into new areas. Just as there was widespread malaise in the 19th century in the face of such adjustments, it was foreseeable that there would be political unrest in this generation.

Since the late 1960s, measured growth in manufacturing productivity has slowed, speeding up in the 1980s during the age of corporate takeovers, only slow again in the recession of 1990–92. It is speeding up again as the restructuring movement motivated by product market competition continues. Productivity measures in the service sector show less improvement, but the measures are so poorly designed that the numbers are seriously misleading.

Income inequality has also risen, particularly since 1979. In addition, real median American family income fell substantially over the 1977–82 period and rose dramatically through 1989 to exceed its earlier level, only to decline again in the recession beginning in 1990. The net result has been that despite rising productivity the median American family was little better off in real terms in our last year of data, 1993, than it was 15 to 20 years ago. The bottom quartile of the distribution is worse off, and the top of the income distribution is substantially better off.

This pattern also manifested itself in the 19th century, when capital reaped many of the immediate gains from the Industrial Revolution, with some of the great fortunes of the world created as a result. Over time, however, an increased supply of capital resulted in an increased demand for (and productivity of) labor, and real wages increased dramatically in the 20th century. This will again occur. But the process takes time, and we must not destroy it in its infancy.

The divergence between the fortunes of labor (Main Street) and capital (Wall Street) have left many on Main Street confused and bitter. In the view of many Americans, company profits seem to come at the expense of social well-being. Thus, it is not surprising that concept of "stakeholder" capitalism—a kinder, gentler corporation taking increased social "responsibility" for its many constituents—is in vogue.

What Downsizing Is All About

Unfortunately, many proponents of this ideology are unthinkingly advocating that we waste resources and handicap our competitiveness to avoid the short-term costs of adjusting to the new world. Increased productivity comes not from relentless growth, but from making better use of the resources we have. This is what downsizing is all about. Traditional, shareholder-based capitalism is not broken, although there are many changes in practices and restrictive regulations that would make it function much better.

These are dangerous times. The economic and social dislocations being caused by the Third Industrial Revolution threaten to undermine the stability of societies—and governments—around the world. Before the revolution concludes, we may witness the failure of one or more Western democracies as extreme brands of political activism find their voice once again and rise up in a bid for control. Faced with a choice between anarchy and non-democratic governments, some societies will opt for the latter. We must not be seduced.

Given the macroeconomic policies we have developed in the last six chapters, these two perspectives present us with a lot to consider. Jensen and Fagan present a case for letting the market proceed, continuing to make sometimes unpopular adjustments. They remind us that the potential for intervention is great, and believe that tampering with market forces is dangerous to capitalism's future. Barnet acknowledges that the unfettered market is creating more workers than jobs and presents a distressing picture of the future for unskilled workers worldwide. He also reports on studies demonstrating that "tinkering" with macroeconomic policy is less effective today than in the past.

Exercises

1. According to Jensen and Fagan, what are the results of these corporate changes from the Third Industrial Revolution? Since 1973, what macroeconomic effects have we seen from this revolution? What are the costs of this revolution? The benefits? How are they distributed among the population?
2. Review Barnet's suggestions for dealing with the job crisis. In what ways are they traditional types of macroeconomic policies? In what ways are they nontraditional? Develop a response to these suggestions using arguments put forth by Jensen and Fagan.
3. In Jensen and Fagan's view, is there a role for macroeconomic policy? Explain.
4. Barnet writes, "The lack of decently compensated jobs under decent working conditions is a global deficit so vast as to require fundamental rethinking about the global economic system itself. The global machine for producing goods and services in ever greater quantities depends upon a growing population of consumers with enough money in their pockets to keep the system going." Do U.S. macroeconomic goals fit into Barnet's call for a "fundamental rethinking about the global economic system"? Explain your answer.
5. List the ways the global nature of capitalism at the millennium hinders traditional macroeconomic policy.
6. Henry Ford said, "If you cut wages, you just cut the number of your customers." Was he right? Explain your answer using macroeconomic theory.
7. Collect recent data on unemployment rates and income distribution worldwide. Review the cases presented by Barnet and Jensen and Fagan. Do your data support either of these two perspectives? In what ways?

INTERNATIONAL ECONOMICS AND FINANCE

With each passing decade, the nations of the world grow increasingly interdependent. When weighing various macroeconomic policy options, U.S. decision makers must consider international economic conditions. In the past economists were primarily concerned with domestic monetary and fiscal policy and any perceived impact international activities might have on these policies. Economist Christopher Colclough noted this over a decade ago:

> This debate therefore has tended to see the choices for economic policy, and the causes of economic problems, in essentially national terms. The monetarist view leads to removing barriers to competition in the context of national monetary restraint; the neo-Keynesian to controlling cost-inflation by keeping down wages and using government intervention to manipulate total domestic demand. If, however, the major causes of inflation are not wholly, or even primarily national, a different perspective on policy has to be allowed. Such a perspective would have to take an analysis of the existing relationships between countries in the international economy as being of central importance to the design of effective national policies for restoring growth without inflation. Here, the current debate embraces, if anything, an even wider ideological spectrum than that which informs the national policy discussion. At the same time, it is more helpful, since it identifies realities in the world economy which tend to be omitted from domestic policy analysis, yet which are crucial to the fortunes of individual countries within it.
>
> —Christopher Colclough, "Lessons from the Development Debate for Western Economic Policy," *International Affairs*, Summer 1982, p. 490.

As far as international issues were concerned, decision makers examined the value of a nation's currency, or its exchange rate; the balance of payments; and perhaps protectionist tendencies that might exist in the world economy. Today, however, more complex questions arise involving volatile exchange rates; the economic power of an increasingly unified Europe; the integration of Eastern Europe and the former Soviet Union into the Western market system; China's rapid economic growth; the changes in various international institutions, such as the IMF; Japanese trade policies; and the overall increase in the level of world trade.

In Chapter 2 we saw how global economic activity has become more integrated by technological change transforming production, finance, trade, information systems, and communications throughout the world. These changes have caused economic and financial markets to become more integrated, and this increased interdependence has affected national political decisions, social and environmental policy, and culture.

By the early 1990s, world trade in goods approached $4 trillion, more than double the level in 1980, and represented almost 17 percent of the world's output. Trade in services surpassed $1 trillion. It is to this global economy that we now turn. First we shall examine the implications of increasing international interdependence and the theory behind international trade. We next survey the often unpredictable arena of international finance. Finally, we shall turn our attention to the developing nations and examine the problems and challenges they face.

20

International Trade and Interdependence

INTRODUCTION

As we have noted previously, interdependence among nations is a major feature of the modern world economy, and this will be a salient theme throughout the remainder of this book. To understand this concept properly and apply it to the problems we will be examining, we must be more specific about it. By the term *economic interdependence*, we mean that all countries are affected by the events of an economic nature that occur in many other countries. For example, many industrialized nations rely on developing nations for raw materials and other resources. In turn, many developing nations import manufactured finished goods from industrialized nations. The degree of interdependence is, of course, different for every nation. For example, the Japanese economy is seriously affected by increased oil prices yet relatively unaffected by Costa Rica's decision to increase banana prices. On the other hand, the Costa Rican economy, also strongly affected by an oil price increase, has the flexibility to shift its imports of steel from the United States to Japan.

Economic interdependence describes the effect of the complex international flow of goods, services, and capital among nations. It helps us understand how individuals, businesses, and nations must first exchange their currencies before exchanging goods and services. To acquire Japanese Toyotas, a U.S. auto importer must first exchange dollars for yen in a currency market. Then the automobile transaction can be completed.

Financial markets are interdependent as well. For example, if real interest rates fall in Germany and at the same time rise in the United States, investors are likely to sell their German bonds and invest the proceeds in U.S. bonds generating a better return. If Mexico experiences political instability or increasing inflation, domestic and foreign investors will likely transfer funds from Mexico to the United States or Europe. Information and communications technology has increased both the magnitude and speed of these transfers and facilitated international interdependence.

The nature of this contemporary interdependence involves not only the exchange of goods and services but technology transfers, financial capital movements, and factors affecting the international division of labor. For the past three centuries, raw materials and resources as well as technology provided the impetus for trade. Indeed, much of the motivation for the geographical explorations of the fifteenth century was the search for trade routes and later for colonies from which raw materials could be exported cheaply. Later, with the Industrial Revolution, the ability to manufacture and export products cheaply became a motivation for trade. While capital has always been highly mobile, seeking the highest profits worldwide, today the transfer of technology has made it very easy to set up operations in places where wages and other production costs are low. Increasingly, industrialized nations are losing jobs and exports to developing countries, which offer an abundance of low-wage labor.

||| 1. What other examples of economic interdependence are there? |

In this chapter, we shall begin to explore various aspects of this interdependence and its implications: the extent of world trade, the role of multinational corporations, and international trade theory and policy.

WORLD TRADE

As shown in Figure 20.1, the total volume of world trade has increased dramatically in the past three decades. In 1965, the total value of international trade was estimated at approximately $200 billion, but by 1995 it had increased to over $4 trillion. Approximately 70 percent of international trade takes place among the industrialized nations, including the United States, Japan, and countries of Europe, Asia, and the Pacific Basin. In 1995 the United States alone accounted for some 12.6 percent of world exports, with Germany accounting for another 12 percent and Japan following with just under 10 percent.

While international trade is important to all countries, the extent of its importance depends in large measure on the relationship of exports to the country's total output. Table 20.1 shows this relationship for several Newly Industrializing Countries. Taiwan's exports accounted for 26.3 percent of its total output in 1970 and 50.5 percent in 1990. Mexican exports accounted for 3.4 percent of total output in 1970 and 18.9 percent in 1990. For Korea, exports grew from 9.4 percent in 1970 to 32.6 percent in 1990. Exports for Hong Kong and Singapore continue to play an important role in the economy, while in Mexico and Argentina exports are becoming increasingly important.

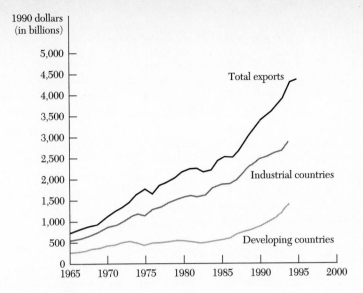

FIGURE 20.1 Growth in World Exports, 1965–1995

Source: International Monetary Fund.

2. Looking at Table 20.1, identify the countries with the most rapidly expanding export sectors.

TABLE 20.1 Newly Industrializing Countries 1965–1990

	Total Exports as a Percentage of Gross Product			
	1970	1975	1980	1990
Taiwan	26.3	34.5	49.4	50.7[a]
Korea	9.4	24.3	28.5	32.6
Hong Kong	56.4	49.0	49.6	50.1
Singapore	81.1	94.5	178.0	132.9
Brazil	6.5	7.1	8.3	6.7
Mexico	3.4	3.5	8.5	18.9
Argentina	8.3	8.4	14.3	15.2

Sources: United Nations, *Handbook of International Trade and Development Statistics* (New York: United Nations, various years); World Bank, *World Debt Tables* (Washington, D.C.: World Bank, 1985, 1992); Council for Economic Planning and Development, Republic of China, *Taiwan Statistical Data Book*, 1984; International Monetary Fund, *World Economic Outlook*, 1992.

[a]Estimate.

WORLD TRADE

MULTINATIONAL FIRMS AND THE INTERNATIONALIZATION OF PRODUCTION

Besides the rapid growth in imports and exports as a percentage of total output, another way to examine economic interdependence is to look at the internationalization of production. We can analyze this dimension of interdependence by examining the capital flows among nations (rather than the flows of trade). Some of these capital movements come from foreign investment and result in the internationalization of capital and labor.

We can understand this process more readily by tracing the history of the operations of multinational corporations. These institutions more than any others have created a new international division of labor on a global scale. In 1776 Adam Smith was well aware that merchants had little loyalty to the home country if profits on capital were greater abroad:

> The capital, however, that is acquired to any country by commerce and manufactures, is all a very precarious and uncertain possession, till some part of it has been secured and realized in the cultivation and improvement of its lands. A merchant, it has been said very properly, is not necessarily the citizen of any particular country. It is in a great measure indifferent to him from what place he carries on his trade; and a very trifling disgust will make him remove his capital, and together with it all the industry which it supports, from one country to another. No part of it can be said to belong to any particular country, till it has been spread as it were over the face of that country, either in buildings, or in the lasting improvement of lands.
>
> —Adam Smith, *The Wealth of Nations*, p. 196.

The modern multinational corporation (MNC), however, is a feature of this century, having matured in the post–World War II period. The history of a typical U.S. multinational corporation might be as follows: The corporation begins its initial production for the U.S. market only, then it exports its products. Next, it creates a factory abroad because of inexpensive labor and the accessibility of raw materials. Finally, the new foreign subsidiary's production is distributed in the local economy, and some is exported back to the United States. When a U.S. firm either builds a production facility or takes over an existing facility in another nation, direct investment occurs.

The incredible growth in world trade since the 1950s has to a large extent been driven by the emergence, growth, and continued transformation of multinational corporations. These firms have provided the mechanism to bring together natural resources, labor, capital, technology, and entrepreneurial ability for the specialization and division of labor to produce goods and services on a global scale. International economist Michael Moffitt, in "Economics Decline, Reagan Style," (*U.S. Policy*; Summer, 1985), has asserted that the rise of the MNC

> represents the central macroeconomic event of the postwar world, the significance of which neither academic analysis nor policy has fully grasped. While most economists and politicians discuss world trade as if individual nations were

engaged in shipping products to and from one another, the rise of multinational corporations has made these conventional concepts of world trade obsolete.

The organizational structure of multinational corporations has changed as well. In the early stages of its development, the MNC might locate its headquarters, housing the financial, strategic planning, and decision-making activities, in a developed country. The MNC might locate its marketing, product development, research and development, and human resource development operations elsewhere. Production might operate in a number of different countries. Historically, MNC production was directed at both export and local markets; the modern expansion of MNC operations has caused production to become internationalized on a global scale. People in many countries depend on decisions made in boardrooms of corporations in New York, Stuttgart, or Tokyo for their jobs and the products they consume. Individual MNCs based in the United States increasingly depend on other countries for their labor, resources, and markets to a far greater extent than that suggested by the U.S. export/GDP ratio of about 10 percent. The continued growth of MNCs directly affects national social, economic, political, and cultural institutions.

||| 3. What implications does the MNC's changing character have for the nation-state and domestic policy making? |

The transformation of global economic and financial systems is changing the way we think and talk about multinational corporations. For example, we may read or hear about the "virtual" or "stateless" MNC. Companies are forming alliances and partnerships with former rivals to take advantage of new opportunities or merely to survive in a more competitive global market system. Today's multinationals are larger and more diverse than ever. They invest and produce throughout the globe, especially in Latin America, in Southeast Asia, and in the transitional countries of Eastern Europe. Figure 20.2 illustrates the flow of foreign direct investment into both developed and developing countries between 1986 and 1995. Over the past few years, foreign direct investment has increased to both developed and developing countries—yet another indication of increased global financial integration.

Multinational corporation–related capital movements gradually transfer control of the accumulation and allocation of capital from institutions that are essentially national in character to financial institutions with a global orientation. Each national economy is more thoroughly integrated into the world capital market and is increasingly affected by events in other national economies. Multinationalization breeds increasing interdependence.

Many policy makers are reluctant to grant so much freedom of operation to one or a combination of private sector institutions. State and provincial governments worldwide have called for the control of MNCs. Others, however, envision with concern one homogenized world of consumers, all with similar tastes and lifestyles. This concern, in fact, is part of the desire of some countries to create a new international economic order.

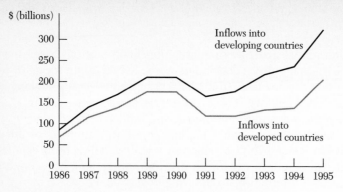

FIGURE 20.2 Foreign Direct Investment, 1986–1995
Source: *Survey of Current Business*, July 1996.

4. Has the multinational corporation changed since Adam Smith's time? Do you think Smith would be surprised at these changes?

THE MODERN THEORY OF INTERNATIONAL TRADE

Modern economic interdependence and the influence of multinational corporations have led to more complex national trade questions in the 1990s. Before examining these questions, however, we need to understand why trade takes place. The simple answer to this question relies on the theory of comparative advantage, which suggests that free trade is most beneficial to world economies. We shall examine the theory behind international trade, a few of the more convincing arguments for protection, and current trends toward free trade as well as the critics of such attempts.

Who Trades What, and Why?

How does an individual nation assume its place in the world economy? Why does one nation specialize in production of groundnuts; a second, textiles; a third, aircraft; and a fourth, financial services? One of the first economists to deal with this question was Adam Smith, and in 1817 David Ricardo refined Smith's ideas to develop the general approach that we still use today. This approach to understanding trade is based on two basic concepts, absolute and comparative advantage.

Some assumptions will greatly facilitate matters by allowing us to deal with the essentials. In our hypothetical world, we have two nations, producing two goods. Perfect competition exists everywhere, there are no transportation costs, and labor cannot move between the two nations. The costs of production in terms of labor hours are assumed to be as follows:

	Cost to Produce 1 Unit (Hours of Labor)	
	Wheat	Cloth
United Kingdom	10	20
France	15	45

Under these assumptions, the United Kingdom can produce both goods with less labor cost than can France. The United Kingdom, therefore, has an absolute advantage in producing both wheat and cloth, and France has an absolute disadvantage in each. Having an **absolute advantage** simply means that a nation can produce goods (in this case, both wheat and cloth) more efficiently than another.

This does not mean, however, that the United Kingdom produces and exports both goods and that France produces neither of them. To find out what production and exchange will take place, we must examine the production trade-off ratios between products within each nation; that is, we must see how much cloth must be given up to produce more wheat. In our example, one unit of wheat is produced in the United Kingdom with half the amount of labor time that it takes to produce a unit of cloth; with other factors constant, one unit of cloth will exchange for two units of wheat. In France—again, because of the relative costs of production—one unit of cloth can be exchanged for three units of wheat. This gives us the following internal rates of exchange of cloth for wheat:

$$\text{United Kingdom} \quad 1 \text{ cloth} = 2 \text{ wheat}$$

$$\text{France} \quad\quad\quad 1 \text{ cloth} = 3 \text{ wheat}$$

or

$$\text{United Kingdom} \quad \tfrac{1}{2} \text{ cloth} = 1 \text{ wheat}$$

$$\text{France} \quad\quad\quad \tfrac{1}{3} \text{ cloth} = 1 \text{ wheat}$$

By comparing the internal rates of exchange in each of the two countries, a trader might reason, "If I could buy one unit of wheat in Paris, ship it to London, and exchange it there for cloth, I could get one-half of a unit of cloth; if I exchanged it in France, I would get only one-third of a unit of cloth. My gain from this trade is one-sixth of a unit of cloth. On the other hand, taking one unit of cloth from Paris to London and exchanging it for wheat would bring me only two units of wheat, whereas I could have gotten three units of wheat at home in France. I lose one unit of wheat in the process." Note that taking one unit of cloth from London to Paris results in a gain of one unit of wheat (two units of wheat in the United Kingdom but three units in France).

Our trader would quickly conclude that France has a comparative advantage in the production and export of wheat, even though France has an absolute disadvantage in both goods. By similar reasoning, we conclude that the United Kingdom has a comparative advantage in the production of cloth. A **comparative advantage** means that one nation can produce a product relatively, not absolutely, more efficiently than another nation. (A nation with an absolute advantage can produce a variety of products more efficiently than another.) Trade is expanded when nations produce products where they possess a comparative advantage.

Although the assumptions underlying this theory are "unreal" in today's world, economists since David Ricardo's time have shown that his comparative advantage model is valid for a world of many nations producing many different goods. Other economists have demonstrated that dropping the assumptions of perfect competition and zero transportation costs reduces the gain from specialization and trade but does not invalidate the theory. The only assumption crucial to these results is labor immobility. If workers migrated freely from country to country, we could have exchanges of labor rather than exchanges of products.

Comparative Advantage and Output

In the following example, we can see what happens to total output of two goods (here, units of wheat and cloth) when trade occurs. We can also use a production possibilities curve to help us understand the effect of trade on total output. Unlike our previous example, we don't know the amount of labor involved in the production of each of these outputs, nor do we know the size of the labor forces. While we cannot calculate total output precisely, the production levels shown in Table 20.2 are consistent with our hypothetical costs and rates of exchange.

For the production levels given, France has the absolute advantage in the production of both products. If neither country is involved in international trade, each must use part of its resources to produce some of each product to meet domestic demand. If France uses half of its resources to produce wheat and half to produce cloth, cloth production will be 400 units and wheat production 1,200 units. If Brazil divides its labor resources so that six-sevenths produce wheat and one-seventh produces cloth, 600 units of wheat and 100 units of cloth will be produced. Total world output will be that shown in Table 20.3. Figure 20.3 shows the production possibilities curves for this example.

5. In what product does Brazil have the comparative advantages? Why would France want to trade with Brazil at all?

TABLE 20.2 Total Country Production

| | Units per Year | | |
	Wheat		Cloth
Brazil	700	or	700
France	2,400	or	800

TABLE 20.3 Total World Output without Trade

	Units per Year	
	Wheat	Cloth
Brazil	600	100
France	1,200	400
Total	1,800	500

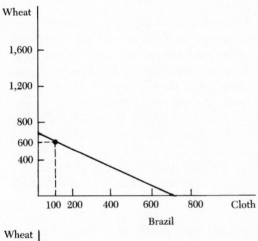

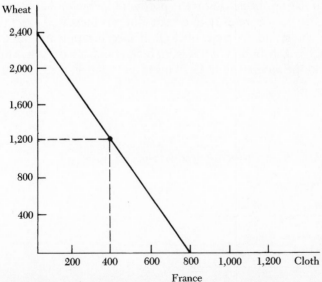

■ FIGURE 20.3 Production Possibilities without Trade

TABLE 20.4 Total World Output with Specialization

| | Units per Year | |
	Wheat	Cloth
Brazil	0	700
France	2,400	0
Total	2,400	700

The two countries can expand total output by specializing. France has a comparative advantage in wheat production, and Brazil has a comparative advantage in cloth. If each country produces only its specialty, world output expands as shown in Table 20.4.

With trade, the countries can exchange some of their expanded output so that both countries have both products. Of the wheat France produces, it uses some for domestic consumption and exports the rest. Of the cloth Brazil produces, it uses some for domestic consumption and exports the rest. After trading, many results are possible, but we might get a result similar to that shown in Table 20.5. In this case, the countries exchange 1,000 units of wheat from France for 500 units of cloth from Brazil. Figure 20.4 shows the production possibilities curves of Brazil and France with trade.

6. Who has gained what through specialization and trade?
7. In the example just given, what are some other possible combinations of exchange?

Thus, if each nation specializes in the product in which it has a comparative advantage, world output of both commodities is increased—in this case by 600 units of wheat and 200 units of cloth. If specialization and trade result in some reasonable distribution of this gain, both countries are better off than they would be in the absence of trade. This is the essence, then, of the argument for free trade.

TABLE 20.5 Total World Output with Specialization and Trade

| | Units per Year | |
	Wheat	Cloth
Brazil	1,000	200
France	1,400	500
Total	2,400	700

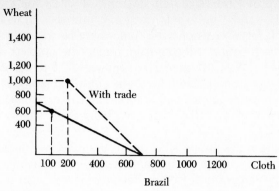

Brazil

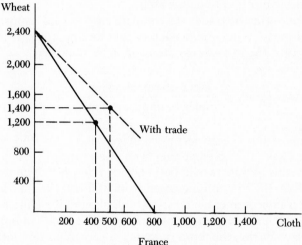

France

— FIGURE 20.4 Production Possibilities with Trade

Terms of Trade

In the example from the previous section, we can not only determine whether Brazil and France can benefit from specialization and trade, we can also examine exchange ratios or a **terms of trade** in which both will gain. By looking at the internal or domestic production ratios within each nation—the production possibilities in Table 20.2—we can determine how much wheat must be given up in order to produce an additional unit of cloth. Brazil can produce 700 units of wheat or 700 units of cloth during a year, so producing an additional unit of wheat necessarily means reducing cloth production by 1 unit. France can produce 2,400 units of wheat or 800 units of cloth, so the internal production trade-off is 3 units of wheat for each additional unit of cloth produced. To produce an additional unit of cloth, French wheat production must be reduced by 3 units.

With the internal production trade-off at 1 unit of wheat for 1 unit of cloth in Brazil (1W:1C) and 3 units of wheat for 1 unit of cloth in France (3W:1C), we can look for a terms of trade somewhere between those two ratios and show that each nation will gain from trade. The simplest trading ratio within that range is 2W:1C. Both nations gain with a 2:1 terms of trade. Brazil is able to exchange 1 unit of cloth for 2 units of wheat (twice as much as domestic production would allow), and France is able to exchange 2 units of its wheat for 1 unit of cloth, rather than sacrificing a full 3 units for an additional unit.

Several other trading ratios are possible in this example. In practice, the final terms of trade will depend on the bargaining strength of each nation as well as other economic and political factors. Each nation will want to negotiate the best possible terms of trade for itself.

To measure the terms of trade, we compare import and export price ratios—that is, we measure the price a country pays for imports and the price it receives for exports. We can express this as an index number:

$$\text{terms of trade} = \frac{\text{index of export prices}}{\text{index of import prices}} \times 100$$

For example, suppose the U.S. export price index was 113 in 1997 and the import price index was 95, both beginning from a base year of 1992 (at 100). In this case, the terms of trade would be $113/95 \times 100 = 119$. The terms of trade over the 1992–1997 period increased from 100 to 119, a 19 percent improvement. This improvement in terms of trade allowed the United States to give up 19 percent less in exports to obtain the same amount of imports.

For developing countries, the terms of trade is a very important influence on their capability to carry out their development plans and strategies. If their terms of trade declines, they have to pay relatively more for imports than they receive for their exports (that is, they must pay greater amounts of exports in return for imports). As we can see in Figure 20.5, the terms of trade for non-oil-exporting developing countries was below 100 from 1979 through the early 1990s.

Problems with the Theoretical Assumptions of Free Trade

This theoretical model of comparative advantage clearly shows that international trade benefits the trading nations. Since the 1800s, this theory has become the rationale for most economists' belief that free trade is good and anything that interferes with it—such as tariffs, quotas, and other protectionist measures—is, by definition, bad. But the theory itself has serious problems. As is often the case in economic analysis, these problems involve the assumptions of the model.

When Ricardo first developed the theory of comparative advantage, he assumed that costs remain constant no matter what the level of production. Therefore, a nation could increase its production to satisfy the needs of other

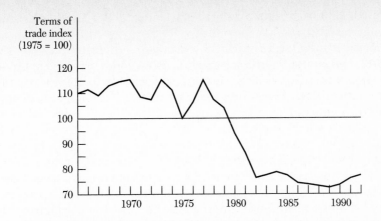

FIGURE 20.5 Terms of Trade of Non-Oil-Exporting Developing Countries

Sources: International Monetary Fund, *International Financial Statistics: Supplement on Trade Statistics* (Washington, D.C.: IMF, 1982), pp. 158–159; United Nations, *World Economic Survey, 1983* (New York: United Nations, 1983), tab. 2-3; International Monetary Fund, *World Economic Outlook, 1992* (Washington, D.C.: IMF, 1992), tab. A28.

nations without increasing its own costs. But modern economics has documented to the satisfaction of most, that since production is subject to diminishing returns, it is also subject to increasing costs—sooner or later, depending on what is being produced. In such a case, the increased costs may cancel out much, if not all, of the benefits of comparative advantage.

Ricardo also did not consider the large transportation costs that may be involved in international trade. These often raise the costs of imported goods considerably over those produced domestically and cancel out some of the benefits of international trade.

Finally, Ricardo assumed that the factors of production that are mobile within a country may be immobile internationally. These days labor still is fairly immobile, but capital funds move freely internationally. It is not so easy, as the modern era has shown, for a country to abandon production of one product and move resources into the production of another without serious reallocation problems. Further, moving resources from one industry to another can cause serious political difficulties beyond the practical economic realities.

Despite these limitations, the theory of comparative advantage does provide a useful perspective for viewing the trading process. However, it cannot alone explain the much more complicated process of the internationalization of world production.

Restrictions to Free Trade: Protectionism

Free trade exists if there are no barriers to the export and import of goods and services. But, historically, when unemployment, job loss, reduced profits, and recession threaten a nation, domestic industry, or region, the predictable response is a call for increased protection of domestic goods and thus domestic jobs.

Nations use several types of trade restrictions, but the most common have been tariffs and quotas. **Tariffs** are simply taxes on goods imported or exported, while **quotas** are limits on the quantities of goods imported or exported. More recently **orderly marketing agreements (OMAs)** have been popular. OMAs are nonmonetary barriers that absolutely or quantitatively limit imports and thus limit the choice between imported and domestic goods. Importers reap the profits from the higher prices commanded by the limited supply (assuming that there is a relatively inelastic demand for the product).

In general, tariffs succeed in their objective—they protect a special interest at the expense of the whole population. In other words, a few people are helped a lot, while all citizens are hurt a little because they pay higher prices for the goods and services on which tariff duties are imposed.

Arguments for Protectionism. Nations establish trade barriers for many reasons. Most often protectionist measures are designed to protect some interest in the home country. Special-interest groups in the United States often appeal to Congress for protection. Industries also seek protection from "unfair trade practices." For example, some governments subsidize particular industries, giving those products a price advantage over other viable producers. Representatives of new industries also use the "infant industries" argument that they need help to gain a foothold in world markets already flush with producers that might "overpower" the infant industry in a competitive marketplace. This argument is common in developing nations hoping to diversify their primarily agricultural base with a new industry. With time, however, particularly in the industrialized countries, the infant industry might grow to be a major competitor in the market, offering a better product at a better price.

Included in the protectionists' argument is another reason for tariff levies—retaliation. Governments have often increased tariffs in response to increases by trading partners. The 1930 Smoot-Hawley tariff, for example, set off a worldwide round of tariff increases. This "do unto others as they have done unto you" philosophy has also been used simply for the sake of self-esteem. As a result, consumers in both nations pay the higher price. At worst, such retaliation can compound recession into worldwide depression. During the 1930s, international trade almost disappeared—one important factor in the length and depth of the Depression. More recently, in the 1990s, the United States threatened retaliatory action against French wine.

At times Congress has considered proposals that it levy tariffs for the purpose of raising revenue, since the proceeds from the tax are collected by the government. This is well and good, but there are many more effective ways of raising revenue. Besides, if the tariff prices the imported good above that of the domestic product, the government will not collect any revenue, since the consumer will be priced out of the import market and will purchase only the domestic product.

Another protectionist argument centers on the need to reduce the competition of cheap foreign labor to protect domestic labor and domestic wage rates.

Protection is also very sensitive to political cycles. For example, during presidential elections, some candidates propose protectionism to win political support from some areas of the United States hurt by exports.

Other arguments on trade policy have run from the rather dry and abstract to the invective. The "national defense" argument falls into both categories. The merchant marine and the oil industry have argued for protection, since they are essential in times of national emergency.

> 8. Congress adopted import quotas to protect the oil industry for "defense" reasons from 1954 to 1973. How did these protective quotas, designed to encourage U.S. oil production, work during the OPEC oil embargo of 1973? As a consequence, what happened to domestic reserves of oil?

Costs of Protectionism. Despite the many arguments in support of protectionist policies, an analysis of the consequences for consumers in each nation and the overall international trading system shows that one group may gain while another loses, and the entire trading system often suffers. The practice of protectionism results in all consumers paying higher prices for goods and services. The higher cost of imported goods may contribute to inflationary pressures. Protected jobs and firms may be sheltered from the competitive dynamics of the market, which would normally force them to allocate their scarce resources more efficiently and more productively.

The costs of protectionism can be high. Australia's Center for International Economics in 1990 concluded that if all regions in the global trading system reduced their tariff and nontariff barriers by 50 percent, the total gains from freer trade, measured in terms of increases in worldwide output, would be around $740 billion (more than $130 per person). A 1988 report issued by the Organization for Economic Cooperation and Development (the OECD, which includes the twenty-two advanced Western countries) concluded that agricultural protectionism cost the OECD countries about $72 billion a year. With free trade in agriculture, the study argues, personal incomes would increase by 1 percent, and less than 1 percent of the workforce would be displaced. The cost per farm job saved was estimated at $20,000 per year. In addition, free trade in agriculture would potentially increase Third World nations' agricultural exports by $30 billion a year.

In the 1997 *Economic Report of the President*, the Clinton administration noted the costs and benefits of free trade:

Defenders of free trade can do it a disservice by promoting it as a way to create more jobs or to reduce bilateral trade deficits. Jobs, the unemployment rate, and the overall balance of payments [see Chapter 21] are ultimately a consequence of macroeconomic policies, not trade barriers. The real objective of free trade is to raise living standards by ensuring that more Americans are working in areas where the United States is comparatively more productive than its trading partners. In a full-employment economy, trade has more impact on the *distribution* of jobs than on the *quantity* of jobs.

—*Economic Report of the President*, 1997, p. 21.

INTERNATIONAL TRADE ISSUES

As the volume of world trade has grown over the past decade, nations have joined together in agreements to reduce trade barriers between them and to move toward freer trade. These agreements have included establishing trading blocs between a group of specific countries to reduce barriers among themselves (increasing both trade and the size of the market), as well as multinational agreements to reduce barriers throughout the world. Among the trade agreements important to the United States (as well as to the other countries involved) are the North American Free Trade Agreement (NAFTA) signed in 1992, the Asia-Pacific Economic Cooperation (APEC) agreements joining twelve Asia-Pacific countries, and the General Agreement on Tariffs and Trade (GATT) ending in 1994, which established the World Trade Organization (WTO) and assigned it the task of monitoring, negotiating, and settling trade disputes. Meanwhile, the integration of Europe continued with the Maastricht Treaty officially establishing the European Union in 1993. While the 1990s have generally been a period of trade liberalization, tension remains as Japan's neomercantilist trade practices are slow to change.

North American Free Trade Agreement (NAFTA)

In 1992 the North American Free Trade Agreement joined Canada, the United States, and Mexico into a multilateral trading bloc. NAFTA provides guiding principles for the reduction of tariffs on goods traded between these countries over fifteen years, until trade barriers no longer exist between the three. The NAFTA agreement was signed by President Bush in 1992 and ratified by Congress in late 1993, despite considerable debate in the 1992 presidential campaign (with Ross Perot opposing NAFTA and Bill Clinton supporting a modified NAFTA agreement). Some changes were negotiated in the areas of the environment and job loss.

NAFTA was hotly debated. Opponents argued that job losses would offset increased profits to manufacturers and lower consumer prices. Supporters argued that more jobs and increased wealth would result for all three nations. Since implementation in 1994, critics point to data validating their predictions. In the first two years of the agreement, Mexico imported fewer U.S. goods than in previous years, at the same time the level of Mexican exports to the United States rose dramatically. Even supporters of the agreement have adjusted their earlier prediction of U.S. job growth. A currency crisis in the Mexican peso complicated interpretation of early results of the treaty. While some argue that the jury is still out on NAFTA, others—politicians and economists alike—look ahead to more free trade agreements in South America and the establishment of a Free Trade Area of the Americas (FTAA).

> 9. How has the United States reacted to NAFTA? Who gains? Who loses? Are there ways to ameliorate the losses? Should the winners share with the losers? Explain.

Asia-Pacific Economic Cooperation (APEC) Agreements

As Pacific Rim countries have continued to grow in importance to the world economy, they have established trade agreements among themselves and with some of their traditional trading partners. In 1989 representatives from twelve Asia-Pacific countries—Australia, Canada, Japan, the Republic of Korea, New Zealand, the United States, Brunei, Indonesia, Malaysia, the Republic of the Philippines, Singapore, and Thailand—met to discuss global and regional economic development, global trade liberalization, regional cooperation, and future economic cooperation in the Asia-Pacific region. These formal discussions continue and are called Asia-Pacific Economic Cooperation (APEC). As U.S. trade with this region increases, we can expect that these negotiations will grow in importance and expand to include other rapidly growing Pacific Rim economies.

General Agreement on Tariffs and Trade (GATT)

While NAFTA promotes free trade among three countries, much of the post–World War II period has seen an overall reduction in the excessive protection of the Depression years. Nations have, of course, disagreed as to which goods should be exempt from tariff reductions and where tariff levels should be set. Protectionist tendencies are particularly prevalent during periods of severe recession as countries compete for shrinking markets. Still, primarily through international negotiations in organizations such as the **General Agreement on Tariffs and Trade (GATT)**, treaties increase trade through agreed-on reductions in tariffs.

Ninety-nine nations participated in the General Agreement on Tariffs and Trade, Multilateral Trade Negotiations, or the Tokyo Rounds, which concluded in 1979 after five years of negotiation over tariff reductions and the elimination of nontariff impediments and distortions to trade. The most recent GATT attempt to reduce barriers was launched in 1986, in Punta del Este, Uruguay, and continued through 1993. Delegates negotiated reductions in both tariff and nontariff barriers, on everything from intellectual property, including patents and copyrights, to services such as telecommunications.

The most controversial part of the Uruguay Round was the agreement to establish the World Trade Organization (WTO) as the institution responsible for governing international trade. The WTO represents over 120 countries. The WTO has the duty of implementing the agreements in the Uruguay Round by administering the agreements and providing a forum for settling disputes. The WTO replaces GATT as the central institution working to eliminate trade barriers. In its few years of existence, the WTO has had its share of critics and supporters. Critics argue that the WTO oversteps its bounds in issues of national sovereignty. As WTO makes more decisions, the organization has come under increased scrutiny from its supporters, who want increased powers and enforcement of those powers, and critics, who wish to reduce WTO's importance.

European Integration

Twelve European nations with a total population of 320 million and a GDP rivaling that of the United States formally merged into the European Union in 1993. (In 1995 three more countries joined the EU, and more are expected to follow.) The latest in a series of European organizational efforts beginning in 1952 with the European Coal and Steel Community, the EU is a trading bloc designed to liberalize trade between member nations, encourage cooperation in intergovernmental and security affairs, and facilitate the movement toward a single currency. The economic goal of the EU is to synchronize economic policies promoting European economic growth and stabilization. Gains from integration are predicted at around 6.2 percent of combined GDP, or $230 billion.

Continued integration efforts are not easy. Strikes by French farmers and German miners emphasize the discord within member nations, as the EU places regional economic decisions above national ones. Questions remain as to whether the EU will open its doors to trade with the rest of the world (thus opening a growing European market to U.S. products), or whether it will instead focus on trade among member nations and construct barriers to trade with other nations. For U.S. trade, the future direction of EU economic policy is an important one.

10. If a nation encourages free trade, what happens to the laborer whose job is threatened by increased domestic demand for imported substitutes?

Japan as a Neomercantilist Trading Partner

While NAFTA, APEC discussions, the WTO, and the European Union aim at reducing the potential for trade wars, fears of such disputes have not vanished. In particular, some concern remains regarding Japan's neomercantilist trade policies. Some policy makers working on Japan trade issues have concluded that prior to the mid-1990s, Japan's trade policies were mercantilist in nature and that free trade interrupted their organized markets.

11. Does it sound as if the Japanese will spread the doctrine of laissez-faire in the near future?

Japanese exports to U.S. markets account for over half of Japan's total trade surplus. Needless to say, there is a great deal of concern over Japanese trade policies, which are generally exclusionary and sometimes violate international trade law. The strategies with which the Japanese encourage strategic industries often puts U.S. domestic competitors at a disadvantage.

U.S. government and trade officials and businesspeople have long been frustrated with the Japanese. Intensive rounds of bilateral trade negotiations have increased the frustration on both sides. Tariff barriers *have* fallen over the past few years, but other restrictive practices have made entry into some Japanese markets difficult.

Some Japanese exporters have created special problems. In the late 1980s, some high-technology industries began feeling a competitive pinch, and Japanese firms were found guilty of dumping semiconductors, computer chips, and telephones on the U.S. market. **Dumping** occurs when an exporting nation sells its product at a lower price in an importing country than it does in its own country. In one case AT&T, the nation's largest manufacturer of telephone equipment, filed an official complaint that accused "Japan, Taiwan, and South Korea of 'dumping,' or selling goods below the cost of production to build market share—a violation of international trade law." In 1987 the United States instituted a protective tariff on $3 billion of Japanese imports to retaliate for semiconductor dumping. Permanent tariff duties were also imposed on the manufacturers of telecommunications equipment after the AT&T decision.

CONCLUSION

With protectionist measures, there is always an undercurrent of possible retaliation and trade wars similar to those of the 1930s, during which time international trade almost disappeared. In the past decade, however, the fear of retaliation seems not to have been an issue. Increasingly more economists are calling for the introduction of trade strategies as an improvement on free trade.

Developing countries are especially concerned about protectionist tendencies. They need to increase their exports in order to earn much-needed dollars and foreign currencies with which to repay the enormous debt that they have accrued during the past decade. A quota on imported steel would greatly affect a nation such as Brazil, which relies heavily on steel exports to earn foreign exchange. These nations have learned to play the game of protection as well. Several of the developing countries are using import controls as well as export subsidies to improve their trade positions. This trend has been caused by a minimal weakening of inflationary activity and the persistence of high unemployment levels.

Protection or free trade? Retaliation? Negotiated trade agreements? Some thirty years ago, in his 1977 presidential address to the twelfth biannual convention of the AFL-CIO, George Meany declared, "Free trade is a joke and a myth, and a government policy dedicated to 'free trade' is more than a joke—it is a prescription for disaster. The answer is fair trade—do unto others as they do unto you—barrier for barrier, closed door for closed door."

There can be no doubt that arguments over free trade will continue in the future, and the effects will be felt on currencies and domestic policies. In the next chapter, we measure international trade and survey the historical development of the institutions that permitted international exchange to develop and flourish in an increasingly interdependent world. We will also see how these institutions sometimes failed to develop appropriate policies for the ever-changing and complex world economy.

Review Questions

1. What linkages among nations have been most important in increasing interdependence in the world economy today?
2. When we say that the world economy is characterized by interdependence, does this mean that all nations are equally dependent on other nations, or are some nations more dominant and others more dependent? Why is that so?
3. How do multinational corporations lead to greater economic interdependence among nations?
4. What is the logic behind the theory of comparative advantage?
5. What is important about the terms of trade for a country?
6. What is the case for and against free trade?
7. The global economy is becoming more and more integrated. There are several trade blocs and efforts toward economic integration. Explain.

21 ═══ International Finance

INTRODUCTION

Having considered the theory and the recent history of international trade, we shall now turn our attention to issues of international finance and accounting for the international exchange of goods, services, investment, and other capital flows. Moneys flow from one nation to another when citizens or institutions of a given nation decide to lend to or borrow from foreigners and to import or export goods and services.

We begin our examination with a discussion of the **balance of payments**, which is the accounting scheme that governments and international organizations use for measuring trade between nations. We shall then move to a discussion of exchange rates and review how they respond to trade and financial transactions. Our discussion of exchange rates includes how international trade flows alter these rates, and how systems of exchange have changed throughout the century.

THE BALANCE OF PAYMENTS

All nations must eventually adjust their national economic policies to meet the demands of the international trading and financial system. Nations commonly keep track of these demands with a mechanism called the balance-of-payments accounting system. A balance-of-payments account is a statement of a nation's aggregate international financial transactions over a period of time, usually one year. The balance of payments is a statement that shows the exchange of a country's currency for foreign currencies for all of the international transactions of a country's citizens, businesses, and government during a year. It helps nations keep track of the flow of goods and services into and out of the country. In this accounting statement, all international economic

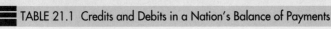

TABLE 21.1 Credits and Debits in a Nation's Balance of Payments

Positive Credits (+)	Negative Debits (−)
1. Any *receipt* of foreign money	1. Any *payment* to a foreign country
2. Any *earnings* of an investment in a foreign country	2. Any *earnings* on domestic investments by a foreign country
3. Any sale of goods or services abroad (*export*)	3. Any purchase of goods and services from abroad (*import*)
4. Any gift or aid *from* a foreign country	4. Any gift or aid *given* abroad
5. Any *sale* of stocks or bonds abroad	5. Any *purchase* of foreign stocks or bonds
6. Any foreign investment in this country	6. Any investment in a foreign country

and financial transactions must have either a positive or a negative effect on a nation's balance-of-payments accounts. Table 21.1 shows the effects of possible transactions.

The balance-of-payments accounting statement is divided into two major classifications: the current account and the capital account. For each of these accounts, payments are subtracted from receipts, and the difference is noted in the *Balance* column.

TABLE 21.2 U.S.International Transactions, 1995 (Millions of Dollars)

	Receipts (+)	Payments(−)	Balance
Current Account			
(1) Merchandise exports	$575,940		
(2) Merchandise imports		$−749,364	
Trade balance (1) + (2)			$−173,424
(3) Net investment income	182,659	−190,674	−8,016
(4) Net services	210,590	−142,230	68,360
(5) Net unilateral transfers			−35,075
Current account balance =			
(1) + (2) + (3) + (4) + (5)			$−148,154
Capital Measures			
(6) Capital outflows (U.S. assets abroad—offical reserve assets)		−298,114	
(7) Capital inflows (Foreign assets in U.S.— foreign official reserve assets)	314,705		
(8) Statistical discrepancy			31,548
Official Reserve Transactions Account =			
(1) + (2) + (3) + (4) + (5) + (6) + (7) + (8)			−$100,015
Method of Financing			
(9) Increase in U.S. official reserve assets		−9,742	
(10) Increase in foreign official assets	109,757		
Total financing of surplus			
Balance of payments =			
(1) + (2) + (3) + (4) + (5) + (6) + (7) + (8) + (9) + (10)			0

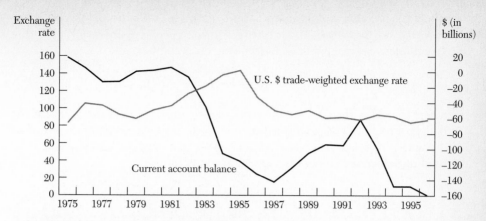

FIGURE 21.1 The U.S. Current Account Balance

The Current Account

The **current account** includes the import and export of all goods and services, investment income, and unilateral transfers during a year. Exports of goods and services create a receipt of income, while imports of goods command payments abroad, resulting in an outflow of income. Table 21.2 shows the magnitude of these components of the current account.

By far the largest category under the current account is the export and import of merchandise—cars, steel, raw materials, machines, and so forth. In 1995 U.S. merchandise exports totaled $575.9 billion, and merchandise imports totaled –$749.4 billion. The merchandise balance, often referred to as the **balance of trade**, for 1995 was –$173.4 billion. The balance of trade was negative because payments were larger than receipts.

Besides merchandise trade, the current account records investment income and services of various types. When we total all of the transactions in the current account, we get the current account balance. For 1995 this balance was –$148.2 billion. In contrast, as shown in Figure 21.1, the 1981 current account balance stood at +$6.9 billion.

Just as we examined the budget deficit within the framework of our leakages and injections model of National Income Accounting, we can look at trade deficits within the same context. In equilibrium, leakages equal injections:

$$\text{leakages} = \text{injections}$$

(1) $$S + Tx + M = I + G + X$$

Next, we can rewrite the equation in terms of the current account balance, which is in deficit in this case:

(2) $$X - M = S - I - G + Tx,$$

where I is domestic investment, G is government expenditures, $X - M$ is net exports (and here serves as a measure of the current account deficit), S is private domestic saving, and Tx is domestic tax receipts.

$$(3) \qquad\qquad (X - M) = S - I - (G - Tx),$$

where $X - M$ is the current account balance and $G - Tx$ is the government deficit. The following excerpt from the 1996 *Economic Report of the President* discusses this relationship and comments on economic policies that might be used to reduce deficits in the current account.

SOURCES OF THE U.S. TRADE DEFICIT

The trade balance is simply the difference between the value of goods and services sold by U.S. residents to foreigners and the value of goods and services that U.S. residents buy from foreigners. Most of what the United States produces (89 percent in 1995) is sold to residents of the United States; the rest is exported. And most of what the United States buys (88 percent in 1995) is produced here; the rest is imported. When we compare total production and total expenditure, those goods and services that we purchase from ourselves net out, and the difference is exports minus imports, or the trade balance. A trade deficit thus results when the Nation's expenditure exceeds its production.

Trade is by far the largest source of foreign income and foreign payments, but there are other external income flows; the main ones are interest and other investment earnings, aid grants, and transfers. Adding these other current flows to the trade balance produces the current account balance, which is the net income that the United States receives from the rest of the world. The current account balance thus represents the bottom line on the income statement of the United States. If it is positive, the United States is spending less than its total income and accumulating asset claims on the rest of the world. If it is negative, as it has been in most recent years, our expenditure exceeds our income, and we are borrowing from the rest of the world.

The net borrowing of the Nation can be expressed as the sum of the net borrowing by each of the principal sectors of the economy: government (Federal, State, and local), firms, and households. In other words, the current account deficit (CAD) is equal to the government's budget deficit ($G - Tx$, or net borrowing by the public sector) plus the difference between private sector investment and private sector saving ($I - S$, or net borrowing by the private sector):

$X - M$	=	I	−	S	+	$(G - Tx)$
current account deficit (CAD)		private investment		private saving		government deficit

The crucial insight of this identity is that the current account deficit is a macroeconomic phenomenon: it reflects an imbalance between national saving and national investment. The fact that the relationship is an identity and always holds true also means that any effective policy to reduce the current account deficit must, in the end, narrow the gap between U.S. saving and U.S. investment. (Note that while the identity is true, we cannot imply causation in these values.)

Source: *Economic Report of the President,* Washington, D.C.: U.S. Government Printing Office, 1996. pp. 250–251.

The Capital Account

The **capital account** includes all capital flows in and out of the United States. U.S. capital outflow represents the purchase of capital assets outside of the United States by the government, citizens, or corporations. The dollars used to purchase these assets flow out of the country. In return, the government, citizen, or business now owns an asset abroad. U.S. citizens or businesses might make bank deposits in other countries, purchase foreign stocks and bonds, or even buy foreign productive facilities (a plant, office, McDonald's franchise, etc.). All of these activities produce an increase in U.S. assets abroad, or an outflow of dollars—a payment in the balance of payments. On the other hand, if U.S. residents were to sell their foreign assets and bring the proceeds back home, this would be recorded as a receipt. In 1995, the net outflow of U.S. private capital amounted to –$270.3 billion, which represented payments in the capital account. Capital inflow into the United States, which occurs when foreign governments, institutions, corporations, or individuals increase their assets in the United States, amounted to $314.7 billion in 1995.

1. What do we lose by foreign direct investment in the United States? What do we gain when it occurs?

Balancing the Accounts

The balance of payments always "balances." Whatever surplus (net inflow) or deficit (net outflow) these transactions generate is offset by the use of official reserve assets of the U.S. government and the statistical discrepancy.

The *statistical discrepancy* category, line (8) in Table 21.2, is in one sense an accounting mechanism for balancing the accounts. It is simply the total of the items in the current and capital measurements—lines (1), (2), (4), (5), (7), and (8)—with the sign reversed. One reason this account is necessary is that the measurement of all international transactions is extremely complex. The government cannot accurately measure all of these transactions, particularly illegal ones; some transactions, both legal and illegal, will escape measurement. For 1995, the $107.4 billion deficit in the U.S. current and capital account items indicates a large outflow of dollars. This number could represent any or a combination of possible activities. The sizable deficit would put downward pressure on the dollar, reducing its value and "balancing" the deficit. Alternatively, other nations could hold on to the dollars that they had

| | Billions of Dollars | |
Year	Trade Surplus or Deficit	Current Account Surplus or Deficit
1975	$+12.4	$+18.1
1976	–6.1	+4.3
1977	–27.3	–14.3
1978	–29.8	–15.1
1979	–24.6	–.285
1980	–19.4	+2.3
1981	–16.1	+5.0
1982	–27.2	–11.4
1983	–57.8	–43.9
1984	–109.1	–98.9
1985	–121.8	–124.2
1986	–140.1	–152.1
1987	–152.9	–167.4
1988	–115.5	–128.4
1989	–91.8	–105.6
1990	–80.3	–94.6
1991	–29.9	–9.6
1992	–38.3	–62.6
1993	–72.0	–99.9
1994	–104.4	–148.4
1995	–105.1	–148.2

Source: *Economic Report of the President,* February 1997, p. 414.

received because of U.S. imports from their countries or U.S. capital flows to their countries. They might want to hold these dollars for future use. Whatever the specifics, to compensate for the imprecision involved in attempting to measure all international economic activities, the statistical discrepancy category mechanically balances the international accounts.

Table 21.3 shows trade and current account surpluses and deficits in the United States between 1975 and 1995.

2. If investment by Canada in the United States results in a "receipt" or positive effect on the U.S. balance of payments in the capital account, is this investment necessarily good for the United States? Why or why not?
3. What would be an example of a merchandise export? A government transfer payment? If you took $1,000 out of your bank account in the United States and put it in a bank in London, what effect would it have in the balance of payments accounts?

Trade Deficits

When reporters, economists, and politicians speak of balance-of-payments deficits (outflows of dollars) and surpluses (inflows of dollars), they may be referring only to the transactions in the current account or the current and capital accounts—and not in the balancing cash, gold, or bond accounts. The *basic balance* includes the balance on the current account added to the long-term capital movements. This basic balance normally shows a payments deficit (payments > receipts) or surplus (receipts > payments).

If we look only at the merchandise balance in the current account (the balance of trade), we find that the U.S. "balance" has historically been a surplus. In every year from 1893 until 1971, merchandise exports exceeded merchandise imports. Beginning in the 1970s, however, the balance of trade has shown deficits—large ones in the late 1970s and even larger through the 1980s, returning to simply large deficits in the 1990s. The trade deficits of the early to mid-1970s resulted primarily from the large increase in the price of imported oil. During the first half of the 1980s, the trade deficits were caused by a very strong dollar, which made U.S. goods much more expensive than imported goods. This price shift decreased U.S. exports and increased foreign imports. In the latter half of the decade, the value of the dollar fell, and the trade deficit began to decrease in 1988, having reached a record $152.9 billion in 1987. Deficits in the trade balance have continued to narrow until 1992. Since 1992 trade deficits climbed to record levels in 1994, 1995, and 1996. Figure 21.2 shows the pattern for international transactions balances between 1971 and 1995.

Trade deficits in the current account have been offset by larger capital inflows into the United States, which have reduced the deficit in the basic balance. The capital account has historically run deficits, since it records U.S. corporate investment in foreign nations. Martin Feldstein, former chair

■ FIGURE 21.2 Trade and Investment Income Balances

Source: *National Economic Trends*, Federal Reserve Bank of St. Louis, March 1997.

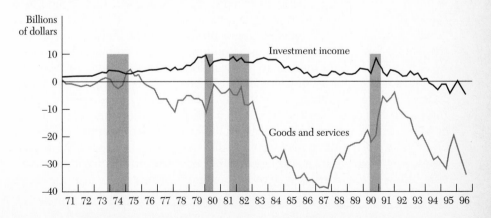

of the Council of Economic Advisors, makes a similar point in relating trade deficits of foreign capital inflows:

> During the period when imports by Americans do exceed our exports to the rest of the world, foreigners must accept additional dollar securities in exchange for our excess imports. In different words, we finance the excess imports by borrowing from the rest of the world or by selling U.S. assets to foreigners. This accommodating flow of credit or capital to the United States is an inevitable corollary of the trade deficit.
>
> —Martin Feldstein, "Why the Dollar Is Strong," *Challenge*,
> January/February 1984.

One of the problems a nation encounters in trade, just as in life, is that it must pay for the goods and services received. An individual can use either cash or an IOU to offset a debt. In the international sphere, several alternatives are available. Payments are accepted in cash (dollars), gold, or Special Drawing Rights (a bookkeeping form of international money).

If a nation's exports exceed its imports, it will have attained a balance-of-payments surplus. The reward for this is increased employment and income at home. The penalty is higher prices. Why? As exports of goods and services rise, income (Y) and hence GDP increase. As income increases, consumption increases. As consumption increases, more dollars are competing for fewer domestic goods, and prices will tend to rise.

A trade deficit (imports greater than exports) earns a nation's economic and political leaders criticism and economic disadvantages. Strains are placed on the value of a nation's currency with respect to other currencies. If these strains become too severe, the country's currency will depreciate (be worth less) with respect to other, stronger currencies, so imported goods will cost more. On the other hand, exports should become cheaper and thus more attractive to foreign nations. In following sections of the chapter, we will see how this happens.

A country cannot do away with a trade deficit simply by removing or reducing a "big" item on the balance-of-payments statement. For example, it is not true that, as opponents of foreign aid have argued, this expenditure caused deficits in the basic trade balance for many years. Much foreign aid is "tied"; that is, it must be spent on goods produced in the United States. So if the United States cut foreign aid by $1 billion, U.S. exports might be reduced by as much as $800 million. The gain would be very small indeed. Many of the items in the balance of payments are related to other items in this way.

It is, however, legitimate to note that when a particular item is in surplus, the country has the freedom to run up a deficit in some other item without creating pressure against its currency. This sort of situation can be created in either of two ways: there may be items that in the working out of "basic economic forces" generate a surplus, or other countries in the world economy may "allow" deficits to exist without exerting pressure for policy measures that would reduce them. An example of the former is the flow of investment income into the United States. In the past, the net income on U.S. investments abroad allowed the United States to, among other things, increase its ownership of factories and mines in other countries and finance military expenditures abroad. An example of the second situation would be the willingness of countries to hold onto dollars accumulated from U.S. deficits because dollars are valuable to them.

EXCHANGE RATES AND THE BALANCE OF PAYMENTS

As we mentioned earlier, trade imbalances can create pressures on a nation's currency. Let's examine how the value (exchange rate) of the dollar is determined and how it influences the balance of payments.

As we saw in Chapter 2, currency prices, like the prices of goods and services, are determined by supply and demand factors. When nations were demanding increasing amounts of German and Japanese products in the 1970s, marks and yen were in demand and were rising in value. At the same time, the United States experienced trade deficits, which, with the exception of 1975, have continued. This is significant, since we would expect that the lower value of the dollar would have stimulated U.S. exports and reduced imports. But high inflation rates of the 1970s in the United States made institutions and investors skeptical about the long-term stability of the currency, so the demand for marks and yen increased as well.

■ Discount store, Tokyo, Japan. *(Eddie Stanger/SuperStock, Inc.)*

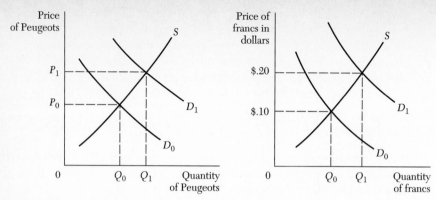

■ FIGURE 21.3 Supply and Demand for Peugeots and Francs

Determinants of Exchange Rates

The value of a nation's currency, or the currency's **exchange rate**, is determined by supply and demand factors. Supply factors are generally controlled by the central bank, but a number of factors influence demand for a nation's currency. The most obvious are the demand for a nation's products and the prices of those products. The lower the price of the products, the greater the demand, and thus the greater the demand for the nation's currency, since currency is needed to purchase the products. Other factors that often influence exchange rates include tastes and preferences for the country's products, productivity increases, the inflation rate and the domestic interest rate relative to other countries' rates. In Figure 21.3, an increased demand in the United States for French-produced Peugeots increases the demand for francs, and thus increases the exchange rate of the franc in terms of dollars. Each dollar will purchase fewer francs as the price of francs in dollars rises.

Given the current U.S. trade deficits, we might expect the value of the dollar to be falling with respect to many other currencies, since the demand for U.S. exports is low and the demand for imported goods is high. But other factors affect the demand for a nation's currency. Nontrade pressures, which are not influenced by the demand for a nation's products, might dramatically influence the value or the exchange rate of the dollar. Currencies are used not only to purchase goods and services, but also to make money—that is, to earn a rate of return, or interest. The Fed's tightening of monetary policy in the fall of 1979 and again in late 1989 and early 1997 did curb the growth rate of the money supply, but the resulting higher interest rate and a growing confidence that the United States was a "safe haven" for assets created a demand for dollars among foreign corporations and investors.

To illustrate this, we will assume that before the Fed initiative, $1 would purchase 5 francs. In Figure 21.4, a Fed reduction in the growth rate of the money supply is shown by the shift in the supply curve of dollars from S_0 to

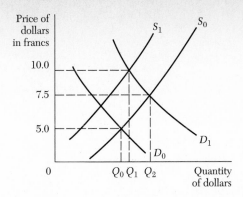

FIGURE 21.4 Supply and Demand for Dollars

S_1. A higher interest rate created by the reduced money supply will attract foreign investment and thus increase the demand for dollars. This is shown by a shift in the demand curve from D_0 to D_1.

In this example, the dollar has become very strong. Therefore, it commands or purchases a larger quantity of other foreign currencies and thus more foreign goods and services. Before the Fed's contractionary monetary policy, $1 would purchase 5 francs, but with increases in demand, $1 purchases 10 francs. French products have become relatively cheaper for U.S. consumers. That will tend to increase French (foreign) imports, which increases the tendency for the U.S. balance of trade to run a deficit. At the same time, 1 franc commands fewer dollars, its buying power having fallen from $.20 worth of U.S. products to only $.10 worth. Therefore, each U.S. product costs French consumers more. Even though the prices of U.S. products have not changed in absolute terms, for a French consumer they are relatively higher, since the franc's dollar-purchasing power has declined. As a result, fewer U.S. goods are exported to France, leading to further deterioration in the balance of trade. In this example, the dollar has **appreciated**, or gained in value with respect to the franc, while the franc has **depreciated**, or lost value with respect to the dollar.

Table 21.4 summarizes the effects of various economic factors on exchange rates.

TABLE 21.4 Factors Affecting Exchange Rates

Factor	Change in Factor	Change in Exchange Rate
Domestic price level	Increase	Depreciation
Import demand	Increase	Appreciation
Export demand	Increase	Depreciation
Productivity	Increase	Appreciation
Domestic interest rate	Increase	Appreciation

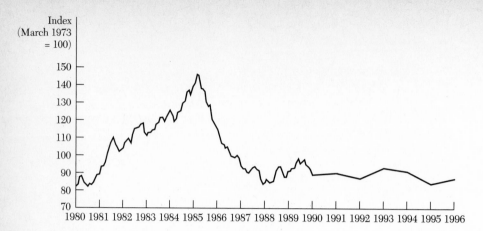

■ FIGURE 21.5 Trade-Weighted Value of the Dollar

The trade-weighted value of the dollar is the value of the dollar with respect to the currencies of the major trading partners of the United States. Data are monthly.

Source: *Economic Report of the President, 1990.*

The Value of the Dollar since the 1970s

During the 1970s the U.S. dollar experienced a spectacular decline in value relative to other major trading currencies. Beginning in the fall of 1979, the dollar began an upward roll, eventually reaching new highs against most European currencies each day in early 1985 (see Figure 21.5). The decline in the 1970s reflected major weaknesses in the U.S. economy: slow growth, an impressive economic challenge by Germany and Japan, and relatively high and continuing inflation in the United States. Factors responsible for sustaining the high dollar value in the 1980s included the high U.S. budget deficits, high real interest rates, and low levels of inflation with respect to those in other industrial nations. The dollar peaked against the yen in 1985 at $1 = 260 yen.

Between 1985 and 1993, the dollar began to drop, particularly in relation to the German mark and the Japanese yen. In September of 1985, the Group of Five (the United States, United Kingdom, France, West Germany, and Japan—also known as G5), agreed in the Plaza Accord* to intervene in foreign exchange markets to lower the value of the soaring dollar in order to promote more even-handed economic growth.† By 1993, the dollar had fallen to its post–World War II low against the yen at $1 = 100.9 yen. The dollar

---

*The Plaza Accord was so named after the location of the September 1985 meeting at New York City's Plaza Hotel.

†Currency intervention occurs when a nation or other nations purchase (or sell) the currency of a particular nation to establish a higher (or lower) rate of exchange. In this case the G5 nations agreed to sell dollars so as to lower the dollar's value with respect to other trading currencies. This is truly a managed float!

had depreciated more than 50 percent from its peak in 1985, as interest rates in the United States and oil prices continued to fall. Since 1993, the dollar strengthened against the yen and many other major currencies, and by early 1997 had moved to 125 yen per dollar.

The period between 1971 and 1997 shows a complete cycle of exchange rate movements that respond to domestic inflation, interest rates, and intervention in currency markets. Some economists argue that the U.S. merchandise trade balance was not reduced by a greater magnitude during the period of dollar decline because many foreign producers cut their profit margins in order to keep export prices low and thus maintain their share of the market. These economists also point out that the dollar depreciation was much greater with respect to the yen and mark than to other currencies. Thus, prices of goods imported from those areas remained attractive to U.S. consumers.

4. What kind of sale on U.S.-produced goods were Japanese consumers and businesses treated to with the fall in the value of the dollar between 1985 and 1993? How would U.S. retailers advertise such a deal?

In 1997 the value of the dollar was again turning upward. The threat of increased inflation caused the Fed to institute a somewhat more restrictive monetary policy and thus an increase in interest rates in the United States. Japanese investors, still concerned with domestic banking and stock market crises, moved some of their funds to the United States and Europe to seek higher yields and perhaps greater stability. If the movement continues, the U.S. trade balance will feel increased pressure as imports become more attractive to U.S. consumers and exports lose their exchange advantage in international markets.

Exchange Rates and the Foreign Exchange Market

Hour by hour and minute by minute, exchange rates shift, largely in response to the demand in foreign exchange markets. Several hundred dealers in foreign exchange (mostly banks) each day purchase and sell deposits denominated in foreign currency. Each transaction must be more than $1 million, and the amount of foreign exchange traded daily in 1997 averaged over $1 trillion. Each day's fluctuations in the foreign exchange market are reported in the *New York Times*, *Wall Street Journal*, and other major newspapers (see Figure 21.6).

In the foreign exchange market, short-run factors contribute to fluctuations in national currencies as banks sell deposits denominated in dollars, francs, and yen to companies, governments, investors, and speculators. In the foreign exchange market, expectations about returns on dollar deposits or franc deposits cause shifts in the exchange rates. If dollar deposits are expected to increase relative to franc deposits, the dollar will appreciate relative to the franc. In this market, interest rate changes as well as *expectations* about

CURRENCY TRADING

EXCHANGE RATES

Friday, August 15, 1997

The New York foreign exchange selling rates below apply to trading among banks in amounts of $1 million and more, as quoted at 4 p.m. Eastern time by Dow Jones and other sources. Retail transactions provide fewer units of foreign currency per dollar.

Country	U.S. $ equiv. Fri	U.S. $ equiv. Thu	Currency per U.S. $ Fri	Currency per U.S. $ Thu
Argentina (Peso)	1.0014	1.0014	.9986	.9986
Australia (Dollar)	.7420	.7416	1.3477	1.3484
Austria (Schilling)	.07814	.07727	12.798	12.942
Bahrain (Dinar)	2.6525	2.6525	.3770	.3770
Belgium (Franc)	.02657	.02629	37.637	38.039
Brazil (Real)	.9195	.9208	1.0875	1.0860
Britain (Pound)	1.6093	1.5910	.6214	.6285
1-month forward	1.6073	1.5890	.6222	.6293
3-months forward	1.6035	1.5852	.6236	.6308
6-months forward	1.5979	1.5798	.6258	.6330
Canada (Dollar)	.7193	.7192	1.3903	1.3905
1-month forward	.7206	.7205	1.3877	1.3879
3-months forward	.7231	.7231	1.3830	1.3829
6-months forward	.7263	.7263	1.3769	1.3769
Chile (Peso)	.002418	.002418	413.65	413.65
China (Renminbi)	.1203	.1202	8.3119	8.3193
Colombia (Peso)	.0008863	.0008884	1128.25	1125.62
Czech. Rep. (Koruna) .				
Commercial rate	.02940	.02960	34.014	33.782
Denmark (Krone)	.1438	.1427	6.9525	7.0075
Ecuador (Sucre)				
Floating rate	.0002472	.0002472	4045.00	4045.00
Finland (Markka)	.1830	.1813	5.4640	5.5153
France (Franc)	.1628	.1612	6.1425	6.2025
1-month forward	.1631	.1615	6.1304	6.1903
3-months forward	.1637	.1622	6.1072	6.1667
6-months forward	.1646	.1631	6.0744	6.1326
Germany (Mark)	.5493	.5435	1.8204	1.8399
1-month forward	.5504	.5446	1.8167	1.8361
3-months forward	.5526	.5468	1.8095	1.8288
6-months forward	.5558	.5500	1.7991	1.8182
Greece (Drachma)	.003500	.003461	285.70	288.94
Hong Kong (Dollar)	.1291	.1291	7.7430	7.7470
Hungary (Forint)	.005049	.005072	198.05	197.16
India (Rupee)	.02796	.02799	35.765	35.725
Indonesia (Rupiah)	.0003472	.0003591	2880.00	2785.00
Ireland (Punt)	1.4635	1.4495	.6833	.6899
Israel (Shekel)	.2836	.2838	3.5265	3.5230
Italy (Lira)	.0005612	.0005565	1782.00	1797.00
Japan (Yen)	.008503	.008485	117.60	117.85
1-month forward	.008541	.008522	117.09	117.34
3-months forward	.008615	.008597	116.07	116.32
6-months forward	.008731	.008712	114.54	114.78
Jordan (Dinar)	1.4094	1.4094	.7095	.7095
Kuwait (Dinar)	3.2776	3.2776	.3051	.3051
Lebanon (Pound)	.0006508	.0006508	1536.50	1536.50
Malaysia (Ringgit)	.3593	.3597	2.7835	2.7800
Malta (Lira)	2.5189	2.4938	.3970	4010
Mexico (Peso)				
Floating rate	.1289	.1289	7.7600	7.7580
Netherland (Guilder)	.4867	.4826	2.0548	2.0719
New Zealand (Dollar)	.6416	.6408	1.5586	1.5605
Norway (Krone)	.1314	.1312	7.6088	7.6243
Pakistan (Rupee)	.02496	.02496	40.070	40.070
Peru (new Sol)	.3800	.3794	2.6318	2.6358
Philippines (Peso)	.03381	.03393	29.575	29.475
Poland (Zloty)	.2860	.2860	3.4965	3.4965
Portugal (Escudo)	.005422	.005361	184.42	186.52
Russia (Ruble) (a)	.0001720	.0001721	5815.50	5809.50
Saudi Arabia (Riyal)	.2666	.2666	3.7505	3.7505
Singapore (Dollar)	.6594	.6577	1.5165	1.5205
Slovak Rep. (Koruna)	.02861	.02861	34.951	34.951
South Africa (Rand)	.2133	.2136	4.6885	4.6821
South Korea (Won)	.001118	.001118	894.85	894.85
Spain (Peseta)	.006495	.006428	153.96	155.58
Sweden (Krona)	.1255	.1244	7.9655	8.0363
Switzerland (Franc)	.6638	.6591	1.5065	1.5173
1-month forward	.6661	.6614	1.5012	1.5120
3-months forward	.6708	.6660	1.4907	1.5014
6-months forward	.6777	.6729	1.4755	1.4861
Taiwan (Dollar)	.03481	.03481	28.724	28.725
Thailand (Baht)	.03125	.03170	32.000	31.550
Turkey (Lira)	.00000612	.00000614	163345.00	162880.00
United Arab (Dirham)	.2723	.2723	3.6725	3.6725
Uruguay (New Peso)				
Financial	.1037	.1037	9.6450	9.6450
Venezuela (Bolivar)	.002021	.002022	494.92	494.68
SDR	1.3518	1.3565	.7397	.7372
ECU	1.0805	1.0683		

Special Drawing Rights (SDR) are based on exchange rates for the U.S., German, British, French , and Japanese currencies. Source: International Monetary Fund.

European Currency Unit (ECU) is based on a basket of community currencies.

a-fixing, Moscow Interbank Currency Exchange.

The Wall Street Journal daily foreign exchange data for 1996 and 1997 may be purchased through the Readers' Reference Service (413) 592-3600.

■ FIGURE 21.6 Daily Fluctuations in Foreign Exchange Markets

Source: Reprinted by permission of The Wall Street Journal, © 1997 Dow Jones & Company, Inc. All Rights Reserved Worldwide.

future productivity, import and export demand, and domestic inflation (perhaps caused by some domestic policy change) cause currency traders to shift from holding one currency to holding another, and thus bid exchange rates up or down.

EXCHANGE RATE SYSTEMS: A HISTORICAL PERSPECTIVE

Some type of international financial system is required to deal with the "imbalances" in the balance-of-payments positions among nations. If the United States, for example, has an overall balance-of-payments deficit with the rest of the world, some mechanism must exist for "balancing" that deficit. Throughout the history of modern world capitalism, several different systems have existed for accomplishing this task, including fixed and fluctuating exchange standards.

The Gold Standard

Gold served as the external form of payment in the international system from the Middle Ages until the twentieth century. Under a gold standard, a country's currency is convertible into gold at a fixed price. The price of the currency expressed in terms of gold is known as its parity value. The United States and the United Kingdom once defined their currencies in terms of gold. As a result, surpluses and deficits in the balance of payments were equivalent to a certain amount of gold.

This mechanism was relatively simple and had some attractive results. The flow of gold from the United Kingdom would reduce the money supply in the United Kingdom and increase it in the United States. As an automatic reaction, prices would fall in the United Kingdom and rise in the United States, since less (more) money would tend to force prices downward (upward) and since gold was a part of the money supply. Consumers in each country would then respond to the price changes. Exports of U.S. goods would tend to fall, and those of the United Kingdom would tend to increase. Consequently, the balance-of-payments surplus of the United States would tend to decline, all without any government intervention.

The concept of liquidity is vital to trade in that transactions require some standard of "moneyness" that is universally accepted, and the trading parties must have this liquidity. Under the gold standard, if countries do not have enough gold reserves (or gold mines) to facilitate trade or if output of goods and services outstrips the output of gold, a liquidity crisis results. The health of domestic economies is therefore at the mercy of the world's ability to produce gold. In practice, the gold standard limited the amount of international trade that could be financed and tended to restrict some domestic economies. As nations and trade grew, the limited gold resources could not satisfy the needs of world trade.

The International Monetary Fund and the Bretton Woods System

Two World Wars separated by the Great Depression dealt fatal blows to the gold standard. The framework for the system that forms the official organizational structure of today's international financial negotiations was formulated in 1944 at a conference in Bretton Woods, New Hampshire, and became known as the Bretton Woods system. The institutional arrangements settled on were to be overseen by a new organization, the **International Monetary Fund (IMF)**. The IMF was established to provide an institutional framework for monetary cooperation and consultation when problems arose. It was charged with facilitating expansion and balanced growth of trade with high levels of domestic income and employment.

To accomplish this goal, the participants established a system of fixed exchange rates. Under the fixed exchange system, currencies were defined in terms of one another. The IMF was to provide for stable exchange rates between currencies. Consistency was assured, with each nation defining its currency in terms of both gold and the U.S. dollar. The U.S. dollar maintained a passive role in the Bretton Woods system because it was chosen to serve as the key or reserve currency, making it as acceptable as gold in international transactions. The Bretton Woods system functioned with this fixed exchange system until 1973.

International Monetary Crisis

The IMF was created and designed to guarantee the working of the Bretton Woods system, but problems sent the fixed exchange system into periods of confusion and disarray, never quite fulfilling the dreams of its creators. According to the design of the Bretton Woods system, exchange rate adjustments should occur in cases of persistent balance-of-payments difficulties. However, because the dollar was the reserve currency and essential for international liquidity, necessary dollar adjustments were avoided. In addition, more serious trouble lay deeper than this. Currency realignments were rare under the Bretton Woods system. Many felt depreciation was a sign of national weakness, while appreciation was viewed not as a sign of strength but as a compromise to a weaker economic position. Many nations' exchange rates were out of kilter, since they remained at essentially the same parity rates that existed at the end of World War II.

With ever-increasing deficits in the balance of payments, U.S. policy remained much the same during the 1960s. During this period, the IMF virtually conceded its operations to the Group of Ten, consisting of the ten most economically powerful countries in the world. At their meetings they discussed and acted at any indication of weakness in currency operations—but prompt realignment of parity rates did not occur. A system of emergency capital flows developed, with funds being shuttled from one weak currency to the next. This led only to greater instability within the Bretton Woods system.

In August 1971, President Nixon introduced the New Economic Policy (NEP), which, along with domestic wage and price controls, called for a temporary 10 percent surcharge on all imports as well as a "temporary" halt in the convertibility of dollars into gold. (This temporary condition still exists, and it is now understood that August 15, 1971, marked the complete end of the gold exchange standard. Although U.S. citizens have not been able to exchange their dollar holdings for gold from the U.S. Treasury since 1934, foreign dollar holders continued to exchange dollars for gold until this suspension.) Under the burden of inflation and the high costs of the war in Vietnam, the U.S. balance-of-payments deficit was larger and more pressing than it had been at any time in the nation's history.

Floating Exchange Rates

On December 18, 1971, President Nixon committed what a few years earlier would have been political suicide and devalued the dollar. The "historic" Smithsonian agreement called for an 8 percent devaluation of the dollar and a realignment of other currencies to reflect the lower value of the dollar. As pressures continued, nations began to let their currencies float (adjust to daily changes in the supply of and demand for each currency).

Since 1973, de facto currency depreciations or appreciations occur without official IMF sanction. The overvalued dollar was allowed to seek its own worth in the somewhat free international currency markets. The IMF was given the power to "oversee the exchange rate regime, adopt principles to guide national policies, and encourage international cooperation."

In the years since the introduction of floating exchange rates, the international monetary system has adjusted surprisingly well, even though the central banks of most major industrial countries have intervened at one time or another to "manage" or intervene in their exchange rates. Floating exchange rates have presented special problems for developing economies, however. Because few of these nations had well-developed currency markets, they tied or pegged their currency to that of their major industrial trading partner. A developing nation whose currency was pegged to the British pound found that its currency, like the pound, depreciated by almost 25 percent between mid-1975 and the end of 1976. These kinds of exchange rate movements can cause severe inflationary pressures in developing countries where inflation is often a persistent problem.

ISSUES IN INTERNATIONAL FINANCE: OPEC AND THE RECYCLING OF PETRODOLLARS

Floating exchange rates were put to the test during the oil embargos of the 1970s. The embargos by OPEC resulted in oil price shocks in 1973–1974 and 1979, quadrupling the price of oil by the end of the decade. These oil shocks contributed to an inflationary spiral throughout the industrialized countries. The international financial system handled this period of economic, political, and financial turmoil by absorbing and recycling "petrodollars"—dollars earned from oil exported by OPEC members. These funds were deposited and invested in the major money centers of Europe and the United States, then loaned to borrowers, often developing countries in need of funds to purchase oil. This recycling of petrodollars ended in the late 1970s and fueled the debt crisis of the 1980s.

The oil price increases of the 1970s also fueled sizable growth of Third World debt. Debt levels of these nations were relatively low until the 1970s. OPEC nations deposited petrodollars in European, Asian, and American banks. Third World nations were forced to borrow funds from these banks to finance their purchases of desperately needed energy supplies. While a strong dollar helps Third World nations increase their exports to the United States, the high interest rates that sustained the value of the dollar further increased the debt burden to the developing nations. These nations became heavily indebted to the banks and to international organizations.

The deep recession of the early 1980s that plagued the economies of the industrial countries caused the export markets of developing nations to collapse at a time when these nations desperately needed export earnings to service their external debt. As borrowers from the International Monetary Fund and commercial banks, these debtor countries had to manage their economic affairs in a manner that met IMF criteria. Developing countries therefore began adopting a neoliberal economic model calling for the adoption of conservative fiscal and monetary policies accompanied by efforts to open up the domestic economy to freer trade and investment flows.

The international community continues to develop creative responses to the developing nations' external debt problems. (We shall explore these in some detail in the next chapter.)

THE FUTURE OF THE INTERNATIONAL FINANCIAL SYSTEM

During the 1990s, as global capital markets became more integrated, economic policy makers and central bankers from all countries realized that their ability to control their respective domestic economies, in the context of rapid global change, was increasingly more difficult and less effective. Capital was highly mobile. It could move quickly. Currency values were increasingly volatile.

The countries with the seven largest industrial economies (the United States, Canada, United Kingdom, France, Germany, Italy, and Japan), together known as the G-7 countries, responded by voluntarily coordinating some of their economic policies. Their ongoing effort to cooperate has been mildly successful. Still, without the discipline of an enforcement mechanism, countries tend to do only what is self-serving and politically expedient. Annual economic summits have served largely to bring together the members of the G-7 for public relations, ritual identification of the problems they face collectively, and only moderate cooperation.

By the mid-1990s, the global economy was marked by rapid and dramatic forces of change. Developing countries in Asia, Latin America, and Africa were moving toward market economies and democratic governments. Other nations in transition in Eastern Europe, Central Europe, and the Commonwealth of Independent States were also following the path toward establishing market economies, drawing enormous attention to the potential opportunities afforded by these emerging market economies. There is a new interest in the stock and bond markets. There have been investment scandals, such as the one in Albania in 1997, which produced riots and a governmental crisis. Increased capital flows in the form of direct private foreign investment in these countries have led many international commercial banks and investment banks to aggressively establish themselves there.

The mid-1990s also found Japan coming out of three years of recession and trying to solve many internal financial and political problems as well as

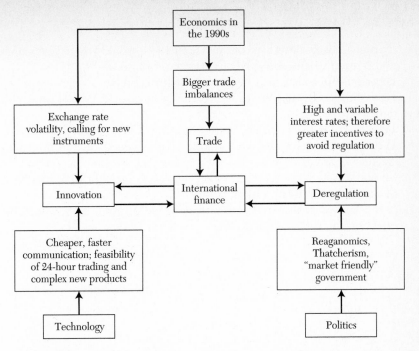

■ FIGURE 21.7 Forces of Change Affecting the International Financial System

confront new competitive pressures in its own backyard. China and India emerged as powerful new players in the global economy. Western Europe struggles to adapt to the changes and challenges of European economic integration and its proposed monetary union. West Germany's integration with East Germany has slowed the locomotive for European economic growth. And, while this is taking place, the competitive pressures of the marketplace are pushing even more rapid change.

CONCLUSION

With all of these changes taking place, what will become of the international financial system? Figure 21.7 shows a number of factors currently driving this system and their interactive effects. The context of these changes is a competitive system characterized by deregulation, free markets, and innovation. The deregulation and innovation have generated exchange rate volatility as financial entities have applied new computer and information system technologies to their operations and the development of new products and services.

Clearly, these issues confound simple Keynesian solutions to macroeconomic problems. As we enter the next millennium, global policy makers will continue to be challenged to find workable solutions that promote worldwide economic stability.

Review Questions

1. If you had been a minister of finance in 1944, would you have encouraged your nation to join the IMF? Explain your reasoning.
2. Is gold useful today, or is it simply a historical relic?
3. How did the United States finance its post–World War II international deficits?
4. Why might nations have a "fear of floating"? Who gains? Who loses?
5. What impacts have the Arab nations had recently on the international financial system?
6. Should the U.S. government more vigorously attempt to lower the value of the dollar? Why or why not?
7. If the United States sold some of its hoard of gold, what would be the effect on the value of the dollar?

22

The Economics of Developing Nations

INTRODUCTION

By the year 2020, according to the United Nations, approximately 80 percent of the world's population (an estimated 8 billion) will be living in developing countries. What will this mean in terms of global poverty? The competition for global resources? The economic growth and development needs of these countries? Relations between the more-developed and less-developed countries?

By the early 1960s, it had become common practice to refer to nations as being part of either the First, Second, or Third World. Those in the First World were the Western industrialized market economies, while those in the Second World were members of the socialist planned economies. The remaining nations fell into the category of the Third World. The member nations of the Third World were the developing nations of Asia, Africa, the Middle East, and Latin America. Most of these nations had achieved political independence by the early 1960s and found themselves caught between the First and Second Worlds in terms of both the Cold War and their own quest for economic development.

By 1960 the economic gap between the developed and developing world had widened to such an extent that the United Nations declared the 1960s to be the "Development Decade." Since then, the global community and many international institutions such as the World Bank and the International Monetary Fund have devoted considerable resources to an attempt to bring about economic development in the Third World. These efforts, as we shall see, have produced mixed results, great controversy, and an emerging consensus on the future direction of development.

COMMON CHARACTERISTICS OF DEVELOPING NATIONS

Despite great diversity among developing nations, they share a set of common characteristics. A developing nation typically has the following attributes:

- Low standard of living
- Low level of labor productivity
- High rate of population growth
- High and rising level of unemployment and underemployment
- Dependency on agricultural production and primary product exports
- Vulnerability in international political, economic, and financial relations

Global Poverty

The World Bank has prepared a classification scheme for nations based on income for 1995. Low-income economies are those with a GDP per capita of $610 or less. Middle-income economies are those with a GDP per capita between $611 and $7,619, and high-income economies are those with GDP per capita of $7,620 or more.

■ FIGURE 22.1 Number of Poor People in Developing Countries
Source: United Nations, *Human Development Report, 1994.*

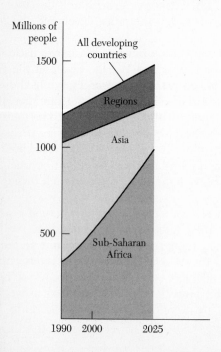

At the end of the twentieth century, about 1.2 billion people live in abject poverty in the developing countries. As shown in Figure 22.1, this figure is expected to rise to 1.5 billion by the year 2025. In 1990, 30 percent of the population of developing countries lived in poverty (with an annual 1990 income of less than $420 per capita), 49 percent of the population of South Asia was classified as living in poverty, and 47 percent of the population of sub-Saharan Africa was classified as poor. By comparison, Latin America and the Caribbean had a poverty rate of 25 percent and East Asia only 11 percent. The projected figures for the year 2000 paint a dismal picture for the developing world in general and for South Asia and sub-Saharan Africa in particular.

Global poverty on such a scale is even more dramatic when looked at in terms of the *distribution* of global income. A 1991 United Nations study revealed that 77 percent of the world's people earn 15 percent of its income. Expressed in GNP per capita, the average income of the high-income countries (commonly referred to as the North) was $12,510, or eighteen times the average for the developing world (the South), which was $710.

Underdevelopment: The Reality and Significance

It is difficult—if not impossible—for those of us living in a modern advanced nation like the United States to understand what it would be like to live in poverty in a developing nation. Denis Goulet, a professor at the University of Notre Dame, has put it eloquently:

> Underdevelopment is shocking: the squalor, disease, unnecessary deaths, and hopelessness of it all! No man understands if underdevelopment remains for him a mere statistic reflecting low income, poor housing, premature mortality, or underemployment. The most empathetic observer can speak objectively about underdevelopment only after undergoing, personally or vicariously, the "shock of underdevelopment." This unique cultural shock comes to one as he is initiated to the emotions which prevail in the "culture of poverty." The reverse shock is felt by those living in destitution when a new self-understanding reveals to them that their life is neither human nor inevitable. The prevalent emotion of underdevelopment is a sense of personal and societal impotence in the face of disease and death, of confusion and ignorance as one gropes to understand change, of servility toward men whose decisions govern the course of events, of hopelessness before hunger and natural catastrophe. Chronic poverty is a cruel kind of hell, and one cannot understand how cruel that hell is merely by gazing upon poverty as an object.
>
> —Denis Goulet, *The Cruel Choice*, Atheneum, 1975.

The condition of underdevelopment in recent years has been improved by some positive developments. The following box identifies areas of progress in several categories, as well as areas in which there is continued deprivation.

BALANCE SHEET OF HUMAN DEVELOPMENT—
DEVELOPING COUNTRIES

Progress	Deprivation

Health
- During 1960–1992, average life expectancy increased by more than a third. By now, 30 countries have achieved a life expectancy of more than 70 years.
- Over the past three decades, the population with access to safe water almost doubled, from 36% to 70%.

- About 17 million people die every year from infectious and parasitic diseases, such as diarrhea, malaria, and tuberculosis.
- More than 90% of the 17 million HIV-infected people live in developing countries.

Education
- Net enrollment at the primary level increased by nearly two-thirds during the past 30 years, from 48% in 1960 to 77% in 1991.

- About 130 million children at the primary level and more than 275 million at the secondary level are out of school.

Food and Nutrition
- Despite rapid population growth, per capita food production rose by more than 20% during the past decade.

- Nearly 800 million people do not get enough food, and about 500 million people are chronically malnourished.

Income and Poverty
- During the past decade, both agriculture and industry expanded at an annual rate of more than 3% in developing countries.

- Almost a third of the population, about 1.3 billion people, live below the poverty line.

Women
- The combined primary and secondary enrollment of girls increased from 38% to 68% during the past two decades.
- During the past two decades, fertility rates declined by more than a third.

- Maternal mortality in developing countries, at 350 per 100,000 live births, is about nine times higher than that in OECD countries.
- Women hold about 10% of parliamentary seats.

Children
- In 1960–1992, the infant mortality rate was more than halved, from 149 per thousand live births to 70.
- During the past two decades, the lives of about three million children were saved every year through the extension of basic immunization.

- More than a third of children are malnourished and underweight.
- The under-five mortality rate, at 100 per thousand live births, is still nearly seven times higher than that in industrial countries.

Environment
- Developing countries' contribution to global emissions is less than a fourth that of industrial countries, even though their population is 3.5 times larger.

- About 200 million people are severely affected by desertification.
- Every year, some 20 million hectares of tropical forest are cleared outright or grossly degraded.

Politics and Conflicts
- More than two-thirds of the population in developing countries live under relatively pluralistic and democratic regimes.

- At the end of 1993, there were more than 13 million refugees in the developing world.

Source: United Nations, *Human Development Report, 1995*, p. 16.

1. Have you ever been to a developing country? Did you see the kind of underdevelopment described in the quotation and table? If not, can you imagine this kind of reality?

Underdevelopment is an economic as well as human condition. In economic terms, we tend to think of an underdeveloped country as having a low per capita income and a low per capita gross domestic product. A developing country usually has a large percentage of its labor force in agriculture. It typically has a shortage of domestic savings, so it must rely on external capital and technology to stimulate investment and economic growth. Such a country usually depends on a small number of primary exports (raw materials and food crops) and some manufactured goods. It typically has balance-of-payments problems that stem from current account deficits (deficits in trade and investment income). In many cases, developing countries suffer from large external debts, which require sizable debt servicing (interest and principal payments). Payment of the debt involves outflows of interest and principal to foreign creditors.

While many economists tend to discuss underdevelopment in economic terms, others have expanded the economic aspect to include categories like productivity, equity, sustainability, and empowerment. The following article, "Components of the Human Development Paradigm," emphasizes each of these categories as a part of a more fully developed definition of what constitutes not just economic development but human development. (This new paradigm has been developed by the United Nations.)

COMPONENTS OF THE HUMAN DEVELOPMENT PARADIGM

The human development paradigm contains four main components:

- *Productivity*—People must be enabled to increase their productivity and to participate fully in the process of income generation and remunerative employment. Economic growth is, therefore, a subset of human development models.
- *Equity*—People must have access to equal opportunities. All barriers to economic and political opportunities must be eliminated so that people can participate in, and benefit from, these opportunities.

- *Sustainability*—Access to opportunities must be ensured not only for the present generations but for future generations as well. All forms of capital—physical, human, environmental—should be replenished.
- *Empowerment*—Development must be *by* people, not only *for* them. People must participate fully in the decisions and processes that shape their lives.

Source: United Nations, *Human Development Report,* 1995.

BASIC ECONOMIC PROBLEMS OF DEVELOPING NATIONS

To complete our basic profile of a developing country, we turn to a more detailed discussion of the basic economic problems of developing nations. These problems include economic growth, population, macroeconomic instability, international trade and finance, and environmental problems.

Economic Growth

The primary consideration for developing countries is increasing the rate of economic growth. The essence of seeking higher levels of economic growth is to produce more goods and services to improve the population's material standard of living. Economic development, in its most basic sense, is the process of improving standards of living and well-being by raising per capita income.

As we have seen, economic growth depends on a number of factors. In a macroeconomic context, it involves increasing consumption, investment, government spending, and trade. In a microeconomic context, it involves physical resources, labor resources, and technology as applied to production. Microeconomic concerns oblige us to think in terms of efficiency and productivity. Macroeconomic issues require us to think in terms of savings flowing to investments in productive activities. Taken separately or together, these two perspectives on economic growth frame a context for understanding the challenges of economic development.

In recent years, the economic growth experience of developing nations has not been encouraging. As Table 22.1 demonstrates, since 1960 developing nations have experienced a decline in real per capita income. Between 1960 and 1980, per capita income grew at an average annual rate of over 3 percent. But the 1980s posted a weak 1.2 percent growth rate. By the early 1990s, economic growth in the Third World fell to a negative 0.2 percent on average. The anemic GDP growth rates in the 1980s pale in comparison with the record of the 1960–1980 period. This, as we shall see, has serious implications for the goal of reducing poverty in the face of enormous environmental and population growth pressures.

Population: Undermining Economic Growth

In 1990 the world's population had reached the 5.3 billion mark. The United Nations and the World Bank projected that global population would reach 6.1 billion by the year 2000 and 8.8 billion by the year 2030. Of these, 7.4 billion (or 84 percent) of humanity will be living in the low- and middle-income countries. In 1991, 79 percent of the world's population lived in low- and middle-income countries, and they produced only 16 percent of the world's gross domestic product. Put differently, in 1990, world GDP was $22 trillion. High-income countries accounted for $19 trillion of that; low- and middle-income countries $3 trillion.

Table 22.2 illustrates the growth of world population from 1965 to 1991 with projections for the years 2000 and 2030. The low- and middle-income

Country group	1960–70	1970–80	1980–90	1990	1991[a]	1990–2000[a]
High-income countries	4.1	2.4	2.4	2.1	0.7	2.1
Developing countries	3.3	3.0	1.2	−0.2	−0.2	2.9
Sub-Saharan Africa	0.6	0.9	−0.9	−2.0	−1.0	0.3
Asia and the Pacific	2.5	3.1	5.1	3.9	4.2	4.8
East Asia	3.6	4.6	6.3	4.6	5.6	5.7
South Asia	1.4	1.1	3.1	2.6	1.5	3.1
Middle East and North Africa	6.0	3.1	−2.5	−1.9	−4.6	1.6
Latin America and the Caribbean	2.5	3.1	−0.5	−2.4	0.6	2.2
Europe	4.9	4.4	1.2	−3.8	−8.6	1.9
Eastern Europe	5.2	5.4	0.9	−8.3	−14.2	1.6

Note: Totals do not include the former U.S.S.R.

[a]estimates

Source: World Bank 1992.

countries have made some progress in reducing the average annual population growth rate from 2.5 percent in the 1965–1973 period to 2.0 by 1990. Yet this reduction has not been enough to halt the rapid increase in population growth from 2.4 billion in 1965 to 4.1 billion in 1990 and a projected 5 billion by the year 2000. The age structure (number of persons in specific age groups) in these countries is such that 40 to 50 percent of the population is under age 15, and the women in this category are in or entering their peak

■ TABLE 22.2 Population

Country group	Population (millions)					
	1965	1975	1980	1990	1991	2000
Low-income	1,776	2,168	2,501	3,058	3,117	3,670
Middle-income	627	755	883	1,088	1,109	1,311
Severely indebted	258	314	370	455	464	546
Sub-Saharan Africa	245	302	366	495	510	668
East Asia and the Pacific	972	1,195	1,347	1,577	1,602	1,818
South Asia	645	781	919	1,148	1,170	1,377
Europe	154	167	182	200	195	217
Middle East and North Africa	125	154	189	256	264	341
Latin America and the Caribbean	243	299	352	433	441	516
Other economies	252	275	294	321	323	345
High-income	671	726	766	816	821	859
OECD members	649	698	733	777	781	814
World	3,326	3,924	4,443	5,284	5,370	6,185

Source: World Bank, *World Development Report 1992*, p. 196.

fertility years. So, even if the average annual population growth rate is declining, say from 2.5 percent to 2 percent, the absolute size of the population is still increasing dramatically.

Even more striking is the situation in much of Africa. In many regions the average annual population growth rate increased in the 1980–1990 period. In sub-Saharan Africa the average annual population growth rate went from 2.7 percent to 3.0 percent. This is a full percentage point above the world average, and more than three times the average for high-income countries, where the population growth rate is less than 1.0 percent.

> 2. What do these data mean in the context of economic develop-
>   ment and the economic growth data examined earlier?

The population growth and pressure in the poorest nations will continue in the context of a projected slowdown in the growth of the global economic system. With more mouths to feed as the number of the world's poor increases, the ability of nations to realistically increase their standard of living by increasing the real per capita GDP will be all the more difficult, if not impossible. Any improvement requires major changes on many different fronts, not the least of which is population control.

The basic issue is that for economic progress to take place, the rate of economic growth has to exceed the rate of population growth. This has not been happening in the Third World.

Macroeconomic Instability

Developing nations share with everyone the same basic overall goal of sustained economic growth with price stability. Yet, unlike the more advanced industrialized countries, their ability to practice traditional Keynesian stabilization policies has proven to be more limited. Many analysts have pointed out that the basic Keynesian theoretical and policy framework evolved out of unique circumstances—the crisis of a well-developed capitalist market economy in the 1930s—and it has been refined in that context ever since. In many developing nations, however, the state of development of free markets and other economic institutions presents unique complexities when it comes to developing policy prescriptions for inflation and unemployment. In other words, traditional Keynesian stimulus policies (increased government spending, lower taxes, lower interest rates, etc.) may not be sufficient to trigger higher growth.

Moreover, in developing nations, inflation rates may be as high as 25 percent to over 1,000 percent. High rates of inflation have the same negative consequences on the economy as in advanced market economies, but to a greater degree. From a policy perspective, developing countries typically resort to conventional Keynesian stabilization policies: reducing government spending, increasing taxes, and reducing government deficits. These usually result in slower growth and higher unemployment, neither of which poor developing countries can tolerate. Contractionary fiscal policy is usually matched with a tight monetary policy, but reducing the growth rate of the

■ Poverty in South Asia: Thai sisters in their primitive village. *(PhotoEdit)*

money supply and increasing interest rates only worsens the contraction of the economy.

Unemployment in developing countries is also a critical problem, and official government unemployment statistics tend to understate its severity. This is a result of political considerations, as well as different methods of determining unemployment than in more advanced market economies. When a country announces that its unemployment rate is only 6 percent, the actual rate may be closer to 30 percent or even more in rural areas. The difficulty in measurement comes from the fact that large numbers of people work outside of formal labor markets. In the informal labor market, there is no official record of work, wages, or taxes. People working in the informal labor market may exchange labor for goods and/or services, or they may work occasionally for cash for which there is no official record.

Furthermore, while formal unemployment is a problem, *underemployment* is a much greater problem. Many people working in the formal labor market are working only a few days or hours a week while seeking full-time employment. In many developing countries, underemployment rates are estimated to be in the range of 40 to 50 percent.

Government policies to address unemployment and underemployment are usually the standard Keynesian expansionary prescription: increase government spending, lower taxes, increase the money supply, and lower interest rates. But these policies are difficult to implement because inflation is severe and governments confront large internal deficits and demanding external debts. For this reason, many leaders champion the growth of the informal sector.

International Trade

In the international sector, developing nations have been trying to reduce their historic current account and balance-of-payments deficits. In addition, virtually all developing countries are trying to diversify their export sectors by moving away from traditional dependence on one or several primary commodity exports (such as oil, coffee, and cotton).

The nations that have been implementing export diversification strategies with some success are called **Newly Industrializing Countries (NICs)**. This group includes Hong Kong, Taiwan, Singapore, Malaysia, the Philippines, South Korea, Brazil, Mexico, and Argentina. These countries have allowed foreign firms to set up operations that have generated a sizable export capability in manufactured goods and hence contributed to increased employment and income.

Policies to promote export growth and reduce imports are designed to improve the overall trade balance. But many developing countries have argued that the terms of trade—the price of *developed* countries' exports relative to the price of *developing* countries' exports—has turned against them. The deteriorating terms of trade, they contend, contributes to their current account deficit and the balance-of-payments deficit. Figures 22.2 and 22.3 illustrate the historical record for nonfuel primary commodities versus manufactured products from 1900 to 1990 and the trends in exports and the terms of trade for developing nations from 1965 to 1988.

International Finance

As we saw in the previous chapter, when a currency is depreciated, exports are cheaper and thus more competitive, and imports are more expensive. The

■ FIGURE 22.2 Relative Price Index for Nonfuel Primary Commodities versus Manufactures

Note: The manufactures price index used is the U.S. wholesale price index.

Source: Michael B. Todaro, *Economic Development,* 5th ed. (Boston: Longman, 1994), p. 418.

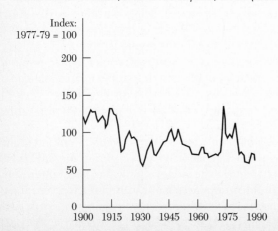

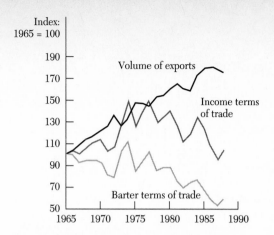

▬ FIGURE 22.3 Exports and the Terms of Trade of Developing Countries

Note: Barter terms of trade are the weighted export unit values of primary commodities deflated by the weighted import unit values of each region. The barter terms of trade multiplied by the actual volume of exports yields the income terms of trade. Data are based on a sample of 90 developing countries.

Source: Michael B. Todaro, *Economic Development,* 5th ed. (Boston: Longman, 1994). p. 418.

theoretical end result is an increase in exports, a decrease in imports, and an improvement in the trade balance, the current account, and the overall balance of payments.

Many developing countries have been and continue to be confronted by a huge external debt. The total external debt of developing countries reached over $2 trillion in 1996 (see Figure 22.4). The debt service on these loans is an enormous burden. Their external debt has put additional pressure on developing countries to increase their export earnings in order to earn the foreign exchange needed to service the external debt. Critics argue that this outflow of scarce foreign exchange hampers governments from spending and investing domestically to produce economic growth.

Since the mid-1980s, private commercial banks in the advanced countries have significantly reduced the level of loans to developing nations. This has created a net resource transfer (the difference between new loans and debt service) on the order of approximately $30 billion a year flowing out of developing nations to the creditors in the advanced countries. In response, creditors and creditor governments have developed initiatives in the early 1990s to reduce the level of debt and debt service without making large new loans. Creditors have done so by renegotiating loans at reduced interest rates or by reducing the amount of the original loan. They have also devised some creative financial schemes like debt-for-equity swaps, which essentially allow creditor banks to sell a portion of a country's debt to a buyer who purchases the debt on the secondary market at a discount and then uses it as investment capital in the country.

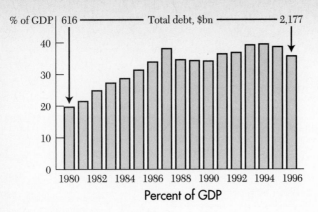

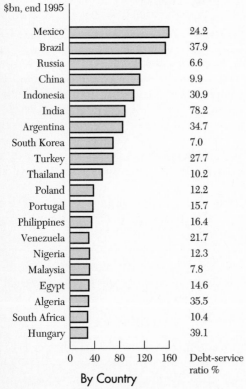

FIGURE 22.4 External Debt of Developing Countries

Source: World Bank, *World Debt Tables*, 1995.

Environmental Problems

Population growth provides several strains on the environment. It increases the demand for goods and services. More people mean more wastes. To feed more people, more land must be put into cultivation, and land currently under cultivation must be farmed more efficiently and productively. This requires more water and often more resource inputs with consequences for human health and the long-term viability of the land itself.

The existence of large numbers of poor people exacerbates the environmental problems. In many countries the pressure to increase nontraditional exports to improve the trade balance and service external debt has resulted in policies that encourage deforestation to permit creation of large cotton and cattle farms. The result is tremendous environmental degradation: not only deforestation, but species extinction, soil depletion and erosion, water contamination, and air pollution.

This issue was one of several addressed at the Earth Summit held in Rio de Janeiro, Brazil, in June 1992. This conference, sponsored by the United Nations, established the link between population growth, poverty, and the environment. It concluded that preservation of the environment and establishment of a framework for sustainable development depend on significantly reducing poverty and population growth in the developing countries. Sustainable development—a goal that had nearly unanimous support at the Earth Summit—is a model of economic growth that respects the integrity of the earth's physical life support system. It means developing a production system that does not degrade or undermine the ability of the earth's life support system to regenerate and cleanse itself. People must use resources in a way that permits renewable resources to renew themselves.

EXPLANATIONS AND SOLUTIONS FOR UNDERDEVELOPMENT

As we saw at the beginning of this text, the basic economic problem is essentially one of producing an economic surplus beyond immediate consumption needs. The more efficient and productive a society, the greater the level of economic surplus or savings for investment. And investment promotes growth in the output of goods and services.

Underdevelopment complicates this problem by creating a cycle of poverty that is hard to break. The existence of high levels of poverty builds a base of people with low incomes, most often subsistence incomes that allow for little if any savings. Yet low-income families tend to have more children. The higher birth rates drive population growth, which slows the rate of economic growth. Higher population growth rates also contribute to higher unemployment and underemployment, especially in a slow-growing economy. Productivity is hampered by other consequences of poverty: poor health and nutrition among the population, a low level of savings (which contributes to the low investment level), and a low level of education. The resulting low level of productivity contributes to the low level of income, and the cycle repeats itself.

||| 3. How can the cycle of poverty be broken? |

While there is widespread agreement among economists about what constitutes development and underdevelopment, there is no consensus with regard to what caused this condition to emerge, what perpetuates it, and what should be done to overcome it. Most economists believe solving underdevelopment requires that the low level of savings be offset by savings injections from external sources. These resources must come from the government in the form of direct income transfers or investment in enterprises and **infrastructure** (roads, bridges, airports, seaports, potable water, electricity, education, etc.). The funds for such investments must come from private foreign investment or from borrowing. This capital and the technology that it would bring can act as the primary stimulus for breaking the cycle of poverty and underdevelopment. With regard to more specific solutions, there are three distinct competing perspectives (schools of thought or paradigms): the neoliberal, structuralist, and dependency models.

The Neoliberal Model

According to the **neoliberal model**, developing nations must adopt modern capital and technology to have strong economic growth. Underdevelopment is assumed to be a natural condition characterized by backward and archaic institutions and values. This condition of underdevelopment must give way to progress and modernization characterized by industrialization, the mechanization of agriculture, urbanization, secular values, and political stability.

This model explains underdevelopment as a consequence of geography, culture, lack of capital and technology, and the vicious cycles of unproductive labor and poverty. In this overall context, the model asserts, a developing nation must create dynamic markets in land, labor, and capital. The emergence of dynamic and smoothly functioning markets along with the expansion of free trade are thus the road to progress. Together, the inflow of foreign capital and the transfer of modern technology are the catalyst necessary to provide the stimulus for sustained growth.

The neoliberal view is that only a free and open private market economy can overcome the vicious cycle of underdevelopment. Because foreign (external) capital, emerging financial markets, and technological change are the stimulants for sustained economic growth in this view, it emphasizes the positive role that multinational firms (corporations) and international financial institutions can and need to play in this process. From the perspective of economic policy, the neoliberal model offers the following prescription:

- A conservative fiscal policy that shrinks domestic deficits by reducing state spending and increasing taxes
- A conservative monetary policy of higher interest rates to reduce inflation
- The promotion of free trade and open-market economic policies that invite the free flow of goods, services, and capital. This will often require an adjustment in the currency's exchange rate through an official devaluation or a commitment to free flexible floating exchange rates.

The Structuralist Model

In the late 1960s and early 1970s, many economists advanced a perspective on underdevelopment that modified the traditional view. This group, led by Raul Prebish, a Brazilian economist then with the United Nations Economic Commission on Latin America, argued that the basic economic problem of underdevelopment exists for all countries but must be understood in the proper historical context. For Latin American, Asian, and African countries, their respective states of underdevelopment had to be understood in the context of their historic relationship to the European countries, which conquered them and transformed them into colonies. These countries' economies were therefore shaped by the economic needs of the colonial powers. Only this historical view explains the inequality in the distribution of income and wealth, the concentration in land ownership, the historic dependence on primary export products, the linking of foreign capital with the industrial and finance capital of domestic elites, and the frequent inappropriateness of Keynesian theories and policies to the circumstances of developing nations.

This **structuralist model** did not deny the basic economic analysis of the traditional view but saw domestic political and economic factors as obstacles to development. The structuralists also viewed the international economic and financial system of the 1960s and 1970s as serving the economic interests of the developed nations while reinforcing the dynamics of underdevelopment for the developing nations.

The contemporary proponents of the structuralist view emphasize the importance of a free and open market economy. They support constructive and responsible foreign investment and the transfer of technology from developed countries. Yet they also emphasize the importance of the following measures:

- A more genuine and equitable distribution of productive land
- A more diversified economy less reliant on primary commodity exports
- Government policies that realistically address the problem of poverty and income distribution
- An active role for government in the economy
- Strong environmental policies
- Relief from the burden of external debt
- Changes in the international trading and financial system designed to bring about a more equitable integration of developing countries into the global economy.

The essence of the structuralist view is that breaking the cycle of underdevelopment requires much more than free and open markets supported by foreign capital and technology.

The Dependency Model

In the 1960s the **depression model** challenged the traditional and structural theories by using Marxian analysis to look at the problem of underdevelopment. The dependency model assumed that we must view underdevelopment as a consequence of the historical evolution of capitalism and the integration of developing countries into the expanding sphere of capitalist production globally. This model is based upon a generalized application of a Marxist methodology drawn from philosophy, history, sociology, political science, and economics. The character and structure of a developing country's economic and political system, as well as its class and social stratification system, are explained by its historical experience with colonialism and the subsequent expansion of capitalism.

Such a historical analysis locates the primary dynamic for change in the economic sphere as it represents at any time a historically specific mode of production. This mode of production characterizes the way in which land, labor, and capital are brought together on a domestic as well as global level.

Dependency analysis argues that development can best be understood as a natural product of the process of capitalist development and expansion worldwide. The theory asserts that as capitalism spread from the European countries in the fifteenth century, it exploited the countries in Latin America, Asia, and Africa. The exploitation of labor and natural resources allowed for a transfer of wealth from the now-developing countries to the then-industrializing European countries. The process of capital accumulation systematically required the exploitation and subjugation of the Third World nations. Colonialism was the political and military dimension that enforced this process. Therefore, dependency analysis argues, this process transformed these countries' economies into vehicles that served the primary needs of the advanced countries. The character of this interdependence produced a dependence, in which the economies of less-developed countries were conditioned by the development and expansion of the advanced country's economy.

Proponents of the dependency view focus their analysis on the way a developing country's economy is integrated with the global economy. Dependency theorists examine everything from the banking system to the communications system to the educational system, focusing on the role and behavior of the direct foreign investment of multinational firms and the role and behavior of multilateral institutions like the International Monetary Fund (IMF) and the World Bank. They argue that these institutions are the instruments and vehicles for the exploitation, domination, and perpetuation of underdevelopment in these countries. They do not deny that some degree of progress, modernization, and economic development result from the spread of capitalism, but they insist that the development is uneven and distorted.

For many years (the 1960s to the 1980s), dependency theorists felt that only a more democratic and socialistically organized society could bring genuine development to these countries by breaking the forms of dependency. The dominating capitalist institutions would need to be replaced. Socialism was seen as one alternative development path. In theory this was attractive to some, but in practice it proved to be difficult, if not impossible. By the late

1990s, whatever the analytical merit of the dependency view, historic events had spelled, for the time being, the end of socialism in practice in Eastern Europe and the Soviet Union (see Chapter 23). Coming off the dismal economic decade of the 1980s, the majority of developing nations entered the 1990s in pursuit of market capitalist development strategies.

ECONOMIC TRENDS IN THE 1990S

Developing countries, confronted with the problems of debt, population, poverty, and the environment, are rapidly adopting variants of the neoliberal model—free and open-market economic strategies for development. Nowhere is this more evident than in Latin America. Among many countries, Mexico is one of the most dramatic examples of the cyclical character of the experience with the neoliberal strategy. The new Mexican development strategy, which began in 1982 and has been in practice since, involves the following actions:

- Privatizing state-owned enterprises
- Opening the economy to foreign investment
- Opening the economy by eliminating tariff and nontariff trade barriers
- Stabilizing the economy by reducing inflation and domestic deficits
- Reducing the level and debt service demands of external debt
- Entering into free-trade agreements with other nations
- Diversifying exports

The success or failure of this strategy will depend on many internal and external factors. It remains to be seen whether enough capital will ultimately flow to these countries to generate rapid development, if the new market-driven economies are efficient and productive enough to compete on a global scale, and if the new democratic governments can manage to maintain political stability and order as their people wait patiently for the results to spill over to them. Much of the implementation of the neoliberal model involves the relationship between the IMF, international commercial banks, and host government. The IMF and commercial banks expect, if not require, governments to implement conservative monetary and fiscal policies in order to provide economic stability (reduce inflation and eliminate budget deficits) and sound economic fundamentals so that capital will flow into the country (and domestic capital will not leave) in order to promote economic growth. In official circles, this kind of economic policy is called "structural adjustment." Many critics of this policy orientation and the IMF's role argue that these policies do not promote growth but induce economic stagnation and reduce the population's standard of living, while serving the vested interests of the domestic financial class and multinational institutions. In some countries, structural adjustment policies have had a major impact on employment and pay, especially for women, as described in the following article.

WOMEN'S EMPLOYMENT AND PAY UNDER STRUCTURAL ADJUSTMENT

The term *structural adjustment* signifies basic structural change in an economy. Two crucial questions: Does this change promote human development? And are women and men affected differently by it?

In many cases, women have been more adversely affected than men. In some instances, they have benefited. Compare the experiences of Mexico and Costa Rica.

Mexico

Since the mid-1980s, Mexico has rapidly altered the structure of its economy. Most trade barriers have been dismantled, state intervention has been drastically reduced, and the economy has been substantially deregulated. The government has focused on combating inflation and attracting capital inflows—and has engineered a drastic fall in wages to cheapen Mexican labour. But there has been little growth and even less job creation.

The human costs have been high. Working men have suffered: many have lost their jobs or seen their real wages cut in half. But working women have faced even greater losses. From 1984 to 1989, the ratio of female wages to male wages for urban workers dropped from 77% to 72%. Even after the economy had begun to recover in 1992, female workers still earned only three-fourths of men's wages. Women's total income declined from 71% of men's in 1984 to 66% in 1992.

Labour market discrimination against women worsened. They became more concentrated in low-wage sectors of the economy and in low-wage jobs within sectors. Export-oriented *maquiladoras* along the U.S. border provided jobs, helping to raise women's share of industrial jobs from 15% in 1984 to 18% in 1992. But the cost was heavy: women's industrial wages plummeted from 80% of men's wages to only 57%. In the meantime, women were laid off in the public sector and in other sectors, and their share of jobs dropped from 42% to 35%. Women in rural areas were hit particularly hard: their share among all income-earners dropped from 28% to 20%.

As recent events attest, Mexico's model of development has had mostly adverse effects on human development—and more so for women than for men.

Costa Rica

Costa Rica is well known for public policies that foster human development. Compared with Mexico, it has had some success in restructuring its economy since the mid-1980s by taking a gradual approach. Non-traditional exports and tourism have increased, helping to spur growth and employment. Export-oriented apparel and electronics assembly firms have created more jobs for women, but not by lowering their pay compared with other private sector jobs. And women have maintained their jobs and pay in the public sector—where they are heavily concentrated.

The government has made an explicit effort to promote gender equality. It has increased paid maternity leave, ratified the ILO convention against all forms of discrimination and toughened its own laws by passing the Law of Equality in 1990. Labour market discrimination against women persists but is on the decline.

As a result, from 1987 to 1993, the ratio of average female wages to male wages rose from 77% to 83%, and women's labour force participation rate also increased.

Much remains to be done. Many women still do not have jobs. And women still predominate in many low-paying jobs, such as domestic work. But thanks to Costa Rica's human development policies and public action, there are clear signs of progress for women—even during structural adjustment.

Source: Gindling 1994 and Alarçon-Gonzalez 1994; United Nations, *Human Development Report,* 1995.

4. Use your library and Internet resources to examine the performance of the Mexican economy since the passage of the North American Free Trade Agreement. What is your diagnosis of the Mexican economy?

Whatever the outcome, it is clear that stimulating economic growth does not in and of itself generate economic development. Economic development involves much more, as suggested by the late E. F. Schumacher, a noted British economist:

Economic development is something much wider and deeper than economics. . . . Its roots lie outside the economic sphere, in education, organization, discipline and, beyond that, in political independence and a national consciousness of self-reliance. It cannot be "produced" by skillful grafting operations carried out by foreign technicians or an indigenous elite that has lost contact with the ordinary people. It can succeed only if carried forward as a broad, popular "movement of reconstruction" with primary emphasis on the full utilization of the drive, enthusiasm, intelligence, and labor power of everyone. Success cannot be obtained by some magic produced by scientists, technicians, or economic planners. It can come only through a process of growth involving the education, organization, and discipline of the whole population. Anything less than this must end in failure.
    —E. F. Schumacher, *Small Is Beautiful,* Harper & Row, 1973, pp. 192–193.

5. Do you agree or disagree with Schumacher? Explain.

CONCLUSION

The Schumacher quotation makes it clear that economic development is a major issue and will involve a multitude of challenges for a developing nation. However, there is no substitute for the reorganization and redirection of the economy to engender increased economic growth that will increase the standard of living for the majority of the society.

Review Questions

1. What are several of the most common characteristics of a developing country?
2. What is the World Bank's classification scheme for the world's nations? Do you think that this is a useful way to group the world's nations?
3. What is the character and magnitude of global poverty? In what ways is poverty more than an economic problem?
4. What are the five basic categories of economic problems of developing nations? How would you rank them in order of importance?
5. What is the relationship between the problems of economic growth and population? Between population and the environment?
6. What is the basic economic explanation for poverty and underdevelopment in the developing world?
7. Of the three competing views of underdevelopment, which do you find to be the most convincing? Why?
8. By the early 1990s, the governments of developing nations apparently were adopting development strategies with a discernable trend. What was this trend? What do you think are the strengths of this strategy? What do you think are or could be some problems with the strategy?
9. At the Earth Summit in 1992, a consensus emerged on the need for all nations to pursue strategies of sustainable development. What does this mean for developing nations? Advanced nations?

23

Economic Systems in Transition

INTRODUCTION

As the twentieth century draws to a close, the centrally planned socialist economies of Eastern Europe and the former Soviet Union have collapsed and are starting the transition to reliance on free markets. In other parts of the world from Latin America to Asia, countries are swiftly moving toward free and open-market economies and away from economies with strong government roles. Why is this happening? What does this mean? Is this the end of socialism and the triumph of capitalism?

In this chapter, we will review the past decades of capitalism and socialism and the economic experiences of the former Soviet Union, China, and Japan. We will also examine the effect of market approaches on global environmental issues.

THE 1990S: LOOKING BACKWARD

At the end of World War II, the Bretton Woods system provided the structure and rules for a new international economic and financial system. The International Monetary Fund oversaw this international monetary system, which positioned the U.S. dollar as the key reserve currency. The system was designed to promote trade and facilitate capital flow between nations, thereby promoting growth. As we saw in the last chapter, the system survived until the early 1970s. Since its creation in 1944, the Bretton Woods system has been challenged to adjust to changes in the global system and its components. This process of constant adjustment has been difficult, yet remarkably successful in many ways.

The most dynamic agents of transformation have been the phenomenal changes in technology—in production of goods and services, communications, transportation, and information—which have dramatically altered the character of the global economic and financial system. These changes have placed enormous pressure on institutions—governments, businesses, financial institutions, and many others—to adapt.

The rapid growth of multinational (transnational) firms in the 1960s was and continues to be fueled by technological change and the pursuit of profit. It is now possible to transfer technology to any part of the globe, utilizing local labor and other resources to produce all or any part of a product. The character of modern production systems in a computer age, combined with the mobility of capital and the interchangeability of human labor, has profoundly changed the character of national economies and the international economic system itself. The globalization of production and the internationalization of capital have pushed the global economic system to a level of development unimaginable fifty years ago.

Financial institutions and financial markets have expanded and changed their roles to deal with this globalization. U.S. banks have branches throughout the world, and foreign banks have offices in the United States. Communication and information technology have allowed these financial markets and institutions to expand their operations. The Group of Seven nations (the United States, Canada, United Kingdom, France, Germany, Italy, and Japan) have—with varying degrees of success—embarked upon a path of voluntary policy coordination. And the group has called upon central banks in these countries to monitor their macroeconomic stabilization policies so as to pursue coordinated stability in the international economic and financial system.

With the conclusion of the General Agreement on Tariffs and Trade negotiations and the establishment of the World Trade Organization, nations have endorsed the goal of freer trade rhetorically but cling to protectionist policies in practice. The past several decades have seen the emergence of Japan and the successful Newly Industrializing Countries as economic powers. Yet, just as GATT and the WTO push for a global free-trade system, the world is splitting into trade blocs—Europe, the Pacific Basin, and North America. The movement toward political democratization and economic liberalization (market economies) in Eastern Europe and the former Soviet Union has created enormous challenges for the global economy. And, finally, the formal economic integration of Western Europe, which began in 1992 with the Treaty of Maastricht, has set into motion forces that will challenge the structure and operation of the European Monetary Union (EMU) and the movement toward a common European currency by the end of the century.

Along with these trade efforts have come significant changes in other dimensions of the economy. The Cold War economic and military tension between the United States and the former Soviet Union has come to an end. Poverty levels in the developing world have continued to expand. And nations have recognized the environmental challenges associated with the need for sustainable development. Together, these changes have brought the international system to a historic turning point. Clearly, the end of the twentieth century marks the end of one era and the beginning of another.

1. Do you agree that the global community is indeed at the end of one era and at the beginning of a new era? Explain.

ECONOMIC SYSTEMS REVISITED: CAPITALISM AND SOCIALISM

Capitalism and socialism have been the two predominant models of economic systems in the twentieth century. But now most nations are attempting to find the right combination of free markets and government policies to achieve stable economic development. Throughout the world, this may produce very different kinds of mixed economies and market-government institutions.

Most would argue that socialism has met with economic and political failure. The desire for individual freedom and political democracy along with the inability of authoritarian and bureaucratic socialist economies to provide for an increased standard of living resulted in widespread revolutionary changes in Eastern Europe and the former Soviet Union in the 1990s. At the end of the century, China, Vietnam, North Korea, and Cuba remain the predominant countries committed to making a variant of market socialism work.

Capitalism, as we have seen, is characterized by the private ownership of the factors of production. This system relies primarily on markets to allocate scarce resources. The free-market system allows prices to be determined by the interaction of supply and demand. Socialism, on the other hand, is characterized by the public (social) ownership of capital and natural resources. The following lists contrast the major characteristics of these two systems.

CAPITALISM AND SOCIALISM

Capitalism
- Private ownership of the means of production
- A market in labor
  a. Workers are divorced from ownership.
  b. Workers are without control over the process of production or choice of product produced.
  c. The price of labor (wage) is determined by the supply and demand for labor.
- A market for land and natural resources
- Income distribution based on market-determined returns to owned factors of production (land, labor, and capital)
- Markets in essential commodities (basic needs)
- Control of the means of production (capital) and the production process by owners of capital or their managerial representatives, with profit as the main objective

Socialism

- Public (social) ownership of the means of production
- Labor markets determined by planning decisions
  a. Workers participate in self-management and/or shared decision making.
  b. The price of labor is determined by planners in accordance with a market wage (supply and demand) in combination with a social wage that incorporates the free provision of many basic needs (health, education, transportation, housing, etc.).
- Government allocation of land and natural resources.
- Income distribution based on a market-determined wage, guided by government planning, in accordance with a social wage and government goals of reducing inequalities in the distribution of income (rather than income related to the ownership of capital or the exploitation of labor)
- Provision of basic needs at no charge or at government-subsidized prices (social wage), with the goal of maximizing public welfare
- Full employment of human resources, utilizing moral and material incentives for increasing output and efficiency, guided by planning

Socialism relies upon social ownership and the process of planning to make decisions about resource allocation. Some socialist countries have utilized both planning and the market system to allocate scarce resources. Such market socialism is intended to utilize the best from each basic system. In practice, this usually produced a mixed economy that included both private and public ownership of the means of production and a private market economy supported by government planning. These ideal—theoretical—types of economic systems do not exist anywhere in the world today. Yet every nation today has an economy that combines some elements of these systems.

The primary distinction between national economies generally comes down to the character of property relations, that is, between private or public ownership of the factors of production and the role of free markets. In capitalism, private ownership prevails, with corporations and other business making decisions about production based on profit expectations. In socialism, the goal of production of enterprises is influenced by state (social) objectives.

THE COLLAPSE OF THE SOVIET UNION

Seventy-four years after the Russian Revolution, the socialist economic system that had evolved in the Soviet Union suffered a virtual collapse. On September 5, 1991, the Congress of People's Deputies transferred power to the new independent republics. The Baltic states of Estonia, Lithuania, and Latvia regained their independence.

The emergence, growth and expansion, and eventual collapse of the Soviet economic system is an important story, but much too long and complicated to tell here. It is important to understand some of the highlights, however, to see what this might mean for the rest of the world.

Early History: 1917–1979

The Bolshevik Revolution in 1917 took place in a semifeudal society made up of great landowners and peasants, all under the domination of a succession of czars. Karl Marx had predicted that socialism (or the first phase of communism) would evolve out of a mature, well-developed, industrial capitalist economy. This revolution would be led by organized industrial workers, who would overthrow the capitalist owners of capital. After a period of transition, Marx thought, full communism would emerge with the elimination of the private ownership of the means of production and usher in a classless society without the exploitation of labor. Thus, the first experience with socialism in the twentieth century took place in a country that lacked Marx's preconditions. Nevertheless, the Russian Marxist revolutionary V. I. Lenin, the early architect of the new Soviet socialist economic system, believed it was possible to construct such a society even in a very undeveloped agricultural nation—the Soviet Union.

The years between 1917 and 1921 were violent and politically chaotic. A civil war ensued and lasted until 1921, after which the Communist Party under the leadership of Lenin set the direction for the development of socialism. Lenin's death in 1924 led to the installation of Joseph Stalin as the new head of the Communist Party. Stalin felt that the key to economic success was to force the Russian peasantry into collectivized state farms. To do this, he first had to nationalize the land belonging to rich landowners. His logic was that collective farms would be more efficient at producing economic surplus, which the state sector, in turn, could use for investment in agriculture and industry.

The economic surplus produced by the agricultural sector allowed for the rapid development of the industrial sector of the Soviet economy, but the savings generated by the Soviet people came at the expense of a decreased standard of living. The legacy of this approach can be seen in the fact that between 1950 and 1980, the Soviet Union allocated less than 60 percent of its GNP to consumption, roughly 25 percent to fixed investments, and about 15 percent to the defense sector.

By 1940 this centrally planned economy had grown into an impressive industrial production system, despite a persistently weak agricultural sector (compounded by geography and climate). World War II devastated the nation and its industrial infrastructure. Yet by the 1950s, the economy had been rebuilt and was back on its impressive economic growth track. But the Cold War tensions between the United States and the Soviet Union in the aftermath of World War II grew into a long and costly arms race for both nations.

The Soviet Planning System

For sixty years the Soviet economy was organized around a series of five-year plans. At the highest levels of the government, economic planners made all the basic decisions about economic growth and output goals. This required decisions related to investment, consumption, prices, and resource inputs. All of the decisions left to the market system in a capitalist economy were being made by planners in a centralized governmental system. The planners even set prices for resources and consumer goods. Obviously, this arrangement placed great power and responsibility in the hands of the bureaucrats who did the planning. In essence, their decisions allocated the resources of the society.

The planning process involved many stages. The initial formulation of the five-year plan by the state economic planning agency, GOSPLAN, involved the integration of thousands of pieces of information. Central planners utilized input-output analysis to determine the resource requirements for the production of specific goods, from shoes to automobiles to tanks. GOSPLAN had to quantify the amount of physical resources, capital resources, and labor necessary to produce a product, then allocate the factors of production to the proper sectors and geographic locations necessary for the final product to be produced.

The system of central planning produced growth rates that averaged over 5 percent a year from 1960 to 1970. But by the mid-1960s, pressure was building to liberalize the planning process in order to overcome what were then recognized to be inefficiencies inherent in centralized planning, which led to shortages, surpluses, and the lack of incentives to harvest crops. These reforms, which involved gradually introducing market practices in pricing, were not widespread. The 1970s witnessed a sharp slowdown in economic growth. Between 1971 and 1975, annual economic growth slowed to 3.7 percent, and by the end of the 1970s, it fell to rates of less than 1 percent.

Crisis and Change: 1980–1986

The early 1980s continued to be difficult times for the Soviet economy. Economic growth rates fluctuated between 2 percent in 1981 and 0.8 percent in 1985. It was becoming increasingly clear that the economy was stagnating and that centralized planning was not working. The poor performance of the economy was related to the inherent inefficiencies of a centralized bureaucratic planning process, and the distortions in the economy were related to the continued allocation of sizable resources to the defense sector. The Soviet people's standard of living was not increasing; more importantly, their expectations were not being met (especially in view of the standard of living in Europe and the United States). In addition, the state bureaucracy had become rigid and resistant to change at a time when political pressures both inside and outside the Communist Party were pushing for political and economic change. This set the stage for the emergence of Mikhail Gorbachev, who became the new General Secretary of the Communist Party in March 1985 with a reform platform.

Gorbachev understood that the economic system would have to be transformed from a centralized planned economy to a more democratic decentralized economy. He also understood the waste of resources involved in the Cold War. Such a new economy would utilize many of the tools and policies of a capitalist market system yet still operate under the basic goals and framework of a socialist system. His plan was to limit GOSPLAN to long-term strategic planning and allow most of the day-to-day economic decisions to be made at the level of the state enterprise. This would allow managers more flexibility.

Perestroika: 1987–1991

By the mid-1980s, a consensus had been reached that the Soviet system was suffering from inadequate technological progress, an overgrown and inefficient centralized planning agency, deficient management of state enterprises, and a distorted price structure. Mikhail Gorbachev described his strategy for economic transformation in his book *Perestroika: New Thinking for Our Country and The World* (1987). The philosophy of perestroika was based on a number of elements but could be reduced essentially to three primary needs of the Soviet economy in the late 1980s:

1. To increase the role of material incentives (wages, salaries, and bonuses)
2. To expand the number of private economic actors (firms)
3. To transform many of the state enterprises into autonomous private enterprises (a process called privatization)

This, Gorbachev thought, would allow for a mixed economy with both public and private ownership. The emergence and expansion of a dynamic private sector would begin to introduce market dynamics in an economy that would be progressively less centralized and planned.

2. What do you think would be some practical operational problems associated with the process of privatization? (Put yourself in the place of a manager having to change from a state-owned enterprise to a market-driven firm.

Gorbachev and his advisers understood that such a transition would be difficult, yet imperative. His policy of glasnost, which increased the openness and democratic character of the political system, was welcomed as a complement to the economic liberalization programs embodied in perestroika. Additionally, the relaxation of Cold War tensions between the United States and the Soviet Union created a climate conducive to transition, as well as freeing up some resources for other uses.

By 1990 the economic reforms of perestroika and the political instability resulting from democratization pushed the Soviet economy into chaos. The nation's gross domestic product dropped from 5 percent in 1988 to a negative 15 percent by the end of 1991. By the end of 1991, the economic crisis and its political impact made it impossible for Gorbachev to govern. After a failed conservative coup in August 1991, one of Gorbachev's major political rivals—Boris Yeltsin—was elected President of the Russian Republic.

The Commonwealth of Independent States

All of Gorbachev's efforts to revive and stabilize the economy from 1990 through 1991 were insufficient. The conservative old guard resisted the liberalization reforms, while the radical reformers wanted to accelerate the economic reforms. By late September 1991, the radical reformers had taken charge. The Congress of People's Deputies transferred power to the republics, and the former Soviet Union ceased to exist. (In terms of size, however, the Russian Republic dominated the other independent republics and the independent Baltic states of Estonia, Latvia, and Lithuania.)

This new Commonwealth of Independent States faced enormous economic and political challenges. What would a new economic federation look like? How would it function? Would there be a single monetary system? How would trade take place? Would there be uniform commercial and civil laws? How would the IMF and the World Bank interact with the independent states? What would be the role of the West with respect to bilateral world aid, technology transfer, and foreign investment? How successful would the privatization efforts be? Would the citizens of these new independent republics be patient for the economic reforms to produce results?

▦ EASTERN EUROPE: ECONOMIC LIBERALIZATION

The nations of Eastern Europe—Albania, Bulgaria, the Czech Republic, Slovakia, Hungary, Poland, Romania, Bosnia and Herzegovina, Croatia, and Yugoslavia—have been in economic transition since the mid-1980s. Many of the economic reforms brought forth by Gorbachev in the former Soviet Union were already under way in Eastern Europe in the 1980s. These economic changes aimed at bringing forth a dynamic market economy in the context of political democratization. It was not only the inefficiency of centralized planning but the rigidity and repressive nature of authoritarian government leaders (often military) that together spelled the collapse of the economies and the political systems of Eastern Europe.

The Eastern European economies had been integrated with the Soviet economy for decades. Even though they had been slowly opening themselves up to the West in terms of trade, loans, and some foreign investment, they were still basically planned economies under the influence of the Soviet Union. Clearly, the changes that took place first in Eastern Europe had a significant economic and political impact on the Soviet Union. By the late 1980s and early 1990s, both Eastern Europe and the former Soviet Union were well along the path to an unprecedented political economic transition.

In Eastern Europe, the economic liberalization strategy called for a number of basic steps to build a market economy. The consensus among government officials and economists was that Eastern Europe needed to lift price controls, reduce subsidies, privatize state enterprises, end monopolies, create a convertible currency, allow unemployment and layoffs, permit bankruptcies, and create a sound banking system.

The fall of the Berlin Wall led to political euphoria and grandiose hopes and dreams with respect to German unification (the merging of West and East Germany, separated after World War II). The early years of German reunification proved to be difficult and costly. But the prospect of a free and open Eastern Europe excited investors all over the world. There was a sense of great anticipation. Many felt that new foreign investment would create jobs and boost production. By late 1992 there was considerable evidence of foreign investment flowing to Eastern Europe, but nothing near the magnitude of what was expected. The recession of 1990–1991 in the Western countries and the economic costs of reform in Eastern Europe did not provide a good climate for a large-scale investment flow.

The challenge of economic integration in Western Europe has also inhibited the economic transition in Eastern Europe. The costs of West Germany's reunification with East Germany have hampered Germany from serving as the "economic locomotive" for Western Europe. The sustained strength and attractiveness of the U.S. economy, as well as the growth and expansion of emerging markets in Latin America and Southeast Asia, have drawn foreign capital from all over the world. Indeed, there is a fierce global competitiveness for foreign capital and investment.

THE PEOPLE'S REPUBLIC OF CHINA

We should not interpret the collapse of socialism in Eastern Europe and the former Soviet Union as the downfall of socialism or communism everywhere. In China, one-fifth of humanity is still living in an economically functioning socialist country—evidence that a variant of socialism is still with us. Economic and foreign policy analysts must consider China's political and economic role in the present and emerging global system.

China has one of the longest cultural, political, and economic histories of any country in the world. It was a relatively developed and sophisticated society centuries before Columbus discovered the New World. Yet, as Europe emerged from the Middle Ages and grew into a modern economy, China stood still. By the time the communist revolutionary Mao Tse-tung came to power in 1949 after a peasant-led revolution, China was still basically a feudalistic agricultural society.

The primary thrust of the Chinese Revolution was to reform the agricultural system. This meant taking land from rich landowners and redistributing it to peasants, who would work the land collectively and share in the fruits of their labor. With economic aid and technology from the Soviet Union in the 1950s, China began to transform both the agricultural and industrial sectors of its economy. These efforts met with mixed results between the late 1950s and the mid-1960s. The debates over economic strategy and policy centered around work incentives. Proponents of moral incentives argued that the workers' revolutionary consciousness ought to be enough to motivate them to produce for the general welfare. Proponents of material incentives argued that workers' revolutionary consciousness alone would not increase economic output for the general social welfare. Higher wages, salaries, bonuses, and promotions would need to be a part of the approach to economic production. Those who argued for material incentives also supported the liberalization of the economy and the introduction of free-market practices. These reforms would have introduced market prices and decentralized the planning process.

Mao regenerated support for the ideals of the socialist revolution and the primacy of moral incentives. From 1965 to the mid-1970s, under Mao's leadership, China entered a period known as the Great Proletarian Cultural Revolution. Those who favored material incentives were denounced. Professionals were sent from urban areas to work in the countryside. Universities were closed down, and students spread out all over the country, carrying the word of Mao. People who resisted the government or were considered enemies of the state were arrested, often tortured, and in some cases murdered. This period of revolutionary upheaval caused the economy to stagnate. The per capita income and production gains made in the 1950s and early 1960s were lost. Only after Mao's death in 1976 did the Cultural Revolution end and the country begin to revive economically.

In 1978 the Chinese Central Committee under the leadership of Deng Xiaoping brought forward dramatic reforms. These reforms took place in agriculture, industry, and the character of property rights. In 1979 Deng ended the agricultural commune system. Workers who did own land individually and worked for the collective welfare were now able to actually own their own parcel of land. They could sell any agricultural surplus they produced and keep the income for themselves. Peasant farm families could work for wages (wage labor) outside the family plot. As a result of these changes, annual increases in farm output averaged 8 percent between 1979 and 1984, compared to only 2 percent a year for the 1958–1978 period. Industrial reforms also produced impressive results. State enterprises were allowed to keep 15 to 25 percent of the profits above those required by the central planners. By the mid-1980s, these firms were able to keep 85 percent of their profits. The use of material incentives generated greater production and began to reduce the role of the state. Finally, Deng's reforms allowed for the emergence of small private enterprises. These new private enterprises were allowed to compete with state enterprises, especially in the retail sector. This change unleashed an entrepreneurial spirit throughout China.

By the late 1970s, the Chinese economy was opened up to Western influences for the first time since 1948. Tourists and those interested in trade and investment opportunities were permitted to travel in China and deal with government officials. Chinese students were permitted to study abroad. A new era had begun.

The Chinese economy continued to grow and expand in the 1980s under Deng's leadership and the leadership of Zhao Ziyang, the prime minister. Their strategy was to rely on centralized economic planning to direct economic activity in the major sectors of the economy, such as heavy industry, but at the same time to introduce elements of a market economy into the economy. The introduction of private ownership in agriculture and in small enterprises set into motion a silent economic revolution that grew rapidly and carried with it the additional demand of political democracy.

Deng's political power base was in the urban centers, where most of the large-scale, heavy industrial state enterprises are located. With his reforms, the state began to change the character and composition of its role, and the state's fiscal role changed radically. In 1978 state government expenditures were almost 35 percent of GNP, and tax revenues were about the same. By 1989 government expenditures had dropped to 23 percent of GNP, and tax revenues to 21 percent of GNP.

In May 1989 thousands of university students and workers gathered in Tiananmen Square in Beijing to challenge the authority of the government. This political unrest was related to the desire for more political freedom and democracy. The protest continued until June 3, when the government sent tanks and troops into the square to clear the demonstrators. Many people were killed, others arrested and tortured, and some executed. World opinion turned against the repressive Chinese government, and the democracy movement was driven underground.

The years after Tiananmen Square have seen political stability and economic growth return to China. In 1991 the real GDP grew at a rate of 10 percent. Yet there is a strong sense among many analysts that China's economic liberalization trend, along with a repressed desire for political democracy, will eventually bring about tremendous changes.

In 1991 state enterprises produced only 50 percent of the nation's industrial output, compared to 80 percent in 1979. The state sector is shrinking, less efficient, and costly to support. The Chinese workforce seems to be infected with new and growing ambitions and expectations with respect to the private economy, especially in rural areas.

The state has less and less revenue with which to maintain the costly state enterprises and their workforce. State workers receive generous benefits for education, housing, and medical care. Over one-third of the government's budget supports subsidies, and almost 50 percent of these subsidies are absorbed by the state-owned enterprises.

The economic tension between the rural agricultural sector and the declining urban industrial sector appears to be on a collision course. The inherent political conflict and consequences seem also to be predictable. In the meantime, China continues to grow and appears stable. Yet this apparent calm cannot erase the fact that, although China's saving rate is 40 percent of its GDP, the country has no financial system capable of utilizing these savings in a productive manner. The nation's infrastructure is in terrible condition and in need of expansion. Energy and raw materials are in short supply all over the country. Other challenges are a growing appetite for consumption goods and an emerging environmental crisis (especially air pollution) in cities.

Will China maintain this unique variant of socialism or in time yield to the economic and political pressures calling for a market economy and political democracy? The rest of the world will be watching with great interest. The following article from *The Wall Street Journal* takes a look at the human consequences of China's transitional economic and political policies.

DESPITE RAPID GROWTH OF CHINA'S ECONOMY, MANY ARE SUFFERING

Craig S. Smith and Marcus W. Brauchli

The causalities of China's economic revolution are rising.

Among them is a thin, 39-year-old worker named Fang. Caught in a financial squeeze, the state-owned medicine factory that employed Mr. Fang stopped paying him early this year. Its once-popular remedies had lost market share to new imports—just as China's government, trying to slash deficits, withdrew subsidies.

In the decade and a half since the national patriarch, Deng Xiaoping, began his historic turn toward market economics, growth in this nominally Communist land has averaged an amazing 10% a year; this year, it is likely to top that again, as it has for three years in a row. Hopes for a modern, technology-driven economy are proudly cited by national leaders.

Yet more and more Chinese are sunk into gloom. Determined to avoid a ruinous bout of inflation, Beijing's economic policy makers have been tightening up for two years. Once-frothy real-estate and securities markets are sluggish. Banks are swamped with nonperforming loans. Unable to obtain fresh capital, many companies, especially state-run behemoths such as Mr. Fang's employer, are in suspended animation. Tens of millions of workers have been idled, if not officially laid off.

The result: heavy pressure on Beijing to open the money spigot again and renew a cycle of tightening, then loosening, controls in a quest for economic stability. Few expect the central bank to start printing cash—the bank's governor vows to keep monetary policy "appropriately tight" in the months ahead—but a selective easing to bolster sagging industries seems likely. Some state companies have won clearance to convert debt into equity to free up new borrowing power. Others are planning international stock issues.

Fast Growth Needed

Unstated, but plainly evident, is a rising consensus that China's economy must race ahead to avoid disaster. "It seems China's economic growth cannot be lower than 10% to keep pace with the demands of society," says Chen Jiagui, a senior research fellow at Beijing's Academy of Social Sciences. Another Beijing economist warns of "political and economic collapse" if growth falls below 7%.

That may sound alarmist, but China's growth centers in its urban and coastal areas, where many people already feel prosperous, and is diluted inland, where 900 million of China's 1.2 billion people live in relative backwardness. There, huge state companies and farms employ three-quarters of the country's workers, and Beijing's austerity drive hurts people whose expectations also have soared. When those expectations aren't met at home, millions go in search of them, in China's cities and abroad. That, according to

Shanghai Academy of Social Sciences economist Zhang Daogen, is why slower growth "could lead to social problems, even rebellion."

President Jiang Zemin tacitly acknowledges the risk. In a major policy address splashed all over major newspapers last week, he laid out a 12-point program calling for "proper handling" of the economy to ensure social stability.

The Pain in 1989

Of course, the Chinese have endured harsher tribulations than the current credit squeeze, and as long as the economy offers any hope of improving their lives, few are likely to act on their frustrations. But the last time Beijing stepped on the brakes hard was 1989, and the resulting pain contributed to the unrest that culminated in the bloody suppression of the Tiananmen Square demonstrations. This year, President Jiang and other leaders visited China's bleak northeast—a sooty rust belt of steel mills and smelters—to assuage factory managers and gauge the mood of idled workers. . . .

Some in Beijing want to revoke the relative autonomy enjoyed by South China's five special economic zones, where speculation in stocks and many commodities was rampant before the credit clampdown. With money tight and corporate profits now squeezed, stock prices are off more than 50% in the past 18 months.

The plunge in financial markets is partly what Beijing wanted, fearing that runaway investments was squandering assets. Now, huge sums are tied up in empty buildings and abandoned construction sites, mostly owned by state companies that financed the projects with bank loans. So, the tight credit is threatening the banks. Because real estate is often sold several times, with each buyer making only a partial down payment, a vacant building can represent a maze of debt—and of lawsuits. Almost every real-estate company in Haikou is suing someone or being sued. Banks won't foreclose because most have already reached the limit on fixed assets they are allowed to carry.

"The banks can't stand it much longer," says a banker in Hainan, where nearly half of outstanding bank loans are nonperforming. Thanks to interest rates that have topped 20% on both loans and deposits, banks are suddenly flush with money. But they have been ordered to suspend almost all lending to battle inflation that a year ago soared above 20% on an annualized basis.

So, while the banks pay more interest to depositors, many squeezed borrowers are no longer making payments on their loans. The result: Three of the country's five major banks lost money in the first half of this year, though inflation has dropped to about 12% in some cities.

The Biggest Danger

Ultimately, the most dangerous fallout of austerity is unemployment. It is especially pernicious in this would-be workers' paradise because there isn't any real social safety net for the jobless. The government says 530,000 enterprises employing 79 million workers now provide some kind of unemployment insurance. But the benefits are scant, sometimes only a fraction of the skimpy $60-a-month salaries most urban workers get at state factories (housing is usually provided with a job).

Instead of outright layoffs, many state companies choose indefinite furloughs with sustenance pay. But the money is barely enough for workers to feed themselves, let alone buy anything else.

Even furloughed workers are being stuck with new bills. At Shanghai's Wuzhou Garment Factory, money is so tight that the factory no longer covers all of its workers' medical bills. "Before we paid everything, but now, if a worker goes to the hospital and has a 5,000 yuan [$602] bill, we'll only pay 2,000, and the worker has to come up with the rest," says the factory's manager, Wang Yaoming. Workers should be reimbursed eventually by the state, he adds, but such payments now take months.

Officially, China's unemployment rate is low: just 3% of its 160 million urban workers. Yet the government admits that up to 80 million people—more than all the people in Germany—have been cut adrift. Most are peasants no longer needed on the increasingly efficient farms; so, they travel to cities—or go abroad—in search of work. Many villages have developed cottage industries to keep them employed, though the work usually is seasonal; starch factories, for example, that depend on corn harvests for raw material.

Companies Relocated

In addition, the government has begun relocating companies to the hinterlands to soak up excess labor. Several Shanghai textile and garment factories have been moved to far-west Xinjiang province, which is nearer China's cotton farms. But moving factories takes jobs from city workers and isn't enough to keep masses of idle rural workers home.

In Fuzhou, the capital of Fujian province, a city official estimates that the number of unemployed itinerants has soared to 25,000 from 10,000 two years ago. The local government tries to send them back home but can't afford the fares. "It's a very big headache," he says.

Moreover, maintaining the credit squeeze could force the beleaguered state sector to close money-losing businesses and cast out another 30 million people, economists say. They think the jobless ranks are swelling by nearly 20% a year—hardly what the government wants.

In Shanghai, where 400 state enterprises have closed in recent months, the city is trying to develop service industries to absorb the idled workers. Right now, it takes an average of 32 months for a laid-off person to find a job. Getting private companies to hire workers is one solution—and another reason China's government, eager to speed the companies' growth, feels pressure to relent on austerity.

Upbeat Examples Scorned

Although Lu Qiwei, deputy division chief of Shanghai's labor bureau, cites approvingly a 48-year-old woman who was laid off by a failing textile company, set up her own tailor shop and "ended up employing others," many Chinese sneer at such upbeat examples. Only young people with energy and entrepreneurial talent can successfully switch to private business, says a furloughed Shanghai factory worker named Zou, who, at 38, is scraping up a living by delivering goods with a tricycle cart. The others, without enough education to get private-sector jobs, stay home. "Some factories have a policy of sending home anyone above the age of 40," admits Han Wei, an administrator at Shanghai No. 2 Textile Machinery Co., which has furloughed 2% of its work force.

With China's frustrated jobless running low on lope, some companies see evidence that the pressures to ease up are getting to Beijing, Shanghai Haixing Shipping Co., whose first-half profit plunged 73%, has noticed a slight pickup in coal shipments along the coast. But loosening credit, says Yang Fan, a Beijing economist, risks a return to the overheated economy of the early 1990s. Unemployment is a "very serious problem," he says, but the government could muster the money for unemployment insurance if it taxed enterprises more aggressively, enforced tariff laws and halted corruption.

That's a tall order for China's unruly bureaucracy, but one that Beijing is trying, gradually, to fill. Until it can, letting money flow faster through the economy may be the only way China's leaders can placate the swelling ranks of people hurt by austerity. Says Zhang Daogen, the Shanghai economist: "As long as people have money, they can tolerate inflation."

Source: *The Wall Street Journal*, October 18, 1995. Reprinted by permission of The Wall Street Journal, © 1995 Dow Jones & Company, Inc. All Rights Reserved Worldwide.

3. What seem to be the most significant human consequences of China's economic policies in the late 1990s?

THE JAPANESE ECONOMY

One of the truly remarkable economic success stories of the past four decades has been the growth and expansion of the Japanese economy. This was a particularly sensitive issue in the 1970s and 1980s as the U.S. economy faltered but the Japanese economy was a consistently solid performer.

Except China, no other country has matched Japan's impressive growth rates during the 1971–1991 period. The period 1971–1975 registered a 4.5 percent annual average, followed by 4.6 percent for the 1976-1980 period, and 3.8 percent for 1981–1985. From 1986 to 1991, while most of the other modern industrial countries experienced sluggish growth rates, the Japanese economy sailed along strongly—only to encounter some serious difficulties throughout the remainder of the 1990s, as we shall see.

Japan, with 123 million people crammed into 378,000 square kilometers (compared to 250 million people in the United States on 9,373,000 square kilometers), has managed to reach a per capita GDP of $25,430 compared to $21,790 for the United States in 1990. Japan's GDP in 1990 was $2.95 trillion compared to $5.40 trillion for the United States. In 1990 Japan exported $286 billion and imported $231 billion of goods and services, leaving it with a current account balance of $40 billion and gross international reserves of $87 billion. The United States in the same year exported $371 billion and imported $515 billion of goods and services, leaving it with a current account deficit of $71 billion and gross international reserves of $173 billion.

The Formula for Success

While there are many competing explanations for the relative success of the Japanese economy, an emerging consensus credits the combination of high saving and investment rates, the ability to develop and implement technology, a well-educated labor force, and government policies that support the unique institutional structure of Japan's private sector.

Saving and Investment Rates. Japanese citizens have the highest domestic saving rate in the world—at around 19 percent of income, compared to less than 6 percent in the United States. As a nation, Japan saved 34 percent of its GDP in 1990, compared to only 15 percent in the United States. On the investment side, Japan in 1990 had a gross domestic investment rate of 33 percent, compared to only 16 percent for the United States.

Technological Innovation. Japan has developed processes and institutions (through support from government policies) that have allowed for the rapid development and implementation of technology. Robert B. Reich, a professor at Harvard University's John F. Kennedy School of Government, has examined the ways in which technology is developed in Japan and applied to the production process. He found that the time periods from the development of the concepts and ideas to the actual use and application of new technologies is about three to four times as fast in Japan as in the United States. This has to do with the lengthy linear process typically used in the United States compared to a faster and more interactive process used in Japan. The difference is probably best characterized in the way the Japanese car manufacturers, especially Toyota, have introduced lean and flexible manufacturing, the core of world-class manufacturing, as we saw in Chapter 2.

Labor Force and Labor-Management Relations. Japan has the most highly trained and skilled workforce in the world. This partially explains why productivity and efficiency are so high and contribute to vibrant economic growth. The workforce is disciplined and displays a strong work ethic. Culturally the workforce is conditioned to cooperative behavior and participatory decision making at the workplace. Also the distribution of income is less uneven than in the United States, and the wage/salary differential between the lowest- and highest-paid workers within enterprises is much less. Many Japanese workers are guaranteed lifetime employment.

Role of the Government. Among the major industrial nations, Japan has a government that is probably the most supportive of the private sector. Government agencies like the Bank of Japan (the central bank), the Economic Planning Agency, the Ministry of Finance, and the Ministry of International Trade and Industry (MITI) work together to create a powerful private corporate sector. The government sector is small (in terms of spending) compared to those of other major industrial nations and does not devote any significant share of its public financial resources to defense.

Industrial Policy and Conglomerate Structure

Before World War II, Japan had a history of large corporate conglomerates, called *zaibatsu*, which were owned by a few rich families. After the war, these were dissolved. Since then, six very strong and powerful corporate groups have emerged: Mitsui, Mitsubishi, Sumitomo, Fuji, Sanwa, and Dai-Ichi Kangyo. These corporate groups are involved in the production, distribution, and financial aspects of the economy by way of *keiretsu* arrangements.

A production **keiretsu** is a stable, mutually beneficial long-term relationship between a large "core" firm and its subcontractors (suppliers). It has allowed for the emergence of the **kanban** ("just-in-time") system, in which suppliers produce and deliver parts required in production precisely when and where they are needed. *Kanban* eliminates costly inventories, in-house production of components, and reliance on unrelated market suppliers. This production system arrangement avoids organizational rigidity and allows for the rapid development and application of technology.

The financial *keiretsu* arrangement provides for two distinct functions: cross-stock holdings, and the main-bank system. The cross-stock holdings system allows huge corporate conglomerates to own each other's stock, thereby solidifying common purpose and interests among companies of a corporate group. For example, the top ten stockholders within a group of companies hold an average of 24 percent of the total stock of companies belonging to the same group. Toyota belongs to the Mitsui group, and the top ten shareholders own 38 percent of Toyota stock. Of these top ten shareholders, five are commercial banks, one is a credit bank, two are life insurance companies, one is a supplier to Toyota, and another is a distributor. By 1990 cross-stock holdings accounted for over 60 percent of the total stock held in Japan. Such a system gives the parent company control over its subsidiaries.

The main-bank system allows the largest bank lender to a firm to monitor the company's financial performance, take an active role in strategic planning, and perform as lender of last resort if the firm falls upon difficult times.

Cross-stock holdings have allowed the separation of management and ownership. Management is protected against the short-term interest of individual stockholders. The main-bank system has permitted firms to implement long-term business strategies for investment and research and development.

The distribution of goods and services takes place within the same kind of *keiretsu* organizational arrangements. Within a conglomerate group of companies, a parent company arranges for the distribution of goods and services for its subsidiaries. By systematizing distribution in this way, firms can achieve great efficiency gains and emphasize service.

Their success is also due in part to the unique relationship between the Japanese government and this *keiretsu* system. Clearly, the Japanese government sees its role as actively promoting the success of the private sector. This is most evident in the operation of the Ministry of International Trade and Industry. MITI's functions are to sponsor research and development activities related to new technologies and products, to strategically use foreign aid to promote the economic and diplomatic interest of Japan, and to direct flows of foreign investment. Robert Ozaki, an expert on Japanese industrial policy, has described MITI's functions as comprehensive and far reaching:

It [MITI] is responsible for shaping the structure of industry and making necessary adjustments for industrial dislocations as they occur, properly guiding the development of specific industries and the production and distribution of their products, managing Japanese foreign trade and commercial relations with other nations, ensuring an adequate supply of energy and raw materials to industry and managing particular areas such as small business policy, patents, and regional development. To achieve these goals, MITI plays many roles ranging from that of broad policy architect to ad hoc working-level problem solver, and from formal regulator to regional policy arbiter or informal administrative guide. In some areas MITI holds strong statutory authority; elsewhere it has only a broad and weak influence. This kind of governmental entity with its powers and functions is a major factor in Japan's success.

> —Robert J. Ozaki, "How Japanese Industrial Policy Works," in *The Industrial World Policy Debate*, edited by Chalmers Johnson, Institute for Contemporary Studies, 1984, p. 54.

Japan in the Late 1990s

Japan's meteoric economic and financial success from the 1970s to the early 1990s has been overshadowed by an uneven economic growth record accompanied by serious banking and financial problems. Banks, long protected by the Japanese government, are reeling under $260 billion in bad debt. The Japanese stock market lost over $2 trillion in value between 1989 and 1997. These economic problems have produced a tense political environment as Japan's leaders move to open the Japanese economy and guide this still strong and powerful nation into the twenty-first century.

SUSTAINABLE DEVELOPMENT AND THE ENVIRONMENTAL CRISIS

As you have seen throughout this book, an unregulated market economy produces market failure, or negative externalities, when it comes to the physical environment. Even a regulated market system only succeeds at setting a particular level of pollution that is determined to be acceptable (based on an assessment of cost and risk). The pollution and degradation of the environment continue nevertheless. Many critics have argued that preventing current and future environmental degradation requires a new world view that focuses on developing environmentally sustainable ways to produce, consume, distribute, and dispose of goods and services. This argument recognizes the need for global economic growth, but in a way that does not violate or degrade our Earth capital—the physical life-support systems of the planet.

Many experts, including Lester Brown from the Worldwatch Institute, argue that we have already pushed beyond critical thresholds in our use and degradation of renewable and nonrenewable resources. As the growth of the global population (particularly in developing countries) continues, we can

— Pedestrians in the shopping district of Macao, China. *(Paul Conklin/PhotoEdit)*

witness many symptoms of damage: early stages of global climate change, or global warming (the greenhouse effect); atmospheric change and ozone depletion; water scarcity; declining water quality; declining per capita grain production; soil erosion; overfishing; overgrazing; air and water pollution; and the loss of species and biodiversity.

While particular environmental problems are unique, they typically stem from economic growth fueled by resources that are nonrenewable, notably petroleum, natural gas, coal, and uranium. Environmental experts believe that the global community is nearing (if it has not already surpassed) many of the earth's physical limits. Their concern is that this kind of industrial economic growth is unsustainable.

This overall perspective is easiest to understand in the context of the following two figures reproduced from a best-selling environmental science textbook, *Living in the Environment* by G. Tyler Miller. In Figure 23.1, Earth capital, in the center of the diagram, is the foundation upon which the earth's life support system is based. Degrading or destroying this foundation undermines the ability to sustain life and the quality of that life. Economic growth that destroys Earth capital is unsustainable. Figure 23.2 identifies the social, political, economic, and environmental problems that derive in part from the earth's environmental and resource problems. Miller takes the position that human beings must adopt a new world view of sustainability and create the kinds of practices and institutions necessary to preserve the earth's biological and physical integrity.

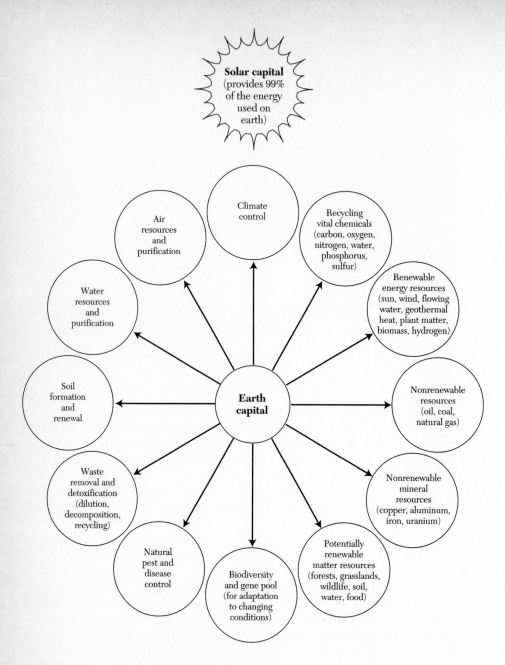

▬ FIGURE 23.1 Solar and Earth Capital

Solar and Earth capital consists of the life-support systems provided by the sun and the planet for use by humans and other species. These two forms of capital support and sustain all life and all economies on the earth.

Source: G. Tyler Miller, *Living in the Environment.*

Chapter 23 ECONOMIC SYSTEMS IN TRANSITION

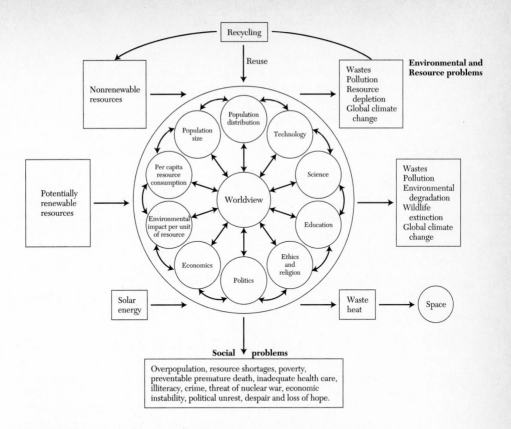

FIGURE 23.2 Factors Causing Environmental and Social Problems

Environmental, resource, and social problems are caused by a complex, poorly understood mix of interacting factors, as illustrated by this simplified model.

Source: G. Tyler Miller, *Living in the Environment.*

GLOBAL RESTRUCTURING AND THE FUTURE OF CAPITALISM

In the face of the economic, political, and environmental challenges confronting the global community in a time of rapid change and transformation, it is predictable that there are many competing perspectives on the character of this change and where it will lead into the next century. Many experts, including Lester C. Thurow in *The Future of Capitalism* (1996), have explored recently the future prospects of global capitalism. Let's examine three distinct perspectives.

Many proponents of the free-market system view this transition, even with its problems, as a necessary adjustment period. The spread of the market system across the world and the global economic and financial integration taking place will lay the foundation for a long period of economic growth for all nations. Their view is that this strong growth will provide the necessary resources to solve many social, economic, health, and environmental problems. This optimistic future anticipates the rapid development of new technologies and the ongoing emergence of political democracy across the globe. This mainstream conservative view sees market capitalism as an economic system that is strong, dynamic, and adaptable.

A more liberal view accepts many of the global changes taking place as necessary and welcome, but recognizes that an unrestrained market system will continue to produce undesirable social, political, economic, and environmental outcomes unless the government (or state) plays a more active role in the domestic economy. This view recognizes the need to yield some economic sovereignty at the international level in order to be able to solve many of the economic, financial, and environmental problems that nation-states confront. This view accepts the basic principles of a capitalist market economy but envisions a very different role for the state to play in the future—a role that would involve greater planning, public investment, and a stronger involvement with the private sector.

A more radical view criticizes market capitalist institutions and blames most of the planet's problems on the unrestrained growth and expansion of industrial and finance capital across the global community. This view holds that global capitalism not only exploits labor but destroys the earth as well, producing poverty and inequality, economic insecurity, and uneven growth and development. Proponents of this perspective advocate a more responsive model of socialism than that which was and currently is practiced throughout the world. This view acknowledges the failures and excesses of a bureaucratic and authoritarian (nondemocratic) socialism but envisions a new kind of democratic and market socialism that would bring forward a sustainable model of economic growth. The radical view sees the current dynamics of economic and financial integration as part of a strategic global restructuring of capitalism. This restructuring is a necessary response on the part of capitalists to adapt and maintain their structures of capital accumulation so that the inherent dynamic of capitalism—capital accumulation—can continue unabated while avoiding the system's tendency to move toward economic crisis.

CONCLUSION

As the twentieth century draws to a close, we have the opportunity to reflect upon our study of introductory economics. What have we learned that helps us to understand our past, our present, and our future? Will the basic economic questions of today always be the basic economic questions? Will the microeconomic tool kit continue to help us make the kinds of decisions we need to make as educated consumers? Will firms be able to make critical decisions using competitive market microeconomic tools and concepts? Will governments be able to adapt traditional macroeconomic policy to the changing microeconomic, macroeconomic, and international realities of a global system challenged by rapid and unprecedented technological change? Can the economic systems of all nations responsibly manage the environmental, energy, and natural resource challenges of the next century? Can human society conduct its economic affairs peacefully?

Review Questions

1. What are the fundamental differences between capitalism and socialism as economic systems?
2. What role did Mikhail Gorbachev play in the economic transformation of the former Soviet Union?
3. What were the essential economic goals and objectives of the economic liberalization strategy of the Eastern European countries in the late 1980s?
4. How would you characterize China's experience with Socialism and its current economic transition? What kinds of economic problems does China face today?
5. Japan has a unique economic system in terms of the government's relationship to the private sector. What is this relationship? By the end of the 1990s, Japan was an economy with two faces. Explain.
6. What is Earth capital? There are two distinct world views in terms of the global environment. What are they? What do you understand sustainable economic growth to be?
7. Global capitalism is in transition. What are three distinct views of this transition? Which do you feel is the most accurate? Why?

THINKING CRITICALLY

GLOBALIZATION IN THE 21ST CENTURY?

As you have seen in Chapters 20 through 23, the international economic and financial system has undergone a profound transformation since the post–World War II days of the late 1940s and the Bretton Woods system. Global trade has exploded and the world of international finance has made it difficult for many nations to manage their own economies. Much of this change has been made possible by rapid technological change. The dominant industrial advanced countries have struggled to adapt to these changes and have in many cases moved in the direction of economic and financial integration. By the late 1980s the socialist experience of the former Soviet Union and the Eastern European countries collapsed and the movement toward market economies began. The developing countries of Asia, Latin America, and Africa found themselves drawn more tightly into this new global system with unique challenges having to do with population pressures, external debt, and balance of payments deficits to name a few. And, surrounding this entire process of change is what many experts argue to be an unprecedented environmental crisis that calls for a new direction toward sustainable development.

In this context, read these two essays. The first by William Greider, author and journalist, "Global Warning: Curbing the Free-Trade Freefall," appeared in the January 13/20, 1997 issue of The Nation. It is a summary of his book, *One World, Ready or Not: The Manic Logic of Global Capitalism* (1997, Simon and Schuster). The other, an editorial by Paul Krugman, professor of economics at MIT, is titled "We Are Not the World," which appeared in the February 13, 1997 issue of the *New York Times*.

Exercises

1. What does Greider believe is the central economic problem of our time?
2. What does Greider mean by "one world"?

3. Greider argues that the imperatives of a new world order can be reduced to a series of six mutually reinforcing propositions. What are these six ideas?
4. Do you think each of these ideas has merit and is desirable? Explain, being careful to identify the consequences of adopting the idea or rejecting it.
5. What do you think would be the consequences and for whom of forgiving the external debt of developing nations?
6. Krugman's essay is written in response to the point of view of Greider and others who share his perspective. What is Krugman's message to them?
7. Do you find Krugman's argument convincing? Explain.
8. Is there any common ground between the two essays?
9. What questions do each of the essays leave you with?
10. What, if anything, is to be done?

GLOBAL WARNING: CURBING THE FREE-TRADE FREEFALL

William Greider

The global system of finance and commerce is in a reckless footrace with history, plunging toward a dreadful reckoning with its own contradictions, pulling everyone along with it. Responsible experts and opinion leaders, of course, do not generally share my sense of alarm. Nor do most political authorities, who, in any case, seem thoroughly intimidated by economic events. Some important voices in business and finance do occasionally express similar anxieties, but multinational enterprise is preoccupied with its own imperatives, finance capital consumed by its own search for returns. Public opinion may be uneasy, even angry, but people generally are confused and rudderless.

The destructive pressures building up within the global system are leading toward an unbearable chaos that, even without a dramatic collapse, will likely provoke a harsh, reactionary politics that can shut down the system. This outcome is avoidable if nations will put aside theory and confront what is actually occurring, if they have the courage to impose remedial changes before it is too late.

If the positive energies of this revolutionary process are to be preserved, it has to be slowed down, not stopped, and redirected on a new course of development that is more moderate and progressive, that promises broader benefits to almost everyone. The economic problem requires governments to discard the hollow abstractions of financial accounting and begin rebuilding the tangible foundations for balanced prosperity, for work and wages, and for greater social equity—not only for older, wealthier nations but for the aspiring poor in the emerging "one world." It is far easier to describe some ways this might be achieved than to imagine that governing elites will act upon them.

The first priority is to reregulate finance capital. Governments will have to reimpose some of the control discarded during the last generation, both to stabilize financial markets and to make capital more responsive to the needs of producing economies. Measures like transaction taxes on foreign exchange would be a beginning. Such controls would take some of the profit out of currency trading and other speculative activities but would not inhibit long-term flows of capital for foreign investment and trade.

The popular belief that governments lack the power to control international finance is simply wrong: to disarm the exaggerated power and random follies of the global bond market, they can tighten terms for easy credit; in some arenas of credit, ceilings on interest rates can be reimposed; prohibitions on accepting transfers of offshore funds could shut down the banking centers where capital hides from securities laws and income taxes. Governments, in essence, must reclaim the ruling obligations of the nation-state from private markets.

The central economic problem of our present Industrial Revolution, not so different in nature from our previous one, is an excess of supply—the growing, permanent surpluses of goods, labor and productive capacity. The supply problem is the core of what drives destruction and instability: accumulation of redundant factories as new ones are simultaneously built in emerging markets, mass unemployment and declining wages, irregular mercantilist struggles for market entry and shares in the industrial base, market gluts that depress prices and profits, fierce contests that lead to cooperative cartels among competitors, and other consequences.

The shocking lesson of economic history—experience that now seems largely forgotten—is that vast human suffering and random destruction of productive capacities are unnecessary. From the crisis and turmoil of the early twentieth century, nations painfully discovered that there is nothing inevitable about these market forces or the social convulsions they sow if societies will act to counter them. A shared prosperity emerges, as Keynes taught, only when people throw off passivity and learn to take control of their fate.

Governments can counter the disorders and ameliorate losses mainly by stimulating consumption, creating more buyers for unsold goods—the rising market demand that activates idle factories and workers. The present regime is fundamentally pathological because it destroys consumer incomes while creating a growing surfeit of goods. Many different measures can push the global system in the opposite direction, but the underlying problem, bluntly stated, requires shifting returns from capital to labor, reversing the maldistribution of incomes generated by the marketplace under the rentier system.

Greater social equity is not only consistent with but required by a sound and expanding economy: When rising incomes are broadly distributed, it creates mass purchasing power—fueling a virtuous cycle of growth, savings and new investment. When incomes are narrowly distributed, as they are now, the economic system feeds upon itself, eroding its own energies for expansion, burying consumers and business, even governments, in impossible accumulations of debt. A relative few become fabulously wealthy, but a healthy economy is not sustained by manic investing. Nothing about modern technologies or the "information age" has altered these ancient fundamentals.

The genuine meaning of "one world" will be tested by how nations answer this question: Can the global system be turned toward a less destructive path without throwing poor people over the side? Older economies may be tempted to revert to insular, self-protective remedies, but this will destroy the promise of the globalizing revolution and could even produce its own implosion of commerce—balkanized struggles for markets that substitute political conflict for the economic disorders. The challenge of "one world" is to create the standards for a progressive system that everyone can trust, that does not leave anyone out.

The imperatives for a new world order can be boiled down to a series of mutually reinforcing propositions, each of which would help to redress the economic imbalances of supply and demand. They include the following ideas:

1. *Tax capital instead of labor.* Even a modest shift in tax structures can stimulate the creation of new jobs and wage incomes while it creates the mechanism for making investors and corporations more accountable for their behavior. The tax codes of most of the advanced industrial nations are tilted against work, focusing regressive payroll taxes on wage earners and their employers, thus raising the real cost for a company that expands its work force. By comparison, financial wealth is lightly taxed and, at least in the United States, is not subject to the property taxes that people pay on real-property assets like homes and businesses.

Reducing the tax barrier to employment can be done in a progressive manner that favors work for the less skilled—lower payroll tax rates on jobs at the lower end of the wage scale, higher taxes at the high end. That would provide a discreet incentive to multiply jobs for those who need them most—a cheaper and more effective approach than social programs that try to help people after they are already poor or unemployed. The same principle could target the common practice, at least among U.S. companies, of escaping the social overhead of doing business by marginalizing workers in piecemeal jobs—the "temporary" or "contract" work that lacks decent wages or benefits. The supposed efficiency of these measures actually involves pushing the social costs—health care or income support for indigent retirees—onto others, mainly the general public.

Direct taxation of financial capital could also create a mechanism for rewarding the firms and investors who take responsibility for broader economic and social consequences while punishing the free riders. Globalizing corporations, which move jobs offshore and arbitrage tax concessions from different governments, ought to be treated less favorably than the enterprises that are conscientiously increasing their domestic employment. Capital investors, likewise, have a financial obligation to the commonweal that protects them.

A direct tax on wealth is not as radical as it may sound to Americans, since eleven other nations in the Organization for Economic Cooperation and Development, including Germany, already have modest versions. The principle is not different from ordinary property taxes or business-license taxes on merchants or professionals, since capital owners benefit from the public domain. For instance, Edward Wolff has proposed that the United States follow the model of Switzerland and adopt a system of modest, graduated rates that would start by exempting the first $100,000 of financial assets, tax the next $100,000 at a rate of only .05 percent and rise to a rate of 0.3 percent above $1 million. He calculates that such a system would have raised only $40 billion in 1994—a lot of money but hardly an onerous burden on the wealthy, nor a solution to the fiscal disorders.

A central purpose of taxing capital, however, is to establish the means for defining the responsibility of capital owners to each nation and its people. If capital wants to enjoy record returns from the global system, it must help pay for the economic and social wreckage it leaves behind. Once that principle is established, the tax code can begin to make distinctions among both corporations and investors, based upon their civic behavior.

"The emerging modern system gives a larger share of income and power to capital, yet the burdens of government and community have steadfastly been shifted to labor," as one financial economist explained to me. "At some point, we have to ask whether utterly free capital is a benefit to everyone. Free capital is certainly a benefit to the people who own the capital. But they couldn't exist if these governments did not exist to protect them. No one wants to locate the Chicago Board of Trade in Bangkok or Jakarta. They want to be in the United States or maybe five or six other countries, where their transactions and their wealth will be safe."

Similar logic could change the strategic calculations of multinational corporations as they disperse production, perhaps by making preferential distinctions in the tax code. If the national objective is to stimulate domestic employment, then capital or corporate stocks might get a reduction or even exemption from capital gains taxation if the corporate balance sheet confirms that the enterprise is increasing jobs by investing at home. Capital should be taxed at the full rate if it is doing the opposite. The global dispersal of industry would not be stopped, but firms and shareholders would have to help pay for what they left behind.

This approach inevitably favors domestic companies over multinationals, but it also discards the fraudulent proposition that any tax break or subsidy to business automatically translates into a benefit for society at large. If that assumption was ever sound, it is clearly suspect in the era of globalizing corporations. Governments promoting the trading fortunes of multinationals have not yet answered the gut question: Who in the nation benefits from this process, owners or workers, capital or citizens?

2. *Reform the terms of trade to insure more balanced flows of commerce, compelling exporting nations to become larger consumers of global production.* The present system is propped up by the persistent trade deficits of wealthier nations, mainly the United States, a condition that cannot endure for much longer. Rhetorical promises notwithstanding, global agreements like the General Agreement on Tariffs and Trade (GATT) and the endless rounds of trade disputes have failed utterly to redress trade imbalances. Indeed, prospects are worsening as China and other major new industrial powers prepare to enter the world market. A fundamental principle , therefore, must be established: An industrial economy cannot expect to construct a vast oversupply of production for export while refusing to accept equivalent volumes of imports form others.

The system, in effect, has to provoke a meaningful showdown with the Japanese model of wealth accumulation—the mercantilist practices that exact zero-sum advantage at the expense of trading partners. Those economies that persist in accumulating huge trading surpluses should lose their cost-free access to foreign markets through emergency tariffs or other measures. On the other hand, nations that practice genuine reciprocity of buying and selling, including the aspiring poor nations, should be rewarded with preferences. In short, Japan and other Asian nations like China that follow Japan's strategic path would face an unsentimental choice: Either expand imports or expect to be stuck with excess productive capacity.

The objective of temporary trading barriers would not be to protect domestic industrial sectors but to force everyone to confront the underlying crisis of surpluses. Every trading nation, including poor nations hoping to become less poor, has a tangible stake in solving the supply problem because it poses a principal obstacle to adapting a pro-growth regime for the world. Under the current system, older economies may actually suffer from faster growth if their rising consumption simply generates a deluge of imports and larger trade deficits, while the foreign markets remain closed to their production. Until this zero-sum condition is corrected, the potential for greater growth will remain stymied. Emergency tariffs to correct a nation's financial disorders are an extreme measure, but not prohibited by GATT. If the United States threatened such measures, other nations might at last face up to the larger global problem of oversupply.

3. *Bring the bottom up—raising wages on the low end as rapidly as possible—by requiring trading nations to honor labor rights.* By defending human freedom, the trading system can establish that the collective right of workers to bid up their wages is sanctioned and protected. Morality aside, the economic objective is straightforward: Raising wages at the bottom enlarges the base of consumption for everyone's goods. Even in the best of circumstances, the downward pressures on high-wage labor markets will not abate soon, given the vast sea of available low-wage workers. But every gain in wage levels at the bottom, even a modest gain, translates into immediate economic benefit for the global system: more purchasing power.

At present, the system functions in reverse, eroding consumption by replacing high-wage labor with cheap labor. To be sure, the new industrial workers in Asia and Latin America have new wage incomes to spend, but overall the system experiences a net loss in the potential for mass consumption. The challenge, roughly speaking, is to create a global system that functions most energetically by pulling the bottom up instead of the top down. Many poorer nations are naturally hostile to the suggestion, fearing that they will lose the comparative advantage of cheap labor or political control over their work forces. But companies or nations that rely on repression and exploitation of the weak for trading advantage are not truly ready for membership in a "one world" economy. They should be penalized, even excluded.

The easiest way to accomplish this reform is to insert an enforceable "social clause" in the global trade agreements requiring all trading nations to honor long-established international rules for labor rights. As a practical matter, that is unlikely to happen at the level of GATT and the World Trade Organization, since both developing countries and multinational corporations are opposed to any labor reform.

The political opening lies in negotiating regional or nation-to-nation compacts that establish networks of social standards and extend trading preferences to those who honor them (the opportunity Bill Clinton failed to act upon when pushing NAFTA). Reciprocal trade agreements that link several rich nations with several poor nations could establish a working model that demonstrates the positive economic energies that flow from labor reform. As participants benefit on both ends, other nations, rich and poor, may see the wisdom of emulating the reform.

Nations are, of course, entitled to their sovereignty—the power to set domestic social standards free of foreigners' interference—but that does not require foreigners to buy their goods. Advanced economies need not meddle in other nations' domestic politics, since they can regulate the behavior of their own multinationals, both at home and abroad. If the national interest lies in bringing up wages worldwide, then governments may withdraw subsidies and tax preferences from companies that, like the U.S. electronics industry in Malaysia, actively seek to block labor rights of their foreign workers.

4. *Forgive the debtors—that is, initiate a general write-off of bad debts accumulated by poorer nations.* Extinguishing failed loans issued by international agencies such as the International Monetary Fund and the World Bank would free desperately poor economies, especially in Africa, to pursue more viable strategies for domestic development. The liquidation of debt obligations is fundamentally a stimulative economic measure since it frees cash for other pursuits, including active consumption, and it is socially enlightened because it eases global poverty.

Writing off these debts is probably inevitable, in any case, since most of the loans can never be repaid. Right now, the interest costs simply bleed the poor nations further each year and often require new loans so they can keep up payments on old loans. Liquidation would free their meager cash flows for genuine development and at least the possibility that they may someday become significant consumers in the global system.

To accompany the debt forgiveness, however, the operating purposes of the international lending institutions must also be reformed. The I.M.F. and World Bank must develop greater respect for indigenous strategies for growth, promoting a more patient development of domestic economies instead of simply enforcing the financial imperatives of the global system. To cite the most obvious contradiction, these institutions routinely use their power to suppress wages and consumption in the developing countries when the advanced nations that finance their lending have an interest in achieving the opposite. If the lending institutions are unable to change direction, then sponsoring governments should withdraw funding and abolish them, writing off their loan portfolios in the process.

5. Reform the objectives of central banks so they will support a pro-growth regime instead of thwarting it. The purposes of monetary policy have to be returned to a more balanced and democratic perspective—an understanding that growth, employment and wages are crucial to a sound economy, no less important that the prerogatives of stored wealth. So long as the Federal Reserve and the central banks of other nations stand in the way of more vigorous growth that might allow a reinflation of wages, the problem of weakening consumption and oversupply is sure to increase, accompanied by compounding debt burdens.

The policy choices embedded in the regulation of money and credit always involve difficult trade-offs between different risks—recession or inflation, idle capacity or overheated activity, failed debtors or financial speculation. But the consequences of these choices are not distributed evenly throughout society, especially when policy is always skewed toward the interests of wealth holders. Most of the leading central banks are ostensibly independent of politics, yet this does not prevent them from adhering faithfully to the narrow constituency of finance capital. Their prejudices are unlikely to change until the competing interests—labor, manufacturing and other sectors—organize counterpressures demanding a more generous policy of economic growth. To make central banks yield, they should be reconstituted as open and accountable governing institutions.

Unfortunately, central banks are stuck in the past, still fighting the last war against inflation when the global system now faces the opposite danger—a massive deflation of prices, economic activity and debt. The trade-offs surrounding monetary policy have been profoundly altered by globalized finance and production. Yet central bankers continue to operate in the traditional manner, as if they were still regulating self-contained domestic economies. This anomaly leads them to err repeatedly on the downside—discouraging domestic economic activity and new investment in the name of stability—even as markets respond to global influences of supply and demand. If a new era of growth is to occur, new theoretical understandings must replace the traditional rules of central banking.

6. Refocus national economic agendas on the priority of work and wages, rather than trade or multinational competitiveness, as the defining issue for domestic prosperity. Obviously, these objectives are intertwined and interacting, but it makes a great difference as to which to put first. If advanced nations, especially the United States, concentrate on promoting employment and more equitable incomes, they can make a great contribution to the global system, in addition to domestic well-being, by boosting mass consumption. If governments continue to be preoccupied with globalization and promotion of the free-market doctrine, then they must inevitably accept the consequences of deepening inequality and deterioration at home.

The actions that governments could take will require new spending, but should focus less on government social aid programs and more on wage realities in private-sector labor markets. Many such measures are traditional forms of intervention: raising minimum wages, strengthening labor laws to encourage companies to share productivity gains with workers, restoring progressive taxation to redistribute income, curbing the luxurious corporate subsidies embedded in the tax code and government programs, underwriting major works projects like high-speed rail systems or urban housing rehabilitation.

If it is true that global pressures will drag down wages and employment for at least another generation, then the economic imperative for large-scale subsidized employment is inescapable. If people cannot find jobs that promise a living wage for families, than all the various social interventions that government undertakes will be futile. Instead, societies will accumulate another generation of dispossessed and alienated citizens.

The same essential question has to be asked of every public measure: Does it genuinely promise to enhance work and wages? In debating that question, people will discover that much of what government currently does is useless or even harmful to broadly shared prosperity. But the answers may also begin to bring the economic future into clearer focus, defining potential new pillars for domestic economic activity. Financial reform, for instance, might direct credit subsidies to sectors like housing or small-scale business enterprises or a national child-care system—new business activity that becomes a significant employer while filling real needs. Every such step, of course, tends to distribute the economic returns more broadly through society and thus creates more buyers for the world's surplus production.

If people can get beyond passivity and insecurity, an era of economic experimentation lies ahead—ventures that explore new social and economic arrangements, projects that can be encouraged by government, not managed by it. Among rich and poor, people are already exploring ideas that may change their destiny, social invention that needs not wait upon market forces.

Source: *The Nation*, January 13/20, 1997. The Nation Company, Inc. Reprinted with permission. William Greider, who writes regularly for *Rolling Stone*, is the author of *Who Will Tell the People* and *Secrets of the Temple* (both Touchstone). This article is adapted from his new book, *One World, Ready or Not: The Manic Logic of Global Capitalism*, published this month by Simon & Schuster.

WE ARE NOT THE WORLD

Paul Krugman

It is a truth universally acknowledged that the growing international mobility of goods, capital and technology has completely changed the economic game. Nations, conventional wisdom tells us, no longer have the power to control their own destinies; governments are at the mercy of international markets.

Some celebrate this development, saying that both rich and poor nations benefit. At the same time, a growing number of journalists, union leaders, politicians of both parties and even businessmen deplore it, blaming globalization for instability, unemployment and declining wages.

But both sides have it wrong. They take the omnipotence of global markets for granted—not realizing that reports of the death of national autonomy are greatly exaggerated.

A certain fascination with the march of globalization is understandable. For half a century, world trade has grown faster than world output, and international capital now moves more quickly than ever before. The rapidly expanding exports of newly industrializing economies have put pressure on less-skilled workers in advanced countries even as they offer unprecedented opportunities to tens of millions in the third world. (The wages of those workers are shockingly low but nonetheless represent a vast improvement on their previous, less visible rural poverty.)

But while global economic integration is increasing, its growth has been far outpaced by that of "global economy" rhetoric. Two recent books by economic journalists, William Greider's *One World, Ready or Not* and Robert Kuttner's *Everything for Sale,* are jeremiads about the evils of unfettered economic globalism. Politicians like Patrick J. Buchanan and Ross Perot have made careers out of assailing open markets. Even the financier George Soros warns, in the current issue of *The Atlantic Monthly*, that global capitalism is now a greater threat than totalitarianism to "open society."

Such oratory has become so pervasive that many observers seem determined to blame global markets for a host of economic and social ills in their countries, even when the facts point unmistakably to mainly domestic—and usually political—causes.

For example, critics of globalization often cite France, whose Government has taken no serious action to reduce its double-digit unemployment rate, as the perfect example of how states have become powerless in the face of impersonal world markets. France cannot act, according to a recent *New York Times* article, because of the demands of "European economic integration—itself partly a response to the competitive demands of the global marketplace."

French policy is indeed paralyzed—not, however, by impersonal market forces but by the determination of its prestige-conscious politicians not to let the franc decline against the German mark. Britain, which has been willing to let the pound sink relative to the mark, has steadily reduced its unemployment rate with no visible adverse consequences.

The cause of France's paralysis, in other words, is political rather than economic. True, the country must meet the conditions laid down by the Maastricht treaty of 1991, which is supposed to lead to a unified European currency. But creating this currency is more a political than an economic project. Its main purpose is to serve as a symbol of European unity, and many economists think that the costs of the common currency will exceed its benefits. It would actually be more accurate to say that French politics has battered markets rather than the other way around.

And what about the United States, where the continuing power of the Government— or at any rate that of the Federal Reserve—to push the economy around can hardly be questioned? Critics of the global economy invariably reply that America may be creating lots of jobs but that they are tenuous because of the prevalence of downsizing, which is a reaction to international competition (a line of reasoning that also provides a good excuse for companies undertaking layoffs).

Come again? *Newsweek* ran a story last year, titled "The Hit Men," about executives responsible for massive layoffs. The chief executives of AT&T, Nynex, Sears, Philip Morris and Delta Air Lines were high on the list. Of course, international competition plays a role in some downsizings, but as *Newsweek's* list makes clear, it is hardly the most important cause of the phenomenon. To my knowledge there are no Japanese keiretsu competing to carry my long-distance calls or South Korean conglomerates offering me local service. Nor have many Americans started buying their home appliances at Mexican stores or smoking French cigarettes. I cannot fly Cathay Pacific from Boston to New York.

What explains this propensity to overstate the importance of global markets? In part, it sounds sophisticated. Pontificating about globalization is an easy way to get attention at events like the World Economic Forum in Davos, Switzerland, and Renaissance Weekends in Hilton Head, S.C.

But there is also a deeper cause—an odd sort of tacit agreement between the left and the right to pretend that exotic global forces are at work even when the real action is prosaically domestic.

Many on the left dislike the global marketplace because it epitomizes what they dislike about markets in general: the fact that nobody is in charge. The truth is that the invisible hand rules most domestic markets, too, a reality that most Americans seem to accept as a fact of life. But those who would like to see us revert to a more managed society in all ways hope that popular unease over the economic influence of people who live in far-off places and have funny-sounding names can be used as the thin end of an ideological wedge.

Meanwhile, many on the right use the rhetoric of globalization to argue that business can no longer be expected to meet any social obligations. For example, it has become standard for opponents of environmental regulations to raise the banner of "competitiveness" and to warn that anything that raises costs for American businesses will price our goods out of world markets.

But even if the global economy matters less than the sweeping assertions would have us believe, does this "globaloney," as the cognoscenti call it, do any real harm? Yes, in part because the public, misguided into believing that international trade is the source of all our problems, might turn protectionist—undermining the real good that globalization has done for most people here and abroad.

But the overheated oratory poses a more subtle risk. It encourages fatalism, a sense that we cannot come to grips with our problems because they are bigger than we are. Such fatalism is already well advanced in Western Europe, where the public speaks vaguely of the "economic horror" inflicted by world markets instead of turning a critical eye on the domestic leaders whose policies have failed.

None of the important constraints on American economic and social policy come from abroad. We have the resources to take far better care of our poor and unlucky than we do; if our policies have become increasingly mean-spirited, that is a political choice, not something imposed on us by anonymous forces. We cannot evade responsibility for our actions by claiming that global markets made us do it.

Source: Paul Krugman, a professor of economics at the Massachusetts Institute of Technology, is the author of *Peddling Prosperity* and *Pop Internationalism*. Reprinted from *The New York Times*, February 13, 1977. Copyright © 1997 by The New York Times Company. Reprinted by permission.

GLOSSARY

Absolute advantage In international trade, a condition in which one nation can produce more of a particular commodity with the same amount of resources as another nation uses for producing that commodity.

Aggregate demand curve The plot of all points corresponding to the total amount of goods demanded in the economy at each overall level of prices.

Aggregate supply curve The plot of all points corresponding to the total amount of goods supplied in the economy at each overall level of prices.

Alienation The condition resulting from the separation of the worker from the means of production. Alienation from the worker's point of view results from no control over the product, no control of the means of producing it, and an antagonistic relationship of workers and owners.

Antitrust policy Laws that attempt to limit the degree of monopoly in the economy and to promote competition. In the United States, the passage, interpretation, and enforcement of antitrust laws have involved varying degrees of emphasis on market performance, market conduct, and market structure. See *Sherman Act*.

Appreciation of currency The relative strengthening of a currency in a flexible exchange rate system. The appreciated currency rises in cost and value relative to the depreciated currency.

Average cost Total cost divided by the number of production units.

Average fixed cost Total fixed cost divided by total units of output.

Average propensity to consume (APC) Total consumption divided by total disposable income. This is the average consumption income ratio.

Average propensity to save (APS) Total savings divided by total disposable income.

Average variable cost (AVC) Total variable cost divided by total output.

Balance of payments A summary record of a country's transactions that typically involves payments and receipt of foreign exchange. Credit items and debit items must balance, since each good that a country buys or sells must be paid for in one way or another.

Balance of trade The difference between the value of exports and the value of imports of visible items (goods and services).

Barriers to entry Obstacles to a firm's entry into new industries or markets. These obstacles may be political (such as tariffs or trade restrictions), economic (economies of scale or limited resources, especially in oligopolies), or legal (patents, copyrights, or monopoly).

Board of Governors A seven-member group appointed by the President and approved by the Congress to head the Federal Reserve. The board coordinates and regulates the nation's money supply. See *Federal Reserve*.

Breakeven point (1) In national income accounting, the amount of income corresponding to consumption of the entire income. There is no saving or dissaving. (2) For an individual business, the amount of revenue corresponding to a production level at which revenues exactly equal costs. There are no profits or losses.

Bretton Woods Agreement (1944) The international agreement that formed the basis for today's international financial organizations.

Bretton Woods Agreement (*continued*)
After World War II, the Allied nations agreed that international financial affairs would be overseen by the International Monetary Fund. Gold became the ultimate means of settling balance-of-payment deficits.

Budget deficit The amount by which government expenditures exceed government revenues during the accounting period.

Built-in stabilizers Automatic, nondiscretionary forms of fiscal policy that compensate for particular trends of aggregate changes in national income.

Business cycle Recurrent ups and downs of business activity, shown in a host of business indicators. Expansion and contraction phases are both thought to have certain cumulative features. They may also contain the seeds of the turning points at the cycle's peak and trough.

Capital account In balance-of-payments accounting, all capital flows other than investment income.

Capital A factor of production, along with labor and land; the stock of a society's produced means of production, including factories, buildings, machines, tools, and inventories of goods in stock.

Capitalism An economic system in which the basic resources and capital goods of the society are privately owned. Decisions are usually made by individual units, which may be relatively small (pure competition) or quite large (monopoly/oligopoly). Decisions tend to be based on profitability in the case of businesses, or economic self-interest in the case of individuals.

Cartel An organization of producers designed to limit or eliminate competition among its members, usually by agreeing to restrict output in an effort to achieve noncompetitive prices. An example is OPEC.

Central bank A Federal Reserve Board operation that serves the nation's banks. Besides its major responsibility—control of the money supply—it conducts some restriction, regulation, and investigation of the banking industry.

Ceteris paribus Literally, "other things being equal"; a term used in economics to indicate that all variables except the ones specified are assumed not to change.

Class In an economic sense, a group of people defined in terms of their relationship to production. For example, under capitalism, one class of people (proletariat) works the means of production, and another class (capitalists, bourgeoisie) owns the means of production. This concept was used largely by Karl Marx.

Classical economics A school of economics that usually refers to the doctrines of the British Classical School of the late eighteenth and early nineteenth centuries, especially those of Adam Smith and followers. They emphasized competition, free trade, and minimal state intervention in the economy.

Collusion Agreements to avoid competition or to set prices.

Commodity Marketable item produced to satisfy wants. Commodities may be either tangible goods or intangible services. Marx considered labor under the wage contract a commodity because it orders wage contracts and responds to supply-and-demand conditions.

Communism An economic system characterized by socialization of labor, centralization of the ownership of the means of production, centralized coordination of production, centralization of credit policy through a central bank, and reduction of alienation and exploitation of the worker.

Comparative advantage In international trade, a country's productive advantage with respect to a particular commodity, based on its ability to give up fewer other commodities to produce a unit of the commodity than another country would have to give up. This relative cost of production is most significant in determining mutually beneficial patterns of trade among nations.

Competition Theoretically, competition exists in a perfect and an imperfect form; the former is known as perfect competition, the latter as monopoly/oligopoly or as monopolistic competition. Perfect competition is characterized by small firms. Adam Smith called competition the "invisible hand" in capitalism. See "*Invisible hand.*"

Concentration ratio The percentage of total sales in an industry that is accounted for by a specific number of firms.

Conglomerate merger Companies in unrelated industries merge.

Conservative economist An economist who advocates classical theory, classical liberalism, and classical economics (i.e., that government should intervene only when necessary, and then only minimally).

Consumer Price Index (CPI) A government statistic that measures inflation in terms of the weighted average composite of goods and services commonly consumed by average families.

Consumption Expenditures by households and individuals on consumer goods.

Corporation A form of business organization with a legal existence separate from that of the owners, in which ownership and financial responsibility are divided, limited, and shared among any number of individual and institutional shareholders.

Cost-push inflation A general increase in prices associated with increases in the cost of production. Categorized as supply inflation.

Crowding out Loss of funding as a result of the competition between economic units for the use of limited funds. The term usually refers to the federal budget deficit and the continuing borrowing of the U.S. Treasury. Funds used to finance government spending deprive businesses of necessary capital, thus crowding out investment.

Currency Any recognized material accepted as national money; almost always paper or coin.

Current accounts In balance-of-payments accounting, the accounts that summarize the flow of goods and services between the United States and the rest of the world.

Cyclical budget deficit The part of the federal deficit that fluctuates with the state of the economy. It increases when there is a downturn of the business cycle.

Cyclical unemployment Measure of unemployment due to decreased demand during the troughs of business cycles, when output is curtailed. Workers who are cyclically unemployed are expected to be reinstated as the cycle moves upward.

Deficit spending Government spending when net government revenues are less than net government expenditures.

Demand curve A hypothetical construction depicting how many units of a particular commodity consumers would be willing to buy over a period of time at all possible prices, assuming that the prices of other commodities, money incomes of consumers, and other factors are unchanged.

Demand deposits Checking accounts in commercial banks. These deposits can be turned into currency "on demand," i.e., by writing a check. Demand deposits are the main form of money in the United States.

Demand, law of A principle concerning the relationship between price and quantity demanded: All other things constant, the lower the price, the higher the quantity demanded. In other words, price and quantity demanded are inversely related.

Demand-pull inflation A general increase in prices arising from increasing excess demand for a given level of output.

Demand (1) Quantity demanded. (2) The whole relationship of the quantity demanded to variables that determine it, such as tastes, income, population, and price. (3) The demand curve.

Dependency model A model that assumes that underdevelopment is a consequence of the historical evolution of capitalism and the integration of developing countries into the expanding sphere of capitalist production globally.

Depreciation (1) Loss of value in capital equipment due to use or obsolescence. (2) The loss of value in any valuable good or commodity due to use or market forces (such as currency exchange rates).

Depression A prolonged downswing of economic activity exemplified by mass unemployment, a level of national income well below the potential level, and great excess capacity. A depression is more severe and longer lasting than a recession. The economic breakdown of the industrialized world in the 1930s was called the Great Depression. See *Recession*.

Derived demand Demand of a good for use in the production of goods and services.

Devaluation A downward revision in the value at which a country's currency is pegged in terms of a foreign currency.

Discount rate Interest rate charged on loans from the Federal Reserve Bank to its member banks; an instrument of Federal Reserve monetary policy.

Discretionary fiscal policy A fiscal policy designed to respond to a particular situation in the macroeconomy. These policies are implemented to achieve specific goals, usually high output, high employment, and stable prices.

Diseconomies of scale The phenomenon of disproportional increasing costs as a firm's long-run productive capacity grows. Simply put, the growth of production costs in an expanding firm outstrips the growth in production.

Disintermediation Resource allocation, particularly investment, by a firm which excluded intermediary institutions such as savings and loan institutions, banks, or brokerage firms.

Disposable income Amount of personal income remaining after payment of various federal, state, and local taxes and other nontax payments.

Dissaving Deficit or negative spending; that is, borrowing or drawing down other financial assets in order to consume.

Distribution of income The division of the total product of a society among its members. The distribution is sometimes described by a classification according to income size or by a classification including factor payments.

Division of labor Subdivision of a productive process into its component parts, which are then handled by specially skilled or trained laborers. Adam Smith believed it was a major source of increased productivity over time.

Dumping Sale by an exporting nation of its product at a lower price in an importing country than in its own country. Dumping tends to ruin the importer's domestic industry while strengthening the exporter's market share.

Economic dependence The relationship of unequal interdependence, endured by the less advanced countries with the developed countries. Theoretically, a country is in a state of economic dependence if the expansion of its economy depends on that of another country. See *Imperialism*.

Economic development Progressive changes in a society's ability to meet its economic tasks of production and distribution. Development is characterized by increasing output and the growth of economic institutions, relationships, and methods that facilitate society's ability to generate economic growth.

Economic growth Increase in productive capabilities beyond the necessary elements of survival. Expansion creates more jobs, goods, and income.

Economic planning The planning of investment, consumption, and similar decisions by one or another bodies. Several variants (among which are corporate planning, command planning, and indicative planning) demonstrate variety in what is to be planned and who does the planning.

Economic profits A return to capital above "normal profit"; profit remaining after opportunity costs have been taken into account.

Economic theory A theory of economics or resource allocation. Examples are Marxist, classical, and Keynesian theory. See *Theory*.

Economics The study of the allocation of resources, the production of goods and services, and their distribution in societies.

Economies of scale The phenomenon of decreasing average costs in large-scale production (usually oligopolistic production). The growth of production in an expanding firm outstrips the growth in costs.

Elasticity A function that describes the sensitivity of demand or supply of a product to changes in its price. Elasticity equals the percentage change in quantity demanded (supplied) divided by the percentage change in price.

Employment Act of 1946 Federal law that created a Council of Economic Advisers to advise the President on the state of the economy and on how best to achieve the goal of full employment.

Enclosure movement In England during the Middle Ages, a series of parliamentary acts by which the feudal nobility fenced off or enclosed lands formerly used for communal grazing, destroying feudal ties and creating a large, new "landless" labor force.

Entrepreneur In the classical liberal sense, an owner of the means of production. In the modern corporate world, a businessperson is often considered an entrepreneur.

Equation of exchange The quantity theory of money, expressed as $MV = PQ$, where M is the money stock, V is velocity of money, P is price level, and Q is real national income. It is a tautology, because V is defined as PQ/M.

Equilibrium A state of balance in which there are no endogenous pressures for change. A market equilibrium is said to exist at the price where the quantity demanded equals the quantity supplied.

Exchange rate The price of a nation's currency in terms of another nation's currency.

Exhaustive spending Governmental purchases of goods and services.

Exports Any unit of production that leaves the country where it was produced for sale in another country.

Externalities Costs of productive activity that the firm is not obliged to bear. The costs are borne by the public as social costs of production. Also known as third-party effect. Externalities may be detrimental (external costs) or beneficial (external benefits).

Factor of production Any implement or agent whose services are used in the production of economic goods and services. Three basic factors are land, labor, and capital.

Federal Reserve (Fed) An independent agency of the federal government and instrumental in determining monetary policy. Its main tools are altering reserve requirements, changing the discount rate, and conducting open-market purchases and sales of governmental securities. See *Monetary policy; Reserve requirements; Discount rate.*

Feudalism The economic system that directly preceded capitalism. Relations of class were between lord and serf. Feudalism existed in a society in which tradition and ceremony played the major roles.

Financial intermediaries Institutions such as banks, savings and loans, insurance companies, mutual funds, pension funds and finance companies that borrow funds from people with savings and then make loans to others (borrowers).

Financial intermediation Use of financial institutions to deposit or acquire funds from the public. Such institutions pool numerous funds and then provide them to businesses, governments, or individuals.

Firm Unit that makes decisions regarding the employment of factors of production and production of goods and services.

Fiscal policy Governmental policy concerned with the tax and expenditure activities of the federal government, including the size of public spending and the balancing or unbalancing of the federal budget. This policy is designed to promote certain macroeconomic objectives, usually full employment, stable prices, economic growth, and balance-of-payments equilibrium.

Fixed exchange rate A rate at which a currency is fixed (set) to establish its price relative either to a universal exchange (gold) or to another currency.

Floating exchange rate A currency exchange rate that rises or falls in response to the forces of international supply and demand. See *Exchange rate.*

Fractional reserve system A banking system under which commercial banks are required to maintain reserves equal to a prescribed percentage of their demand or other deposits. See *Reserve requirements.*

Free trade A situation in which all commodities can be freely imported and exported without special taxes or restrictions being levied because of their status as imports or exports.

Frictional unemployment Loss of jobs caused by temporary mismatching of laborers with jobs due to differences between the needs of business and skills of labor.

Full employment A condition under which those who wish to work at the prevailing wage are able to find work. In the United States, full employment is defined as 4 percent unemployment.

General Agreement on Tariffs and Trade (GATT) An association of countries that "sets and regulates the code of international trade conduct and promotes free trade."

Gini coefficient A measure of inequality in income distribution derived from the Lorenz curve. To calculate it for a population, find the difference in area between a 45° line and the population's Lorenz curve, and divide the difference by the entire area below the 45° line.

Gross domestic product (GDP) The market value of all final goods and services produced in an accounting period by factors of production located within a country.

Gross national product (GNP) The market value of all final goods and services produced in an accounting period by factors of production owned by citizens of that country.

Historical materialism Developed by Karl Marx, an in-depth historical study of material relations of people. The basis of social and economic change resides in class relations of people. The base of a society is its mode of production, and all class struggle emanates out of the relations of people to the mode of production. The superstructure, which is determined by the base, includes the philosophy, religion, ideology, etc. of the specific epoch.

Horizontal merger Companies in the same industry merge.

Imperialism One country's economic, social, political, and cultural dominance over another country. Imperialism, as developed by Lenin, Sweezy, Baran, Magdoff, and many others, is a historical problem and directly related to the growth and development of capitalism.

Imports Goods brought into a country for sale, having been produced elsewhere.

Income flow The path that income follows in the economy. Businesses pay rents, wages, interest, and profits to households, which in turn spend their incomes to continue the flow.

Incomes policy A governmental policy designed to limit inflation by instituting direct and indirect controls over prices, wages, profits, and other types of income.

Income velocity of money The rate of turnover of money in the economy. From the equation of exchange, velocity is GDP divided by the money supply. See *Equation of exchange.*

Index number A weighted average of a given variable with a specified base number, usually 100.

Indirect business taxes Taxes imposed on the production and sale of goods. Examples include sales tax, excise tax, custom duties, and property taxes.

Industry The collective group of producers of a single good or service or closely related goods or services.

Inefficiency in production A condition in a noncompetitive market in which output is not at minimum average cost.

Inefficiency in resource allocation A condition in a noncompetitive market in which the good's price does not equal marginal cost.

Infant industry An industry that has recently been established in a country and has not yet had time to exploit possible economies of scale and other efficiencies. Such industries provide one of the traditional arguments for tariff protection.

Inflation A general rise in the average level of all prices in an economy as defined by some index (Consumer Price Index, wholesale price index, or GDP price deflator).

Infrastructure Necessary supports for development, such as transportation routes and social services.

Innovation A change for the better in technology or production. A change is considered "better" if it involves higher efficiency and/or lower production costs.

Interest rate The amount of interest expressed as a percentage of the initial sum.

Interest (1) The price of borrowing money. (2) The rate of return to owners of financial capital.

International Monetary Fund (IMF) International organization founded with the goal of encouraging trade by establishing an orderly procedure for stabilizing foreign exchange rates and for altering those rates in the case of fundamental balance-of-payments disequilibrium.

International trade Buying and selling of goods and services across national borders. The country that sells is the exporter, and the country that buys is the importer.

Inventories Stocks of goods kept on hand to meet orders from other producers and customers.

Investment An addition to a firm's or society's stock of capital (machines, buildings, inventories, etc.) in a certain period of time.

"Invisible hand" Term coined by Adam Smith to suggest that individuals who are motivated only by private (not social) interest will nevertheless be guided invisibly by the market to actions and decisions beneficial to the welfare of society.

Kanban The "just-in-time" system in which services and supplies are produced and delivered only when needed.

Keiretsu A production relation between a large core firm and its subsidiaries that allows for a stable, mutually beneficial long-term relationship.

Keynesian economics Theory characterized by its emphasis on macroeconomic problems, the special role of aggregate expenditure in determining national income, and the possibility of unemployment equilibrium; its attempt to synthesize real and monetary analysis; and its argument for a greater government intervention in the economy.

Keynesian multiplier The number of dollars by which a \$1 increase in spending (C, I, G) will raise the equilibrium level of national income. Represented as k, it can be expressed mathematically in relation to the marginal propensity to consume (MPC) or the marginal propensity to save (MPS):

$$k = \frac{1}{1 - MPC} \qquad k = \frac{1}{MPS}$$

Labor The physical and mental contributions of humans to the production process. Collectively, labor refers to all workers.

Labor force participation rate Percentage of actual civilians participating in the labor force compared with the total number of civilians of working age.

Labor theory of value Theory held by Marx (and Ricardo in differing form) that the value of a commodity is proportional to the labor embodied in its production.

Laissez-faire A doctrine that the state should largely leave the economy to its own devices. Associated with Adam Smith.

Land A means of production that includes raw materials and the land upon which productive activity takes place (i.e., factory, farm).

Law of diminishing returns Principle that in the production of any commodity, as more units of a variable factor of production are added to a fixed quantity of other factors of production, the amount that each additional unit of the variable factor adds to the total product will eventually begin to diminish.

Liquidity The ease with which an asset can be converted into cash. Considerations in measuring liquidity include the time necessary to acquire cash, the cost of conversion, and the predictability of the asset's value.

Liquidity preference Demand for money as a function of the interest rate; the willingness to hold money on hand.

Liquidity trap In Keynesian theory, the point in the economy when all economic agents desire to keep each additional dollar on hand. To them, the existing interest rate does not warrant the acquisition of bonds. The demand for money is thus perfectly elastic or horizontal, and monetary policy is completely ineffective in stimulating aggregate expenditures.

Long run Any extended period, usually longer than three to five years. For a firm, the time necessary to effect changes in "fixed" resources. Economists view the long run as the period in which equilibrium is reached.

Lorenz curve Graphs the extent of income inequality by charting the cumulative percentage of income against the cumulative percentage of families.

Macroeconomics The branch of economics concerned with large economic aggregates such as GDP, total employment, overall price level, and how these aggregates are determined.

Malthus, Thomas Economist who developed a theory that population tends to grow at a geometric rate while food supplies can, at best, grow at an arithmetic rate. Thus, in Malthus's eyes, extreme poverty, famine, plague, and war would continually beset humanity.

Marginal cost (MC) The increase in total cost resulting from raising the rate of production by one unit.

Marginal factor cost The cost of an additional resource or factor of production (which in competition equals the price of the resource).

Marginal physical product The additional output realized when one more unit of a variable input is used, assuming all other input levels are held constant.

Marginal propensity to consume (MPC) The change in consumption divided by the change in income (MPC = $\Delta C / \Delta Y$).

Marginal propensity to save (MPS) The change in saving divided by the change in income that brought it about (MPS = $\Delta S / \Delta Y$).

Marginal revenue (MR) The change in a firm's total revenue arising from the sale of one additional unit.

Marginal revenue = marginal cost In microeconomics, the point at which profits are maximized for a firm.

Marginal revenue product The additional revenue realized when one more unit of a variable input is used, assuming all other input levels are held constant.

Market economy An economy functioning largely through market forces (supply, demand, etc.).

Market failure The inability of the market to produce an efficient (or acceptable) result.

Market power A condition in which the firm can exercise control over the price of a good or service because the firm supplies the total quantity.

Market (1) An area over which buyers and sellers negotiate the exchange of a well-defined commodity. (2) From the point of view of a household, the firms from which it can buy a well-defined product. (3) From the point of view of the firm, the buyers to whom it can sell a well-defined product.

Marxian economics School of economics aimed at understanding the class system (or private property system), the methods of production and commodity exchange under capitalism.

Medium of exchange The function of money as intermediary. Since money is accepted in payment for goods and services and is valued for the goods and services it buys, money is a medium of exchange.

Mercantilism A characteristic European economic doctrine in the sixteenth to seventeenth centuries, emphasizing the role of money and trade in economic life and the desirability of active state intervention in the economy.

Microeconomics Branch of economics that deals with the interrelationships of individual businesses, firms, industries, consumers, laborers, and other factors of production that make up the economy. Focuses on markets.

Mixed economy An economy in which there are substantial public and private sectors, in which private enterprise and the market are significant determining factors, but in which the state also takes on certain basic economic responsibilities (e.g., full employment and business regulation). See *Capitalism*.

Monetary aggregates Various measures of the money supply used by the Federal Reserve System and include M_1, M_2, M_3, and L.

Monetary policy Governmental policy concerned with the supply of money and credit in the economy and the rate of interest. This policy is designed to promote certain macroeconomic objectives, usually full employment, stable prices, economic growth, exchange rates, and balance-of-payments equilibrium.

Money Anything that is generally accepted in payment for goods and services and in the repayment of debts.

Monopolistic competition A market structure in which each firm is relatively small, but each has a monopoly on its particular version of the product in question. Competition in such a framework assumes the form of advertising, product differentiation, and other forms of non-price competition.

Monopoly capitalism An economy that marks the dominance of imperfect competition; productive forces or factors are extremely concentrated, and markets are imperfect. See *Capitalism*.

Monopoly A market structure in which there is a single seller of a commodity or service that has no close substitutes.

Multinational corporation A corporation that operates within more than one country.

Multiplier See *Keynesian multiplier; Transfer multiplier*.

National debt The net accumulation of federal budget deficits; the total indebtedness of the federal government.

National income The total income of factors of production in the current productive period.

Neoliberal model A model that assumes that developing nations must adopt modern capital and technology to have strong economic growth.

Net national product (NNP) Total output of final goods and services produced in an economy in a given period of time, including net rather than gross investment. NNP = GDP – depreciation or capital consumption allowances.

Newly Industrializing Countries (NIC) A group of countries (Hong Kong, Taiwan, Singapore, Malaysia, the Philippines, South Korea, Brazil, Mexico, and Argentina) that have allowed foreign firms to set up operations favorably and have generated sizable export capabilities.

Oligopoly A market structure in which a few large firms dominate the industry. Some of these industries produce an undifferentiated product, others a differentiated product. In either case, a special feature of oligopoly is that the firms recognize their interdependence.

Open-market operations Federal Reserve purchases and sales of government securities on the open market. These activities are an important instrument of monetary policy because sales of government securities reduce the money supply, while purchases increase it. See *Federal Reserve.*

Opportunity cost The cost of an economic good as measured in terms of the alternative goods one must forgo to secure it.

Organization of Petroleum Exporting Countries (OPEC) Organization of oil-producing nations, largely in the Middle East, that have joined together for the purpose of controlling the production, export, and price of petroleum.

Paradox of thrift Economic principle, identified by Keynes, that an increase in the desire to save decreases output, even though investment may also increase.

Peak (of business cycle) The height of the business cycle; characterized by greatest economic activity and followed by contracting economic activity.

Per capita income Total national income divided by total population.

Petrodollars Dollars and currency in the form of monetary reserves controlled by the oil-exporting (largely OPEC) nations, accumulated by selling petroleum.

Phillips curve Graph showing the relationship between inflation and unemployment.

Political business cycle Distortion of the basic business cycle caused by the actions and policies of politicians bidding for reelection. Usually a four-year cycle in sequence with presidential elections.

Political economy Social science dealing with political policies and economic processes, their interrelationships, and their mutual influence on social institutions.

Possessions Personal items people own and use, including home, farm, or tools. Private property, in contrast, reflects ownership of impersonal property used by the owner only to collect rent on land, interest, and profits on capital; it is used (worked) by others.

Postindustrial society A society that has encountered the processes of industrialization and has gone beyond industrialization in terms of benefits accruing to the people. Some people consider the United States a postindustrial society.

Praxis Practical activity with an added twist, i.e., the dialectical interrelation of thought and practice. The term was used by the young Hegelians and especially Marx.

Precautionary demand for money Holding money in order to cover unexpected or temporary expenses or losses of income.

Present value The value today of a sum to be received or paid in the future, adjusted by a prevailing or assumed interest rate.

Price elasticity of demand The sensitivity of demand for a product to changes in its price.

Price elasticity of supply The sensitivity of supply of a product to changes in its price.

Price index See *Consumer Price Index; Index.*

Price leadership The practice of a single firm in an industry announcing a price change and other firms following suit.

Price stability Price policy that aims to counter wide fluctuations in aggregate price levels. During a period of high inflation, for example, governments seeking price stability adopt anti-inflationary measures such as credit withdrawal, higher interest rates, and decreased government spending (or increased taxes).

Price wars Progressive price cutting to increase sales.

Price An amount of money that guides resource allocation and reflects the value of a good or service. Prices are transmitted by markets through which producers make decisions about what factors of production to use, and consumers decide what to consume.

Primitive accumulation A way of accumulating wealth that fuels class conflict. In particular, the early formation of capital that accompanied the development of capitalism, often characterized by piracy and plunder.

Product differentiation Business strategy in which substitute products retain some distinctive difference. Means of differentiating products include brand names, coloring, packaging, or advertising.

Production possibilities curve Graph that illustrates scarcity and opportunity cost by showing that whenever society chooses to have more of one type of good, it must sacrifice some of another type of good.

Productivity (of labor) The output produced per unit of input (output per hour of work).

Profits Excess of revenues over costs. Normal profits are equal to the opportunity costs of management. Economic profits are the profits above the normal profit. Theoretically, in pure competition, economic profits equal zero in the long run. However, in imperfect market structures, they do not.

Progressive income tax Tax that claims an ever-increasing percentage of income as the income level rises.

Property rights In capitalism, where productive property is privately owned, owners' rights to control the use of these productive resources. See *Possessions*.

Property Tangible or intangible possession that may be used to produce some product or aid in the selling of the product. Certain legal rights are attached to this "private property."

Protectionism Policy that institutes high tariffs on incoming goods, so as to preserve domestic industry. Protectionism was prevalent during mercantilism. See *Infant industry; Tariff*.

Public debt The amount of outstanding federal debt held by individuals, corporations, and nonfederal government agencies.

Public goods Goods or resources that benefit the general public and are not necessarily directly paid for by all those who use them. Examples are street signs and public schools.

Public sector Local, state, and federal governmental offices, organizations, and institutions.

Putting-out system Labor system in which an owner would give workers the necessary materials and pay the worker to make a finished product. Replaced the handicraft type of industry and marked the emergence of private capital.

Quantity demanded The specific number of units of a product in the economy that is desired by economic agents at a given price level.

Quantity supplied The specific number of units of a product in the economy that is provided by producers at a given price level.

Quantity theory of money Theory that the quantity of money in the economy largely determines the level of prices. Stated as $MV = PQ$, where M is the quantity of money, V is the income velocity of money, P is the price level, and Q is real national income. The theory postulates that V is largely determined by institutional factors and Q is determined by factor supplies and technology; hence changes in M will be reflected in proportionate changes in P.

Quotas Limits on the quantities of goods imported or exported.

Radical economists Economists who are critical of classical and neoclassical theory and view economic problems as resulting directly from the capitalist system itself. Thus, the only serious relief to these problems is a change of economic system.

Rational expectations An economics-based theory about the nature of economic agents, stating that all agents are rational, logical, and aware of what is best for them and what the consequences of decisions and developments in the economy will mean for their well-being. Agents will act logically to take advantage of changes in the economy and enhance their position.

Real wages Wages measured from a specific point; wages that reflect the rate of inflation. If a worker's wage level increases 10 percent and inflation increases 10 percent in the same period of time, then we say that the real wage remains the same. Usually contrasted with money wages, which in the example would reflect only the 10 percent increase in the worker's wage.

Recession A slowing down of economic activity, resulting in an increase in unemployment and in excess industrial capacity. Less severe than a depression. Sometimes defined in the United States in terms of a decline in GDP for two or more successive quarters of a year.

Regulation Q Federal regulation placing a ceiling on interest rates payable by banks on deposits. This regulation has been phased out.

Rent (1) Payment for the services of a factor of production. (2) Payment for the use of land.

Reserve army (industrial) A term developed by Marx to describe the functioning of capitalism in which worker strength was greatly decreased, in propoprtion to the amount of unemployment.

Reserve currency A currency that is accepted in settlement of international exchanges.

Reserve requirements In banking, the fraction of public deposits that a bank holds in reserves.

Ricardo, David One of the reformers of classical liberalism, developed by Adam Smith. Ricardo's analysis was based on an economy composed of many small enterprises.

Savings All income received by households and not spent on the consumption of goods and services.

Say's law The doctrine (named after J. B. Say) that "supply creates its own demand." The production of one good adds to both aggregate supply and aggregate demand. In this non-monetary world, depression and mass unemployment are not possible.

Scarcity Inability of a society to produce or secure enough goods to satisfy all the wants, needs, and desires people have for these goods.

Seasonal unemployment Joblessness created by changing seasonal conditions or demand.

Services Duties (or work) for others that do not necessarily render a good but are nevertheless worth payment.

Sherman Antitrust Act A major U.S. antitrust law passed in 1890 prohibiting "every contract, combination in the form of trust or otherwise or conspiracy, in restraint of trade or commerce," and prescribing penalties for monopoly.

Shortage Disequilibrium situation wherein quantity demanded exceeds quantity supplied. In such a situation, price will tend to rise until it reaches an equilibrium level (where quantity supplied equals quantity demanded).

Smith, Adam Economist who in 1776 published *The Wealth of Nations*, noting the foundation of a new individualist philosophy, classical liberalism.

Special Drawing Rights (SDRs) A bookkeeping device created by the International Monetary Fund to increase international liquidity. SDRs may be drawn by each country in proportion to its original contribution.

Specialization (of labor) Methods of production in which individual workers specialize in particular tasks rather than making everything for themselves.

Speculative demand for money Function that describes the amount of assets held by households and firms in the form of money, relative to the interest rate.

Stagflation Term coined in the 1970s to describe the coexistence of unemployment (stagnation) and inflation afflicting the United States and other countries.

Standard of deferred payment Acceptability as future payment; a characteristic of money.

Stock Shares of ownership in a corporation. May be common stock and/or preferred stock.

Store of value An asset that holds value into the future. Money has this characteristic.

Structural budget deficit The federal budget deficit which remains if the economy were at full employment.

Structural unemployment Type of permanent unemployment that stems from shifting demand and/or technological changes requiring new skills for workers. Disparities in geographic locations of workers and jobs also contribute to this phenomenon.

Structuralist model A model that assumes that domestic political and economic factors affect development.

Supply curve The set of all points representing the amount of goods or services that will be offered at different price levels.

Supply shock Events that are unexpected and that affect the aggregate supply of goods and services.

Supply, law of Economic principle that says the lower the price, the lower the quantity supplied, all other things being constant. Price and quantity supplied are positively related.

Supply The amount of goods or services produced and available for purchase.

Surplus value In Marxian terms, the amount by which the value of a worker's output exceeds his or her wage. Hence, a source of profit for the capitalist.

Surplus A state of disequilibrium wherein quantity supplied exceeds quantity demanded. Price will tend to fall until it reaches an equilibrium (where quantity supplied equals quantity demanded).

Tariff A tax applied to imports.

Terms of trade The prices of a country's exports in relation to its imports. Any improvement in a country's terms of trade means a relative increase in its export prices, while a deterioration in its terms of trade indicates a relative increase in its import prices.

Theory A cogently expressed group of related propositions declared as principles for explanation of a set of phenomena.

Total cost The cost of all factors of production involved in producing one good.

Total fixed costs The sum of all costs that do not change with varying output (in the short run). A firm incurs these costs regardless of production levels.

Total revenue The amount of funds credited to the firm for sales of its output; price multiplied by units sold.

Total variable costs The sum of all costs that fluctuate in relation to the activity of the firm and the productive process. The two major variable costs are labor and resources.

Transactions demand for money Function that indicates the amount of money balances that individuals desire for purchasing purposes. Considered relatively constant, given a level of income and consumption pattern.

Transfer multiplier The ratio that relates the change in the equilibrium level of income (Y_y) to a change in government transfer payments.

Transfer payments Government payments to individuals that are not compensation for currently productive activity.

Trough (of business cycle) The low point of the business cycle, representing the slowest level of business activity. Following this low point, the cycle begins an upward swing.

Unemployed A person 16 years of age or older who is not working and is available for work and has made an effort to find work during the previous four weeks.

Unemployment rate The number of people unemployed expressed as a percentage of the total number of people in the labor force.

Unemployment A condition wherein workers who are ordinarily part of the labor force are unable to find work at prevailing wages. May take any of five specific forms: (1) Frictional unemployment arises from workers changing jobs, etc.; all labor markets have this kind. (2) Seasonal unemployment results from changing seasonal demand and supply for labor. (3) Structural unemployment results from changing or shifting product demand; i.e., it is a function of geographic and job skill mobility. (4) Cyclical unemployment arises from changes in demand of labor during the business cycle. (5) Hidden unemployment consists of frustrated potential workers who have given up looking for a job.

Unit of account A measure of value or the standard way of quoting prices and keeping accounts in an economy.

Value added Strictly, the value of a final product less the cost of production. Loosely, the increase in value due to the labor input.

Variable costs Costs that fluctuate due to the activity of the firm and the productive process. The two major variable costs are labor and resources.

Vertical merger Companies in different stages of an industry merge.

Wage and price controls Mandatory regulation of wages and prices by the government in order to contain inflation. The U.S. government applied such controls to certain segments of the economy with varying force from 1971 to 1974.

Wages The price paid for units of labor or service supplied in the market per unit of time.

World Bank A bank that assists poor countries by lending or by insuring private loans to finance development projects. Officially the International Bank for Reconstruction and Development (IBRD) established after World War II to promote postwar reconstruction and development of underdeveloped countries.

NAME INDEX

SUBJECT INDEX

Relations of production, 97
Rent, 79
Reserve asset account in balance-of-payment account, 464–467
Reserve currency, 478
Reserve for balance-of-payment fluctuations. *See* Reserve currency
Reserve requirements, 378
    criticism of, 384
Resource allocation, 123
    efficiency in, 182
    inefficiency in, 193
Revaluation. *See* Exchange rates
Revenues
    average, 173
    marginal, 173
    total, 163, 173
Robber barons, 64
Roman Empire, 52

Saving, 325, 328
Saving function, 328–329
Say's Law, 10, 82, 91, 317–318
Scarcity, 119
    economic choice, 122, 131
    energy, 36–37
    of resources, 122
Selective credit controls, 383
Self-interest, 77. *See also* Assumptions of self-interest
Serfs, 53–54
Sex and income distribution, 228
Sherman Antitrust Act, 277
Shortages, 147
Size distribution of income, 220
Smithsonian agreement, 479
Smoot-Hawley Tariff, 321, 456
Social change, Marxian model of, 102–103
Social revolution, 102
Social science, 3
Social Security contributions, 308–309
Socialism, 95
    characteristics of, 506
    market, 506
Socialist critique, 88
Sole proprietorship, 233
Soviet Union
    basic problems of, 508
    decentralization of, 508

economy of, 507
negative growth rates, 508–509
opportunity costs, 508–509
planning system, 508
problems with reform, 508–510
Special drawing rights, 470
Specialization, 75
Speculative demand for money, 367
Spending multiplier, 342–343
Stabilization policy, 428–429
    monetarists and, 429
    New Classical School of Macro-economics and, 430
    post-Keynesians and, 431
    radical economists and, 431
    rational expectations school and, 431
Stagflation, 419
Standard of deferred payment, money as, 366
The State
    Adam Smith on need for civil government, 78–79
    and corporations, 244
    and income distribution, 220
    Marx's theory of, 102–103
    the rise of laissez-faire, 82–85
    the rise of the nation-state, 60
Stock. *See* Capital
Stock Market Crash of October 19, 1987, 304
Store of value, money as, 366
"Strong" dollar, 474
Structural crisis, 431–432
Structural deficit, 363
Structuralist model, 497
Superstructure, 97
Supply, 14, 136
    change in, 149, 150
    curve or schedule, 144
    determinants of, 149–150
    quantity supplied, 143, 150
    of a resource, 123
Supply and demand analysis, 161
Supply shocks, 410
    OPEC embargo and, 410
Supply-side economics, 415–417
    critique of, 416–417
    and inflation, 430

support for, 416
theory vs. Keynesian theory, 416
Surplus value, 99, 106
Surpluses, 146
    and equilibrium prices, 146

Taft-Hartley Act, 246
Tariffs, 27
    arguments for, 456
    defined, 456
    Smoot-Hawley, 321, 456
Tastes and preferences, 137
Tax(es) and taxation
    corporate income in GDP, 353
    effect on income, 343–344
    fiscal policy and, 356–358
    personal income in GDP, 310
    and supply-side economics, 416
Tax multiplier, 344
Tax Reform Act (1986), 353
Teapot Dome, 64
Technological Revolution, 30
Technology, 33, 34
    as a determinant of supply, 142
    and feudalism, 505
Third World, 483–501
    consequences of debt, 493
    and the debt crisis, 493
    size of debt, 483
Three-sector model, 335
Thrifts, 373–374
    cost of bail-out, 374
    instability of, 373
    savings and loan crisis, 373–374
Time deposits, reserve requirements and, 379
Time lags. *See* Lags
Tokyo Round, 459
Trade
    absolute advantage in, 449
    balance, 465
    formula for, 465
    comparative advantage in, 22, 26, 450
    consumer cost of restrictions, 27
    currency values and, 471–474
    deficits, 469
    free. *See* Free trade